Burrawang
Fitzroy Falls Reservoir
Moss Vale
FITZROY FALLS
BELMORE FALLS
MANNING LOOKOUT
FITZROY FALLS
Mount Carralao
HAMPDEN BRIDGE
Kangaroo Valley

ESSENTIAL
ATLAS
OF AUSTRALIA

Contents

NEW SOUTH WALES AND AUSTRALIAN CAPITAL TERRITORY

VICTORIA

IN AND AROUND
THE CAPITAL
CITIES

Inner Urban Map Legend

Freeway, with tunnel	River, creek
Highway, with tunnel	Lake, reservoir
M31 — 51 Highway, with National Highway Route Marker	SANDY BAY Suburb
A1 — 1 Highway, with National Route Marker	TARONGA ZOO ✪ Place of Interest
5 Highway, with Metroad Route Marker	■ Hospital, university, college
Toll road	✈ Airport
Through route	★ Lighthouse
Arterial road, with tunnel	+ Hill, mountain, peak
C141 — 26 Arterial road, with State Route Marker	National park
Collector road	Other reserve
Local road, vehicle track	Aboriginal land
Railway / Tram line, with station	Prohibited area
Ferry route	

Maps are in a Lamberts Conformal Conic Projection

Geocentric Datum Australia, 1994 (GDA94)

SYDNEY

Australia's largest city stretches from the shores of the Pacific Ocean to the foot of the Blue Mountains. Along with outstanding natural assets – stunning beaches, extensive parklands and the vast expanse of the harbour – Sydney boasts an impressive list of urban attractions, including world-class shopping and a host of superb restaurants and nightclubs.

Sydney began life in 1788 as a penal colony, a fact long considered a taint on the city's character. Today, echoes of those bygone days remain in areas such as The Rocks, Macquarie Street and the western suburb of Parramatta.

Since those early days, the one-time prison settlement has become one of the world's great cities. Home to two of Australia's most famous icons, the Sydney Harbour Bridge and the Sydney Opera House, Sydney attracts more than two million international visitors a year. For a true Sydney experience, try watching a Rugby League Grand Final at ANZ Stadium with a crowd of 80 000 cheering fans. Or if good food and fine wine are more your style, sample the waterfront dining at Circular Quay or Darling Harbour, and multicultural flavours in inner-city Darlinghurst.

With a population of 4 500 000, Sydney offers a multitude of activities. Surf the breakers at Bondi Beach or jump on a Manly ferry and see the harbour sights. Whatever you do, Sydney is a great place to explore.

Sydney's Top Ten

Bondi
Not only is the suburb home to one of the world's most famous beaches it also has many restaurants, clothing boutiques and a weekend market.

Circular Quay and the Sydney Opera House
A public transport junction and home to many cafes and bars, the quay is also home to one of the great buildings of the 20th century, the Sydney Opera House.

Elizabeth Bay House
This elegant villa, built in 1839, is one of Australia's finest colonial mansions and is now a Historic Houses Trust museum.

Elizabeth Farm
This lovely sandstone building, surrounded by gardens, is now a museum. Nearby in Parramatta is Old Government House, Australia's oldest public building.

Manly Ferry
The ferry, which travels to and from Circular Quay, is a great way to see many of Sydney Harbour's waterside suburbs, picturesque coves and famous attractions.

Queen Victoria Building (QVB)
Originally built in 1898 and restored in 1984, QVB is one of Sydney's most cherished landmarks and is considered by some to be the most beautiful shopping centre in the world.

Aerial view of Royal Botanic Gardens and Sydney Opera House

Sydney Aquarium and Sydney Wildlife World

This world-class aquarium features underwater tunnels, a Great Barrier Reef exhibition and a Seal Sanctuary. Next door is Sydney Wildlife World, home to over 250 different Australian species, all living within their natural habitats.

Sydney Harbour Bridge

This Australian icon was opened in 1932 and is the fourth longest single-span steel arch bridge in the world. The Pylon Lookout offers one of the best views of Sydney and contains an exhibition detailing the bridge's history.

Taronga Zoo

This world-class institution houses over 2000 animals; visitors can enjoy animal feeding, keeper talks, and displays as well as a Skyline Safari.

The Rocks

A historic site by the water that features a weekend market, galleries, parks, cafes, craft shops and the Sydney Visitor Centre.

Visitor information

Sydney Visitor Centre
Level 1, cnr Argyle and Playfair sts
The Rocks
(02) 9240 8788 or 1800 067 676

Sydney Visitor Centre
33 Wheat Rd
Darling Harbour
(02) 9240 8788 or 1800 067 676
www.sydneyvisitorcentre.com

Manly Visitor Information Centre
Manly Wharf Forecourt
(02) 9976 1430

Motoring organisation
NRMA 13 1122

Getting around

Travelling through Sydney can be daunting. The traffic is dense, the peak 'hour' lasts for several hours and some of the traffic lanes are narrow. However, with some planning, Sydney is not a difficult city to negotiate. Carefully choose a main through-route and then navigate using the route signs. Main routes are generally clearly signposted. The South Western Motorway (Route 5), the Eastern Distributor (Route 1) and the Hills Motorway (Route 2) are all toll roads with attended toll gates.

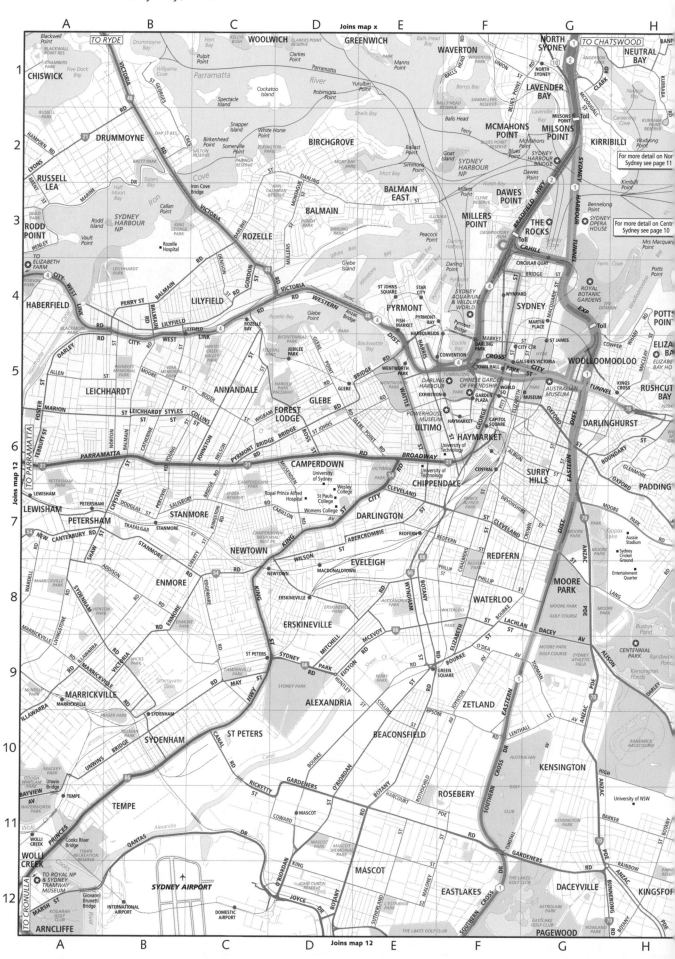

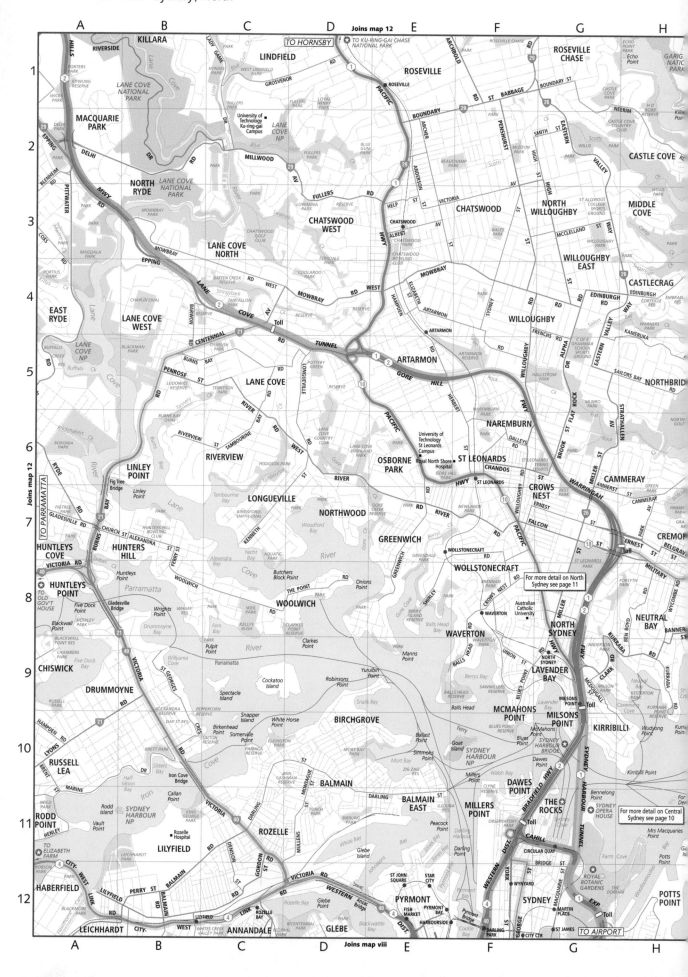

0   1   2 km

Joins map 12

I   J   K   L   M   N   O   P

1

KILLARNEY HEIGHTS
GARIGAL NATIONAL PARK
WAKEHURST
ALLAMBIE HEIGHTS
TO MONA VALE
NORTH MANLY
WILLIAM ST
CORRIE RD
BRIGHTON ST
BENNETT ST
CURL CURL
JOHN FISHER PARK
CURL CURL LAGOON
FLORA & RICHIE ROBERTS RESERVE
Dee Why Head

GARIGAL NATIONAL PARK
MANLY WAR MEMORIAL PARK
GUMBOOYA RESERVE
MANLY DAM RESERVE
WAKEHURST GOLF CLUB
BANTRY RESERVE
Manly Reservoir
KENTWELL
DAVID THOMAS RESERVE
MILLERS RD
WARRINGAH GOLF CLUB
NOLAN RESERVE
PITTWATER
HARBORD
HARBORD PARK
JACKA PARK
McKILLOP PARK

2

Harbour
Yeoland Point
H C PRESS PARK
NORTH SEAFORTH GARDEN & RECREATION
NORTH BALGOWLAH
URUNGA ST
WOODBINE
SEAFORTH OVAL
PKWY
CLONTARF ST
BLIGH ST
NORTH BALGOWLAH RESERVE
MANLY VALE
PARK
CAMPBELL PDE
CONDAMINE
QUIRK
KENNETH
LAWRENCE
OLIVER RD
QUEENSCLIFF
ALBERT ST
EVANS ST
CARRINGTON
PARK
QUEENSCLIFF

Sugarloaf Bay
Sugarloaf Point
Pickering Point
FRENCHS FOREST
BANGAROO ST
NORTH BALGOWLAH
BROOK RD
BURNT RD
BRIDGE
CK
DEVIATION
10
BALGOWLAH
CONDAMINE ST
MANLY WEST PARK
MANLY GOLF CLUB
WEEROONA PARK
BALGOWLAH RD
LAGOON
KEIRLE PARK
LAGOON PARK
STEYNE
North Steyne Beach
Queenscliff Bay
TASMAN

3

Pinnacle
SEAFORTH
22
BALGOWLAH GOLF CLUB
BALGOWLAH OVAL
SYDNEY
ETHEL
SYDNEY RD
FAIRLIGHT
PITTWATER
NTH STEYNE PARK
KANGAROO PARK
IVANHOE PARK
MANLY OVAL
SEA

Powder Hulk Bay
SANGRADO ST
PONSONBY
CRES
PDE
NEW ST
WANGANELLA ST
WHITE ST
LAUDERDALE AV
SYDNEY RD
TOWER HILL PARK
WEST ESPL
STH STEYNE
Manly Beach

4

The Pinnacle
SEAFORTH CRES
MANLY
FISHER BAY RESERVE
Fisher Bay
WEST ST
SOUTH
BRIMBECOM PARK
NORTH HARBOUR RESERVE
LAUDERDALE AV
ESPLANADE PARK
ESPL
EAST
ASHBURNER ST
DARLEY RD
Cabbage Tree Bay

Middle
Beauty Point
Bradys Point
Sandy Bay
PEROUSE
WOODLAND
BAREENA PARK
Manly Cove
ESPLANADE PARK
LITTLE MANLY RESERVE
MANLY
SYDNEY HARBOUR NATIONAL PARK

5

CLIVE PARK
Quakers Hat
Quakers Hat Bay
SPIT RES
THE SPIT
CLONTARF RESERVE
BEATRICE
CLONTARF
BALGOWLAH HEIGHTS
PARK
TANIA PARK
North
Harbour
Smedleys Point
Little Manly Cove
Little Manly Point
SCENIC DR
Blue Fish Point

ELIZABETH PARK
Fig Tree Point
BEAUTY POINT
Pearl Bay
Parriwi Head
Clontarf Point
CUTLER RD
Crater Cove
Manly Point
Spring Cove
NORTH HEAD
SYDNEY HARBOUR FEDERATION TRUST

6

Long Bay
Quakers Hat Bay
RD
Shell Cove
ROSHERVILLE RESERVE
Chinamans Beach
Wy-ar-gine Point
WYARGINE RESERVE
Dobroyd Head
Cannae Point
Q STATION

Folly Point
BALMORAL
PARK
GROTTO POINT RESERVE

7

ORTH MORNE
OURIMBAH
ST
MACPHERSON
RD
RD
AWABA
SPIT
ST
THE ESPLANADE
HUNTER PARK
Hunters Bay
Rocky Point
The Bar
Grotto Point
The Sound
Manly
Quarantine Head
SYDNEY HARBOUR NATIONAL PARK

MILITARY
BELMONT
MOSMAN ROWLING CLUB
Balmoral Beach
Middle Head
NORTH HEAD

8

MILITARY
SPOFFORTH ST
COMLES
MOSMAN
RAGLAN
ST
RD
RAGLAN
MIDDLE
ILAWSON PARK
GEORGES HEIGHTS
MIDDLE HEAD OVAL
Obelisk Bay
SYDNEY HARBOUR NATIONAL PARK
JACKSON

REID PARK
HARNETT PARK
BRADLEYS HEAD RD
GEORGES HEIGHTS OVAL
CLIFTON GARDENS
Georges Head
South Head
Hornby Lighthouse
Lady Bay

9

Mosman
RAGLAN
AVENUE
SIRIUS COVE RESERVE
SYDNEY HARBOUR NP
Little Sirius Cove
CLIFTON GARDENS
Chowder Bay
SYDNEY HARBOUR NP
SYDNEY HARBOUR NP
HMAS WATSON NAVAL BASE
Camp Cove
WATSONS BAY

MORNE OINT
Little Sirius Point
CREMORNE RESERVE
TARONGA ZOO
RD
Taylors Bay
Chowder Head
Green Point
GREEN POINT RESERVE
ROBERTSON PARK
Gap Bluff
The Gap
GAP PARK

10

Robertsons Point
ATHOL WHARF RD
Ferry
SYDNEY HARBOUR NATIONAL PARK
Watsons Bay
76
Vaucluse Point
Village Point
AV
Dunbar Head
Outer South Head

Bradleys Head
PORT
Steel Point
Shark Bay
Vaucluse Bay
PARSLEY BAY RESERVE
Parsley Bay
CAMBRIDGE AV
LIGHTHOUSE RESERVE
HEAD RD

11

Manly
SYDNEY HARBOUR
SYDNEY HARBOUR NATIONAL PARK
Shark Island
SYDNEY HARBOUR NP
HERMITAGE FORESHORE RESERVE
WENTWORTH
VAUCLUSE HOUSE
VAUCLUSE PARK
VAUCLUSE
HOPETOUN
Macquarie Lighthouse
CHRISTISON PARK
TASMAN SEA

SYDNEY HARBOUR NP
Clarke Island
Hermit Bay
Hermit Point
VAUCLUSE
NEW SOUTH
OLD SOUTH
DIAMOND BAY RESERVE

12

SYDNEY HARBOUR NP
Point Piper
Felix Bay
Woollahra Point
Rose Bay
76
Diamond Bay

DARLING POINT
Darling Point
McKELL PARK
Double Bay
WYUNA
POINT PIPER
ROSE BAY
TOWNS RD
TO BONDI

Joins map ix

I   J   K   L   M   N   O   P

N

MELBOURNE

Melbourne is renowned as Australia's cultural capital. The city has a decidedly European feel, with neo-Gothic banks and cathedrals, much-loved department stores, art galleries and theatres around every corner. And hidden among these buildings is a string of vibrant laneways given over to cafe culture and boutique shopping. Yet Melbourne wouldn't be Melbourne without sport – seeing a footy match at the MCG is a must.

Melbourne was born in 1835, and quickly became a city. With the boom of Victoria's goldfields, unbelievable wealth was poured into public buildings and tramways, grand boulevards and High Victorian masterpieces.

Today Melbourne's population of just over 4 000 000 still enjoys the good life, at the very centre of which is a love of good food and fine dining. You can find comfort food in a cosy corner pub or meals with a view and a waterfront setting – a trend in so many of the country's coastal cities. Southbank, the shopping and eating precinct on the Yarra River, has become an extension of the city centre, while Docklands is the city's latest waterside area.

You might come to Melbourne for the dining and the shopping; the gardens and the architecture; the arts and music; the football, cricket and tennis. The city has as much diversity as it has suburbs, and at last check these were marching right down the Mornington Peninsula.

Melbourne's Top Ten

Eureka Skydeck 88
Melbourne's tallest building, Eureka Tower (92 storeys high), offers breathtaking 360-degree views from its observation deck on the 88th floor. Try out The Edge, a 3-metre glass cube that projects out of the building, 285 metres above the city!

Federation Square
An open public space containing not only cafes and bars but also the Ian Potter Centre: NGV Australia and the Australian Centre for the Moving Image (ACMI).

Gothic Bank
Erected between 1883 and 1887, the old ANZ Bank is one of the most outstanding examples of gothic architecture in Melbourne and Australia.

Lanes and arcades
Explore the darkened, narrow city laneways and you will find hidden galleries, cafes, shops and even charming arcades such as Australia's oldest, the Royal Arcade.

MCG and National Sports Museum
A football or cricket match at the MCG would have to be one of Melbourne's top experiences; alternatively, you can take a tour of the MCG and include a visit to the National Sports Museum.

Melbourne Zoo
Take the Trail of the Elephants, where elephants live in a re-created Asian rainforest, or visit the Butterfly House, a perennial favourite at Australia's oldest zoo.

Yarra River in Melbourne's CBD

Queen Victoria Market

This famous market is spread across 7 hectares under the shelter of a massive shed. It offers a large range of fresh fish, meat, fruit, vegetables, delicatessen items, clothing and general merchandise.

Royal Botanic Gardens Melbourne

These magnificently landscaped gardens spread over 36 hectares and incorporates lakes, lawns, pavilions, the Melbourne Observatory and over 50 000 plant species.

Royal Exhibition Building

This is Melbourne's most significant historical building – and arguably Australia's, now that it has become the country's first man-made structure to achieve World Heritage status.

Shrine of Remembrance

Originally built as a memorial to those who died in World War I, an Eternal Flame was added to the forecourt of this imposing monument to commemorate the fallen of World War II. The Remembrance Garden honours servicemen and women of more recent conflicts.

Visitor information

Melbourne Visitor
Information Centre
Federation Square
Cnr Swanston and Flinders sts
(03) 9658 9658

www.visitmelbourne.com
www.visitvictoria.com

Motoring organisation
RACV 13 7228, roadside
assistance 13 1111

Getting around

The city centre is easy to explore, with its wide streets laid out in a grid system. Parking in the centre consists of mainly short-term parking meters and undercover carparks, which at peak times can be difficult to find or expensive. Outside the centre there is usually no problem finding a parking spot.

If you wish to use the tollways CityLink or EastLink, either an e-TAG or a day pass is required (there are no tollbooths, but day passes can be purchased over the phone either before or after making a journey; call CityLink 13 2629 or EastLink 13 5465).

0   1   2 km

I J K L M N O P

1 2 3 4 5 6 7 8 9 10 11 12

TO EPPING

COBURG

BRUNSWICK WEST

BRUNSWICK

BRUNSWICK EAST

THORNBURY

PRESTON

NORTHCOTE

PARKVILLE

PRINCES HILL

CARLTON NORTH

FITZROY NORTH

CLIFTON HILL

FAIRFIELD

TO MONTSALVAT & HEIDE MUSEUM OF MODERN ART

CARLTON

FITZROY

COLLINGWOOD

ABBOTSFORD

KEW

TO HEALESVILLE SANCTUARY & YARRA VALLEY

Royal Childrens Hospital
University of Melbourne Western Precinct
The Royal Melbourne Hospital
Ormond College
St Hildas College
Queens College
Trinity College
Newman College
University of Melbourne Parkville Campus

Melbourne Zoo
Royal Park
Melbourne Cemetery
Melbourne Museum
Royal Exhibition Building Carlton Gardens
St Vincents Hospital

RMIT University
Queen Victoria Market
Melbourne Central

MELBOURNE

EAST MELBOURNE

RICHMOND

HAWTHORN

BURNLEY

SOUTHBANK

TO ST KILDA

Flagstaff
Flagstaff Gardens
Parliament
Fitzroy Gardens
Treasury Gardens
St Vincents & Mercy Private Hospital
Gothic Bank
Southern Cross
Federation Square
Flinders Street
Melbourne Aquarium
Eureka Tower
Queen Victoria Gardens
Kings Domain
Olympic Blvd
Toll
Birrarung Marr
Jolimont
MCG & National Sports Museum

Studley Park Boathouse
Yarra Bend Park
Studley Park Golf Course
Yarra Bend Golf Course

For more detail on Central Melbourne see page 39

Studley Park
Eastern Fwy
M3
TO RINGWOOD

0   1   2 km

Joins map xv

I J K L M N O P

1
NORTH MELBOURNE
CARLTON
FITZROY
COLLINGWOOD
ABBOTSFORD
Melbourne Museum
Queensberry St
Royal Exhibition Building
Carlton Gardens
St Vincents Hospital
Queen Victoria Market
RMIT University
GERTRUDE ST
GIPPS ST
PARK
GAHAN RESERVE
Collingwood
Browns Reserve
Andrews Reserve
Studley Park
YARRA
Studley Park Golf Course
WALMER ST
STUDLEY PARK RD
KING ST
PEEL ST
SWANSTON ST
LYGON ST
RATHDOWNE ST
NICHOLSON ST
BRUNSWICK ST
SMITH ST
WELLINGTON ST
LANGRIDGE ST
Yarra
KEW
TO HEALESVILLE SANCTUARY & YARRA VALLEY

2
FLAGSTAFF GARDENS
MELBOURNE CENTRAL
PARLIAMENT
FITZROY GARDENS
EAST MELBOURNE
St Vincents & Mercy Private Hospital
Treasury Gardens
NORTH RICHMOND
VICTORIA PDE
VICTORIA ST
DUDLEY ST
WILLIAM ST
ELIZABETH ST
QUEEN ST
BOURKE ST
SPRING ST
LANSDOWNE ST
ALBERT ST
MACARTHUR ST
CLARENDON ST
HODDLE ST
POWLETT RESERVE
Darling Gardens
NELSON ST
BAKER ST
ELIZABETH ST
BARKERS RD
For more detail on Central Melbourne see page 39

3
SOUTHERN CROSS
GOTHIC BANK
MELBOURNE
COLLINS ST
BOURKE ST
FEDERATION SQUARE
FLINDERS STREET
Birrarung Marr
River
Melbourne Aquarium
Eureka Tower
SOUTHBANK
WELLINGTON PDE
JOLIMONT RESERVE
JOLIMONT
BRUNTON AV
BRIDGE RD
MCG & NATIONAL SPORTS MUSEUM
RICHMOND
WEST RICHMOND
HIGHETT ST
City Reserve
Richmond Union Bowling Club
HAWTHORN
Yarra Bank Res
CHURCH ST
BURWOOD RD
PRIDMORE PARK

4
WEST GATE FWY
NORMANBY RD
CLARENDON ST
KINGS WAY
CITY RD
POWER ST
SOUTHBANK BLVD
ST KILDA RD
Queen Victoria Gardens
Kings Domain
Alexandra Gardens
DOMAIN
ALEXANDRA AV
OLYMPIC BLVD
BURNLEY
Melbourne Park
Yarra Park
Toll
Toll
RICHMOND
EAST RICHMOND
SWAN ST
LENNOX ST
COPPIN ST
BURNLEY
CITYLINK
Burnley Park
River Yarra
Yarra Bank Res
Mazda Reserve
Victoria University
M1
DOMAIN TUNNEL
PUNT RD
Burnley Tunnel
TO CHADSTONE

5
SOUTH MELBOURNE
KINGS WAY
SHRINE OF REMEMBRANCE
Edmund Herring Memorial Oval
ROYAL BOTANIC GARDENS
Ornamental Lake
DOMAIN RD
CREMORNE
ALEXANDRA AV
CHURCH ST
BARKLY AV
Barkly Gardens
Ryan Reserve
Athol Brown Reserve
Allan Bain Reserve
BURNLEY
Toll
McConchie Reserve
Herring Island
Como Park North
Burnley Golf Course
University of Melbourne Burnley Campus
CITYLINK
GEORGES RD
Sol Green Reserve
DORCAS ST
CECIL ST
CLARENDON ST
FERRARS ST

6
TOORAK RD
DOMAIN RD
SOUTH YARRA
WEST TOORAK RD
DARLING ST
SOUTH YARRA
KENSINGTON RD
BRUCE ST
Como Park
Royal South Yarra Tennis Club
Winifred Crescent Reserve
ORRONG RD
TOORAK
ALBERT RD
CANTERBURY RD
QUEENS WAY
ST KILDA RD
Fawkner Park
Gunn Island
Albert Park Lake
ALBERT PARK
Joins map 40

7
ALBERT PARK
Albert Park Golf Course
COMMERCIAL RD
Albert Cricket Ground
CHAPEL ST
CROMWELL RD
TOORAK RD
GRANGE RD
ST GEORGES RD
TOORAK
ALBANY RD
Argo Reserve
Fairbairn Reserve
Brookville Gardens
TO THE DANDENONG & PUFFING BILLY RAILWAY
ALBERT PARK
St Vincent Gardens
Plantation Reserve
Crescent Reserve
KERFERD RD
PAGE ST
Alfred Hospital

8
MIDDLE PARK
MOUBRAY ST
Wesley College
GREVILLE ST
PUNT RD
HIGH ST
PRAHRAN
MALVERN RD
SURREY RD
WILLIAMS RD
MATHOURA RD
CLENDON RD
MALVERN
KOOYONG RD
Hawksburn
Grattan Reserve
Princes Gardens
KING ST
HIGH ST
Victoria Gardens
Toorak Park
Swinburne University of Technology Prahran Campus
Harry Gregory Reserve
Orrong Park
TOORAK
MIDDLE PARK ST
AUGHTIE DR
BEACONSFIELD PDE
MILLS ST

9
ST KILDA WEST
JUNCTION OVAL
WELLINGTON ST
WINDSOR
DANDENONG RD
Windsor
Melbourne Bowling Club
Gladstone Gardens
Ross Gregory Oval
Windsor Siding
Lumley Park
ARMADALE
Armadale
Chomley ST
ORRONG RD
WATTLETREE RD
UNION STREET RES
ALT 1
ST KILDA RD
PRINCES ST
ALMA RD
JACOBY RESERVE
Albert Park
TO DANDENONG

10
ST KILDA
ACLAND ST
GREY ST
FITZROY ST
Catani Gardens
St Kilda Harbour
St Kilda Pier
INKERMAN ST
PRINCES ST
ALMA RD
ST KILDA RD
J Duggan Reserve
Grey Street Reserve
Recreation Reserve
Alma Park West
Alma Park East
ST KILDA EAST
CHAPEL ST
ALMA RD
Amsdale Reserve
Alma Bowling Club
PARK ST
WESTBURY ST

11
THE ESPLANADE
JACKA BLVD
CARLISLE ST
INKERMAN ST
Peanut Farm Reserve
St Kilda Botanical Gardens
BRIGHTON RD
CHAPEL ST
PARK
BALACLAVA
INKERMAN ST
BALACLAVA ST
CAULFIELD NORTH
HOTHAM ST
Balaclava
ORRONG RD
KOOYONG RD
HAWTHORN RD

12
St Kilda Marina
M.O. Moran Reserve
ELWOOD
BROADWAY
J L Dawkins Reserve
Renfrey Gardens
BARKLY ST
MITFORD ST
GLEN EIRA RD
RIPPONLEA
Rippon Lea
Ripponlea Park
Ripponlea
Greenmeadows Gardens
TO RIPPON LEA ESTATE
ARGONA
KOOYONG RD
HAWTHORN RD
TO FRANKSTON
Joins map 40

ADELAIDE

One of the best-planned cities in the world, Adelaide remains testament to the work of its first surveyor, Colonel William Light, whose statue stands on Montefiore Hill, overlooking Adelaide Oval.

Settled in 1836, Adelaide was Australia's first free settlement. Like other well-planned cities around the world, Adelaide has few skyscrapers and its architecture blends both heritage and contemporary styles, retaining a 'human scale'.

Since the 1970s Adelaide has been famous for food and wine. The state is the powerhouse of the booming Australian wine industry, producing almost 60 per cent of the total output, while Adelaide Central Market is possibly the finest fresh-produce market in Australia. The city is renowned for its restaurants – from the fish cafes of Gouger Street to the many gourmet eateries dotted around the CBD, and tucked away in quiet corners.

Adelaide also knows how to throw a party, and with a population of 1 200 000 the city is compact enough to generate a feeling of all-over revelry. First on the calendar is the Adelaide Festival of Arts, one of the world's great arts festivals. During February and March every second year, the festival and the now annual Adelaide Fringe take over the city.

Adelaide's Top Ten

Adelaide Festival Centre
This centre is an architectural landmark and consists of four theatres, including the large Festival Theatre and the outdoor amphitheatre.

Adelaide Oval
With its charming blend of historic and contemporary grandstand architecture this oval is regarded as one of the most beautiful sporting arenas in the world.

Art Gallery of South Australia
The gallery's permanent collection is grouped into three major categories: Australian, European and Asian. There is also a program of changing exhibitions.

Ayers House
One of Australia's finest examples of Regency architecture, the home of former state Premier Henry Ayres has been painstakingly restored and one wing has been transformed into a luxurious restaurant.

Central Railway Station
Built in the 1920s to a Neo-Classical design, the building was restored and refurbished in the 1980s and SKYCITY Adelaide casino now occupies much of the station's upper floors.

Migration Museum
This museum details immigrant life from pioneering days up to today.

River Torrens
The river provides a scenic setting for a host of leisure activities including walking, cycling, paddling, cruising and even a Venetian gondola ride.

View of St Peter's Cathedral and Adelaide skyline

South Australian Museum

The museum has played a crucial role in researching, documenting and exhibiting every facet of Aboriginal culture; the Australian Aboriginal Cultures gallery contains over 3000 objects and is the world's most comprehensive Aboriginal cultural exhibition.

State Library of South Australia

The complex is a blend of charming 19th-century buildings and modern technology.

The most notable attraction is the Bradman Collection, featuring memorabilia belonging to the famous cricketer.

Tandanya

Tandanya aims to exhibit the contemporary culture, art, and lifestyles of Australia's Indigenous people while still acknowledging the traditions the culture was built on.

Visitor information

South Australian Visitor and Travel Centre
18 King William St
(08) 8303 2220 or 1300 764 227

www.southaustralia.com

Motoring organisation
RAA (08) 8202 4600, roadside assistance 13 1111

Getting around

Adelaide's city centre is compact and easily negotiated on foot. The Explorer Tram offers visitors the chance to tour the city's attractions at a leisurely pace and with the benefit of a recorded commentary. A fleet of Popeye motor launches cruise the River Torrens and also provide an ideal means of transport to the Adelaide Zoo. The historic Glenelg tram departs Victoria Square regularly for a return trip to Adelaide's premier seaside suburb. Car travel is recommended for touring some of the further-flung regions; the roads are excellent and navigation should not be a problem.

0   1   2 km

I   J   K   L   M   N   O   P

TO ELIZABETH   *TO HIGHBURY*   A11

1
PROSPECT
NAILSWORTH   BROADVIEW   KLEMZIG   NEWTON
A1   PROSPECT OVAL   RD   GOLF COURSE   NEWTON SPORTS GROUND
COLLINSWOOD   A10   A17   VALE PARK   River   CAMPBELLTOWN LEISURE CENTRE   CAMPBELLTOWN
OSPECT   MEDINDIE GARDENS   WALKERVILLE   MARDEN   FELIXSTOW   LOWER NORTH EAST
FITZROY THORNGATE PARK   NOTTAGE TCE   LOWER   FELIXSTOW RESERVE   RD   MONTACUTE
DREGE RES   PATTERSON SPORTS GROUND   MONTACUTE

2
FITZROY   MEDINDIE   GLYNDE   HECTORVILLE   ROSTREVOR RESERVE
THORNGATE   FITZROY   TCE   A10   GILBERTON   ROYSTON PARK   PAYNEHAM   GLYNDE   MAGILL   ROSTREVOR   AV
NORTH ADELAIDE PARK   ROBE   A21   NORTHCOTE   JOSLIN   PAYNEHAM OVAL   REID
JEFFCOTT   TCE   PARK

3
NORTH ADELAIDE PARK   A21   ST PETERS   A11   EVANDALE   PAYNEHAM SOUTH   FIRLE   TRANMERE   MAGILL   WOODFORDE   GLEN STUART
O'CONNELL   WELLINGTON SQUARE   MANN   ST PETERS PARK   A17   THE GUMS RECREATION GROUND   University of South Australia Magill Campus   RESERVE   SUMMIT   NORTON   RD
PALMER GARDENS   PARK   MELBOURNE   MARIAN   PARK   RD   MOULES   RD   TERINGIE

4
BROUGHAM GARDENS   PRINCE ALFRED COLLEGE SPORTS GROUND   COLLEGE PARK   MAYLANDS   TRINITY GARDENS   ST MORRIS   KENSINGTON PARK   OLD NORTON SUMMIT RD
KING   FROME   University of Adelaide Sports Ground   ZOOLOGICAL GARDENS   HACKNEY   STEPNEY   MAGILL   KENSINGTON GARDENS   AULDANA
WILLIAM   Botanic Gardens   University of South Australia   Botanic Gardens of Adelaide   NORTH   A11   FULLARTON   BEULAH PARK   HASLAM OVAL   PENFOLDS MAGILL ESTATE

5
ADELAIDE FESTIVAL CENTRE   ART GALLERY OF SOUTH AUSTRALIA   AYERS HOUSE   RUNDLE   KENT TOWN   NORWOOD   PARADE   KENSINGTON PARK SPORTS FIELD   PARADE   ROSSLYN PARK
MONTEFIORE RD   RD   RUNDLE MALL   TANDANYA   DEQUETTEVILLE TCE   KENT TOWN PARK   KENSINGTON   KENSINGTON GARDENS   SKYE
A11   ADELAIDE   KING   GRENFELL   BARTELS RD   RD   KENSINGTON   TCE   RD
RRIE   PULTENEY   HUTT   FLINDERS TCE

6
MORPHETT   VICTORIA SQUARE   WAKEFIELD   ST   ROSE PARK   MARRYATVILLE   LEABROOK   ERINDALE   WATTLE PARK
ADELAIDE   ADELAIDE CENTRAL MARKET   For more detail on Central Adelaide see page 65   St Andrew's Hospital   HEATHPOOL   FERGUSON PARK
ROTE   ST   PARK   FULLARTON   TOORAK GARDENS   TUSMORE PARK   STONYFELL
PARK LANDS   VICTORIA PARK RACECOURSE   DULWICH   TUSMORE   HAZELWOOD PARK

7
SOUTH   SIR LEWIS COHEN   VEALE GARDENS   OSMOND GARDENS   UNLEY   A1   GLEN   PARK LANDS   GREENHILL   GREENHILL   HAZELWOOD PARK   BURNSIDE   HORSNELL GULLY
GOODWOOD   PEACOCK   RD   HUTT RD   OSMOND   A21   EASTWOOD   Glenside Hospital   GLENSIDE   PORTRUSH   LINDEN PARK   GLYNBURN   GREENHILL RECREATION PARK
A21   GREENHILL   TRAMWAY   HAIGH'S CHOCOLATES FACTORY   PARKSIDE   RD   ST GEORGES RESERVE   MILLER RESERVE   GREENHILL RD

8
WAYVILLE   GLENELG   SOUTER PARK   UNLEY   DUTHY   FULLARTON   FREWVILLE   GLENUNGA RESERVE   BEAUMONT   GREENHILL RD   GREENHILL
GOODWOOD   UNLEY OVAL   GLEN   GLENUNGA   ST GEORGES   DASHWOOD   RD
MILLSWOOD   MILLSWOOD   HYDE PARK   FISHER   FULLARTON   WOOTOONA   TCE   CLELAND CONSERVATION PARK

9
KINGS PARK   HYDE PARK   HYDE PARK RESERVE   MALVERN   HEYWOOD PARK   HIGHGATE   MYRTLE BANK   RESERVE   RIDGE PARK   GLEN OSMOND   MOUNT OSMOND GOLF COURSE   WATERFALL GULLY
UNLEY PARK   A3   RD   CROSS   ST   MYRTLE BANK   A17   RD   RESERVE   CLELAND
UNLEY PARK   HAWTHORN PLAYING FIELDS   BELAIR   FULLARTON   WAITE   A3   GLEN OSMOND   MOUNT OSMOND   CLELAND WILDLIFE PARK

10
WESTBOURNE PARK   HAWTHORN   HAWTHORN   KINGSWOOD   University of Adelaide Waite Campus   URRBRAE   M1   EASTERN   LEAWOOD GARDENS   CLELAND CONSERVATION PARK
RLAND PARK   WESTBOURNE PARK OVAL   HAWTHORN RESERVE   NETHERBY   CLAREMONT   AV   RESERVE   SOUTH   MOUNT   BARKER
BATCHELOR RESERVE   TUTT   RD

11
MITCHAM   SPRINGFIELD   BROWN HILL CREEK   FWY
READE PARK   LOWER MITCHAM   PARK
COLONEL LIGHT GARDENS   TORRENS PARK   BLYTHEWOOD   RD   MITCHAM   OLD BELAIR   M1   TO HAHNDORF

12
MORTLOCK PARK   CLAPHAM   TORRENS PARK   CRAFERS WEST   TO ADELAIDE HILLS
SPRINGBANK   CLAPHAM   RD   BROWNHILL CREEK RECREATION PARK   RANDELL PARK
GOODWOOD   PANORAMA   LYNTON   JAMES RD   TO BELAIR NATIONAL PARK   BELAIR

I   J   K   L   M   N   O   P

Joins map 66

PERTH

Perth is the most isolated capital city in the world, closer to Singapore than it is to Sydney. Its nearest neighbour, Adelaide, is 2700 kilometres away by road. Yet it is exactly this isolation that has allowed Perth to retain a feeling of space and relaxed charm.

Claimed to be the sunniest state capital in Australia, Perth has a Mediterranean climate: hot and dry in summer, cool and wet in winter. This climate, and the city's proximity to both river and ocean, fosters a relaxed lifestyle for the population of 1 696 000. One of Perth's great attributes is that its water frontages are public land, accessible to everyone. Picnicking is a popular pastime, while cafes and bars spill their tables and chairs out onto pavements to make the most of the glorious weather.

Yet for all Perth's coastal beauty, it is the Swan River that defines the city. North of the river is Kings Park and the old-money riverside suburbs with their grand homes; further on are the beaches and the newer northern beach suburbs stretching up the coast. At the mouth of the Swan is the historic port city of Fremantle, with its rich maritime history, creative community and street cafe culture. Upstream from Perth – where the river dwindles to a meandering waterway – is the Swan Valley, the state's oldest wine district.

Perth's Top Ten

Aquarium of Western Australia (AQWA)
The highlight of this attraction is an incredible 98-metre underwater tunnel offering views of thousands of marine creatures.

Hillarys Boat Harbour
This ocean-side complex houses a marina, a world-class aquarium, and Sorrento Quay – a 'village' of shops, cafes, restaurants and resort apartments.

His Majesty's Theatre and Museum of Performing Arts
Perth's premier arts venue and Australia's only remaining Edwardian theatre. The 1904 theatre also houses the museum featuring an extensive collection of photographs and costumes.

Kings Park and Botanic Garden
A 400-hectare bushland reserve with landscaped gardens, walkways, lakes, a war memorial and good city views from the top of Mount Eliza. The botanic garden is set over 17 hectares and planted with approximately 3000 native species.

Malls and arcades
Perth's central shopping precinct is made up of three main blocks which house two malls, a series of arcades and underground walkways.

Swan Bells
The Swan Bells consist of 18 'change-ringing' bells, which form the largest set in the world. The bell tower offers galleries from which to view the bell ringers and the bells in action.

Barrack Street Jetty and Perth skyline

The Perth Mint

Australia's oldest operating mint offers displays of historic and rare coins, regular tours and gold-pouring demonstrations. Visitors can also see the world's largest collection of natural gold specimens.

University of Western Australia

With its distinctive Mediterranean-style architecture and landscaped gardens, the university is renowned as one of Australia's most beautiful campuses. The Berndt Museum of Anthropology and the Lawrence Wilson Art Gallery are located within its grounds.

WACA

This is the home of cricket in Western Australia. The museum provides a fascinating insight into cricketing, sporting and social history from the 1800s to the present day.

Western Australian Museum

Housed in a group of contemporary and historic buildings this fine museum offers a comprehensive collection as well as an interactive Discovery Centre for kids.

Visitor information

Western Australian Visitor Centre
Cnr Forrest Pl and Wellington St
1300 361 351 or
1800 812 808 or
(08) 9483 1111
www.westernaustralia.com
www.wavisitorcentre.com

Fremantle Visitor Centre
Town Hall
Kings Square
High St
(08) 9431 7878
www.fremantlewa.com.au

Motoring organisation
RAC of WA (08) 9301 3113
or 13 1703

Getting around

The city centre is compact and easy to explore. A free, regular bus service known as the CAT (Central Area Transit) System operates around central Perth. You can also travel free on Transperth buses and trains within the Free Transit Zone in the city centre. Transperth produces a handy tourist guide and map that shows the Free Transit Zone.

A good way to discover the city is on the Perth Tram Co. tours, which operate daily. These replicas of the city's first trams extend east to Burswood International Resort Casino and west to the University of Western Australia. On weekdays Fremantle Tram Tours operates a 'tram' tour (the vehicle is actually a bus) around the streets of historic Subiaco and out to Lake Monger.

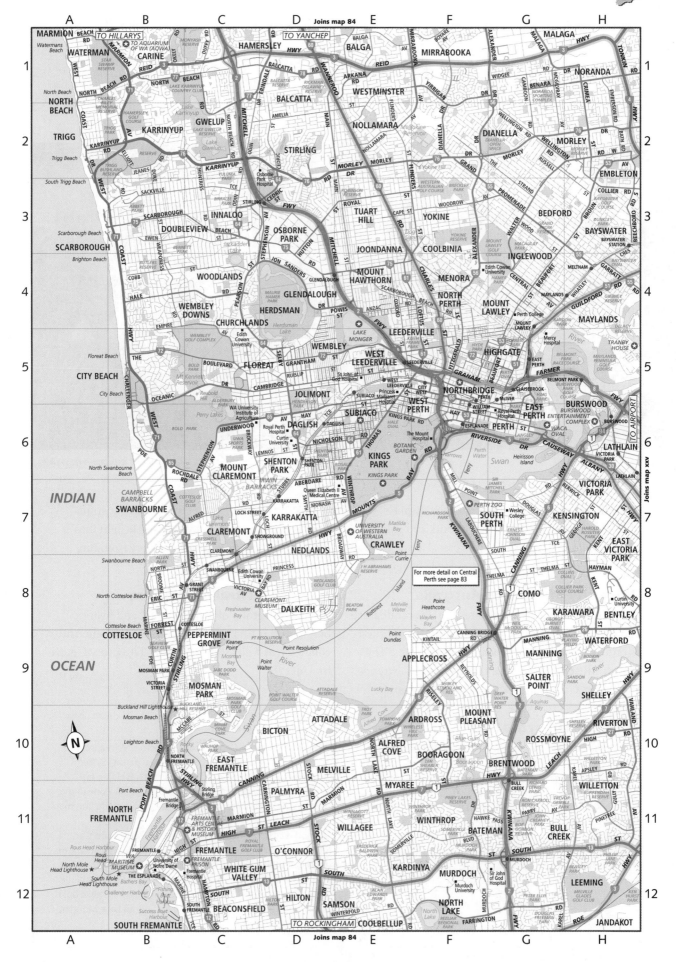

0 1 2 3 4 5 km

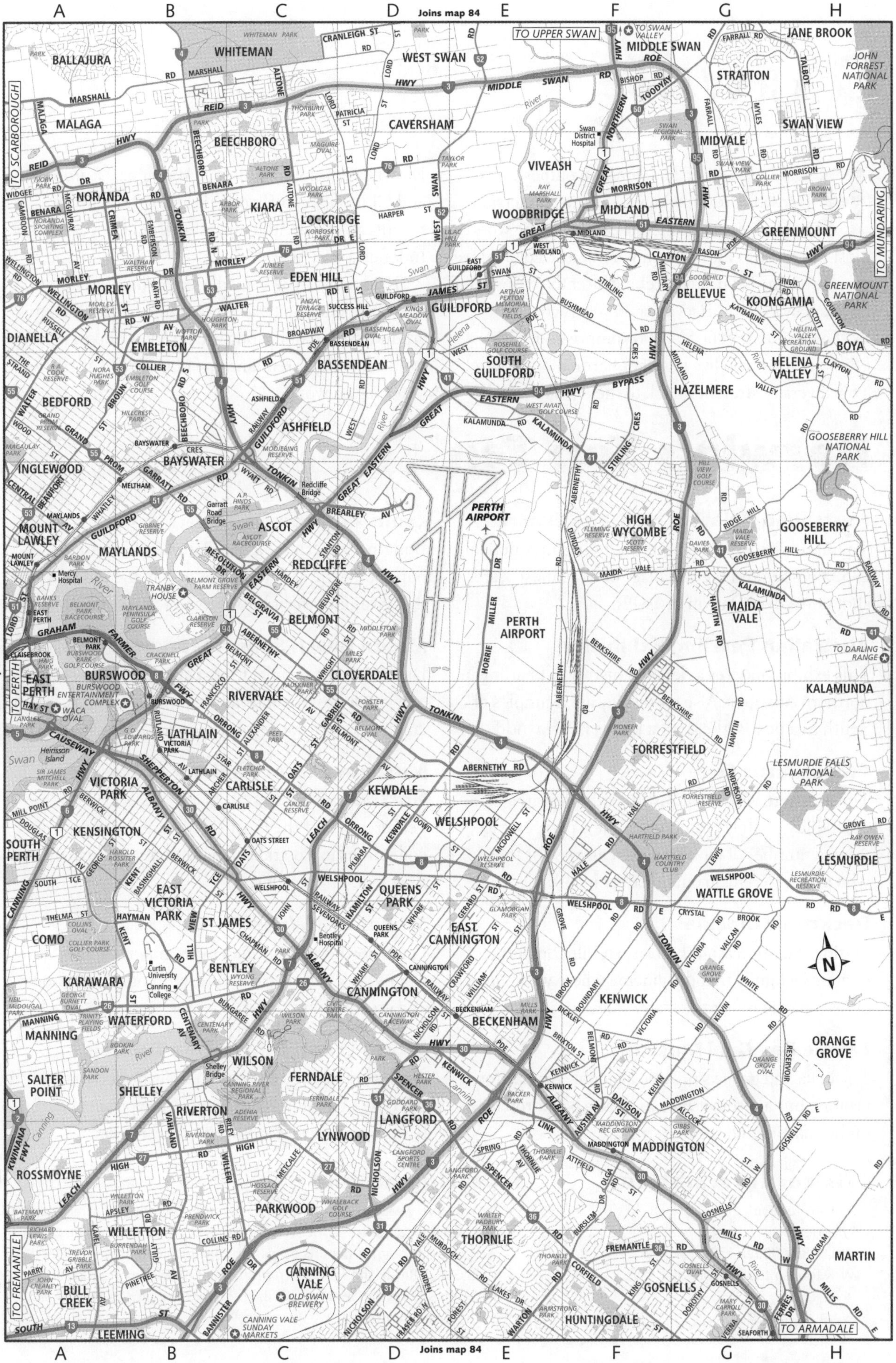

A B C D E F G H

Joins map 84

TO UPPER SWAN

BALLAJURA
WHITEMAN
WEST SWAN
TO SWAN VALLEY
MIDDLE SWAN
JANE BROOK
STRATTON
JOHN FORREST NATIONAL PARK

MALAGA
BEECHBORO
CAVERSHAM
VIVEASH
Swan District Hospital
SWAN REGIONAL PARK
MIDVALE
SWAN VIEW

NORANDA
KIARA
LOCKRIDGE
WOODBRIDGE
MIDLAND
GREENMOUNT

MORLEY
EDEN HILL
BASSENDEAN
GUILDFORD
WEST MIDLAND
BELLEVUE
KOONGAMIA
BOYA
GREENMOUNT NATIONAL PARK

DIANELLA
EMBLETON
SOUTH GUILDFORD
HELENA VALLEY

BEDFORD
ASHFIELD
HAZELMERE
GOOSEBERRY HILL NATIONAL PARK

INGLEWOOD
BAYSWATER
ASCOT
REDCLIFFE
BELGRAVIA
BELMONT
HIGH WYCOMBE
GOOSEBERRY HILL

MOUNT LAWLEY
MAYLANDS
Mercy Hospital
PERTH AIRPORT
MAIDA VALE
KALAMUNDA

EAST PERTH
BURSWOOD
RIVERVALE
CLOVERDALE
Burswood Entertainment Complex
WACA OVAL

VICTORIA PARK
LATHLAIN
FORRESTFIELD

KENSINGTON
CARLISLE
KEWDALE
LESMURDIE FALLS NATIONAL PARK

SOUTH PERTH
CARLISLE
WELSHPOOL
LESMURDIE

COMO
EAST VICTORIA PARK
ST JAMES
WELSHPOOL
QUEENS PARK
EAST CANNINGTON
WATTLE GROVE

KARAWARA
BENTLEY
Curtin University
Canning College
CANNINGTON
KENWICK

MANNING
WATERFORD
WILSON
BECKENHAM
ORANGE GROVE

SALTER POINT
SHELLEY
FERNDALE
LANGFORD
MADDINGTON

ROSSMOYNE
RIVERTON
LYNWOOD
THORNLIE
MARTIN

BULL CREEK
WILLETTON
PARKWOOD
CANNING VALE
Old Swan Brewery
GOSNELLS
HUNTINGDALE

LEEMING
Canning Vale Sunday Markets

TO SCARBOROUGH
TO FREMANTLE
TO PERTH
Joins map xxiv
TO MUNDARING
Joins map 84
TO DARLING RANGE
TO ARMADALE

Joins map 84

N

DARWIN

Regarded as Australia's northern outpost, Darwin's proximity to Asia and its immersion in Aboriginal culture make it one of the world's most interesting cities. It retains a tropical, colonial feel despite having been largely rebuilt after the devastation wreaked by cyclone Tracy over 30 years ago.

The population of 127 000 comprises over 50 ethnic groups who live together harmoniously here. This diversity stretches back to the early days of Darwin's development when Aboriginal, European and Chinese people worked side by side. More recent arrivals include migrants from Greece, Timor, Indonesia and Africa.

Evidence of the early days remain, but Darwin is also a modern city. With so much natural beauty around its harbour, along the beaches and in its tropical parks, it remains one of the most attractive cities in the world.

Darwin's Top Ten

Australian Aviation Heritage Centre
An impressive list of exhibits including an American B-52 bomber and the wreckage of a Japanese Zero shot down over Darwin in 1942.

Australian Pearling Exhibition
This exhibition gives a detailed history of pearling in northern Australia. Also on display are examples of South Sea pearls, the largest pearls in the world.

Crocosaurus Cove
This is where visitors can swim with saltwater crocodiles – safely protected inside a perspex cage! A large number of reptiles are on display for those who prefer to remain outside the enclosure.

Deckchair Cinema
During the dry season the Darwin Film Society operates a family friendly cinema where you can enjoy a movie under the starry skies.

Fannie Bay Gaol Museum
The cells and gallows provide a gloomy display for visitors, but are sometimes used as a backdrop for dinner parties and social events.

Lyons Cottage
Built in 1925, this classic example of colonial bungalow-style architecture is now home to a collection that gives an insight into Darwin's rich cultural history.

Mindil Beach Sunset Markets
Darwin's most popular tourist attraction (dry season only) includes live entertainment, exotic foods, art and craft, a tropical sunset and occasional beach fireworks.

Museum and Art Gallery of the Northern Territory
Features one of the most significant Aboriginal art collections in Australia, a natural history display, and a cyclone Tracy gallery.

Stokes Hill Wharf
Once northern Australia's most important port, now a popular leisure area with restaurants, bars, shops and great fishing.

World War II Oil Storage Tunnels
A network of five concrete tunnels buried beneath the city; two tunnels are open to the public and feature historical displays of the war years.

Visitor information

Tourism Top End
6 Bennett St
(08) 8980 6000 or 1300 138 886
www.tourismtopend.com.au

Motoring organisation
AANT (08) 8925 5901, roadside assistance 13 1111

Getting around

Darwin is very easy to negotiate either by car or on foot. The streets are well signed and traffic is light even at peak times. The Tour Tub bus tour of the city's top sights departs daily from the north end of Smith Street Mall. Cullen Bay Marina is the departure point for cruises around Fannie Bay, Stokes Hill Wharf and Frances Bay, and for ferry trips to Mandorah on the Cox Peninsula.

0 1 2 3 4 5 km

TIMOR SEA

A B C D E F G H

1
2
3
4
5
6
7
8
9
10
11
12

N

Lee Point

CASUARINA COASTAL RESERVE

BUFFALO Ck RD

RD

LEE POINT

BUFFALO CREEK MANAGEMENT AREA

Dariba Rock

CASUARINA COASTAL RESERVE

Royal Darwin Hospital

LYONS

SHOAL BAY PENINSULA

MUIRHEAD

Beagle Gulf

ROCKLANDS DR

HENBURY AV

FITZMAURICE DR

TROWER

TIWI GARDENS

TIWI PARK

TIWI

NAKARA
NAKARA PARK

TAMBLING TCE

WANGURI
WANGURI PARK

V.R.D.

LEANYER

CASUARINA COASTAL RESERVE

Charles Darwin University Casuarina Campus

BRINKIN

ELLENGOWAN DR

CASUARINA

VANDERLIN

LEANYER DR

RAPID CREEK

CASUARINA DR

NIGHTCLIFF

BANKSIA ST

ARALIA

NIGHTCLIFF RD

NIGHTCLIFF OVAL

RYLAND

RAPID

DRIPSTONE RD

ALAWA OVAL

LAKESIDE DR

ALAWA

WAGAMAN
WAGAMAN PARK

WULAGI
WULAGI PARK

DR

LEANYER RECREATION PARK

VANDERLIN DR

PROGRESS DR

DICK WARD

BAGOT RD

TROWER RD

SABINE RD

CREEK

RAPID CREEK PARK

MILLNER

JINGILI
JINGILI PARK

DARWIN WATER GARDENS

ROTHDALE RD

MOIL PARK

MOIL

LEE POINT RD

UNION

WULAGI TCE

ANULA
YANYULA PARK

CRES

PATTERSON

MALAK CRES

MALAK PARK

MALAK

VANDERLIN DR

KARAMA

COCONUT GROVE

MCMILLANS

BAGOT PARK

RD

HENRY RD

WRIGLEY

MARRARA

MARRARA SPORTING COMPLEX

DARWIN GOLF COURSE

MCMILLANS RD

KALYMNOS DR

MUELLER

HOLMES JUNGLE NATURE PARK

EAST POINT MILITARY MUSEUM

East Point

EAST POINT

EAST POINT RESERVE

Lake Alexander

Ludmilla Ck

BAGOT ABORIGINAL COMMUNITY

TOTEM RD

DICK WARD DR

RD

RAAF GOLF COURSE

DARWIN AIRPORT

AUSTRALIAN AVIATION HERITAGE CENTRE

AMY JOHNSON AV

BERRIMAH

VANDERIM DR

CROCODYLUS PARK

Joins map 102

Dudley Point

WARATAH OVAL

FANNIE BAY OVAL

LUDMILLA

BAGOT RD

BUKATILLA RD

BILLEROY RD

RAAF BASE

THE NARROWS

DWYER PARK

RICHARDSON PARK

STUART HWY

WINNELLIE

WINNELLIE PARK

WINNELLIE

HOOK RD

STUART HWY

AMY JOHNSON AV

KNUCKEY LAGOON

KMUCKEY LAGOONS CONSERVATION RESERVE

FANNIE BAY GAOL MUSEUM

FANNIE BAY

ROSS SMITH AV

LUDMILLA OLYMPIC POOL

DOUGLAS

PARAP RD

BISHOP ST

STUART

WOOLNER

TIGER

BENISON

COONAWARRA RD

BRENNAN

BENNAN

NAVAL BASE

COONAWARRA

BERRIMAH DR

PRUEN RD

TO PALMERSTON

Fannie Bay

MUSEUM & ART GALLERY OF THE NORTHERN TERRITORY

Bullocky Point

Vesteys Beach
Vesteys Lake

THE GARDENS

PARAP

STUART ST

BAYVIEW

Sadgroves Ck

CHARLES DARWIN NATIONAL PARK

HIDDEN VALLEY

DR

TO HOWARD SPRINGS & DARWIN CROCODILE FARM

Myilly Point

MINDIL BEACH SUNSET MARKETS

Mindil Beach

GEORGE BROWN DARWIN BOTANIC GARDENS

GARDENS PARK GOLF COURSE

STUART PARK

Oinah Oval

BRENNAN

CHARLES DARWIN

Reichardt Creek

Ferry to Mandorah

Emery Point

CULLEN BAY MARINA

Park

KAHLIN OVAL

GILRUTH

SMITH

MITCHELL

MCMINN

TIGER

Dinah Beach

WISHART RD

DR

LARRAKEYAH

Elliott Point

LARRAKEYAH ARMY BASE

Patrol Boat Harbour

Doctors Gully

ESPLANADE

ALLEN AV

KNUCKEY ST

CROCOSAURUS COVE

STUART ST

Small Boat Harbour

Fishermans Wharf

RAILWAY

DARWIN

BERRIMAH RD

ALICE SPRINGS RD

EAST ARM

Lameroo Beach
DECKCHAIR CINEMA

DARWIN

Darwin Harbour

WWII OIL STORAGE TUNNELS

AUSTRALIAN PEARLING EXHIBITION

STOKES HILL WHARF

Fort Hill Wharf

Frances Bay

Bleesers Ck

Hudson Creek

For more detail on Central Darwin see page 101

PORT

DARWIN

East Arm

BRISBANE

The subtropical climate may be warm, but Brisbane is decidedly cool. The population has doubled in the last two decades, and as a result, Brisbane has been busily reinventing itself. There's a lively young arts scene and the city has been ranked among the hottest places in the world for new music. Its young fashion designers are making a name for themselves, and the Gallery of Modern Art is bringing blockbuster exhibitions down under. But while the CBD skyline may be spiked by glittering high-rise buildings, and the river lined with big boats, thankfully, the city has lost little of its friendliness in the make-over. Life is as relaxed as ever, and firmly focused on the outdoors.

Brisbane's hilly terrain provides breathing space and a beautiful backdrop to the CBD. Step into the nearby suburbs and you'll find stately Moreton Bay fig trees standing sentinel in the suburban streets and mango trees blooming in the backyards of those distinctive weatherboard houses on stilts known as 'Queenslanders'. With their shady verandahs and tin roofs just made for the patter of summer rain, you can still find them within walking distance of the CBD.

From the coast to the suburbs, the year-round warm climate means that Brisbane is tops for a holiday – whether you want city parks or national parks, markets or museums, nightlife or wildlife, you'll find it's all here.

Brisbane's Top Ten

ANZAC Square
A grassy public square that houses the Shrine of Remembrance and a pedestrian tunnel which doubles as the World War II Shrine of Memories.

Brisbane River
A boat trip on the Brisbane River is a must. Plenty of tours are available to riverside attractions and there is an excellent commuter ferry and catamaran service.

City Botanic Gardens
Established in 1855 in the heart of the city, Queensland's oldest public gardens are known for both their natural and historic heritage.

Commissariat Stores
Built by convicts in 1829, one of Brisbane's oldest buildings is now home to the offices, library and museum of the Royal Historical Society of Queensland.

Customs House
Built in 1889, this magnificent building is now a cultural and educational facility of the University of Queensland.

Newstead House
Built in 1846, this is Brisbane's oldest residence. Beautifully restored, with its spacious verandahs, formal gardens and lawns down to the river, it offers an image of the quintessential Australian homestead.

Parliament House
This French Renaissance style building, constructed in 1868, is still home to the Queensland parliament; tours run on demand except when parliament is sitting.

St Johns Cathedral and Chapel
A striking example of Gothic Revival architecture that was built in three stages beginning in 1906 and completed a century later.

Shrine of Remembrance with eternal flame, ANZAC Square

South Bank Cultural Precinct

This riverfront site is home to the Queensland Cultural Centre, the Queensland Performing Arts Centre and museum, the Queensland Museum, Queensland Art Gallery, the Gallery of Modern Art and the State Library.

Story Bridge

The city's best-known landmark and the largest steel cantilever bridge in Australia. For a unique adventure and amazing 360-degree views, try a bridge climb.

Visitor information

Brisbane Visitor Information Centre
Cnr Albert and Queen sts
Queen Street Mall
(07) 3006 6290
www.visitbrisbane.com.au

South Bank Visitor Centre
South Bank House
Stanley Street Plaza
(07) 3867 2051

Redlands Tourism Information
Centre
Shop 2, Raby Bay Harbour
152 Shore St West, Cleveland
(07) 3821 2730
1300 667 386

Wynnum Manly Tourism and
Visitor Centre
42A Cambridge Pde, Manly
(07) 3348 3524

Redcliffe Visitor Information Centre
111 Hornibrook Espl, Clontarf
(07) 3284 3500
1800 659 500

Motoring organisation
RACQ 13 1905, roadside assistance
13 1111

Getting around

Brisbane has well-signed roads and little traffic congestion, yet it is not an easy city for the first-time visitor to negotiate. There is a crisscrossing network of major motorways and a number of one-way streets. Brisbane's best through-routes are all multilane motorways with staffed tollgates.

The Gateway Motorway also provides excellent access to Brisbane Airport. The transport system (bus, rail, catamaran and ferry) is efficient, with a couple of excellent bus routes specifically for tourists. A boat trip on the Brisbane River is a must, and there is a very good commuter ferry and catamaran (CityCat) service that stops at key destinations around the city.

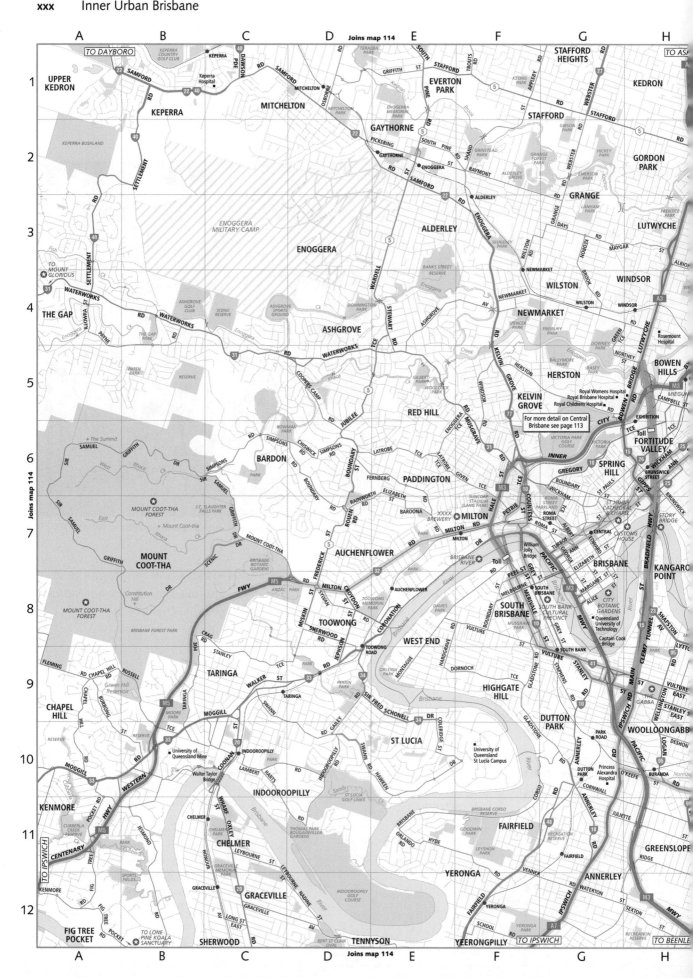

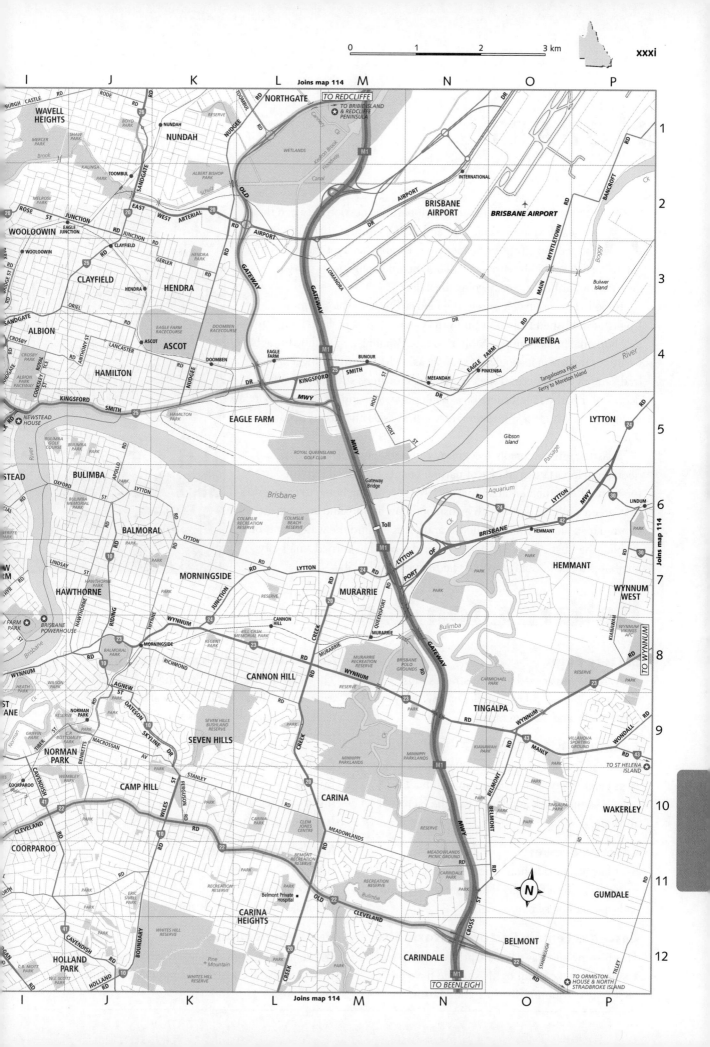

HOBART

At the southern tip of Australia, Hobart lies nestled between the slopes of Mount Wellington and the Derwent estuary. It was the second city after Sydney to be established, yet today it is the smallest of the capitals with just 214000 people enjoying its glorious location and unhurried, easy-going lifestyle.

Impelled to set up colonies in the face of French exploration, the English established Hobart at Sullivans Cove in 1804 on land known to its Aboriginal inhabitants as Nibberloonne. Whaling and sealing brought wealth to the town, its dockside soon awash with taverns doing a brisk trade among seafarers and traders. Hobart's fortunes still centre on its deep-water harbour, but these days fishing trawlers and freighters moor alongside tourist ferries, Antarctic research vessels and luxury ocean liners.

Boasting internationally recognised temperate wilderness on its doorstep, Hobart's abundance of natural beauty propelled it to the forefront of environmental politics in 1972, becoming home to the world's first 'green' political party. With a cosmopolitan literary and arts culture centred on a handful of hip galleries and cafes around the waterfront, but without the hustle-bustle of bigger cities, Hobart has turned small-city attributes to its advantage with its laid-back friendly vibe.

Hobart's Top Ten

Battery Point
This area is considered to be Australia's most complete colonial village with its narrow, hilly streets, corner pubs and quaint cottages.

Cadbury Visitor Centre
While the factory produces the 90 million Freddo frogs eaten every year, visitors can watch a DVD, enjoy a sample pack and indulge in the factory shop and cafe.

Cascade Brewery
Beer has been made here since 1824, making it Australia's oldest brewery. There are several tours daily and samples are included.

Cascades Female Factory Historic Site
This historic site was a female prison for 50 years. Visitors can take a tour of the site and have a 1830s-style 'Morning Tea with the Matron'.

Constitution and Victoria docks
The heart of Sullivans Cove; there are several excellent seafood restaurants nearby, as well as dockside punts offering takeaway fish and chips in paper cones – a Hobart tradition.

Government House
Built in 1857, this Neo-Gothic building is one of the finest vice-regal residences in the Commonwealth. It is open to the public one Sunday each year.

Mount Wellington
Rising 1270 metres above the city's rolling foothills, this is a Hobart icon. The 20-minute drive to the Pinnacle is a must for all visitors.

Parliament House
Originally a customs house designed by John Lee Archer and constructed by convicts in the late 1830s.

Parliament House

Royal Tasmanian Botanical Gardens

These superb botanic gardens, spread over 13.5 hectares in the Queens Domain, were established in 1818.

Salamanca Place

These historic sandstone warehouses are packed with interesting shops and galleries. Hobart's famous Salamanca Market is also held here every Saturday.

Tasmanian Museum and Art Gallery

This historic museum and gallery complex is home to Australia's finest collection of colonial art, as well as fascinating displays on whaling and convict histories, and a collection of Aboriginal artefacts.

Visitor information

Tasmanian Travel and Information Centre
20 Davey St
(03) 6238 4222 or 1800 900 440
www.discovertasmania.com
www.hobarttravelcentre.com.au

Motoring organisation
RACT 13 2722, roadside assistance 13 1111

Getting around

Traffic flows freely throughout Hobart; however, be warned that many of the streets are one way. Metered street parking is readily available and the Council operates several carparks at modest rates. Metro Tasmania operates a bus service that runs frequently during business hours, with a limited evening/weekend timetable. Ferries and cruise boats leave regularly from Franklin Wharf and Brooke Street Pier at Sullivans Cove. During summer, sailing vessels run charter tours as far afield as Port Arthur and Bruny Island. There are also a number of coach tours, including a daily tour of the city and suburbs.

0   1   2 km

Joins map 137

Joins map 137

Joins map 1

Joins map 137

Joins map 1

TO NEW NORFOLK
TO DERWENT VALLEY

CLAREMONT
Claremont College
Claremont Reserve
Claremont Golf Course

CADBURY SCHWEPPES CHOCOLATE FACTORY

Windermere Bay
Knights Point
Windermere Beach
Connewarre Bay
McCarthys Point
Lowestoft Bay

Dogshear Point
Woodville Bay
Restdown Point
PARK

OLD BEACH

B32

Mount Direction

OTAGO

MEEHAN RANGE NATURE RECREATION AREA

GRASSTREE HILL

BERRIEDALE
MOORILLA ESTATE
Eliss Point
Berriedale Reserve
Berriedale Bay
Frying Pan Island

River

Derwent Haven

Wilkinsons Point

Derwent

RISDON

MEEHAN RANGE NATURE RECREATION AREA

Risdon Brook Reservoir

C324
GRASSTREE HILL RD
TO RICHMOND

ROSETTA

MARYS HOPE RD

MAIN HWY
BROOKER
PARK
GOODWOOD RD

Elwick Bay
ELWICK RACECOURSE

DOWSING POINT

B35

Bowen Bridge

EAST RD

Cleburne Point
Risdon Cove
Church Point

B32

DERWENT HWY

RISDON VALE

MONTROSE
Islet Rivulet
PITCAIRN
BRENT

King George V Park
EADY ST
ELWICK RD
TASMANIAN TRANSPORT MUSEUM
Bivulet

GOODWOOD

Dowsings Point

Prince of Wales Bay

Store Point
Porter Point

EAST RISDON NATURE RESERVE

GEILSTON BAY

B32

GLENORCHY
CHAPEL ST
TOLOSA ST
VIESTE ST

Guilford Young College

DERWENT PARK
DERWENT PARK RD
GORMANSTON RD
MAIN RD

LUTANA

NEW TOWN BAY GOLF COURSE
Stanhope Point
Shag Bay Point
Woodman Point
Rock Cod Point

Shag Bay

Bedlam Walls Point

GEILSTON BAY PARK

Geilston

NATONE HILL

LINDISFARNE

CLYDESDALE AV
FOURTH AV
SPRINGFIELD AV
BARROSSA RD
DEVINES RD
TOLOSA
Lower Glenorchy Reservoir
CHAPEL

MOONAH
HOPKINS ST
ALBERT RD
CENTRAL AV
BENJAFIELD RD
DR TENTH AV

WEST MOONAH
PARK

ASHBOLT ST
BOWEN RD
RISDON RD
SELFS POINT RD

New Town Bay
Selfs Point

Limekiln Point
Koomela Bay
Beltana Point
Beauty Bay
Lindisfarne Point
Lindisfarne Bay
ANZAC PARK

KALANG
Barrossa
WELLINGTON PARK
LENAH VALLEY RD
AUGUSTA RD
JOHN TURNBULL PARK
NEW TOWN OVAL
TOWER RD
NEW TOWN RD

NEW TOWN
RUNNYMEDE

FORSTER ST
GIBLIN ST
Sacred Heart College
CLARE ST
CLARE STREET OVAL
Calvary Hospital
DOYLE
MONTAGU
AUGUSTA

River

Rugby Park
GAS RD
Cornelian Bay Point
Cornelian Bay

ROSE BAY
Rose Bay

DOMAIN
B36

QUEENS DOMAIN

Pavilion Point
TASMAN HWY
A3
Tasman Bridge

MONTAGU BAY
TO AIRPORT

ROSE BAY

LENAH VALLEY
VALLEY
LENAH
POTTERY RD
Brushy
Pottery

MOUNT STUART

NORTH HOBART
NORTH HOBART OVAL
ARGYLE ST
BROOKER HWY

ROYAL TASMANIAN BOTANICAL GARDENS
QUEENS DOMAIN
Government House

GLEBE

Ross Bay

TASMAN HWY
A3

For more detail on Central Hobart see page 136

Macquarie Point
Rosny Point

ROSNY

WELLINGTON PARK
MAIN RD
FIRE TRAIL

Knocklofty
Knocklofty
Gully

WEST HOBART

ELIZABETH ST
BURNETT ST
MURRAY ST
HARRINGTON ST
ARTHUR ST
HILL ST
WARWICK ST
Elizabeth College
St Marys College
Guilford Young College
St Helens Hospital
MOLLE ST

GLEBE AV

HOBART
CAMPBELL ST
BATHURST ST
COLLINS ST
Royal Hobart Hospital
TASMANIAN MUSEUM & ART GALLERY
A6
VICTORIA & CONSTITUTION DOCKS

DOMAIN HWY
TASMAN HWY

Derwent

Ferry

SOUTH HOBART
Rivulet

TO MOUNT WELLINGTON, CASCADES FEMALE FATORY HISTORIC SITE & CASCADE BREWERY

TO HUONVILLE

B64

TO KINGSTON

MACQUARIE ST
DAVEY ST
University of Tas Conservatorium of Music
B68

SALAMANCA PLACE
PRINCES PARK
Battery Point
Sullivans Cove

BATTERY POINT

Joins map 1

Joins map 137

0   1   2 km

Joins map xxxiv

A   B   C   D   E   F   G   H

TO GAGEBROOK

B32

RISDON VALE

SUGARLOAF

Sugarloaf Hill

RISDON

DERWENT PARK

Store Point

Porter Point

EAST RISDON NATURE RESERVE

Tommys Bight

GEILSTON BAY

Faggs PARK

CAMBRIDGE

LUTANA

Stanhope Point

Shag Bay Point   Shag Bay

Woodman Point

GEILSTON BAY PARK

MEEHAN RANGE NATURE RECREATION AREA

NEW TOWN BAY GOLF COURSE

Rock Cod Point

Bedlam Walls Point

NATONE HILL

Flagstaff Gully Reservoir

PARK

Joins map xxxiv

New Town Bay

NEW TOWN

Selfs Point

Limekiln Point

Koomela Bay

LINDISFARNE

FLAGSTAFF GULLY

MEEHAN RANGE NATURE RECREATION AREA

Rugby Park

GAS

Cornelian Bay Point

Beltana Point

ANZAC PARK

Beauty Bay

GORDONS HILL

WARRANE

Cornelian Bay

Lindisfarne Point

Shore Street Point

B32

PARK

TASMAN

A3

TO RICHMOND

DOMAIN

QUEENS DOMAIN

B36

Rose Bay

ROSE BAY

Warrane Recreation Reserve

LINK

CAMBRIDGE

B33

TO AIRPORT

BROOKER

NORTH HOBART OVAL

Pavilion Point

EAST DERWENT

GORDONS HILL NATURE RECREATION AREA

CAMBRIDGE

Mackillop College

ARGYLE

ROYAL TASMANIAN BOTANICAL GARDENS

Montagu Point

HWY

ROSNY PARK GOLF COURSE

PARK

MORNINGTON

NORTH HOBART

SOUNDY PARK

GOVERNMENT HOUSE

Montagu Bay

MONTAGU BAY

KELLIATE

ROSNY HILL

ROSNY PARK

Mornington Reservoir

SOUTH ARM

QUEENS DOMAIN

Queens Domain

ROSNY HILL NATURE RECREATION AREA

Rosny College

WAVERLEY FLORA PARK

KNOPWOOD HILL NATURE RECREATION AREA

GLEBE

Ross Bay

BASTICK

ORMOND

WAVERLEY

ELIZABETH

BURNETT

CAMPBELL

HOBART

ROSNY

Sheoak Point

CAMBRIDGE

BELLERIVE

Joins map 137

MURRAY

WARWICK

Elizabeth College

Macquarie Point

Rosny Point

CLARENCE

ST

St Marys College

BATHURST

Royal Hobart Hospital

Bellerive Oval

MORNINGTON PARK

CLARENCE

HARRINGTON

COLLINS

A6

TASMANIAN MUSEUM & ART GALLERY

South St

Bellerive Beach

WENTWORTH PARK

WEST HOBART

St Helens Hospital

VICTORIA & CONSTITUTION DOCKS

Sullivans Cove

Ferry

KANGAROO BLUFF HISTORIC SITE

Second Bluff

Howrah Beach

University of Tasmania Conservatorium of Music

SALAMANCA PLACE

PRINCES PARK

Battery Point

For more detail on Central Hobart see page 136

Kangaroo Bluff

Howrah Point

B33

ROKEBY RD

TO HUONVILLE

MACQUARIE

DAVEY

B68

BATTERY POINT

Sandy Bay

Little Howrah Beach

HOWRAH

A6

FITZROY GARDENS

REGENT

Short Beach

HOWRAH

TRANMERE

KING ST

SANDY BAY

University of Tasmania Teaching & Learning

Mt Carmel College

Proctors Ck

University of Tasmania Sandy Bay Campus

Christ College

University of Tasmania Hytten Hall

WREST POINT CASINO

Wrest Point

DYNNYRNE

University of Tasmania Horticulture

Lords Beach

B68

Joins map 137

Red Chapel Beach

Nutgrove Beach

LONG BEACH RESERVE

NELSON

SANDY BAY

AV

CHURCHILL

Sandy Bay Point

Long Beach

Little Sandy Bay

OLINDA GV

MT NELSON

SIGNAL STATION

SKYLINE RESERVE

ALEXANDRA BATTERY PARK

Blinking Billy Point

Blinking Billy Beach

Derwent

C643

MOUNT NELSON

RESERVE

Mount Nelson

CHURCHILL

SANDY BAY

TRUGANINI CONSERVATION AREA

TO KINGSTON

B68

TO D'ENTRECASTEAUX CHANNEL

Tranmere Point

TRANMERE

N

1 2 3 4 5 6 7 8 9 10 11 12

OVERVIEW MAP & MAP SYMBOLS

Inter-City Route Maps

The inter-city route maps and distance charts will help you plan your route between major cities. As well, you can use the maps during your journey, since they provide information on distances between towns along the route, roadside rest areas and road conditions. The table below provides an overview of the routes mapped. The inter-city route maps can be found on pages 6–8.

INTER CITY ROUTES	DISTANCE	TIME
Sydney–Melbourne via Hume Hwy/Fwy	879 km	12 hrs
Sydney–Melbourne via Princes Hwy/Fwy	1039 km	15 hrs
Sydney–Brisbane via New England Hwy	995 km	14 hrs
Melbourne–Adelaide via Western & Dukes hwys	729 km	8 hrs
Melbourne–Adelaide via Princes Hwy	911 km	11 hrs
Melbourne–Brisbane via Newell Hwy	1676 km	20 hrs
Darwin–Adelaide via Stuart Hwy	3026 km	31 hrs
Adelaide–Perth via Eyre & Great Eastern hwys	2700 km	32 hrs
Adelaide–Sydney via Sturt & Hume hwys	1415 km	19 hrs
Perth–Darwin via Great Northern Hwy	4032 km	46 hrs
Sydney–Brisbane via Pacific Hwy	936 km	14 hrs
Brisbane–Darwin via Warrego Hwy	3406 km	39 hrs
Brisbane–Cairns via Bruce Hwy	1703 km	20 hrs
Hobart–Launceston via Midland Hwy	197 km	3 hrs
Hobart–Devonport via Midland & Bass hwys	279 km	4 hrs

Legend

	Freeway, with toll
M31 31	Highway, sealed, with National Highway Route Marker
A1 1	Highway, sealed, with National Route Marker
5	Highway, sealed, with Metroad Route Marker
	Highway, unsealed
C141 26	Main road, sealed, with State Route Marker
	Main road, unsealed
	Connector road, on central city maps only
→	Other road, with traffic direction, on central city maps only
	Other road, sealed
	Other road, unsealed
	Vehicle track
	Walking track
	Mall, on central city maps only
	Railway, with station
	Underground railway, with station
▼ 114	Total kilometres between two points
▼ 45	Intermediate kilometres
	State border
	Fruit fly exclusion zone boundary
	River, with waterfall
	Lake, reservoir
	Intermittent lake
	Coastline, with reefs and rocks

SYDNEY ○	State capital city
GEELONG ○	Major city / town
Deniliquin ○	Town
Caldwell ○	Other population centres / localities
Rorruwuy ○	Aboriginal community
Karoonda Roadhouse ▣	Roadhouse
Nullagong ▢	Pastoral station homestead
ESSENDON	Suburb, on suburbs maps only
Unley	Suburb, on central city maps only
THE TWELVE APOSTLES ⊕	Place of interest
✈	Airport
✛	Landing ground
★	Lighthouse
+	Hill, mountain, peak
•	Gorge, gap, pass, cave or saddle
•	Waterhole
⚒	Mine site
	National park
	Other reserve
	Aboriginal / Torres Strait Islander land
	Other named area
	Prohibited area

Maps are in a Lamberts Conformal Conic Projection
Geocentric Datum Australia, 1994 (GDA94)

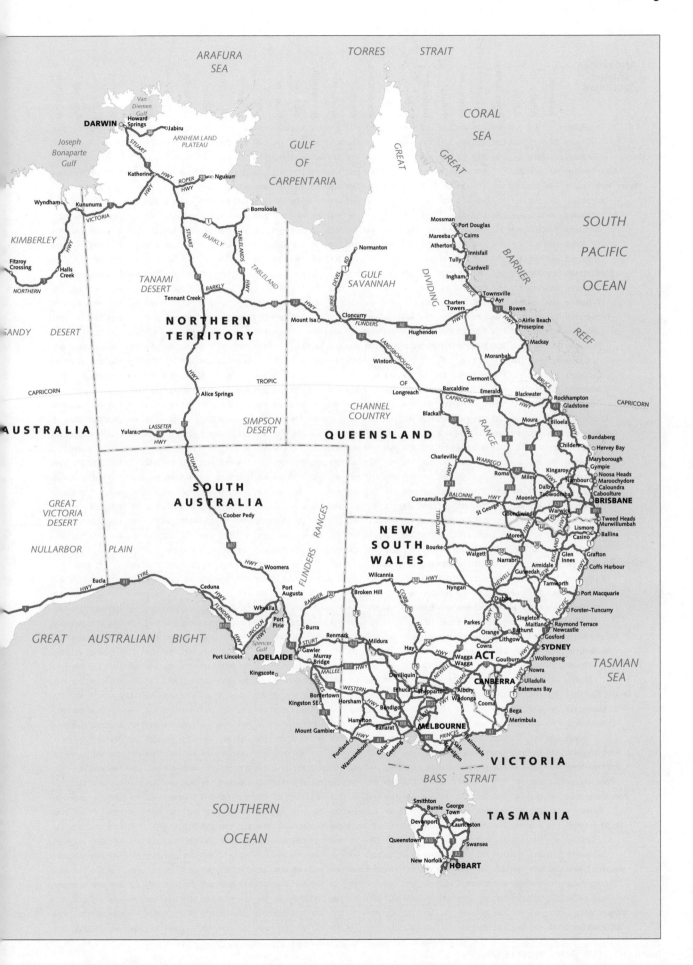

Approximate Distances AUSTRALIA	Adelaide	Albany	Albury	Alice Springs	Ayers Rock/Yulara	Bairnsdale	Ballarat	Bathurst	Bega	Bendigo	Bordertown	Bourke	Brisbane	Broken Hill	Broome	Bunbury	Cairns	Canberra	Carnarvon	Ceduna	Charleville	Coober Pedy	Darwin	Dubbo	Esperance	Eucla	Geelong	Geraldton
Adelaide		2662	965	1537	1578	1010	625	1198	1338	640	274	1129	2048	514	4268	2887	3207	1197	3568	772	1582	847	3026	1194	2183	1267	711	3086
Albany	2662		3487	3585	3626	3672	3287	3720	4000	3302	2936	3388	4310	2773	2626	335	5466	3719	1300	1890	3841	2895	4428	3526	479	1395	3373	818
Albury	965	3487		2362	2403	336	412	466	427	313	679	779	1407	865	5093	3712	2764	348	4393	1597	1232	1672	3851	553	3008	2092	382	3911
Alice Springs	1537	3585	2362		443	2547	2162	2595	2875	2177	1811	2263	2979	1648	2731	3810	2376	2594	4114	1695	2320	690	1489	2401	3106	2190	2248	4009
Ayers Rock/Yulara	1578	3626	2403	443		2588	2203	2636	2916	2218	1852	2304	3226	1689	3174	3851	2819	2635	4532	1736	2763	731	1932	2442	3147	2231	2289	4050
Bairnsdale	1010	3672	336	2547	2588		388	802	328	423	736	1115	1743	1119	5278	3897	3100	455	4578	1782	1568	1857	4036	863	3193	2277	349	4096
Ballarat	625	3287	412	2162	2203	388		878	716	124	351	996	1747	754	4893	3512	3104	760	4193	1397	1449	1472	3651	893	2808	1892	86	3711
Bathurst	1198	3720	466	2595	2636	802	878		531	779	1180	569	1000	958	5011	3945	2416	309	4626	1830	1022	1905	3769	205	3241	2325	848	4144
Bega	1338	4000	427	2875	2916	328	716	531		751	1064	994	1399	1447	5436	4225	2910	222	4906	2110	1447	2185	4364	630	3521	2605	677	4424
Bendigo	640	3302	313	2177	2218	423	124	779	751		366	872	1623	696	4908	3527	2980	661	4208	1412	1325	1487	3666	769	2823	1907	210	3726
Bordertown	274	2936	679	1811	1852	736	351	1180	1064	366		1138	1922	788	4542	3161	3257	1071	3842	1046	1591	1121	3300	1068	2457	1541	437	3360
Bourke	1129	3388	779	2263	2304	1115	996	569	994	872	1138		922	615	4442	3613	2078	772	4294	1498	453	1573	3200	364	2909	1993	1082	3812
Brisbane	2048	4310	1407	2979	3226	1743	1747	1000	1399	1623	1922	922		1537	4648	4535	1703	1241	5216	2420	742	2495	3406	854	3831	2915	1745	4734
Broken Hill	514	2773	865	1648	1689	1119	754	958	1447	696	788	615	1537		4379	2998	2693	1097	3679	883	1068	958	3137	753	2294	1378	840	3197
Broome	4268	2626	5093	2731	3174	5278	4893	5011	5436	4908	4542	4442	4648	4379		2417	4045	5214	1451	3750	3989	3421	1870	4806	2745	3255	4979	1921
Bunbury	2887	335	3712	3810	3851	3897	3512	3945	4225	3527	3161	3613	4535	2998	2417		5691	3944	1091	2115	4066	3120	4219	3751	664	1620	3598	609
Cairns	3207	5466	2764	2376	2819	3100	3104	2416	2910	2980	3257	2078	1703	2693	4045	5691		2619	5428	3576	1625	3066	2803	2211	4987	4071	3102	5890
Canberra	1197	3719	348	2594	2635	455	760	309	222	661	1071	772	1241	1097	5214	3944	2619		4625	1829	1225	1904	3972	408	3240	2324	730	4143
Carnarvon	3568	1300	4393	4114	4532	4578	4193	4626	4906	4208	3842	4294	5216	3679	1451	1091	5428	4625		2796	4747	3801	3253	4432	1628	2301	4279	482
Ceduna	772	1890	1597	1695	1736	1782	1397	1830	2110	1412	1046	1498	2420	883	3750	2115	3576	1829	2796		1951	1005	3184	1636	1411	495	1483	2314
Charleville	1582	3841	1232	2320	2763	1568	1449	1022	1447	1325	1591	453	742	1068	3989	4066	1625	1225	4747	1951		2026	2747	817	3362	2446	1500	4265
Coober Pedy	847	2895	1672	690	731	1857	1472	1905	2185	1487	1121	1573	2495	958	3421	3120	3066	1904	3801	1005	2026		2179	1711	2416	1500	1558	3319
Darwin	3026	4428	3851	1489	1932	4036	3651	3769	4364	3666	3300	3200	3406	3137	1870	4219	2803	3972	3253	3184	2747	2179		3564	4547	3679	3737	3723
Dubbo	1194	3526	553	2401	2442	863	893	205	630	769	1068	364	854	753	4806	3751	2211	408	4432	1636	817	1711	3564		3047	2131	891	3950
Esperance	2183	479	3008	3106	3147	3193	2808	3241	3521	2823	2457	2909	3831	2294	2745	664	4987	3240	1628	1411	3362	2416	4547	3047		916	2894	1160
Eucla	1267	1395	2092	2190	2231	2277	1892	2325	2605	1907	1541	1993	2915	1378	3255	1620	4071	2324	2301	495	2446	1500	3679	2131	916		1978	1819
Geelong	711	3373	382	2248	2289	349	86	848	677	210	437	1082	1745	840	4979	3598	3102	730	4279	1483	1500	1558	3737	891	2894	1978		3797
Geraldton	3086	818	3911	4009	4050	4096	3711	4144	4424	3726	3360	3812	4734	3197	1921	609	5890	4143	482	2314	4265	3319	3723	3950	1160	1819	3797	
Grafton	1845	4177	1184	3052	3093	1397	1544	825	1069	1420	1719	808	330	1404	4975	4402	2033	911	5083	2287	1069	2362	3733	651	3698	2782	1542	4601
Horsham	433	3095	531	1970	2011	577	192	997	905	218	159	1067	1841	599	4701	3320	3145	879	4001	1205	1520	1280	3459	987	2616	1700	278	3519
Kalgoorlie–Boulder	2184	886	3009	3107	3148	3194	2809	3242	3522	2824	2458	2910	3832	2295	2338	779	4988	3241	1460	1412	3363	2417	4140	3048	407	917	2895	978
Katherine	2712	4114	3537	1175	1618	3722	3337	3455	3880	3352	2986	2886	3092	2823	1556	3905	2489	3658	2939	2870	2433	1865	314	3250	4233	3365	3423	3409
Kununurra	3224	3602	4049	1687	2130	4234	3849	3967	4392	3864	3498	3398	3604	3335	1044	3393	3001	4170	2427	3382	2945	2377	826	3762	3721	3877	3935	2897
Longreach	2098	4357	1748	1804	2247	2084	1965	1538	1963	1841	2107	969	1175	1584	3473	4582	1109	1741	4856	2467	516	2494	2231	1333	3878	2962	2016	4781
Mackay	2670	4932	2029	2451	2894	2365	2369	1681	2106	2245	2544	1544	968	2159	4120	5157	735	1884	5503	3042	1091	3141	2878	1476	4453	3537	2367	5356
Meekatharra	3055	1159	3880	3978	4019	4065	3680	4113	4393	3695	3329	3781	4703	3166	1467	950	5444	4112	627	2283	4234	3288	3269	3919	1278	1788	3766	541
Melbourne	733	3395	313	2270	2311	277	111	779	605	146	459	978	1676	842	5001	3620	3033	661	4301	1505	1431	1580	3759	822	2916	2000	72	3819
Mildura	394	2916	571	1791	1832	825	460	804	956	402	417	870	1654	294	4522	3141	2948	803	3822	1026	1323	1101	3280	800	2437	1521	546	3340
Moree	1567	3829	926	2704	2745	1262	1294	578	1003	1141	1482	441	481	1056	4608	4054	1838	781	4735	1939	702	2014	3366	373	3350	2434	1264	4253
Mount Gambier	452	3114	721	1989	2030	697	309	1187	1025	433	186	1324	2098	856	4720	3339	3402	1069	4020	1224	1777	1299	3478	1244	2635	1719	365	3538
Mount Isa	2706	4754	2383	1169	1612	2719	2600	2173	2598	2476	2742	1604	1810	2219	2838	4979	1207	2736	4221	2864	1151	1859	1596	1968	4275	3359	2651	4691
Newcastle	1553	3930	704	2805	2846	917	1116	338	589	1017	1427	768	821	1157	5111	4155	2341	431	4836	2040	1205	2115	3869	404	3451	2535	1086	4354
Perth	2700	410	3525	3623	3664	3710	3325	3758	4038	3340	2974	3426	4348	2811	2230	187	5504	3757	904	1928	3879	2933	4032	3564	738	1433	3411	422
Port Augusta	307	2355	1132	1230	1271	1317	932	1365	1645	947	581	1033	1955	418	3961	2580	3111	1364	3261	465	1486	540	2719	1171	1876	960	1018	2779
Port Hedland	3921	2025	4746	3264	3707	5100	4546	4979	5259	4561	4195	4647	5181	4032	601	1816	4578	4978	850	3149	4522	3954	2403	4785	2144	2654	4632	1320
Port Lincoln	647	2289	1472	1570	1611	1657	1272	1705	1985	1287	921	1373	2295	758	4149	2514	3451	1704	3195	399	1826	880	3059	1511	1751	894	1358	2713
Port Macquarie	1804	4136	942	3011	3052	1155	1354	565	827	1255	1665	859	584	1363	5150	4361	2287	669	5042	2246	1244	2321	3908	610	3657	2741	1324	4560
Renmark	250	2772	715	1647	1688	969	604	948	1100	546	269	1014	1798	438	4378	2997	3092	947	3678	882	1467	957	3136	944	2293	1377	690	3196
Rockhampton	2336	4598	1695	2486	2929	2031	2035	1347	1772	1911	2210	1210	634	1825	4155	4823	1069	1550	5504	2708	831	3176	2913	1142	4119	3203	2033	5022
Sydney	1414	3936	565	2811	2852	759	977	211	431	878	1288	780	966	1169	5222	4161	2479	292	4842	2046	1233	2121	3980	416	3457	2541	947	4360
Tamworth	1534	3866	893	2741	2782	1186	1233	457	858	1109	1408	589	573	1093	4880	4091	2110	700	4772	1965	974	2051	3638	340	3387	2471	1231	4290
Tennant Creek	2043	4091	2868	531	949	3053	2668	2836	3261	2683	2317	2267	2473	2154	2225	4316	1870	3039	3608	2201	1814	1196	983	2631	3612	2696	2754	4078
Toowoomba	1921	4183	1280	2852	3099	1616	1620	956	1357	1496	1795	795	127	1410	4521	4408	1705	1199	5089	2293	615	2368	3279	727	3704	2788	1618	4607
Townsville	2862	5121	2419	2061	2504	2755	2759	2071	2496	2635	2871	1733	1358	2348	3730	5346	345	2274	5113	3231	1280	2751	2488	1866	4642	3726	2757	5545
Wagga Wagga	948	3470	145	2345	2386	481	550	321	402	426	822	711	1262	848	5076	3695	2619	249	4376	1580	1164	1655	3834	408	2991	2075	527	3894
Warrnambool	649	3311	567	2186	2227	534	174	1052	862	298	383	1170	1933	829	4917	3536	3278	987	4217	1421	1623	1496	3675	1067	2832	1916	185	3735

Distances on this chart have been calculated over main roads and do not necessarily reflect the shortest route between towns.
Refer to page 135 for distance chart of Tasmania.

Approximate Distances AUSTRALIA

	Grafton	Horsham	Kalgoorlie–Boulder	Katherine	Kununurra	Longreach	Mackay	Meekatharra	Melbourne	Mildura	Moree	Mount Gambier	Mount Isa	Newcastle	Perth	Port Augusta	Port Hedland	Port Lincoln	Port Macquarie	Renmark	Rockhampton	Sydney	Tamworth	Tennant Creek	Toowoomba	Townsville	Wagga Wagga	Warrnambool
Adelaide	1845	433	2184	2712	3224	2098	2670	3055	733	394	1567	452	2706	1553	2700	307	3921	647	1804	250	2336	1414	1534	2043	1921	2862	948	649
Albany	4177	3095	886	4114	3602	4357	4932	1159	3395	2916	3829	3114	4754	3930	410	2355	2025	2289	4136	2772	4598	3936	3866	4091	4183	5121	3470	3311
Albury	1184	531	3009	3537	4049	1748	2029	3880	313	571	926	721	2383	704	3525	1132	4746	1472	942	715	1695	565	893	2868	1280	2419	145	567
Alice Springs	3052	1970	3107	1175	1687	1804	2451	3978	2270	1791	2704	1989	1169	2805	3623	1230	3264	1570	3011	1647	2486	2811	2741	531	2852	2061	2345	2186
Ayers Rock/Yulara	3093	2011	3148	1618	2130	2247	2894	4019	2311	1832	2745	2030	1612	2846	3664	1271	3707	1611	3052	1688	2929	2852	2782	949	3099	2504	2386	2227
Bairnsdale	1397	577	3194	3722	4234	2084	2365	4065	277	825	1262	697	2719	917	3710	1317	5100	1657	1155	969	2031	759	1186	3053	1616	2755	481	534
Ballarat	1544	192	2809	3337	3849	1965	2369	3680	111	460	1294	309	2600	1116	3325	932	4546	1272	1354	604	2035	977	1233	2668	1620	2759	550	174
Bathurst	825	997	3242	3455	3967	1538	1681	4113	779	804	578	1187	2173	338	3758	1365	4979	1705	565	948	1347	211	457	2836	956	2071	321	1052
Bega	1069	905	3522	3880	4392	1963	2106	4393	605	956	1003	1025	2598	589	4038	1645	5259	1985	827	1100	1772	431	858	3261	1357	2496	402	862
Bendigo	1420	218	2824	3352	3864	1841	2245	3695	146	402	1141	433	2476	1017	3340	947	4561	1287	1255	546	1911	878	1109	2683	1496	2635	426	298
Bordertown	1719	159	2458	2986	3498	2107	2544	3329	459	417	1482	186	2742	1427	2974	581	4195	921	1665	269	2210	1288	1408	2317	1795	2871	822	383
Bourke	808	1067	2910	2886	3398	969	1544	3781	978	870	441	1324	1604	768	3426	1033	4647	1373	859	1014	1210	780	589	2267	795	1733	711	1170
Brisbane	330	1841	3832	3092	3604	1175	968	4703	1676	1654	481	2098	1810	821	4348	1955	5181	2295	584	1798	634	966	573	2473	127	1358	1262	1933
Broken Hill	1404	599	2295	2823	3335	1584	2159	3166	842	294	1056	856	2219	1157	2811	418	4032	758	1363	438	1825	1169	1093	2154	1410	2348	848	829
Broome	4975	4701	2338	1556	1044	3473	4120	1467	5001	4522	4608	4720	2838	5111	2230	3961	601	4149	5150	4378	4155	5222	4880	2225	4521	3730	5076	4917
Bunbury	4402	3320	779	3905	3393	4582	5157	950	3620	3141	4054	3339	4979	4155	187	2580	1816	2514	4361	2997	4823	4161	4091	4316	4408	5346	3695	3536
Cairns	2033	3145	4988	2489	3001	1109	735	5444	3033	2948	1838	3402	1207	2341	5504	3111	4578	3451	2287	3092	1069	2479	2110	1870	1705	345	2619	3278
Canberra	911	879	3241	3658	4170	1741	1884	4112	661	803	781	1069	2736	431	3757	1364	4978	1704	669	947	1550	292	700	3039	1199	2274	249	987
Carnarvon	5083	4001	1460	2939	2427	4856	5503	627	4301	3822	4735	4020	4221	4836	904	3261	850	3195	5042	3678	5504	4842	4772	3608	5089	5113	4376	4217
Ceduna	2287	1205	1412	2870	3382	2467	3042	2283	1505	1026	1939	1224	2864	2040	1928	465	3149	399	2246	882	2708	2046	1965	2201	2293	3231	1580	1421
Charleville	1069	1520	3363	2433	2945	516	1091	4234	1431	1323	702	1777	1151	1205	3879	1486	4522	1826	1244	1467	831	1233	974	1814	615	1280	1164	1623
Coober Pedy	2362	1280	2417	1865	2377	2494	3141	3288	1580	1101	2014	1299	1859	2115	2933	540	3954	880	2321	957	3176	2121	2051	1196	2368	2751	1655	1496
Darwin	3733	3459	4140	314	826	2231	2878	3269	3759	3280	3366	3478	1596	3869	4032	2719	2403	3059	3908	3136	2913	3980	3638	983	3279	2488	3834	3675
Dubbo	651	987	3048	3250	3762	1333	1476	3919	822	800	373	1244	1968	404	3564	1171	4785	1511	610	944	1142	416	340	2631	727	1866	408	1067
Esperance	3698	2616	407	4233	3721	3878	4453	1278	2916	2437	3350	2635	4275	3451	738	1876	2144	1751	3657	2293	4119	3457	3387	3612	3704	4642	2991	2832
Eucla	2782	1700	917	3365	3877	2962	3537	1788	2000	1521	2434	1719	3359	2535	1433	960	2654	894	2741	1377	3203	2541	2471	2696	2788	3726	2075	1916
Geelong	1542	278	2895	3423	3935	2016	2367	3766	72	546	1264	365	2651	1086	3411	1018	4632	1358	1324	690	2033	947	1231	2754	1618	2757	527	185
Geraldton	4601	3519	978	3409	2897	4781	5356	541	3819	3340	4253	3538	4691	4354	422	2779	1320	2713	4560	3196	5022	4360	4290	4078	4607	5545	3894	3735
Grafton		1638	3699	3419	3931	1502	1298	4570	1473	1451	367	1895	2137	491	4215	1822	5436	2162	254	1595	964	638	311	2800	431	1688	1059	1718
Horsham	1638		2451	3145	3657	2036	2463	3322	300	305	1360	257	2671	1235	3133	740	4188	1080	1462	428	2129	1096	1327	2476	1714	2800	644	230
Kalgoorlie–Boulder	3699	2451		3826	3314	3879	4454	871	2917	2438	3351	2636	4276	3452	582	1877	1737	1811	3658	2294	4120	3458	3388	3613	3705	4643	2992	2833
Katherine	3419	3145	3826		512	1917	2564	2955	3445	2966	3052	3164	1282	3556	3718	2405	2089	2745	3594	2822	2599	3666	3324	669	2965	2174	3520	3361
Kununurra	3931	3657	3314	512		2429	3076	2443	3957	3478	3564	3676	1794	4067	3206	2917	1577	3257	4106	3334	3111	4178	3836	1181	3477	2686	4032	3873
Longreach	1502	2036	3879	1917	2429		791	4750	1947	1839	1135	2293	635	1638	4395	2002	4006	2342	1677	1983	682	1749	1407	1298	1048	764	1680	2139
Mackay	1298	2463	4454	2564	3076	791		5325	2298	2276	1103	2720	1282	1606	4970	2577	4653	2917	1552	2420	334	1744	1375	1945	970	390	1884	2543
Meekatharra	4570	3322	871	2955	2443	4750	5325		3788	3309	4222	3507	4237	4323	763	2748	866	2682	4529	3165	5524	4329	4259	3624	4576	5129	3863	3704
Melbourne	1473	300	2917	3445	3957	1947	2298	3788		548	1195	420	2582	1017	3433	1040	4823	1380	1255	692	1964	878	1162	2776	1549	2688	458	257
Mildura	1451	305	2438	2966	3478	1839	2276	3309	548		1173	562	2474	1159	2954	561	4175	901	1397	144	1942	1020	1140	2297	1527	2603	554	535
Moree	367	1360	3351	3052	3564	1135	1103	4222	1195	1173		1627	1770	503	3867	1474	5088	1814	542	1317	769	641	272	2433	354	1493	781	1449
Mount Gambier	1895	257	2636	3164	3676	2293	2720	3507	420	562	1627		2928	1425	3152	759	4373	1099	1663	455	2386	1286	1584	2495	1971	3057	901	197
Mount Isa	2137	2671	4276	1282	1794	635	1282	4237	2582	2474	1770	2928		2273	4792	2399	3371	2739	2312	2618	1317	2384	2042	663	1683	892	2315	2774
Newcastle	491	1235	3452	3556	4067	1638	1606	4323	1017	1159	503	1425	2273		3968	1575	5189	1915	249	1303	1272	158	289	2936	788	1996	605	1271
Perth	4215	3133	582	3718	3206	4395	4970	763	3433	2954	3867	3152	4792	3968		2393	1629	2327	4174	2810	4636	3974	3904	4129	4221	5159	3508	3349
Port Augusta	1822	740	1877	2405	2917	2002	2577	2748	1040	561	1474	759	2399	1575	2393		3614	340	1781	417	2243	1581	1511	1736	1828	2766	1115	956
Port Hedland	5436	4188	1737	2089	1577	4006	4653	866	4823	4175	5088	4373	3371	5189	1629	3614		3548	5395	4031	4688	5195	5125	2758	5054	4263	4729	4570
Port Lincoln	2162	1080	1811	2745	3257	2342	2917	2682	1380	901	1814	1099	2739	1915	2327	340	3548		2121	757	2583	1921	1851	2076	2168	3106	1455	1296
Port Macquarie	254	1462	3658	3594	4106	1677	1552	4529	1255	1397	542	1663	2312	249	4174	1781	5395	2121		1541	1218	396	270	2975	630	1942	843	1509
Renmark	1595	428	2294	2822	3334	1983	2420	3165	692	144	1317	455	2618	1303	2810	417	4031	757	1541		2086	1164	1284	2153	1671	2747	698	652
Rockhampton	964	2129	4120	2599	3111	682	334	5524	1964	1942	769	2386	1317	1272	4636	2243	4688	2583	1218	2086		1410	1041	1980	636	724	1550	2209
Sydney	638	1096	3458	3666	4178	1749	1744	4329	878	1020	641	1286	2384	158	3974	1581	5195	1921	396	1164	1410		427	3047	926	2134	466	1132
Tamworth	311	1327	3388	3324	3836	1407	1375	4259	1162	1140	272	1584	2042	289	3904	1511	5125	1851	270	1284	1041	427		2705	499	1765	748	1407
Tennant Creek	2800	2476	3613	669	1181	1298	1945	3624	2776	2297	2433	2495	663	2936	4129	1736	2758	2076	2975	2153	1980	3047	2705		2346	1555	2851	2692
Toowoomba	431	1714	3705	2965	3477	1048	970	4576	1549	1527	354	1971	1683	788	4221	1828	5054	2168	630	1671	636	926	499	2346		1360	1135	1794
Townsville	1688	2800	4643	2174	2686	764	390	5129	2688	2603	1493	3057	892	1996	5159	2766	4263	3106	1942	2747	724	2134	1765	1555	1360		2274	2933
Wagga Wagga	1059	644	2992	3520	4032	1680	1884	3863	458	554	781	901	2315	605	3508	1115	4729	1455	843	698	1550	466	748	2851	1135	2274		724
Warrnambool	1718	230	2833	3361	3873	2139	2543	3704	257	535	1449	197	2774	1271	3349	956	4570	1296	1509	652	2209	1132	1407	2692	1794	2933	724	

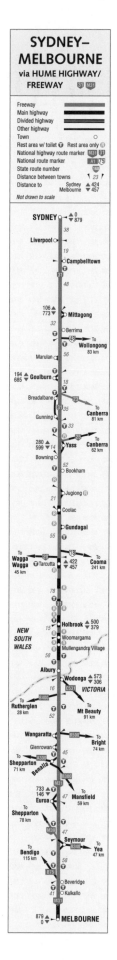

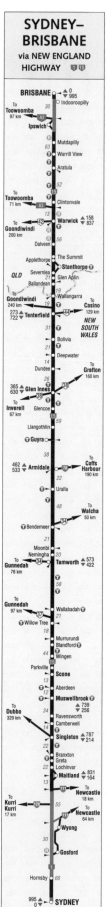

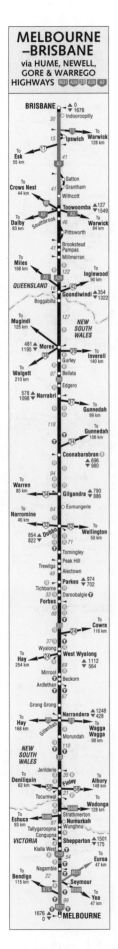

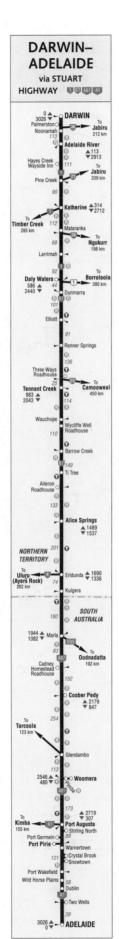

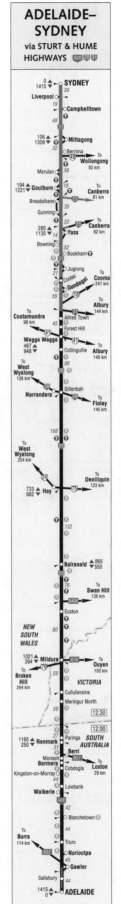

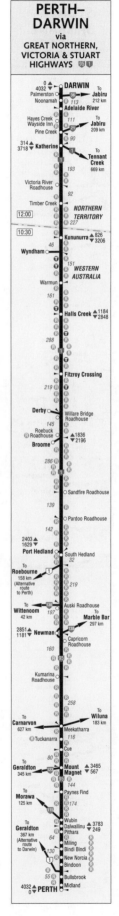

SYDNEY–BRISBANE
via PACIFIC HIGHWAY

BRISBANE–DARWIN
via WARREGO, LANDSBOROUGH, BARKLY & STUART HIGHWAYS

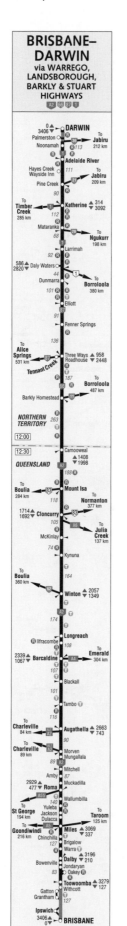

BRISBANE–CAIRNS
via BRUCE HIGHWAY

HOBART–LAUNCESTON
via MIDLAND HIGHWAY

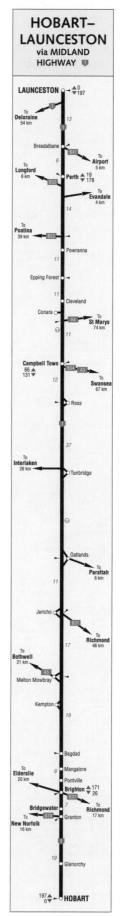

HOBART–DEVONPORT
via MIDLAND & BASS HIGHWAYS

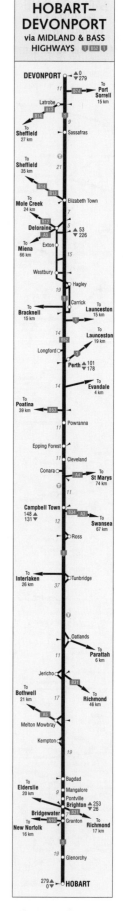

MAPS

NEW SOUTH WALES and AUSTRALIAN CAPITAL TERRITORY

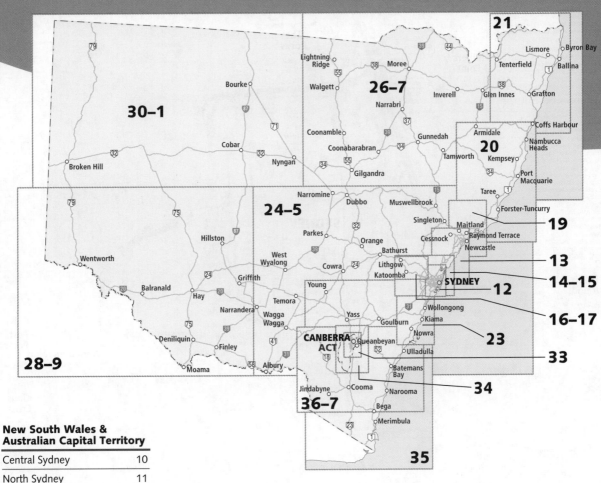

INTER-CITY ROUTES		DISTANCE
Sydney–Melbourne via Hume Hwy/Fwy	31 M31	879 km
Sydney–Melbourne via Princes Hwy/Fwy	1 A1 M1	1039 km
Sydney–Brisbane via New England Hwy	15	995 km
Sydney–Brisbane via Pacific Hwy	1 1 M1	936 km
Sydney–Adelaide via Hume & Sturt hwys	31 20 A20	1415 km

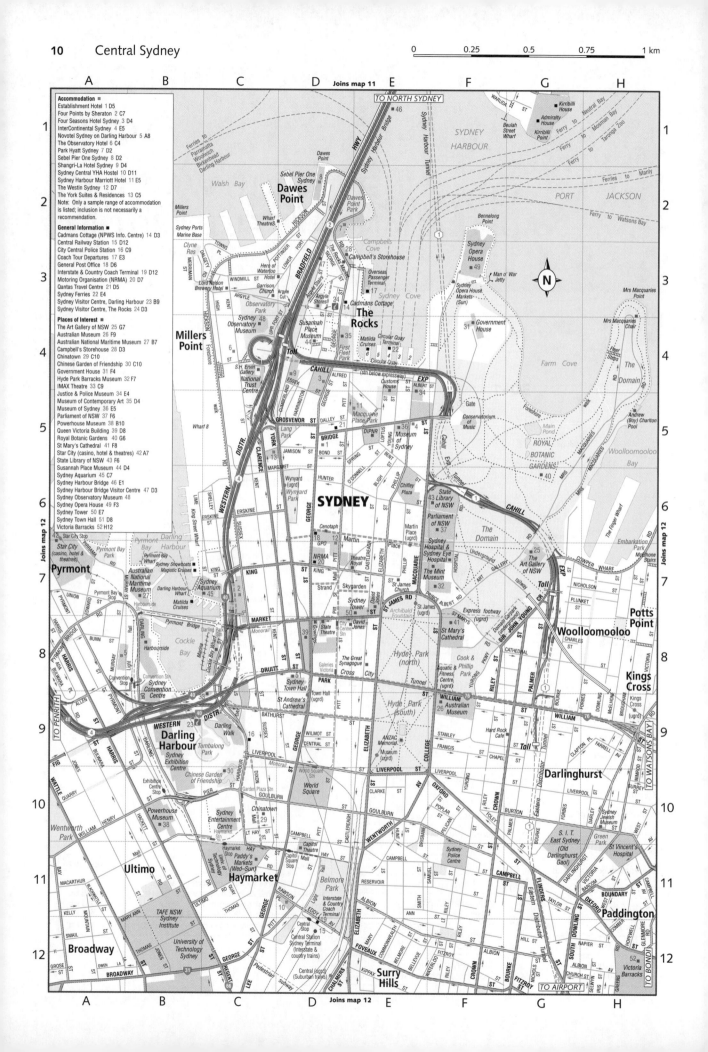

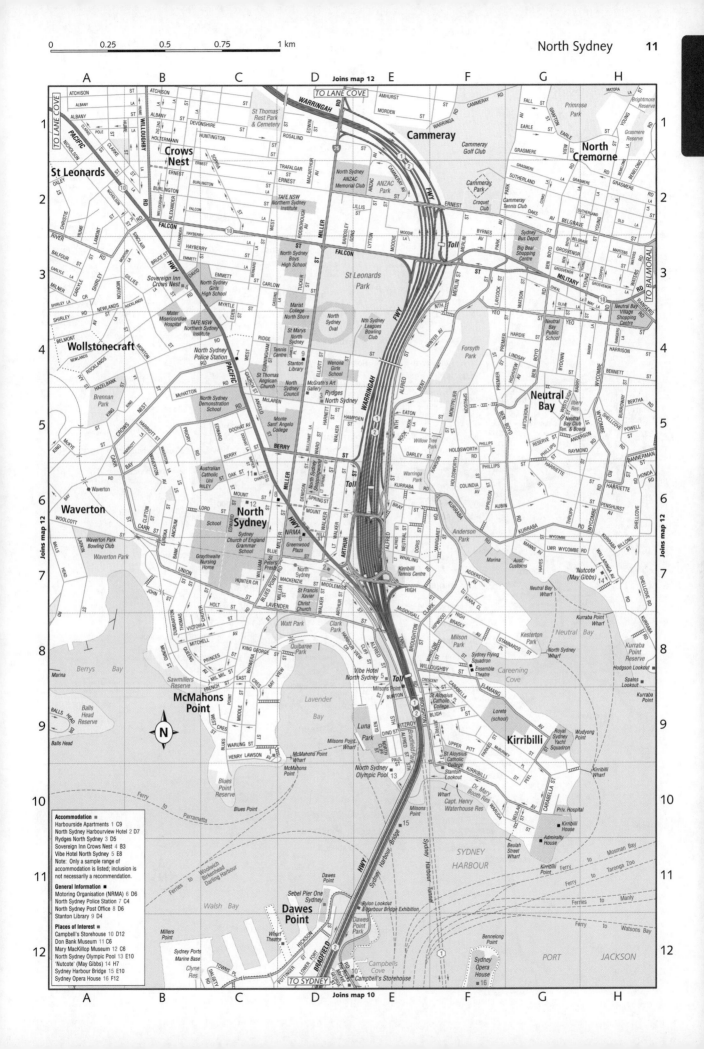

0   0.25   0.5   0.75   1 km

TO LANE COVE
WARRINGAH RD
TO LANE COVE

Cammeray

St Thomas'
Rest Park
& Cemetery

Crows
Nest

North
Cremorne

St Leonards

Primrose
Park

Cammeray
Golf Club

North Sydney
ANZAC
Memorial Club

ANZAC
Park

Cammeray
Park

Cammeray
Tennis Club

TAFE NSW
Northern Sydney
Institute

Sydney
Bus Depot

Big Bear
Shopping
Centre

North Sydney
Boys
High School

FALCON   ST

Sovereign Inn
Crows Nest 4

North Sydney
Girls
High School

St Leonards
Park

MILITARY   RD

TO BALMORAL

Wollstonecraft

Mater
Misericordiae
Hospital

TAFE NSW
Northern Sydney
Institute

North Sydney
Demonstration
School

North Sydney
Police Station 7

North Sydney
Council

Marist
College
North Shore

St Marys
North
Sydney

North
Sydney
Oval

Nth Sydney
Leagues
Bowling Club

Forsyth
Park

Neutral Bay
Village
Shopping
Centre

Brennan
Park

St Thomas
Anglican
Church

Tennis
Centre

Stanton
Library

McGrath's Art
Gallery

Rydges
North Sydney

Wenona
Girls
School

Neutral Bay
Public
School

Neutral
Bay

Monte
Sant' Angelo
College

North Sydney
Shoppingworld

Australian
Catholic
Uni
Riley

BERRY   ST

Warringa
Park

Neutral
Bay Club
Ten. & Bowls

Waverton

North
Sydney

NRMA

Greenwood
Plaza

'Nutcote'
(May Gibbs) 14

Waverton Park
Bowling Club

School

Sydney
Church of England
Grammar School

Kirribilli
Tennis Centre

Neutral Bay
Wharf

Waverton Park

Graythwaite
Nursing Home

St Peters'
Presb.

North
Sydney

Anderson
Park

Kurraba Point
Wharf

Berrys
Bay

Sawmillers
Reserve

St Francis
Xavier
Christ Church

Marina

Aust.
Customs

Kesterton
Park

Neutral   Bay

Kurraba
Point
Reserve

Kurraba
Point

McMahons
Point

Watt Park

Clark
Park

Vibe Hotel
North Sydney

North Sydney
Wharf

Sydney Flying
Squadron

Ensemble
Theatre

Careening
Cove

Hodgson Lookout

Spains
Lookout

Balls
Head
Reserve

Quibaree
Park

Milson
Park

St Aloysius
Catholic
College

Loreto
(school)

Royal
Sydney
Yacht
Squadron

Wudyong
Point

Balls Head

Lavender
Bay

Luna
Park

North Sydney
Olympic Pool 13

St Aloysius
Catholic
College

Kirribilli

Stanton
Lookout

Dr. Mary
Booth Res.

Kirribilli
Wharf

McMahons Point
Wharf

Milsons Point
Wharf

Wharf
Capt. Henry
Waterhouse Res

Priv. Hospital

Kirribilli
House

McMahons
Point

Milsons
Point

Beulah
Street
Wharf

Admiralty
House

Blues
Point
Reserve

Kirribilli
Point

to
Mosman Bay

to
Taronga Zoo

Blues Point

Parramatta

Woolwich/
Birkenhead/
Darling Harbour

SYDNEY
HARBOUR

to
Manly

Ferries to

Walsh Bay

Dawes
Point

Sebel Pier One
Sydney

Dawes
Point Park

PORT

JACKSON

Millers
Point

Bennelong
Point

to
Watsons Bay

Wharf
Theatre

Sydney Ports
Marine Base

Campbells
Cove

Campbell's Storehouse

Sydney
Opera
House 16

Clyne
Res

TO SYDNEY

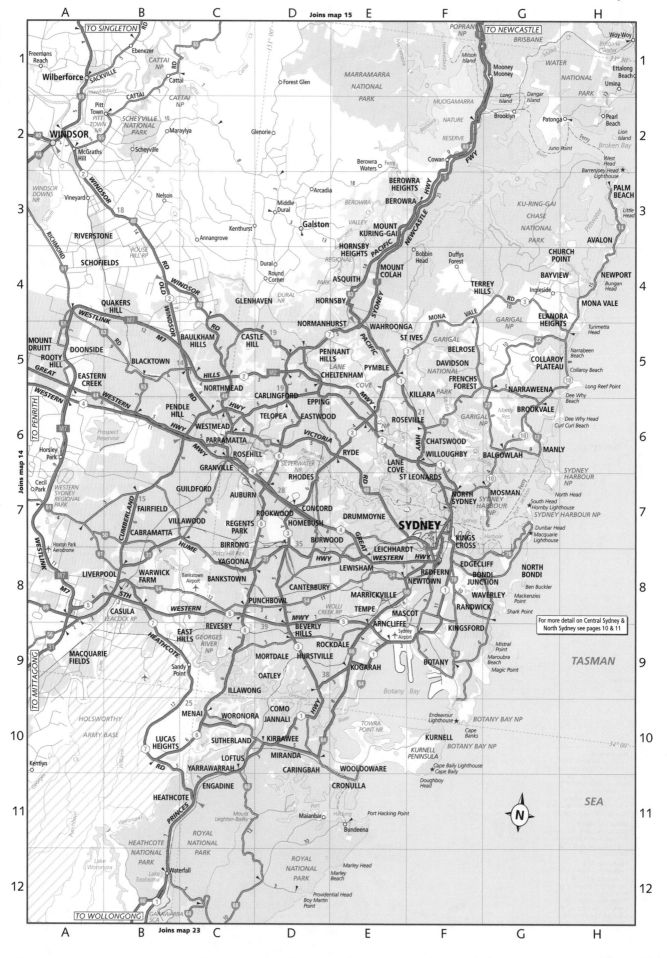

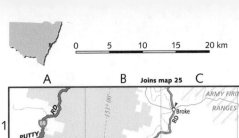

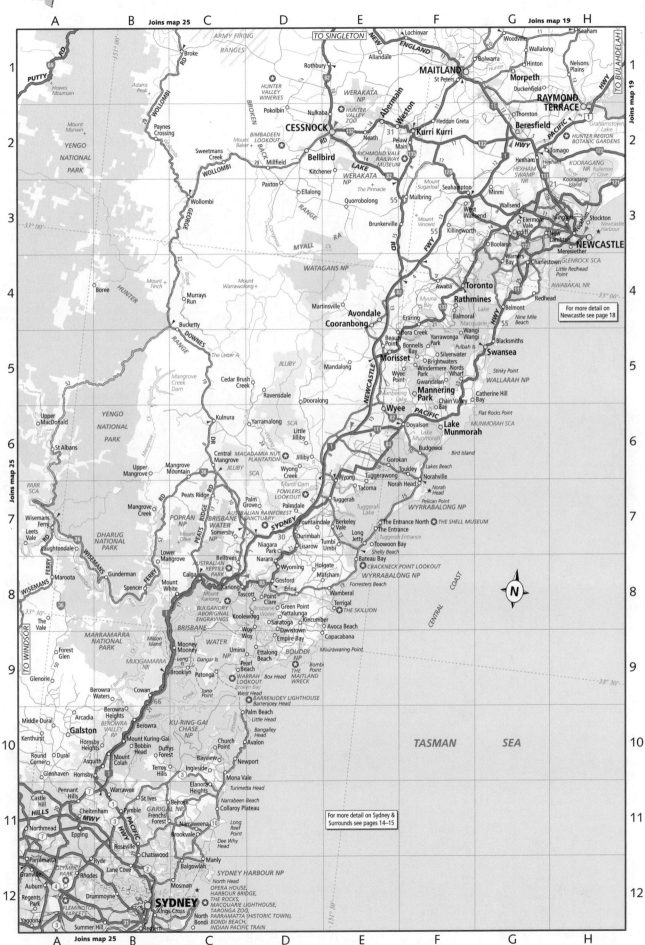

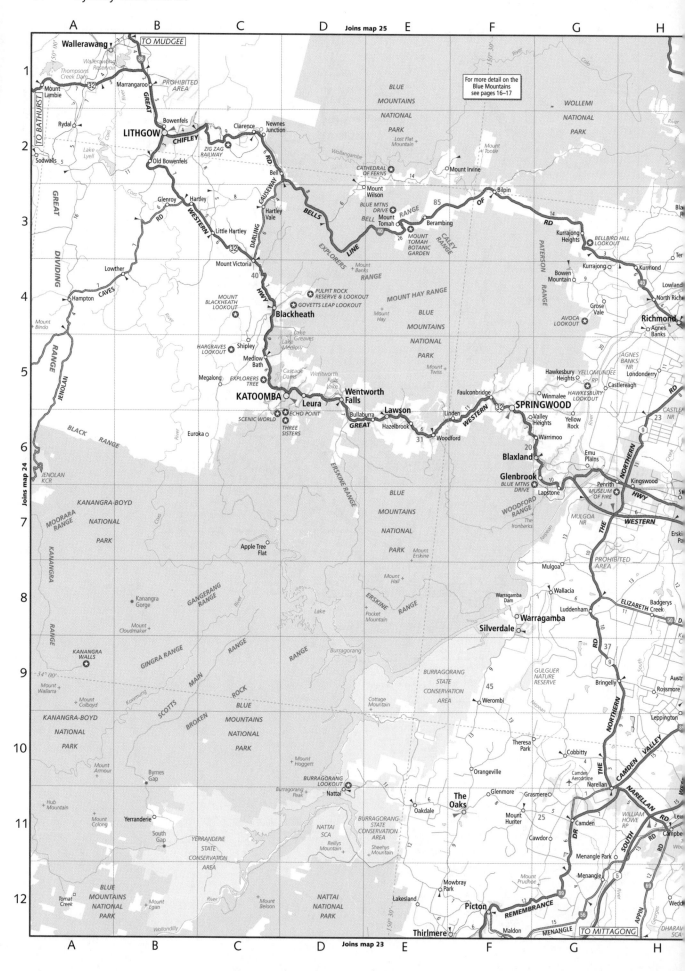

Joins map 25

For more detail on the
Blue Mountains
see pages 16–17

Joins map 24

Joins map 23

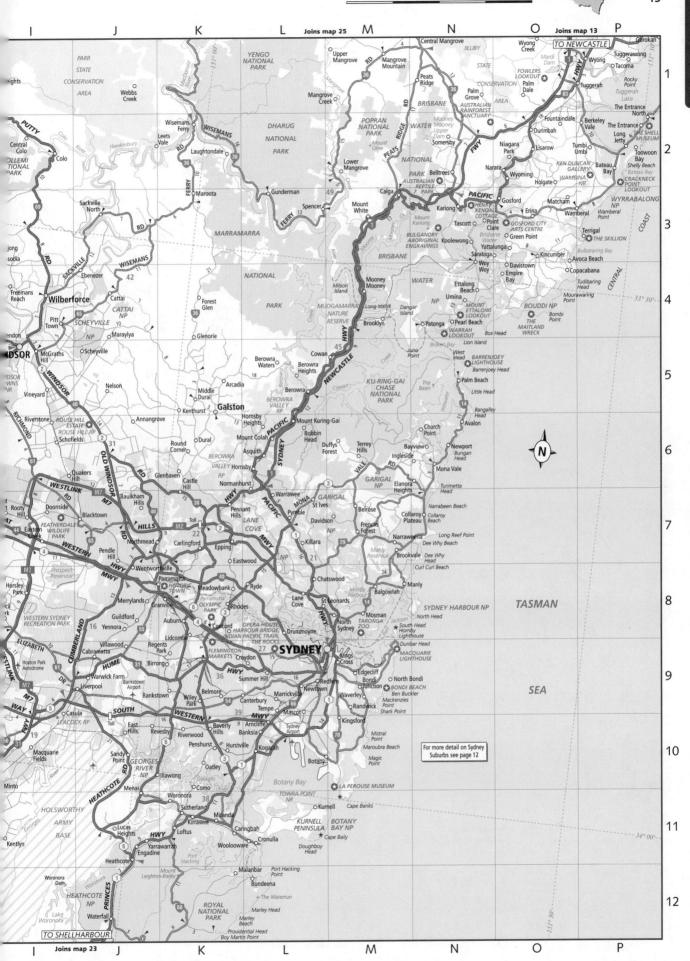

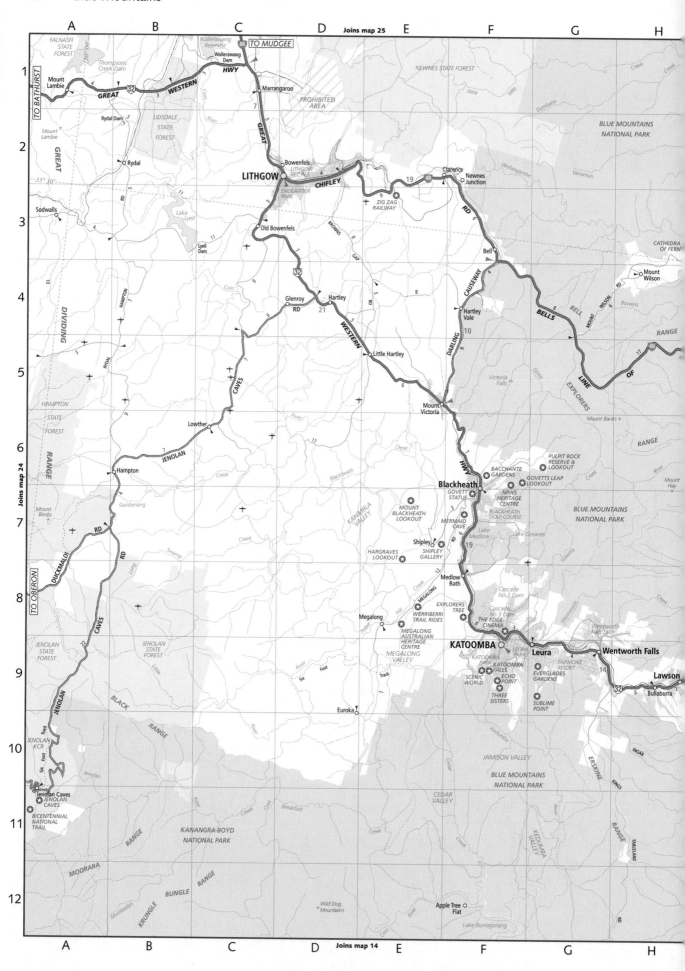

Joins map 25

Joins map 24

Joins map 14

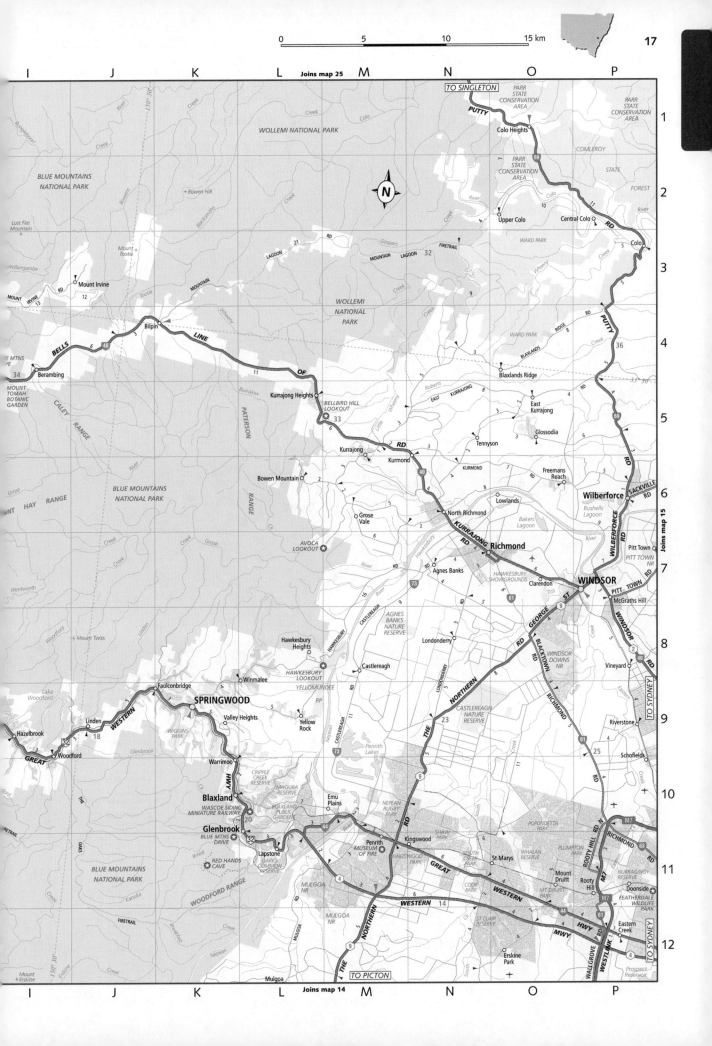

0   5   10   15 km

Joins map 25

I   J   K   L   M   N   O   P

TO SINGLETON

PARR STATE
CONSERVATION
AREA

PUTTY

PARR
STATE
CONSERVATION
AREA

Colo Heights

WOLLEMI NATIONAL PARK

COMLEROY

69

BLUE MOUNTAINS
NATIONAL PARK

+ Bowen Hill

River

Colo

STATE

River

FOREST

Lost Flat
Mountain

Mount +
Tootie

Upper Colo

WARD PARK

Central Colo

Colo

RD

River

Mount Irvine

RD

LAGOON

21

MOUNTAIN LAGOON 32

FIRETRAIL

Wollangambe

MOUNT
IRVINE
13

RD

12

MOUNTAIN

WOLLEMI
NATIONAL
PARK

RD

PUTTY

8

BELLS

6

40

3

Bilpin

LINE

WARD PARK

RIDGE

36

BE MTNS
E
34

Berambing

OF

11

Blaxlands Ridge

BLAXLANDS

69

MOUNT
TOMAH
BOTANIC
GARDEN

Burralow

Kurrajong Heights

Roberts

EAST KURRAJONG

East
Kurrajong

RD

CALEY RANGE

BELLBIRD HILL
LOOKOUT

33

PATERSON

Little

Wheeny

RD

3

Glossodia

Kurrajong

6

Kurmond

40

Tennyson

KURMOND

SACKVILLE

Grose

BLUE MOUNTAINS
NATIONAL PARK

Bowen Mountain

2

3

Freemans
Reach

Wilberforce

RD

NT HAY RANGE

RIVER RANGE

Grose
Vale

Lowlands

North Richmond

Bakers
Lagoon

Bushells
Lagoon

WILBERFORCE

WINDSOR

RD

Pitt Town

PITT TOWN
NR

AVOCA
LOOKOUT

KURRAJONG

6

Richmond

River

RD

Wentworth

RD

Agnes Banks

HAWKESBURY
SHOWGROUNDS

73

Clarendon

61

WINDSOR

PITT TOWN

McGraths Hill

GEORGE

9

Windsor

RD

+ Mount Twiss

16

AGNES
BANKS
NATURE
RESERVE

RP

Londonderry

RD

BLACKTOWN

WINDSOR
DOWNS
NR

Vineyard

40

RD

Woodford

Hawkesbury
Heights

HAWKESBURY
LOOKOUT

Castlereagh

THE

LONDONDERRY

NORTHERN

CASTLEREAGH
NATURE
RESERVE

RICHMOND

Riverstone

WESTERN

Faulconbridge

SPRINGWOOD

YELLOMUNDEE

RP

73

Penrith
Lakes

23

61

Schofields

Lake
Woodford

Linden

18

WIGGINS
PARK

Valley Heights

Yellow
Rock

CASTLEREAGH

RD

Hazelbrook

32

GREAT

Woodford

Glenbrook

Warrimoo

HWY

CRIPPLE
CREEK
RESERVE

MAGURA
RESERVE

Emu
Plains

NEPEAN
RUGBY
PARK

RD

SHAW
PARK

POPONDETTA
PARK

RD

M7

RICHMOND

63

THE

OAKS

Blaxland

WASCOE SIDING
MINIATURE RAILWAY

20

BLAXLAND
PUBLIC
GARDENS

44

Penrith

PENRITH
MUSEUM
OF FIRE

Kingswood

SOUTH

CREEK
PARK

St Marys

WHALAN
RESERVE

PLUMPTON
PARK

ROOTY HILL

NURRAGINGY
RESERVE

Doonside

FEATHERDALE
WILDLIFE
PARK

Glenbrook
BLUE MTNS
DRIVE

32

Lapstone

RED HANDS
CAVE

BLAXLAND
COMMON
RESERVE

KINGSWOOD

GREAT

6

Kingswood
Park

Mount
Druitt

M7

Rooty
Hill

61

BLUE MOUNTAINS
NATIONAL PARK

WOODFORD RANGE

4

MULGOA
NR

RD

ST CLAIR
RESERVE

COOK
PARK

WESTERN

MT DRUITT
PARK

44

Eastern
Creek

TO SYDNEY

FIRETRAIL

Kanuka

MULGOA
NR

THE

NORTHERN

WESTERN

HWY

MWY

WALLGROVE

WESTLINK

RD

61

4

Prospect
Reservoir

Mount
+ Erskine

Mulgoa

8

TO PICTON

Erskine
Park

+

I   J   K   L   M   N   O   P

Joins map 14

Joins map 15

1   2   3   4   5   6   7   8   9   10   11   12

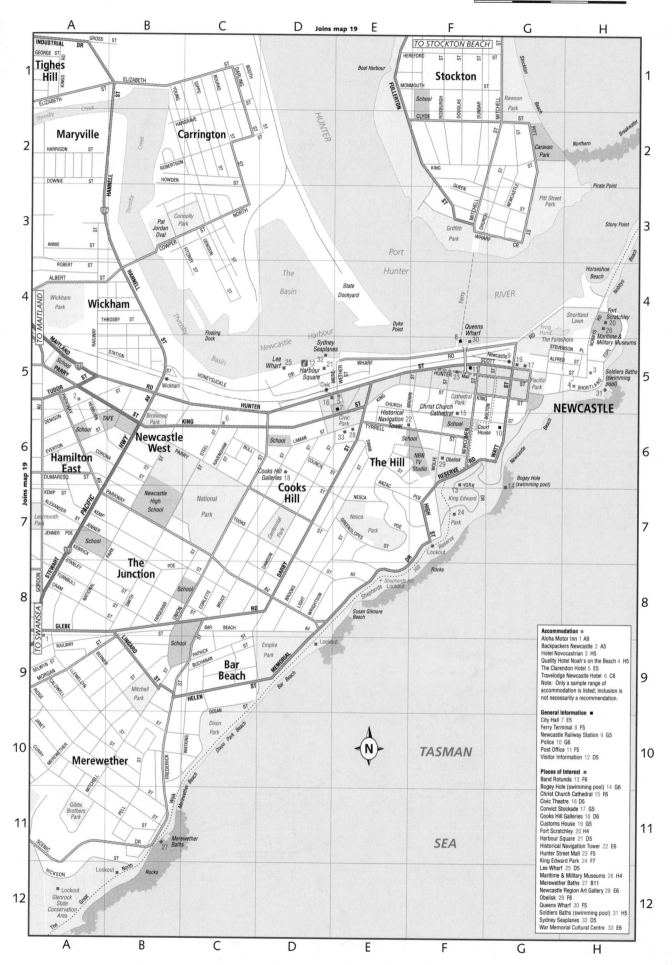

0   0.25   0.5   0.75   1 km

A   B   C   D   Joins map 19   E   F   G   H

Tighes Hill
INDUSTRIAL DR
GEORGE ST RD
KINGS ST
GROSS ST
ELIZABETH ST
Throsby Creek
ELIZABETH ST

Maryville
HARRISON ST
DOWNIE ST
HANNELL ST
124
Throsby Creek

Carrington
YOUNG ST
GIPPS ST
BOURKE ST
DARLING ST
BOOTH ST
HARGRAVE ST
ST
ROBERTSON ST
HOWDEN ST
NORTH ST
Pat Jordan Oval
Connolly Park
COWPER
DENISON ST
FITZROY ST

HUNTER
Boat Harbour

Stockton
TO STOCKTON BEACH
HEREFORD ST
MONMOUTH ST
School
ROXBURGH
CLYDE ST
DOUGLAS
DUNBAR
MITCHELL
FULLERTON
KING ST
QUEEN ST
MITCHELL
CHURCH
WHARF
Griffith Park
Caravan Park
NEWCASTLE
PITT ST
Pitt Street Park
Rawson Park
Beach
Northern
Breakwater
Pirate Point
Stony Point

Port Hunter

The Basin
State Dockyard
ANNIE ST
ROBERT ST
ALBERT ST
Wickham Park
Wickham
HANNELL ST
THROSBY ST
RAILWAY
STATION
Floating Dock
Throsby Basin
Newcastle Harbour
HONEYSUCKLE
Dyke Point

RIVER
Ferry
Horseshoe Beach
Nobbys Beach
Shortland Lawn
Frog Pond
The Foreshore
STEVENSON
ALFRED
Fort Scratchley 20
26
Maritime & Military Museums
Soldiers Baths (swimming pool)
31

TO MAITLAND
MAITLAND RD
111
School
PARRY ST
TUDOR ST
PARKWAY
HEBBURN ST
TAFE HWY
DENISON ST
Birdwood Park
KING ST
Wickham
HUNTER ST
Civic Park
2
6
16 7
Lee Wharf 25
Sydney Seaplanes
Harbour Square
12 32 21
Civic
WETHER ST
WHARF
KING ST
BROWN ST
CHURCH ST
Historical Navigation Tower 22
Christ Church Cathedral 15
Cathedral Park
School
NBN TV Studio
Obelisk 29
Queens Wharf 8 30
SCOTT ST
HUNTER ST 23 Mall 11
King ST
Court House 10
NEWCOMEN ST
BOLTON ST
WATT ST
Newcastle 9
19
17
Pacific Park
Beach
NEWCASTLE
SHORTLAND
3
4

Newcastle West
Hamilton East
DUMARESQ ST
KEMP ST
ALEXANDER ST
JENNER ST
JENNER PDE
PACIFIC HWY
PARKWAY
KEMP ST
School
KENRICK ST
STANLEY ST
TURNBULL
CRAM ST
PARK
PDE
The Junction
School
NATIONAL
SMITH ST
Cooks Hill
Cooks Hill Galleries 18
Newcastle High School
National Park
Centennial Park
TOOKE ST
DARBY ST
LINDSON
BROOKS ST
LIGHT ST
WRIGHTSON
UNION ST
CORLETTE ST
BRUCE ST
BAR BEACH RD
LAMAN ST
COUNCIL ST
BULL ST
STEEL ST
RAVENSHAW ST
School
SWAN ST
TYRRELL ST
ANZAC
NESCA
Nesca Park
GREENSLOPES
PDE
The Hill
War Memorial Cultural Centre 33
Newcastle Region Art Gallery 28
HIGH ST
RESERVE RD
YORK 13
Band Rotunda
King Edward Park 24
PDE
Reserve
Lookout
Bogey Hole (swimming pool) 14
Rocks
Shepherds Hill Lookout
Hill DR

Joins map 19
TO SWANSEA
GORDON AV
STEWART AV
111
GLEBE RD
Learmonth Park
RAILWAY
SELWYN ST
MORGAN
CALDWELL
LLEWELLYN
BERNER
LINDSAY ST
Mitchell Park
School
PATRICK ST
BUCHANAN
HELEN ST
OCEAN ST
Bar Beach
Empire Park
MEMORIAL DR
Bar Beach
Lookout
Susan Gilmore Beach

Merewether
JANET ST
CURRY ST
MEREWETHER
RIDGE ST
MITCHELL
PELL ST
Gibbs Brothers Park
FREDERICK ST
WATKINS ST
Dixon Park
Dixon Park Beach
Merewether Beach
Merewether Baths 27

SCENIC DR
HICKSON ST
Lookout
North Rocks
Glenrock State Conservation Area
The Great

N

TASMAN

SEA

Accommodation ■
Aloha Motor Inn 1 A9
Backpackers Newcastle 2 A5
Hotel Novocastrian 3 H5
Quality Hotel Noah's on the Beach 4 H5
The Clarendon Hotel 5 E5
Travelodge Newcastle Hotel 6 C6
Note: Only a sample range of accommodation is listed; inclusion is not necessarily a recommendation.

General Information ■
City Hall 7 E5
Ferry Terminal 8 F5
Newcastle Railway Station 9 G5
Police 10 G6
Post Office 11 F5
Visitor Information 12 D5

Places of Interest ■
Band Rotunda 13 F6
Bogey Hole (swimming pool) 14 G6
Christ Church Cathedral 15 F6
Civic Theatre 16 D5
Convict Stockade 17 G5
Cooks Hill Galleries 18 D6
Customs House 19 G5
Fort Scratchley 20 H4
Harbour Square 21 D5
Historical Navigation Tower 22 E6
Hunter Street Mall 23 F5
King Edward Park 24 F7
Lee Wharf 25 D5
Maritime & Military Museums 26 H4
Merewether Baths 27 B11
Newcastle Region Art Gallery 28 E6
Obelisk 29 F6
Queens Wharf 30 F5
Soldiers Baths (swimming pool) 31 H5
Sydney Seaplanes 32 D5
War Memorial Cultural Centre 33 E6

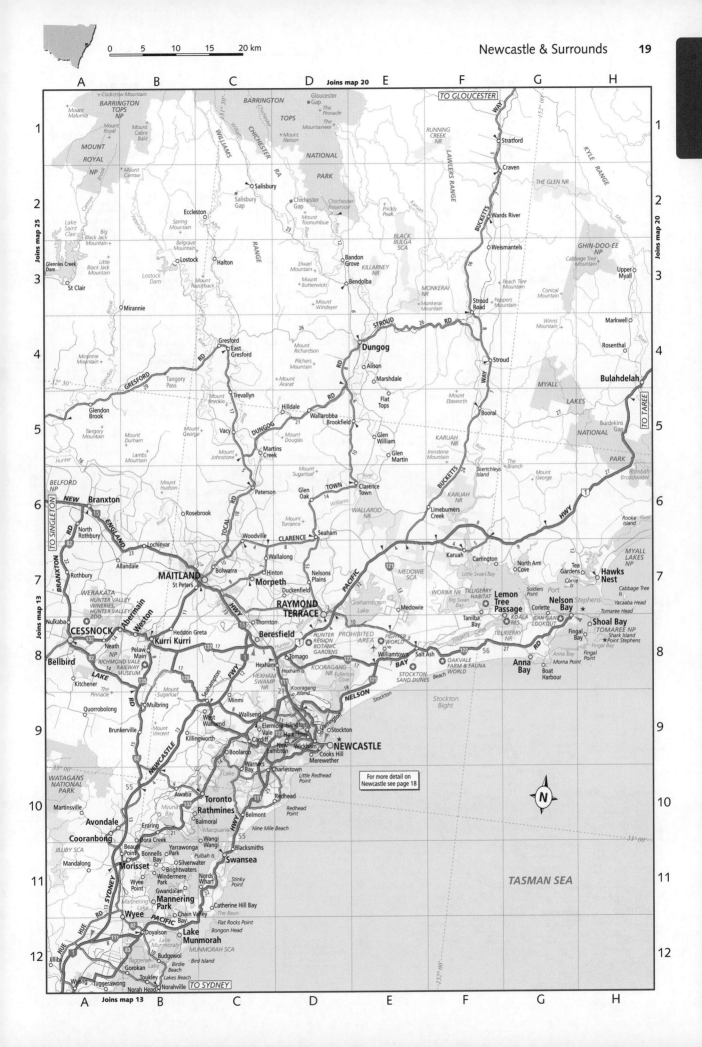

0   5   10   15   20 km

A   B   C   D   E   F   G   H

TO GLOUCESTER

1

BARRINGTON TOPS NP
Mount Malumla
Cockcrow Mountain
Mount Royal
Mount Cabre Bald
MOUNT ROYAL NP
BARRINGTON TOPS
Gloucester Gap
The Pinnacle
The Mountaineer
Mount Nelson
RUNNING CREEK NR
Stratford
Craven
THE GLEN NR
KYLE RANGE
LAWLERS RANGE
WAY
BUCKETTS

2
Joins map 25
Lake Saint Clair
Big Black Jack Mountain
Mount Carrow
Brook
Salisbury
Eccleston
Salisbury Gap
Spring Mountain
Belgrave Mountain
WILLIAMS
CHICHESTER
RANGE
CHICHESTER
Mount Toonumbue
Chichester Gap
Mount
Chichester Reservoir
NATIONAL PARK
Prickly Peak
BLACK BULGA SCA
Wards River
Weismantels
GHIN-DOO-EE NP
Cabbage Tree Mountain
Joins map 20
Myall

3
Glennies Creek Dam
St Clair
Little Black Jack Mountain
Lostock
Halton
Lostock Dam
Mount Razorback
Elwari Mountain
Mount + Butterwicki
Bandon Grove
Bendolba
KILLARNEY NR
MONKERAI NR
Peach Tree Mountain
Monkerai Mountain
Stroud Road
Peppers Mountain
Conical Mountain
Upper Myall
Markwell
Rosenthal

4
Mirannie
Mirannie Mountain
GRESFORD
RD
Gresford
East Gresford
Tangory Pass
Mount Windeyer
Mount Richardson
Pilchers Mount
Mount Ararat
Dungog
Alison
Marshdale
STROUD
RD
WAY
Stroud
Winns Mountain
MYALL LAKES
Bulahdelah
TO TAREE

5
Glendon Brook
Tangory Mountain
Mount Durham
Lambs Valley
Trevallyn
Hilldale
Vacy
Mount Douglas
Wallarobba
Brookfield
Flat Tops
Glen William
Glen Martin
Mount Ebsworth
Booral
KARUAH NR
Ironstone Mountain
The Branch
Mount George
Burdekins Gap
Bombah Broadwater
NATIONAL PARK

6
BELFORD NP
NEW
Branxton
North Rothbury
ENGLAND
Rosebrook
Martins Creek
Paterson
Glen Oak
TOWN
Clarence Town
WALLAROO NR
Limeburners Creek
BUCKETTS
Skertchleys Island
KARUAH NR
Mount George
HWY
Rooke Island
MYALL LAKES NP

7
Joins map 13
Nulkaba
WERAKATA NP
HUNTER VALLEY WINERIES, HUNTER VALLEY ZOO
Weston
Abermain
Lochinvar
Allandale
Rothbury
Bolwarra
Woodville
Hinton
MAITLAND
St Peters
Morpeth
Duckenfield
Nelsons Plains
RAYMOND TERRACE
Thornton
Seaham
CLARENCE
Grahamstown Lake
MEDOWIE SCA
Medowie
WORIMI NR
TILLIGERRY HABITAT
Big Swan Bay
Little Swan Bay
North Arm Cove
Carrington
Tea Gardens
Corrie Is
Hawks Nest
Cabbage Tree
Yacaaba Head
Tomaree Head
Soldiers Point
Lemon Tree Passage
KOALA RES
Nelson Bay
Port Stephens
Shoal Bay
TOMAREE NP
Shark Island
Point Stephens
Fingal Bay

8
CESSNOCK
Bellbird
Kitchener
Neath
Pelaw Main
RICHMOND VALE RAILWAY MUSEUM
Kurri Kurri
Heddon Greta
Beresfield
Hexham
Tomago
Williamtown
Salt Ash
BAY
OAKVALE FARM & FAUNA WORLD
Anna Bay
Boat Harbour
Morna Point
Fingal Point
GAN GAN LOOKOUT
Corlette
TILLIGERRY NR
Tanilba Bay
HUNTER REGION BOTANIC GARDENS
PROHIBITED AREA
FIGHTER WORLD
LAKE
The Pinnacle
Mount Sugarloaf
Seahampton
Minmi
Hexham Is
HEXHAM SWAMP NR
Kooragang Island
KOORAGANG NR
Fullerton Cove
STOCKTON SAND DUNES
Beach

9
Quorrobolong
Mount Vincent
Brunkerville
Killingworth
West Wallsend
Wallsend
Elermore Vale
Islington
Hamilton
Cardiff
New Lambton
Wickham
Boolaroo
Warners Bay
Charlestown
Merewether
Cooks Hill
NEWCASTLE
Carrington
Stockton
Stockton Bight

10
Martinsville
WATAGANS NATIONAL PARK
Awaba
Toronto
Rathmines
Balmoral
Belmont
Little Redhead Point
Redhead
Redhead Point
Nine Mile Beach
For more detail on Newcastle see page 18
N

11
Avondale
Cooranbong
Eraring
Dora Creek
JILLIBY SCA
Mandalong
Beauty Point
Bonnells Bay
Yarrawonga Park
Silverwater
Brightwaters
Windermere Park
Morisset
Wyee Point
Gwandalan
MANNERING PARK
Wangi Wangi
Pulbah Is
Blacksmiths
Swansea
Nords Wharf
Stinky Point
Macquarie
TASMAN SEA

12
Jilliby
Wyong
Tuggerawong
Norah Head
Toukley
Norahville
Gorokan
Budgewoi
Birdie Beach
Bird Island
Lakes Beach
MUNMORAH SCA
Doyalson
Lake Munmorah
Wyee
PACIFIC
HUE HUE RD
Catherine Hill Bay
The Basin
Chain Valley Bay
Flat Rocks Point
Bongon Head
TO SYDNEY

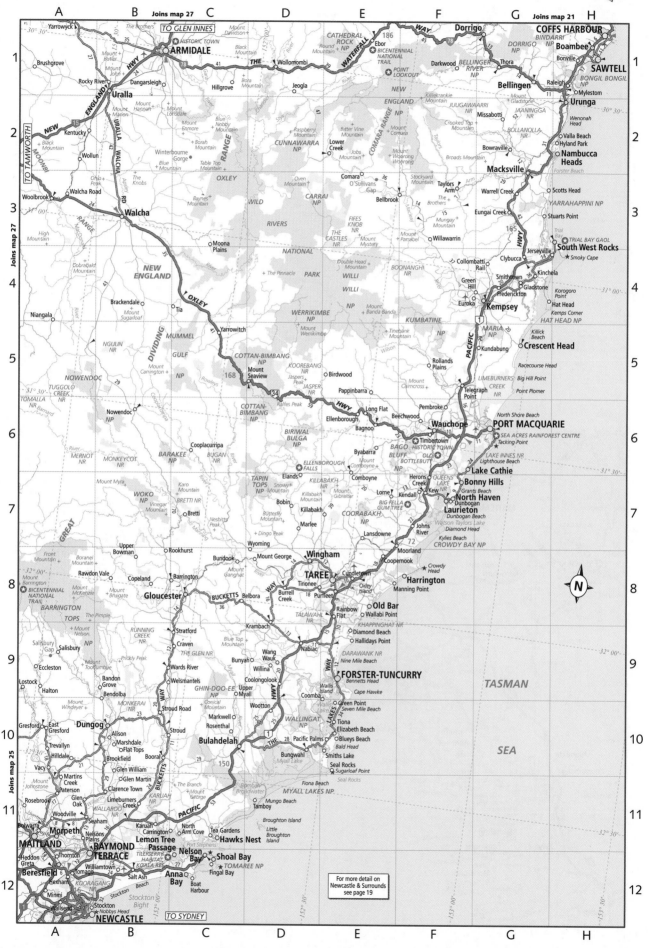

0   20   40   60 km

A | B | Joins map 27 | C | D | E | F | G | Joins map 21 | H

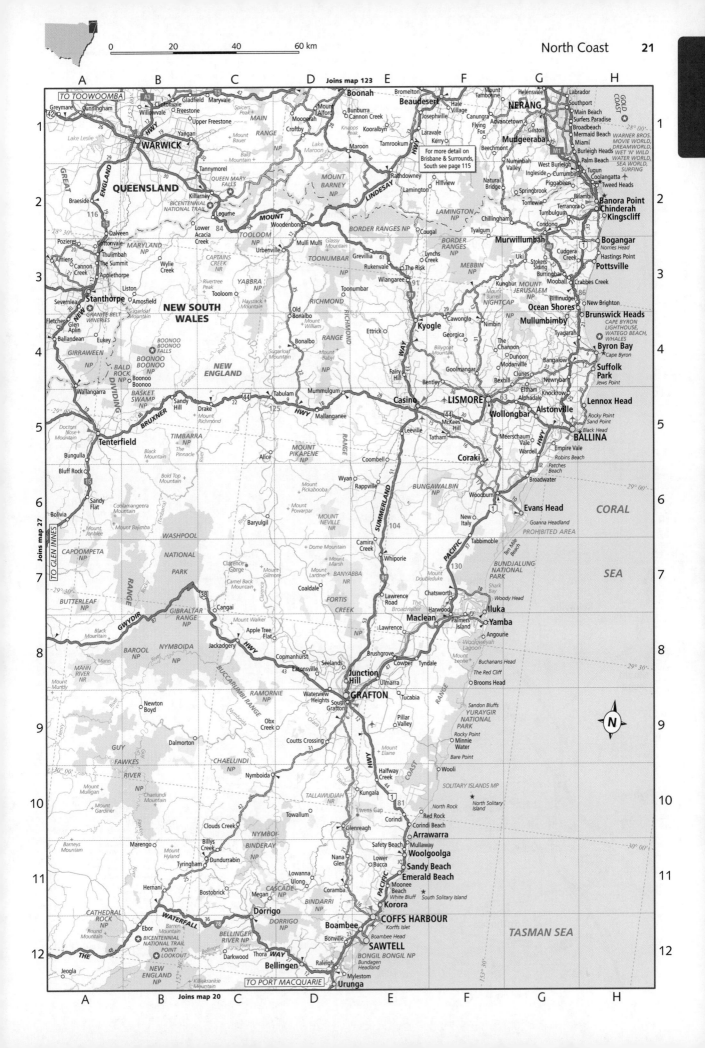

0   20   40   60 km

Joins map 123

TO TOOWOOMBA

QUEENSLAND

WARWICK

NEW SOUTH WALES

NEW ENGLAND

Tenterfield

Stanthorpe

CORAL

SEA

NERANG

Mudgeeraba

Murwillumbah

Banora Point
Chinderah
Kingscliff

Bogangar
Pottsville

Ocean Shores
Brunswick Heads
Byron Bay
Suffolk Park

Mullumbimby

Lennox Head

Alstonville
BALLINA

Kyogle

Casino
LISMORE
Wollongbar

Coraki

Evans Head

Maclean
Iluka
Yamba

Junction Hill
GRAFTON
South Grafton

Coutts Crossing

Dorrigo

Bellingen

Arrawarra
Woolgoolga
Sandy Beach
Emerald Beach
Korora

COFFS HARBOUR
Boambee
SAWTELL

Urunga

TASMAN SEA

TO PORT MACQUARIE

Joins map 20

Joins map 27
TO GLEN INNES

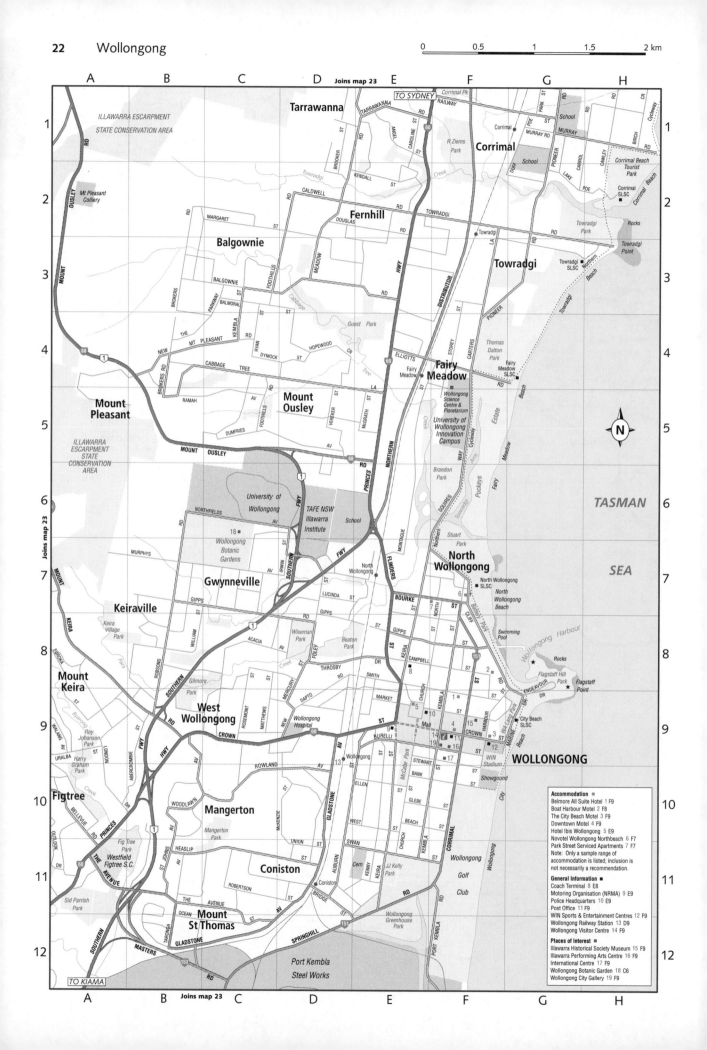

0   0.5   1   1.5   2 km

Joins map 23

ILLAWARRA ESCARPMENT
STATE CONSERVATION AREA

Tarrawanna

TO SYDNEY

Corrimal Pk

Corrimal

Fernhill

Balgownie

Towradgi

Mount
Pleasant

Fairy
Meadow

Mount
Ousley

ILLAWARRA
ESCARPMENT
STATE
CONSERVATION
AREA

Wollongong
Science
Centre &
Planetarium

University of
Wollongong
Innovation Campus

TASMAN

University of
Wollongong

TAFE NSW
Illawarra
Institute

Brandon
Park

Gwynneville

North
Wollongong

SEA

Keiraville

Wollongong
Botanic
Gardens

Stuart
Park

North Wollongong
Beach

Wollongong Harbour

Mount
Keira

West
Wollongong

Flagstaff Hill
Park

Flagstaff
Point

Wollongong Hospital

WOLLONGONG

WIN
Stadium

Figtree

Mangerton

Coniston

Wollongong
Golf
Club

Mount
St Thomas

Wollongong
Greenhouse
Park

TO KIAMA

Port Kembla
Steel Works

Joins map 23

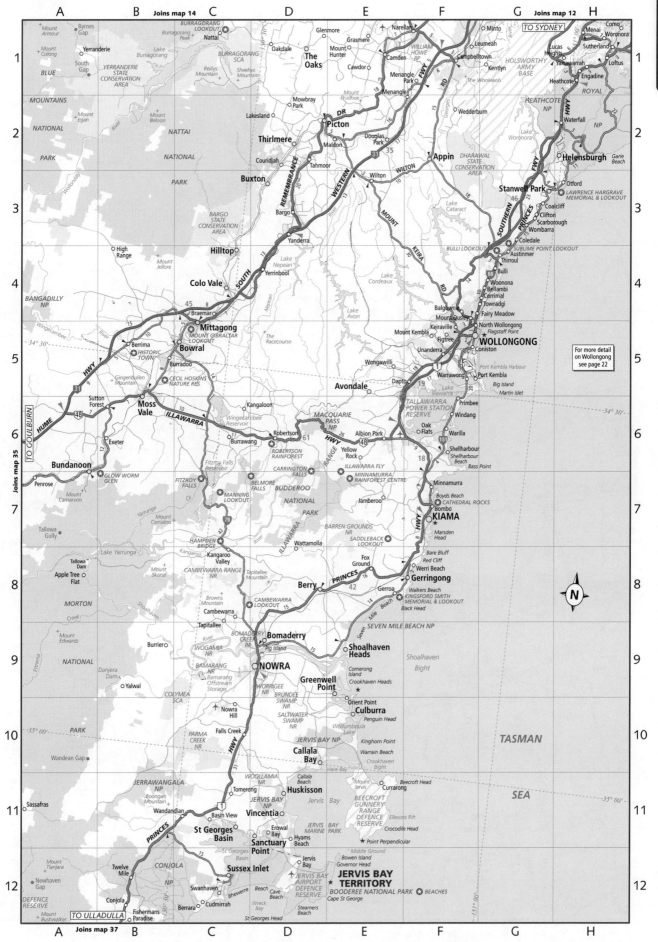

Joins map 14
Joins map 12
TO SYDNEY
For more detail on Wollongong see page 22
Joins map 35
TO GOULBURN
Joins map 37
TO ULLADULLA

0 5 10 15 20 km

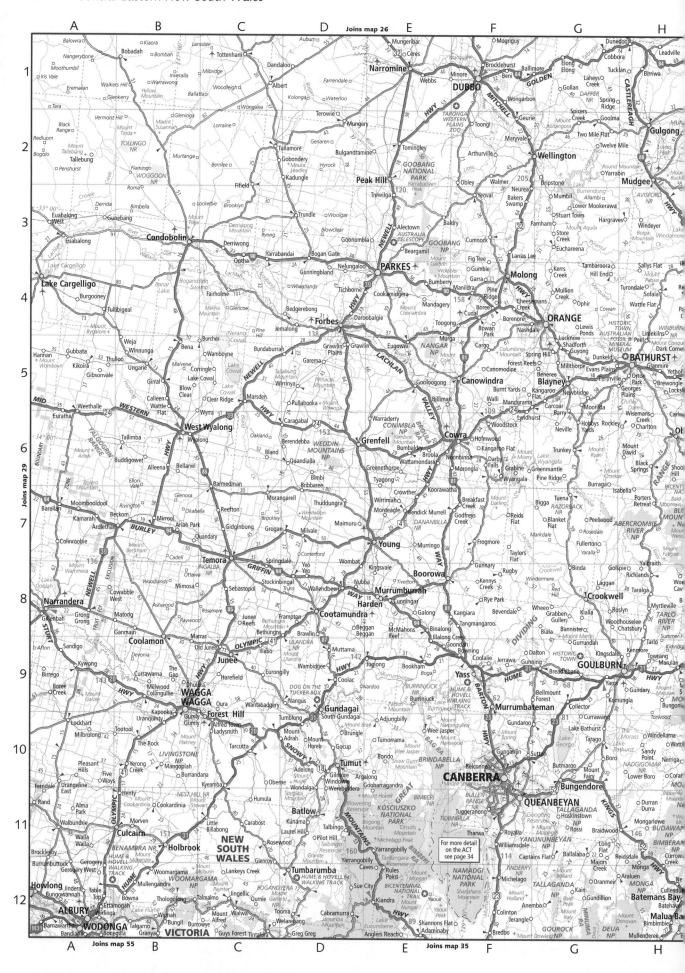

Joins map 29

Joins map 55

Joins map 35

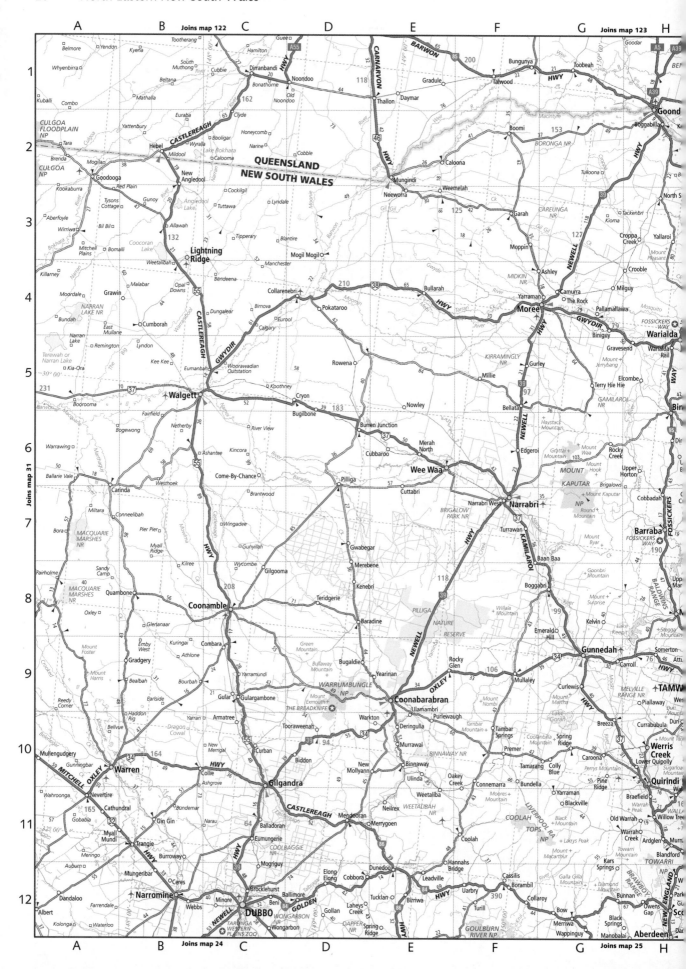

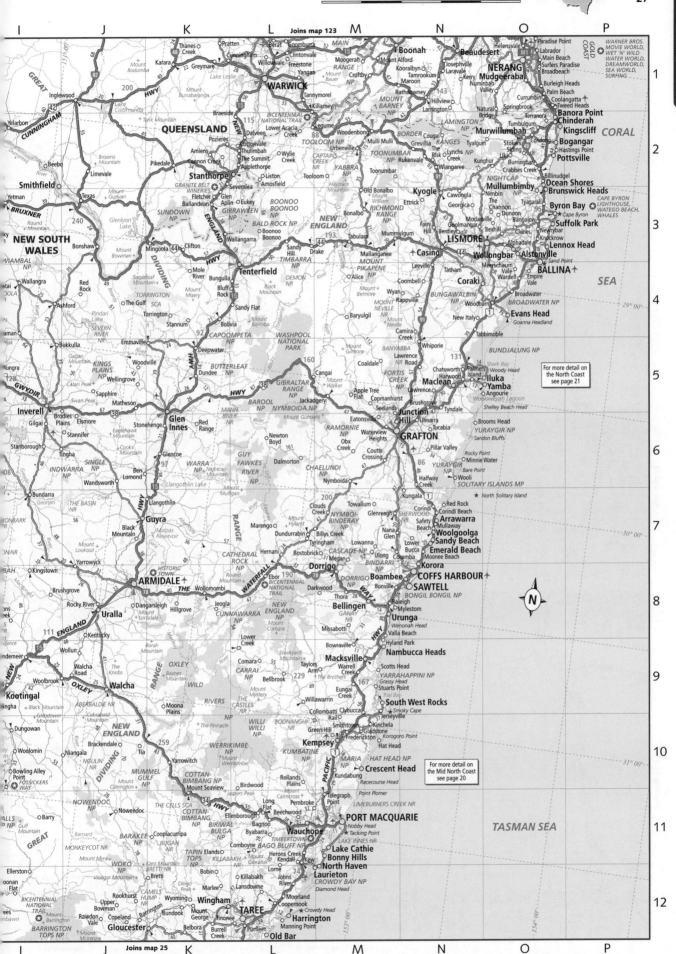

0 20 40 60 80 100 km

Joins map 123

WARNER BROS.
MOVIE WORLD,
WET 'N' WILD
WATER WORLD,
DREAMWORLD,
SEA WORLD,
SURFING

GREAT

CUNNINGHAM

Inglewood

Yelarbon

Smithfield

Yetman

BRUXNER

NEW SOUTH
WALES

QUEENSLAND

WARWICK

Stanthorpe

GRANITE BELT
WINERIES

Tenterfield

SUNDOWN
NP

BALD ROCK NP

GIRRAWEEN
NP

NEW
ENGLAND

BOONOO
BOONOO
NP

TIMBARRA

DEMON
NR

Ashford

TORRINGTON
SCA

Emmaville

Deepwater

CAPOOMPETA
NP

Bolivia

WASHPOOL
NATIONAL
PARK

GIBRALTAR
RANGE
NP

BAROOL NP

Glen
Innes

MANN
RIVER
NR

NYMBOIDA NP

Inverell

KINGS
PLAINS
NP

GWYDIR

SINGLE
NP

INDWARRA
NP

WARRA
NP

GUY
FAWKES
RIVER
NP

Guyra

Llangothlin

Marengo

NYMBOI-
BINDERAY
NP

Dundurrabin

CATHEDRAL
ROCK
NP

NEW
ENGLAND
NP

Hernani

CASCADE NP

BINDARRI
NP

Dorrigo

DORRIGO NP

ARMIDALE

Uralla

ENGLAND

Kentucky

Wollun

OXLEY

Walcha

NEW

Kootingal

NGULIA
NR

NEW
ENGLAND

WERRIKIMBE
NP

COTTAN-
BIMBANG NP

WILLI
WILLI
NR

MUMMEL
GULF
NP

CARRAI
NP

THE
CASTLES
NR

Kempsey

KUMBATINE
NP

MARIA
NR

BIRIWAL
BULGA
NP

BAGO BLUFF NP

WAUCHOPE

PORT MACQUARIE

CORAL

NERANG
Mudgeeraba

Beaudesert

Boonah

Murwillumbah

Mullumbimby

Byron Bay

Suffolk Park

LISMORE

Casino

Coraki

BALLINA

Evans Head

Maclean
Yamba
Iluka

GRAFTON

Junction
Hill

COFFS HARBOUR

SAWTELL

Woolgoolga
Sandy Beach
Emerald Beach
Korora

Boambee

Bellingen

Urunga

Nambucca Heads

Macksville

South West Rocks

Crescent Head

SEA

For more detail on
the North Coast
see page 21

For more detail on
the Mid North Coast
see page 20

TASMAN SEA

Lake Cathie
Bonny Hills
North Haven
Laurieton

Wingham

TAREE

Harrington

Gloucester

Old Bar

Joins map 25

PACIFIC

HWY

1

2

3

4

5

6

7

8

9

10

11

12

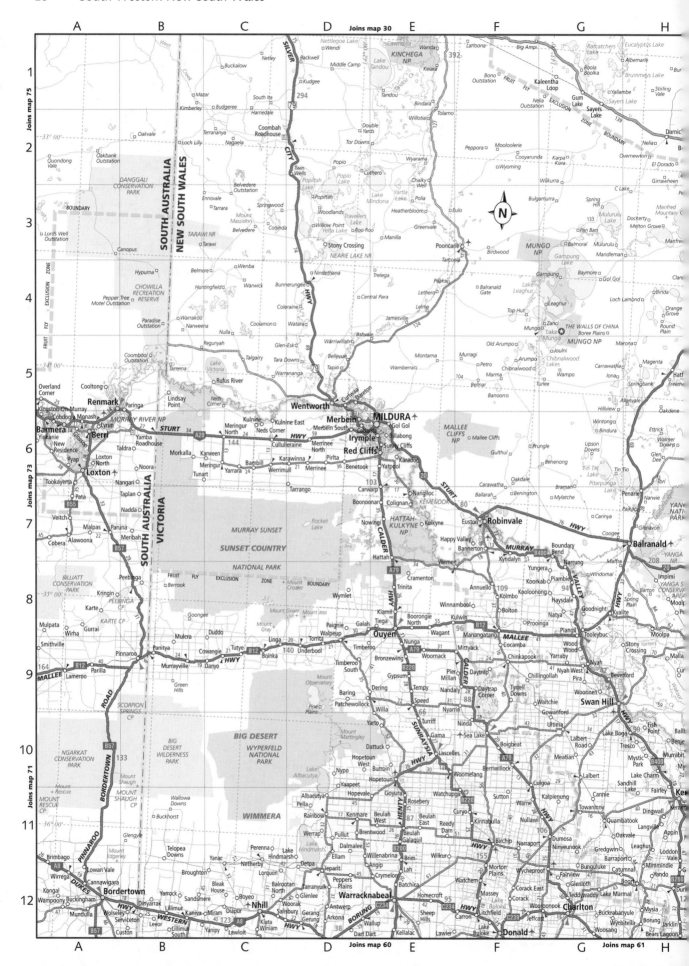

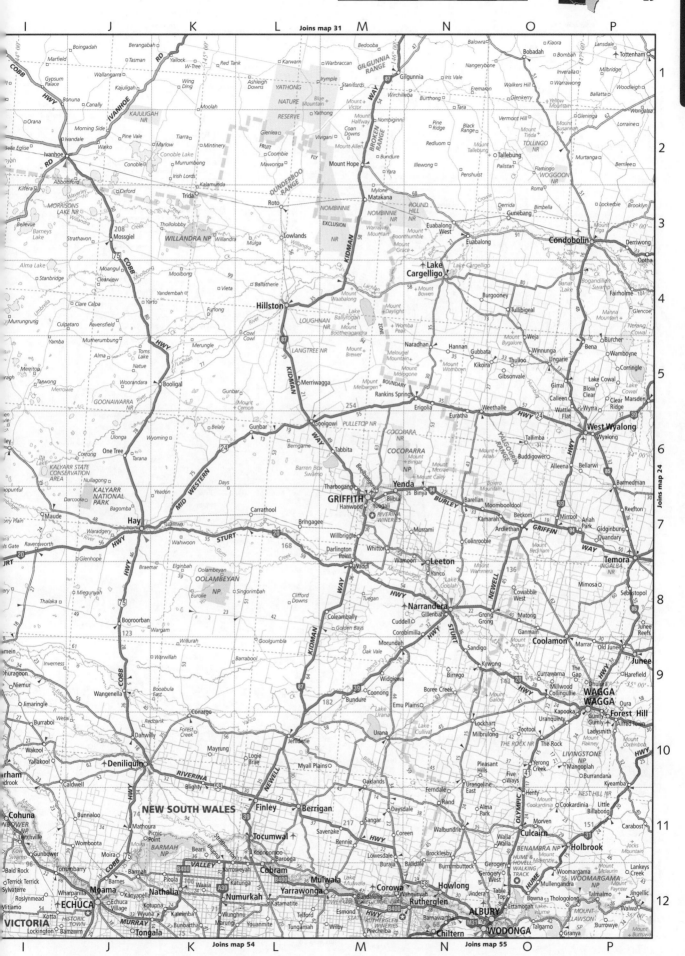

Joins map 31

Joins map 54

Joins map 55

Joins map 24

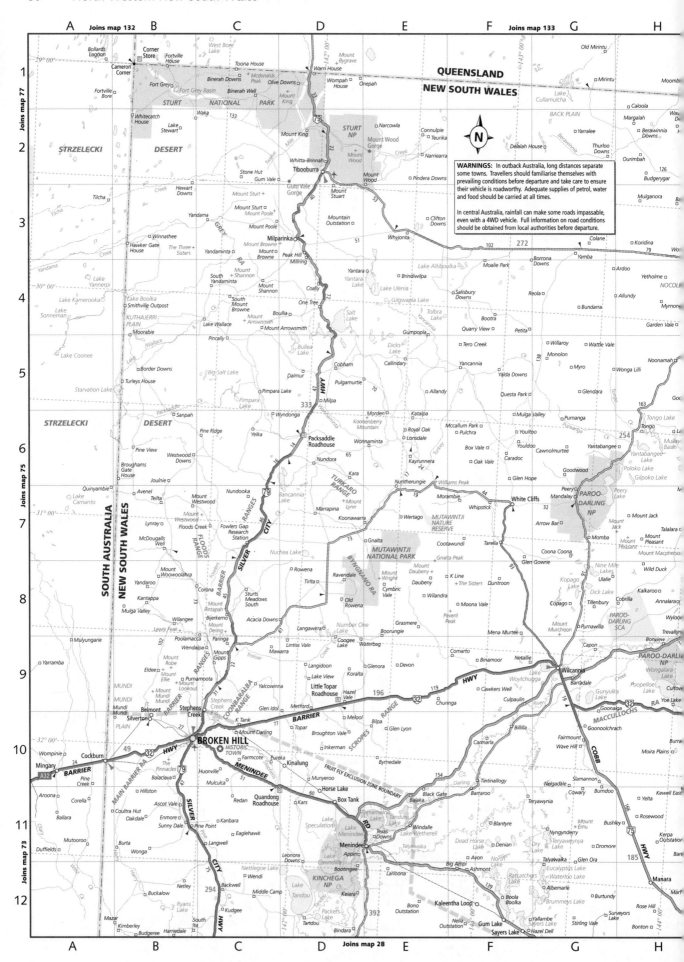

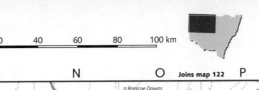

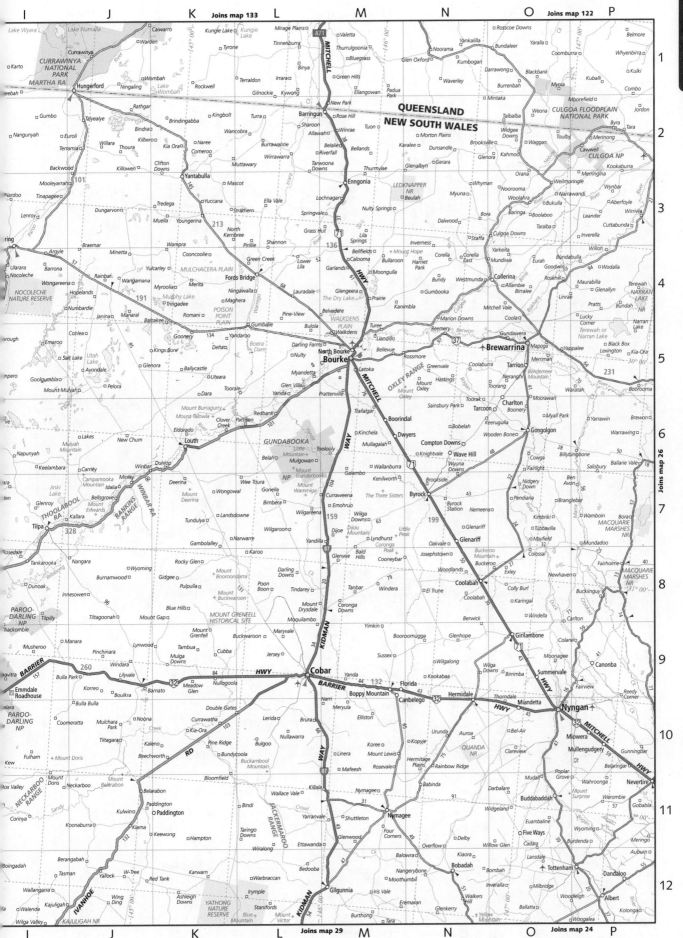

0   20   40   60   80   100 km

I   J   K   L   M   N   O   P

QUEENSLAND
NEW SOUTH WALES

I   J   K   L   M   N   O   P

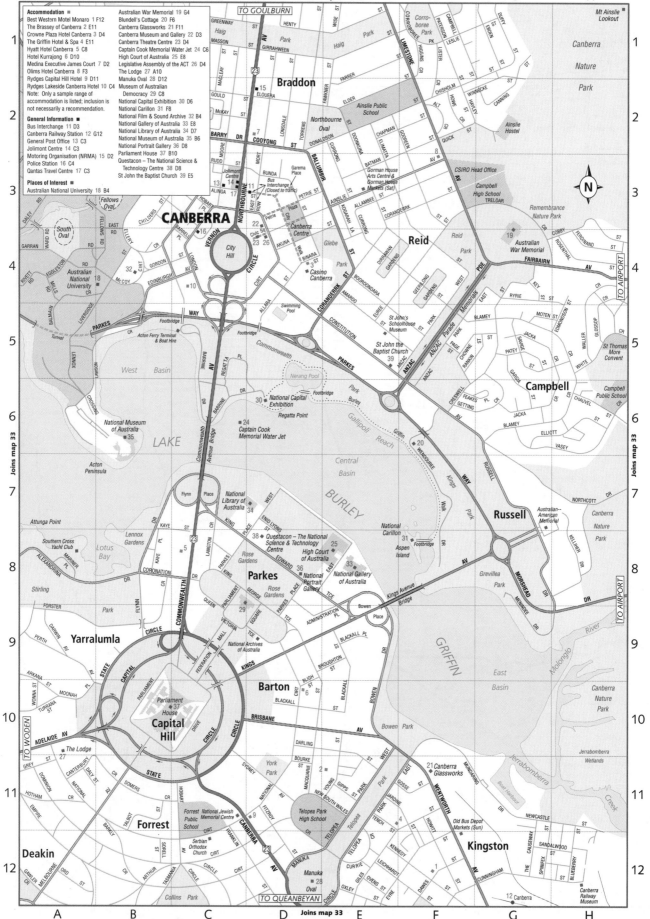

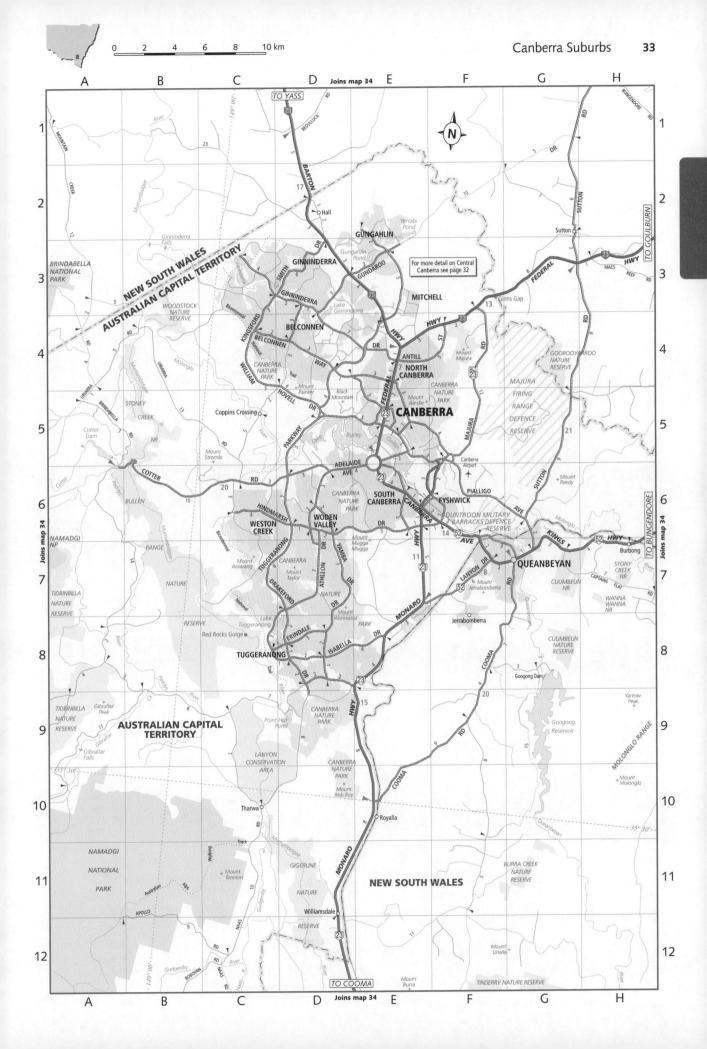

0 5 10 15 20 km

Joins map 35

A B C D E F G H

1

Lake Burrinjuck
Bloomfield
Ravensworth
Spring Creek
Pine Dale
Carmody
Hilltop
Willow Vale
High Knoll
Roseglen
Murrumbateman
Keswick
Beralston
OAK CREEK NATURE RESERVE
Mount Boombolo
Ruthfield

2

Mount Narrangullen
WADDYS PLAIN
RANGE
YASS
Mount Spring
Gundaroo
Geary Gap
Lake George
Wee Jasper
WEE JASPER NR
Mount Hartwood
BARTON HWY
SUTTON RD
Brooks

3

BRINDABELLA BAG RA
BRINDABELLA NATIONAL PARK
NEW SOUTH WALES
Ginninderra Falls
Hall
GOLD CREEK VILLAGE
Gungahlin
Sutton
FEDERAL
LAKE GEORGE RANGE
HISTORIC BYWONG GOLDMINING TOWN

4

BRINDABELLA NATIONAL PARK
AUSTRALIAN CAPITAL TERRITORY
Devils Peak
Mount Blundell
WOODSTOCK NR
Ginninderra
Belconnen
Mitchell
Ginns Gap
GOOROOYARROO NR
Mount Majura
Mount Ainslie
Mount Painter
Black Mountain
MAJURA FIRING RANGE DEFENCE RESERVE
Bungendore
HWY

5

Mount Coree
Cotter Dam
CASUARINA SANDS
MOUNT STROMLO OBSERVATORY
Coppins Crossing
CANBERRA
Lake Burley Griffin
Canberra Airport
Mount Reedy
TURALLO NR
BRINDABELLA
COTTER
BULLEN
HINDMARSH
CANBERRA
Fyshwick
MARKETS
KINGS
Mount Lickhole
Brindabella Mountain
NAMADGI NATIONAL PARK

6

KOSCIUSZKO NATIONAL PARK
BIMBERI NATURE RESERVE
TIDBINBILLA RANGE
CANBERRA DEEP SPACE COMMUNICATION COMPLEX
KAMBAH POOL
Mount Arawang
Mount Taylor
Mount Mugga Mugga
Mount Jerrabomberra
QUEANBEYAN
Burbong
STONY CREEK NR
CUUMBEUN NR
WANNA WANNA NR
TALLAGANDA NATIONAL PARK
Mount Aggie
TIDBINBILLA VISITOR CENTRE
Tidbinbilla Peak
Bendora Dam
TIDBINBILLA
Red Rocks Gorge
Tuggeranong
Mount Wanniassa
Jerrabomberra
Googong Dam
CUUMBEUN NR
TURALLO RA

7

Ginini Falls
Mount Franklin
CORIN FOREST
Gibraltar Peak
Gibraltar Falls
TUGGERANONG HOMESTEAD
Point Hut Pond
LANYON CA
Mount Rob Roy
COOMA
Mount Molonglo
LONDON BRIDGE LIMESTONE FORMATION
MOLONGLO RANGE
YANUNUNBEYAN NR
Hoskinstown
Rossi
Little Ginini Mountain
Mount Ginini
Smokers Gap
LANYON
Tharwa
CUPPACUMBALONG CRAFT CENTRE
Royalla
TALLAGANDA NP

8

NATURE RESERVE
Mount Gingera
Corin Dam
FORMER SPACE TRACKING STATION
NAMADGI VISITOR CENTRE
GIGERLINE NATURE RESERVE
Mount Tennent
Williamsdale
MONARO
BURRA CREEK NR
YANUNUNBEYAN NATIONAL PARK
Mount Foxlow
Harrisons Peak
GOUROCK RANGE
GREAT DIVIDING
Blackfellows Gap
Cotter Gap
Mount McKeahnie

9

Leura Gap
Bimberi Gap
Bimberi Peak
Coronet Peak
FORMER SPACE TRACKING STATION
OLD ORRORAL HOMESTEAD
NAMADGI NATIONAL PARK
BILLY RANGE
Mount Burra
Mount Michelago
TINDERRY
Mount Bullongong
Captains Flat
KOSCIUSZKO RA
Mount Murray
Australian Alps Walking

10

KOSCIUSZKO NATIONAL PARK
Mount Kelly
Mount Scabby
SCABBY RANGE NR
Mount Gudgenby
BOBOYAN
BOOTH RANGE
NAAS RANGE
ACT NSW
Mount Yarara
Michelago
TINDERRY TWIN PEAK
Tinderry Peak
NATURE RESERVE
Mount Woolpack
TALLAGANDA
Mount Bollard
Parkers Gap
Tumatbulla Mountain
Kain
Half Moon Peak
Mount Morgan

11

Mount Ash Hill
Yaouk
BICENTENNIAL NATIONAL TRAIL
Sentry Box Mountain
NAMADGI NATIONAL PARK
CLEAR RANGE
MONARO HWY
BURNT SCHOOL NATURE RESERVE
STRIKE-A-LIGHT NATURE RESERVE
Mount Holland
Mount Tumanang
Anembo
NATIONAL PARK
Bald Peak
Tumannang Mountain
Yaouk Peak
YAOUK NATURE RESERVE
DOG PLAIN
Shanahans Mountain
Mount Wangrah

12

YAOUK BILL RA
YAOUK NR
Black Cow Peak
Shannons Flat
BOBOYAN
Mount Clear
Colinton
Gungoandra Gap
Jerangle
GOUROCK
Mount Anembo
Mount Italy
GREAT DIVIDING PARK

Joins map 36
Joins map 36
Joins map 37

A B C D E F G H

N

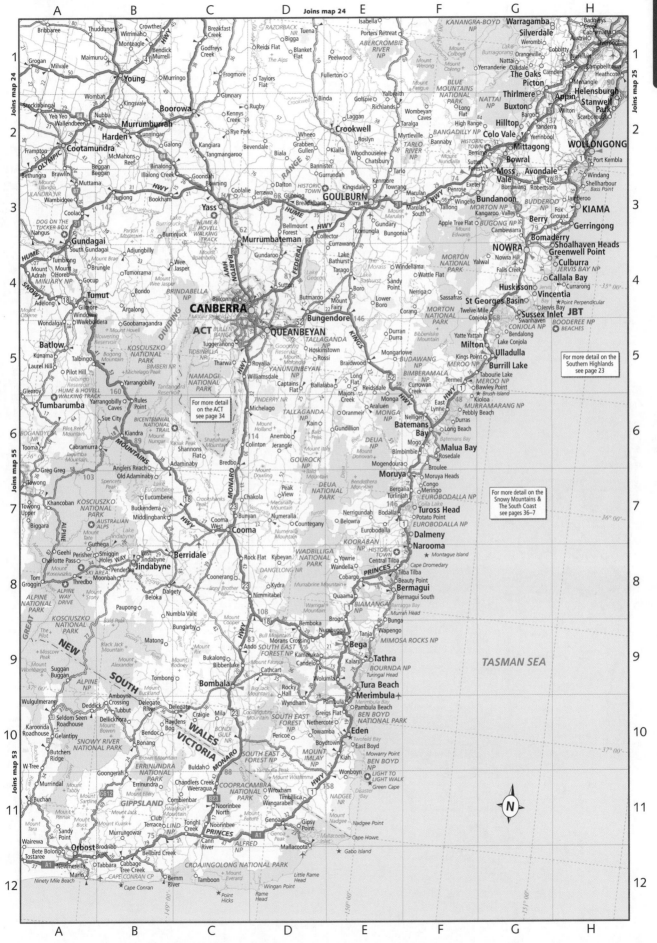

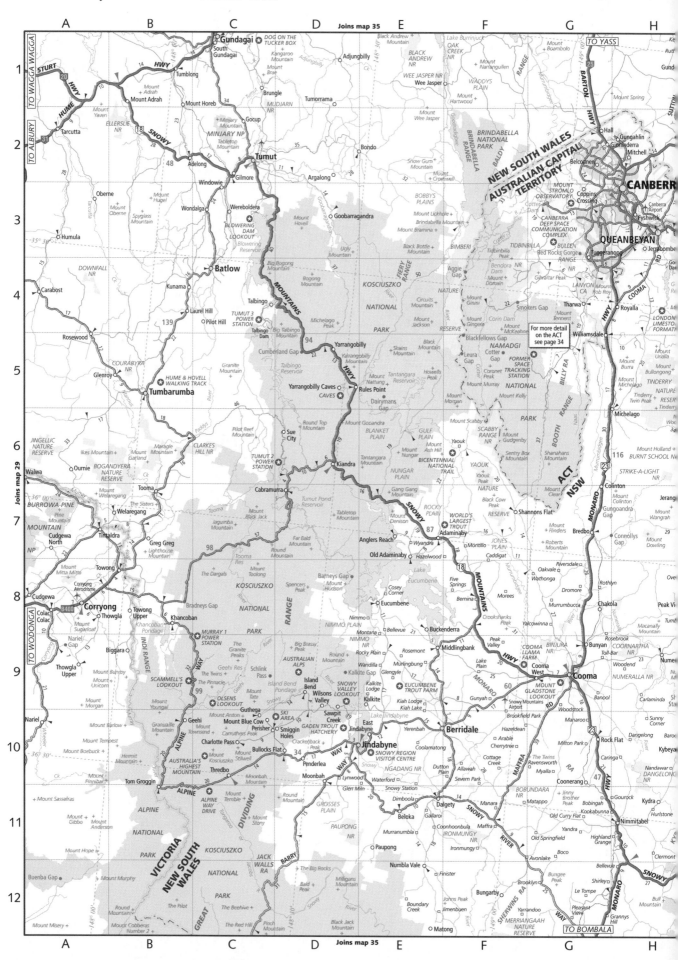

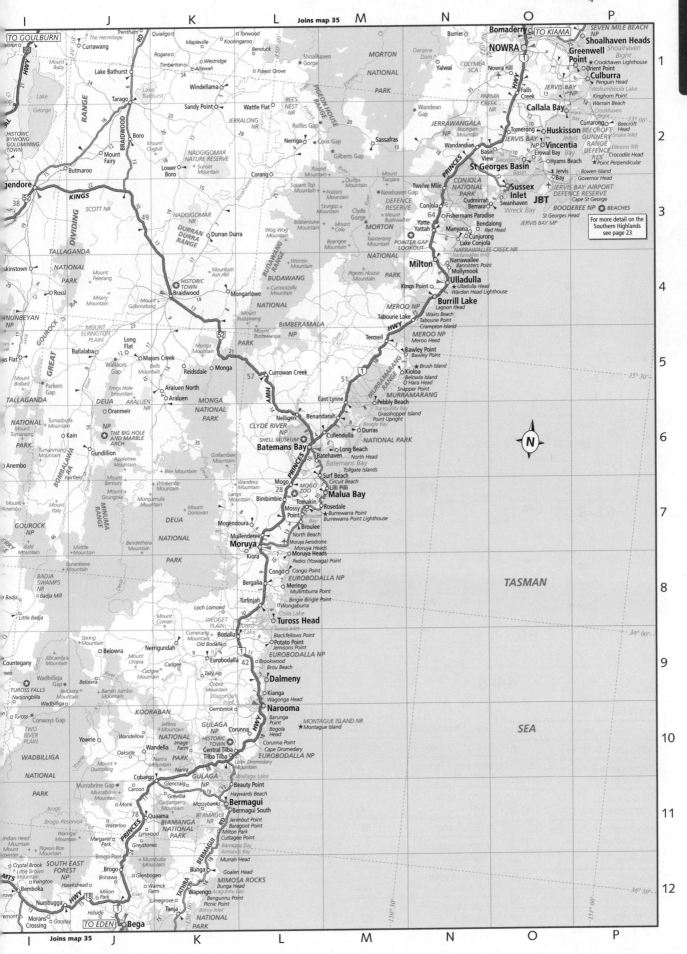

0 10 20 30 40 km

I J K L M N O P

TO GOULBURN

Trentham
Quialigo
The Hermitage
Currawang
Torwood
Kooringaroo
Mount
Baby
Mapleville
Benduck
Rogara
Timberton
Westridge
Allawah
Forest Grove
Shoalhaven
Gorge
Danjera
Dam
Burrier
Bomaderry
TO KIAMA
SEVEN MILE BEACH
NP
Shoalhaven Heads
NOWRA
Greenwell
Point
Shoalhaven
Bight
Crookhaven Lighthouse
Nowra Hill
Orient Point
Culburra
Penguin Head
Wollumboula Lake
Kinghorn Point
Warrain Beach

Lake Bathurst
Windellama
Sandy Point
Wattle Flat
BEES
NEST
NR
MORTON
NATIONAL
PARK
Yalwal
Yalwal
COLYMEA
SCA
Falls
Creek
Wandean
Gap
Callala Bay
Huskisson
Vincentia

Mount
Fairy
Boro
Lower
Boro
Corang
Nerriga
Coris Gap
Gilberts Gap
Sassafras
Wandandian
Erowal Bay
Hyams Beach
St Georges Basin
Jervis
Bay
Bowen Island
Governor Head
Point Perpendicular

JERRALONG
NR
NADGIGORAR
NATURE RESERVE
Mount
Coghill
Rolfes Gap
JERRAWANGALA
NP
Basin
View
Georges
Basin
JERVIS BAY AIRPORT
DEFENCE RESERVE
Cape St George
BOOEREE NP BEACHES

Braidwood
Boro
Mount
Palerang
NADGIGORAR
NR
DURRAN
DURRA
RANGE
Durran Durra
Square Top
Mountain
Fosters
Mountain
Clyde
Gorge
Mount
Tianjara
Twelve Mile
Conjola
Yatte Yattah
Cudmirrah
Swanhaven
Fishermans Paradise
Sussex
Inlet
JBT
For more detail on the
Southern Highlands
see page 23

TALLAGANDA
NATIONAL
PARK
Mount
Gillamatong
BUDAWANG
RANGE
BUDAWANG
NATIONAL
Currockbilly
Mountain
Wog Wog
Mountain
Bibbenluke
Mountain
Byangee
Mountain
MORTON
NATIONAL
Talaterang
Mountain
POINTER GAP
LOOKOUT
Bendalong
Red Head
Manyana
Cunjurong
Lake Conjola
CONJOLA
NATIONAL
PARK
Manyana
Narrawallee
Bannisters Point
Mollymook
Milton

Rossi
Misery
Ridge
Braidwood
Mongarlowe
PARK
Mount
Ash Hill
Mount
Budawang
BIMBERAMALA
NP
Pigeon House
Mountain
Termeil
MEROO NP
Meroo Head
NARRAWALLEE CREEK NR
Narrawallee Inlet
Ulladulla
Ulladulla Head
Warden Head Lighthouse
Kings Point
Burrill Lake
Lagoon Head

DIVIDING
RANGE
GREAT
KINGS
SCOTT NR
Long
Flat
Monga
Mountain
Monga
Currowan Creek
Tabourie Lake
Wairo Beach
Tabourie Point
Crampton Island
Bawley Point
Bawley Point

Ballalaba
Majors Creek
Reidsdale
Monga
East Lynne
Termeil
MURRAMARANG
NP
Brush Island
Kioloa
Belowla Island
O'Hara Head
Snapper Point
Pebbly Beach

Wallaces
Gap
Araluen North
Araluen
MONGA
NATIONAL
PARK
Nelligen
Benandarah
MURRAMARANG
NATIONAL PARK
Tranquility Bay
Grasshopper Island
Point Upright
Beagle Bay
Pebbly Beach

DEUA
ARALUEN
NP
THE BIG HOLE
AND MARBLE
ARCH
Oranmeir
Kain
CLYDE RIVER
NP
SHELL MUSEUM
Durras
Long Beach
North Head
Batemans Bay
Tollgate Islands

Gundillion
Appletree
Mountain
Bier Mountain
Gollambee
Mountain
Batemans Bay
Batehaven
Surf Beach

Fairfield
Winbenby
Mountain
Mount
Grungola
Mogo
MOGO
ZOO
Circuit Beach
Lilli Pilli
Malua Bay
Tomakin
Rosedale
Burrewarra Point
Burrewarra Point Lighthouse

GOUROCK
NP
Bald
Mountain
DEUA
NATIONAL
Wandera
Mountain
Larrys
Mountain
Bimbimbie
Mossy
Point
Broulee
North Beach
Moruya Aerodrome

Middle
Mountain
Bendethera
Mountain
PARK
Mogendoura
Mullenderee
Moruya
Kiora
Moruya Heads
Pedro (Yowaga) Point

Buranbene
Mountain
Bergalia
Congo
Congo
EUROBODALLA NP
Mullimburra Point

BADJA
SWAMPS
NR
Badja
Badja Mill
Little Badja
MINUMA
RANGE
Turlinjah
Meringo
Bingie Bingie Point
Wongaburra
Coila Lake

Loch Lomond
WEDGET
PLAIN
Tuross Head
Coila
TASMAN

Spring
Mountain
Belowra
Nerrigundah
Comerong
Mountain
Old Bodalla
Bodalla
Blackfellows Point
Potato Point
Jemisons Point

Countegany
Wadbilliga
Gap
Belowra
Barren Jumbo
Mountain
Cadgee
Cadgee
Eurobodalla
Tally Ho
Brookwood
Brou Beach
EUROBODALLA NP

TUROSS FALLS
Nadjongbilla
Wadbilliga
Cobra
Mountain
Wagonga
Inlet
Dalmeny
Kianga
Wagonga Head

Tuross
Conways Gap
TWO
RIVER
PLAIN
KOORABAN
NATIONAL
PARK
Jeffers
Image
Farm
Gembrook
Narooma
Barunga
Point
Bogola
Head
MONTAGUE ISLAND NR
Montague Island
SEA

Yowrie
Wandello
Oakside
Wandella
GULAGA
NP
Corunna
Corunna Point
Cape Dromedary
EUROBODALLA NP

WADBILLIGA
Mount
Dumpling
Narira
PARK
Central Tilba
Tilba Tilba
Little Dromedary
Mountain
Wallaga Lake

NATIONAL
Murrabrine Gap
Murrabrine
Mountain
Caroon
Monk
Cobargo
Glencraig
Grevillia
Cadjangarry
Mountain
GULAGA
NP
Beauty Point
Haywards Beach
Mossybanks
Bermagui

PARK
Brogo
Brogo Reservoir
Waterloo
Quaama
BIAMANGA
NATIONAL
BERMAGUI
NR
Bermagui South
Jerimbut Point
Baragoot Point
Milton Park
Cuttage Point

Indian
Mountain
Warrigal
Mountain
Pigeon Box
Mountain
Margaret
Park
Lynwood
Greystones
PARK
Barraga Bay
Armands Bay
Barragga Bay
Murrah Head

Crystal Brook
Little Brown
Mountain
Brogo
Brinawa
Glenbogen
Brogo Pass
Mumbulla
Mountain
Bunga
Goalen Head
MIMOSA ROCKS
Bunga Head
Aragunnu Point

SOUTH EAST
FOREST
NP
Bemboka
Irvington
Hawkshead
Warrick
Park
Milion
Park
Limegrove
TATHRA
Wapengo
Bengunnu Point
Picnic Point
Bithry Inlet

Numbugga
Morans
Gourlay
Crossing
Hillside
Tanja
TO EDEN
Bega
NATIONAL
PARK

MAPS

VICTORIA

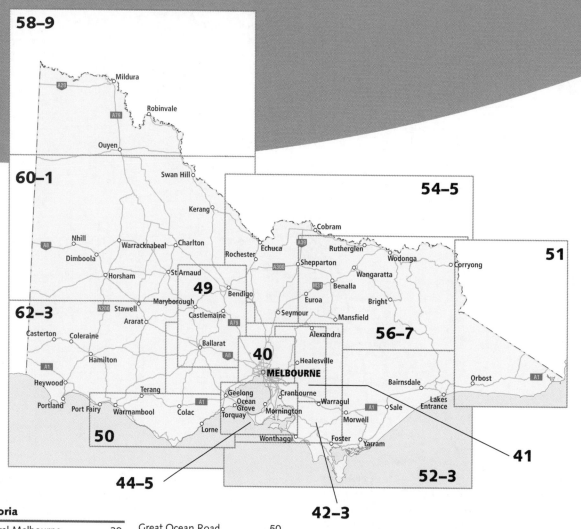

58–9

Mildura
Robinvale
A20
A79
Ouyen

60–1

Swan Hill
Kerang

54–5

Cobram
Echuca
Rochester
A39
Rutherglen
Shepparton
Wodonga
Corryong
51

Nhill
Warracknabeal
Charlton
A8
Dimboola
Horsham
St Arnaud
A300
Wangaratta
Benalla
Euroa
Bright
M31
Seymour
Mansfield

49
Bendigo
Maryborough
Castlemaine
A79

62–3
A200 Stawell
Ararat
Casterton
Coleraine
Ballarat
A6
40
Alexandra
56–7
Hamilton
A1
Healesville
MELBOURNE
Heywood
Terang
Geelong
Ocean
Grove
Cranbourne
Warragul
Bairnsdale
Orbost
A1
Portland
Port Fairy
Warrnambool
Colac
Torquay
Mornington
A1 Sale
Lakes
Entrance
A1

50
Lorne
Wonthaggi
Morwell
Foster
Yarram
41

44–5
42–3
52–3

INTER-CITY ROUTES		DISTANCE
Melbourne–Sydney via Hume Hwy/Fwy	M31 31	879 km
Melbourne–Sydney via Princes Hwy/Fwy	M1 A1 1	1039 km
Melbourne–Adelaide via Western & Dukes hwys	M8 A8 M1	729 km
Melbourne–Adelaide via Princes Hwy	M1 A1	911 km
Melbourne–Brisbane via Newell Hwy	M31 A39 39 A39 A2	1676 km

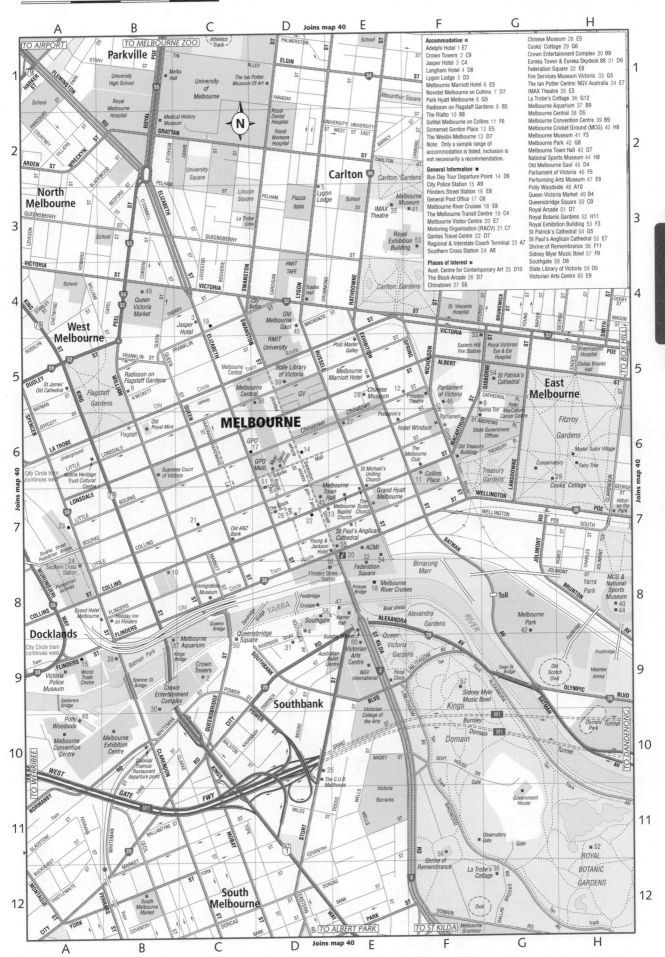

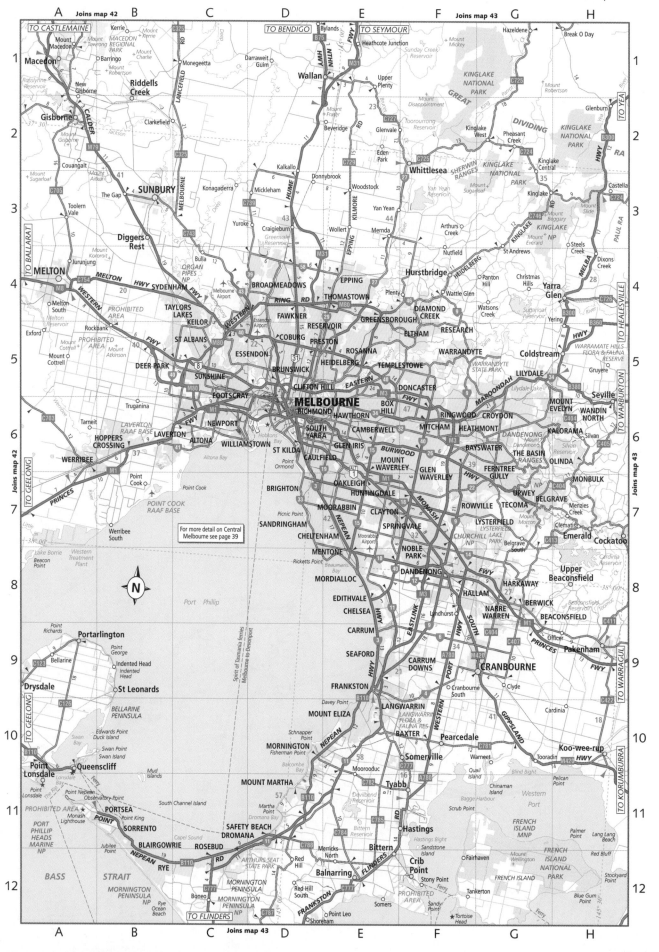

0   5   10   15   20 km

A Joins map 42 **B**   **C**   **D**   **E**   **F** Joins map 43 **G**   **H**

TO CASTLEMAINE

Kerrie
Mount Macedon
Mount Macedon
New Gisborne
Macedon

Riddells Creek
Barringo
Mount Charlie
Monegeetta
Clarkefield

Gisborne
Mount Gisborne
Couangalt
Mount Aitken

SUNBURY
The Gap
Toolern Vale

Diggers Rest
Jurunjung

MELTON
Melton South
Melton Reservoir
Rockbank
Exford
Mount Cottrell

DEER PARK
Truganina
Tarneit
SUNSHINE
ST ALBANS

HOPPERS CROSSING
WERRIBEE
LAVERTON
ALTONA
WILLIAMSTOWN
FOOTSCRAY
NEWPORT

Point Cook
Werribee South

POINT COOK RAAF BASE

For more detail on Central Melbourne see page 39

Lake Borrie
Beacon Point
Western Treatment Plant

N

Port Phillip

Point Richards
Portarlington
Point George
Indented Head
Bellarine
Drysdale
St Leonards

BELLARINE PENINSULA

Edwards Point Duck Island
Swan Bay
Swan Point
Swan Island

Point Lonsdale
Queenscliff
Mud Islands

Point Lonsdale
Point Nepean
Observatory Point
South Channel Island

PROHIBITED AREA
Monash Lighthouse
PORTSEA
Point King
SORRENTO
BLAIRGOWRIE
Jubilee Point
ROSEBUD
Capel Sound
RYE
Boneo

PORT PHILLIP HEADS MARINE NP

BASS STRAIT

MORNINGTON PENINSULA NP
Rye Ocean Beach

TO BENDIGO   *TO SEYMOUR*

Bylands
Heathcote Junction
Hazeldene
Break O Day

TO CASTLEMAINE
Upper Plenty
Mount Mickey
Mount Robertson
Glenburn

Wallan
Mount Fraser
Sunday Creek Reservoir

KINGLAKE NATIONAL PARK

Beveridge
Glenvale
Toorourrong Reservoir
Kinglake West
Pheasant Creek
Mount Slide

Kalkallo
Eden Park
Whittlesea
Kinglake Central
Castella

Donnybrook
Woodstock
Yan Yean
Mernda
Nutfield
St Andrews
Kinglake
Mount Beggary
KINGLAKE NP

Konagaderra
Mickleham
Wollert
EPPING
Plenty
Hurstbridge
Panton Hill
Christmas Hills
Steels Creek
Dixons Creek

Craigieburn
Greenvale Reservoir
Bulla
BROADMEADOWS
THOMASTOWN
DIAMOND CREEK
Wattle Glen
Watsons Creek

Melbourne Airport
Essendon Airport
EPPING
GREENSBOROUGH
ELTHAM
RESEARCH
WARRANDYTE
Coldstream

TAYLORS LAKES
KEILOR
FAWKNER
RESERVOIR
HEIDELBERG
TEMPLESTOWE

ESSENDON
COBURG
PRESTON
ROSANNA

BRUNSWICK
HEIDELBERG
DONCASTER
LILYDALE
Gruyere

CLIFTON HILL
BOX HILL
Lilydale Lake
Seville
MOUNT EVELYN
WANDIN NORTH

MELBOURNE
Richmond
HAWTHORN
RINGWOOD
CROYDON
KALORAMA
Silvan

FOOTSCRAY
SOUTH YARRA
CAMBERWELL
MITCHAM
HEATHMONT
BAYSWATER
THE BASIN
OLINDA

GLEN IRIS
BURWOOD
MOUNT WAVERLEY
GLEN WAVERLEY
FERNTREE GULLY
MONBULK

ST KILDA
CAULFIELD
OAKLEIGH
HUNTINGDALE
ROWVILLE
UPWEY
BELGRAVE
TECOMA

BRIGHTON
MOORABBIN
CLAYTON
SPRINGVALE
LYSTERFIELD
Menzies Creek
Clematis

SANDRINGHAM
Moorabbin Airport
NOBLE PARK
CHURCHILL NP
LYSTERFIELD LAKE PARK
Belgrave South
Emerald
Cockatoo

CHELTENHAM
MENTONE
DANDENONG
HARKAWAY
Upper Beaconsfield

MORDIALLOC
HALLAM
NARRE WARREN
BERWICK
BEACONSFIELD

EDITHVALE
CHELSEA
Lyndhurst
Officer
Pakenham

CARRUM
CARRUM DOWNS
CRANBOURNE
Clyde

SEAFORD
Cranbourne South
Cardinia

FRANKSTON
Davey Point
LANGWARRIN
LANGWARRIN FLORA & FAUNA RES
Pearcedale
Koo-wee-rup

MOUNT ELIZA
BAXTER
Warneet
Tooradin

Schnapper Point
MORNINGTON
Fisherman Point
SOMERVILLE
Quail Island
Pelican Point

Balcombe Bay
Moorooduc
TYABB
Chinaman Island
Western Port

MOUNT MARTHA
Martha Point
Dromana Bay
HASTINGS
Bagge Harbour
Scrub Point

SAFETY BEACH
DROMANA
Bittern
BITTERN
Sandstone Island
FRENCH ISLAND MNP

Arthurs Seat State Park
Red Hill
CRIB POINT
Fairhaven
Mount Wellington
Palmer Point
Lang Lang Beach

Balnarring
Stony Point
FRENCH ISLAND NATIONAL PARK
Red Bluff

Red Hill South
Somers
Sandy Point
Blue Gum Point
Stockyard Point

TO FLINDERS   Shoreham   Point Leo   Tankerton

Joins map 43

A   **B**   **C**   **D**   **E**   **F**   **G**   **H**

TO BALLARAT
TO GEELONG
Joins map 42
TO GEELONG

TO YEA
TO HEALESVILLE
TO WARBURTON
Joins map 43
TO WARRAGUL
TO KORUMBURRA

0 5 10 15 20 km

TO SEYMOUR

Joins map 43

TO MANSFIELD

Alexandra

TO MELBOURNE

Joins map 40

Joins map 43

TO WOODS POINT

For more detail on Mornington & Bellarine Peninsulas see pages 44–5

TO PHILLIP ISLAND

Joins map 43

TO WARRAGUL

Tyaak
Strath Creek
Reedy Creek
Murchison Gap
Little Falls
Strath Falls
Flowerdale
Hazeldene
Break O Day
Mount Mickey
Sunday Creek Reservoir
KINGLAKE NATIONAL PARK
Mount Disappointment
Toorourrong Reservoir
Kinglake West
Pheasant Creek
Humevale
WHITTLESEA
SHERWIN RANGES
Mount Sugarloaf
Strathewen
Kinglake Central
Kinglake
Kinglake East
Castella
Toolangi
Arthurs Creek
Nutfield
St Andrews
Steels Creek
Dixons Creek
Cottles Bridge
Smiths Gully
Christmas Hills
Hurstbridge
Panton Hill
Rob Roy
Wattle Glen
Diamond Creek
Research
Warrandyte
GULF STATION
Yarra Glen
Yarra Valley Wineries
Yering
Coldstream
Gruyere
Seville
Lilydale
Mooroolbark
Croydon
Mount Evelyn
Wandin North
Woori Yallock
Yellingbo
Launching Place
Yarra Junction
Nunawading
Mitcham
Ringwood
Heathmont
Bayswater
Boronia
Kalorama
Silvan
Ferntree Gully
Upper Ferntree Gully
Sassafras
Olinda
The Basin
Sherbrooke
The Patch
Kallista
Monbulk
Macclesfield
Nangana
Rowville
Tecoma
Belgrave
Selby
Menzies Creek
Clematis
Avonsleigh
Emerald
Cockatoo
Gembrook
Lysterfield
Narre Warren North
Harkaway
Upper Beaconsfield
Beaconsfield
Officer
Pakenham
Noble Park
Dandenong
Hallam
Hampton Park
Narre Warren
Berwick
Maryknoll
Lyndhurst
CRANBOURNE
Cranbourne South
Clyde
Cardinia
Nar Nar Goon
Tynong
Garfield
Bunyip
Cora Lynn
Iona
Longwarry
Yea
Limestone
Murrindindi
Mount Caroline
Glenburn
Mount Despair
GREAT DIVIDING RANGE
Wilhelmina Falls
Mount Mitchell
Mount Klondyke
Mount Tanglefoot
St Fillans
Narbethong
YARRA RANGES
Donnelly's Weir Park
Maroondah Reservoir Park
Healesville
BICENTENNIAL NATIONAL TRAIL
Badger Weir Park
Don Valley
Millgrove
Wesburn
Warburton
Gladysdale
Hoddles Creek
Three Bridges
Powelltown
THE BLUE RA
Tomahawk Gap
The Three Sisters
KURTH KILN REGIONAL PARK
BUNYIP STATE PARK
Bunyip Gap
BLACK SNAKE RA
Tonimbuk
Mount Towt
Garfield North
Tonimbuk
Drouin West
Labertouche
Jindivick
Neerim South
Tarago
Rokeby
Brandy Creek
Buln Buln
Buln Buln East
Crossover
Neerim East
Neerim
Neerim Junction
Nayook
MT BAW BAW RD
ALPINE TROUT FARM
Noojee
NOOJEE
Mount Beenak
Mount Myrtalia
Alexandra
Acheron
Thornton
Taggerty
Buxton
BUXTON TROUT FARM
Marysville
LADY TALBOT FOREST DRIVE
STEVENSON FALLS
Cambarville
LAKE MOUNTAIN
SKI AREA
Lake Mountain
CERBEREAN RANGES
THE CATHEDRAL
CATHEDRAL RANGE STATE PARK
South Jawbone Peak
Mount Sugarloaf
Snobs Creek
Rubicon
BLUE RANGE
Mount Margaret Gap
Royston Gap
Dudley Saddle
FEDERATION RANGE
Snobs Gap
Eildon
Eildon Dam
LAKE EILDON
LAKE EILDON NATIONAL PARK
Mount Enterprise
Haines Saddle
Skyline
Survey Peak
GOULBURN
EILDON
JAMIESON
YARRA RANGES NATIONAL PARK
WOODS POINT RD
O'Shannassy Reservoir
Upper Yarra Reservoir
Upper Yarra Dam
McMahons Creek
Warburton East
Big Pats Creek
La-La Falls
Gifford Saddle
The Big Rock
MAROONDAH
WARBURTON HWY
MELBA HWY
YEA HWY
PAUL RA
PRINCES HWY
MONASH FWY
STH GIPPSLAND HWY
WESTERN PORT HWY
EASTLINK
BURWOOD HWY
WARRANDYTE STATE PARK
SUGARLOAF RESERVOIR PARK
DANDENONG RANGES NATIONAL PARK
WILLIAM RICKETTS SANCTUARY
DANDENONG RANGES DRIVE
PUFFING BILLY
PUFFING BILLY STEAM MUSEUM
CHURCHILL NP
LYSTERFIELD LAKE PARK
CARDINIA RESERVOIR
HEALESVILLE SANCTUARY
HEDGEND MAZE
YARRA VALLEY DAIRY
YARRA GLEN RACECOURSE
MALLESONS LOOKOUT
Mount Toole-Be-Wong
BLACK SPUR
Carter Gap
Mount Vinegar
Mount Juliet
Mount Riddell
Boobyalla Saddle
Mount Boobyalla
Donna Buang
Mount Victoria
TOMMY FINN'S TROUT FARM
Mount Bride
Mount Donna Buang
ACHERON WAY
MARYSVILLE WOODS POINT RD
GRANITE RA
Mount Gordon
Mount Strickland
Mount Kitchener
Mount Edgar
Mount Stinton
Cora Lynn Falls
Keppel Falls
Mount Observation
Mount Arnold
Cumberland Falls
Royston Gap
TORBRECK RA
Mount Torbreck
Mount Nibo
Mount Cunningham
WHANREGARWEN
Mount Pleasant
Rubicon
Mount Robertson
Kinglake
Reedy Creek

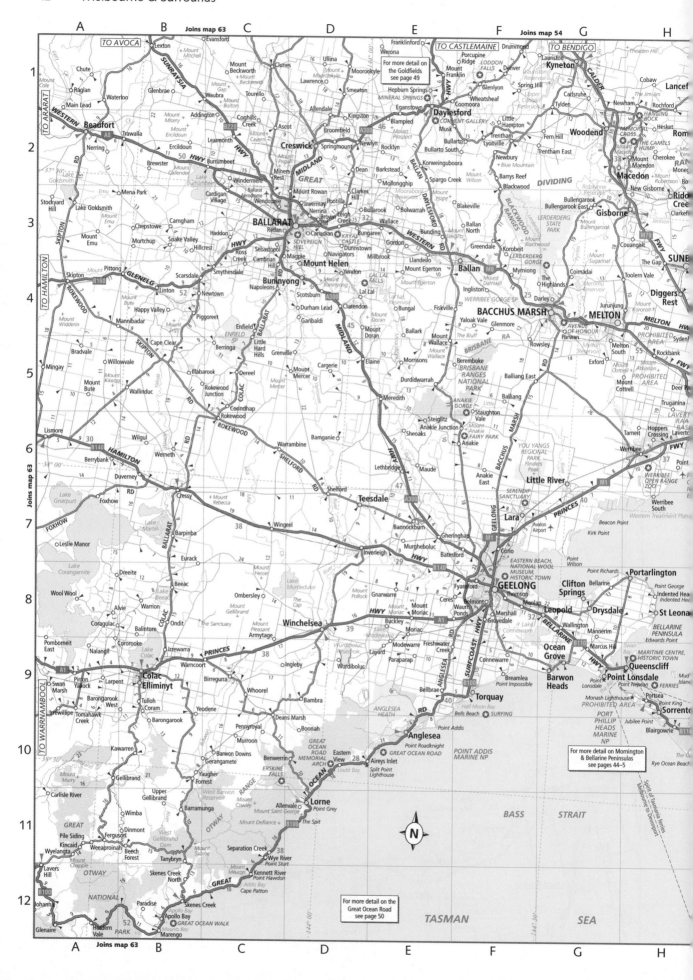

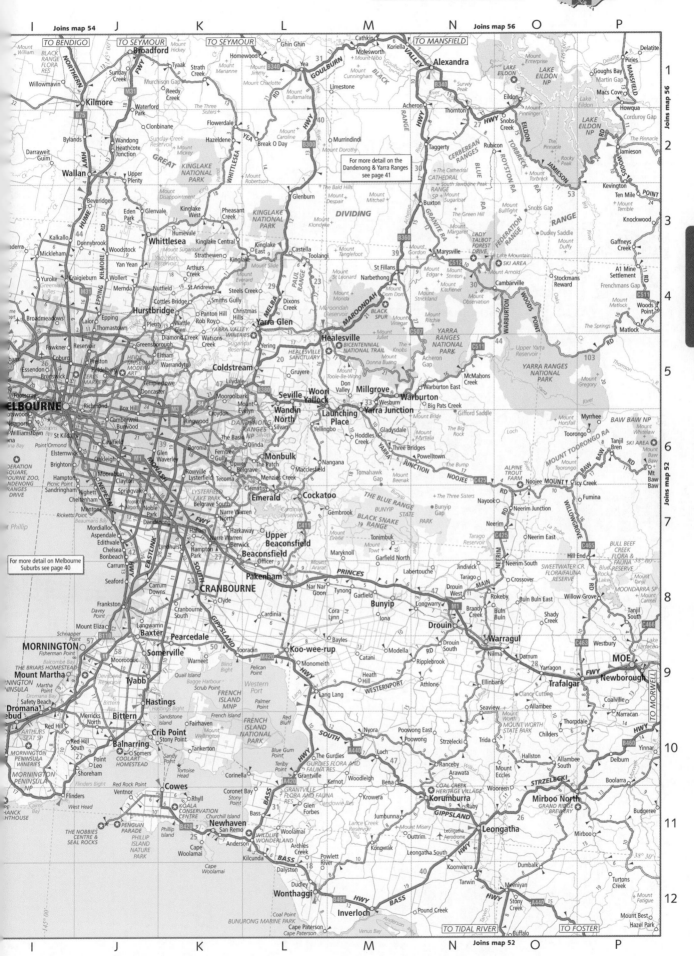

Joins map 42

TO WERRIBEE

For more detail on Geelong see page 46

Joins map 42

Werribee South

Rothwell

SERENDIP SANCTUARY

AVALON RACEWAY

Lara

Lara Lake

Hovell Park

Rosewall

Lovely Banks

Moorabool

Batesford

Norlane

Corio

Bell Park

North Shore

Avalon

Point Lillias

Avalon Airport

LIMEBURNERS LAGOON NATURE RESERVE

WILDLIFE RESERVE

Beacon Point

Western Treatment Plant

Kirk Point

Point Wilson

Port Phillip

POINT RICHARDS CHANNEL

Point Richards

Port Bellarine

Portarlington

Point George

PORTARLINGTON GOLF COURSE

Indented Head

Indented Head

Hamlyn Heights

Ripplesid

Geelong North

Drumcondra

Fyansford

GEELONG

Geelong East

Geelong South

Thomson

Highton

Belmont

Breakwater

Moolap

St Albans Park

Marshall

Grovedale

Mount Dunned

Connewarre

Breamlea

Point Impossible

Corio Bay

Stingaree Bay

EASTERN BEACH, NATIONAL WOOL MUSEUM, HISTORIC TOWN

Outer Harbour

WILSON SPIT

Point Henry

Clifton Springs

CLIFTON SPRINGS GOLF COURSE

Bellarine

Drysdale

Murradoc

St Leonards

DRYSDALE REC RES

Leopold

Curlewis

BELLARINE PENINSULA RAILWAY

BELLARINE PENINSULA

Mannerim

Marcus

Marcus Hill

Edwards Point

Duck Island

LOWER BLUFF WILDLIFE RESERVE

PORT PHILLIP HEADS MARINE NP

Swan Bay

Swan Island

Swan Point

ADVENTURE PARK

Wallington

Lake Connewarre

A MAZE 'N GAMES

Fenwick

WILDLIFE RESERVE

JIRRAHLINGA KOALA & WILDLIFE RESERVE

Barwon Heads

Ocean Grove

Collendina

Lake Victoria

Lonsdale Bay

MARITIME CENTRE, BELLARINE PENINSULA RAILWAY & HISTORIC TOWN

Queenscliff

PORT PHILLIP HEADS MARINE NP

Mud Islands

PINNACE CHANNEL

SYMONDS CHANNEL

BLACK LIGHTHOUSE, FORT QUEENSCLIFF, WHITE LIGHTHOUSE

BARWON HEADS GOLF CLUB

Barwon Head

Point Lonsdale

Point Lonsdale

PORT PHILLIP HEADS MARINE NP

Point Nepean

FORT NEPEAN

PORT PHILLIP HEADS MARINE NP

FERRIES

Observatory Point

SOUTH CHANNEL

South Channel Island

The Rip

PROHIBITED AREA

Monash Lighthouse

LONDON BRIDGE

Portsea

Point King

Sorrento

Capel Sound

COLLINS SETTLEMENT HISTORIC SITE

MORNINGTON PENINSULA

NATIONAL PARK

Jubilee Point

Blairgowrie

Rye

Tootgarook

Rosebud West

Rosebud

McCrae

ROSEBUD COUNTRY CLUB

MORNINGTON PENINSULA

Rye Ocean Beach

Saint Andrews Beach

MORNINGTON PENINSULA

Fingal

Boneo

MORNINGTON PENINSULA NATIONAL PARK

Gunnamatta Beach

NATIONAL PARK

Cape Schanck

CAPE SCHANCK LIGHTHOUSE

Cape Schanck

SURFWORLD AUSTRALIA

Torquay

Jan Juc

Half Moon Bay

SURFING

POINT DANGER MARINE SANCTUARY

BUCKLEY FALLS

Wandana Heights

BARWON VALLEY GOLF COURSE

Spirit of Tasmania ferries Melbourne to Devonport

Spirit of Tasmania ferries Melbourne to Devonport

TO WERRIBEE

TO BALLARAT

TO HAMILTON

TO COLAC

TO LORNE

GEELONG BACCHUS MARSH RD

MIDLAND HWY

PRINCES HWY

HAMILTON HWY

RING RD

BELLARINE HWY

BARWON HEADS RD

SURFCOAST HWY

GEELONG RD

PRINCES FWY

PRINCES HWY

GEELONG PORTARLINGTON RD

PORTARLINGTON RD

QUEENSCLIFF RD

OCEAN GROVE RD

DRYSDALE RD

BELLARINE HWY

NEPEAN HWY

POINT NEPEAN RD

ROSEBUD FLINDERS RD

FLINDERS RD

BASS STRAIT

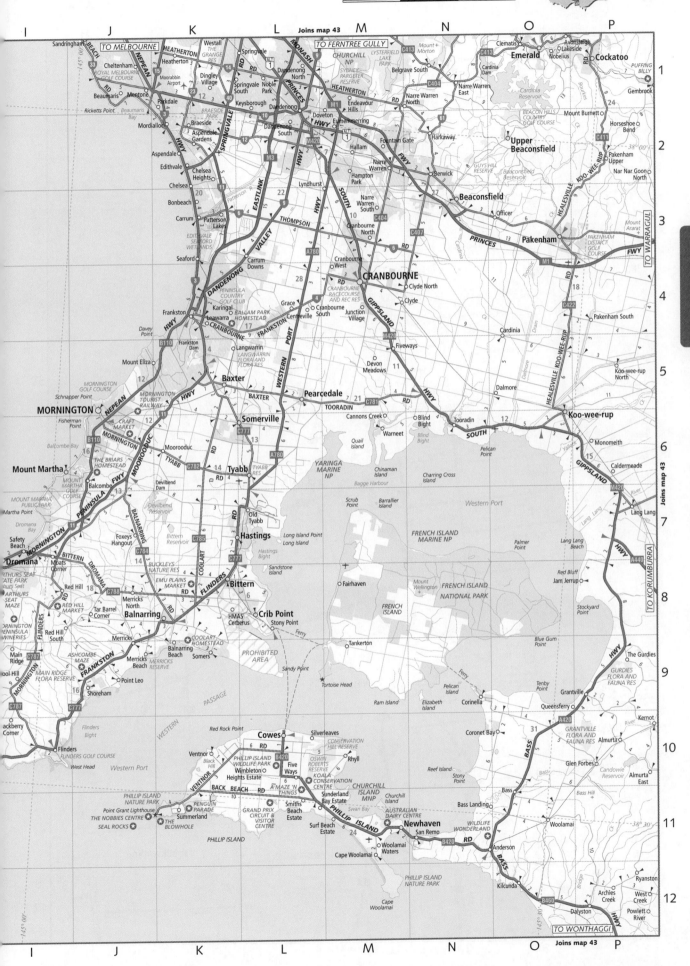

0   5   10   15 km

TO MELBOURNE
TO FERNTREE GULLY

Sandringham

Cheltenham
Heatherton
Heatherton
Westall
THE GRANGE RES
Springvale
Springvale
Dandenong North
Springfield
LYSTERFIELD
LAKE PARK
CHURCHILL
NP
Mount
Morton
Clematis
Avonsleigh
Lakeside
Nobelius
Emerald
Nobelius
Cockatoo
PUFFING
BILLY
ROYAL MELBOURNE
GOLF COURSE
Beaumaris
Mentone
Moorabbin
Airport
Dingley
Village
Springvale
South
Noble
Park
Keysborough
Dandenong
Dandenong
South
Doveton
Eumemmerring
Endeavour
Hills
Belgrave South
Narre Warren
North
Narre Warren
East
CARDINIA
Reservoir
Cardinia
Dam
BEACON HILLS
COUNTRY
GOLF COURSE
Mount Burnett
Gembrook
Horseshoe
Bend
Parkdale
Ricketts Point
Beaumaris
Bay
Braeside
Aspendale
Gardens
BRAESIDE
PARK
Hallam
Fountain Gate
Harkaway
Upper
Beaconsfield
GUYS HILL
RESERVE
Beaconsfield
Reservoir
Mount
Ararat
Pakenham
Upper
Nar Nar Goon
North
Mordialloc
Aspendale
Edithvale
Chelsea
Heights
Lyndhurst
Narre
Warren
Hampton
Park
Narre Warren
South
Berwick
Beaconsfield
Officer
Pakenham
PAKENHAM
DISTRICT
GOLF COURSE
Chelsea
Bonbeach
Carrum
Patterson
Lakes
EDITHVALE
SEAFORD
WETLANDS
Carrum
Downs
Cranbourne
North
Cranbourne
West
PRINCES
Pakenham
TO WARRAGUL
Seaford
CRANBOURNE
Clyde North
Clyde
Koo-wee-rup
North
Pakenham South
Frankston
Karingal
Leawarra
BALLAM PARK
HOMESTEAD
Grace
Centreville
Cranbourne
South
CRANBOURNE
RACECOURSE
AND REC RES
Junction
Village
Cardinia
Davey
Point
Frankston
Dam
PENINSULA
COUNTRY
GOLF CLUB
Langwarrin
LANGWARRIN
FLORA AND
FLORA RES
Fiveways
Dalmore
Mount Eliza
Baxter
Baxter
Devon
Meadows
MORNINGTON
GOLF COURSE
Schnapper Point
MORNINGTON
TOURIST
RAILWAY
Somerville
Pearcedale
Tooradin
Cannons Creek
Blind
Bight
Tooradin
Koo-wee-rup
Monomeith
MORNINGTON
Fisherman
Point
CRAFT
MARKET
Moorooduc
Warneet
Blind
Bight
SOUTH
Caldermeade
Balcombe Bay
THE BRIARS
HOMESTEAD
Tyabb
TYABB
RES
Quail
Island
Pelican
Point
Lang Lang
Mount Martha
Balcombe
Devilbend
Dam
Old
Tyabb
YARINGA
MARINE
NP
Chinaman
Island
Bagge Harbour
Charring Cross
Island
Western Port
Lang Lang
Beach
MOUNT
MARTHA
PUBLIC PARK
MOUNT MARTHA
GOLF COURSE
Devilbend
Reservoir
Hastings
Long Island Point
Long Island
Scrub
Point
Barrallier
Island
FRENCH ISLAND
MARINE NP
Palmer
Point
Martha Point
Dromana
Bay
Safety
Beach
Foxeys
Hangout
Bittern
Reservoir
Hastings
Bight
Sandstone
Island
FRENCH ISLAND
NATIONAL PARK
Red Bluff
Jam Jerrup
Dromana
ARTHURS SEAT
STATE PARK
Mpats
Corner
BUCKLEYS
NATURE RES
Bittern
EMU PLAINS
MARKET
FLINDERS
Fairhaven
Mount
Wellington
FRENCH
ISLAND
Stockyard
Point
ARTHURS
SEAT
MAZE
Red Hill
RED HILL
MARKET
Merricks
North
Tar Barrel
Corner
Balnarring
HMAS
Cerberus
Crib Point
Stony Point
Tankerton
Blue Gum
Point
The Gurdies
GURDIES
FLORA AND
FAUNA RES
MORNINGTON
PENINSULA
WINERIES
Red Hill
South
Merricks
COOLART
HOMESTEAD
Somers
Ferry
Main
Ridge
Main Ridge
FLORA RESERVE
Merricks
Beach
Balnarring
Beach
MERRICKS
RESERVE
PROHIBITED
AREA
Sandy Point
Pelican
Island
Ferry
Elizabeth
Island
Corinella
Tenby
Point
Grantville
GRANTVILLE
FLORA AND
FAUNA RES
Shoreham
Point Leo
Tortoise Head
Ram Island
Queensferry
Kernot
Blackberry
Corner
Flinders
Bight
Red Rock Point
Cowes
Silverleaves
CONSERVATION
HILL RESERVE
Coronet Bay
Almurta
Flinders
FLINDERS GOLF COURSE
Ventnor
Black
Hill
PHILLIP ISLAND
WILDLIFE PARK
Wimbleton
Heights Estate
Five
Ways
OSWIN
ROBERTS
RESERVE
Rhyll
KOALA
CONSERVATION
CENTRE
Reef Island
Glen Forbes
Almurta
East
West Head
Western Port
PHILLIP ISLAND
NATURE PARK
BACK BEACH
A'MAZE 'N
THINGS
Smiths
Beach
Estate
Sunderland
Bay Estate
CHURCHILL
ISLAND MNP
Churchill
Island
Bass
Bass Landing
Point Grant Lighthouse
THE NOBBIES CENTRE
SEAL ROCKS
PENGUIN
PARADE
Summerland
THE
BLOWHOLE
GRAND PRIX
CIRCUIT &
VISITOR
CENTRE
Surf Beach
Estate
Swan Bay
AUSTRALIAN
DAIRY CENTRE
Newhaven
San Remo
PHILLIP ISLAND
WILDLIFE
WONDERLAND
Woolamai
PHILLIP ISLAND
PHILLIP ISLAND
NATURE PARK
Cape Woolamai
Woolamai
Waters
Anderson
Ryanston
Cape
Woolamai
Kilcunda
Dalyston
Archies
Creek
West
Creek
Powlett
River
TO WONTHAGGI
TO KORUMBURRA

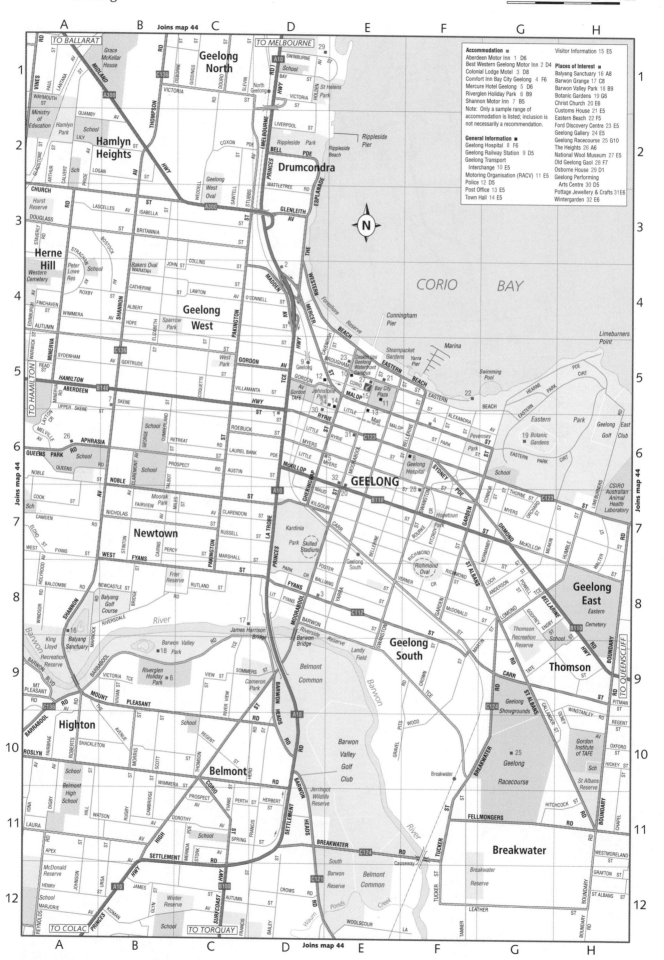

Accommodation ■
Aberdeen Motor Inn 1 D6
Best Western Geelong Motor Inn 2 D4
Colonial Lodge Motel 3 D8
Comfort Inn Bay City Geelong 4 F6
Mercure Hotel Geelong 5 D6
Riverglen Holiday Park 6 B9
Shannon Motor Inn 7 B5
Note: Only a sample range of
accommodation is listed; inclusion is
not necessarily a recommendation.

General Information ■
Geelong Hospital 8 F6
Geelong Railway Station 9 D5
Geelong Transport
  Interchange 10 E5
Motoring Organisation (RACV) 11 E5
Police 12 D5
Post Office 13 E5
Town Hall 14 E5

Visitor Information 15 E5

Places of Interest ■
Balyang Sanctuary 16 A8
Barwon Grange 17 C8
Barwon Valley Park 18 B9
Botanic Gardens 19 G6
Christ Church 20 E6
Customs House 21 E5
Eastern Beach 22 F5
Ford Discovery Centre 23 E5
Geelong Gallery 24 E5
Geelong Racecourse 25 G10
The Heights 26 A6
National Wool Museum 27 E5
Old Geelong Gaol 28 F7
Osborne House 29 D1
Geelong Performing
  Arts Centre 30 E5
Pottage Jewellery & Crafts 31 E6
Wintergarden 32 E6

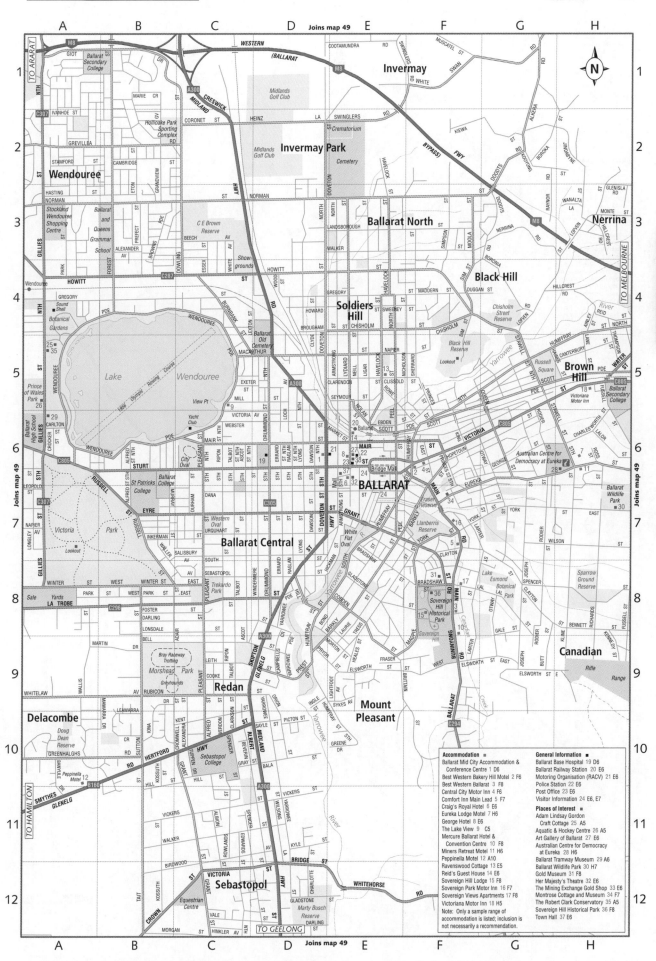

Scale: 0 0.5 1 1.5 2 km

N

Accommodation ■
Ballarat Mid City Accommodation &
    Conference Centre 1 D6
Best Western Bakery Hill Motel 2 F6
Best Western Ballarat 3 F8
Central City Motor Inn 4 F6
Comfort Inn Main Lead 5 F7
Craig's Royal Hotel 6 E6
Eureka Lodge Motel 7 H6
George Hotel 8 E6
The Lake View 9 C5
Mercure Ballarat Hotel &
    Convention Centre 10 F8
Miners Retreat Motel 11 H6
Peppinella Motel 12 A10
Ravenswood Cottage 13 E5
Reid's Guest House 14 E6
Sovereign Hill Lodge 15 F8
Sovereign Park Motor Inn 16 F7
Sovereign Views Apartments 17 F8
Victoriana Motor Inn 18 H5
Note: Only a sample range of
accommodation is listed; inclusion is
not necessarily a recommendation.

General Information ■
Ballarat Base Hospital 19 D6
Ballarat Railway Station 20 E6
Motoring Organisation (RACV) 21 E6
Police Station 22 E6
Post Office 23 E6
Visitor Information 24 E6, E7

Places of Interest ■
Adam Lindsay Gordon
    Craft Cottage 25 A5
Aquatic & Hockey Centre 26 A5
Art Gallery of Ballarat 27 E6
Australian Centre for Democracy
    at Eureka 28 H6
Ballarat Tramway Museum 29 A6
Ballarat Wildlife Park 30 H7
Gold Museum 31 F8
Her Majesty's Theatre 32 E6
The Mining Exchange Gold Shop 33 E6
Montrose Cottage and Museum 34 F7
The Robert Clark Conservatory 35 A5
Sovereign Hill Historical Park 36 F8
Town Hall 37 E6

TO ARARAT · TO MELBOURNE · TO HAMILTON · TO GEELONG

Wendouree · Invermay · Invermay Park · Ballarat North · Black Hill · Nerrina · Soldiers Hill · Brown Hill · Lake Wendouree · BALLARAT · Ballarat Central · Mount Pleasant · Canadian · Redan · Delacombe · Sebastopol · Victoria Park

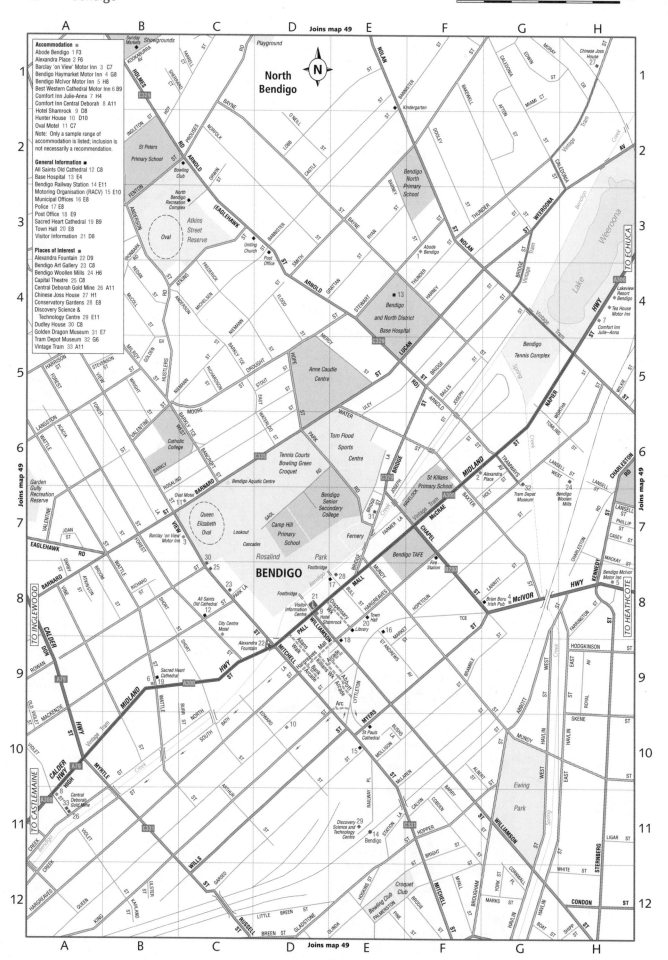

0   200   400   600 m

A   B   C   D   Joins map 49   E   F   G   H

**North
Bendigo**

N

BENDIGO

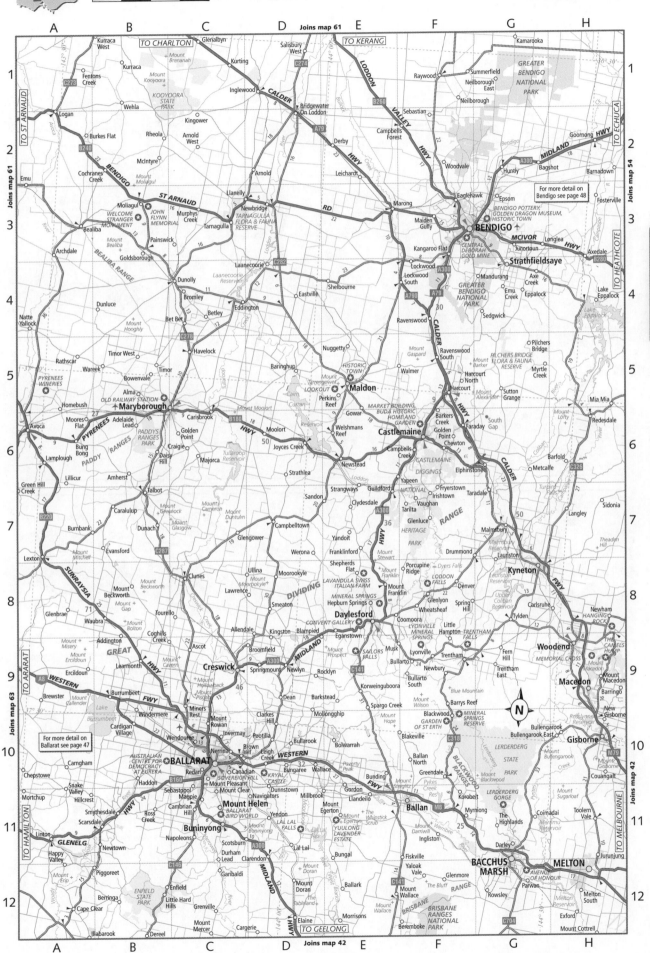

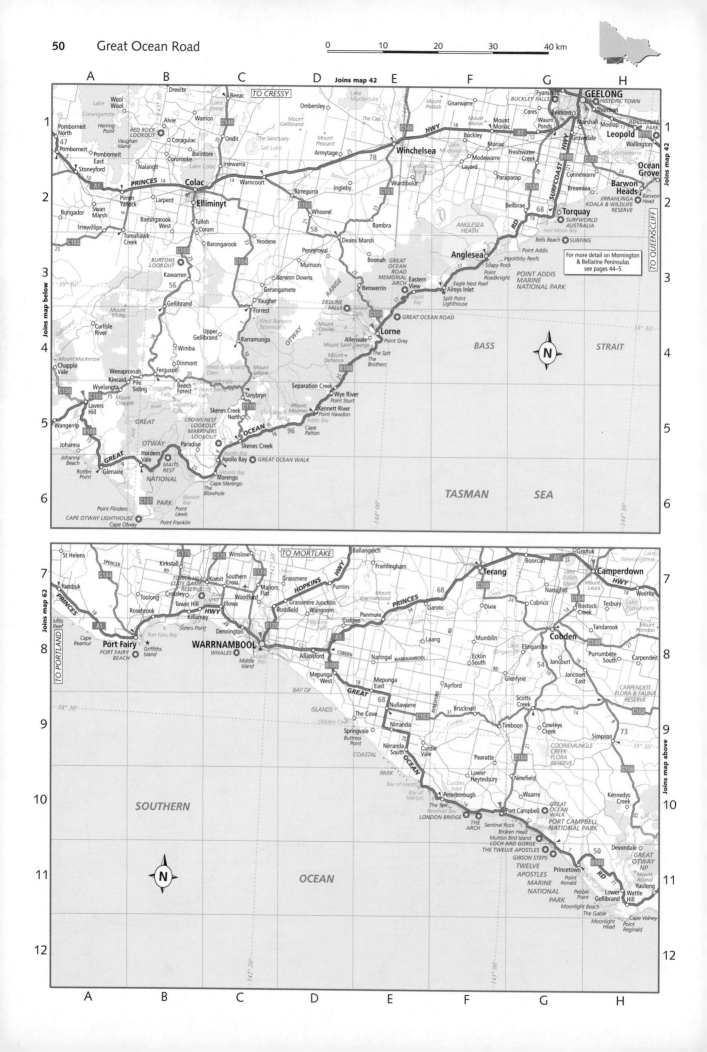

0   10   20   30   40 km

A   B   C   D   Joins map 42   E   F   G   H

1

Wool Wool
Dreeite
Beeac
TO CRESSY
Ombersley
Lake Murdeduke
The Cap
Mount Pollock
Gnarwarre
BUCKLEY FALLS
Fyansford
GEELONG
HISTORIC TOWN
Thomson
ADVENTURE PARK
Moolap
Pomborneit North
Herring Point
RED ROCK LOOKOUT
Alvie
Warrion
C146
Lake Beeac
Mount Gellibrand
C145
HWY
18
Mount Monac
Mount Moriac
Ceres
Buckley
Belmont
Marshall
Grovedale
A1
12
SURFCOAST
HWY
B110
Leopold
Wallington
Pomborneit
47
Coragulac
Balintore
Ondit
The Sanctuary
Salt Lake
Armytage
25
Winchelsea
78
Modewarre
Moriac
Freshwater Creek
Waurn Ponds
Connewarre
C121
24
Lake Connewarre
Ocean Grove

2

Pomborneit East
Stoneyford
Nalangil
Cororooke
Lake Colac
Warncoort
14
Birregurra
Ingleby
C151
Wurdiboluc
Wurdiboluc Reservoir
Layard
Paraparap
C134
Breamlea
Barwon Heads
Barwon Head
Bungador
PRINCES
14
Colac
Larpent
Elliminyt
C152
Whoorel
Bambra
Bellbrae
68
Torquay
SURFWORLD AUSTRALIA
Half Moon Bay
Bells Beach
JIRRAHLINGA KOALA & WILDLIFE RESERVE

3

Swan Marsh
Pirren Yallock
Barongarook West
Tulloh
Coram
21
58
Deans Marsh
ANGLESEA HEATH
19
SURFING
Irrewillipe
C163
Tomahawk Creek
Yeodene
Barongarook
Pennyroyal
Boonah
GREAT OCEAN ROAD MEMORIAL ARCH
Eastern View
Anglesea
11
Soapy Rock
Point Addis
Ingoldsby Reefs
POINT ADDIS MARINE NATIONAL PARK
25
BURTONS LOOKOUT
Murroon
Benwerrin
Eagle Nest Reef
Point Roadknight
Kawarren
56
Barwon Downs
Gerangamete
RANGE
Aireys Inlet
Split Point Lighthouse

4

Carlisle River
Gellibrand
Yaugher
Forrest
ERSKINE FALLS
Straw Falls
C151
GREAT OCEAN ROAD
38° 30'
BASS
STRAIT
Mount Mirry
River
16
Upper Gellibrand
Barramunga
West Barwon Reservoir
Mount Cowley
Lorne
Point Grey
N
Chapple Vale
Mount Mackenzie
Wimba
Dinmont
West Gellibrand Dam
Mount Sabine
Allenvale
Mount Saint George
The Spit
Mount Defiance
The Brothers

5

Kincaid
Pile
Weeaproinah
Ferguson
20
B100
Separation Creek
Wye River
Point Sturt
Lavers Hill
Wyelangta
Siding
Congram Falls
Beech Forest
Beauchamp Falls
Hopetoun Falls
Mount Meuron
Kennett River
Point Hawdon
Addis Bay
Wangerrip
B100
15
Mount Chapple
OTWAY
Paradise
Skenes Creek North
C119
OCEAN
Carisbrook Falls
16
96
Cape Patton
CROWS NEST LOOKOUT
MARRINERS LOOKOUT
TASMAN
SEA

6

Johanna
GREAT
Hordern Vale
Skenes Creek
Johanna Beach
MAITS REST
Apollo Bay
GREAT OCEAN WALK
Rotten Point
Glenaire
Marengo
NATIONAL
C157
PARK
Point Flinders
Cape Marengo
The Blowhole
Mounts Bay
Blanket Bay
Point Lewis
CAPE OTWAY LIGHTHOUSE
Cape Otway
Point Franklin

7

St Helens
SPENCER
G184
Kirkstall
C178
C175
Winslow
TO MORTLAKE
Ballangeich
Framlingham
A1
Boorcan
Gnotuk
Lake Weerangamuk
Camperdown
Yambuk
Toolong
Crossley
Koroit
Southern Cross
C174
Grassmere
Purnim
Mount Warrnambool
Terang
C156
Naroghid
HWY
Weerite
PRINCES
TOWER HILL STATE GAME RESERVE
Rosebrook
Tower Hill
Woodford
Illowa
Mailors Flat
Grassmere Junction
Wangoom
PRINCES
Garvoc
Dixie
Cobrico
Bostock Creek
Tesbury
Lake Purrumbete

8

Cape Reamur
A1
Port Fairy
Killarney
HWY
Bushfield
Cudgee
Panmure
34
Mumblin
Lake Elingamite
Cobden
C149
TO PORTLAND
PRINCES
Mills Reef
PORT FAIRY BEACH
Griffiths Island
Sisters Point
Dennington
B120
WARRNAMBOOL
WHALES
Middle Island
COBDEN
Naringal
WARRNAMBOOL
Laang
Ecklin South
Elingamite
Jancourt
54
Purrumbete South
Carpendeit
Jancourt East

9

PRINCES
38° 30'
Allansford
12
Lady Bay
Mepunga West
B100
18
Mepunga East
GREAT
68
Ayrford
Glenfyne
Scotts Creek
19
CARPENDEIT FLORA & FAUNA RESERVE
C164
BAY OF
ISLANDS
The Cove
Nullawarre
C164
Brucknell
Timboon
Cowleys Creek
Simpson
73
C156
Childers Cove
Nirranda
Curdies
COASTAL
Nirranda South
Curdie Vale
Paaratte
Lower Heytesbury
Newfield
C164
COORIEMUNGLE CREEK FLORA RESERVE

10

SOUTHERN
PARK
Bay of Islands
Bay of Martyrs
Peterborough
The Spit
Newfield Bay
LONDON BRIDGE
Springvale
Buttress Point
14
Waarre
Port Campbell
GREAT OCEAN WALK
PORT CAMPBELL NATIONAL PARK
Kennedys Creek
Devondale
GREAT OTWAY NP

11

N
OCEAN
THE ARCH
Sentinel Rock
Broken Head
Mutton Bird Island
LOCH ARD GORGE
THE TWELVE APOSTLES
GIBSON STEPS
TWELVE APOSTLES MARINE NATIONAL PARK
7
50
Princetown
B100
Point Ronald
Pebble Point
Lower Gellibrand
Mount Acland
Yuulong
Wattle Hill
Moonlight Beach
The Gable
Moonlight Head
Point Reginald
Cape Volney

12

142° 30'   142° 00'   143° 00'   143° 30'

A   B   C   D   E   F   G   H

Joins map 42
Joins map below
Joins map above
Joins map 62
For more detail on Mornington & Bellarine Peninsulas see pages 44–5

TO QUEENSCLIFF

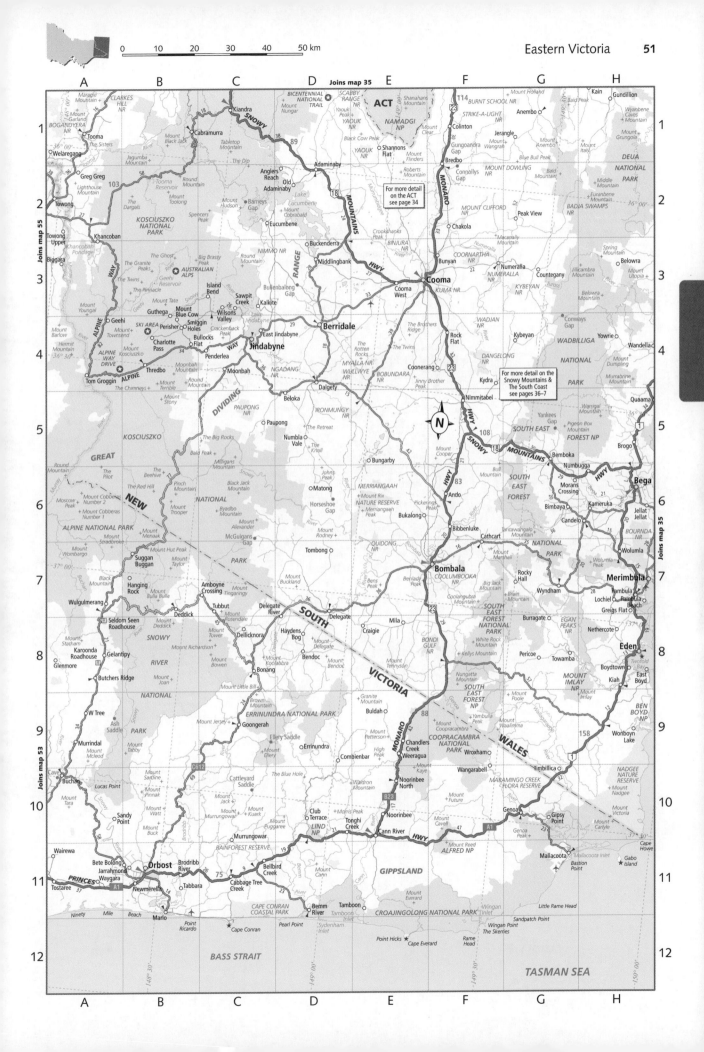

0 10 20 30 40 50 km

Joins map 35

ACT

For more detail on the ACT see page 34

For more detail on the Snowy Mountains & The South Coast see pages 36–7

N

Joins map 55

Joins map 53

Joins map 35

BASS STRAIT

TASMAN SEA

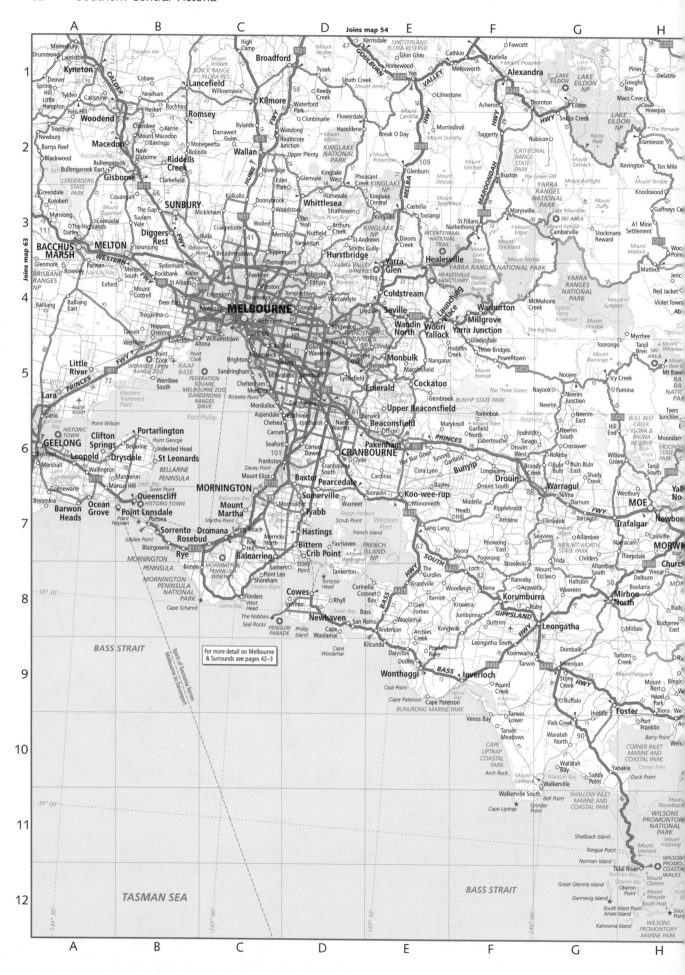

Joins map 54

Joins map 63

For more detail on Melbourne & Surrounds see pages 42–3

BASS STRAIT

TASMAN SEA

BASS STRAIT

0 10 20 30 40 50 km

I J K L M N O P

Joins map 51

1 2 3 4 5 6 7 8 9 10 11 12

Mount Cobbler
Mount Selwyn
AUSTRALIAN ALPS
The Twins
Hotham Heights
SKI AREA
Dinner Plain
Anglers Rest
Benambra
Mount Bung Bung
Mount Stradbroke
Mount Wombargo
Suggan Buggan

The Pinnacle
The Monument
Mount Buller SKI AREA
Mount Bullet No 3+
Mirimbah
ALPINE
Mount Despair
Mount Freezeout
Mount Tabletop
112
GREAT RANGE
Cobungra
C543
Hinnomunjie
ALPINE
Mount Tambo
NATIONAL
Mount Wombargo
Black Mountain
Hanging Rock

Mount Stirling
Mount Thorn
Mount Speculation
DIVIDING
Dargo High Plains
B500
ALPINE
Omeo
Mount Cook
Mount Shaw
Mount Simson
PARK
Wulgulmerang

Mount Darling
Mount Howitt
Wombat Gap
Mount Sarah
NATIONAL
Mount Parslow
21
Mount Livingstone
Mount George
Bindi
Mount Deception
Seldom Seen Roadhouse

NATIONAL PARK
Mount Clear
GREAT
Mount Darling
RANGE
70
BICENTENNIAL NATIONAL TRAIL
Mount Phipps
Mount Mungobala
Tongio
Mount Stawell
Mount Hopeless
Glenmore
Mount Stewart
Karoonda Roadhouse
21
Gelantipy

The Nobs Spur
Mount Von Guerard
Mount Short
Mount Larrit
Mountain Ash
SNOWY RANGE
PARK
Woonnangatta
Dargo
Cassilis
Tongio West
Swifts Creek
Mount Nugong
Mount Statham
Butchers Ridge

Mount McKinty
RANGE
Mount Lookout
The White Ladies
The Two Creeks
The Walnuts
Doctors Flat
Mount Hopeful
Timbarra
NATIVE GRASSLAND CONSERVATION RESERVE
W Tree
SNOWY RIVER NATIONAL PARK

(WONNANGATTA MOROKA UNIT)
Crooked River
Mount Ewen
Mount Delusion
Brookville
Ensay North
Mount Dawson
Ash Saddle

The Horrell Top
The Sisters
Mount Dawson
Mount Kent
The Farm
Mount Baldhead
Ensay South
Ensay
Reedy Flat
Glenmore
Mount Dawson
Murrindal

Mount Lookout
MOROKA
Mount Tamboritha
The Long Spur
Dargo
Mount Thomson
Stirling
ROAD
121
Battle Point
Mount Victoria
Mount Johnston
Mount Mcleod

The Crinoline
RANGE
The Pinnacles
Waterford
Hells Gate
B500
Tambo Crossing
Mount Elizabeth
Buchan
Mount Tabby

Primrose Gap
AVON
The Razorback
The Sentinels
Mount Djoandah
Morris Peak
Mount Sugarloaf
Buchan Caves
Mount Pinnak

Licola
Mount Margaret
Mount Wellington
Tabberabbera
The Two Sisters
Mount Welcome
ALPINE
Buchan South
Mount Tara

Mount Eliza
Mount Hump
WILDERNESS
Castleburn
Cobbannah
The Basin
Deptford
Mount Little Dick
FLORA RESERVE MOTTLE RANGE

Burgoyne Gap
PARK
Mount Blomford
Bullumwaal
Mount Alfred
33
Sandy Point

BLACK RANGE
Mount Useful
MITCHELL RIVER NATIONAL PARK
Mount Difficulty
28
Mount Taylor
Clifton Creek
Wiseleigh
Bruthen
Mount Nowa Nowa
Wairewa

C488
Mount Gog
GIPPSLAND
Mount Ray
Woodglen
Wuk Wuk
Mount Lookout
24
Mount Taylor
Sarsfield
Mossiface
Nowa Nowa
Bete Bolong

HISTORIC TOWN Walhalla
Mount
Culloden
Glenaladale
Walpa
Lindenow
Calulu
GREAT
Tambo Upper
29
Colquhoun
Waygara
Jarrahmond
Newmerella

Glenmaggie
Valencia Creek
Stockdale
Coongulmerang
Lindenow South
BAIRNSDALE
Wy Yung
Lucknow
Nicholson
Swan Reach
A1
Tostaree
37
A1 HWY

Lake Glenmaggie
Briagolong
Hillside
20
East Bairnsdale
Johnsonville
14
Kalimna West
Lake Tyers

Seaton
Coongulla
Boisdale
Bushy Park
Fernbank
Harrow
Eagle Point
Metung
Kalimna
Nungurner
Lake Tyers

Thomson
Newry
Munro
32
PROVIDENCE PONDS FLORA & FAUNA RESERVE
Forge Creek
Raymond Island
Kalimna
Lakes Entrance
Ninety Mile Beach

Dawson
Heyfield
Tinamba
Maffra
69
A1
PRINCES
Perry Bridge
14
Goon Nure
Paynesville
GIPPSLAND LAKES

Cowwarr
Denison
Stratford
HWY
Airly
Bengworden
Sperm Whale Head
Rotomah Island

Winnindoo
Nambrok
Bundalaguah
Montgomery
Clydebank
Meerlieu
Loch Sport
THE LAKES NATIONAL PARK

Toongabbie
21
Fulham
SALE
Cobains
The Heart
GIPPSLAND LAKES COASTAL PARK
38° 00'

Glengarry
PRINCES
Kilmany
26
Longford
Seacombe
Lake Wellington
Lake Reeve

TRARALGON
A1
65
Rosedale
Kilmany South
28
Dutson
26
Lake Coleman
Reeve Beach

Flynn
HOLEY PLAINS STATE PARK
Paradise Beach
Golden Beach

Flynns Creek
Willung
Delray Beach
The Wreck Beach
TASMAN

Callignee North
Gormandale
STRADBROKE FLORA AND FAUNA RESERVE
Stradbroke
Flamingo Beach
Glomar Beach

Callignee
C482
Willung South
GIFFARD FLORA RESERVE
A440
The Island
The Honeysuckles

Carrajung
Carrajung South
Seaspray

Blackwarry
MULLUNGDUNG FOREST
Giffard
SOUTH GIPPSLAND

Macks Creek
Won Wron
Darriman
McGauran Beach

Devon
HYLAND
Greenmount
Woodside
Ninety

Yarram
Hunterston
Woodside Beach

Alberton West
Alberton
McLoughlins Beach

163
Tarraville
St Margaret Island

Langsborough
Manns Beach

Port Albert
Sunday Island
NOORAMUNGA MARINE AND COASTAL PARK

Townsend Point
N
SEA

Seal Island
Notch Island
Rag Island
Cliffy Island

BASS STRAIT
39° 00'

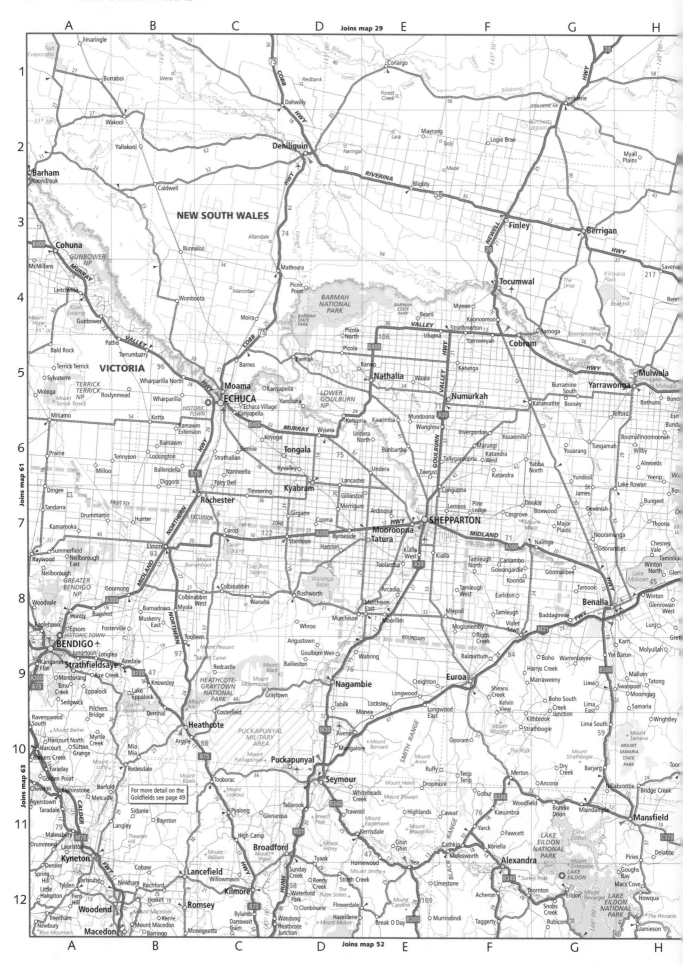

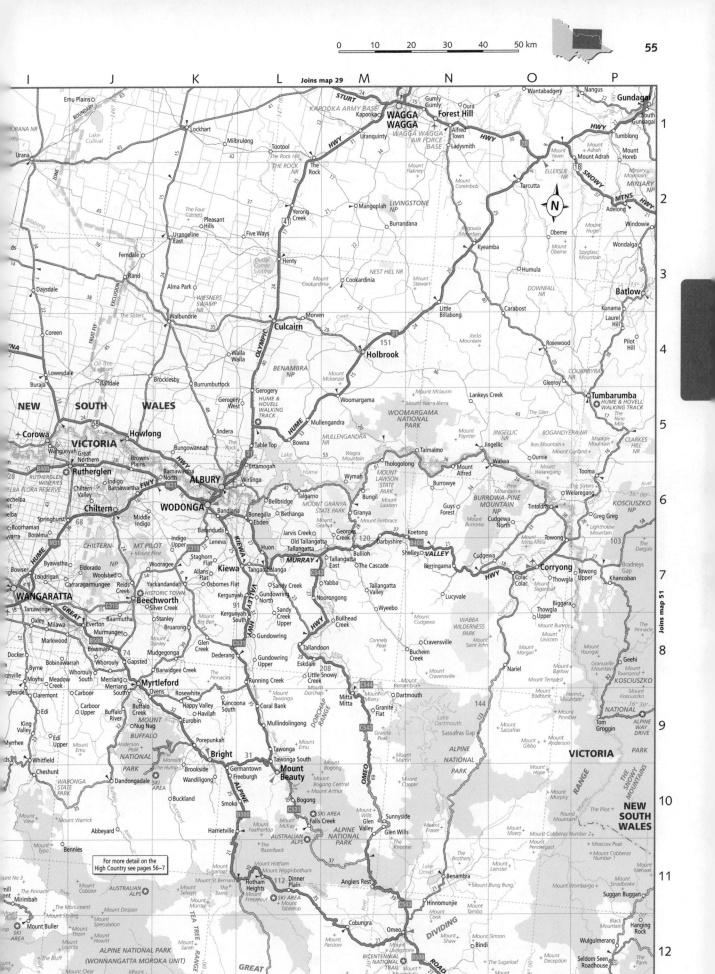

0   10   20   30   40   50 km

Joins map 51

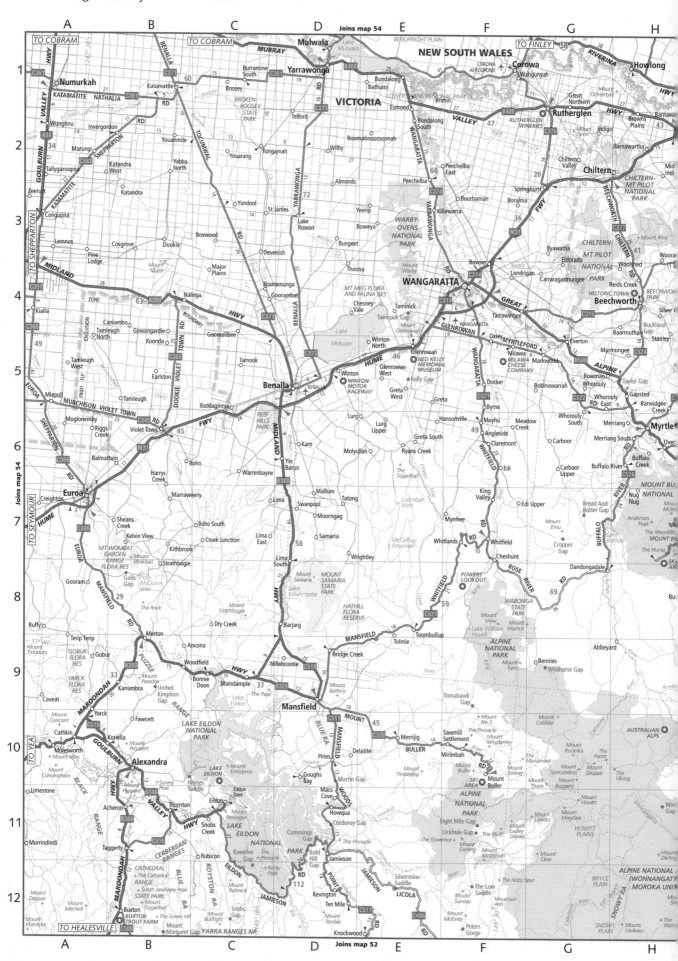

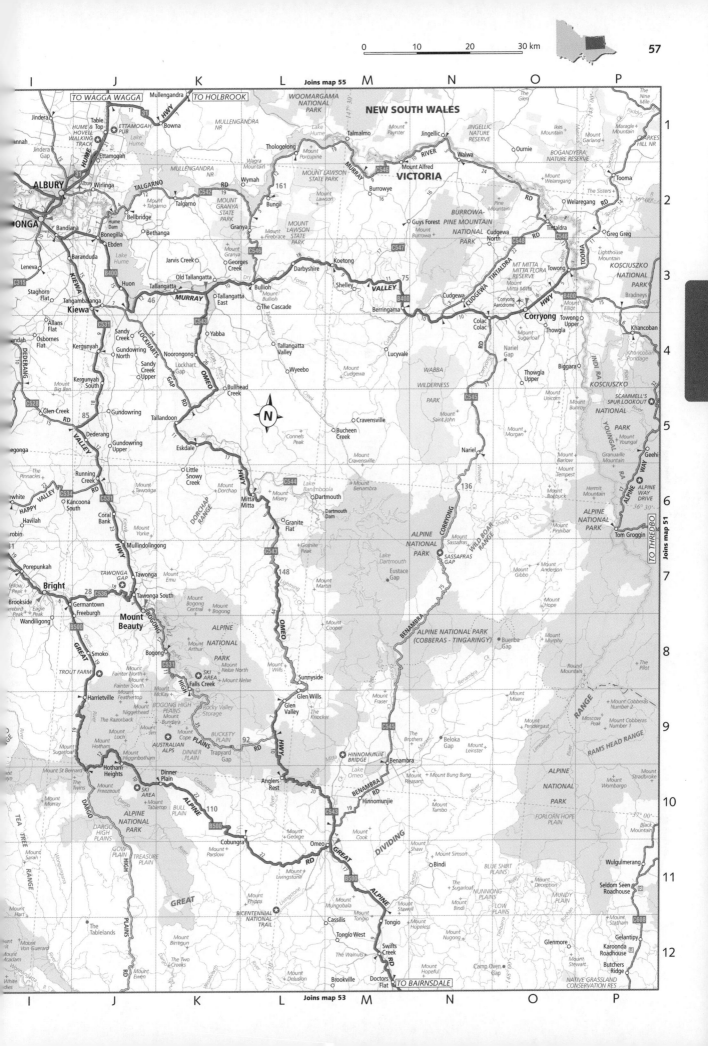

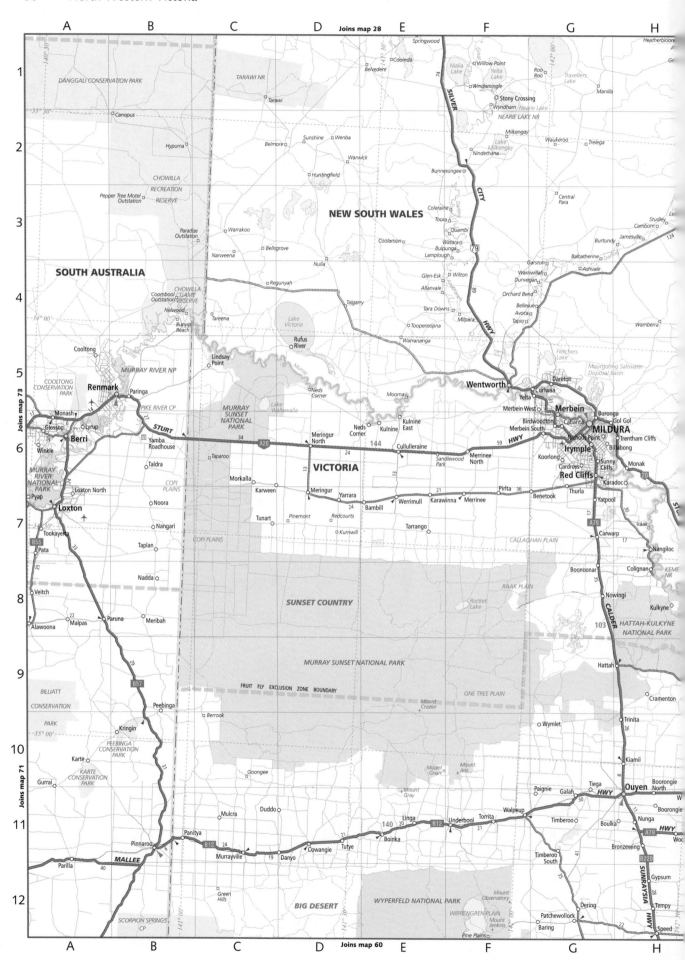

Joins map 28
Joins map 73
Joins map 71
Joins map 60

Joins map 28
Joins map 29
Joins map 61

0 10 20 30 40 50 km

I J K L M N O P

Column grid rows: 1 2 3 4 5 6 7 8 9 10 11 12

131

Carinya
Bellevue
Dockerty
Manfred Mountain
Melton Grove
Hartshorns
Barneys Lake
Clarebank
Manfred
Claremont
Clare Corner
Killarney
Clare
Alma Lake
Stanbridge
Moolbong Creek

Pooncarie
Birdwood
Balmoral
Pan Ban
Mulurulu Lake
Mulurulu
Mandleman
133
Tarcoola
Akuna
Incourt
ngwood

MUNGO
Garnpung
Baymore
Gol Gol
Balranald Gate
Leaghur
Lake Leaghur
NATIONAL
Binda
Loch Lamond
Rosalind Park
The Ridge
Min Min
Clare Calpa

Top Hut
Zanci
PARK
THE WALLS OF CHINA
Mungo
Lake Mungo
Orange Grove
Murrungrung
Culpataro

Old Arumpo
Joulni
Boree Plains
Round Plain
The Vale
Til Til
Palari
Yamba

Murragi
Petro
Arumpo
Chibnalwood
Wampo
Carrawatha
Magenta
South Winter
Blue Bush
Lake House
Curragh
Merritop

104
Bellnar
Marma
Turlee
Iona
Springbank
Hatfield
Rata
Freemount
Tarwong
Merrowie Creek

Banoon
Hillview
Wintong
Llanover Downs
Allanvale
Oakdene
Beliamong
Chillichil
Glen Alvie
34° 00'

MALLEE CLIFFS NATIONAL PARK
Mallee Cliffs
Prungle
Bindura
The Oaks
Upson Downs
Glen Emu
Box
Walmer Downs
Bunumburt
Oxley
Corrong
Thelangerin

Gulthul
Benenong
Koolaman
LILY PLAIN
Tin Tin Lake
Tin Tin
The Peppers
Glen Dee
BULL PLAIN
KALYARR STATE CONSERVATION AREA
Ita Lake

Carawatha
Oakdale
Benington
Mylatche
Bramah
Cringadale
Karra
Pitarpunga Lake
Lake Marimley
Tori
Yanga
Murrum Valley
Mungery
Toopuntul
KALYARR NATIONAL PARK

Ballarah
Model Farm
TOPRA PLAIN
Lake Benanee
Penarie
Jindeena
Athen
Narwie
YANGA NATIONAL PARK
Nap Nap
Newmarket

HWY
20
Euston
Robinvale
MURRAY
Meilman
Pine Hills
Glen Ewan
76
Hazelwood
Coogee
Paika
28
Tangrambally
Wynburn
Glenavon
Talpee
Torry Plain
Maude
34° 30'

Prill Park
Happy Valley
Bannerton
13
Kyndalyn
VALLEY
22
Boundary Bend
Manie
Kungie
Waldaira
Benongal
Balranald
YANGA NATIONAL PARK
Auley
Kia Ora
Uara
Warwaegae
Hells Gate
Ravensworth
HWY
20

Tammit
18
Margooya
Yungera
94
Narrung
Weimby
Canally
Willow Isles
Maffra
Yanga
Yanga NR
208
Oakhampton
Willow Vale
Jeraly
St Pauls
Glenhope

Wemen
VICTORIA
Koorkab
B400
Piambie
Windomal
Hit Or Miss
Redgate
Yanga Lake
Condoulpe
Myall Farm
The Willows
Millicent

Annuello
Koolooong
Wilga Park
Norwood
Impimi
Impini
YANGA STATE CONSERVATION AREA
Tchelery
Miegunyah
Thalaka

112
Koimbo
Haysdale
Thistlebank
Tralee
Spring Plain
Condoulpe Lake
Barton
Moolpa
Merwein
Kingfe
Baldon

Mowat-Ville
Winnambool
Bolton
Natya
Goodnight
Kyalite
Yal Yal
84
Perekerten
49

MALLEE
96
Kulwin
B12
Prooinga
Mileu
MALLEE
Edward
Liewah
Moolpa
Yarrein
35° 00'

EXCLUSION
Manangatang
41
Piangil North
Tooleybuc
18
Stony Crossing
Billabong

Cocamba
B12
Piangil
Miralie
HWY
Mallan
Moulamein
61

Mittyack
88
CALDER
Chinkapook
41
Yarraby
Wood Wood
70
Wakool
Niemur River
34
Inverness
23

Millan
24
Daytrap
Ryanby
Nyah West
Vinifera
Nyah
Pira
Beverford
Speewa
Beverford
Cunninyeuk
Dhuragoon

Nandaly
ZONE
BOUNDARY
Chillingollah
Nowie North
Woorinen North
Tyntynder Central
Tyntynder South
Niemur
Jimaringle
55

Nyarrin
A79
Daytrap Corner
Lake Wahpool
Tyrrell Downs
Waitchie
Woorinen
Swan Hill
MULLIGANS PLAIN
Noorong

Lake Timboram
40
31
144° 00'
144° 30'

NEW SOUTH WALES
STURT
DEADMAN PLAIN
Tillara East

HWY
MURRAY
VALLEY
MALLEE
HWY
CALDER
HWY

N

69
67
62
37
84
62
38
39
24
27
16
21

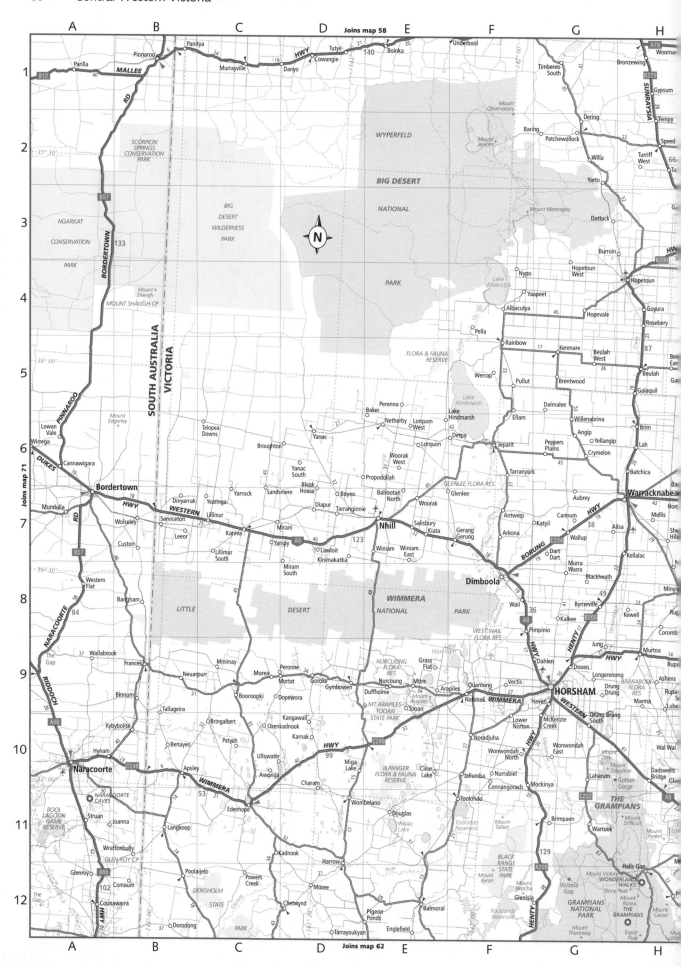

Joins map 58
Joins map 71
Joins map 62

Joins map 59
Joins map 54
Joins map 63

0 10 20 30 40 50 km

VICTORIA

NEW SOUTH WALES

MULLIGANS PLAIN

Mittyack · Pier Millan · Nandaly · Daytrap Corner · Nyarrin · Ninda · Sea Lake · Woomelang · Watchupa · Curyo · Kinnabulla · Reedy Dam · Birchip · SUNRAYSIA · Morton Plains · Watchem · Massey · Corack East · Corack · Carron · Litchfield · Lake Buloke · Donald · Laen · Rich Avon · Burrereo · Lawler · Laen North · Banyena · Burrum · WIMMERA · Marnoo · Wallaloo · Wallaloo East · Callawadda · Stawell · Bridge Inn · Joel Joel · Greens Creek · Tulkara · Campbells Bridge · Great Western · Dunneworthy · Armstrong · Norval · Rhymney Reef · Ararat · Warra Yadin · Warrak · Ben Nevis · Eversley

Miralie · Wood Wood · Yarraby · Nyah · Nyah West · Ryanby · Nowie North · Pira · Woorinen North · Woorinen · Chillingollah · Chinkapook · Daytrap · Fruit Fly Exclusion Zone · Tyrrell Downs · Long Plains · Waitchie · Gowanford · Lake Tyrrell · Lake Timboram · Lake Wahpool · Boigbeat · Berriwillock · Culgoa · Meatian · Lalbert Road · Lalbert · Ultima · Sutton · Warne · Jil Jil · Nullawil · Towaninny · Kalpienung · Tittybong · Cannie · Whirily · Dumosa · Narraport · Ninyeunook · Wycheproof · Fairview · Bunguluke · Glenloth · Narrewillock · Lake Marmal · Teddywaddy · Wooroonook · Barrakee · Buckrabanyule · Wychitella · Charlton · CALDER · Catumnal · Mount Kerang · Mount Egbert · Woosang · Borung · Nine Mile · Wedderburn · Wedderburn Junction · Korong Vale · Fiery Flat · Mount Korong · Coonooer Bridge · Yeungroon · RICHMOND PLAINS · Berrimal · Kurraca West · Kurraca · Glenalbyn · Serpentine · Gooroc · Slaty Creek · Gowar East · Fentons Creek · KOOYOORA STATE PARK · Inglewood · Salisbury West · Bears Lagoon · Swanwater West · Avon Plains · Cope Cope · St Arnaud · Kooreh · Logan · Wehla · Rheola · Kingower · Bridgewater On Loddon · Traynors Lagoon · Gre Gre · Carapooee · Burkes Flat · Cochranes Creek · McIntyre · Arnold West · Arnold · Derby · Campbells Forest · Sebastian · Neilborough · Neilborough East · Summerfield · Beazleys Bridge · Emu · Moliagul · Murphys Creek · Llanelly · Newbridge · Leichardt · Marong · Woodvale · Rostron · Stuart Mill · Winjallok · Paradise · Tottington · Kanya · Bealiba · Goldsborough · Painswick · Tarnagulla · Maiden Gully · Eaglehawk · Morri Morri · Archdale · Dunolly · Laanecoorie · Lockwood · BENDIGO · Navarre · Barkly · Moyreisk · Bromley · Shelbourne · Lockwood South · Kangaroo Flat · Strathfieldsaye · Landsborough · Shays Flat · ST ARNAUD RANGE NP · Redbank · Moonambel · Natte Yallock · Dunluce · Betley · Eddington · Eastville · Nuggetty · Walmer · Emu Creek · Sedgwick · Mandurang · Axe Creek · Joel South · Moonlight · Rathscar · Timor West · Timor · Havelock · Bet Bet · Baringhup · Ravenswood · Ravenswood South · Mount Barker · Harcourt · Harcourt North · Sutton Grange · Pilchers Bridge · Knowsley · Glenlofty · Tanwood · Warrenmang · Percydale · Homebush · Wareek · Bowenvale · Alma · Carisbrook · Maryborough · Maldon · Gower · Barkers Creek · Faraday · Elphinstone · Lake Eppalock · Derrinal · Heathcote · Crowlands · Glenshee · Glenpatrick · Avoca · Moores Flat · Amherst · Adelaide Lead · Golden Point · Craigie · Moolort · Welshmans Reef · Campbells Creek · Chewton · Castlemaine · Myrtle Creek · Argyle · Mia Mia · Redesdale · Elmhurst · Amphitheatre · Green Hill Creek · Lillicur · Caralulup · Talbot · Daisy Hill · Majorca · Joyces Creek · Strathlea · Newstead · Yapeen · Guildford · Fryerstown · Taradale · Metcalfe · Sidonia · Barfold · Mount Avoca · Mount Lonarch · Burnbank · Dunach · Campbelltown · Sandon · Clydesdale · Vaughan · Irishtown · Glenluce · Malmsbury · Langley · Baynton · Glengower · Yandoit · Guildford

Swan Hill · Murray Downs · Lake Boga · Tresco West · Tresco · Kunat · Beauchamp · Fish Point · Benjeroop · Nooring · Mystic Park · The Marsh · Lake Tutchewop · Gonn Crossing · Murrabit · Capels Crossing · Myall · Koondrook · Barham · Caldwell · Sandhill Lake · Lake Bael Bael · Fairley · Westby · Kerang · Koroop · Cohuna · Leitchville · Bunnaloo · Normanville · Dingwall · Langville · Kerang East · Kerang South · Tragowel · McMillans · GUNBOWER NP · Womboota · Oakvale · Gredgwin · Leaghur · Canary Island · Canary Island South · Macorna · Mincha · Mount Hope · Kow Swamp · Gunbower · Patho · Mimmindie · Yando · Loddon Vale · Gladfield · Bald Rock · Torrumbarry · Boort · Durham Ox · Sylvaterre · Pyramid Hill · TERRICK TERRICK NP · Mount Terrick Terrick · Roslynmead · Wharparilla North · Wharparilla · Jarlin · Yarrawalla South · Mologa · Mitiamo · Kotta · Mysia · Fernihurst · Raywood · Calivil · Prairie · Dingee · Tandarra · Tennyson · Lockington · Bamawm Extension · Bamawm · Drummartin · Kamarooka · Hunter · Diggora · Ballendella · Milloo · Pompapiel · FRUIT FLY EXCLUSION ZONE · Elmore · Huntly · Epsom · Bagshot · Barnadown · Myola · Longlea · Muskerry East · Fosterville · Toolleen · Goornong · Neilborough · Kurting · Bridgewater · Sebastian · GREATER BENDIGO NP · Marong · Woodvale · Annorton · Kennington · Flagstaff · Lockwood · Strathfieldsaye · Emu Creek · Axedale · Sedgwick · Knowsley · Mandurang · Eppalock · Axe Creek · Lake Eppalock

Mallan · Moulamein · Inverness · Cunninyeuk · Dhuragoon · Niemur · Wakool · Noorong · Jimaringle · Werai · Burraboi · Ballbank · Wakool · Yallakool · Caldwell

For more detail on the Goldfields see page 49

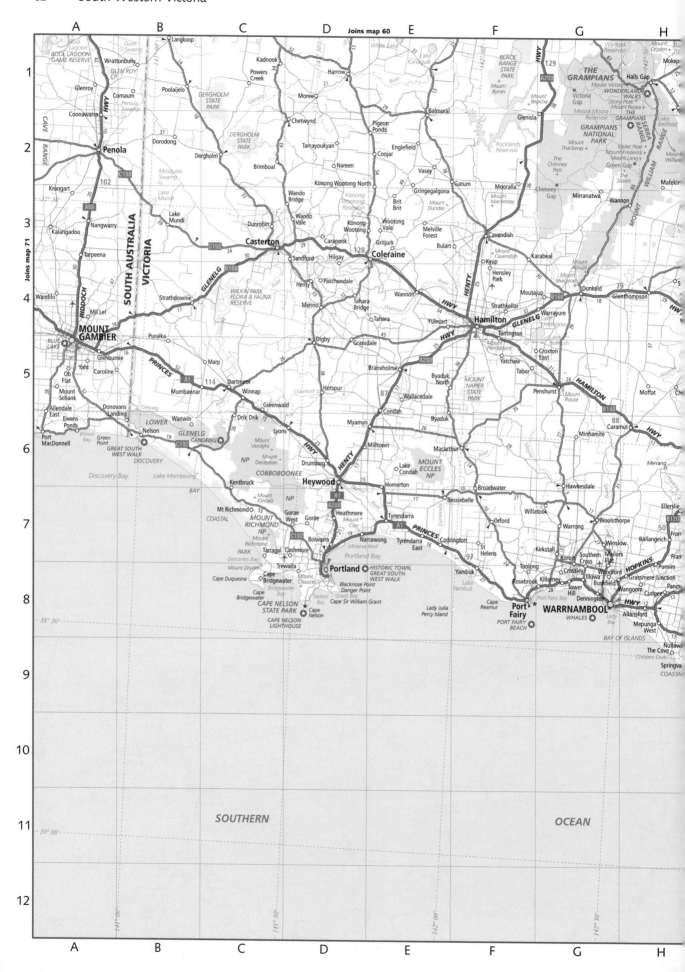

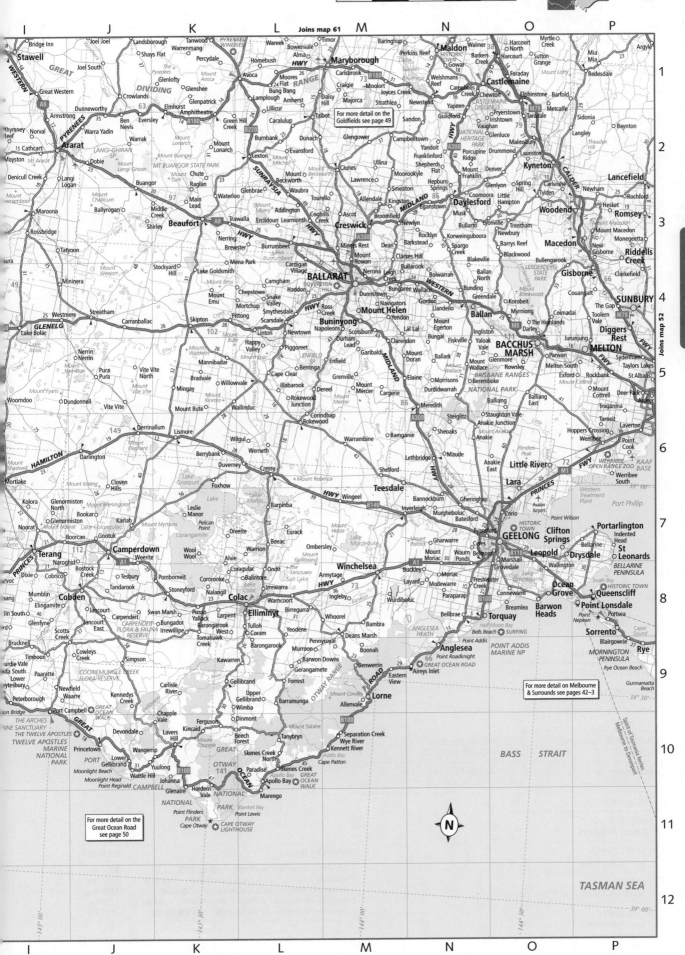

0   10   20   30   40   50 km

Stawell

GREAT

Bridge Inn
Joel Joel
Landsborough
Tanwood
Pyrenees
Wineries
Wareek
Bowenvale
Timor
Baringhup
Maldon
Walmer
Harcourt
North
Myrtle
Creek
Mia
Mia
Argyle

Great Western
Joel South
Shays Flat
Warrenmang
Alma
Maryborough
Perkins Reef
Gowar
Barkers
Creek
Harcourt
Sutton
Grange
Redesdale

WESTERN
DIVIDING
The
Pyrenees
Percydale
Homebush
Moores
Flat
Carisbrook
Campbells
Reef
Welshmans
Reef
Castlemaine

Dunneworthy
Glenlofty
Glenshee
Avoca
Bung Bong
Craigie
Moolort
Joyces Creek
Chewton
Elphinstone
Barfold
Mount
Lofty

Armstrong
Crowlands
Glenpatrick
Lamplough
Amherst
Strathlea
Newstead
Faraday
Taradale
Metcalfe

Rhymney
Reef
Norval
Ben
Nevis
Elmhurst
Amphitheatre
Green Hill
Creek
Burnbank
Dunach
Campbelltown
Yandoit
Fryerstown
Irishtown
Sidonia

Cathcart
Ararat
Warra Yadin
Warrak
Lexton
Evansford
Glengower
Franklinford
Shepherds
Flat
Guildford
Vaughan
Baynton

Moyston
Mt Ararat
Langi
Logan
Dobie
Mount
Lonarch
Clunes
Ullina
Moorookyle
Mount
Franklin
Denver
Glenlyon
Malmsbury
Langley
Theaden
Hill

Denicull Creek
Buangor
Raglan
Mount
Mitchell
Smeaton
Kingston
Hepburn
Springs
Musk
Kyneton
Newham
Rochford

Mount
Langi Ghiran
Chute
Waubra
Lawrence
Allendale
Coomoora
Daylesford
Trentham
Lauriston
Carlsruhe
Woodend
Hesket
Romsey

Main
Lead
Glenbrae
Ascot
Broomfield
Bullarto
Lyonville
Newbury
Spring
Hill
Tylden

Maroona
Middle
Creek
Waterloo
Tourello
Newlyn
Rocklyn
Korweinguboora
Barrys Reef
Macedon
New
Gisborne
Monegeetta

Ballyrogan
Shirley
Beaufort
Trawalla
Creswick
Dean
Barkstead
Spargo
Creek
Blackwood
Gisborne
Riddells
Creek

Nerring
Burrumbeet
Minrs Rest
Clarkes Hill
Blakeville
Ballan
North
Bullengarook
Clarkefield

Rossbridge
Tatyoon
Brewster
Cardigan
Village
Nerrina
Leigh
Creek
Bullarook
Bolwarrah
Greendale
Couangalt
Sunbury

Mininera
Stockyard
Hill
Lake Goldsmith
Mena Park
BALLARAT
Dunnstown
Bungaree
Wallace
Bunding
Ballan
The Gap

Mount
Weejort
Carngham
Haddon
Ross
Creek
Mount Helen
Gordon
Llandeilo
Korobeit
Myrniong
Coimadai
Diggers
Rest

Westmere
Streatham
Skipton
Mount
Emu
Chepstowe
Buninyong
Napoleons
Scotsburn
Mount
Egerton
Darley
The Highlands
MELTON

Glenelg
Lake Bolac
Carranballac
Pittong
Linton
Newtown
Happy
Valley
Clarendon
Fiskville
Yaloak
Vale
BACCHUS
MARSH
Parwan
Sydenham
Taylors Lakes

Nerrin
Nerrin
Piggoreet
Enfield
Mount
Doran
Ballark
Mount
Wallace
Glenmore
Rowsley
Melton South
Exford
Rockbank
St Albans

Mount
Hamilton
Pura
Pura
Vite Vite
North
Mannibadar
Cape Clear
Berringa
Grenville
Elaine
Morrisons
Durdidwarrah
Beremboke
Balliang
Melton
Cottrell
Deer Park

Mount Fyans
Bradvale
Willowvale
Illabarook
Dereel
Mount
Mercer
Cargerie
Meredith
Balliang
East
Truganina

Woorndoo
Dundonnell
Mingay
Mount Bute
Rokewood
Junction
Durham
Lead
Steiglitz
Staughton Vale
Tarneit

Mount
Kinross
Wallinduc
Rokewood
Mount
Mercer
Anakie Junction
Hoppers Crossing
Werribee

Mount
Shadwell
Derrinallum
Lismore
Wilgul
Warrambine
Lethbridge
Maude
Anakie
Sheoaks
Anakie
East
Werribee
South

HAMILTON
Darlington
Berrybank
Werneth
Shelford
Little River
Lara
Point
Cook

Mortlake
Cloven
Hills
Duverney
Cressy
Teesdale
Bannockburn
Gheringhap
Corio
RAAF
BASE

Kolora
Glenormiston
North
Bookaar
Kariah
Foxhow
Wingeel
Inverleigh
Murgheboluc
Batesford
GEELONG
Avalon
Airport

Noorat
Glenormiston
Gnotuk
Leslie
Manor
Dreeite
Barpinba
Ceres
Clifton
Springs
Portarlington
Indented
Head

Terang
Boorcan
Camperdown
Weerite
Pelican
Point
Eurack
Ombersley
Gnarwarre
Belmont
Leopold
Bellarine
St
Leonards

Naroghid
Wool
Wool
Beeac
Armytage
Winchelsea
Buckley
Moriac
Grovedale
Wallington
Drysdale

Dixie
Cobrico
Bostock
Creek
Tesbury
Pomborneit
Warrion
Alvie
Coragulac
Ondit
Irrewarra
Layard
Modewarre
Connewarre
Ocean
Grove
Queenscliff

Mumblin
Tandarook
Stoneyford
Nalangil
Balintore
Ingleby
Paraparap
Breamlea
Barwon
Heads
Point Lonsdale

Elingamite
Jancourt
Carpendeit
Bungador
Colac
Warncoort
Wurdiboluc
Bellbrae
Torquay

Cobden
Jancourt
East
Irrewillipe
Pirron
Yallock
Larpent
Birregurra
Whoorel
Deans Marsh
Bells Beach
SURFING
Point
Nepean
Sorrento

Scotts
Creek
Carlisle
River
Barongarook
West
Tulloh
Coram
Yeodene
Bambra
Anglesea
Point Addis
Blairgowrie
Rye

Brucknell
Cowleys
Creek
Simpson
Tomahawk
Creek
Barongarook
Murroon
Barwon Downs
Boonah
Aireys Inlet
Great Ocean Road

Timboon
Paaratte
Kawarren
Gerangamete
Benwerrin
Eastern
View
Rye Ocean Beach

Newfield
Waarre
Kennedys
Creek
Gellibrand
Forrest
Lorne

Peterborough
Port Campbell
GREAT OCEAN
WALK
Carlisle
Upper
Gellibrand
Barramunga
Allenvale

THE ARCHES
MARINE SANCTUARY
THE TWELVE APOSTLES
Chapple
Vale
Wimba
Dinmont
Mount Sabine
Separation Creek
Wye River
Kennett River

TWELVE APOSTLES
MARINE
NATIONAL
PARK
Devondale
Ferguson
Kincaid
Beech
Forest
Tanybryn

Princetown
Lower
Gellibrand
Wangerrip
Lavers
Hill
Skenes Creek
North
Addis Bay
Cape Patton

PORT
Moonlight Beach
Yuulong
Johanna
Paradise
Skenes Creek
Apollo Bay
GREAT OCEAN WALK

Moonlight Head
Point Reginald
CAMPBELL
Glenaire
Hordern
Vale
Marengo

OTWAY
NATIONAL
Point Flinders
PARK
Blanket Bay
Point Lewis

For more detail on the
Great Ocean Road
see page 50

Cape Otway
CAPE OTWAY
LIGHTHOUSE

N

BASS   STRAIT

TASMAN SEA

For more detail on Melbourne
& Surrounds see pages 42–3

For more detail on the
Goldfields see page 49

MAPS

SOUTH AUSTRALIA

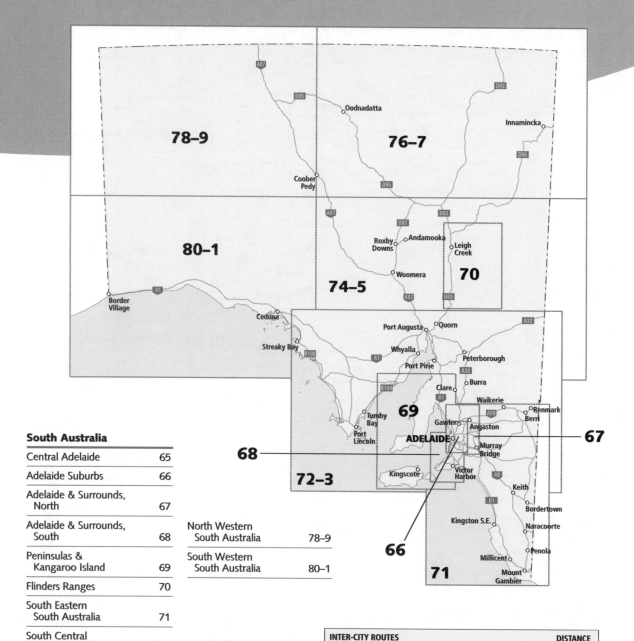

INTER-CITY ROUTES	DISTANCE
Adelaide–Darwin via Stuart Hwy	3026 km
Adelaide–Perth via Eyre & Great Eastern hwys	2700 km
Adelaide–Sydney via Sturt & Hume hwys	1415 km
Adelaide–Melbourne via Dukes & Western hwys	729 km
Adelaide–Melbourne via Princes Hwy	911 km

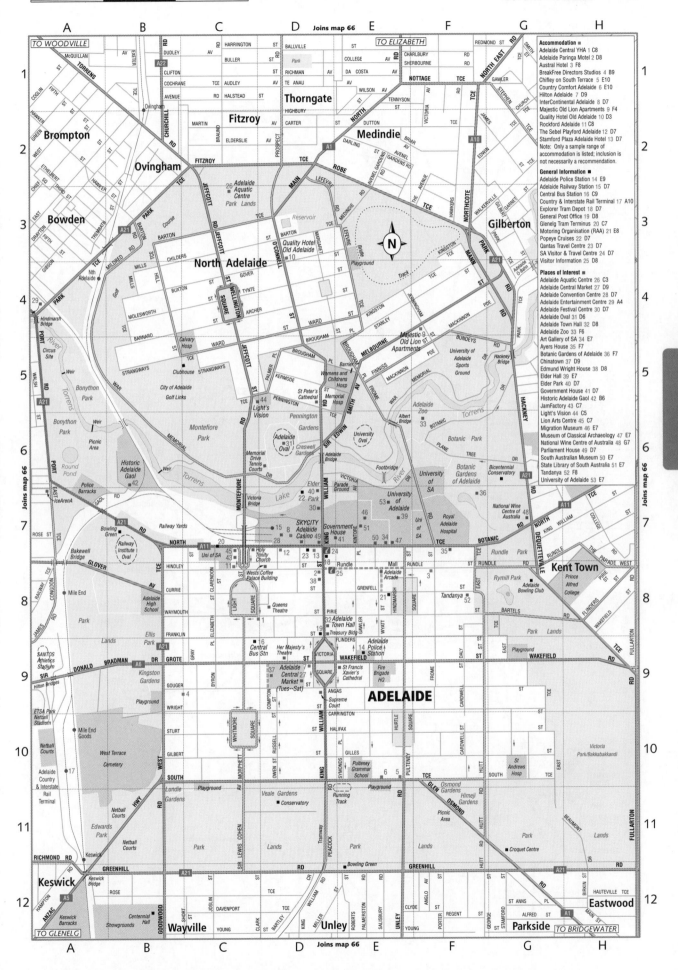

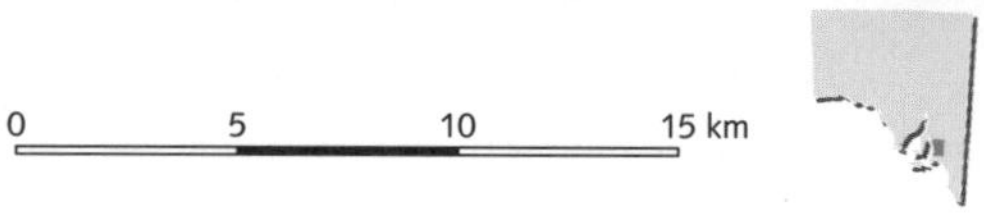

0 5 10 15 km

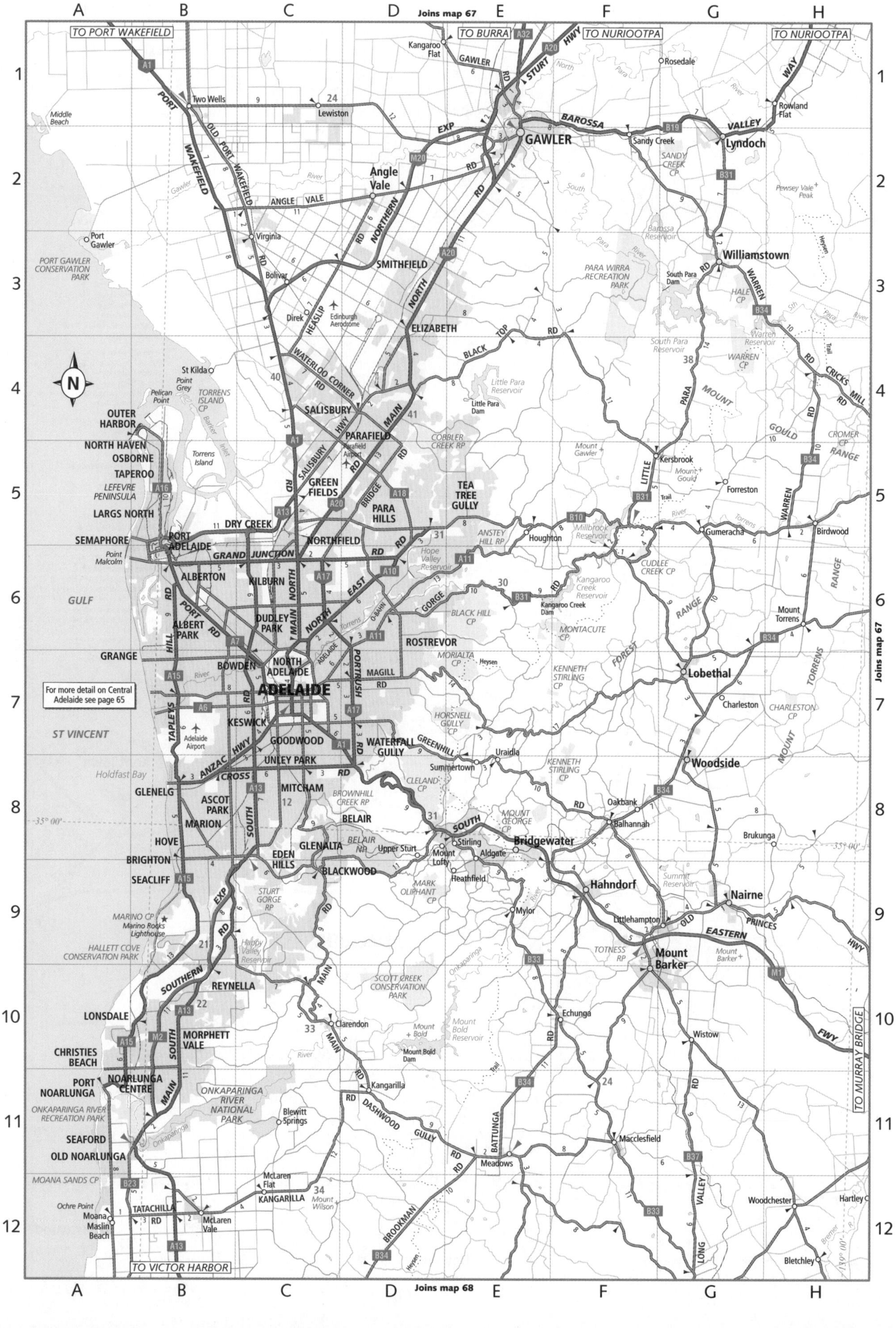

Joins map 67

TO PORT WAKEFIELD
TO BURRA
TO NURIOOTPA
TO NURIOOTPA

Kangaroo Flat
GAWLER
Rosedale
Two Wells
Lewiston
24
EXP
STURT HWY
BAROSSA
Sandy Creek
Lyndoch
VALLEY
Middle Beach
PORT
OLD PORT WAKEFIELD
NORTHERN
GAWLER
Angle Vale
South Para
Williamstown
Pewsey Vale Peak
Port Gawler
Virginia
ANGLE VALE
SMITHFIELD
Para Wirra Recreation Park
South Para Dam
WARREN CP
PORT GAWLER CONSERVATION PARK
Bolivar
NORTH
ELIZABETH
South Para Reservoir
WARREN Reservoir
WARREN CP
CRICKS MILL
Direk
Edinburgh Aerodrome
BLACK
TOP
38
St Kilda
Point Grey
Pelican Point
WATERLOO CORNER
40
Little Para Reservoir
Little Para Dam
Mount Gawler
Kersbrook
Mount Gould
Forreston
CROMER CP
RANGE
TORRENS ISLAND CP
SALISBURY
MAIN
41
COBBLER CREEK RP
GOULD
OUTER HARBOR
NORTH HAVEN
OSBORNE
TAPEROO
PARAFIELD
Parafield Airport
TEA TREE GULLY
B10
Millbrook Reservoir
Gumeracha
Birdwood
WARREN
RANGE
SALISBURY HWY
GREEN FIELDS
BRIDGE
PARA HILLS
ANSTEY HILL RP
Houghton
LARGS NORTH
DRY CREEK
NORTHFIELD
Hope Valley Reservoir
30
Kangaroo Creek Reservoir
Mount Torrens
SEMAPHORE
PORT ADELAIDE
GRAND JUNCTION
EAST
31
Kangaroo Creek Dam
CUDLEE CREEK CP
RANGE
Point Malcolm
ALBERTON
KILBURN
NORTH
GORGE
BLACK HILL CP
MONTACUTE CP
GULF
ALBERT PARK
DUDLEY PARK
Torrens
ROSTREVOR
MORIALTA CP
Heysen
FOREST
Lobethal
GRANGE
BOWDEN
NORTH ADELAIDE
MAGILL
KENNETH STIRLING CP
Charleston
CHARLESTON CP
ST VINCENT
ADELAIDE
For more detail on Central Adelaide see page 65
KESWICK
PORTRUSH
HORSNELL GULLY CP
MOUNT
Adelaide Airport
GOODWOOD
WATERFALL GULLY
GREENHILL
Uraidla
Summertown
KENNETH STIRLING CP
Woodside
Holdfast Bay
ANZAC HWY
UNLEY PARK
CLELAND CP
TORRENS
MITCHAM
BROWNHILL CREEK RP
Mount George
Oakbank
GLENELG
ASCOT PARK
BELAIR
SOUTH
Balhannah
Brukunga
HOVE
MARION
GLENALTA
BELAIR NA
Upper Sturt
Stirling
Bridgewater
BRIGHTON
EDEN HILLS
BLACKWOOD
Mount Lofty
Aldgate
SEACLIFF
Heathfield
Hahndorf
Nairne
MARINO CP
Marino Rocks Lighthouse
STURT GORGE RP
MARK OLIPHANT CP
Mylor
PRINCES
EASTERN
HWY
HALLETT COVE CONSERVATION PARK
EXP
Happy Valley Reservoir
Littlehampton
SCOTT CREEK CONSERVATION PARK
TOTNESS RP
Mount Barker
REYNELLA
MAIN
Mount Bold Reservoir
Mount Barker
FWY
LONSDALE
SOUTHERN
21
22
Clarendon
Mount Bold Dam
Echunga
Wistow
TO MURRAY BRIDGE
CHRISTIES BEACH
MORPHETT VALE
33
ONKAPARINGA RIVER NATIONAL PARK
Kangarilla
B34
24
PORT NOARLUNGA
NOARLUNGA CENTRE
Blewitt Springs
DASHWOOD GULLY
Macclesfield
ONKAPARINGA RIVER RECREATION PARK
SEAFORD
OLD NOARLUNGA
McLaren Flat
34
Mount Wilson
BATTUNGA
Meadows
B37
MOANA SANDS CP
KANGARILLA
Woodchester
Hartley
Ochre Point
Moana
Maslin Beach
TATACHILLA
McLaren Vale
BROOKMAN
VALLEY
LONG
Bletchley

TO VICTOR HARBOR

0   5   10   15   20 km

TO CLARE   TO BURRA

Joins map 73

Joins map 69

Joins map 71

TO PORT WAKEFIELD

TO WAIKERIE

TO TAILEM BEND

Erith, Salter Springs, Giles Corner, Hamilton, Eudunda, Kooninderie, Neales Flat, Brownlow, The Watchers, Pinery, Owen, Alma, Tarlee, Taylor Gap, Mount Allen, Hansborough, Mount Rufus, Frankton, Long Plains, Barabba, Stockport, Linwood, Kapunda Museum, **Kapunda**, St Kitts, Dutton, Stonefield, Mallala, Hamley Bridge, Fords, Greenock, Stockwell, The Gap, Truro, The Basin, Redbanks, Wasleys, Templers, **Freeling**, Seppeltsfield, **Nuriootpa**, Luhrs Pioneer German Cottage, Penrice, Moculta, Mount Karinya, Angas Park Fruit Co, Vintners Bar & Grill, **Angaston**, Reeves Plains, Roseworthy, **Tanunda**, Barossa Historical Museum, The Keg Factory, Barossa Wineries, Towitta, Long Plain, Two Wells, Kangaroo Flat, Rosedale, Sandy Creek, Mengler Hill Scenic Drive & Lookout, Collingrove Homestead, Keyneton, Lewiston, **GAWLER**, **Lyndoch**, Rowland Flat, Kaiserstuhl Conservation Park, Pewsey Vale Peak, Eden Valley, Sedan, Port Gawler, Port Gawler Conservation Park, Virginia, Bolivar, Angle Vale, Whispering Wall, Goldfields Walk, Barossa Reservoir, **Williamstown**, Lyndoch Lavender Farm, Marne, Cambrai, Middle Beach, Direk, Smithfield, Para Wirra Recreation Park, Hale CP, Warren CP, Springton, Karl Seppelt Grand Cru Estate, St Kilda, Point Grey, Pelican Point, Edinburgh Aerodrome, Elizabeth, Little Para Res, South Para Reservoir, Warren Reservoir, Mount Pleasant, Sanderston, Angas Valley, Outer Harbor, North Haven, Osborne, Taperoo, Salisbury, Parafield, Cobbler Creek Recreation Park, Mount Gawler, Kersbrook, Mount Gould, Forreston, Punthari, Largs North, Parafield Gardens, Green Fields, Tea Tree Gully, Millbrook Reservoir, Birdwood, National Motor Museum, Tungkillo, Peterhead, Semaphore, Point Malcolm, Dry Creek, Pooraka, Northfield, Houghton, Gumeracha, The Toy Factory, Mount Torrens, Palmer, Apamurra, South Australian Maritime Museum, Kilburn, Woodville, Hope Valley Res, Anstey Hill Rec Park, Black Hill CP, Kangaroo Creek Reservoir, Adelaide Hills, Cleland Wildlife Park, Indian Pacific Train, The Ghan, Junction Markets, R.M. Williams Outback Heritage Museum, Hendon, Albert Park, Croydon, Ovingham, North Adelaide, Rostrevor, Morialta CP, Montacute CP, **Lobethal**, Charleston, Charleston CP, Mount Beevor, Harrogate, Rockleigh, **Mannum**, Ponde, Grange, Penfolds Magill Estate, Horsnell Gully CP, Summertown, Uraidla, Kenneth Stirling CP, **Woodside**, Caloote, Adelaide Airport, Keswick, Goodwood, Unley Park, Cleland NP, Petaluma's Bridgewater Mill Winery, Oakbank, Harrogate, Tepko, Glenelg, Mitcham, Torrens Park, Belair, Stirling, **Bridgewater**, Balhannah, Brukunga, Holdfast Bay, Edwardstown, Marion, Belair NP, Upper Sturt, Mount Lofty, Aldgate, **Hahndorf**, Historic Town, **Nairne**, Mypolonga, Warradale, Hove, Eden Hills, Glenalta, Blackwood, Heathfield, Littlehampton, Kanmantoo, Brighton, Seacliff, Clovelly Park, Mark Oliphant Conservation Park, Mylor, Marino CP, Marino Rocks Lighthouse, Sturt Gorge Recreation Park, Happy Valley Reservoir, Scott Creek CP, **Mount Barker**, Mount Barker, Monarto, **MURRAY BRIDGE**, Hallett Cove Conservation Park, Reynella, Kangarilla, Jupiter Creek Goldfields, Mount Bold, Echunga, Wistow, Callington, Monarto South, Swanport, Lonsdale, Morphett Vale, Clarendon, Mount Bold Reservoir, Monarto Conservation Park, Christie Downs, Christies Beach, Port Noarlunga, Noarlunga Centre, Onkaparinga River Rec Park, Blewitt Springs, Seaford, McLaren Flat, Macclesfield, Woodchester, Hartley, Bletchley, Brinkley, Ferries-McDonald Conservation Park, Old Noarlunga, Ochre Point, Maslin Beach, McLaren Vale, McLaren Vale Wineries, Mount Wilson, Meadows, Soldiers Memorial Gardens, **Strathalbyn**, Port Willunga, Aldinga, **Willunga**, Kyeema Conservation Park, **Aldinga Beach**

TO VICTOR HARBOR

For more detail on Adelaide Suburbs see page 66

Joins map 68   Joins map 71

0   5   10   15   20 km

Joins map 67

A B C D E F G H

1

LEFEVRE PENINSULA
Taperoo
Largs North
Peterhead
Semaphore
Point Malcolm
Port Adelaide
MARITIME MUSEUM
Dry Creek
TO TWO WELLS   TO GAWLER
Tea Tree Gully
Pooraka
Northfield
Cheltenham
Woodville
Kilburn
Hope Valley Res
B10
Houghton
Anstey Hill REC PARK
B31
Millbrook Reservoir
Forreston
Gumeracha
THE TOY FACTORY

For more detail on Adelaide Suburbs see page 66

Hendon
Albert Park
Croydon
Bowden
Ovingham
North Adelaide
Rostrevor
MORIALTA CP
MONTACUTE
Kangaroo Creek Reservoir
BLACK HILL CP
30
FOREST

Grange
ADELAIDE HILLS, CLELAND WILDLIFE TRAIN, INDIAN PACIFIC TRAIN, THE GHAN, JUNCTION MARKETS, R.M. WILLIAMS OUTBACK HERITAGE MUSEUM

2

ADELAIDE
Keswick
Adelaide Airport
Goodwood
Unley Park
Waterfall Gully
Summertown
CLELAND CP
PENFOLDS MAGILL ESTATE
HORSNELL GULLY
PETALUMA'S BRIDGEWATER MILL WINERY
Uraidla
KENNETH STIRLING CP
Oakbank
B34
Lobethal
Charleston
Woodside
Balhannah

Holdfast Bay
Glenelg
Edwardstown
Marion
Mitcham
Torrens Park
Belair
BELAIR N.P.
Mount Lofty
Stirling
Aldgate
Bridgewater
Hahndorf
HISTORIC TOWN
Littlehampton
Nairne
Summit Res

3

MARINO CP
Marino Rocks Lighthouse
HALLETT COVE CONSERVATION PARK
Warradale
Hove
Brighton
Seacliff
Clovelly Park
Eden Hills
Glenalta
Upper Sturt
Blackwood
Heathfield
STURT GORGE RECREATION PARK
MARK OLIPHANT CONSERVATION PARK
Mylor
EASTERN
Echunga
Wistow
Mount Barker
B33
M1
FWY
TO MURRAY BRIDGE
Joins map 67

4

Lonsdale
M2
Reynella
Morphett Vale
Clarendon
SCOTT CREEK CP
Mount Bold
JUPITER CREEK GOLDFIELDS
Mount Bold Reservoir
B34
Meadows
Macclesfield
Christie Downs
Christies Beach
Port Noarlunga
Noarlunga Centre
Kangarilla
Happy Valley Reservoir
ONKAPARINGA RIVER NP
River
ONKAPARINGA RIVER RECREATION PARK

5

Seaford
Old Noarlunga
MOANA SANDS CP
Ochre Point
Maslin Beach
McLaren Flat
McLaren Vale
McLAREN VALE WINERIES
Mount Wilson
VICTOR
HILL
A15
BROOKMAN RD
KYEEMA CONSERVATION PARK
RANGE
RANGES
SOLDIERS MEMORIAL GARDENS
Strathalbyn
LONG
VALLEY
24
18
B33

6

Port Willunga
Aldinga
Aldinga Beach
ALDINGA SCRUB CONSERVATION PARK
Silver Sands
Aldinga Bay
Sellicks Beach
LOOKOUT
B23
27
SOUTH
SELLICKS
Willunga
B34
38
Mount Compass
Yundi
MOUNT MAGNIFICENT CP
Ashbourne
FINNISS CP
COX SCRUB CP
Nangkita
35
B37
Sandergrove
THE STEAM RANGER TOURIST RAILWAY
LOOKOUT

7

Myponga Beach
Myponga Reservoir
Myponga
PAGES FLAT RD
LOOKOUT
49
Mount Compass
Tooperang
SCOTT CP
Finniss
CURRENCY CREEK WINERY
Gilberts
Haycock Point
Carrickalinga
B23
14
MYPONGA CP
YULTE CP
MOUNT
29
HINDMARSH FALLS
A13
MIDDLETON WINERY
Currency Creek
CANOE TREE

8

Normanville
Yankalilla
Yankalilla Bay
34
SOUTH
SPRING MOUNT CP
MOUNT
GLACIER ROCK
Hindmarsh Valley
MOUNT BILLY CP
URIMBIRRA WILDLIFE PARK, GREENHILLS ADVENTURE PARK
CROWS NEST LOOKOUT
Goolwa Aerodrome
MALLEEBAA WOOLSHED
Middleton
Goolwa
COCKLE TRAIN
Clayton
Hindmarsh Island
Rapid Head
Rapid Bay
Second Valley
Rapid Bay
Mount Rapid
FLEURIEU
33
13
Goolwa or Lower Murray
35° 30'

9

HEYSEN TRAIL
CAPE JERVIS LIGHTHOUSE
Delamere
B37
SOUTH
RANGE
MAIN
62
12
RD
B37
Waitpinga
Victor Harbor
Granite Island
FAIRY PENGUINS
Wright Island
Rosetta Head (The Bluff)
King Head
West Island
HORSE-DRAWN TRAM, S.A. WHALE CENTRE
Port Elliot
Pullen Island
SIR RICHARD PENINSULA
LOOKOUT
Mundoo Island
COORONG NATIONAL PARK
Cape Jervis Lands End
Cape Jervis
B23
Fishery Beach
TALISKER CP
PENINSULA
DEEP CREEK CONSERVATION PARK
NEWLAND HEAD CONSERVATION PARK
Encounter Bay

10

BACKSTAIRS PASSAGE
Tunkalilla Beach
Tunk Head
Parsons Beach
Waitpinga Beach
Newland Head
Porpoise Head

11

Cuttlefish Bay
Snapper Point
Cape Coutts
LASHMAR CP
Antechamber Bay
Red House Bay
Cape St Albans
Cape Saint Alban Lighthouse
THE PAGES CONSERVATION PARK
North Page
South Page
The Pages
SOUTHERN   **OCEAN**
Joins map 71

KANGAROO ISLAND
Joins map 69
Moncrieff Bay
Cape Willoughby Lighthouse
Cape Willoughby
Windmill Bay

12

LESUEUR CONSERVATION PARK
SIMPSON CP
MACDONNELL (DUDLEY) PENINSULA
Cape Hart

GULF

ST VINCENT

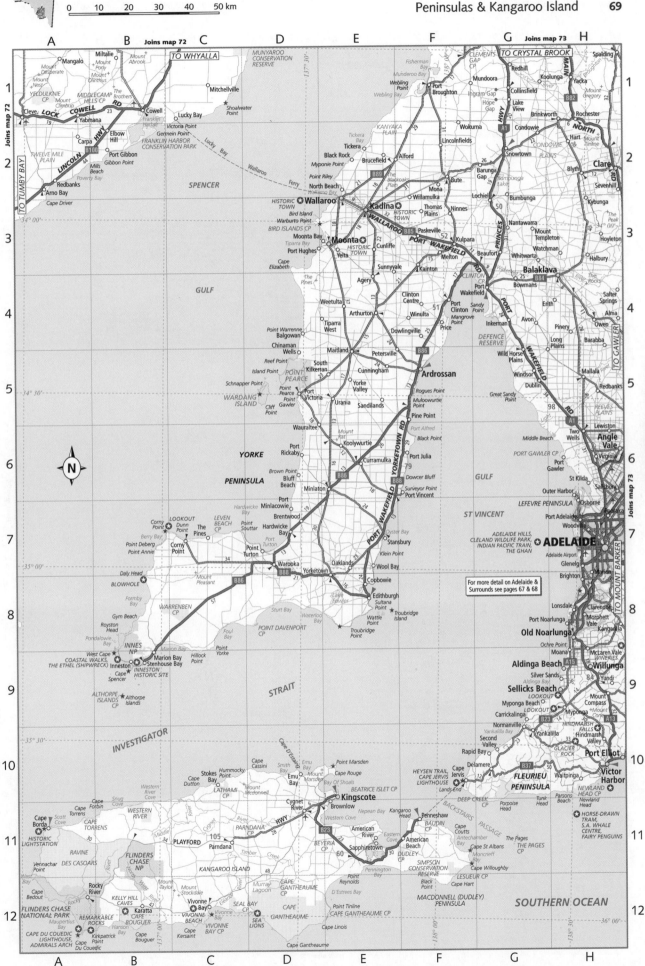

0   10   20   30   40   50 km

Joins map 72
TO WHYALLA
Joins map 73
TO CRYSTAL BROOK
Joins map 72
Joins map 73

For more detail on Adelaide &
Surrounds see pages 67 & 68

0   10   20   30   40 km

A   B   C   D   E   F   G   H

1   2   3   4   5   6   7   8   9   10   11   12

Joins map 75
Joins map 74
Joins map 75

TO MARREE
TO INNAMINCKA
TO PORT AUGUSTA
TO PETERBOROUGH

STRZELECKI TRACK

Place names and features:

Minagoona Lake, Leigh Creek, Mundy Creek, Ochre Cliffs, Avondale, Mount Lyall, Mount Lyndhurst, Mount Lyndhurst, Ilyteena Gap, Yerelina, Mount Saturday, Mount Harris, Mount Crocker, Mount Neil, Pepegoona Gorge

Lyndhurst, Mount Ogilvie, Mount Burr, Mount Clive, Mount Curtis, Mount Thomas, Mount MacDonnell, Mount Ward, Mount Pitt, Yudnamutana Gorge, North Mulga

FLINDERS RANGES, NORTH FLINDERS RANGES, The Armchair, NOOLDOONOOLDOONA & BOLLA BOLLANA WATERHOLES, Umberatana, The Needles, The Pinnacles, East Painter Gorge, Mount Painter, American Gap, Mount Dickinson, Paralana Outstation

Mount Playfair, Mount Parry, Myrtle Springs Gorge, Myrtle Springs, Mount Hutto, COALFIELD, Mount Telford, Jacob Gap, Burr Well, WEEDNA PLAINS, RED RANGE, Mount Rose, Mount Serle, VULKATHUNHA-GAMMON RANGES NATIONAL PARK, Compass Pass, Yankaninna, Idninha, Arkaroola, ARKAROOLA WILDERNESS SANCTUARY, BARARRANA GORGE, Mount Oliphant, Arkaroola, Tillite Gorge, Mount Jacob, Mount Hastings, Mount Warren Hastings

YANKANINNA RANGE, GAMMON RANGES, Owieandana, The Plateau, Changeweather, Mount John Roberts, Cleft Peak, Bunyip Chasm, Mount Mctaggart, Balcanoona Gorge, WEETOOTLA GORGE, Mount McCallum, Nepouie Peak, Wooltana, COPLEY

Copley, Leigh Creek, Mount Coffin, Depot Springs, Camel Gap, Silver Gap, Mount Serle, Mount Serle, Angepena, The Wall, Italowie Gap, Balcanoona, The Bluff, PARK HEADQUARTERS, Balcanoona Gorge

Mount Aroona, Copley, The Cutaway, Mountain of Light, Mount Jeffery, Red Gorge, Frome Gap, Mudlapena, Nepabunna, Oocabolina Outstation, COPLEY, ITALOWIE GORGE, 135, 24

Leigh Creek, Leigh Creek Aerodrome, Mount Scott, Manners Well, Mount Morris, Mount Wallace, Evans Outstation, Mulka Gap, Mount McKinlay, Mount Rowe, CAMPBELL, BALD HILL RANGE, McKinlay Ck, Wertaloona, VULKATHUNHA-GAMMON RANGES NATIONAL PARK

Mount Deception, Mount Deception, Puttapa Gap, Mount Bayley (Puttapa), Warrawena, Mount Goddard, Mount Greig, Mount Hack, Mount Uro, Mount Waukawoodna, NANTAWARRINNA, Mount Dorner, BIG MORO GORGE, Mount Comet, Arrowie Gorge, LAKE FROME RECREATION RESERVE

Trebilcock Gap, Beltana, SLIDING ROCK MINE (RUINS), Puttapa, Warrawena Gap, Main Gap, Mount Gill, Mount Tilley, Mount Stuart, Waukawoodna Gap, Nantawarrina, Deep Bore Gap, STIRRUP IRON RA, Mount Robert, Lake Frome

Beltana Roadhouse, Moorillah, Hannigan Gap, Mount McFarlane, Mount Andre, Pinda Springs, Mount Roebuck, Mulga View, WEARING GORGE, Teatree Outstation, MOUNT CHAMBERS GORGE

RED RA, NORTH RANGE, Mooloolooo, Patawarta Gap, Point Well, Narrina, Rose Ck, Mount Brooke, Mount John, Mount Chambers, Mount Chambers

Nilpena, GLASS GORGE, Mount Lucius, Mount Lyall, Mount Frome, Wyambana Outstation, Frome Downs

Mount Samuel Proper, Breakneck Gorge, Oratunga, Angorigina, Nildottie Gap, EREGUNDA VALLEY, Balcoracana Ck

Parachilna, 156, HEYSEN TRAIL, PARACHILNA GORGE, Mount Falkland, Mount Mary, Mount Elkington, Blinman, Alpana, GREAT WALL OF CHINA, Wirrealpa, Wirrealpa, Bendieuta Ck

Motpena, ANGORICHINA TOURIST VILLAGE, Mount Falkland, SOUTH RA, Kanyaka Peak, Gum Creek, Mount Emily, SECOND PLAIN, GRINDSTONE RA

Commodore, ABC RA, Mount Barloo, Mount Barbara, AROONA VALLEY (RUINS), Bulls Gap, FLINDERS RANGES, The Bunkers

Lake Station, Mount Hayward, BRACHINA GORGE, Walkandi Peak, FLINDERS RANGES NATIONAL PARK, Mount, Billy Ck

Brachina Gap, Mount Rupert, Oraparinna, Mount Well, Mount Sunderland, Mount Caernarvon, Mount Mantell, LOVES MINE RA, Martins Well, Erudina

BUNYEROO GORGE, Edeowie, Bunyeroo Valley, Mount Abrupt, St Mary Peak, Upalinna Outstation, Willow Springs, BUNKERS CONSERVATION RESERVE, Buffalo Ck

WESTERN PLAIN, Mount Burns, Edeowie Gorge, Wilpena, Upalinna, STOKES HILL LOOKOUT, Wilpena Ck

MORALANA PLAIN, Moralana, Mount Boorong, Mount Ohlssen Bagge, Pound Gap, WILPENA POUND, Binya Peak, WILPENA

Merna Mora, Mount Palmerston, Greig Peak, WANGARRA LOOKOUT, Mount Karawarina, SCARED CANYON

Hells Gate, Mernmerna, Mount Aleck, RAWNSLEY PARK STATION, Moonarie Gap, ARKAROO ROCK, Mount Prelinna, 55

THREE SISTERS RANGE, Woolyana, MORALANA SCENIC DRIVE, Ulowdna, Mount Havelock, Mount Neville, Mount Josephine, Curnamona

Three Sisters, Mount Little, Arkaroola, ELDER RANGE, Arkaba, White Gap, SOUTH FLINDERS RANGES, FLINDERS CHACE RA, Mount Desire, Red Gap, Warcowie, Shaggy Ridge, BLACK RA, Mount Davidson, Willipa, Bibliando

Worro Downs, WONOKA HISTORIC SITE (RUINS), Wonoka, Black Gap, Glen Lyle, Glen Oak, The Bluff, Killawarra Outstation

HODKINA (RUINS), Wild Dog Glen, Yappala, Pine Flat, Fairleigh, Fairview, WILLOW PLAINS, Mount Craig, Mount Plantagenet, Holowiliena, Siccus Ck, Glenorchy

JARVIS HILL LOOKOUT, Hawker, Echo, Mount Ernest, Niggly Gap, Worumba, Holowiliena South, Mount Sims

Mount Elm, Gum Vale, The Oaks, YOURAMBULLA CAVES, Mount Elm, Yourambulla Peak

B83, B80, D83, D96

0   20   40   60   80   100 km

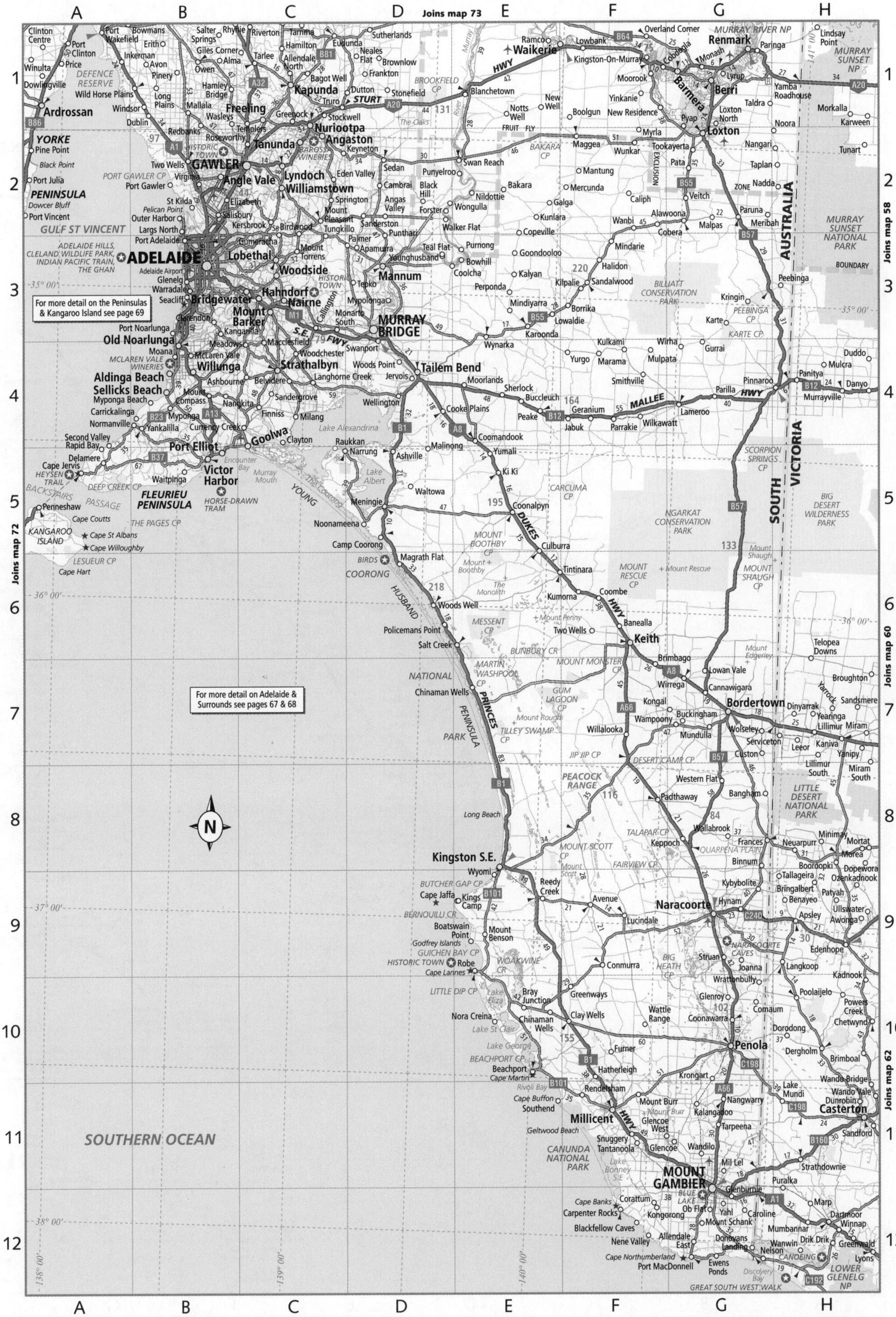

Joins map 73

Joins map 58

Joins map 60

Joins map 62

Joins map 72

SOUTH AUSTRALIA

VICTORIA

SOUTHERN OCEAN

GULF ST VINCENT

YORKE PENINSULA

FLEURIEU PENINSULA

KANGAROO ISLAND

For more detail on the Peninsulas & Kangaroo Island see page 69

For more detail on Adelaide & Surrounds see pages 67 & 68

ADELAIDE

MURRAY BRIDGE

MOUNT GAMBIER

MURRAY SUNSET NATIONAL PARK

BIG DESERT WILDERNESS PARK

LITTLE DESERT NATIONAL PARK

N

Major places:
Ardrossan, Port Clinton, Port Wakefield, Kapunda, Nuriootpa, Tanunda, Angaston, Gawler, Freeling, Lyndoch, Williamstown, Woodside, Hahndorf, Nairne, Mount Barker, Old Noarlunga, Willunga, Aldinga Beach, Sellicks Beach, Strathalbyn, Goolwa, Port Elliot, Victor Harbor, Cape Jervis, Penneshaw, Waikerie, Renmark, Berri, Barmera, Loxton, Swan Reach, Mannum, Tailem Bend, Meningie, Coonalpyn, Tintinara, Keith, Bordertown, Kingston S.E., Robe, Beachport, Millicent, Naracoorte, Penola, Casterton, Mount Gambier, Port MacDonnell

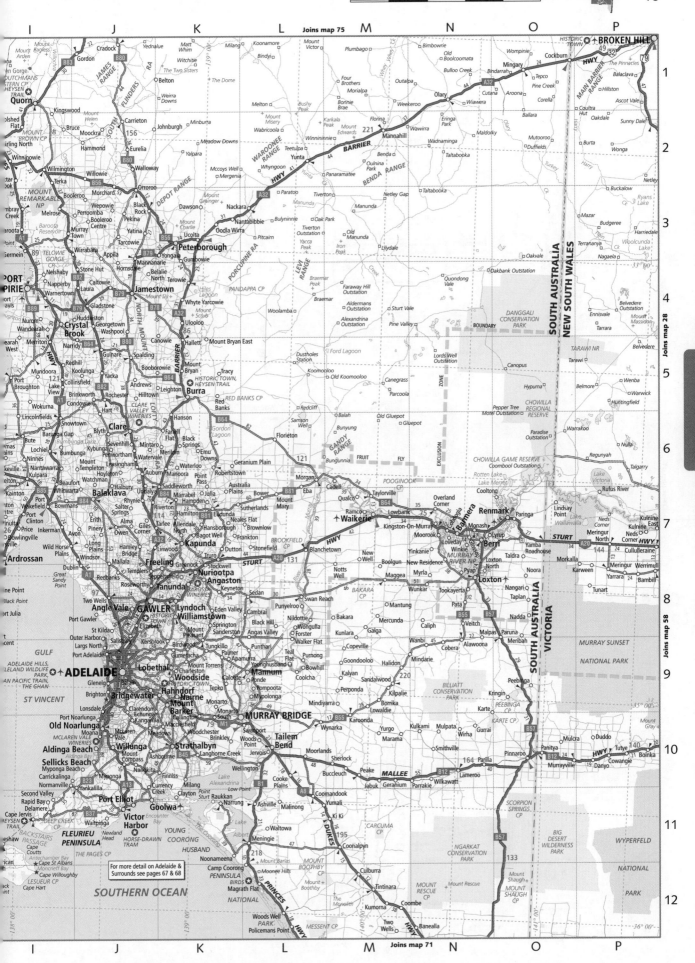

0   20   40   60   80   100 km

Joins map 28

Joins map 58

Broken Hill

HISTORIC TOWN

Quorn

PORT PIRIE

Crystal Brook

Peterborough

Jamestown

Burra

Clare

Balaklava

Kapunda

Nuriootpa
Angaston

Tanunda

GAWLER

Lyndoch
Williamstown

ADELAIDE

Lobethal

Woodside

Hahndorf

Bridgewater

Mount Barker

Nairne

Murray Bridge

Old Noarlunga

Willunga

Strathalbyn

Aldinga Beach

Sellicks Beach

Tailem Bend

Port Elliot

Victor Harbor

Goolwa

Waikerie

Barmera

Renmark

Berri

Loxton

SOUTH AUSTRALIA
NEW SOUTH WALES

SOUTH AUSTRALIA
VICTORIA

MURRAY SUNSET
NATIONAL PARK

BIG DESERT WILDERNESS PARK

WYPERFELD

NATIONAL PARK

NGARKAT CONSERVATION PARK

BILLIATT CONSERVATION PARK

CHOWILLA GAME RESERVE

DANGGALI CONSERVATION PARK

TARAWI NR

FLEURIEU PENINSULA

YOUNG HUSBAND PENINSULA

COORONG

SOUTHERN OCEAN

GULF ST VINCENT

For more detail on Adelaide & Surrounds see pages 67 & 68

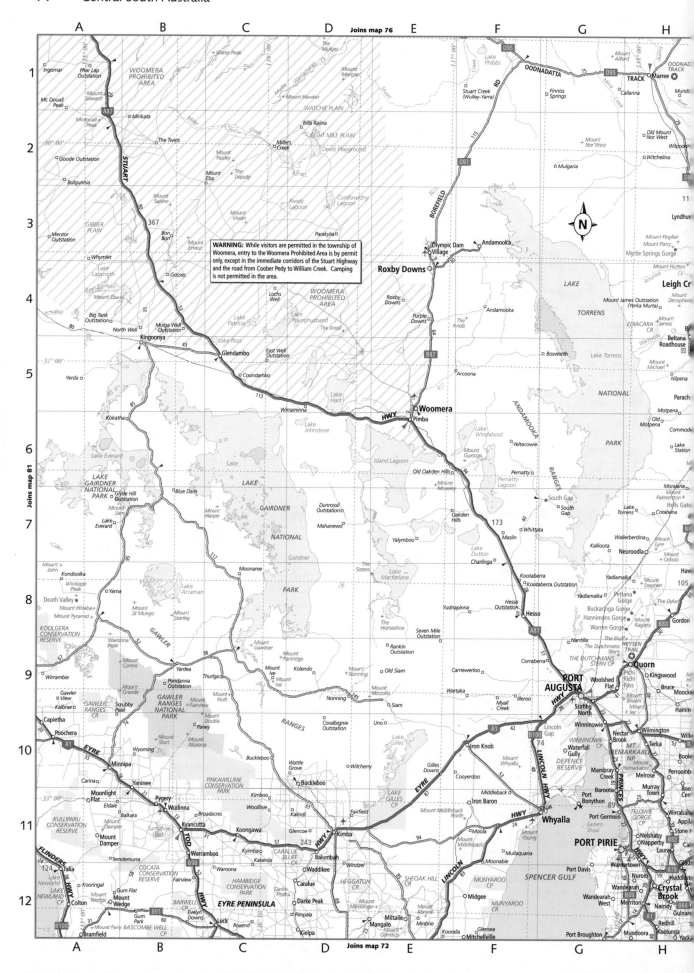

Joins map 76

A   B   C   D   E   F   G   H

1

Ingomar · Phar Lap Outstation · WOOMERA PROHIBITED AREA · Wares Peak · The Mulgas · Mount Morgan · Lake Phibbs · D95 · OODNADATTA · Mount Alford · TRACK · Marree · OODNAD TRACK · Callanna · Mundo

2

McDouall Peak · Minkata · Mount Seward · McDouall Peak · The Twins · Mount Hawker · WATCHIE PLAIN · Billa Kalina · EIGHT MILE PLAIN · Millers Creek · Devils Playground · Stuart Creek (Wulley-Yarra) · Finniss Springs · Mount Nor West · Old Mount Nor West · Wilpolinna · Witchelina

Goode Outstation · Mount Pauley · Mulgaria

Bulgunnia · Mount Eba · The Deputy · Reedy Lagoon · Curdlawidny Lagoon · D97 · Mulgaria

3

GIBBER PLAIN · Mount Sabine · Mount Vnsan · Parakylia · BOREFIELD RD · LAKE · 11 · Lyndhu

Mentor Outstation · 367 · Bon Bon · Mount Ernest · Olympic Dam Village · Andamooka · Mount Playfair · Mount Parry · Myrtle Springs Gorge · Mount Hutton · Arrunta · Leigh Cr

Whymlet · WARNING: While visitors are permitted in the township of Woomera, entry to the Woomera Prohibited Area is by permit only, except in the immediate corridors of the Stuart Highway and the road from Coober Pedy to William Creek. Camping is not permitted in the area. · Roxby Downs · Mount James Outstation (Yerka Murta) · Mount Deception

4

Lake Labyrinth · 35 · Gosses · Lochs Well · WOOMERA PROHIBITED AREA · Lake Younghusband · The Knoll · Roxby Downs · Andamooka · Purple Downs · The Knob · TORRENS · EDIACARA CR · Mount James · Be · Beltana Roadhouse

Big Tank Outstation · North Well · Mulga Well Outstation · Lake Patricia · 897 · 64 · Bosworth · Lake Torrens · Mount Michael

Kingoonya · 43 · Glendambo · East Well Outstation · Lake Ross · Arcoona · NATIONAL · Nilpena · Parach

5

Yerda · 85 · Coondambo · 113 · Lake Hart · HWY · Woomera · Pimba · Motpena · Old Motpena · Commode

Kokatha · Wirraminna · Lake Johnstone · ANDAMOOKA · Yeltacowie · Lake Windabout · RANGES · Lake Station

6

LAKE GAIRDNER NATIONAL PARK · Lake Everard · Lake · LAKE · Island Lagoon · Old Oakden Hills · Mount Gunson · Mount Moseley · Pernatty · Pernatty Lagoon · South Gap · Moralana · Mount Palmerton · Hells Gate · Cotabena

Blue Dam · GAIRDNER · Dunrossil Outstation · Oakden Hills · South Gap · Lake Torrens · B8

Clyde Hill Outstation · Mount Sam · Mount Harper · Mahanewo · NATIONAL · Yalymboo · Maslin · Whittata · 173 · 40 · Kallioota · Wallerberdina · Mount Eyre · Neuroodla · Mount Orkolo

7

Lake Everard · 95 · 117 · Gairdner · Lake Dutton · Charlinga · Kootaberra · Kootaberra Outstation · Yadlamalka · 105

8

Mount John · Kondoolka · Winlippie Peak · Yarna · Moonaree · Lake Acraman · The Sisters · Lake Macfarlane · Yudnapinna · Hesso Outstation · Hesso · Yadlamalka CP · Pettana Gorge · The Dyke · Mount Stephen · Buckaringa Gorge · Hannimans Gorge · Warren Gorge · Mount Ragless · B83 · Gordon

Death Valley · Mount Hiltaba · Mount St Mungo · Mount Stanley · The Horseshoe · Seven Mile Outstation · A87 · Nantilla · The Bluff · The Dutchmans Stern · HEYSEN TRAIL

KOOLGERA CONSERVATION RESERVE · GAWLER · Waroona Peak · Mount Gardner · Mount Partridge · Rankin Outstation · Corraberra · THE DUTCHMANS STERN CP

9

Wirrambie · 67 · Yardea · Pondanna Outstation · Thurlga · Mount Ive · Mount Ive · Kolendo · Old Siam · Carrierwerloo · PORT AUGUSTA · Pichi Richi Pass · Kingswood · Quorn · Bruce · Moocke

Gawler View · Kalbree · Mount Granite · Scrubby Peak · Mount Fairview · Mount Nott · Nonning · 145 · Mount Miccollo · Siam · Wartaka · Illeroo · Stirling North · Mount Brown · Mount Jay · Hamm

10

Capietha · Poochera · A1 · EYRE · GAWLER RANGES CR · GAWLER RANGES NATIONAL PARK · Paney · Mount Double · Coralbignie Outstation · Uno · Myall Creek · A1 · 42 · Lincoln Gap · B100 · 74 · WINNINOWIE CP · DEFENCE RESERVE · Winninowie · Nectar Brook · Wilmington · Willi

Minnipa · Wyoming · Mount Sturt · Mount Allakine · Buckleboo · Wattle Grove · Wilcherry · Lake Gilles · Gilles Downs · Iron Knob · Mount Whyalla · Waterfall Gully · Terka · Boole

Carina · Yaninee · Woollinie · Kimboo · Buckleboo · Fairfield · LAKE GILLES CP · Cooyerdoo · Mount Young · Mambray Creek · Melrose · Perroomb

11

Moonlight Flat · Eldale · Pygery · Wudinna · Broadacres · Kalindi · 33 · Middleback · Iron Baron · Mount Middleback North · Moola · 24 · Whyalla · Port Bonython · Baroota · Murray Town · Boo · Cen

Kyancutta · TOD · 31 · Koongawa · Glencoe · Kimba · 94 · Moonabie · Mount Middleback · Port Germein · PORT PIRIE · Nelshaby · Napperby · Appila · Stone H

12

FLINDERS · 124 · Talia · Kooringal · Gum Flat · Fairview · COCATA CONSERVATION PARK · Warrambo · Kyimba · Karanda · Waddikee · CARALUE BLUFF CR · 243 · Balumbah · Windzel · SHEOAK HILL CP · MUNYAROO CP · Port Davis · Warnertown · Telowie Gorge · B82 · Laura · Nurom · 19 · Glad · Crystal Brook · B84

Colton · Mount Wedge · Gum Park · Evelyn Downs · Lock · Roxend · Caralue · Darke Peak · HAMBIDGE CONSERVATION PARK · HEGGATON CR · Mount Messenger · Midgee · MUNYAROO CR · Port Broughton · Redhill · Koolunga · Mundoora · A1 · Narridy · Gulnare

B100 · Bramfield · Mount Fairy · BASCOMBE WELL CP · BARWELL CR · B91 · EYRE PENINSULA · Pimpala · Kielpa · Mangalo · Mount Olinthus · Miltalie · Minbrie · Kooralla · Mitchellville · Glensea

Joins map 81 · 30° 00' · 31° 00' · 33° 00'

Joins map 72

A   B   C   D   E   F   G   H

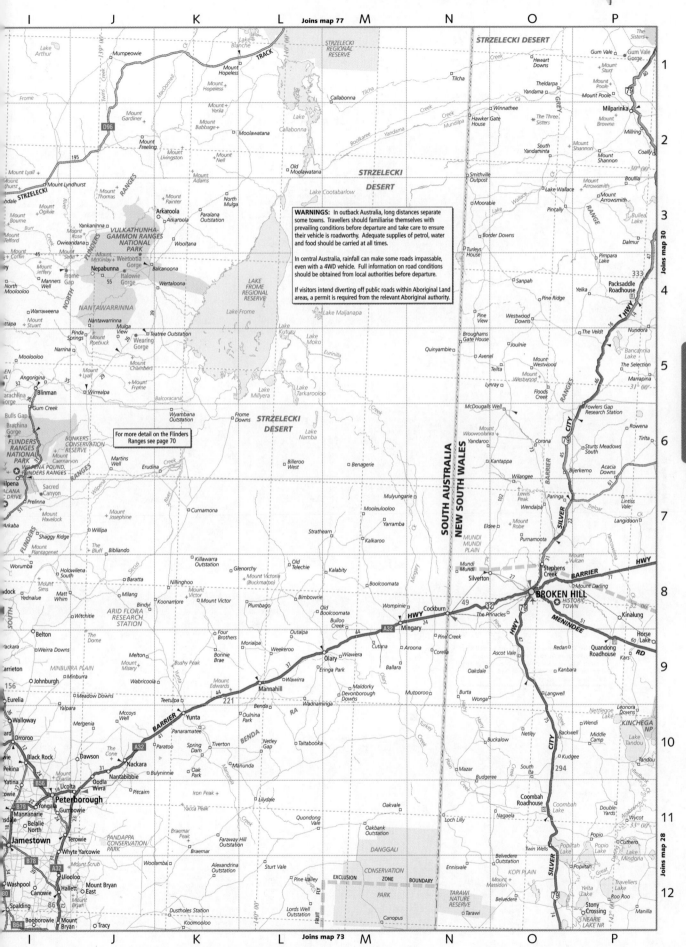

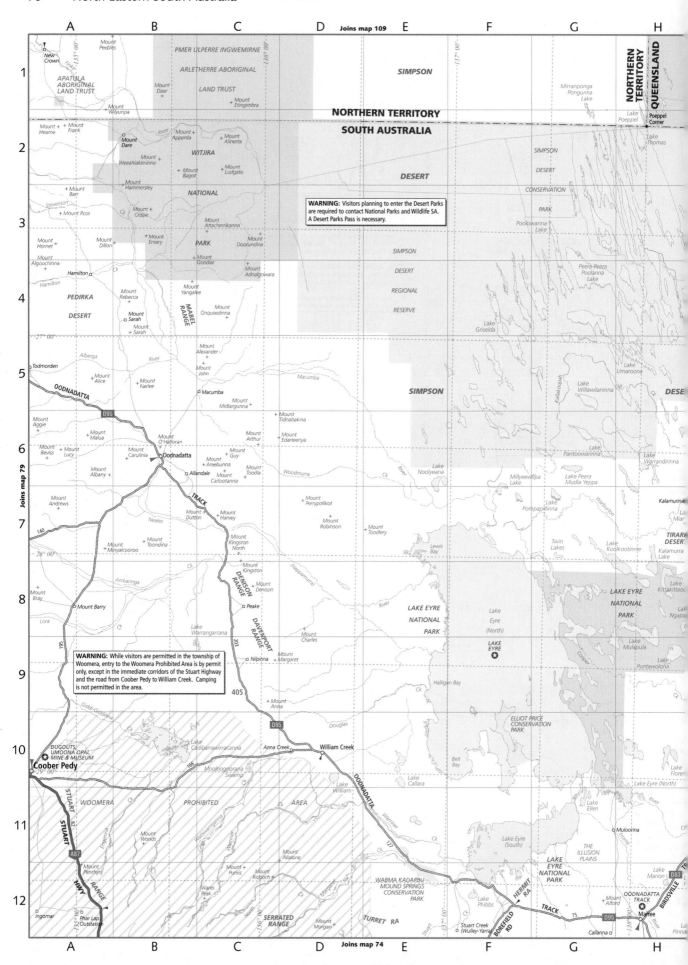

WARNING: Visitors planning to enter the Desert Parks are required to contact National Parks and Wildlife SA. A Desert Parks Pass is necessary.

WARNING: While visitors are permitted in the township of Woomera, entry to the Woomera Prohibited Area is by permit only, except in the immediate corridors of the Stuart Highway and the road from Coober Pedy to William Creek. Camping is not permitted in the area.

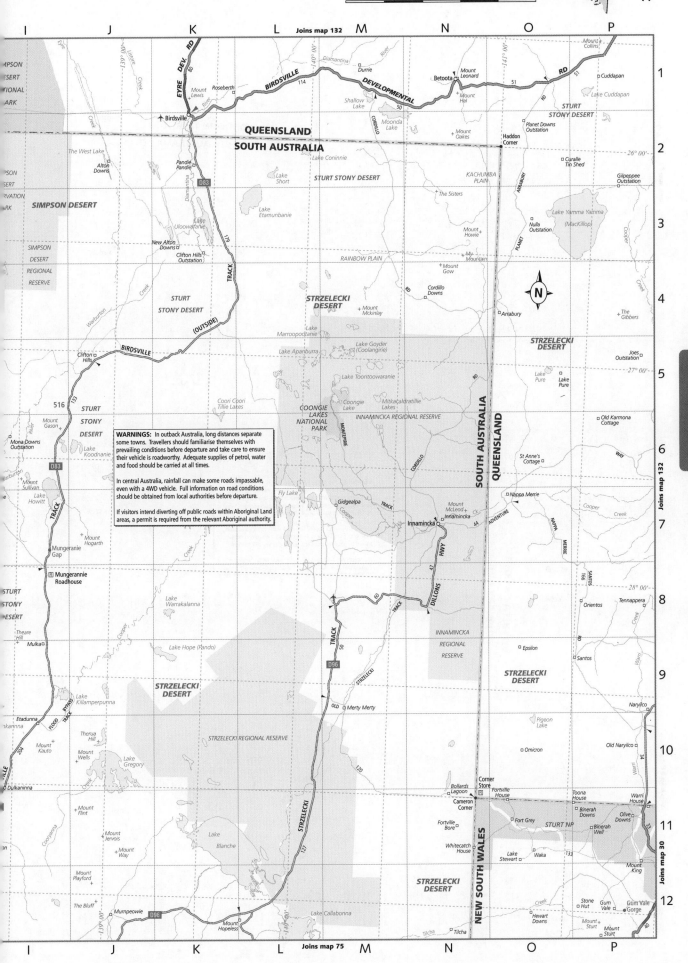

0   20   40   60   80   100 km

I   J   K   L   M   N   O   P

Joins map 132

1

EYRE DEV. RD
BIRDSVILLE
DEVELOPMENTAL
RD

Diamantina River
Durrie
Mount Collins
Cuddapan
Betoota
Mount Leonard
51
Lake Cuddapan
Birdsville
Mount Lewis
Roseberth
Warburton River
114
Shallow Lake
Mount Hal
STURT STONY DESERT
Moonda Lake
Mount Oakes
Haddon Corner
Planet Downs Outstation

QUEENSLAND
SOUTH AUSTRALIA

2

The West Lake
Alton Downs
Pandie Pandie
D83
Lake Coninnie
Lake Short
STURT STONY DESERT
The Sisters
KACHUMBA PLAIN
AIRBURY
Curalle Tin Shed
Gilpeppee Outstation
26° 00'

3

SIMPSON DESERT
SIMPSON DESERT REGIONAL RESERVE
New Alton Downs
Clifton Hills Outstation
Lake Uloowaranie
Lake Etamunbanie
Mount Howie
RAINBOW PLAIN
Mount Mountain
PLANET
Nulla Outstation
Lake Yamma Yamma (MacKillop)
Cooper Creek

4

Warburton Creek
STURT STONY DESERT (OUTSIDE) TRACK
Lake Marroopodtanie
STRZELECKI DESERT
Mount Mckinlay
Mount Gow
RD
Cordillo Downs
Arrabury
STRZELECKI DESERT
The Gibbers
N

5

Clifton Hills
BIRDSVILLE
516
133
Lake Apanburra
Lake Goyder (Coolangine)
Lake Toontoowaranie
Coori Coori Tillie Lakes
RD
Lake Pure
Lake Pure
Joes Outstation
27° 00'

6

Mona Downs Outstation
Mount Gason
Lake Koodnanie
D83
STURT STONY DESERT
COONGIE LAKES NATIONAL PARK
Coongie Lake
Mitkacaldratillie Lakes
INNAMINCKA REGIONAL RESERVE
MONTEPIRE
CORDILLO
St Anne's Cottage
Old Karmona Cottage
WAY

WARNINGS: In outback Australia, long distances separate some towns. Travellers should familiarise themselves with prevailing conditions before departure and take care to ensure their vehicle is roadworthy. Adequate supplies of petrol, water and food should be carried at all times.

In central Australia, rainfall can make some roads impassable, even with a 4WD vehicle. Full information on road conditions should be obtained from local authorities before departure.

If visitors intend diverting off public roads within Aboriginal Land areas, a permit is required from the relevant Aboriginal authority.

7

Warburton
Mount Sullivan
Lake Howitt
TRACK
Fly Lake
Gidgealpa
Cooper Creek
TRACK
Innamincka
Mount McLeod
Innamincka
44
ADVENTURE
Nappa Merrie
NAPPA MERRIE
Cooper Creek

8

STURT STONY DESERT
Mount Hogarth
Mungeranie Gap
Lake Warrakalanna
TRACK
TRACK
50
HWY
47
DILLONS
60
SANTOS
166
Orientos
Tennappera
28° 00'

9

Mungerannie Roadhouse
Theare Hill
Mulka
Lake Hope (Pando)
Cooper Creek
TRACK 50
D96
STRZELECKI
INNAMINCKA REGIONAL RESERVE
STRZELECKI DESERT
Epsilon
Santos

10

Etadunna
FLOOD BYPASS TRACK
Mount Kauto
Therua Hill
Mount Wells
Lake Gregory
Lake Killamperpunna
STRZELECKI DESERT
OLD Merty Merty
STRZELECKI REGIONAL RESERVE
120
Pigeon Lake
Omicron
Naryilco
Old Naryilco
34

11

Dulkaninna
Mount Flint
Mount Jervois
Mount Way
Lake Blanche
STRZELECKI
127
Bollards Lagoon
Corner Store
Fortville House
Cameron Corner
Fortville Bore
Fort Grey
STURT NP
Toona House
Binerah Downs
Binerah Well
Warri House
Olive Downs
33

12

The Bluff
Murnpeowie
D96
Mount Hopeless
Lake Callabonna
Whitecatch House
Lake Stewart
Waka
133
Mount King

NEW SOUTH WALES
STRZELECKI DESERT
Hewart Downs
Stone Hut
Gum Vale
Gum Vale Gorge
Mount Sturt
Mount Sturt
40

Tilcha Creek
Tilcha

I   J   K   L   M   N   O   P

Joins map 75

Joins map 132

Joins map 30

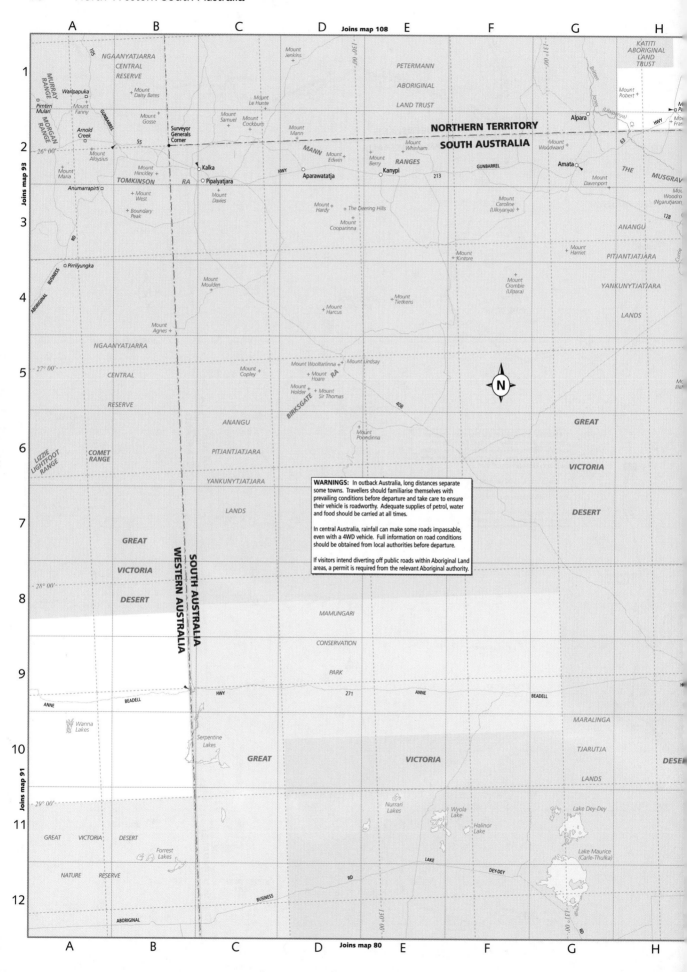

Joins map 93

Joins map 91

A B C D E F G H

NGAANYATJARRA
CENTRAL
RESERVE

105

MURRAY RANGE

Warlpapuka

Pirntirri Mulan

Mount Fanny

MORGAN RANGE

Arnold Creek

26° 00'

Mount Aloysius

Mount Maria

Anumarrapirti

Mount Daisy Bates

Mount Gosse

55

Surveyor Generals Corner

GUNBARREL

Kalka

TOMKINSON RA

Pipalyatjara

Mount Hinckley

Mount West

Boundary Peak

Mount Davies

RD

Pirrilyungka

BUSINESS

ABORIGINAL

Mount Moulden

NGAANYATJARRA

Mount Agnes

CENTRAL

27° 00'

RESERVE

Mount Copley

ANANGU

PITJANTJATJARA

COMET RANGE

YANKUNYTJATJARA

LIZZIE LIGHTFOOT RANGE

LANDS

GREAT

VICTORIA

SOUTH AUSTRALIA / WESTERN AUSTRALIA

28° 00'

DESERT

Mount Jenkins

Mount Le Hunte

Mount Samuel

Mount Cockburn

130° 00'

Mount Mann

MANN

HWY

Aparawatatja

Mount Hardy

Mount Cooparinna

Mount Tietkens

Mount Harcus

Mount Woolfarlinna

Mount Lindsay

Mount Hoare

BIRKSGATE RA

Mount Holder

Mount Sir Thomas

408

Mount Poondinna

PETERMANN

ABORIGINAL

LAND TRUST

Mount Whinham

Mount Berry

Mount Edwin

Kanypi

RANGES

213

Mount Caroline (Ulkiyanya)

Mount Kintore

Mount Crombie (Ulpara)

The Deering Hills

131° 00'

Britten

Jones (Ulainanya)

Mount Robert

NORTHERN TERRITORY

SOUTH AUSTRALIA

Alpara

GUNBARREL

Mount Woodward

Amata

Mount Davenport

Mount Harriet

ANANGU

PITJANTJATJARA

YANKUNYTJATJARA

LANDS

N

GREAT

VICTORIA

DESERT

KATITI ABORIGINAL LAND TRUST

HWY

63

THE MUSGRAV

Mount Woodro (Ngarutjaran)

128

Mc Ellit

WARNINGS: In outback Australia, long distances separate some towns. Travellers should familiarise themselves with prevailing conditions before departure and take care to ensure their vehicle is roadworthy. Adequate supplies of petrol, water and food should be carried at all times.

In central Australia, rainfall can make some roads impassable, even with a 4WD vehicle. Full information on road conditions should be obtained from local authorities before departure.

If visitors intend diverting off public roads within Aboriginal Land areas, a permit is required from the relevant Aboriginal authority.

ANNE

BEADELL

Wanna Lakes

Serpentine Lakes

HWY

271

MAMUNGARI

CONSERVATION

PARK

ANNE

BEADELL

MARALINGA

TJARUTJA

DESE

9

GREAT

10

VICTORIA

GREAT VICTORIA DESERT

29° 00'

11

NATURE RESERVE

Forrest Lakes

BUSINESS

ABORIGINAL

12

130° 00'

Nurrari Lakes

LAKE

RD

Wyola Lake

Halinor Lake

DEY-DEY

Lake Dey-Dey

Lake Maurice (Carle-Thulka)

131° 00'

80

A B C D E F G H

0   20   40   60   80   100 km

I   J   K   L   M   N   O   P

74

Mount Maparey
Mount Falconer
NEWLAND
Lilla
Ck
Mount Gordon
Mount Peterswald
34
36
Mount Daniel +
Mount Mcgowan
31
New Crown
Finke River
Mount Peebles
1

Kulgera
Mount Reynolds +
Kulgera
51
+ Mount Cavenagh
19
RAILWAY
Mount Cecil +
22
Mount Hopetoun
147
Goyder
60
RANGES
+ Mount Beddome
Mount Grundy
BEDDOME RANGE
APATULA ABORIGINAL LAND TRUST
Mount Wilyunpa

NORTHERN TERRITORY
SOUTH AUSTRALIA

Victory Downs
AYERS RANGE
AUSTRALIA
Mount Darling
Mount Parkee
Mount Mead
Coglin
Mount Anderson +
Mount + Hearne
Mount + Frank
Mount Dare
2

New Well
Mount Cuthbert +
Mount + Everard
Marryat
Birthday
Tietkens
RANGES
Mount Howe +
Hamilton
Tieyon
Mount Anthony +
Mount Treloar
Abminga
WITJIRA
Mount Hammersley
NATIONAL

A87
180
Sundown Outstation
Mount Tieyon
Mount + Pair

Mount + Spec
Mount + Warrabillinna
Agnes Creek
Mount Irwin
+ Mount Ross
PARK
3

ANANGU
Eaerengnma
STUART
CENTRAL
Alberga
River
Mount Walter +
Akoolatunna
BAGOT RA
+ Mount Britton
Mount Hornet +
Mount Dillon

PITJANTJATJARA
Mount Mair +
+ Mount Aigoochinna
Hamilton
Hamilton +
Mount Rebecca +
4

YANKUNYTJATJARA
Fregon
LANDS
Tarcoonyinna
River
Lambina
Alberga
PEDIRKA DESERT
Mount Deane +
+ Mount Isabel
Mount Sarah +

Granite Downs
Mount Mystery +
Mount Alberga +
27° 00'

Iwantja (Indulkana)
143
Chandler
INDULKANA RANGE
Christmas Well
Mount Randolph +
Todmorden
River
Mount Alice +
5

Mimili
Wallatalleena Peak
Mount + Illbillee
Mount + Cammeena
THE EVERARD RA
Mount Etitinna
Taddy Peak
Mount John +
Mount Weir +
Coongra
Ck
D95
Mount Herbert North
Mount Jane North
212
TRACK
Mount Naklee +

Mintabie
Mount Byilicaoora +
Marla
OODNADATTA TRACK
Mount Gordon +
+ Mount Todmorden
Mount Aggie +
Mount Malua +
Neales

onna
Officer
COMALCO SURVEY
Wallatinna
Welbourn Hill
Hamenta
Mount Brougham +
South
+ Mount Beviss
Mount Lucy +
River
Mount Carulinia +
6

SURVEY
TRACK
GREAT
A87
83
HWY
SURVEY TRACK
Branch
Kyber Pass
+ Mount Willoughby
Mount Andrews +
+ Mount Albany
7

COMALCO SURVEY
VICTORIA
Wintinna
Mount Marron +
Mount Waddikee +
Mount Arckaringa +
140
Mount Minyalcooroo +
28° 00'

DESERT
Cadney Homestead
Copper Hill
32
Arckaringa
Ck
7

TRACK
Mount Willoughby
Mount Furner +
Mount Evelyn +
Mount Bray +

WOOMERA
235
Mount Gillen +
Evelyn Downs
Mcdonald Peak +
Mount Barry
8

PROHIBITED
Mount Barry +

Lake Meramangye
AREA
Pootnoura
Pootnoura
Mount Euee +
9

MARALINGA
STUART
Algebullcullia
48

ANNE
TJARUTJA
TALLARINGA
CENTRAL
Ck
Giddi-Giddinna
Lake Cadibarrawirracanna

LANDS
CONSERVATION
HWY
Mount Clarence +
DUGOUTS UMOONA OPAL MINE & MUSEUM
Oolgelima
10

BEADELL
284
HWY
PARK
BEADELL
Mabel Creek
Manguri
STUART
23
Coober Pedy

RD
WOOMERA
ANNE
AUSTRALIA
RANGE
29° 00'

PROHIBITED
WARNING: While visitors are permitted in the township of Woomera, entry to the Woomera Prohibited Area is by permit only, except in the immediate corridors of the Stuart Highway and the road from Coober Pedy to William Creek. Camping is not permitted in the area. Note the overlap with Aboriginal Land where you need additional seperate permits.
WOOMERA PROHIBITED AREA
A87
82
11

EMU
AREA
GREAT
VICTORIA
DESERT
Lake Woorong
Lake Phillipson
HWY
Mount Perirhyn +

Mount Igy
Wirrida
Lake Wirrida
Phar Lap Outstation
12

Garford
Sandstone
RAILWAY
Ingomar
135° 00'

Wilkinson Lakes

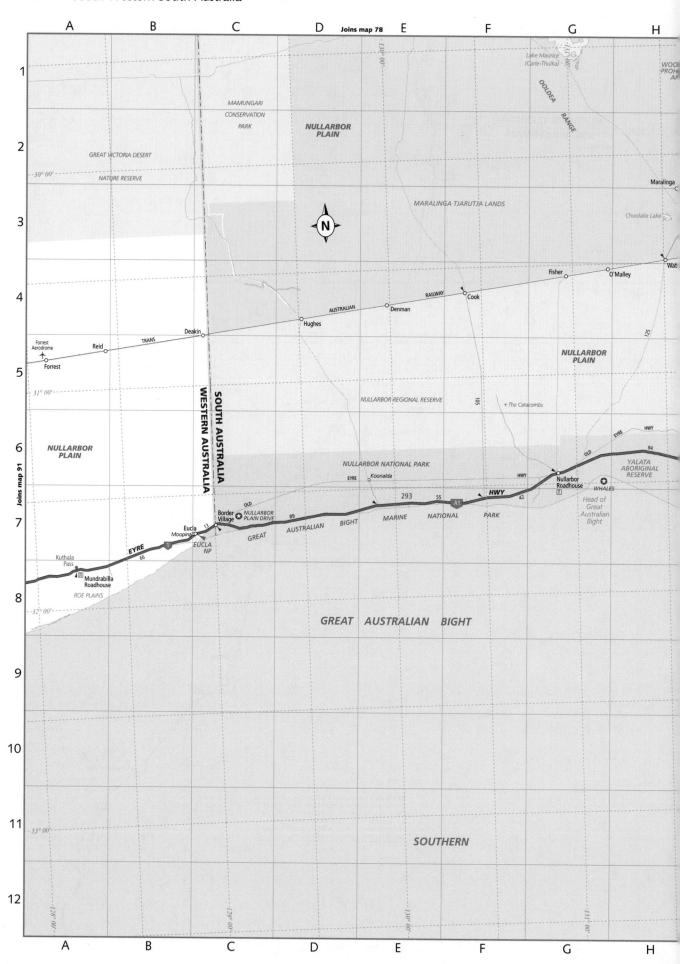

Joins map 78

MAMUNGARI
CONSERVATION
PARK

**NULLARBOR
PLAIN**

Lake Maurice
(Carle-Thulka)

OOLDEA

RANGE

WOO
PROH
A

GREAT VICTORIA DESERT

-30° 00'-

NATURE RESERVE

Maralinga

MARALINGA TJARUTJA LANDS

Choolalie Lake

N

Wat

Fisher   O'Malley

RAILWAY   Cook

AUSTRALIAN   Denman

Hughes

Deakin

TRANS

Reid

Forrest
Aerodrome

Forrest

**NULLARBOR
PLAIN**

-31° 00'-

125

NULLARBOR REGIONAL RESERVE

105

+ The Catacombs

EYRE   HWY

94

OLD

**NULLARBOR
PLAIN**

Joins map 91

**NULLARBOR
PLAIN**

NULLARBOR NATIONAL PARK

EYRE

Koonalda

293   55   A1   42

HWY

HWY

Nullarbor
Roadhouse

YALATA
ABORIGINAL
RESERVE

WHALES

Head of
Great
Australian
Bight

Border
Village

OLD
NULLARBOR
PLAIN DRIVE

89

GREAT   AUSTRALIAN   BIGHT   MARINE   NATIONAL   PARK

Eucla
Moopina

13

EUCLA
NP

EYRE

66

Kuthala
Pass

Mundrabilla
Roadhouse

ROE PLAINS

-32° 00'-

GREAT   AUSTRALIAN   BIGHT

SOUTHERN

SOUTH AUSTRALIA
WESTERN AUSTRALIA

-128° 00'-   *-129° 00'-*   *-130° 00'-*   *-131° 00'-*

0   20   40   60   80   100 km

I   J   K   L   M   N   O   P

Joins map 79

WARNING: While visitors are permitted in the township of
Woomera, entry to the Woomera Prohibited Area is by permit
only, except in the immediate corridors of the Stuart Highway
and the road from Coober Pedy to William Creek. Camping
is not permitted in the area. Note the overlap with Aboriginal
Land where you need additional seperate permits.

Wirrida

Lake
Wirrida

RAILWAY

Ingomar

Phar Lap   Mount
Outstation   Sandy

STUART

62

1

Wilkinson
Lakes

MARALINGA
TJARUTJA
LANDS

ALINGA
ENCE
AND
HIBITED
REA)

Comet

McDouall Peak

Mount
Soward

Mirikata

A87

Indooroopilly
Outstation

Jumbuck

Commonwealth
Hill

Gina
Outstation

WOOMERA
PROHIBITED
AREA

HWY

2

Lake Anthony

WOOMERA
PROHIBITED
AREA

Half Moon
Lake

Irria
Outstation

Muckanippie
Outstation

Bradman
Outstation

Goode
Outstation

367

Lake Bring

Mulgathing

Carne
Outstation

Ooraminna Outstation

3

Mount
Christie

Durkin
Outstation

Gibraltar
Outstation

Ambrosia
Outstation

Johns
Outstation

Ealbara
Outstation

Mentor
Outstation

AUSTRALIAN

Warrior
Outstation

CENTRAL

Whymlet

Ooldea

Bates

Wynbring

Carnding Road
Outstation

Lake
Labyrinth

TRANS

AUSTRALIAN

Lyons
Camp

Malbooma
Outstation

RAILWAY

Tarcoola

Lake
Moolira

Mount
Eba

4

30° 00'

OR
AL
VE

Wilgena

North
Well

Big Tank
Outstation

Lake Ifould

Mount +
Finke

80

Kingoonya

YELLABINNA REGIONAL RESERVE

Lake Tallacootra

143

Yerda

Lake
Harris

5

32° 00'

YALATA
ABORIGINAL
RESERVE

Kokatha

Yalata

LAKE GAIRDNER
NATIONAL PARK

6

Joins map 74

ata
use

AHGUNYAH
CONSERVATION
PARK

YUMBARRA
CR

Lake Everard

Glyde Hill
Outstation

55

EYRE

YUMBARRA CONSERVATION PARK

Lake
Everard

7

EAL
AN
HT
E NP

Nundroo
Roadhouse

39   202

Bookabie

Cundilippy

Northedge

YUMBARRA CR

Mount John +

Kondoolka

-32° 00'

Lake
Acraman

56

Nundroo

Pintumba
Coorabie

35

Koonibba

PUREBA
CR

PUREBA CONSERVATION PARK

Mount
Wallaby

Mount
Pollard

Yarna

Wookata

CHADINGA
CR

Penong

A1

73

Corrong

Winilippe Peak

Mount
Hiltaba

Mount
St Mungo

8

FOWLERS
BAY CR

Fowlers Bay

26

CHADINGA CR

NULLARBOR
PLAIN DRIVE

Watchbrae

Mount
Pyramid

Cape Adieu
Cheetima Beach

Cape
Nuyts

Fowlers Bay
Point Fowler

SURFING
Cactus Beach
Point Sinclair

Lake MacDonnell
+ Black Peak

Marbra

Theyenard

Ceduna

EYRE

Mudamuckla

92

NUNNYAH
CR

Oak Valley

Chinbingina

KOOLGERA CR

Waroona
Peak

NUYTS REEF CP

POINT BELL CR

Point
Bell

Point Peter

Denial
Bay

FLINDERS

Nunjikompita

Mount Centre

Point
Bell
Purdie Islands

St Peter Island

Goat Island

Cape D'Estrees

Kara-Pine

Carawa

Wallala

9

Lacy Island

Evans
Island

Franklin
Islands

Smoky Bay

Smoky
Bay

30

222

109

Wirrulla

61

Wirrambie

GAWLER
RANGES
NP

NUYTS ARCHIPELAGO CP

Point Dillon

ACRAMAN CREEK
CP

Flagstaff

A1

Petina

Yantanabie

Gawler
View

GAWLER
RANGES
CR

Scrubby
Peak

ISLES OF
ST FRANCIS CP

St Francis Island

St Mary Bay
Point Brown

Gascoigne Bay

Haslam

B100

Chilpanunda

Cungena

Kalbrae

Mount
Granite

Point
Collinson

Streaky
Bay

HWY

Coolgrana

Capietha

Poochera

74

Cape Bauer

Eba Island

The Bald Hills

Mount Jane

Chandada

Wyoming

10

Corvisart Bay

36

Maryvale

Parla Peak

62

HWY

Minnipa

16

Streaky Bay

33

Point Westall

Yanerbie Beach

SCEALE BAY CR

ALPATANNA
WATERHOLE
CP

Tootla

Carina

Yandra

Congima

Moonlight
Flat

Yaninee

Sceale Bay

Calca

Mount
Cooper+

Colley

Lake
Yaninee

11

Slade Point

Searcy Bay

Mount Hall

Mount Misery

FLINDERS

KULLIPARU
CP

+ Mount Damper

Mount
Damper

Point Labatt

Cape Radstock

Baird
Bay

Port
Kenny

124

VENUS BAY CP

Venus Bay

24

Talia

COCATA
CP

OCEAN

Anxious Bay

Talia Beach

B100

Kooringal

98

Mount
Wedge

Mount
Wedge

12

34° 00'

Lake Newland

LAKE
NEWLAND
CP

HWY

Colton

WALDEGRAVE
ISLANDS

+ Mount Fairy

Bramfield

B91

I   J   K   L   M   N   O   P

Joins map 72

MAPS

WESTERN AUSTRALIA

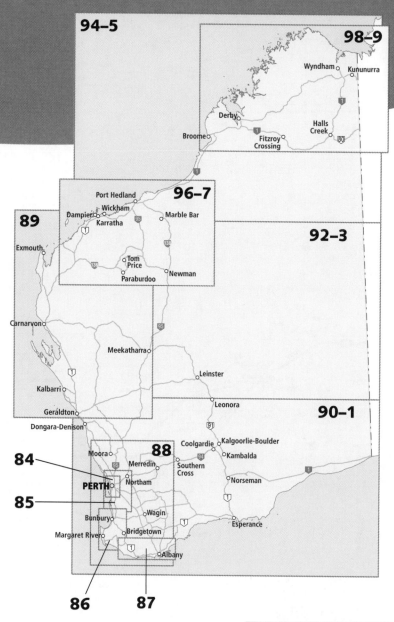

Western Australia	
Central Perth	83
Perth Suburbs	84
Perth & Surrounds	85
South-West Coast	86
South Coast	87
South Western Western Australia	88
Central Western Western Australia	89
Southern Western Australia	90–1
Central Western Australia	92–3
Northern Western Australia	94–5
Pilbara	96–7
Kimberley	98–9

INTER-CITY ROUTES		DISTANCE
Perth–Adelaide via Great Eastern & Eyre hwys	94 1 A1	2700 km
Perth–Darwin via Great Northern Hwy	1 95	4032 km

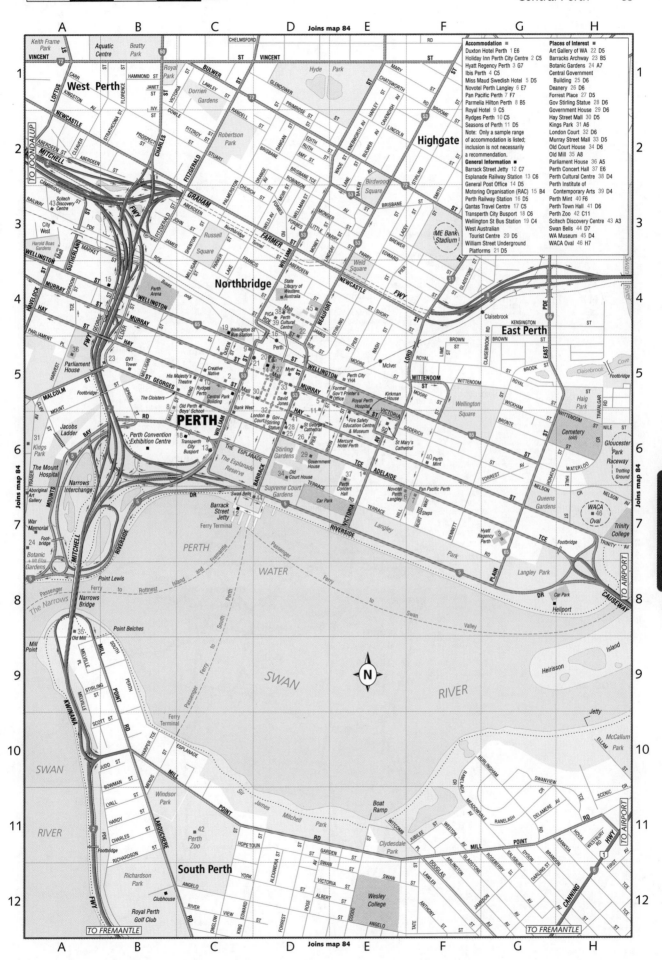

Joins map 84

Scale

0   0.25   0.5   0.75   1 km

Accommodation ■
Duxton Hotel Perth 1 E6
Holiday Inn Perth City Centre 2 C5
Hyatt Regency Perth 3 G7
Ibis Perth 4 C5
Miss Maud Swedish Hotel 5 D5
Novotel Perth Langley 6 E7
Pan Pacific Perth 7 F7
Parmelia Hilton Perth 8 B5
Royal Hotel 9 C5
Rydges Perth 10 C5
Seasons of Perth 11 D5
Note: Only a sample range
of accommodation is listed;
inclusion is not necessarily
a recommendation.

General Information ■
Barrack Street Jetty 12 C7
Esplanade Railway Station 13 C6
General Post Office 14 D5
Motoring Organisation (RAC) 15 B4
Perth Railway Station 16 D5
Qantas Travel Centre 17 C5
Transperth City Busport 18 C6
Wellington St Bus Station 19 C4
West Australian
Tourist Centre 20 D5
William Street Underground
Platforms 21 D5

Places of Interest ■
Art Gallery of WA 22 D5
Barracks Archway 23 B5
Botanic Gardens 24 A7
Central Government
Building 25 D6
Deanery 26 D6
Forrest Place 27 D5
Gov Stirling Statue 28 D6
Government House 29 D6
Hay Street Mall 30 D5
Kings Park 31 A6
London Court 32 D6
Murray Street Mall 33 D5
Old Court House 34 D6
Old Mill 35 A8
Parliament House 36 A5
Perth Concert Hall 37 E6
Perth Cultural Centre 38 D4
Perth Institute of
Contemporary Arts 39 D4
Perth Mint 40 F6
Perth Town Hall 41 D6
Perth Zoo 42 C11
Scitech Discovery Centre 43 A3
Swan Bells 44 D7
WA Museum 45 D4
WACA Oval 46 H7

0   5   10   15   20 km

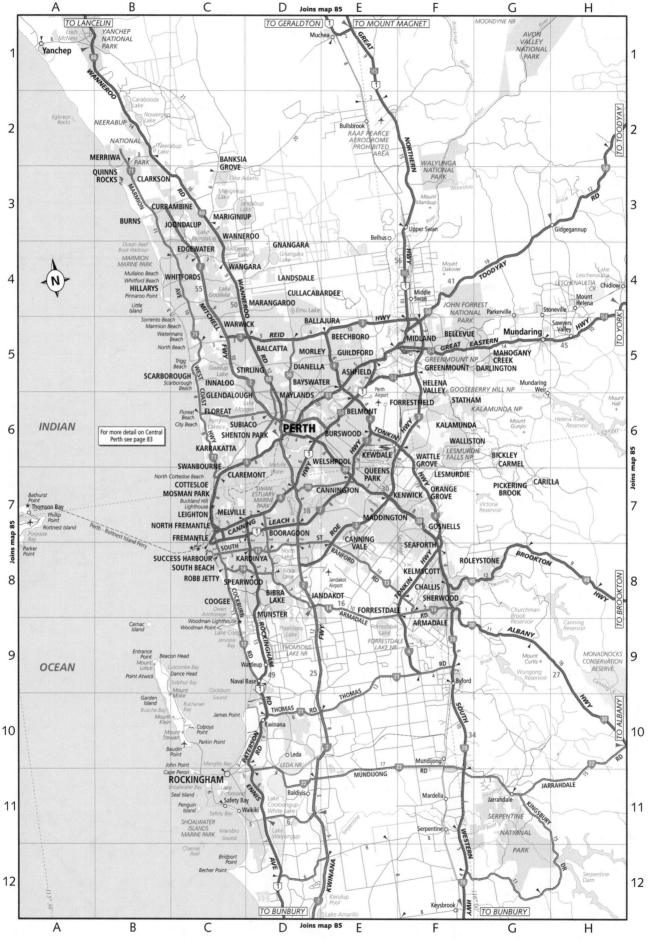

A   B   C   D   E   F   G   H

Joins map 85

TO LANCELIN

TO GERALDTON

TO MOUNT MAGNET

TO TOODYAY

TO YORK

MOONDYNE NR

AVON VALLEY NATIONAL PARK

Yanchep
YANCHEP NATIONAL PARK
Loch McNess

WANNEROO

Carabooda Lake

Nowergup Lake

Eglinton Rocks

NEERABUP

NATIONAL

PARK

Neerabup Lake

Muchea

Bullsbrook
RAAF PEARCE AERODROME PROHIBITED AREA

Brockman River

WALYUNGA NATIONAL PARK

Wooroloo

MERRIWA
QUINNS ROCKS
CLARKSON

BANKSIA GROVE

Lake Adams

Mount Mambup

Upper Swan

Belhus

NORTHERN

HWY

Brook

RD

Gidgegannup

Mount Oakover

TOODYAY

Lake Leschenaultia

CURRAMBINE
BURNS
JOONDALUP

MARIGINIUP

Mariginup Lake

Joondabup Lake

Chidlow

LESCHENAULTIA CR

Mount Helena

MARMION

EDGEWATER
WANGARA

Lake Joondalup

Badgerup Lake

GNANGARA

Gnangara Lake

LANDSDALE

Middle Swan

Stoneville

Parkerville

JOHN FORREST NATIONAL PARK

Ocean Reef Boat Harbour
MARMION MARINE PARK
Mullaloo Beach
Whitford Beach
HILLARYS
Pinnaroo Point
Little Island

WHITFORDS

Lake Goollelai

CULLACABARDEE

MARANGAROO

Emu Lake

BALLAJURA

HWY

Swan

MIDLAND
BELLEVUE

Mundaring
Sawyers Valley

HWY

Sorrento Beach
Marmion Beach
Watermans Beach
North Beach

WARWICK

REID

BEECHBORO

GREAT

EASTERN

MAHOGANY CREEK
GREENMOUNT
DARLINGTON

GREENMOUNT NP

Mundaring Weir

Trigg Beach

BALCATTA

MORLEY

GUILDFORD

Helena

Mount Hall

SCARBOROUGH
Scarborough Beach

STIRLING

DIANELLA

ASHFIELD

HELENA VALLEY

STATHAM

GOOSEBERRY HILL NP

INNALOO
GLENDALOUGH
FLOREAT

BAYSWATER

MAYLANDS

Perth Airport

FORRESTFIELD

KALAMUNDA NP

Mount Gunjin

Helena River Reservoir

INDIAN

Lake Monger

Lake Joondalup

BELMONT

KALAMUNDA

Floreat Beach
City Beach

SUBIACO
SHENTON PARK

PERTH

BURSWOOD

WELSHPOOL

KEWDALE

WALLISTON

LESMURDIE FALLS NP

Mount Gunjin

For more detail on Central Perth see page 83

KARRAKATTA

Melville Water

WATTLE GROVE

LESMURDIE

BICKLEY
CARMEL

SWANBOURNE

QUEENS PARK

ORANGE GROVE

PICKERING BROOK

CARILLA

North Cottesloe Beach
COTTESLOE
MOSMAN PARK
Buckland Hill Lighthouse

CLAREMONT

CANNINGTON

KENWICK

Victoria Reservoir

Bathurst Point
Thomson Bay
Phillip Point
Rottnest Island
Rottnest Island
Porpoise Bay
Parker Point

LEIGHTON
NORTH FREMANTLE
FREMANTLE

MELVILLE

SWAN ESTUARY MARINE PARK

LEACH

BOORAGOON

MADDINGTON

SEAFORTH

GOSNELLS

ROLEYSTONE

BROOKTON

Perth - Rottnest Island Ferry

CANNING

ST

ROE

CANNING VALE

RANFORD

KELMSCOTT

HWY

TO BROOKTON

SUCCESS HARBOUR
SOUTH BEACH
ROBB JETTY

KARDINYA

SPEARWOOD

North Lake

Bibra Lake

Jandakot Airport

CHALLIS
SHERWOOD

Canning

Churchman Brook Reservoir

ALBANY

COOGEE

BIBRA LAKE

JANDAKOT

FORRESTDALE

ARMADALE

Canning Reservoir

Carnac Island

MUNSTER

COCKBURN

ROCKINGHAM

Thomsons Lake

ARMADALE

FORRESTDALE LAKE NR

Mount Curtis

MONADNOCKS CONSERVATION RESERVE

OCEAN

Entrance Point
Mount Lotus
Point Atwick

Woodman Lighthouse
Woodman Point

Lake Coogee

Jervoise Bay

THOMSONS LAKE NR

Wattleup

Wungong Reservoir

Canning

Luscombe Bay
Dance Head
Sulphur Bay

Naval Base

Thomas

Byford

Mount Curtis

Garden Island
Buache Bay
Mount Klein

Cockburn Sound

James Point

THOMAS

RD

SOUTH

Baudin Point

Buchanan Bay

Colpoys Point
Parkin Point

Kwinana

Leda

Mundijong

Mundijong

WESTERN

JARRAHDALE

John Point
Cape Peron
ROCKINGHAM
Shoalwater Bay
Seal Island
Penguin Island

Mangles Bay

LEDA NR

MUNDIJONG

RD

Mardella

Jarrahdale

KINGSBURY

Safety Bay
Waikiki

Lake Richmond

Baldivis

SERPENTINE NATIONAL PARK

SHOALWATER ISLANDS MARINE PARK

Lake Coolongup
Lake Walyungup

Serpentine

DR

Channel Reef

Warnbro Sound

Serpentine Dam

Bridport Point
Becher Point

HWY

Kerulup Pool

Keysbrook

Lake Amarillo

TO ALBANY

TO BUNBURY

Keysbrook

TO BUNBURY

Joins map 85

0 10 20 30 km

A B C D E F G H

1
TO LANCELIN
TO GERALDTON
TO MOUNT MAGNET
Joins map 88
TO GOOMALLING
Gingin
Needoonga
Bindoon
BINDOON
DEWARS POOL RD
FLAT ROCK GULLY NR
Dewars Pool
Dewars Pool
TOODYAY RD
Jennacubbine
Yarramony
NORTHAM PITHARA HWY
31° 30'
WALLINGUP PLAIN
Wilbinga Peak
'YEAL NATURE RESERVE
Lake Chittering
Chittering
Brockman River
Julimar
Mount Dick

2
Two Rocks
The Spot
Yanchep
YANCHEP NATIONAL PARK
CRYSTAL & YONDERUP CAVES
Muchea
Lower Chittering
MOONDYNE NATURE RESERVE
CARTREF PARK COUNTRY GARDEN
Toodyay
GOOMALLING RD
Windmill Hill Cutting
Mount Pleasant
Ringa
Mount Nardie
NORTHAM TOODYAY RD
Northam
Mount Ommane
Quellington
TO MERREDIN
AVON VALLEY NATIONAL PARK
MORANGUP NR
CLACKLINE NATURE RESERVE
EASTERN HWY

3
Eglinton Rocks
NEERABUP NATIONAL PARK
MARMION
Quinns Rocks
Burns
Joondalup
RAAF PEARCE AERODROME PROHIBITED AREA
Jandabup Lake
WANNEROO MARKETS
Bullsbrook
NORTHERN HWY
Mount Mambup
WALYUNGA NP
DARLING RANGE
Gidgegannup
TOODYAY
Wooroloo
Wundowie
Clackline
Bakers Hill
WOONDOWING NATURE RESERVE
KWOLYININE NATURE RESERVE
Mokine
Hamersley
Mount Mackie
York
HISTORIC TOWN
Mount Bright
TO BRUCE ROCK
DYLOTT RA
Mount Bakewell

4
Mullaloo Beach
Hillarys
HILLARYS BOAT HARBOUR, AQUARIUM OF WA (AQWA), SORRENTO BEACH
Pinnaroo Point
Edgewater
Wangara
Gnangara
Landsdale
Belhus
Upper Swan
Henley Brook
Middle Swan
Whiteman
Ballajura
JOHN FORREST NP
Parkerville
Stoneville
Chidlow
Mount Helena
LESCHENAULTIA CONSERVATION RESERVE
GREAT EASTERN HWY
SOUTHERN
Mount Clifford
Mount Observation
MITCHELL FWY
REID HWY
Marangaroo

5
North Beach
Trigg Beach
Scarborough
Floreat Beach
City Beach
PERTH ZOO, INDIAN PACIFIC TRAIN, SWAN VALLEY WINERIES, BIBBULMUN TRACK, WILDFLOWERS, ADVENTURE WORLD
Stirling
Glendalough
Floreat
Subiaco
Karrakatta
Swanbourne
Claremont
PERTH
Dianella
Maylands
Ashfield
Belmont
Burswood
Midland
Guildford
Hazelmere
Greenmount
C.Y. O'CONNOR MUSEUM
Darlington
Mundaring
Mundaring Weir
MUNDARING WEIR
KALAMUNDA NP
Mount Gungin
Mount Hall
Helena River Reservoir
WANDOO CONSERVATION RESERVE
Mount Yetar
Mount Gorrie
Mount Talbot
Mount Billy
North Point
Bathurst Point

6
Thomson Bay
Porpoise Bay
Cape Vlamingh
Strickland Bay
Parker Point
ROTTNEST ISLAND
Rottnest Island
North Fremantle
Fremantle
HISTORIC TOWN
Catherine Point
Spearwood
STOCK ROAD MARKETS
Owen Anchorage
Melville
Bicton
Bibra Lake
Kardinya
Jandakot
ARMADALE RD
Cockburn Sound
Welshpool
Cannington
Kenwick
Orange Grove
Maddington
Gosnells
SWAN BREWERY, CANNING VALE MARKETS
Kelmscott
Armadale
Roleystone
ARALUEN BOTANIC PARK
Churchman Brook Res
Canning Reservoir
DARLING
Mount Dale
BROOKTON
WANDOO CONSERVATION RESERVE
WANDOO CONSERVATION RESERVE
WESTDALE RD
BEVERLEY RD
Wattle Grove
Kalamunda

7
Garden Is
Collins Point
Mount Moke
Sulphur Bay
Buache Bay
Mount Stewart
Beacon Head
Woodman Point
Munster
Wattleup
Naval Base
Kwinana
Leda
ROCKINGHAM
Shoalwater Bay
Safety Bay
Penguin Island
Waikiki
Baldivis
Mundijong
Byford
TUMBULGUM FARM
Wungong Reservoir
JARRAHDALE RD
Jarrahdale
Mount Randall
MONADNOCKS
Mount Cuthbert
Mount Vincent
Mount Cooke
BOYAGARRING CONSERVATION RESERVE
STRANGE ROAD NR
BROOKTON HIGHWAY NR
LUPTON CONSERVATION RESERVE
TO BROOKTON
Westdale
FREMANTLE RD
ENNIS AVE
THOMAS RD
ROE
Channel Reef
Wambro Sound

8
INDIAN
Bridport Point
Becher Point
Comet Bay
Singleton
Madora
Keysbrook
Serpentine
SERPENTINE NP
Lake Amarillo
Guanarup Pool
Serpentine Dam
Mount Solus
WESTERN HWY
32° 30'
Mount Cooke
RESERVE

9
32° 30'
OCEAN
MANDURAH
Blue Bay
Halls Head
Furnissdale
Falcon Bay
PINJARRA RD
North Pinjarra
North Dandalup
North Dandalup Dam
Yatbanerup Pool
O'Neill
RANGE
Mount Wells
NTH BANNISTER
Bannister
Wandering
WANDERING RD
Peel Inlet
Robert Bay
Austin Bay
Austin Bay NR
Yunderup

10
Florida
Melros
Cape Bouvard
KOOLJERRENUP NATURE RESERVE
Pinjarra
HOTHAM VALLEY TOURIST RAILWAY
Meelon
Marrinup
Dwellingup
Amphion
Etmilyn
ETMILYN FOREST TRAMWAY
ALCOA SCARP LOOKOUT
Lake Banksiadale
Dandalup River
Curara
WILLIAMS RD
Crossman
Dwarda
Ranford
Boddington
Marradong
MOORADUNG NATURE RESERVE
TO ALBANY
OLD COAST RD
KWINANA FWY
SOUTH WESTERN HWY
BUNBURY
PINJARRA RD
LANE-POOLE RESERVE
LANE POOLE

11
YALGORUP NATIONAL PARK
Boundary Lake
Lake Clifton
Lake Clifton
Martins Tank Lake
Mount John
Coolup
Hamel
Waroona
Lake Navarino
Lake Moyanup
Lake Kabbanup
Mount Keats
CONSERVATION
Nanga
Mount William
PINJARRA RD
WILLIAMS RD
Mount Saddleback
33° 00'
Quindanning
Lyndhurst
RD

12
Preston Beach
Lake Preston
YALGORUP NATIONAL PARK
Wagerup
Yarloop
South Yalup Upper Dam
Lake Brockman
RESERVE
TO BUNBURY
TO BUNBURY
Joins map 86
Joins map 88

N

A B C D E F G H

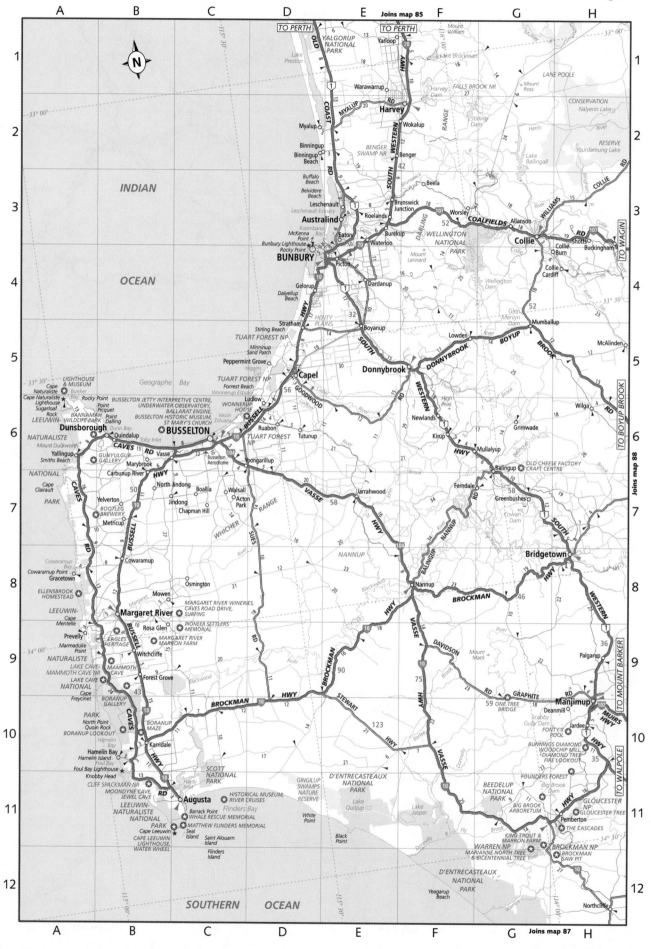

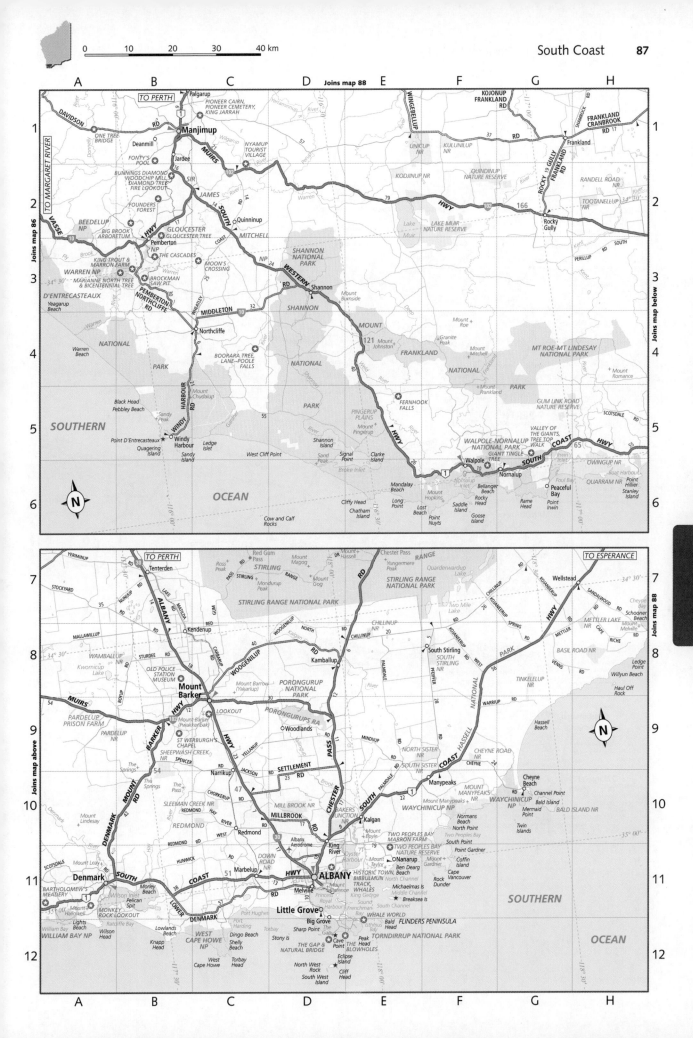

Joins map 88

0 10 20 30 40 km

A   B   C   D   E   F   G   H

Joins map 86

TO MARGARET RIVER

TO PERTH

Palgarup
PIONEER CAIRN,
PIONEER CEMETERY,
KING JARRAH
KOJONUP
FRANKLAND
RD
FRANKLAND
CRANBROOK
RD 17

DAVIDSON
RD
ONE TREE
BRIDGE
Deanmill
Manjimup
Jardee
Wilgan River
NYAMUP TOURIST
VILLAGE
Yerraminnup River
WINGEBELLUP
Frankland

VASSE
Donnelly River
FONTY'S
POOL
MUIRS
RD
102
SIR
57
UNICUP
NR
KULUNILUP
NR
KODJINUP NR
37
RD
QUINDINUP
NATURE RESERVE
RANDELL ROAD
NR
34° 30'

BUNNINGS DIAMOND
WOODCHIP MILL,
DIAMOND TREE
FIRE LOOKOUT
JAMES
14
Warren River
79
HWY
166
ROCKY
GULLY
FRANKLAND
RD
River
TOOTANELLUP
NR

BEEDELUP
NP
BIG BROOK
ARBORETUM
FOUNDERS
FOREST
17
SOUTH
Quinninup
River
Lake
Muir
LAKE MUIR
NATURE RESERVE
107
Rocky
Gully
PERILLUP
RD
Kent
RD
SOUTH

WARREN NP
KING TROUT &
MARRON FARM
Pemberton
NP
Gloucester
GLOUCESTER TREE
THE CASCADES
MITCHELL
COAST
NP 24
SHANNON
NATIONAL
PARK
WESTERN
Shannon
Mount
Burnside
Kent River
Perillup

MARIANNE NORTH TREE
& BICENTENNIAL TREE
BROCKMAN
SAW PIT
PEMBERTON
NORTHCLIFFE
RD
WHEATLEY
MIDDLETON
10 32
RD
SHANNON
Mount
Roe
MOUNT
121
Mount
Johnston
Granite
Peak
Mount
Mitchell
MT ROE–MT LINDESAY
NATIONAL PARK
Mount
Romance

D'ENTRECASTEAUX
Yeagarup
Beach
Warren
Beach
NATIONAL
6
Northcliffe
BOORARA TREE
LANE–POOLE
FALLS
NATIONAL
PARK
FRANKLAND
FERNHOOK
FALLS
Mount
Frankland
NATIONAL
PARK
GUM LINK ROAD
NATURE RESERVE
SCOTSDALE
RD
Mount

SOUTHERN
Black Head
Pebbley Beach
HARBOUR
RD
WINDY
Mount
Chudalup
55
PINGERUP
PLAINS
Mount
Pingerup
HWY
VALLEY OF
THE GIANTS,
TREE TOP
WALK
COAST
65
HWY
55

Point D'Entrecasteaux
Quagering
Island
Windy
Harbour
Sandy
Island
Ledge
Islet
West Cliff Point
Shannon
Island
Broke Inlet
Sand
Peak
Signal
Point
Clarke
Island
26
Walpole
10
GIANT TINGLE
TREE
WALPOLE-NORNALUP
NATIONAL PARK
Nornalup
SOUTH
Irwin
Inlet
OWINGUP NR
Boat Harbour

OCEAN
Mandalay
Beach
Long
Point
Cliffy Head
Chatham
Island
Mount
Hopkins
Lost
Beach
Point
Nuyts
Saddle
Island
Rocky
Head
Goose
Island
Nornalup
Inlet
Bellanger
Beach
Rame
Head
Peaceful
Bay
Point
Irwin
Foul Bay
QUARRAM NR
Point
Hillier
Stanley
Island

Cow and Calf
Rocks

N

A   B   C   D   E   F   G   H

TO PERTH
Tenterden
Red Gum
Pass
STIRLING
Ross
Peak
Mount
Magog
Mount+
Hassell
DR
Mount
Gog
Chester Pass
RANGE
Yungermere
Peak
Quarderwardup
Lake
STIRLING RANGE
NATIONAL PARK
Wellstead
TO ESPERANCE

YERIMINUP
30
STOCKYARD
NUMJUP
RD
35
LAKE
RD
STIRLING
RANGE
Mondurup
Peak
STIRLING RANGE NATIONAL PARK
CHILLINUP
RD
Two Mile
Lake
KOJANERUP
26
SANDALWOOD
HWY
Cheyne
Bay
Schooner
Beach

MALLAWILLUP
WAMBALLUP
NR
STURDEE
RED
CARRABUP
Kendenup
40
WOOGENILLUP
NORTH
Kalgan River
RD
20
CHILLINUP
South Stirling
5
SOUTH
STIRLING
NR
KOJANERUP
SPRING
RD
METTLER LAKE
NR
CAPE
RICHE
METTLER
BASIL ROAD NR

ALBANY
Kwornicup
Lake
18
Mount Barrow
(Yakarlup)
WOOGENILLUP
PORONGURUP
NATIONAL
PARK
Kambalup
RD
72
PALMDALE
28
56
VENNS
RD
TINKELELUP
NR
Ledge
Point
Willyun Beach

MUIRS
HWY
54
OLD POLICE
STATION
MUSEUM
Mount
Barker
12
LOOKOUT
Mount Barker
(Pwakkenbak)
PORONGURUPS RA
Woodlands
HWY
23
PASS
RD
MINDUNP
NORTH SISTER
NR
COAST
WARRIUP
CHEYNE ROAD
NR
Hassell
Beach

PARDELUP
PRISON FARM
PARDELUP
NR
BARKER
102
ST WERBURGH'S
CHAPEL
SHEEPWASH CREEK
SPENCER
YELLANUP
SETTLEMENT
RD
23
CHESTER
SOUTH SISTER
NR
SOUTH
PALMDALE
CHEYNE
24
Manypeaks
MOUNT
MANYPEAKS
Cheyne
Beach
Channel Point
Bald Island
BALD ISLAND NR

DENMARK
The
Springs
54
The
Pass
The
Springs
Narrikup
JACKSON
CHORKERUP
47
MILL BROOK NR
BAKERS
JUNCTION
NR
Kalgan
22
1
Mount Manypeaks+
WAYCHINICUP NP
WAYCHINICUP
NP
Mermaid
Point
Twin
Islands
SOUTHERN

Mount
Lindesay
MOUNT
RD
SLEEMAN CREEK NR
REDMOND
HAY
RIVER
MILLBROOK
17
RD
Mount
Boyle
19
TWO PEOPLES BAY
MARRON FARM
Normans
Beach
North Point
South Point
Coffin
Island
Point Gardner
Cape
Vancouver

Denmark
SCOTSDALE
Mount Leaf+
REDMOND
WEST
Redmond
30
Albany
Aerodrome
DOWN
ROAD
RD
King
River
Oyster
Harbour
Mount
Taylor
Ben Dearg
Beach
TWO PEOPLES BAY
NATURE RESERVE
Mount+
Gardner
Nanarup
Rock
Dunder

BARTHOLOMEW'S
MEADERY
35° 00'
Mount
Hallowell+
SOUTH
51
Marbelup
COAST
13
HWY
Melville
ALBANY
HISTORIC TOWN,
BIBBULMUN
TRACK,
WHALES
North Channel
Mount
Clarence
Michaelmas Is
Breaksea Is

MONKEY
ROCK LOOKOUT
Morley
Beach
Pelican
Spit
Wilson Inlet
1
LOWER
DENMARK
57
Port Hughes
Little Grove
Big Grove
Princess
Royal
Harbour
Frenchman
Bay
King George
Sound
Middle Channel
South Channel
Bald
Head
FLINDERS PENINSULA

WILLIAM BAY NP
Lights
Beach
Wilson
Head
Ratcliffe Bay
Lowlands
Beach
Knapp
Head
WEST
CAPE HOWE
NP
Dingo Beach
Shelly Beach
Stony Is
Sharp Point
THE GAP &
NATURAL BRIDGE
Cave
Point
Peak
Head
THE
BLOWHOLES
TORNDIRRUP NATIONAL PARK
OCEAN

West
Cape Howe
Torbay
Head
North West
Rock
South West
Island
Eclipse
Island
Cliff
Head

N

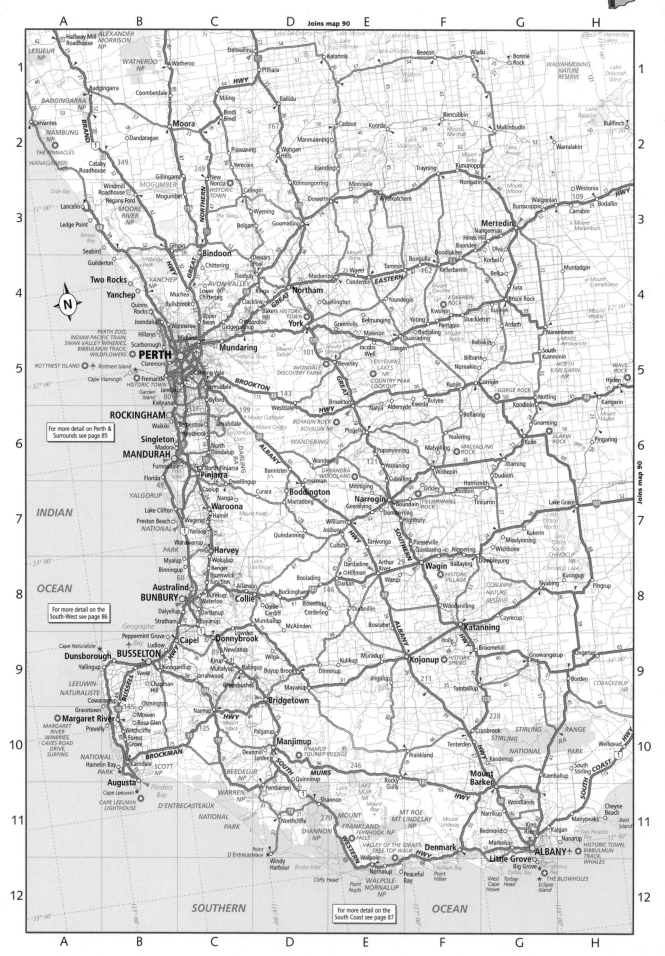

0   20   40   60   80 km

For more detail on Perth &
Surrounds see page 85

For more detail on the
South-West see page 86

For more detail on the
South Coast see page 87

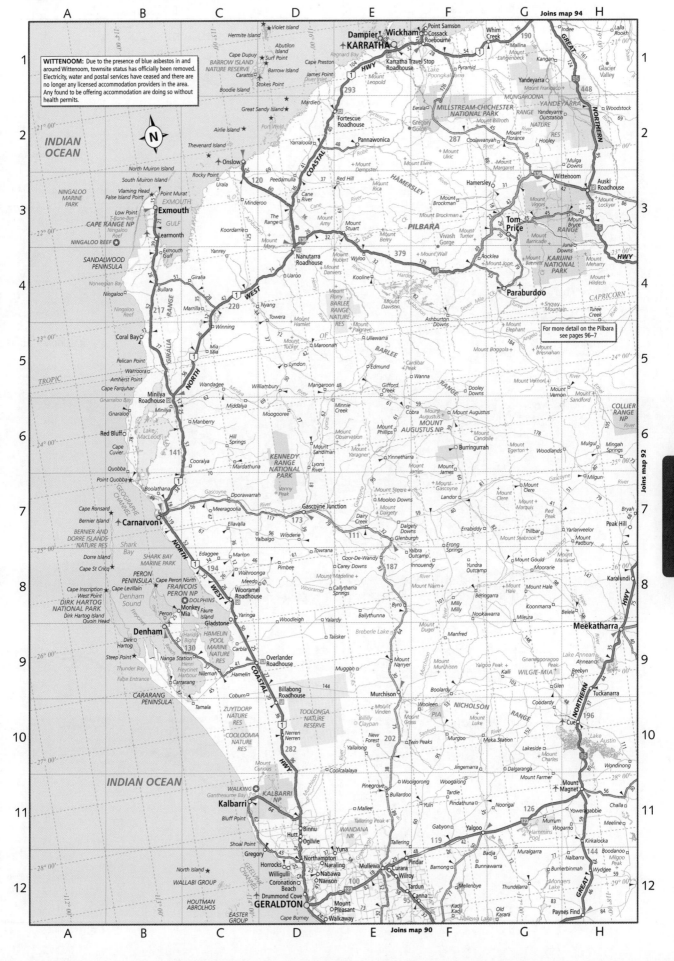

0   50   100   150   200 km

WITTENOOM: Due to the presence of blue asbestos in and around Wittenoom, townsite status has officially been removed. Electricity, water and postal services have ceased and there are no longer any licensed accommodation providers in the area. Any found to be offering accommodation are doing so without health permits.

INDIAN OCEAN

N

NINGALOO MARINE PARK

CAPE RANGE NP

SANDALWOOD PENINSULA

Exmouth
Learmonth

EXMOUTH GULF

Onslow

Nanutarra Roadhouse

PILBARA

HAMERSLEY

MILLSTREAM-CHICHESTER NATIONAL PARK

MUNGAROONA RANGE NATURE RES

YANDEYARRA

NORTHERN

Dampier Wickham
KARRATHA
Roebourne

Whim Creek

GREAT

Tom Price

KARIJINI NATIONAL PARK

Paraburdoo

RANGE

CAPRICORN

COLLIER RANGE NP

For more detail on the Pilbara see pages 96–7

BARLEE RANGE NATURE RES

GIRALIA RANGE

NORTH

WEST

Coral Bay

Minilya Roadhouse

Red Bluff

Carnarvon

KENNEDY RANGE NATIONAL PARK

MOUNT AUGUSTUS NP

Gascoyne Junction

BARLEE RANGE

Meekatharra

NORTHERN

WILGIE-MIA

NICHOLSON

Cue

TROPIC

BERNIER AND DORRE ISLANDS NATURE RES

Shark Bay

SHARK BAY MARINE PARK

PERON PENINSULA

FRANCOIS PERON NP

DIRK HARTOG NATIONAL PARK

Denham
Monkey Mia

HAMELIN POOL MARINE NATURE RES

Overlander Roadhouse

Billabong Roadhouse

Wooramel Roadhouse

Murchison

Karalundi

Tuckanarra

GREAT

Mount Magnet

CARARANG PENINSULA

ZUYTDORP NATURE RES

COOLOOMIA NATURE RES

TOOLONGA NATURE RESERVE

INDIAN OCEAN

KALBARRI NP
Kalbarri

WANDANA NR

Yalgoo

Kirkalocka

Paynes Find

WALLABI GROUP

HOUTMAN ABROLHOS

EASTER GROUP

GELVINK CHANNEL

Northampton

GERALDTON

Mullewa

Joins map 92

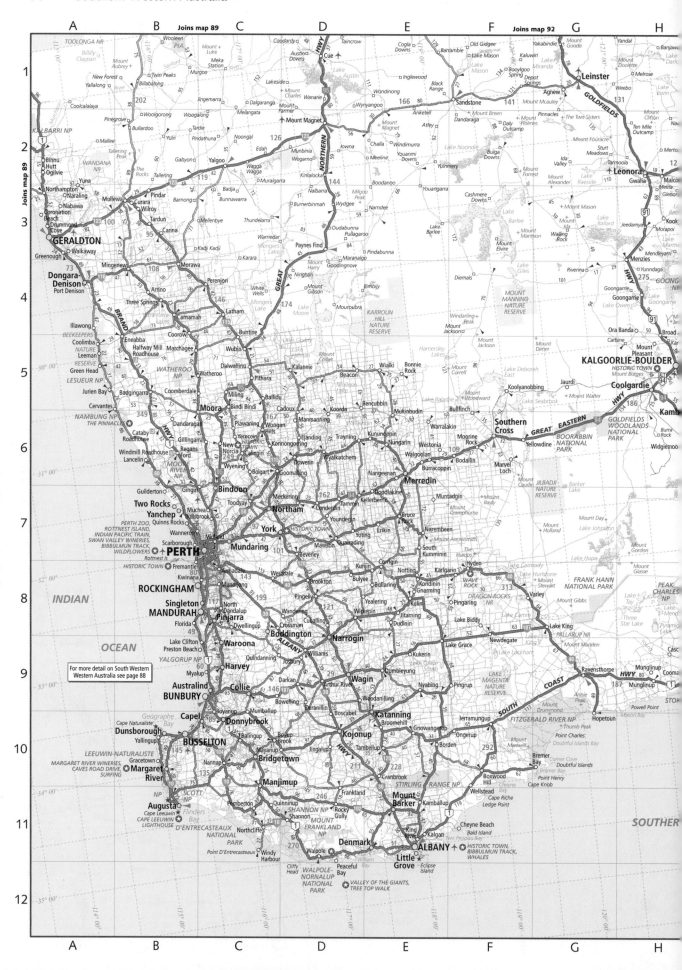

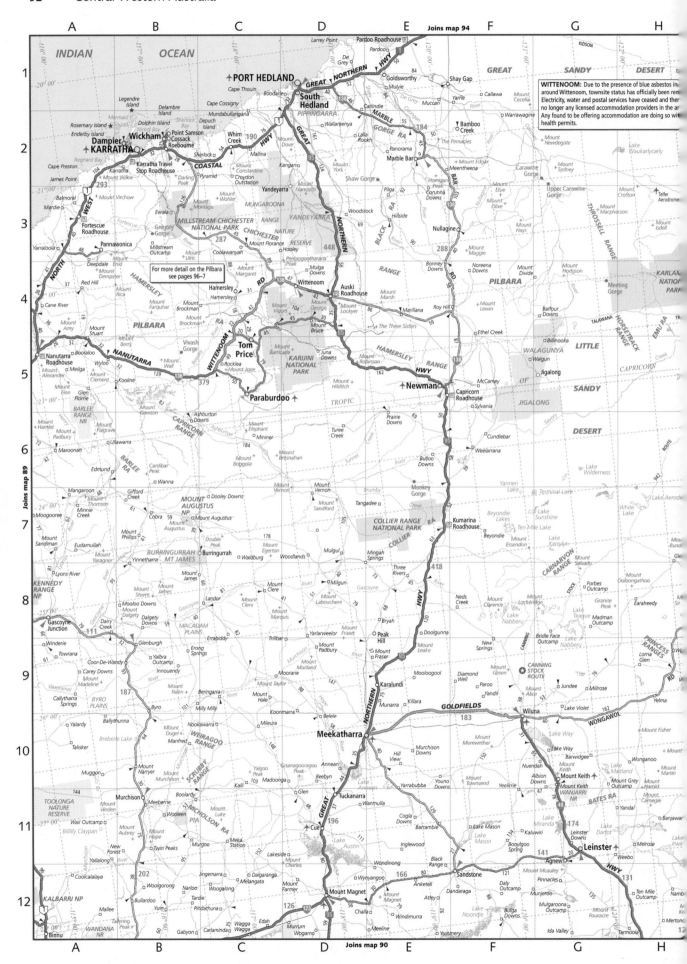

Joins map 94

Joins map 89

Joins map 90

WITTENOOM: Due to the presence of blue asbestos in and around Wittenoom, townsite status has officially been removed. Electricity, water and postal services have ceased and there are no longer any licensed accommodation providers in the area. Any found to be offering accommodation are doing so without health permits.

For more detail on the Pilbara see pages 96-7

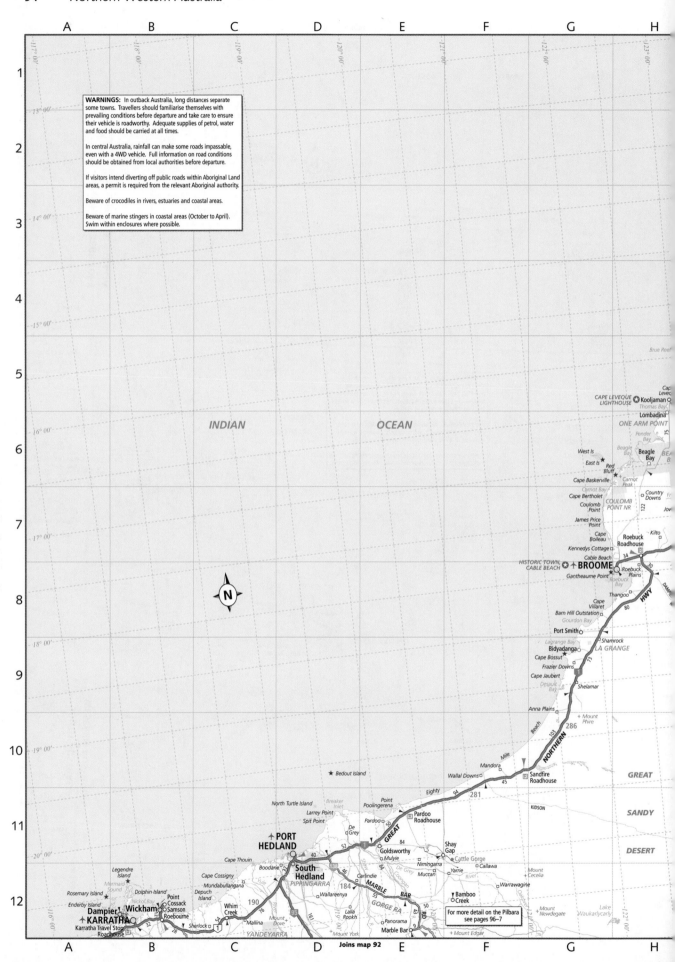

WARNINGS: In outback Australia, long distances separate some towns. Travellers should familiarise themselves with prevailing conditions before departure and take care to ensure their vehicle is roadworthy. Adequate supplies of petrol, water and food should be carried at all times.

In central Australia, rainfall can make some roads impassable, even with a 4WD vehicle. Full information on road conditions should be obtained from local authorities before departure.

If visitors intend diverting off public roads within Aboriginal Land areas, a permit is required from the relevant Aboriginal authority.

Beware of crocodiles in rivers, estuaries and coastal areas.

Beware of marine stingers in coastal areas (October to April). Swim within enclosures where possible.

INDIAN   OCEAN

Brue Reef

Cape Leveque
CAPE LEVEQUE Kooljaman
LIGHTHOUSE   Thomas Bay
Lombadina
ONE ARM POINT
Pender Bay
West Is   Beagle Bay
East Is   Red   Beagle Bay
Bluff
Cape Baskerville
Carnot Peak
Carnot Bay
Cape Bertholt   Country Downs
Coulomb   COULOMB
Point   POINT NR   Jov
James Price   122
Point
Cape   Kilto
Boileau   Roebuck
Kennedys Cottage   Roadhouse
Cable Beach   3A
HISTORIC TOWN,   BROOME
CABLE BEACH   Roebuck
Gantheaume Point   Plains
Roebuck
Bay
Thangoo   HWY
Cape   80
Villaret
Barn Hill Outstation   DAMPIER
Gourdon Bay
Port Smith   Shamrock
Lagrange Bay   LA GRANGE
Bidyadanga   73
Cape Bossut
Frazier Downs
Cape Jaubert   Shelamar
Desault
Bay
Anna Plains
+ Mount
Phire
286
Mile
Mandora   NORTHERN
Wallal Downs   GREAT
45   Sandfire
Eighty   Roadhouse
94   281
KIDSON   SANDY
Point
Poolingerena
North Turtle Island   Pardoo
Larrey Point   Pardoo   GREAT   84   DESERT
Spit Point   Roadhouse
De
Grey   Shay
Goldsworthy   Gap
PORT   Mulyie   Cattle Gorge
HEDLAND   84   Nimingarra
Cape Thouin   52   De Grey   Yarrie   Callawa
40   River
Boodarie   South   46   Carlindie   Muccan   Mount
Legendre   Hedland   188   Cecelia
Island   Cape Cossigny   PIPPINGARRA   MARBLE   Warrawagine
Mundabullangana   184   55
Rosemary Island   Depuch   BAR   Bamboo
Mermaid   Island   Wallareenya   GORGE RA   50   Creek   Mount
Sound   190   RD   Newdegate
Dolphin Island   Whim   Lalla   43   Lake
Enderby Island   Point   Creek   76   Rookh   For more detail on the Pilbara   Waukarlycarly
Nickol Bay   Cossack   Mount   see pages 96-7
Dampier   Wickham   Samson   Dove   Panorama
KARRATHA   Roebourne   Mallina   Marble Bar
Karratha Travel Stop   32   Sherlock   54   + Mount Edgar
Roadhouse   28   YANDEYARRA

N

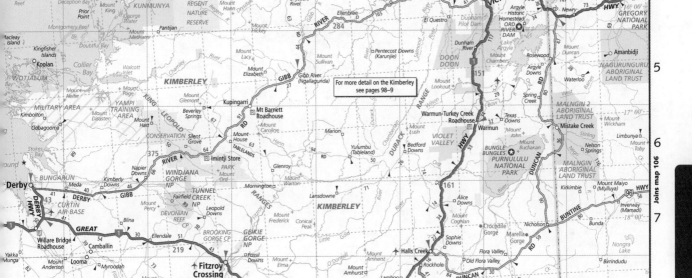

Joins map 104
Joins map 106
Joins map 108
Joins map 93

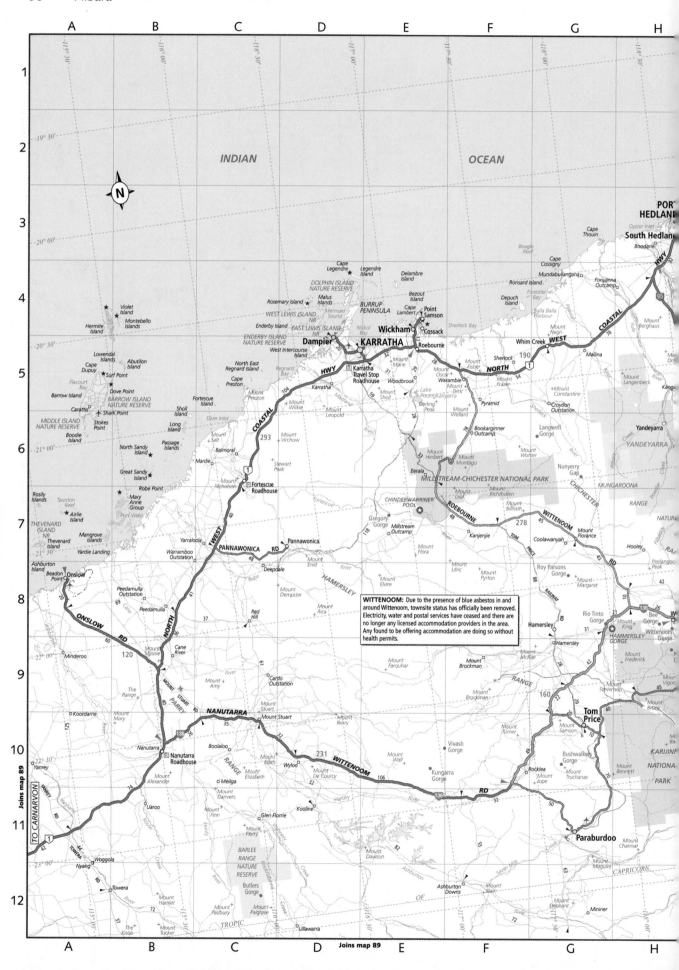

WITTENOOM: Due to the presence of blue asbestos in and around Wittenoom, townsite status has officially been removed. Electricity, water and postal services have ceased and there are no longer any licensed accommodation providers in the area. Any found to be offering accommodation are doing so without health permits.

INDIAN   OCEAN

Joins map 89

Joins map 89

0   20   40   60   80   100 km

Joins map 94
Joins map 94
Joins map 92
Joins map 92

TO BROOME

Bedout Island

Mandora
Sandfire Roadhouse

Wallal Downs
Beach
45
Eighty Mile
HWY
KIDSON
NORTHERN
94
241
BORELINE

Turtle
Breaker Inlet
Poissonnier Point
Cartaminia Point
Point Poolingerena
Cape Keraudren
Pardoo Outcamp
GREAT

Larrey Point
spit Point
Red Point
Mount Blaze
Pardoo Roadhouse
GREAT SANDY

De Grey
Ripon Island
Pardoo
CAPE KERAUDREN
50
70

Mount St George
Goldsworthy
84
Shay Gap
Cattle Gorge
kennedy Gap
Kimberley Gap
Caliawa
DESERT

Mount Grant
Mount Goldsworthy
52
Nimingarra
Cundaline Gap
Muccan
Yarrie
Warrawagine

Mulyie
Mount Woodhouse
DeGrey
RD

MARBLE
138
46
Carlindie
144
Kittys Gap
Coppin Gap
Bamboo Creek
Warrawagine

ARRA
BAR
55
Talga Peak
50
The Pinnacles
RD
HILLS

Wallareenya
RANGE
Doolena Peak
Doolena Gap
The Sisters
RIPON
Mount Newdegate
Lake Waukarlycarly

Lalla Rookh
GORGE
Panorama
Mount Edgar
GREGORY
TELFER
MINE

Mount York
Strelley Gorge
Marble Bar
Limestone
Meentheena
Warrawoona Peak
Horrigan Peak
WOODIE
RANGE
RD
Mount Sydney

Glacier Valley
The Island Hill
Old Corunna Downs
92
Carawine Gorge
RD
Mount Crofton

Shaw Gorge
Pilga
Corunna Downs
Emu Creek
103
Mount Elsie
Upper Carawine Gorge
RD
THROSSELL

Warrery Gap
138
Mount Olive
Mount Macpherson
RANGE

Woodstock
Mount Webber
Hillside
Beaton Gorge
201
SKULL
Mount Hays
Mount Edgar

NORTHERN
69
Nullagine
40
SPRINGS
Hallcomes Peak
Mount Maggie
Mount Cooke
Davis
Coonarie

PILBARA
BLACK
90
Mount Edgar
Mount Rudall
Mount Hodgson
Meeting Gorge
KARLAMILYI

Yule
RANGE
Bonney Downs
Noreena Downs
NATIONAL

HWY
95
Warrie
RD
Mount McKay
Mount Divide
PARK

Auski Roadhouse
MUNJINA
145
Mount Marsh
Roy Hill
Lynn Peak
Mount Lewin
Balfour Downs
Talawana
HORSETRACK RANGE
TRACK

Mount George
Munjina Gorge
Mount Lockyer
86
ROY HILL RD
59
LITTLE

DALES GORGE
35
Marillana
Ethel Creek
WALAGUNYA
Talawana

Mount Windell
95
HAMERSLEY
The Three Sisters
87
Billinooka
SANDY

GREAT
34
RANGE
WEELI WOLLI SPRING
89
PUNDA POOL
138
Waigun

Downs
Mount Meharry
HANCOCK RANGE
Mount Robinson
WANNA MUNNA ROCK ART SITE
EAGLE ROCK FALLS
KALGANS POOL
Jigalong
CAPRICORN

The Governor
194
NORTHERN
90
HWY
Cathedral Gorge
MARBLE
OF
DESERT

Mount Ella
Mount Newman
35
BAR
JIGALONG

Newman
Ophthalmia Dam
McCamey
Sylvania
TROPIC
Capricorn Roadhouse
RD

Spearhole
50
138

Turee Creek
Prairie Downs
69

KUNDERONG RANGE
95
Cundlebar
Weelarrana

TO MEEKATHARRA

WARNINGS: In outback Australia, long distances separate some towns. Travellers should familiarise themselves with prevailing conditions before departure and take care to ensure their vehicle is roadworthy. Adequate supplies of petrol, water and food should be carried at all times.

In central Australia, rainfall can make some roads impassable, even with a 4WD vehicle. Full information on road conditions should be obtained from local authorities before departure.

If visitors intend diverting off public roads within Aboriginal Land areas, a permit is required from the relevant Aboriginal authority.

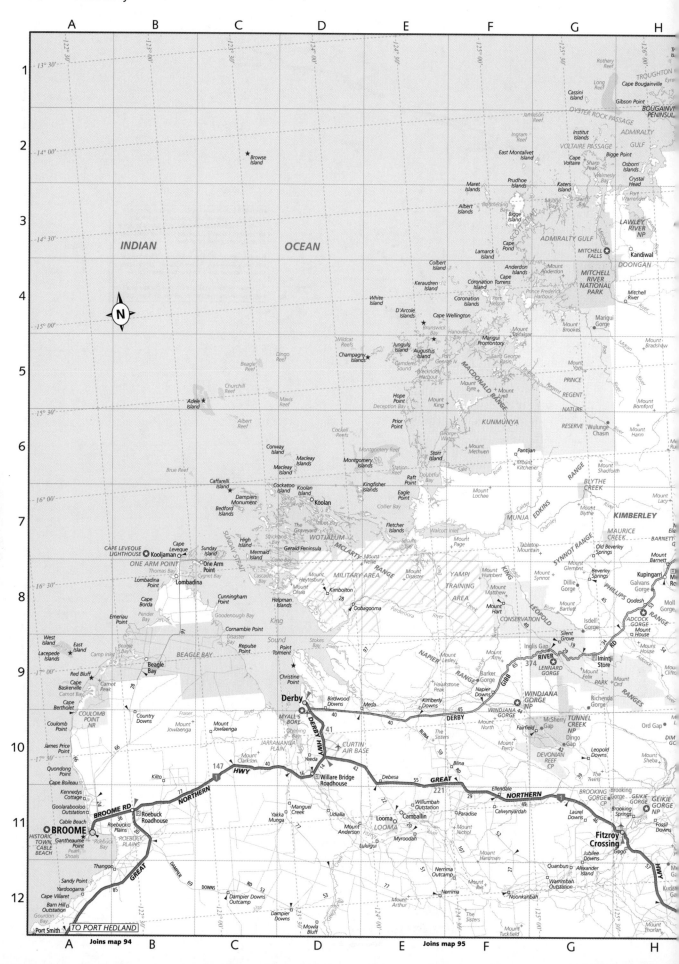

Joins map 94

Joins map 95

0 20 40 60 80 100 km

Joins map 104

Joins map 106

TIMOR SEA

JOSEPH BONAPARTE GULF

Cape Londonderry
Cape Talbot
Graham Moore Islands
Governor Islands
Glycosmis Bay
Lesueur Island
Koolama Bay
Cape Rulhieres
Cape Bernier
Cape Whiskey
Cape St Lambert
Reveley Island
Buckle Head
Thurburn Bluff
Cape Dussejour
Lacrosse Island
Cape Domett
Rocky Island
Pelican Island
Sharp Peak
Turtle Point
Cape Hay
Port Keats Kuy
Cape Dombey
Hyland Bay
Tree Point Kuy
Yederr
Un-Marr
Moyle
Kubuyirri
Peppimenarti
Merrepen
Emu Point
MOYLE PLAIN
Injin Beach
Old Mission
Ditchi
Nangu
Kultchill
Wudapuli
Port Keats (Wadeye)
Nganinthi
Fossil Head
Treachery Bay
New Moon Inlet
Swamp Point
Quoin Island
Keyling Inlet
Queens Channel
Fitzmaurice
DALY RIVER / PORT KEATS ABORIGINAL LAND TRUST
TABLE PLAIN
MACADAM RANGE
BRADSHAW FIELD TRAINING AREA
Bradshaw The Tombs
Legune
Marralum
Kneebone
Spirit Hill
Bucket Springs (Doojum)
Bullo Gorge
Bullo River
Auvergne
Bulla
East Baines Gorge
Karrauumby
RANGE

Cape Broome Bluff
Red Bluff
Napier-Broome Bay
Deep Bay
Cone Mountain
KALUMBURU
Barton Plains
Kalumburu
BARTON PLAIN
KIMBERLEY
Carson River
Mount Leeming
Mount Connelly
OOMBULGURRI
DRYSDALE RIVER NATIONAL PARK
Glider Gorge
Euro Gorge
Mount Keating
Worriga Gorge
Wongaroodoo Gorge
HMAN RANGE
ASHTON RANGE
MILLIGAN RANGES
FORREST RIVER
Mount Nicholls
Mount Booton
Mount Burns
Mount Fraser
Drysdale River
Berkeley River
Mount Mongona
Oombulgurri
Adolphus Island
Drayton Peak
CAMBRIDGE GULF
NINGBING RANGE
Knob Peak
Cave Spring Gap
Carlton Hill
PARRYS LAGOONS NR
PARRY CREEK
Buttons Gap
PALM SPRINGS NR
The Grotto
Kununurra
ZEBRA ROCK GALLERY
CARR BOYD RANGES
Policemans Hole
KEEP RIVER NATIONAL PARK EXTENSION (PROPOSED)
KEEP RIVER NP
Bubble Bubble
Desmonds Passage
Wyndham
PRISON TREE
Home Valley
Mount Lawley
Mount Beatrice
Durack River
Mount Edith
EMMA GORGE
El Questro
VOYAGES EL QUESTRO WILDERNESS PARK
Dunham Pilot Dam
Carlton Gorge
Argyle Historic Homestead
ORD RIVER DAM LAKE ARGYLE TOURIST VILLAGE
Lake Argyle
The Twins
Newry
VICTORIA
GREGORY
NATIONAL PARK
MINERS POOL
Ellenbrae
Palmer Pass
Grimwood Gap
Salmond Gorge
Mount Todd
Dunham River
DOON DOON
Mount Evelyn
Argyle Downs
Rosewood
Mount Duncan
Waterloo
Amanbidji
NAGURUNGURU ABORIGINAL LAND TRUST
Pimple Peak
Scotty-Salmond Gorge
Pentecost Downs (Karunjie)
Salmond
GLEN HILL
ARGYLE DIAMOND MINE
Bow River
Spring Creek
Mount Close
Bamboo Springs
Mistake Creek
MALNGIN 2 ABORIGINAL LAND TRUST
Mount Kimon
Mount Wickham
Limbunya
Gibb River Jagunda
Gordons Gorge
Chamberlain River
RANGE
Mount Jarrad
Mount John
Mount Elder
Nelson Springs
Stirling
Mount Besley
Mount Toby
DAGARAGU ABORIGINAL LAND TRUST
Warmun-Turkey Creek Roadhouse
Warmun
Texas Downs
MALNGIN ABORIGINAL LAND TRUST
Patterson Gorge
Mabel Downs
VIOLET VALLEY CONSERVATION RESERVE
Mount Remarkable
Mount Ranford
BUNGLE BUNGLES
PURNULULU NATIONAL PARK
Mount Buchanan
DUNCAN RD
Mount Napier
Mount Maiyo (Mulluya)
Kirkimbie
Limbunya
Riveren
HOOKER CREEK ABORIGINAL LAND TRUST
TABLELANDS
Yulumbu (Tableland)
Bedford Downs
Mount Wells
Crocodile Gorge
NARRIE RANGE
JOHN GORGE
ngton
Lansdowne
Tunganary Gorge
Alice Downs
Mount Forster
Nicholson
Inverway (Mamadi)
Mount Farquharson
Mount Archie
Bunda
Nongra Lake
Birrindudu
BUNTINE HWY
NORTHERN TERRITORY
WESTERN AUSTRALIA
KIMBERLEY
LEOPOLD RANGES
O'Donnell River Gorge
Pyra Gorge
One Palm Tree Gorge
Neville Gorge
Mount Coghlan
Crocodile Gorge
Sophie Downs
Marella Gorge
Flora Valley
Frederick
Mount Cummings
Mount Amhurst
Moola Bulla
Halls Creek
CHINA WALL
Old Flora Valley
Flora Valley
HOOKER CREEK
Mount Winifred
Crowhurst Gorge
Koongie Park
Rockhole
OLD HALLS CREEK
Mount Flora
Saw Tooth Gorge
DUNCAN RD
DENISON PLAINS
Margaret Gorge
Mount Huxley
Lamboo
Eagle Hawk Crossing Gorge
Old Lamboo
Ruby Plains
GORDON DOWNS (RINGERS SOAK)
YINGUALYALYA ABORIGINAL LAND TRUST
CENTRAL DESERT ABORIGINAL LAND TRUST
Mount Ramsay
Margaret River
Louisa Downs
Mount Dockrell
TANAMI DESERT
BALLARA RD
GREAT NORTHERN HWY
TANAMI RD
MUELLER RANGE
NICHOLSON PLAIN
DURACK RANGE
BIRRINDUDU RANGE
STURT CREEK

WARNINGS: In outback Australia, long distances separate some towns. Travellers should familiarise themselves with prevailing conditions before departure and take care to ensure their vehicle is roadworthy. Adequate supplies of petrol, water and food should be carried at all times.

In central Australia, rainfall can make some roads impassable, even with a 4WD vehicle. Full information on road conditions should be obtained from local authorities before departure.

If visitors intend diverting off public roads within Aboriginal Land areas, a permit is required from the relevant Aboriginal authority.

Beware of crocodiles in rivers, estuaries and coastal areas.

Beware of marine stingers in coastal areas (October to April). Swim within enclosures where possible.

TO TIMBER CREEK

MAPS

NORTHERN TERRITORY

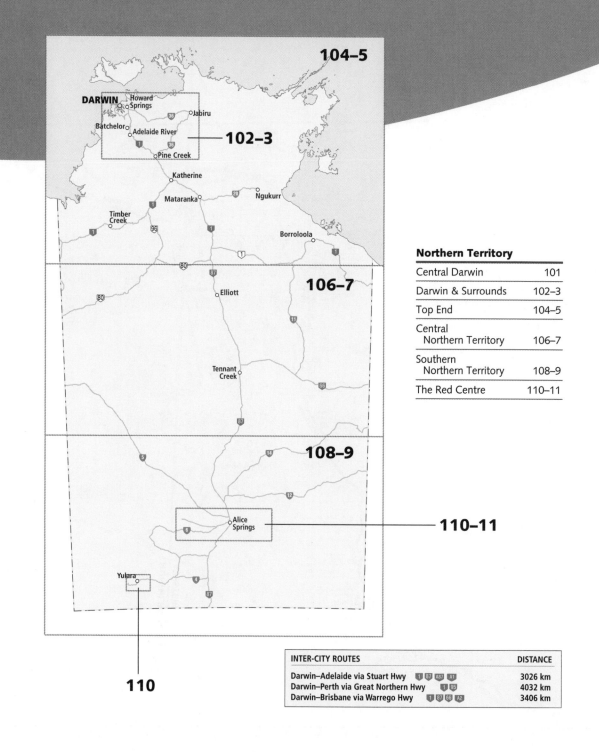

INTER-CITY ROUTES	DISTANCE
Darwin–Adelaide via Stuart Hwy	3026 km
Darwin–Perth via Great Northern Hwy	4032 km
Darwin–Brisbane via Warrego Hwy	3406 km

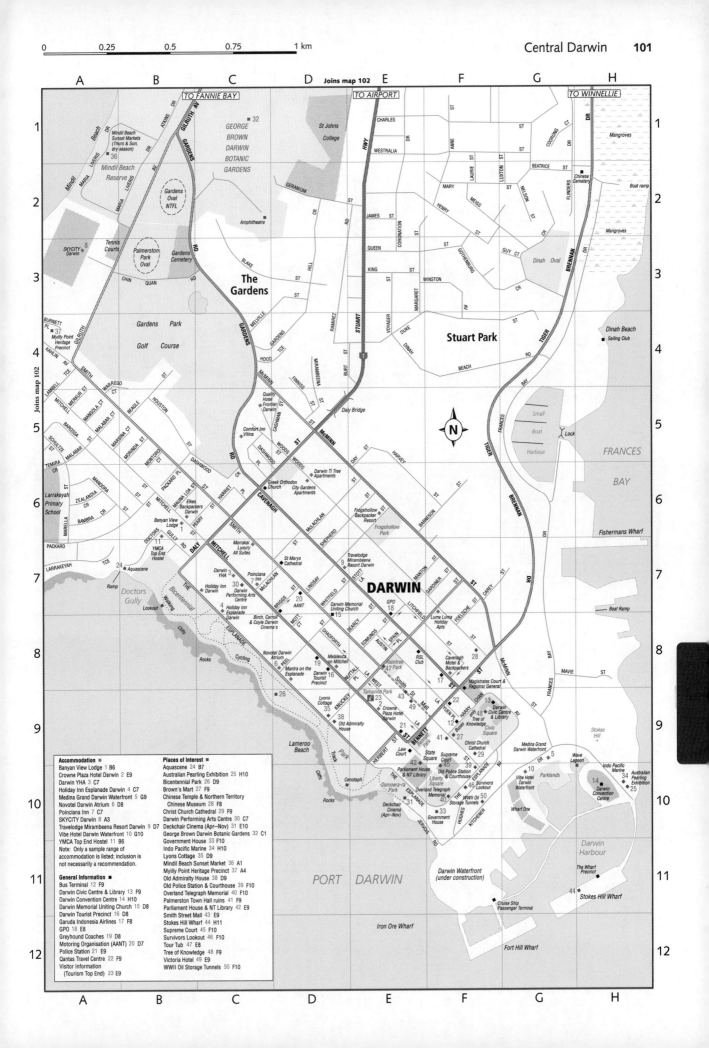

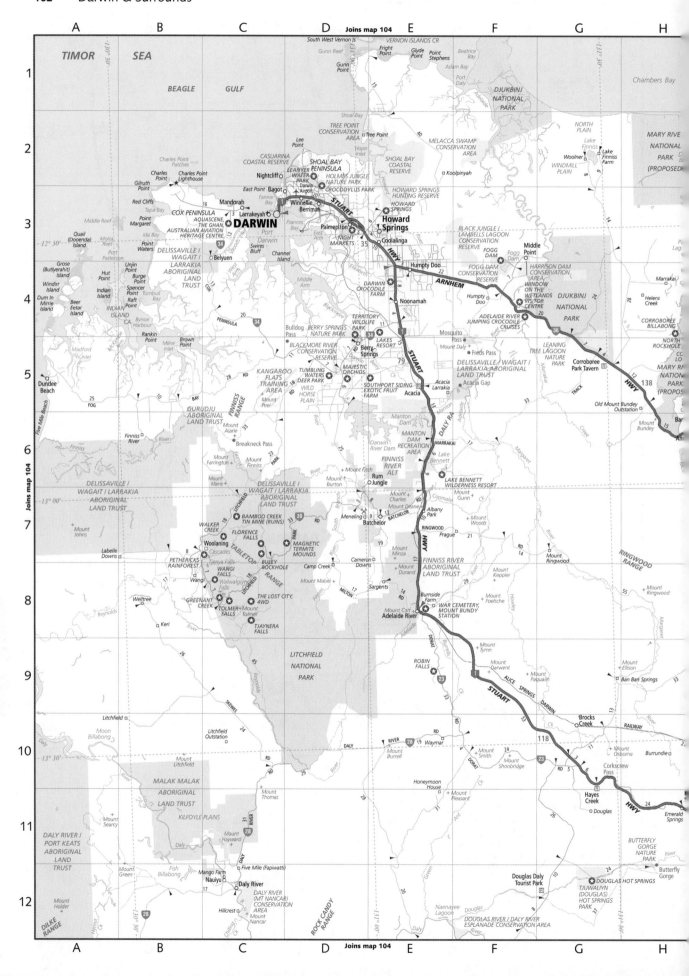

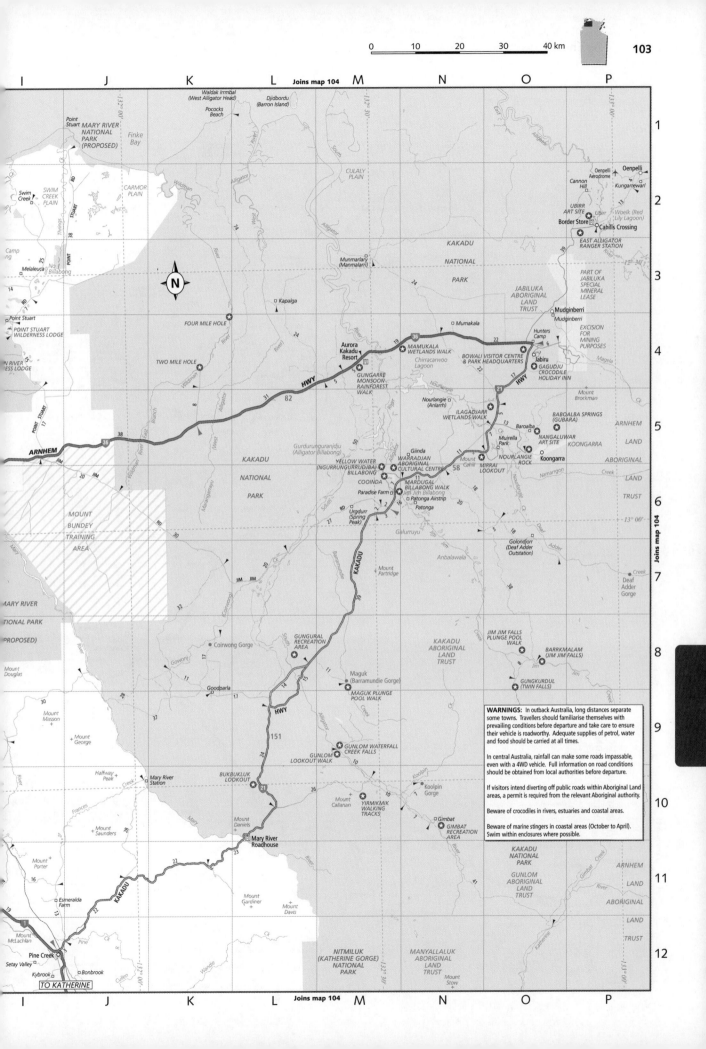

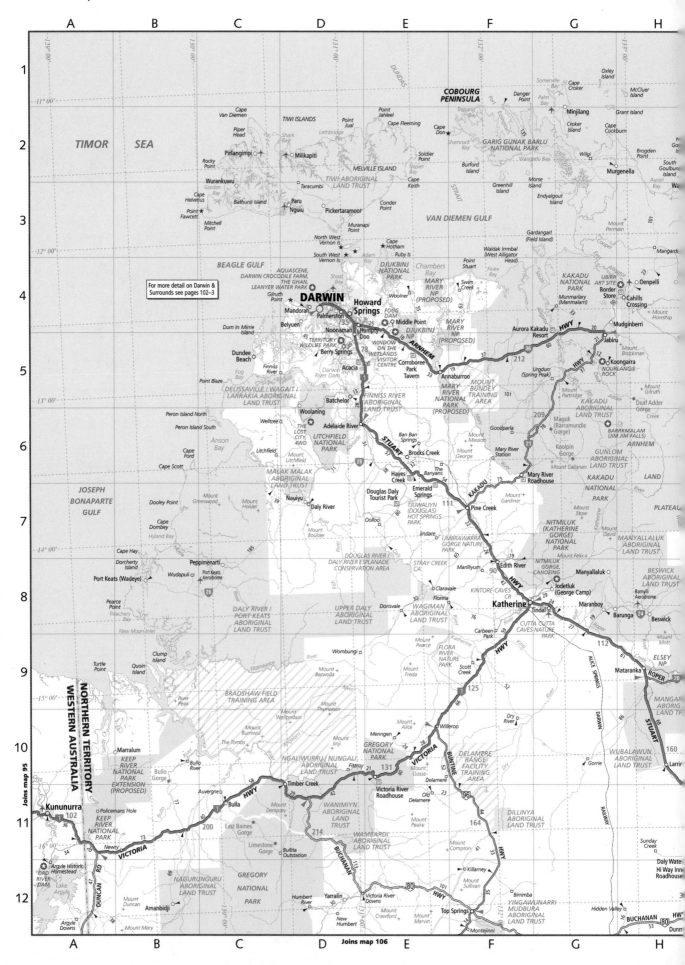

For more detail on Darwin & Surrounds see pages 102–3

Joins map 95

Joins map 106

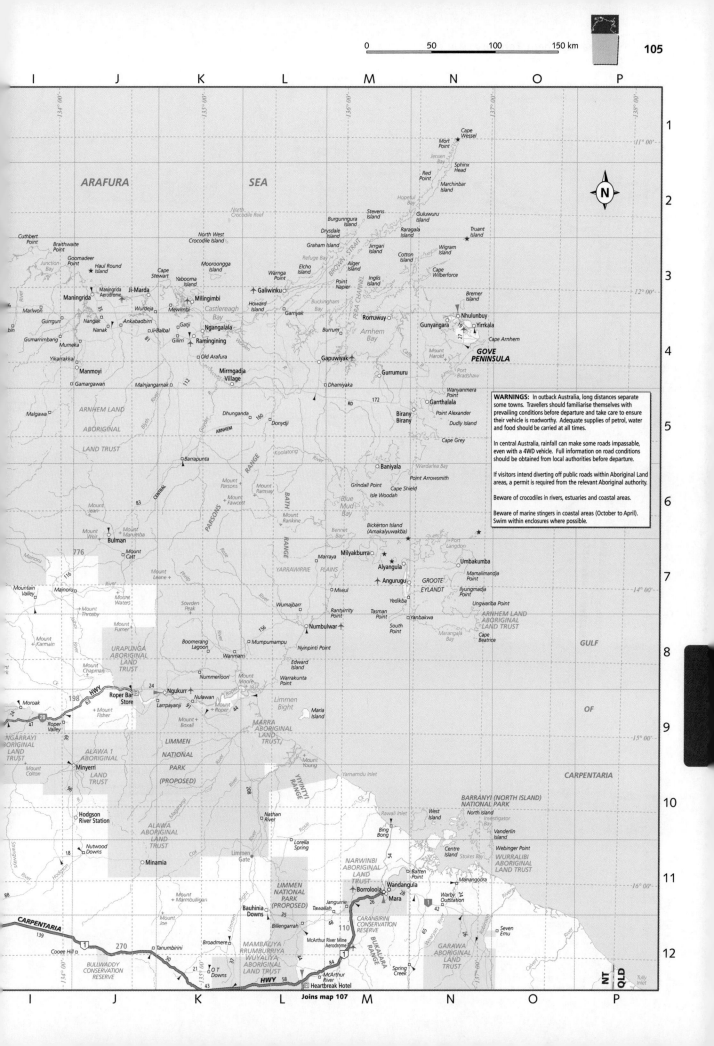

Joins map 107

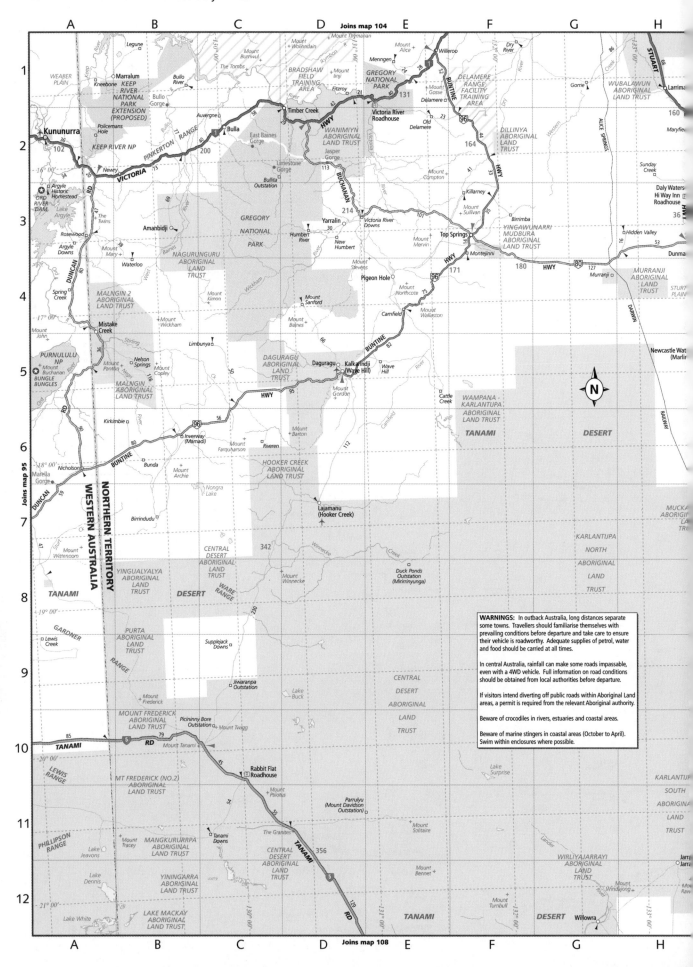

WARNINGS: In outback Australia, long distances separate some towns. Travellers should familiarise themselves with prevailing conditions before departure and take care to ensure their vehicle is roadworthy. Adequate supplies of petrol, water and food should be carried at all times.

In central Australia, rainfall can make some roads impassable, even with a 4WD vehicle. Full information on road conditions should be obtained from local authorities before departure.

If visitors intend diverting off public roads within Aboriginal Land areas, a permit is required from the relevant Aboriginal authority.

Beware of crocodiles in rivers, estuaries and coastal areas.

Beware of marine stingers in coastal areas (October to April). Swim within enclosures where possible.

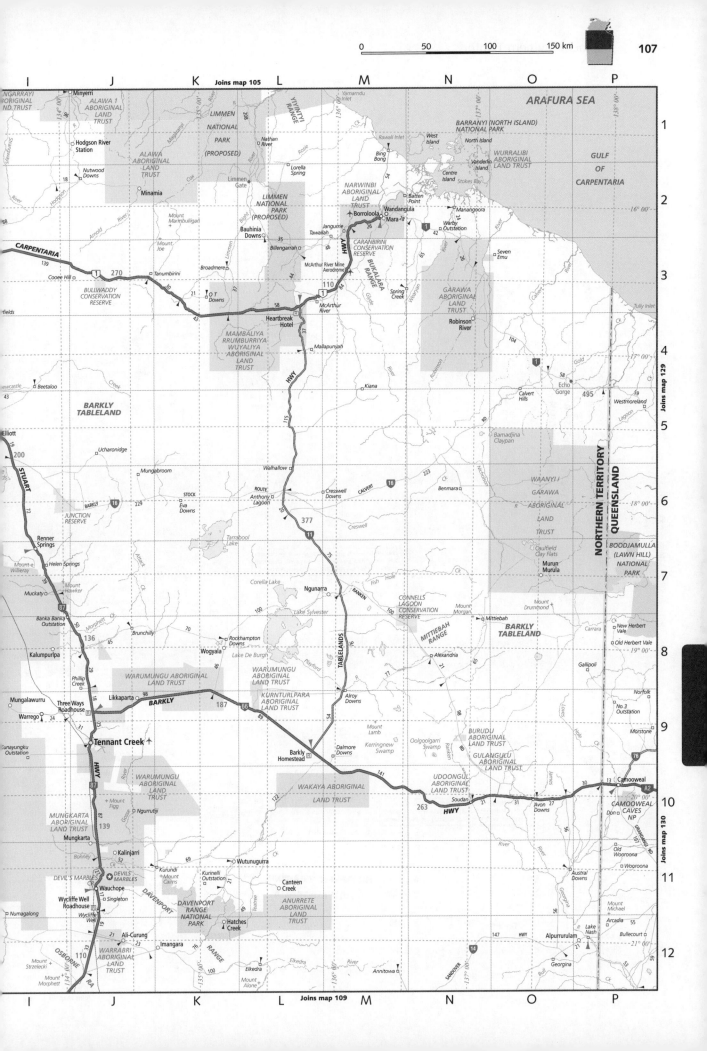

0   50   100   150 km

ARAFURA SEA

Joins map 105

I   J   K   L   M   N   O   P

NGARRAYI
ORIGINAL
ND TRUST
Minyerri
ALAWA 1
ABORIGINAL
LAND
TRUST

Hodgson River
Station

Nutwood
Downs
18

Minamia

CARPENTARIA
139
Cooee Hill

BULLWADDY
CONSERVATION
RESERVE

270
Tanumbirini

20

O T
Downs
21

37

43

Beetaloo
Newcastle
43

BARKLY
TABLELAND

Elliott
19
200

STUART

72

BARKLY 16
229

Renner
Springs

Mount
Willieray
Helen Springs

Muckaty

Banka Banka
Outstation
50
87

136
45
Brunchilly

Kalumpurlpa
29

Phillip
Creek
18

Mungalawurru
Three Ways
Roadhouse
Warrego
24
31
25

Tennant Creek

HWY
87

MUNGKARTA
ABORIGINAL
LAND TRUST
139
Mungkarta

Numagalong

Mount
Strzelecki
Mount
Morphett

OSBORNE
RA
110
33

ALAWA
ABORIGINAL
LAND
TRUST

Mount
Marmbulligan

LIMMEN
NATIONAL
PARK
(PROPOSED)
208

Limmen
Gate

Bauhinia
Downs
35
Billengarrah

Mount
Joe

Broadmere

58

Heartbreak
Hotel

MAMBALIYA
RRUMBURRIYA
WUYALIYA
ABORIGINAL
LAND
TRUST

HWY

115

Walhallow

ROUTE
Anthony
Lagoon

STOCK
Eva
Downs

Ucharonidge

Mungabroom

JUNCTION
RESERVE

Mount
Hawker

Morphett

70

Rockhampton
Downs
Wogyala
46

WARUMUNGU ABORIGINAL
LAND TRUST

Likkaparta
98

BARKLY
187

Kurundi
+Mount
Cairns

WARUMUNGU
ABORIGINAL
LAND
TRUST

Ngurrutji

Kalinjarri
52
Bonney
69

DEVIL'S MARBLES
DEVILS
MARBLES
Wauchope
Singleton

Wycliffe Well
Roadhouse
Wycliffe
Well
21
Ali-Curung
23

WARRABRI
ABORIGINAL
LAND
TRUST

Imangara

DAVENPORT
RANGE

100

KURNTURLPARA
ABORIGINAL
LAND TRUST
89
66

WARUMUNGU
ABORIGINAL
LAND TRUST

Lake De Burgh
Playford

Lake Sylvester

Corella Lake

Ngunarra

100

TABLELANDS

RANKEN

Fish Hole

Barkly
Homestead

WAKAYA ABORIGINAL
LAND TRUST
122

Kurinelli
Outstation

Canteen
Creek

Teatree

ANURRETE
ABORIGINAL
LAND TRUST

Wutunugurra

Hatches
Creek
89

Elkedra

Mount
Alone

Elkedra
100

YYINTYI
RANGE

LIMMEN
NATIONAL
PARK
(PROPOSED)
136

Nathan
River
Lorella
Spring
Rosie

Ck

Yarnarndu
Inlet

Janguirie
Tawallah
48

McArthur River Mine
Aerodrome
1

McArthur
River
37

Mailapunjah

Kiana

Cresswell
Downs
20

CALVERT

377
11
75

Ck

Bing
Bong

Borroloola
Mara 28
Wandangula
26

NARWINBI
ABORIGINAL
LAND
TRUST

CARANBIRINI
CONSERVATION
RESERVE

BUKALARA
RANGE

Spring
Creek

Glyde
River

Walawa

Robinson
River

Rawali Inlet

West
Island

Batten
Point

1
42

CALVERT

16
223

Benmara

Creswell

Murun
Murula

CONNELLS
LAGOON
CONSERVATION
RESERVE

100

MITTIEBAH
RANGE

76

77

Dalmore
Downs

Kerringnew
Swamp

58

Alroy
Downs

Mount
Lamb

263
HWY

Oolgoolgarri
Swamp

Ranken

BURUDU
ABORIGINAL
LAND
TRUST

GULANGULU
ABORIGINAL
LAND TRUST

141

Soudan

UDOONGUL
ABORIGINAL
LAND TRUST

21

BARRANYI (NORTH ISLAND)
NATIONAL PARK

North Island

Vanderlin
Island

Centre
Island
Stokes Bay

Manangoora
Warby
Outstation

76

Seven
Emu

Calvert
Hills

Echo
Gorge
58
495

Bamadjina
Claypan

Caulfield
Clay Flats

Mount
Morgan
Mittiebah

BARKLY
TABLELAND

Alexandria
21

98

99

Avon
Downs

Austral
Downs

30

31
27

13

Camooweal

A2

WURRALIBI
ABORIGINAL
LAND TRUST

GARAWA
ABORIGINAL
LAND
TRUST

104

GULF
OF
CARPENTARIA

Tully Inlet

Westmoreland
59

WAANYI
GARAWA
ABORIGINAL
LAND
TRUST

NORTHERN TERRITORY
QUEENSLAND

BOODJAMULLA
(LAWN HILL)
NATIONAL
PARK

Carrara

New Herbert
Vale
Old Herbert Vale

Gallipoli

Norfolk

No 3
Outstation

Morstone

78

CAMOOWEAL
CAVES
NP
Don
Old
Wooroona
Wooroona

Mount
Michael

Arcadia
55
Bullecourt

Lake
Nash

Gold

ARAFURA SEA

16° 00'
17° 00'

18° 00'

19° 00'

20° 00'

21° 00'

Joins map 129

Joins map 130

Alpurrurulam
147
HWY
21

Georgina

SANDOVER

Annitowa

14

I   J   K   L   M   N   O   P

Joins map 109

Joins map 106

A B C D E F G H

PHILLIPSON RANGE
Lake Jeavons
Lake Dennis
Lake White
Lake Wills
Lake Hazlett
Mount Russell
+ Mount Tracey
Tanami Downs
The Granites
MANGKURURRPA ABORIGINAL LAND TRUST
YININGARRA ABORIGINAL LAND TRUST
KARLANTIJPA SOUTH ABORIGINAL LAND TRUST
WIRLIYAJARRAYI ABORIGINAL LAND TRUST
CENTRAL DESERT ABORIGINAL LAND TRUST
Mount Bennet
Mount Theo
Mount Tumbull
Mount Patricia
Willowra
Mount Rennie
Mount Peake

TANAMI
Puyurru
Chilla Well
356 179
TANAMI
Mount Barkly
Mount Parkinson
PAWU ABORIGINAL LAND TRUST
DESERT
Anningie
Mount Leichhardt
AHAKEYE ABORIGINAL LAND TRUST
Mount Finniss

DESERT
MALA ABORIGINAL LAND TRUST
WABUDALI RANGE
Mount Farewell
Mount Singleton
Mount Doreen
Mount Campbell
Mount Hardy
Djagamara Peak
Vaughan Springs
Yuendumu
Yuelamu
Mount Denison
Mount Allan
GILES RA
Coniston
Mount Stafford
Mount Gardiner
LAKE MACKAY ABORIGINAL LAND TRUST
Lake Mackay
Ethel Ck
Mount Nicker
Mount Davenport
Mount Eclipse
YUNKANJINI ABORIGINAL LAND TRUST
TANAMI
Mount Hammond
Laramba
Mount Freeling
YALPIRAKINU ABORIGINAL LAND TRUST
YALYIRIMBI RA

WILBRUNGA RANGE
NORTHERN TERRITORY / WESTERN AUSTRALIA
Nyirripi
Mount Carey
Mount Redvers
Mount Morris
Mount Cockburn
Newhaven
STUART
Lake Bennett
BLUFF
Central Mount Wedge
Owl Gorge
NGALURRTJU ABORIGINAL LAND TRUST
Lake Lewis
Central Mount
Tilmouth Well Roadhouse
Mount Harris
289
BURT PL

Joins map 93
TROPIC OF CAPRICORN
Ininti
Mount Lindsay
Kintore
Mount Leisler
Tinki
KINTORE
Mount Russell
Mount Lyell Brown
Mount Kuta-Kuta
Mount Udor
273
Warren Creek
Mount Liebig
Illili
Papunya
Derwent
Ulambaura
Haasts Bluff
Glen Helen
Mount Zeil
Narwietooma
Milton Park
LARAPINTA TRAIL
WEST MACDONNELL
Mount Hay
REDBANK GORGE
Mount Sonder
ORMISTON GORGE
NAMATJIRA
Mount Mein
Yuwalki
Mount Rennie
Mount Stirling
Mount Musgrave
RANGE
IDIRRIKI
Glen Helen Resort
GLEN HELEN GORGE
SERPENTINE GORGE
NAMATJIRA DRIVE
NATIONAL

EMERY RANGE
Lake MacDonald
SIR FREDERICK RANGE
HAASTS BLUFF ABORIGINAL LAND TRUST
WATSON RANGE
Mount Solitary
LARAPINTA
MISSIONARY PLAIN
TNORALA (GOSSE BLUFF)
Ipolera
Hermannsburg
PALM VALLEY
LARAPINTA
130

WARNING: Visitors planning to travel along the Larapinta Drive through Aboriginal Land require a permit. Check road conditions before departing; 4WD vehicle may be required.

Mount Murray
Mount Olifent
Mount Tucker
Kings Canyon Resort
KINGS CANYON
WATARRKA NATIONAL PARK
Areyonga
URRAMPINYI ILTJILTJARRI ABORIGINAL LAND TRUST
Tempe Downs
FINKE GORGE NATIONAL PARK
ELLIS RANGE
Lake Hopkins
Mount Cowle
Lake Neale
Mount Unapproachable
LURITJA
WATARRKA LEASEBACK AREA
Kings Creek
358
Mount Levi
ERNEST GILES
Wallara Ranch
HENBURY METEORITES
Mount Barlee
Mount Johnno
BLOODS RANGE
Mount Ant
Mount Deering
Mount Harts
Mount Carruthers
Mount Bowley
Lake Amadeus
KATITI ABORIGINAL LAND TRUST
LURITJA
Angas Downs
BASEDOW RA
Warakurna
Warakurna Roadhouse
Kutjurntari
Kaltukatjara (Docker River)
TJUKARURU
Mount Bearteaux
231
PETERMANN RANGES
Mount Currie
Yulara
LASSETER
ULURU
Mutitjulu
Curtin Springs
Imanpa
Mount Ebenezer Roadhouse
Erldunda
GREAT CENTRAL RD
GUNBARREL
Mount Conner
Lyndavale

WARNING: Visitors planning to travel along the Tjukaruru Road through Aboriginal Land require a permit. A second permit is required for those venturing over the WA border.

For more detail on Uluru–Kata Tjuta National Park see page 110

KATA TJUTA (THE OLGAS)
ULURU-KATA TJUTA NATIONAL PARK
PETERMANN ABORIGINAL LAND TRUST
Mount Holt
Warlpapuka
Mount Jenkins
Mount Le Hunte
NORTHERN TERRITORY
Mount Robert
Alpara
Mulga Park
Victory Downs
Mount Cavenagh
Arnold Creek
Mount Gosse
Surveyor Generals Corner
Mount Cockburn
Mount Edwin
SOUTH AUSTRALIA
New Well
Mount Cuthbert
Marryat
Sundown Outstation
Tjwupalya
Mount Aloysius
Mount Hinckley
Kalka
Pipalyatjara
MANN RANGES
GUNBARREL
Aparawatatja
Kanypi
213
Amata
GUNBARREL HWY
THE MUSGRAVE RANGES
Agnes Creek
TOMKINSON RA
NGAANYATJARRA CENTRAL RESERVE
Boundary Peak
ANANGU PITJANTJATJARA YANKUNYTJATJARA LANDS
Mount Cooparinna
Mount Caroline (Ulkiyana)
Mount Davenport
Mount Woodroffe (Ngarutjaranya)
Mount Warrabilinna
Mount Kintore
Mount Crombie (Ulpara)
Mount Harriet
Mount Mair

A B C D E F G H

0   50   100   150 km

RLANTIJPA
SOUTH
ABORIGINAL
LAND TRUST
Numagalong

Wauchope
Singleton
DAVENPORT
DAVENPORT
RANGE
NP
Hatches Creek

Canteen Creek

ANURRETE
ABORIGINAL
LAND
TRUST

Wycliffe Well
Roadhouse

Ali-Curung
Imangara

WARRABRI
ABORIGINAL
LAND
TRUST

Elkedra
Elkedra
River

Mount
Alone

Annitowa

Mount Michael
Arcadia
Bullecourt

Mount
Strzelecki
Mount
Morphett

Mount
Nelson

Tara
Barrow Creek

Wilora

Mount
Tops

Mount
Octy

SPRING
RANGE

Indiranginya

Ampilatwatja
Ammaroo

Sandover
River

Ermarne
Argadargada

IRRMARNE
ABORIGINAL
LAND TRUST

Mount
Hogarth

Alpurrurulam
Georgina

Lake
Nash

BARRY   PLAIN

Headingly

Urandangi

AHAKEYE
ABORIGINAL
LAND
TRUST

Irrwelty
Arawerr

Peretty
Derry
Downs

ANGARAPA
ABORIGINAL
LAND TRUST

Atneltyey

Ooratippra

Mount
Stott

Arapunya

ANATYE
ABORIGINAL
LAND
TRUST

Manners
Creek

Mount
Skinner
Mount
Skinner

Woolla
Downs

Atartinga

Utopia

Waite
River

Delmore
Downs

MacDonald
Downs

Lucy
Creek

Warlpeyangrere

Tobermorey

Mount
Pozieres

DONOHUE   HWY

Chianina

Delny
Dneiper

DULCIE
RANGE
NATIONAL
PARK

DULCIE
RA

Mount
Sainthill

Arthur
River

Orrtipa-
Thurra

PLENTY

Mount
Cornish

Tarlton
Downs

Mount Guide

Mount
Brown

Marqua
Marqua

TOKO

Mount
stwart

Engawala

Mount
Swan

Mount
Swan

Huckitta

Jinka

HWY

Jervois

Mount
Ewing

ADAM

Mount
Reinecke

Mount
Woods

RANGE

Bushy
Park

Gemtree

PLENTY

Atitjere

Marshall
River

486

Plenty

Akarnenehe

ATNETYE

Mount
Wilnecke

Mount
Knuckey

Mount
Gardner

Mount
Harriet
Mount
Alfred

TOOMBA
RA

Yambah

Mount
Riddock

Mount
Palmer

Mount
Brassey

HARTS   RA

Mount
Bird

Fluckitta

Indiana

Mount Lloyd

Atula

ABORIGINAL

LAND

TRUST

TROPIC

OF

CAPRICORN

Mount
Beck

Ethabuka

MACDONNELL

RANGES

TREPHINA GORGE
NATURE
PARK

Claraville

ARLTUNGA
HISTORICAL
RESERVE

Arltunga
Bush
Hotel

RUBY GAP GORGE
RUBY GAP
NATURE PARK

Illogwa
Hale
Ck

Mount
Isabel

Lake
Caroline

HISTORIC TOWN,
LARAPINTA TRAIL,
THE GHAN

ALICE
SPRINGS

ROSS

Ross
River

N'DHALA GORGE
NATURE PARK

Ringwood

NORTHERN TERRITORY

QUEENSLAND

STANDLEY
CHASM

Iwupataka
wen
prings

Amoonguna

SANTA
TERESA
ABORIGINAL
LAND
TRUST

Todd
River

Limbla

URETYINGKE ABORIGINAL
LAND TRUST

Numery

River

Mount
Polhi

OLD GHAN
RAILWAY

Mount
Ooraminna

Santa Teresa
(Ltyente Purte)

River

Little Well
(Alurakwa)

SIMPSON

DESERT

SIMPSON

DESERT

NATIONAL

RAINBOW
VALLEY
CR
tuarts CR
Well
nge Creek

Deep
Well

Allambi

RODINGA
RA

PMERE
NYENTE
ABORIGINAL
LAND TRUST

Todd River Downs

Mount
Peachy

Titjikala

Mount
Rodinga

YEWERRE
ABORIGINAL
LAND
TRUST

The
Twins

PARK

Mount
Gloaming

River

CHAMBER'S PILLAR
HISTORICAL RES

Idracowra

Mount
Thodia

Mount
Casuarina

Horseshoe
Bend

APATULA
ABORIGINAL
LAND
TRUST

MAC CLARK
(ACACIA PEUCE)
CONSERVATION
RESERVE

Finke

Mount
Watt

Finke

Mount
Musgrave

Mount
Rumbalara

Andado

PMER
ULPERRE
INGWEMIRNE
ARLETHERRE
ABORIGINAL
LAND TRUST

Mirranponga
Pongunna
Lake

Poeppel
Corner

Mount
Kingston

Lilla Creek

New
Crown

Mount
Peebles

Umbeara
lgera

Mount
Gordon

Mount
Grundy

Goyder

Mount Wilyunpa

Mount
Etingimbra

NORTHERN TERRITORY

SOUTH AUSTRALIA

Lake
Thomas

SIMPSON
DESERT

unt Cecil
Mount
Darling

Mount
Parlee
Mount
Mead

Mount
Hearne

Mount
Dare

Mount
Apperda

SIMPSON

DESERT

SIMPSON   DESERT

CONSERVATION

Tieyon

Stevenson
River

Mount Iirn
Mount
Treloar

Mount
Hammersley

WITJIRA

NATIONAL

PARK

DESERT

PARK

NANGU
TJANTJATJARA
ANKUNYTJATJARA
NDS

BAGOT
RA

Mount
Deane

Mount
Barr

Mount
Ross

Mount
Emey

Mount
Attacherrikanna

RECREATION

RESERVE

Lake
Griselda

Poolowannal
Lake

Peera Peera
Poolanna
Lake

WARNINGS: In outback Australia, long distances separate
some towns. Travellers should familiarise themselves with
prevailing conditions before departure and take care to ensure
their vehicle is roadworthy. Adequate supplies of petrol, water
and food should be carried at all times.

In central Australia, rainfall can make some roads impassable,
even with a 4WD vehicle. Full information on road conditions
should be obtained from local authorities before departure.

If visitors intend diverting off public roads within Aboriginal Land
areas, a permit is required from the relevant Aboriginal authority.

For more detail on Alice Springs
& the MacDonnell Ranges
see page 110–11

Joins map 130

Joins map 132

N

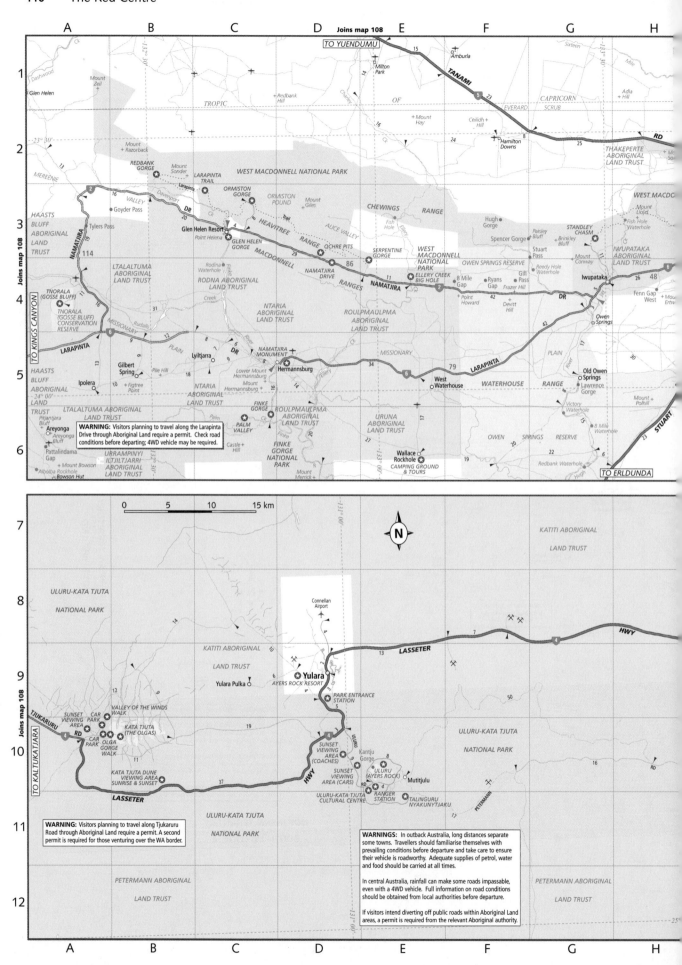

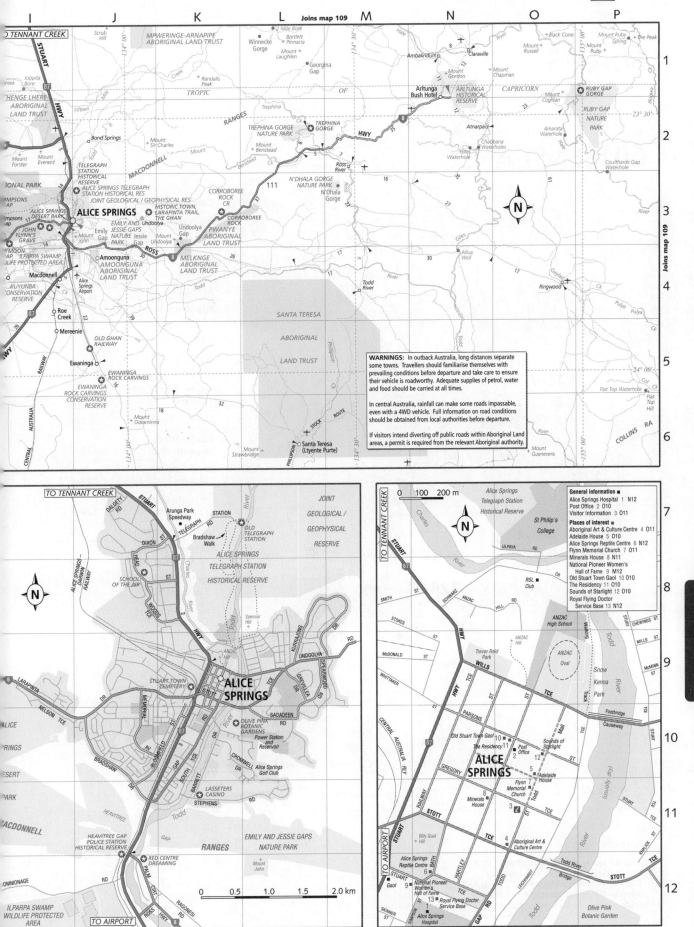

WARNINGS: In outback Australia, long distances separate some towns. Travellers should familiarise themselves with prevailing conditions before departure and take care to ensure their vehicle is roadworthy. Adequate supplies of petrol, water and food should be carried at all times.

In central Australia, rainfall can make some roads impassable, even with a 4WD vehicle. Full information on road conditions should be obtained from local authorities before departure.

If visitors intend diverting off public roads within Aboriginal Land areas, a permit is required from the relevant Aboriginal authority.

General information ■
Alice Springs Hospital 1 N12
Post Office 2 O10
Visitor Information 3 O11
Places of interest ■
Aboriginal Art & Culture Centre 4 O11
Adelaide House 5 O10
Alice Springs Reptile Centre 6 N12
Flynn Memorial Church 7 O11
Minerals House 8 N11
National Pioneer Women's
    Hall of Fame 9 N12
Old Stuart Town Gaol 10 O10
The Residency 11 O10
Sounds of Starlight 12 O10
Royal Flying Doctor
    Service Base 13 N12

MAPS

QUEENSLAND

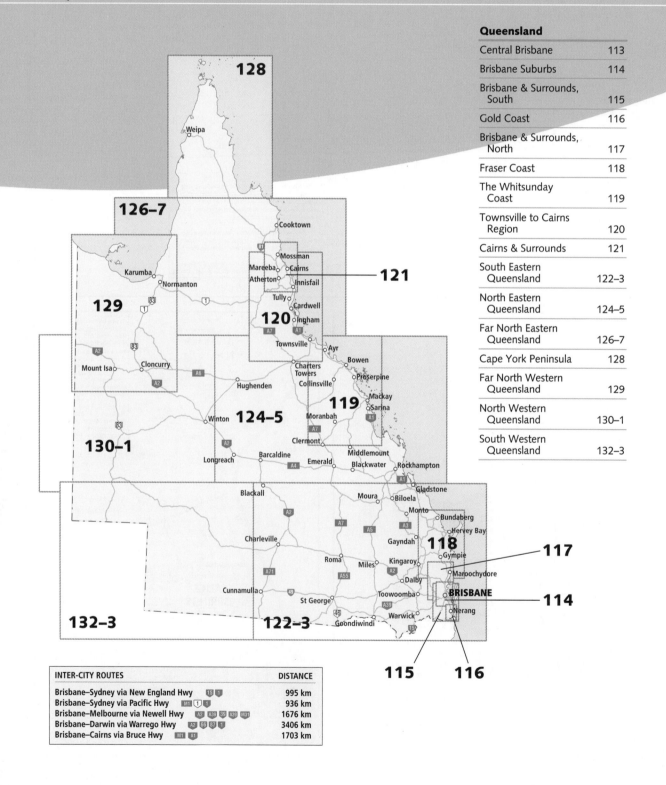

INTER-CITY ROUTES	DISTANCE
Brisbane–Sydney via New England Hwy	995 km
Brisbane–Sydney via Pacific Hwy	936 km
Brisbane–Melbourne via Newell Hwy	1676 km
Brisbane–Darwin via Warrego Hwy	3406 km
Brisbane–Cairns via Bruce Hwy	1703 km

0   0.25   0.5   0.75   1 km

Joins map 114

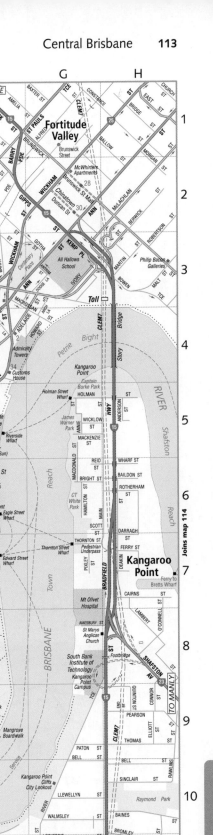

Accommodation
BASE Backpacker Central 1 D5
Brisbane Marriott Hotel 2 F4
Chifley at Lennons 3 D6
Hilton Brisbane 4 E6
Holiday Inn Brisbane 5 C5
Hotel Grand Chancellor Brisbane 6 C3
Mantra on Queen 7 F3
Mercure Hotel Brisbane 8 C6
Novotel Brisbane 9 E4
Park Regis North Quay 10 B5
Rydges South Bank Hotel 11 C9
The Sebel Suites Brisbane 12 E7
Sofitel Brisbane 13 E4
Stamford Plaza Brisbane Hotel 14 F7
Treasury Heritage Hotel 15 D7
Urban Brisbane 16 C4
Note: Only a sample range of accommodation is listed; inclusion is not necessarily a recommendation.

General Information
Brisbane Transit Centre 17 B5
Central Railway Station 18 E5
City Police Station 19 E7
General Post Office 20 E5
RACQ 21 E5
Qantas Travel Centre 22 E5

Roma Street Station 23 B4
Visitor Information 24 D9,D6

Places of Interest
Arbour 25 D9
Brisbane City Hall 26 D6
Brisbane Cricket Ground (The Gabba) 27 H12
Brunswick Street Mall 28 G2
Cathedral of St Stephen 29 E6
Chinatown 30 G2
City Botanic Gardens 31 F8
Commissariat Store 32 D8
Conrad Treasury Casino 33 D7
Customs House 34 F4
Eagle Street Pier 35 F6
Museum of Brisbane 36 D5
Old Government House 37 E8
Old Windmill 38 D5
Parliament House 39 E8
Queen Street Mall 40 D6
Queensland Art Gallery 41 B7
Queensland Maritime Museum 42 D11
Queensland Museum South Bank 43 B7
Queensland Performing Arts Centre 44 C8
St John's Cathedral 45 F4
State Library of Qld 46 B7
Streets Beach 47 D9

Joins map 114

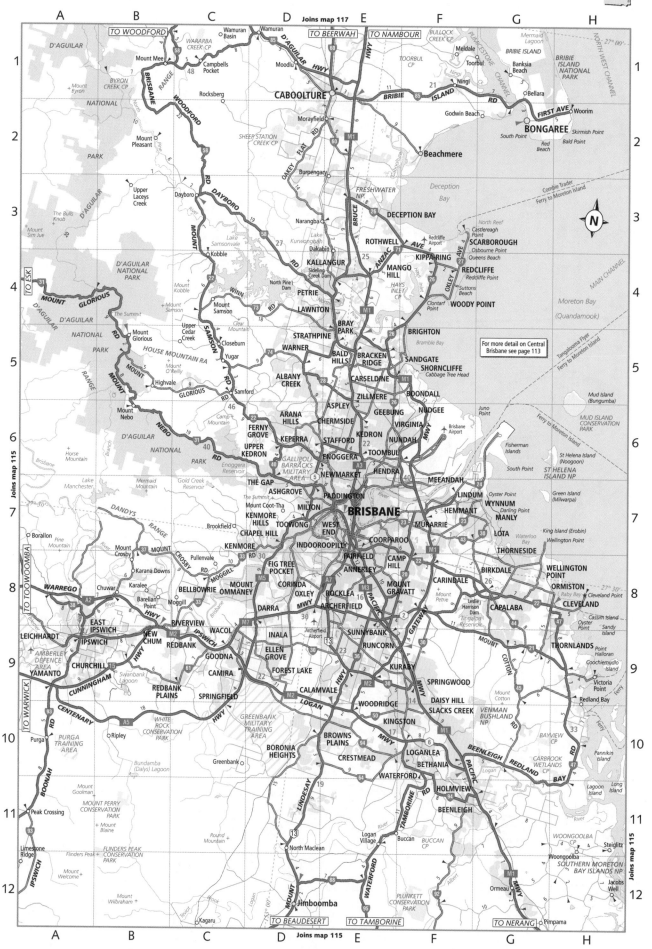

Joins map 117
Joins map 115
Joins map 115

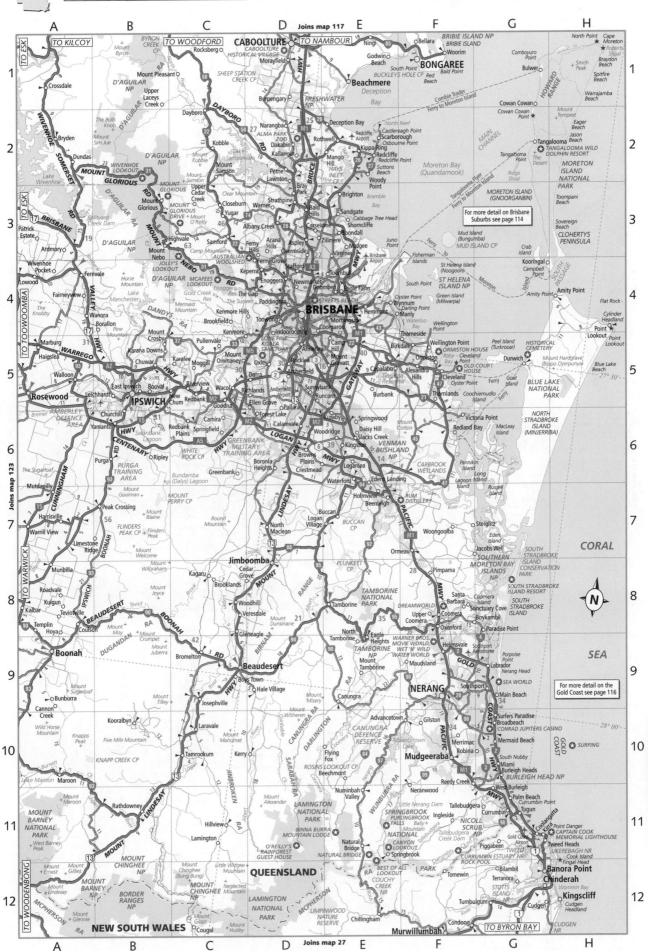

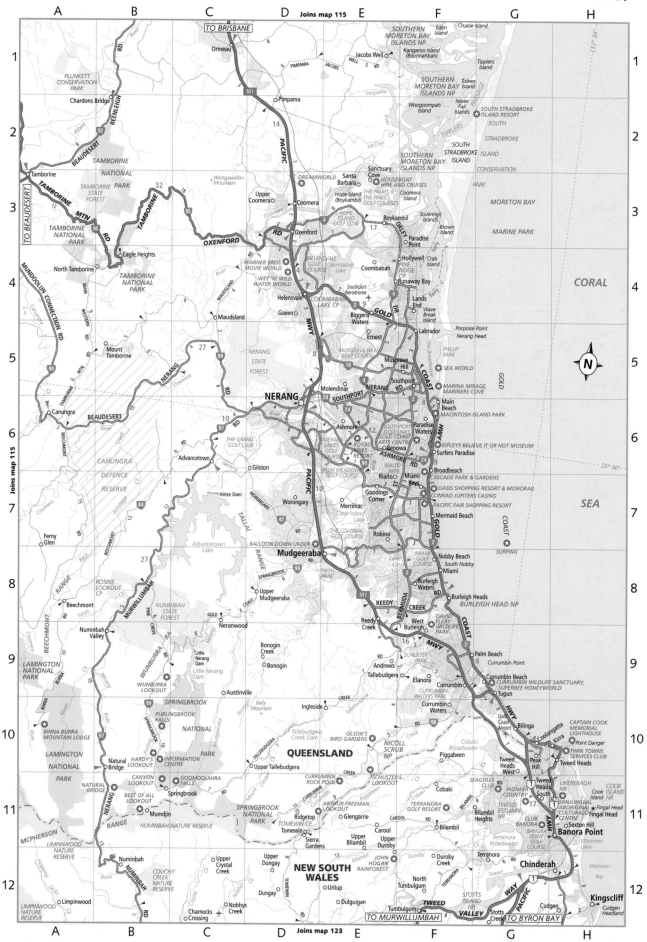

0 2 4 6 8 10 km

0   10   20   30 km

GREAT SANDY NATIONAL PARK

TO GYMPIE   **TO GYMPIE**

Gallangowan
Kandanga
Mount Coorooa
Pomona
Lake MacDonald
Big Shell
Noosa Head
Alexandria Bay
Tewantin
Noosa Heads
BEACHES
Sunshine Beach
NOOSA
Marcus Beach
Imbil
Brooloo
North Arm
Eumundi
VILLAGE MARKETS
Noosaville
Peregian Beach
NATIONAL PARK
KANDANGA RANGE
AMAMOOR RANGE
HERITAGE RAILWAY
Mount Kandanga
Borumba Dam
Borumba Mountain
KENILWORTH
TUCHEKOI CP
MOUNT EERWAH
Yandina
Mount Ninderry
Coolum Beach
Point Arkwright
MOUNT COOLUM NATIONAL PARK
Marcoola
Mount Gibbanee
Diaper Mountain
Kenilworth
EUMUNDI
BLACKALL RANGE
THE GINGER FACTORY, NUTWORKS
SUNSHINE CASTLE
FERNTREE CREEK NP
Bli Bli
Maroochydore Aerodrome
Jimna
JIMNA RANGE
MURGON
Summer Mountain
Mount Monsildale
MAPLETON FALLS NP
Mapleton
Flaxton
NAMBOUR
TRIUNIA NP
Woombye
THE BIG PINEAPPLE, MACADAMIA NUT FACTORY
Mudjimba
MAROOCHYDORE
MAROOCHY RIVER CP
CONONDALE NATIONAL PARK
Mount Langley
Conondale
KENILWORTH
THE MINIATURE ENGLISH VILLAGE
KONDALILLA NP
Montville
Baroon Pocket Dam
Lake Baroon
Palmwoods
EUDLO CREEK NP
Forest Glen
SUPERBEE HONEY FACTORY
BUDERIM
Point Cartwright
MOOLOOLABA
UNDERWATER WORLD
Buddina
Mount Pascoe
Yednia
Eudlo
AUSSIE WORLD & ETTAMOGAH PUB, HOUSE OF HERBS, OPALS DOWN UNDER
MOOLOOLAH RIVER NP
Warana
CORAL
Mount Spencer
Linville
Mount Miner
CONONDALE RANGE
McCARTHYS LOOKOUT
Maleny
Mooloolah
PALMVIEW CP
CURRIMUNDI LAKE CP
The Round Mountain
Mount Lional
Mount Moore
Mount Kilcoy
Mount Marysmokes
Mount McLean
Landsborough
Peachester
BILARCHA NP
CALOUNDRA CP
Moffat Head
CALOUNDRA
Moore
D'AGUILAR
Mount Pine View
BEERWAH WAY
Beerwah
AUSTRALIA ZOO
BIG KART TRACK
IRWIN HWY
QUEENSLAND AIR MUSEUM
Caloundra Head
Deep Water Point
Nurinda
Gregors Creek
Kilcoy
Coochin Creek
Mount Beerwah
GLASS HOUSE MOUNTAINS
Glass House Mountains
BRIBIE ISLAND NP
SEA
Harlin
Yimbun
Woodford
GLASS HOUSE MOUNTAINS NATIONAL PARK
Beerburrum
BRIBIE ISLAND
BRISBANE RD
CRESSBROOK CONSERVATION PARK
D'AGUILAR
STEVE IRWIN HWY
BRIBIE ISLAND NATIONAL PARK
Ivory Creek
Biarra
Delaneys Creek
Wamuran Basin
WARARBA CREEK NP
Wamuran
Elimbah
CABOOLTURE HISTORICAL VILLAGE
Donnybrook
Meldale
Toorbul
Banksia Beach
Toogoolawah
D'AGUILAR NP
Mount Mee
Campbells Pocket
Moodlu
Ningi
Bellara
Mount Beppo
BYRON CREEK NP
Mount Byron
Rocksberg
CABOOLTURE
BRIBIE ISLAND RD
Woorim
Caboonbah
Somerset Dam
Crossdale
Morayfield
South Point
Godwin Beach
BONGAREE
Bald Point
The Gap
Coal Creek
Murrumba
Mount Esk
Mount Pleasant
Upper Laceys Creek
SHEEP STATION CREEK CP
Beachmere
BUCKLEYS HOLE CP
Red Beach
Mount Tin Tin
Gallanani
Esk
Bryden
Dayboro
DAYBORO
Burpengary
FRESHWATER CP
Deception Bay
Combie Trader Ferry to Moreton Island
Mount Hallen
Moombra
Dundas
WIVENHOE LOOKOUT
Kobble
Mount Kobble
Narangba
Deception Bay
Castlereagh Point
Redcliffe Airport
Scarborough
Osbourne Point
For more detail on Brisbane Suburbs see page 114
Buaraba
WIVENHOE NP
MOUNT GLORIOUS
MOUNT GLORIOUS
Upper Cedar Creek
Mount Samson
Lake Samsonvale
Dakabin
Kallangur
Kippa-Ring
Redcliffe
Redcliffe Point
MAIN CHANNEL
Mount Mulgowie
Mount Hallen
Splityard Creek Dam
Mount Glorious
MOUNT GLORIOUS DRIVE & Mount O'Reilly
Closeburn
Yugar
Clear Mountain
Petrie
Lawnton
Strathpine
Mango Hill
Suttons Beach
Woody Point
Moreton Bay (Quandamook)
Coominya
Patrick Estate
Ardmory
Fernvale
Highvale
Samford
Warner
Bray Park
Bald Hills
Brighton
Sandgate
Bramble Bay
Tangalooma Flyer Ferry to Moreton Island
Clarendon
Wivenhoe Pocket
Mount Nebo
JOLLYS LOOKOUT
Camp Mountain
AUSTRALIAN WOOLSHED
Ferny Hills
Arana Hills
Albany Creek
Aspley
Carseldine
Zillmere
Shorncliffe
Cabbage Tree Head
Boondall
Nudgee
Juno Point
Mud Island (Bungumba)
MUD ISLAND CP
Lowood
Tarampa
Fairney View
Wanora
MCAFEES LOOKOUT
NEBO RD
Keperra
Enoggera
Stafford
Chermside
Virginia
Brisbane Airport
Fisherman Islands
St Helena Island (Noogoon)
ST HELENA ISLAND NP
Glenore Grove
Prenzlau
Coolana
Borallon
Pine Mountain
Mount Crosby
Enoggera Res
The Gap
Paddington
Newmarket
Doomben
Eagle Farm
BRISBANE
STREETS BEACH
Hemmant
Wynnum
Darling Point
Manly
Green Island (Milwarpa)
Plainland
Minden
Karana Downs
Kenmore Hills
Brookfield
Kenmore
Pullenvale
Toowong
Indooroopilly
Morningside
Cooparoo
Thorneside
Wellington Point
ORMISTON HOUSE
Peel Island (Turkroar)
Forest Hill
Hatton Vale
Marburg
Haigslea
Chuwar
Karalee
Moggill
LONE PINE KOALA SANCTUARY
Annerley
Camp Hill
Carina
Birkdale
Cleveland Point
OLD COURT HOUSE
Laidley
Rosewood
Walloon
East Ipswich
Booval
Riverview
Wacol
Richlands
Darra
Oxley
Rocklea
Mount Gravatt
Capalaba
Alexandra Hills
Cleveland
Oyster Point
Grandchester
Calvert
Leichhardt
Churchill
Yamanto
IPSWICH
New Chum
Redbank
Goodna
Camira
Archerfield Airport
Ellen Grove
Inala
Pallara
Durack
Acacia Ridge
Sunnybank
Runcorn
Burbank
Thornlands
Coochiemudlo Island
Victoria Point
MacLeay Island
TO WARWICK   **TO BEAUDESERT**   **TO NERANG**

Joins map 118
Joins map 123
Joins map 115
TO KINGAROY
TO TOOWOOMBA
GATTON
Joins map 123

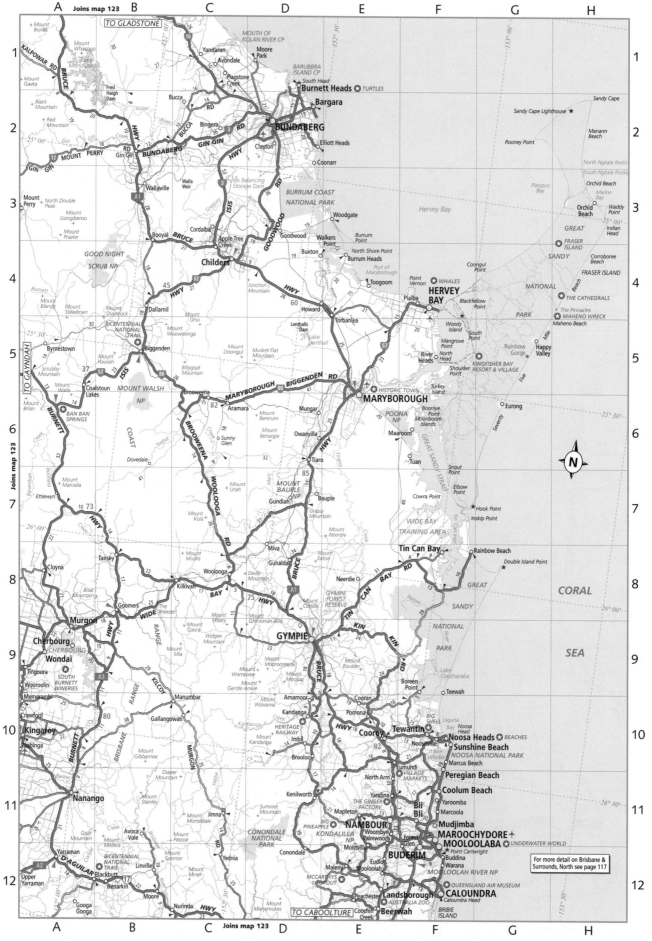

0 10 20 30 40 50 km

TO GLADSTONE

MOUTH OF
KOLAN RIVER CP

Mount Borilla
Mount Wharoo
Lake Monduran
Mount Gaeta

BARUBBRA
ISLAND CP

Yandaran
Avondale
Moore
Park

South Head
Burnett Heads TURTLES

Sandy Cape

Sandy Cape Lighthouse ★

Black Mountain
Fred Haigh Dam
Bucca

Flagstone
Creek

Bargara

Manann
Beach

Red Mountain

Kolan
River

Bingera

BUNDABERG

Rooney Point

North Ngkala Rocks
South Ngkala Rocks

Mount Perry
North Double Peak

Wallaville
Walla
Weir

Clayton

Elliott Heads

Hervey Bay

Orchid Beach

Platypus
Bay

Marloo
Bay

Mount Gongiberoo

Coonarr

Mount Prazier

Isis Balancing
Storage Dam

BURRUM COAST
NATIONAL PARK

Woodgate

Orchid
Beach

Waddy
Point

Indian
Head

GREAT

Cordalba
Booyal

Apple Tree
Creek

Goodwood

Walkers
Point

North Shore Point

SANDY

FRASER
ISLAND

Corroboree
Beach

FRASER ISLAND

GOOD NIGHT
SCRUB NP

Childers

Buxton

Burrum Heads

Port of
Maryborough

Coongul
Point

NATIONAL

THE CATHEDRALS

Mount
Blandy

Junction
Mountain

Howard

Toogoom

Point
Vernon

WHALES

HERVEY
BAY

Blackfellow
Point

The Pinnacles
MAHENO WRECK

Maheno Beach

Mount
Steadman

Dallarnil

Mount
Orzo

Lenthalls
Dam

Torbanlea

Pialba

Woody
Island

PARK

Mount
Shamrock

Mount
Woowonga

Lake
Lenthall

South
Point

Mount
Havilah

Biggenden

Mangrove
Point

Rainbow
Gorge

Happy
Valley

Byrnestown

Scrubby
Mountain

Billygoat
Mountain

Mount
Doongul

Musket Flat
Mountain

North Head
Shoulder
Point

KINGFISHER BAY
RESORT & VILLAGE

Mount
Brian

Coalstoun
Lakes

MOUNT WALSH
NP

Brooweena

MARYBOROUGH

BIGGENDEN RD

HISTORIC TOWN
MARYBOROUGH

Turkey
Island

Eurong

BAN BAN
SPRINGS

Aramara

Mungar

Boonlye
Point
Moonboom
Islands

Ettiewyn

Dovedale

Sunny
Glen

Mount
Bererum

Owanyilla

POONA
NP

Maaroom

Mount
Marcella

Mount
Benargie

Mount
Urah

Tiaro

Tuan

Snout
Point

Mount
Kola

MOUNT
BAUPLE
NP

Gundiah

Bauple

Grassy
Mountain

Cowra Point

Elbow
Point

Tansey

Mount
Mudlo

Miva

Mount
Eaton

Mount
Neerdie

Hook Point
Inskip Point

WIDE BAY
TRAINING AREA

Cloyna

Boat
Mountain

Kilkivan

Woolooga

Devils
Mountain

Gunaldai

Neerdie

Tin Can Bay

Rainbow Beach

Double Island
Point

CORAL

Goomeri

The Breezer

Mount
Coora

Mount
Misery

Mount
Ghrooman Hills

GYMPIE FOREST
RESERVE

GREAT

Murgon

Mount
Corella

SANDY

SEA

Cherbourg
CHERBOURG

Mount
Mia

GYMPIE

Mount
Boulder

Boreen
Point

NATIONAL

Wondai

SOUTH
BURNETT
WINERIES

Mount
Moorooral

Teewah

Lake
Cootharaba

Tingoora
Wooroolin

Mount
Warawee

Mount
Mooloo

PARK

Laguna
Bay

BIG
SHELL

Memerambi

Mount
Gentle Annie

Amamoor

Cooran

Noosa
Head

Noosa Heads BEACHES

Crawford

Mount
Wilwarrel

Kandanga

Pomona

Cooroy

Noosaville

Sunshine Beach

NOOSA NATIONAL PARK

Kingaroy

Manumbar

Heritage
Railway

Imbil

Tewantin

Lake
Weyba

Marcus Beach

Nabinga

Gallangowan

Brooloo

Eumundi
VILLAGE
MARKETS

Peregian Beach

Mount
Gibbarnee

Kenilworth

North Arm

Yandina

Coolum Beach

Nanango

Diaper
Mountain

Mapleton

THE GINGER
FACTORY

Yaroomba
Marcoola

Mount
Stanley

Jimna

Summer
Mountain

BIG
PINEAPPLE
KONDALILLA
NP

Bli
Bli

Mudjimba

Avoca
Vale

CONONDALE
NATIONAL
PARK

NAMBOUR

Woombye
Palmwoods

MAROOCHYDORE

Yarraman

Linville

Mount
Monsildale

Montville

Forest
Glen

MOOLOOLABA

Point Cartwright

UNDERWATER WORLD

Upper
Yarraman

Blackbutt

BICENTENNIAL
NATIONAL
TRAIL

Mount
Spencer

Conondale

BUDERIM

Buddina
Warana

MOOLOOLAH RIVER NP

Benarkin

Mount
Miner

Yednia

Maleny
Eudlo
Mooloolah

QUEENSLAND AIR MUSEUM

For more detail on Brisbane &
Surrounds, North see page 117

Moore

Nurinda

MCCARTHYS
LOOKOUT

Peachester

Landsborough

CALOUNDRA

Caloundra Head

Googa
Googa

Mount
Maroonmokes

TO CABOOLTURE

Coochin
Creek

AUSTRALIA ZOO

Beerwah

BRIBIE
ISLAND

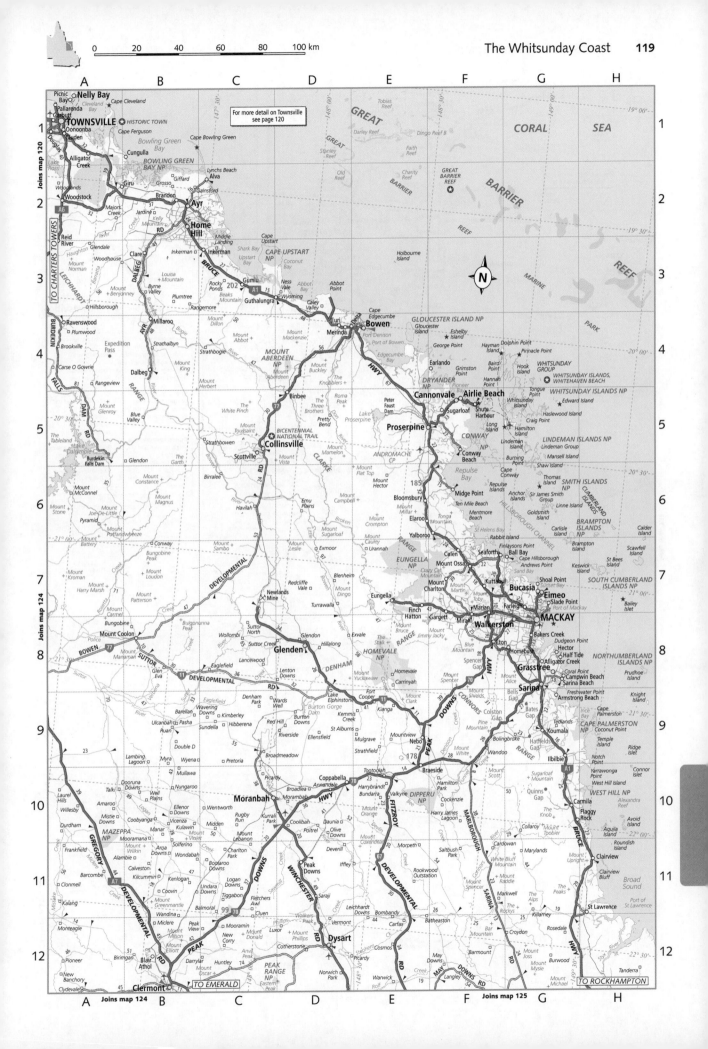

For more detail on Townsville see page 120

Joins map 120

Joins map 124

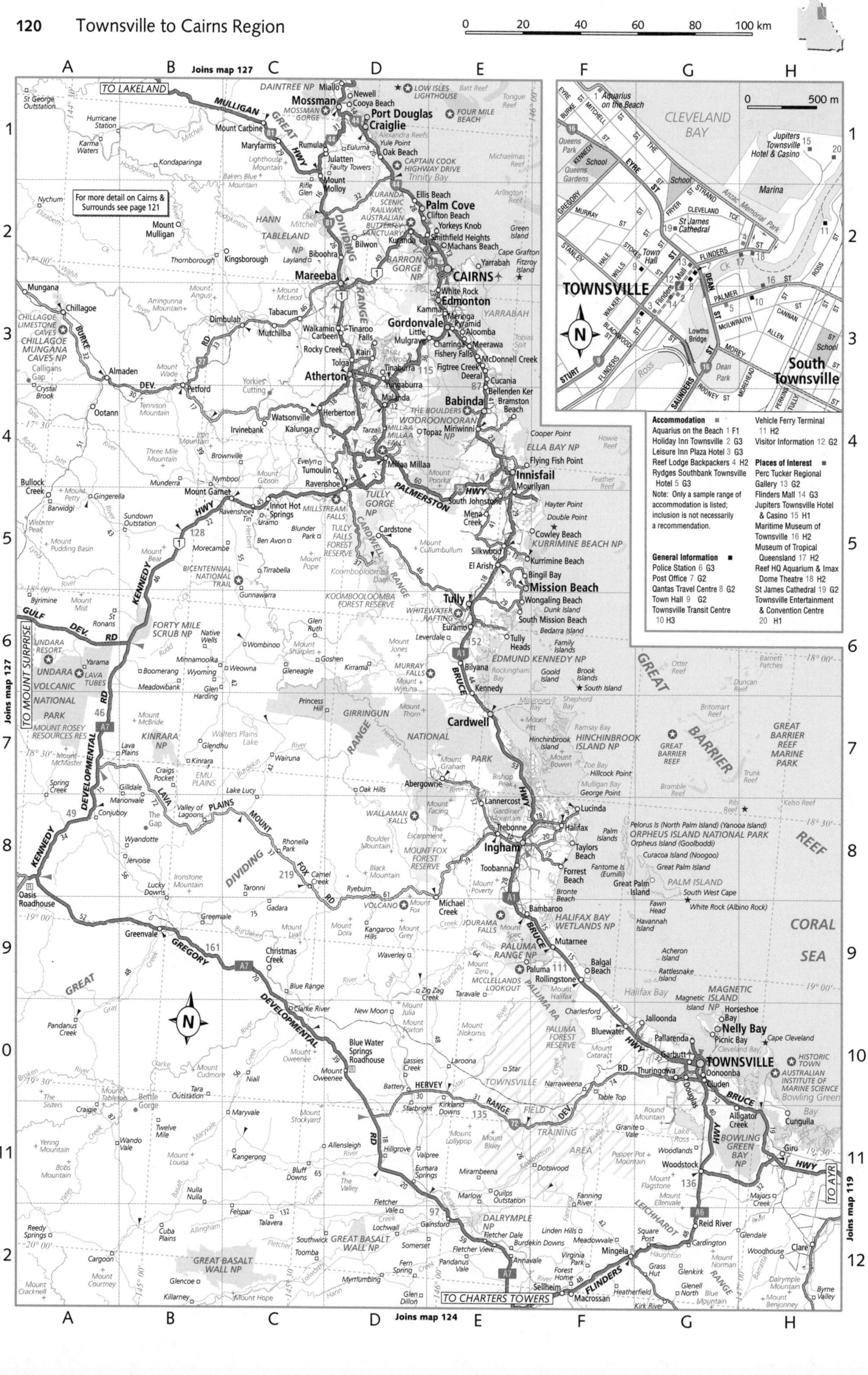

0 20 40 60 80 100 km

Joins map 127
Joins map 127
Joins map 124
Joins map 119

For more detail on Cairns & Surrounds see page 121

0 500 m

TOWNSVILLE inset

Accommodation
Aquarius on the Beach 1 F1
Holiday Inn Townsville 2 G3
Leisure Inn Plaza Hotel 3 G3
Reef Lodge Backpackers 4 H2
Rydges Southbank Townsville Hotel 5 G3
Note: Only a sample range of accommodation is listed; inclusion is not necessarily a recommendation.

General Information
Police Station 6 G3
Post Office 7 G2
Qantas Travel Centre 8 G2
Town Hall 9 G2
Townsville Transit Centre 10 H3

Vehicle Ferry Terminal 11 H2
Visitor Information 12 G2

Places of Interest
Perc Tucker Regional Gallery 13 G2
Flinders Mall 14 G3
Jupiters Townsville Hotel & Casino 15 H1
Maritime Museum of Townsville 16 H2
Museum of Tropical Queensland 17 H2
Reef HQ Aquarium & Imax Dome Theatre 18 H2
St James Cathedral 19 G2
Townsville Entertainment & Convention Centre 20 H1

0 10 20 30 40 km

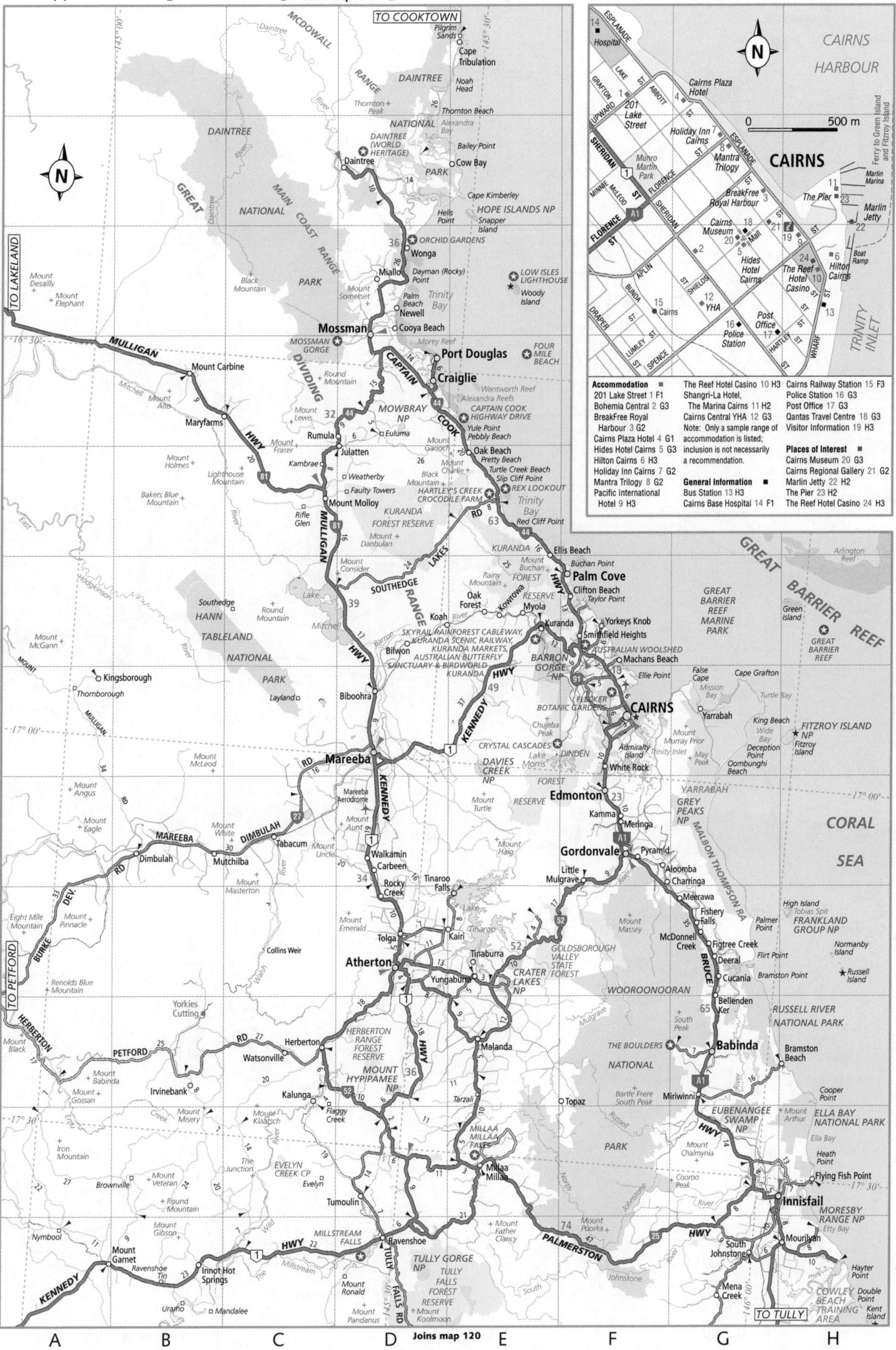

Joins map 127

TO COOKTOWN

CAIRNS & SURROUNDS MAP

Joins map 127
TO LAKELAND
Joins map 120
TO PETFORD

CAIRNS HARBOUR

CAIRNS (inset)

ESPLANADE
Hospital
Cairns Plaza Hotel
201 Lake Street
Holiday Inn Cairns
Cairns Museum
Mantra Trilogy
BreakFree Royal Harbour
Munro Martin Park
Hides Hotel Cairns
YHA
Post Office
Police Station
The Reef Hotel Casino
The Pier
Marlin Marina
Marlin Jetty
The Reef Hotel Cairns
Hilton Cairns
Boat Ramp
TRINITY INLET

Accommodation
201 Lake Street 1 F1
Bohemia Central 2 G3
BreakFree Royal Harbour 3 G2
Cairns Plaza Hotel 4 G1
Hides Hotel Cairns 5 G3
Hilton Cairns 6 H3
Holiday Inn Cairns 7 G2
Mantra Trilogy 8 G2
Pacific International Hotel 9 H3

The Reef Hotel Casino 10 H3
Shangri-La Hotel, The Marina Cairns 11 H2
Cairns Central YHA 12 G3
Note: Only a sample range of accommodation is listed; inclusion is not necessarily a recommendation.

General Information
Bus Station 13 H3
Cairns Base Hospital 14 F1

Cairns Railway Station 15 F3
Police Station 16 G3
Post Office 17 G3
Qantas Travel Centre 18 G3
Visitor Information 19 H3

Places of Interest
Cairns Museum 20 G3
Cairns Regional Gallery 21 G2
Marlin Jetty 22 H2
The Pier 23 H2
The Reef Hotel Casino 24 H3

Map place names (main map)

Pilgrim Sands
Cape Tribulation
Noah Head
Thornton Beach
Thornton Peak
DAINTREE NATIONAL PARK
DAINTREE (WORLD HERITAGE)
Alexandra Bay
Bailey Point
Cow Bay
Daintree
Cape Kimberley
HOPE ISLANDS NP
Hells Point
Snapper Island
ORCHID GARDENS
Wonga
Dayman (Rocky) Point
LOW ISLES LIGHTHOUSE
Woody Island
Miallo
Palm Beach Newell
TRINITY BAY
Cooya Beach
Morey Reef
Mossman
MOSSMAN GORGE
Port Douglas
FOUR MILE BEACH
Craiglie
Wentworth Reef
CAPTAIN COOK HIGHWAY DRIVE
Round Mountain
Mount Carbine
MOWBRAY NP
Yule Point
Pebbly Beach
Maryfarms
Rumula
Euluma
Oak Beach
Pretty Beach
Turtle Creek Beach
Julatten
Black Mountain
HARTLEY'S CREEK CROCODILE FARM
Weatherby
Kambrae
Faulty Towers
REX LOOKOUT
Mount Molloy
TRINITY BAY
Red Cliff Point
Rifle Glen
KURANDA FOREST RESERVE
KURANDA
Ellis Beach
Buchan Point
SOUTHEDGE
Mount Consider
Mount Buchan NP
Palm Cove
Clifton Beach
Taylor Point
HANN TABLELAND NATIONAL PARK
Round Mountain
Rainy Mountain
Oak Forest
Kowrowa
Myola
GREAT BARRIER REEF MARINE PARK
Green Island
GREAT BARRIER REEF
Southedge
Kingsborough
Thornborough
Koah
Kuranda
Yorkeys Knob
Smithfield Heights
AUSTRALIAN WOOLSHED
Machans Beach
Layland
SKYRAIL RAINFOREST CABLEWAY, KURANDA SCENIC RAILWAY, KURANDA MARKETS, AUSTRALIAN BUTTERFLY SANCTUARY & BIRDWORLD KURANDA
Bilwon
BARRON GORGE NP
Ellie Point
Mount McLeod
Biboohra
False Cape
Cape Grafton
Mission Bay
Turtle Bay
BOTANIC GARDENS
Chujeba Peak
FLECKER
CAIRNS
Yarrabah
FITZROY ISLAND NP
Fitzroy Island
Mount Angus
Mareeba
Mareeba Aerodrome
CRYSTAL CASCADES
DAVIES CREEK NP
Lake Morris
DINDEN FOREST RESERVE
Admiralty Island
King Beach
Wide Bay
Deception Point
Oombunghi Beach
Mount Eagle
Mount White
DIMBULAH
Tabacum
Mount Aunt
Mount Turtle
White Rock
Edmonton
GREY PEAKS NP
CORAL SEA
Dimbulah
Mutchilba
Walkamin
Mount Uncle
Mount Haig
Kamma
Meringa
Carbeen
Gordonvale
Pyramid
MALBON THOMPSON RA
Rocky Creek
Tinaroo Falls
Little Mulgrave
Aloomba
Charringa
High Island
Tobias Spit
FRANKLAND GROUP NP
Collins Weir
Mount Emerald
Tinaroo
Meerawa
Fishery Falls
Palmer Point
Tolga
Kairi
Tinaburra
McDonnell Creek
Figtree Creek
Normanby Island
Russell Island
Atherton
Yungaburra
CRATER LAKES NP
GOLDSBOROUGH VALLEY STATE FOREST
Deeral
Flint Point
Cucania
Bramston Point
Yorkies Cutting
WOOROONOORAN
South Peak
Bellenden Ker
RUSSELL RIVER NATIONAL PARK
PETFORD
Herberton
HERBERTON RANGE FOREST RESERVE
MOUNT HYPIPAMEE NP
Malanda
THE BOULDERS
Babinda
Bramston Beach
Watsonville
Mount Babinda
Irvinebank
Kalunga
Tarzali
Bartle Frere South Peak
NATIONAL
Miriwinni
Cooper Point
Flaggy Creek
Topaz
Mount Chalmynia
EUBENANGEE SWAMP NP
ELLA BAY NATIONAL PARK
Ella Bay
Brownville
Mount Veteran
EVELYN CREEK CP
Evelyn
MILLAA MILLAA FALLS
Millaa Millaa
PARK
Heath Point
Flying Fish Point
Tumoulin
Mount Father Clancy
Cooroo Peak
Innisfail
MORESBY RANGE NP
Etty Bay
Nymbool
Mount Gibson
MILLSTREAM FALLS
Ravenshoe
TULLY GORGE NP
Mount Poorka
PALMERSTON HWY
South Johnstone
Mourilyan
Mount Garnet
Ravenshoe Tin
Innot Hot Springs
Uramo
Mandalee
Mount Ronald
TULLY FALLS FOREST RESERVE
Mount Koolmoon
Mount Pandanus
Mena Creek
COWLEY BEACH TRAINING AREA
Double Point
Kent Island
Hayter Point

KENNEDY
TO TULLY

Joins map 120

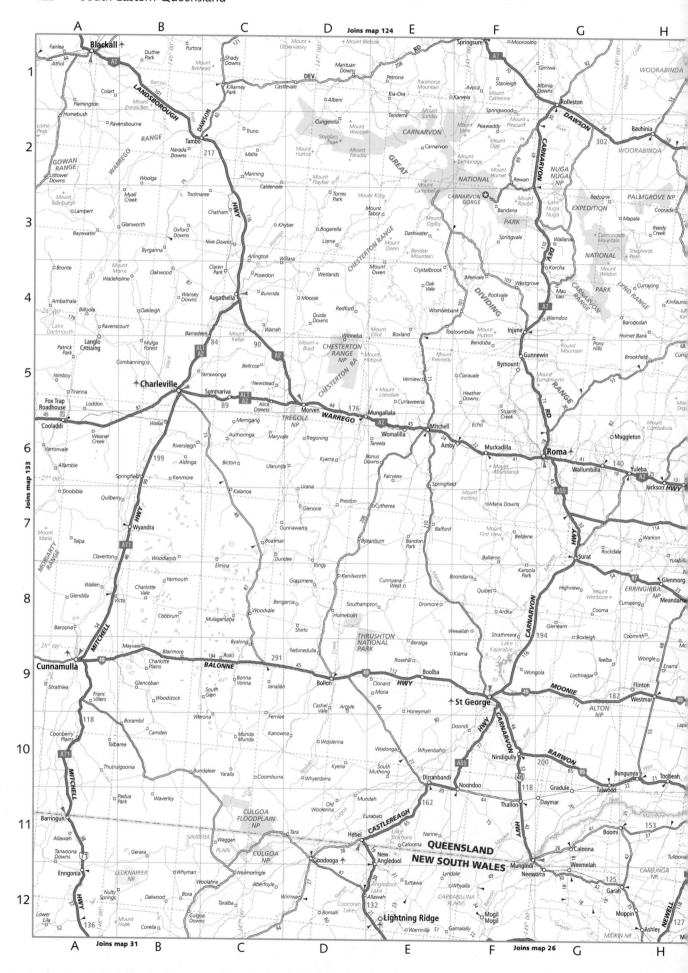

Joins map 124
Joins map 133
Joins map 31
Joins map 26

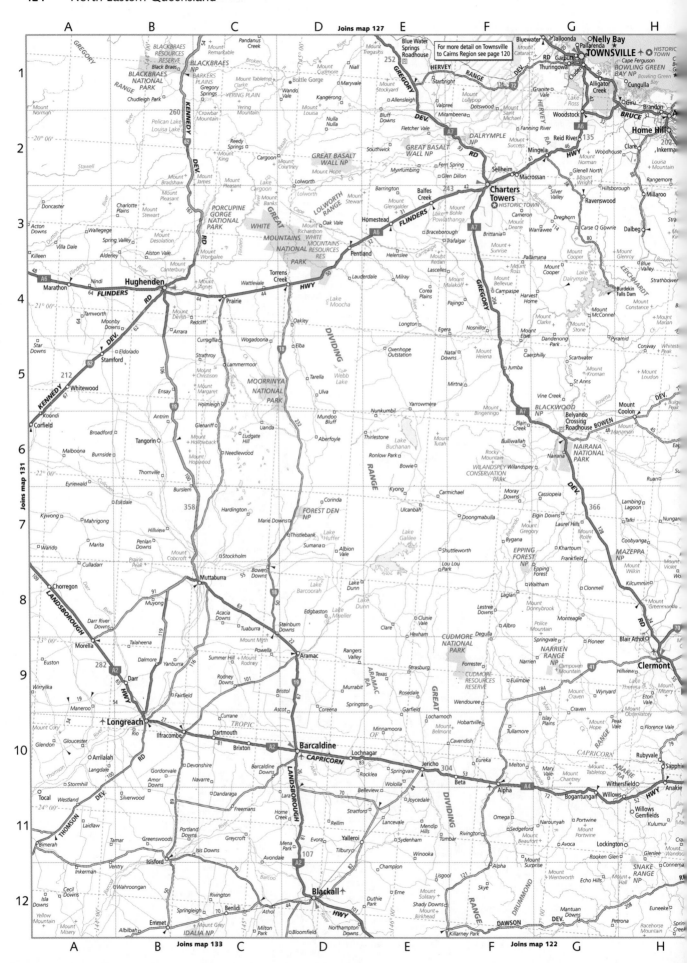

Joins map 127

Joins map 131

Joins map 133

Joins map 122

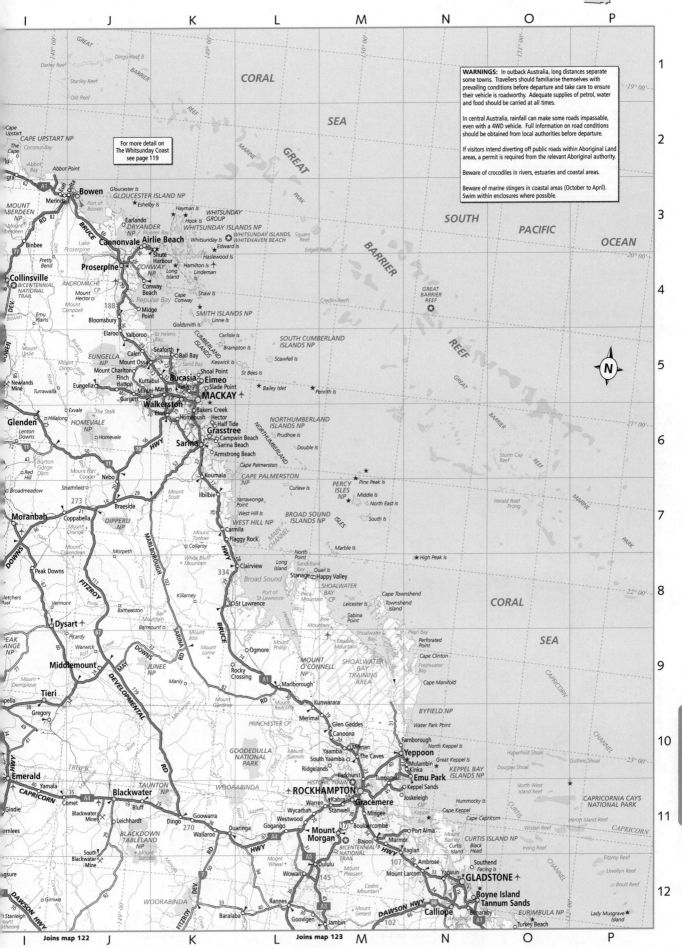

A B C D E F G H

Joins map 128

WARNINGS: In outback Australia, long distances separate some towns. Travellers should familiarise themselves with prevailing conditions before departure and take care to ensure their vehicle is roadworthy. Adequate supplies of petrol, water and food should be carried at all times.

In central Australia, rainfall can make some roads impassable, even with a 4WD vehicle. Full information on road conditions should be obtained from local authorities before departure.

If visitors intend diverting off public roads within Aboriginal Land areas, a permit is required from the relevant Aboriginal authority.

Beware of crocodiles in rivers, estuaries and coastal areas.

Beware of marine stingers in coastal areas (October to April). Swim within enclosures where possible.

ARAFURA SEA

CAPE YORK PENINSULA

ERRK OYKANGAND NP

Strathgordon
Strathgordon
Strathmay
Strathhaven
Glen Garland
New Dixie
Sefton
Oriners
Imooya
Killa
Kin

Pormpuraaw

Kowanyama

RUTLAND PLAINS
Rutland Plains

GULF COUNTRY

Koolatah
Strathleven
Dunbar
Drumduff
DEVELOPMENTAL
Staaten
Clark
Highbury
AERODROME PLAIN
GAMBOOLA

WELLESLEY ISLANDS
White Cliffs
Mornington Island
Lingnoonganee (Wallaby) Island
Cape Van Diemen
Weediah Bay
Sydney Island
Bountiful Islands
Bentinck Island
Sweers Island
SOUTH WELLESLEY ISLANDS
Tarrant Point

GULF OF CARPENTARIA

Macaroni Outstation
Dorunda Outstation
STAATEN RIVER NATIONAL PARK
Vanrook
Bulimba

Delta Downs
Point Austin
Myra Vale
Lotus Vale
Vanrook
Accident Inlet
Double Lagoon
Stirling
Smithburne
TWELVE MILE PLAIN

Pasco Inlet
Kangaroo Point
FINUCANE ISLAND NP
Disaster Inlet
Morning Inlet

Karumba
Maggieville
BURKE
Glencoe
Miranda Downs
Old Miranda Homestead
Minnies Outstation
Einasleigh
Abingdon Downs
Mount Emu

Escott
Burketown
Yarrum
JOHNNIES PLAIN
Mutton Hole
Normanton
Shady Lagoon
Fish
Hole
Eden Vale
Camp Mount
Dagworth

Magowra
Glenore Crossing
Timora
Catron
NARDOO
Armraynald
Inverleigh
GULF
Blackbull
Wallabadah Outstation
Strathmore

Wernadinga
ARMSTRONG PLAIN
NORMANTON
Milgarra
Gum Creek
Ellavale
Guildford
Belmore
DEVELOPMENTAL
Tabletop
Gilbert River
Huonfels
Ironhur

BURKETOWN
Floraville
McAllister
Belmore
Yappar Station
Florence Holding
Croydon
Inorunie
Lake Calo
Langlo Vale
Malacura
Georgetown
Alexandra
Mount Victoria
Warren Vale
GULF COUNTRY
Alehvale
GREGORY
Mount Little
Idalia
Mount Tabletop
Law

Fiery Downs Outstation
Augustus Downs
SIMPSON
Bang Bang
Wondoola
Vena Park
Claraville
Mittagong
Paddys
Mount Clark
Forsayth

Nardoo
Talawanta
PLAIN
Donors Hill
Iffley
Clara
Perpendicular Peak
North Head
Bald Mountain

Lorraine
WILLS
DEVELOPMENTAL
Cowan Downs
Momba
Prospect
Esmeralda
South Head
Glenora
Agate Creek

Burke & Wills Roadhouse
Myola
Pioneer
Victoria Vale
Nara
Iona
RANGE

White Gorge
American Gorge
Kamileroi
Ten Mile Waterhole
Lyriah Waterhole
Taldora
Bellfield
Perryvale

Gleeson
MADCAP PLAIN
Canobie
Mount Fort Bowen
Numil Downs
Malpas
Waitan
Strathpark

Mount Fox
BURKE
The Knob
Alcala
WALLA PLAIN
Violet Vale
Mount Brown
Mount Norman

Mount Stanley
The Nobbles
Etta Plains
Baalootha
Millungera
Saxby Downs

Mount Mckeon
Coolullah
Kajabbi
Granada
Bendigo Park
Clonagh
Dalgonally
Bunda Bunda

Lake Julius
Gereta
Mount Rose Bee

A B C D E F G H

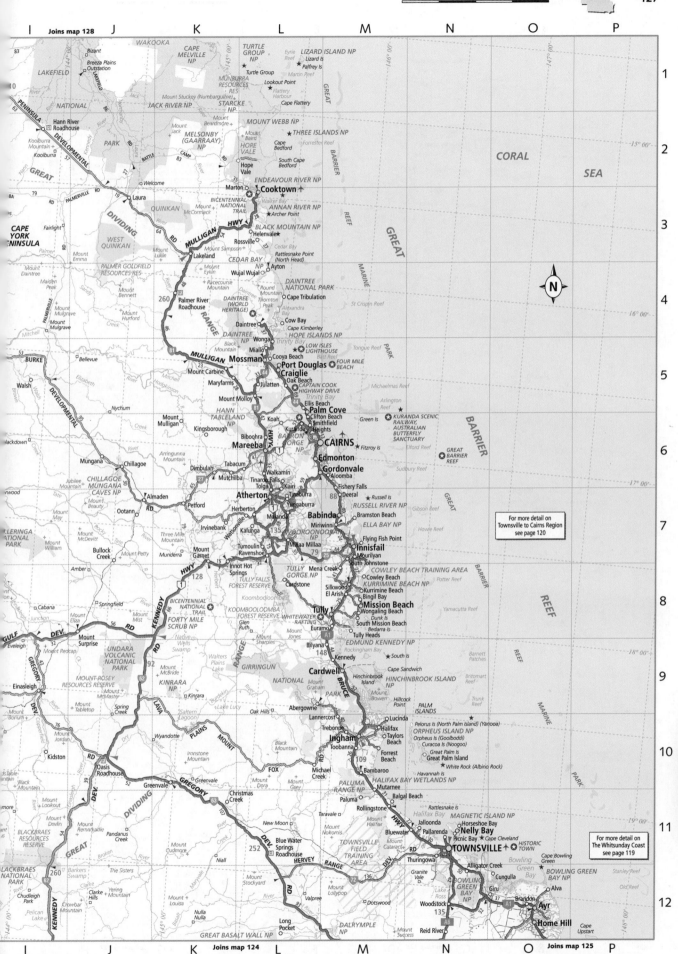

0   25   50   75   100 km

WARNINGS: In outback Australia, long distances separate some towns. Travellers should familiarise themselves with prevailing conditions before departure and take care to ensure their vehicle is roadworthy. Adequate supplies of petrol, water and food should be carried at all times.

In central Australia, rainfall can make some roads impassable, even with a 4WD vehicle. Full information on road conditions should be obtained from local authorities before departure.

If visitors intend diverting off public roads within Aboriginal Land areas, a permit is required from the relevant Aboriginal authority.

Beware of crocodiles in rivers, estuaries and coastal areas.

Beware of marine stingers in coastal areas (October to April). Swim within enclosures where possible.

N

TORRES STRAIT

ARAFURA SEA

Mabuiag Island
Kulku Pad Reef
Badu (Mulgrave) Island
Moa Island
Sassie Island
Sassie Island Reefs
Bet Reef
Derder Reef
Rugged Point
St Pauls
Pabi Point
Long Reef
Warral (Hawkesbury) Is
North Torres Reef
North West Reef
Wednesday Island
Twin Is
East Strait Is
Hammond Is
Booby Is ★
Thursday Island
Horn (Narupai) Is
Mount Adolphus (Mori) Is
Prince of Wales (Muralag) Island
Punsand Bay
Cape York
Kai-Damun Reef
Albany Island
ENDEAVOUR STRAIT
Seisia
Newcastle Bay
Kennedy Inlet
Crab Island
Injinoo
Bamaga
Turtle Head Is
Sharp Point
GULF
GREAT
Vrilya Point
Sanamere Lagoon
JARDINE RIVER RESOURCES RESERVE
Reid Point
River
Ussher Point

OF
GREAT
DENHAM
JARDINE RIVER NATIONAL PARK
Orford Bay
False Orford Ness
GROUP
CORAL

CARPENTARIA
INJINOO
Hunter Point
NP
HEATHLANDS RESOURCES RESERVE
Captain Billy Landing

LANDS
Duyfung
Middle Peak
SAUNDERS ISLANDS NP
Bird Is
BARRIER
GREAT BARRIER REEF
SEA

Mapoon
OLD MAPOON
442
Shelburne Bay
Round Point
Cape Grenville
Red Beach
Spencers
SIR CHARLES HARDY GROUP NP

Bramwell Junction Roadhouse
Bramwell
DIVIDING
Bolt Head
Temple Bay
Nomad Reef
Gallon Reef
Wishbone Reef
BARRIER

OLD MAPOON
Bertiehaugh
Coolibah
Bramley
Mosquito Point
Fair Cape
Forbes Islands A
Mantis Reef
REEF

Myerfield
Weymouth
Wattle Hill
Long Sandy

Duyfken Point
Albatross Bay
Weipa
RAAF BASE SCHERGER PROHIBITED AREA
WEIPA
Batavia Downs
FRENCHMANS RD
Mount Nelson
IRON RANGE NP
Portland Roads
Cape Weymouth
Cape Griffith
IRON RANGE RR

Wooldrum Point
Napranum
Sudley
PENINSULA
Iron Range
Lockhart River
Lloyd Bay
Cape Direction
MARINE

Boyd Point
FOUR WHEEL DRIVE (TO CAPE YORK)
Mount Bowden
LOCKHART
Bligh Reef

Thud Point
North Camp
245
Meluna
Iguana Mountain
North Peak

False Pera Head
Picaninny Plains
Mount Carter
Nundah
First Red Rocky Point
Tijou Reef

Worbody Point
AURUKUN
Watson River
Wolverton
Chester Peak
RIVER
Bobardt Point
Eve Peak

Aurukun
MUNGKAN KANDJU NATIONAL PARK
Archer River Roadhouse
Table Mountain
Friendly Point
Cape Sidmouth
REEF

Peret Outstation
DEVELOPMENTAL
Birthday Mountain
Plant Peak
Campbell Point

Kenchering Camp
Kendall River
Merapah
Rokeby
MUNGKAN
RANGE
SILVER PLAINS
Round Mountain
Magpie Reef

Cape Keerweer
KANDJU
Jabaroo Outstation
NATIONAL
Coen Aerodrome
Mount Croll
KULLA (MCILWRAITH RANGE) NATIONAL PARK (CYPAL)
SILVER PLAINS
Hay Is
Lytton Reef

Ti-Tree Outstation
CAPE
PARK
Coen
Roberts Point
Burkitt Is
Hedge Reef

Kuchendoopen Outstation
YORK
Crystal Vale
53
Silver Plains
Claremont Point
Corbett Reef
Scooterboot Reef

Holroyd River
Port Stewart
Stanley Is ★
King Is
Pipon Is
Cape Melville

PENINSULA
Cliff Islands
Flinders Island
FLINDERS GROUP NP

Southwell
Strathburn
Emu Swamp
Strathbun
Yarraden
Mount Newberry
Mount Walsh
Running Creek
Princess Charlotte Bay
Bathurst Head
Abbey Peak
Ninian Bay
Barrow Point
HOWICK GROUP NP

Mount Ryan
LAMA LAMA NP (CYPAL)
Lily Vale
Marina Plains
Bathurst Head Outstation
CAPE MELVILLE
Cape Bowen
Bewick Is

Pormpuraaw
STRATHGORDON
Strathgordon
227
Strathmay
Strathhaven
Astrea
New Bamboo
Aloszville
Bizant
LAKEFIELD
Breeza Plains Outstation
Cone Peak
Howick Is
WAKOOKA

Wallaby Island
310
Artemis
Mary Valley
Morehead River
Pelican Lake
NATIONAL
Lakefield
Jack Lakes
JACK RIVER NP
Mount Norkwa

New Dixie
Musgrave Roadhouse
LILYVALE RD
PARK
Brown Peak

0 25 50 75 100 km

A B C D E F G H

N

ARAFURA SEA

WELLESLEY ISLANDS

Rocky Is
White Cliffs
Lingnoonganee (Wallaby) Is
Cape Van Diemen
Mornington Island
Gee Wee
Gubungura
Denham Is
Sydney Is
Gerrigroo Point
Bountiful Islands
Forsyth Is
Bayley Is
Oaktree Point
Bentinck Island
Allen Island
Sweers Island

GULF

OF

CARPENTARIA

Point Austin
Accident Inlet

Bidgagun Ck
Massacre Inlet
Tully Inlet
Gold
Nicholson Creek

OLD DOOMADGEE

GULF COUNTRY

Tarrant Point
Pasco Inlet
Kangaroo Point
FINUCANE ISLAND NP
Gore Point
Morning Inlet

495
59
Westmoreland
Hells Gate Roadhouse
Cliffdale
Corinda
Bowthorn
Doomadgee
72
Brinawa
113
Almora
Kunkulla
Yeldham
74
Gregory Downs
Kamarga
Nardoo
141
Lorraine

DOOMADGEE
80
Lily

Escott
Burketown
Tirranna Roadhouse
26
Armraynald
74
Wernadinga
229
Floraville
BURKETOWN
Alexandra
Augustus Downs
Neumayer Valley
Talawanta
73
Wombool
Donors Hill
Coolibah Outstation
Kamileroi

WAANYI GARAWA ABORIGINAL LAND TRUST

BARKLY TABLELAND

Mount Oscar

BOODJAMULLA (LAWN HILL) NATIONAL PARK

Highland Plains
New Herbert Vale
Old Herbert Vale
Gallipoli

Lawn Hill
Lawn Hill Gorge
74
Adels Grove
RIVERSLEIGH FOSSIL SITE
Riversleigh
76
Mount Merlin
Norfolk

Karumba
Bynoe Inlet
Maggieville
Mutton Hole
27
Normanton
Shady Lagoon
Magowra
Glenore Crossing
Inverleigh
155
McAllister
195
Milgarra
Warren Vale
Bang Bang
Wondoola
Cowan Downs
61
Vena Park
Iffley

BURKE DEV.
Glencoe
Delta Downs
Lotus Vale
Double Lagoon
Gum Creek
Timora
Yappar Station
GULF COUNTRY
Claraville
Myola
Saxby Roundup
Earles Camp Waterhole
Lyrian Waterhole
Ten Mile Waterhole
Canobie
Mount Fort Bowen
Arizona
Numil Downs
Mount Little
Millungera
Baloortha
Dalgonally
Manfred Downs
Alva Downs
Kamerooka
Coolreagh
Eulolo

NORTHERN TERRITORY
QUEENSLAND

GREGORY
91
Undilla
Morstone
Thornton
Mount Oxide
Gunpowder
Mount Fox

BARKLY TABLELAND

Camooweal
CAMOOWEAL CAVES NP
30
13
71
URANDANGI RD

Burke & Wills Roadhouse

Boomarra
Gleeson
Dobbyn
Coolullah
Mount Mckeon
Kajabbi
Gereta
Granada
Alcala
The Nobbies
Bellman
Violet Vale
Brinard
Kalmeta
Etta Plains
182
250
Clonagh
Mount Margaret

Yelvertoft
188
73
Barkly Downs
Old Wooroona
Wooroona
107
Mingera
Mount Michael
55
Bullecourt
Lake Nash
Headingly
Bull Creek

Calton Hills
Glenroy
New May Downs
44
Lake Moondarra
MOUNT ISA
Lake Mary Kathleen
The Three Sisters
Mount Philip
Mount Woodhouse
Sheila Outstation
78
Bushy Park
Ashover
Duchess

Mount Remarkable
Mount Roseby
Quamby
45
Corella Park
BARKLY HWY
118
Roxmere
Mount Connor
Malbon Vale
Black Mountain
99
Mount Collis
Devoncourt
66
37
Kuridala
Mount Tracey

Mount Maggie
Gereta
Cloncurry
Oorindi
Mount Norna
SEDAN DIP
Ernestina Plains
FLINDERS
112
Gilliat
Julia Creek
25
Rutchillo
Mount Boolgal
McKinlay
105
129

FLINDERS HWY
LANDSBOROUGH HWY
141° 00'
27° 00'

DIAMANTINA DEV. RD
URANDANGI NORTH RD

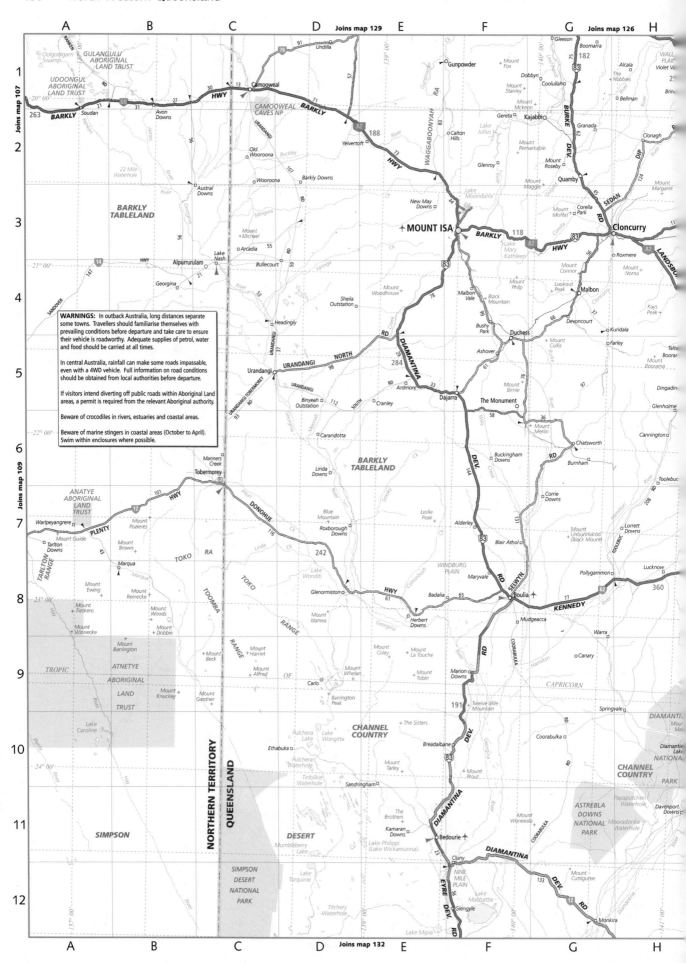

WARNINGS: In outback Australia, long distances separate some towns. Travellers should familiarise themselves with prevailing conditions before departure and take care to ensure their vehicle is roadworthy. Adequate supplies of petrol, water and food should be carried at all times.

In central Australia, rainfall can make some roads impassable, even with a 4WD vehicle. Full information on road conditions should be obtained from local authorities before departure.

If visitors intend diverting off public roads within Aboriginal Land areas, a permit is required from the relevant Aboriginal authority.

Beware of crocodiles in rivers, estuaries and coastal areas.

Beware of marine stingers in coastal areas (October to April). Swim within enclosures where possible.

0   25   50   75   100 km

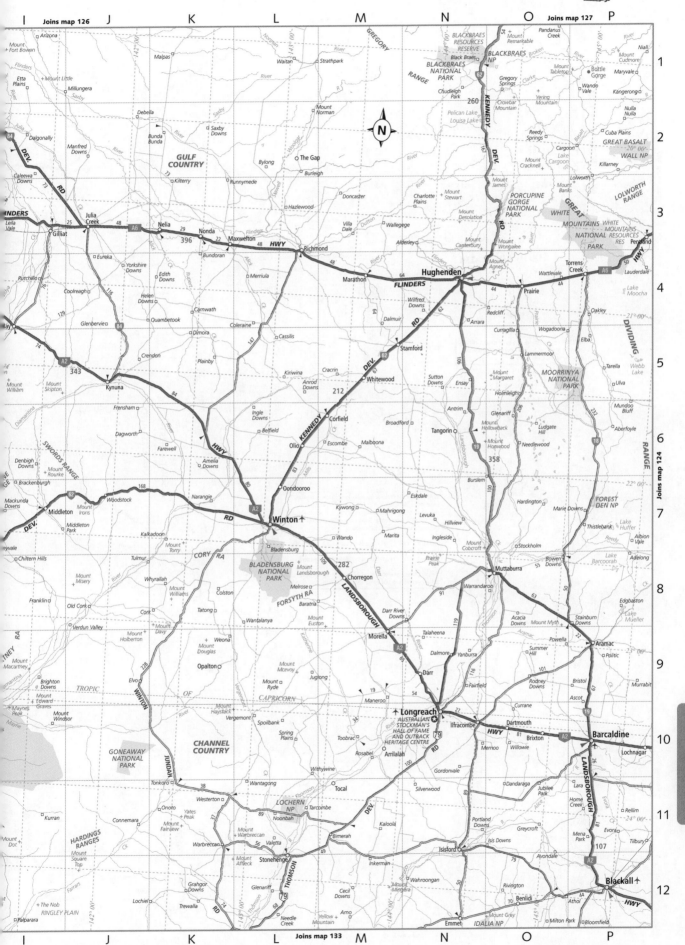

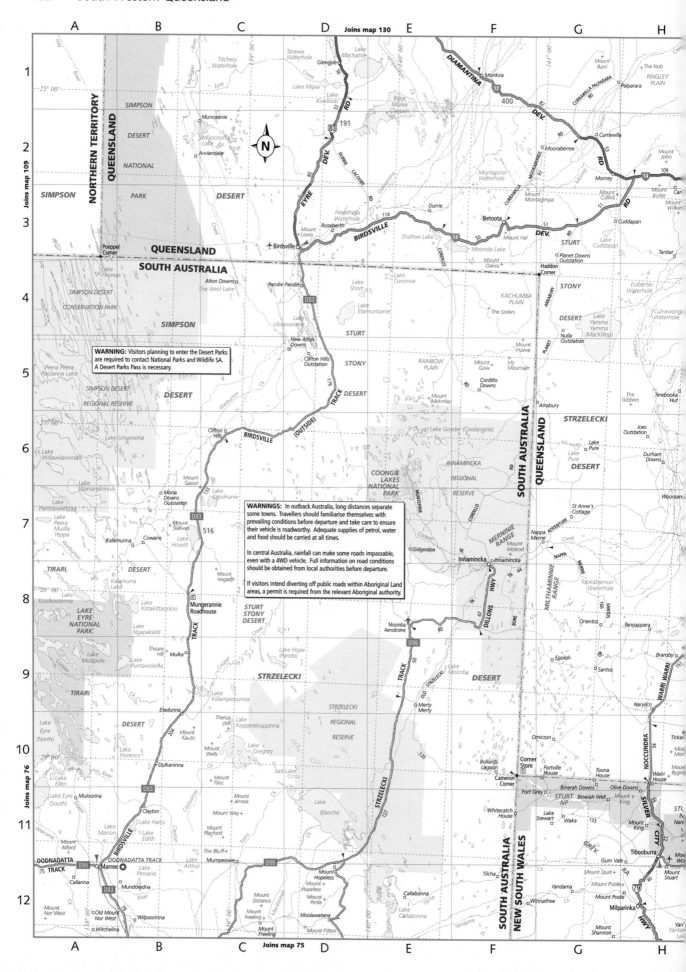

WARNING: Visitors planning to enter the Desert Parks are required to contact National Parks and Wildlife SA. A Desert Parks Pass is necessary.

WARNINGS: In outback Australia, long distances separate some towns. Travellers should familiarise themselves with prevailing conditions before departure and take care to ensure their vehicle is roadworthy. Adequate supplies of petrol, water and food should be carried at all times.

In central Australia, rainfall can make some roads impassable, even with a 4WD vehicle. Full information on road conditions should be obtained from local authorities before departure.

If visitors intend diverting off public roads within Aboriginal Land areas, a permit is required from the relevant Aboriginal authority.

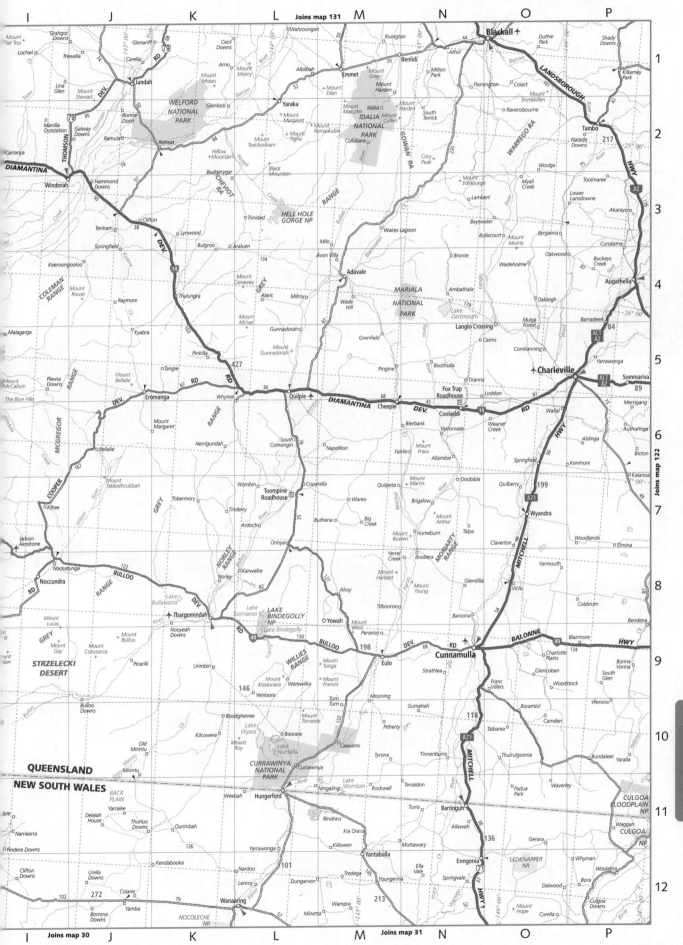

0 25 50 75 100 km

133

Joins map 131

Joins map 122

Joins map 30

Joins map 31

I J K L M N O P

1
2
3
4
5
6
7
8
9
10
11
12

MAPS

TASMANIA

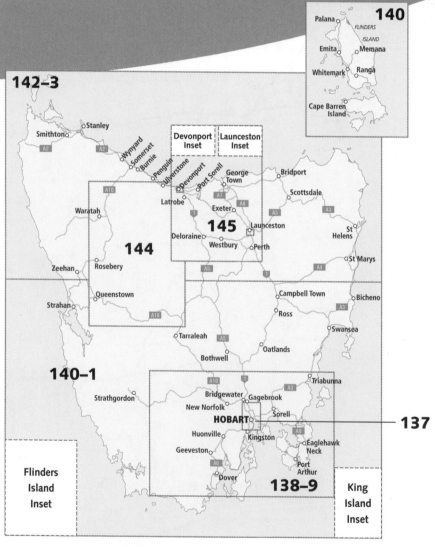

Egg
Lagoon
KING
ISLAND
Currie
Grassy
141

Palana   *FLINDERS* **140**
          ISLAND
Emita   Memana
Whitemark   Ranga

Cape Barren
Island

142–3

Smithton   Stanley

Wynyard
Somerset
Burnie
Penguin
Ulverstone
Devonport
Port Sorell

Devonport
Inset   Launceston
        Inset

George
Town   Bridport

Scottsdale

Latrobe   A7

Exeter   A8
Deloraine   **145**   Launceston
Westbury   Perth

St
Helens

Waratah

144

Zeehan   Rosebery

St Marys

Queenstown   A10   A4

Strahan   Campbell Town   Bicheno
          Ross   A3
          Swansea

Tarraleah   A5
Bothwell   Oatlands

140–1

Strathgordon   A10   Triabunna
               A3
Bridgewater   Gagebrook
New Norfolk   Sorell

HOBART ————————— **137**

Huonville   Kingston
Geeveston   A9   Eaglehawk
                 Neck
            Port
            Arthur
Dover   **138–9**

Flinders
Island
Inset

King
Island
Inset

Tasmania

INTER-CITY ROUTES		DISTANCE
Hobart–Launceston via Midland Hwy	1	200 km
Hobart–Devonport via Midland & Bass hwys	1 B52 1	286 km

Approximate Distances TASMANIA	Burnie	Campbell Town	Deloraine	Devonport	Geeveston	George Town	Hobart	Launceston	New Norfolk	Oatlands	Port Arthur	Queenstown	Richmond	Rosebery	St Helens	St Marys	Scottsdale	Smithton	Sorell	Strahan	Swansea	Ulverstone
Burnie		200	101	50	391	204	333	152	328	247	432	163	304	110	300	263	222	88	318	185	267	28
Campbell Town	200		99	150	191	119	133	67	128	47	232	304	104	357	122	85	137	288	118	344	67	172
Deloraine	101	99		51	290	103	232	51	227	146	331	207	203	211	199	162	121	189	217	247	166	73
Devonport	50	150	51		341	154	283	102	278	197	382	213	254	160	250	213	172	138	268	235	217	22
Geeveston	391	191	290	341		310	58	258	95	144	157	308	85	361	313	276	328	479	84	348	197	363
George Town	204	119	103	154	310		252	52	247	166	351	310	223	314	182	182	83	292	237	350	186	176
Hobart	333	133	232	283	58	252		200	37	86	99	250	27	303	265	228	270	421	26	290	139	305
Launceston	152	67	51	102	258	52	200		195	114	299	258	171	262	167	130	70	240	185	298	134	124
New Norfolk	328	128	227	278	95	247	37	195		81	136	213	64	266	250	213	265	416	63	253	176	300
Oatlands	247	47	146	197	144	166	86	114	81		175	257	57	310	169	132	184	335	71	297	125	219
Port Arthur	432	232	331	382	157	351	99	299	136	175		349	87	402	312	275	369	520	73	389	186	404
Queenstown	163	304	207	213	308	310	250	258	213	257	349		277	53	426	389	328	253	276	40	389	191
Richmond	304	104	203	254	85	223	27	171	64	57	87	277		330	226	189	241	392	14	317	123	276
Rosebery	110	357	211	160	361	314	303	262	266	310	402	53	330		410	373	332	222	329	75	442	138
St Helens	300	122	199	250	313	182	265	167	250	169	312	426	226	410		37	99	388	240	466	126	272
St Marys	263	85	162	213	276	182	228	130	213	132	275	389	189	373	37		136	351	203	429	89	235
Scottsdale	222	137	121	172	328	83	270	70	265	184	369	328	241	332	99	136		310	255	368	204	194
Smithton	88	288	189	138	479	292	421	240	416	335	520	253	392	222	388	351	310		406	275	355	116
Sorell	318	118	217	268	84	237	26	185	63	71	73	276	14	329	240	203	255	406		316	113	290
Strahan	185	344	247	235	348	350	290	298	253	297	389	40	317	75	466	429	368	275	316		429	213
Swansea	267	67	166	217	197	186	139	134	176	125	186	389	123	442	126	89	204	355	113	429		239
Ulverstone	28	172	73	22	363	176	305	124	300	219	404	191	276	138	272	235	194	116	290	213	239	

Distances on this chart have been calculated over main roads and do not necessarily reflect the shortest route between towns.

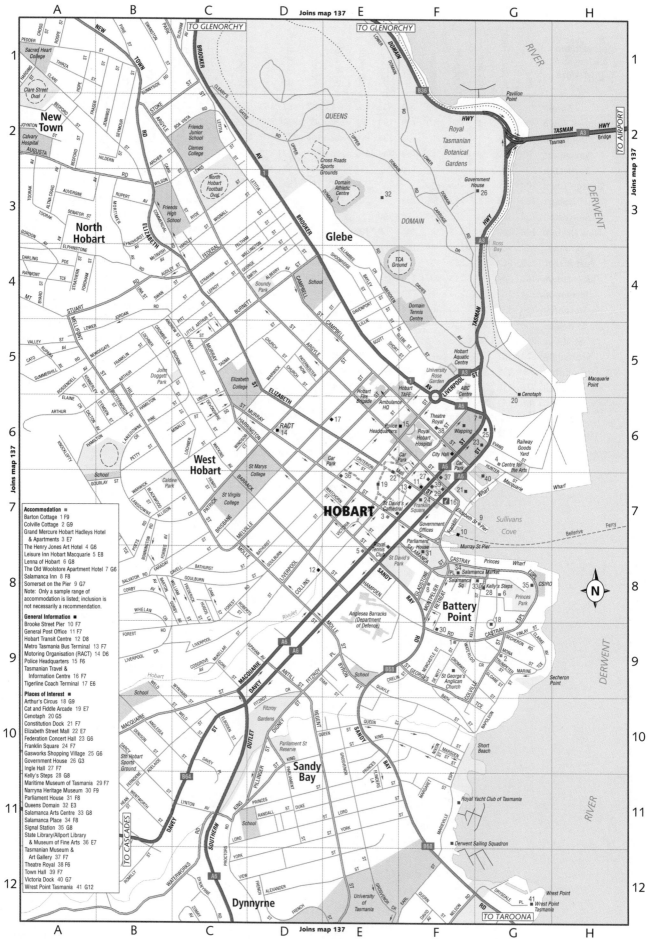

0   0.25   0.5   0.75   1 km

A   B   C   D   E   F   G   H

Joins map 137

TO GLENORCHY

TO GLENORCHY

TO AIRPORT

Joins map 137

New Town

North Hobart

Glebe

West Hobart

HOBART

Battery Point

Sandy Bay

Dynnyrne

TO CASCADES

TO TAROONA

Joins map 137

Joins map 137

DERWENT RIVER

Accommodation ■
Barton Cottage 1 F9
Colville Cottage 2 G9
Grand Mercure Hobart Hadleys Hotel
 & Apartments 3 E7
The Henry Jones Art Hotel 4 G6
Leisure Inn Hobart Macquarie 5 E8
Lenna of Hobart 6 G8
The Old Woolstore Apartment Hotel 7 G6
Salamanca Inn 8 F8
Somerset on the Pier 9 G7
Note: Only a sample range of
accommodation is listed; inclusion is
not necessarily a recommendation.

General Information ■
Brooke Street Pier 10 F7
General Post Office 11 F7
Hobart Transit Centre 12 D8
Metro Tasmania Bus Terminal 13 F7
Motoring Organisation (RACT) 14 D6
Police Headquarters 15 F6
Tasmanian Travel &
 Information Centre 16 F7
Tigerline Coach Terminal 17 E6

Places of Interest ■
Arthur's Circus 18 G9
Cat and Fiddle Arcade 19 E7
Cenotaph 20 G5
Constitution Dock 21 F7
Elizabeth Street Mall 22 E7
Federation Concert Hall 23 G6
Franklin Square 24 F7
Gasworks Shopping Village 25 G6
Government House 26 G3
Ingle Hall 27 F7
Kelly's Steps 28 G8
Maritime Museum of Tasmania 29 F7
Narryna Heritage Museum 30 F9
Parliament House 31 F8
Queens Domain 32 E3
Salamanca Arts Centre 33 G8
Salamanca Place 34 F8
Signal Station 35 G8
State Library/Allport Library
 & Museum of Fine Arts 36 E7
Tasmanian Museum &
 Art Gallery 37 F7
Theatre Royal 38 F6
Town Hall 39 F7
Victoria Dock 40 G7
Wrest Point Tasmania 41 G12

N

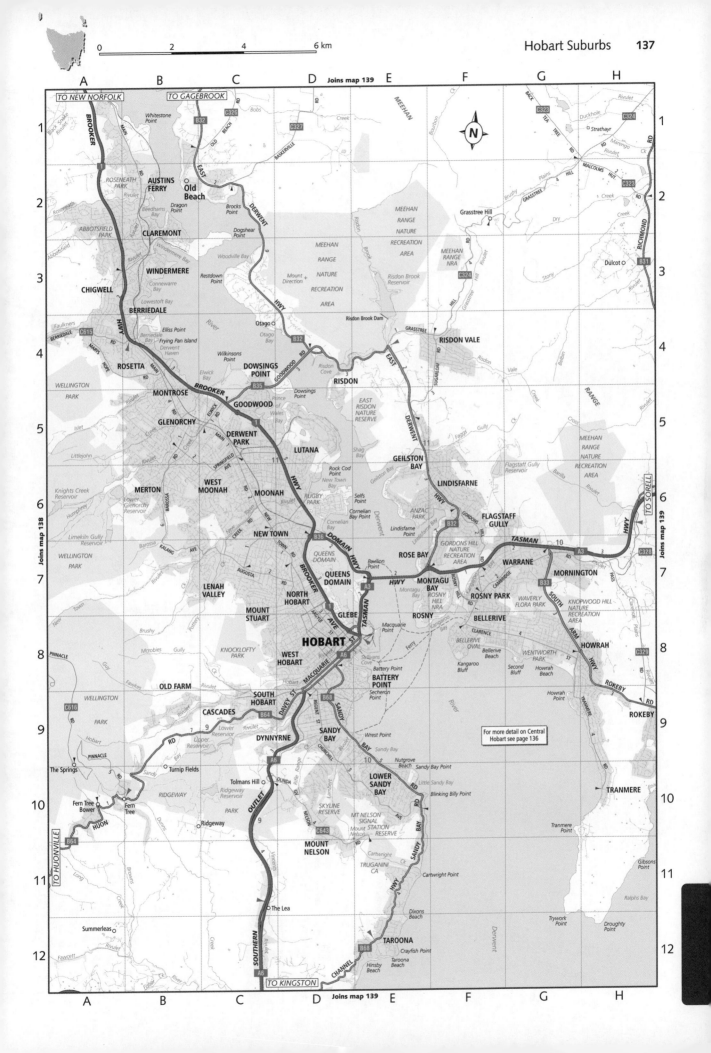

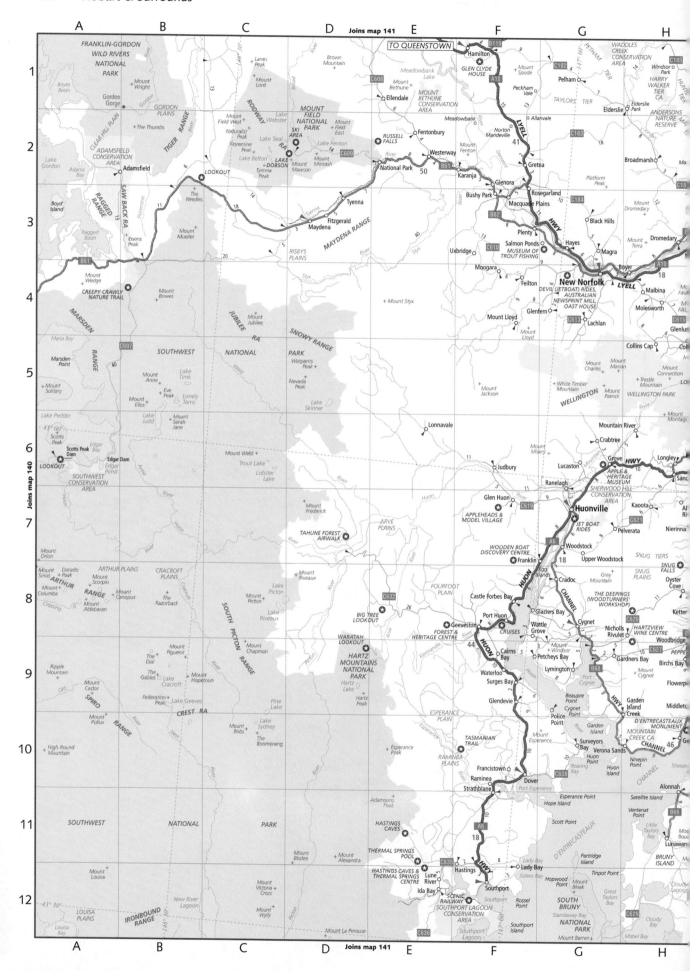

0 5 10 15 20 km

Joins map 141

TO LAUNCESTON

TO SWANSEA

Eldon
Colebrook
Quoin Mountain
Fair View
Craigbourne Dam
GRAVELLY RIDGE CONSERVATION AREA
Mount Hobbs
Levendale
Mount Douglas
BUCKLAND MILITARY PROHIBITED AREA
Triabunna
Woodstock
Rostrevor Reservoir
Cape Bougainville

Chauncy Vale
Bagdad
Mount Bains
The Cobs
Stonehurst
Louisville
Point Home Lookout Lighthouse
Point Home Lookout
Lords Bluff
Okehampton

Mangalore
Lowdina
Brown Mountain
Buckland
Court Farm
Orford
Shelly Beach
Quarry Point
Spring Beach
Ile Du Nord
Cape Boullanger
Fossil Bay
Darlington
HISTORIC PENAL SETTLEMENT

Pontville
PONTVILLE RIFLE RANGE PROHIBITED AREA
Campania
Campania House
Runnymede
Whitemarsh
Mount Calvary
HISTORIC CHURCH
Sally Peak
Rheban
Carrickfergus
Johnsons Point
PAINTED CLIFFS
MARIA ISLAND NATIONAL PARK
Mistaken Cape

Tea Tree
BONORONG WILDLIFE PARK
Rekuna
Mount Phipps
Mount Morrison
Ringrove
Earlham Lagoon
Earlham
Sandspit Point
Point Lesueur
Perpendicular Mountain
Little Raggedy Head

Old Beach
CADBURY VISITOR CENTRE
Gagebrook
Richmond
HISTORIC TOWN
Orielton
Pawleena
Nugent
Mount Walter
CAPE BERNIER NATURE RESERVE
Cape Bernier
Point Des Galets
Point Maugé
Shoal Bay
Riedle Bay
MARIA ISLAND
Cape Des Tombeaux
Cape Bald

Claremont
BASKERVILLE RACEWAY
Strathayr
Park View
Penna
Sorell
Wattle Hill
Hillcrest
Mount Reuben
Mount Jacob
Cape Boullanger
Barren Head
Cape Maurouard

Berriedale
Otago
Grasstree Hill
Mount Lord
Mount Elizabeth
Forcett
Kellevie
WOODVINE NATURE RESERVE
ILES TIER
Point Du Ressac
Point Peron

Risdon Vale
Risdon
PITT WATER NR
Cambridge Aerodrome
Midway Point
Lewisham
Bream Creek
Marion Bay
LONG SPIT PRIVATE NR
Long Spit
Cape Paul Lamanon
Visscher Island
Marion Bay

HOBART
New Town
Moonah
Lindisfarne
Rosny Park
BELLERIVE OVAL
Mount Rumney
Cambridge
Hobart Airport
Copping MUSEUM
Marion Bay
Cape Frederick Hendrick

Rokeby
Seven Mile Beach
Sandy Point
Park Beach
Dodges Ferry
Carlton
Connellys Marsh
Dunalley
Bangor Point
Swan
North Bay
BLACKMAN PLAINS
Kelly Islands
Humper Bluff

Taroona
MT NELSON SIGNAL STATION
Sandy Bay
Howrah
Lauderdale
Mays Point
Carlton Bluff
Primrose Sands
Fulham Point
Fulham Island
DENISON CANAL
Mount Forestier
Mount Reynolds
TASMAN
High Yellow Bluff

Kingston
Blackmans Bay
SHOT TOWER
Gellibrand Point
Cremorne
Green Head
LIME BAY STATE RES
Dunbabin
Murdunna
FORESTIER PENINSULA
PENINSULA TRAIL DRIVE
NATIONAL

Howden
SOUTH ARM CA
South Arm
Clifton Beach
Gwandalan
Coal Mines HISTORIC SITE
Norfolk Bay
EAGLEHAWK BAY-FLINDERS BAY CONSERVATION AREA
Cape Surville
Deep Glen Bluff
View Peak
Macgregor Peak

Opossum Bay
Cape Deslacs
North West Head
Mount Wilmot
Deer Point
Saltwater River
Heather Point
Eaglehawk
PIRATES BAY LOOKOUT
TESSELLATED PAVEMENT

Tinderbox
Cape Contrariety
Sloping Island
Whitehouse Point
Smooth Island
Dunbabin Bay
Eaglehawk Neck
TASMAN BLOWHOLE
TASMANS ARCH
DEVIL'S KITCHEN
Waterfall Bay

Dennes Point
Iron Pot
Betsey Island
Premaydena
Koonya
Taranna
Penzance
Doo Town
Clemes Peak
O'Hara Bluff
TASMAN NATIONAL

Barnes Bay
Little Betsey Island
Outer North Head
Nubeena
Mount Koonya
Mount Clark
Oakwood
TASMAN PENINSULA
Thumbs Point

Yellow Bluff
White Beach
Wedge Island
Mount Tonga
BUSH MILL STEAM RAILWAY
Dolomieu Point
Hippolyte Rocks
The Lanterns
Fortescue Bay

Killora
Trumpeter Bay
Storm Bay
Highcroft
Mount Spaulding
Two Island Bay
Mount Arthur
PALMERS LOOKOUT
Port Arthur
HISTORIC TOWN
TUNAH PLAINS
Cape Hauy

Chuckle Head
Variety Point
Curio Bay
Stormlea
Black Mountain
Safety Cove
Mount Fortescue
TASMAN NATIONAL

MORELLA ISLAND RETREAT
Coal Point
Penguin Island
CAPTAIN COOK'S LANDING PLACE
Cookville
Fluted Cape
SOUTH BRUNY
Salters Point
REMARKABLE CAVE
Mount Raoul
Mount Brown
Mount West Arthur Head
Budget Head
Haines Bight
Black Head
Cape Pillar
TASMAN SEA

Grass Point
BLIGH MUSEUM OF PACIFIC EXPLORATION
Mount Cook
Cape Connella
Raoul Bay
Maingon Bay
Cape Raoul
Tasman Island
Tasman Island Lighthouse
TASMAN PASSAGE

N

Mangana Bluff
Arched Island
Bay of Islands
NATIONAL PARK

For more detail on Hobart Suburbs see page 137

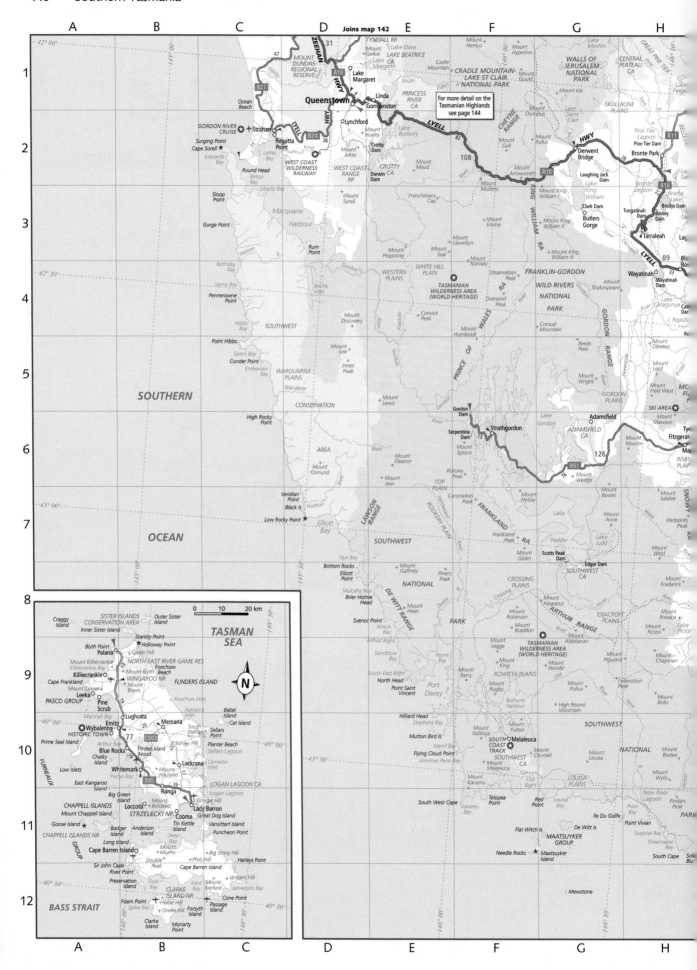

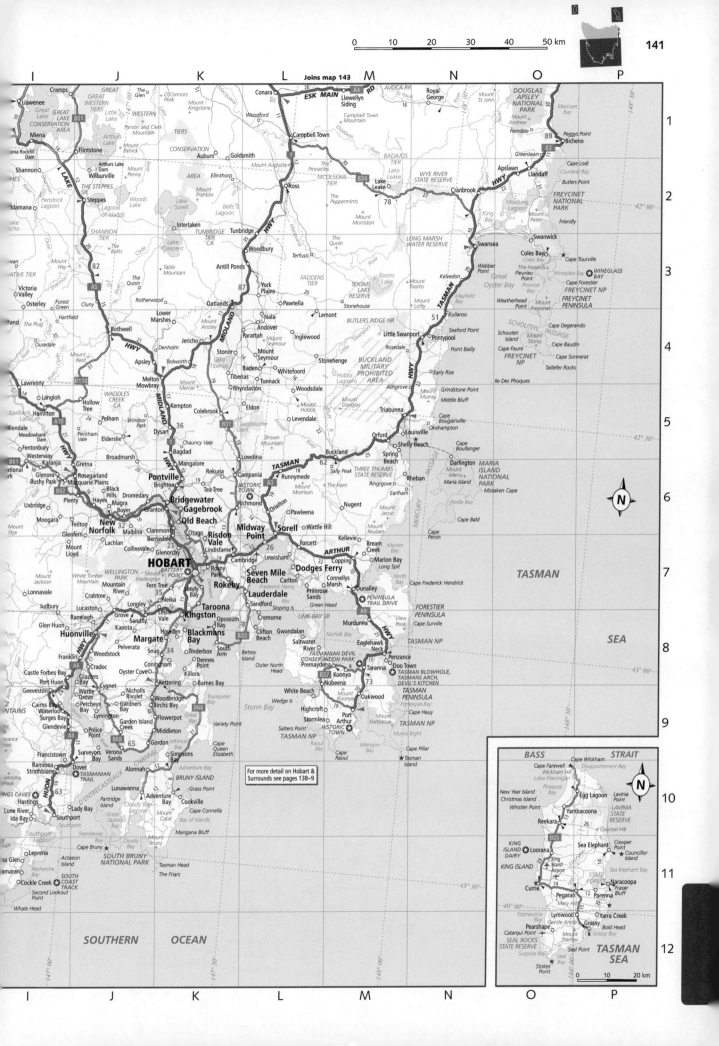

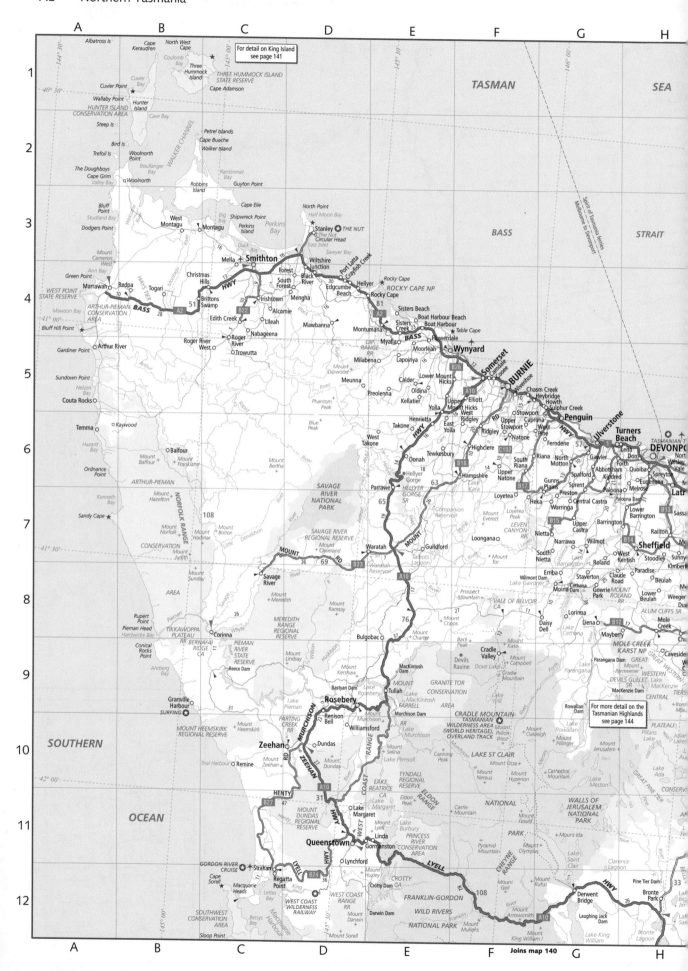

For detail on King Island see page 141

For more detail on the Tasmanian Highlands see page 144

Joins map 140

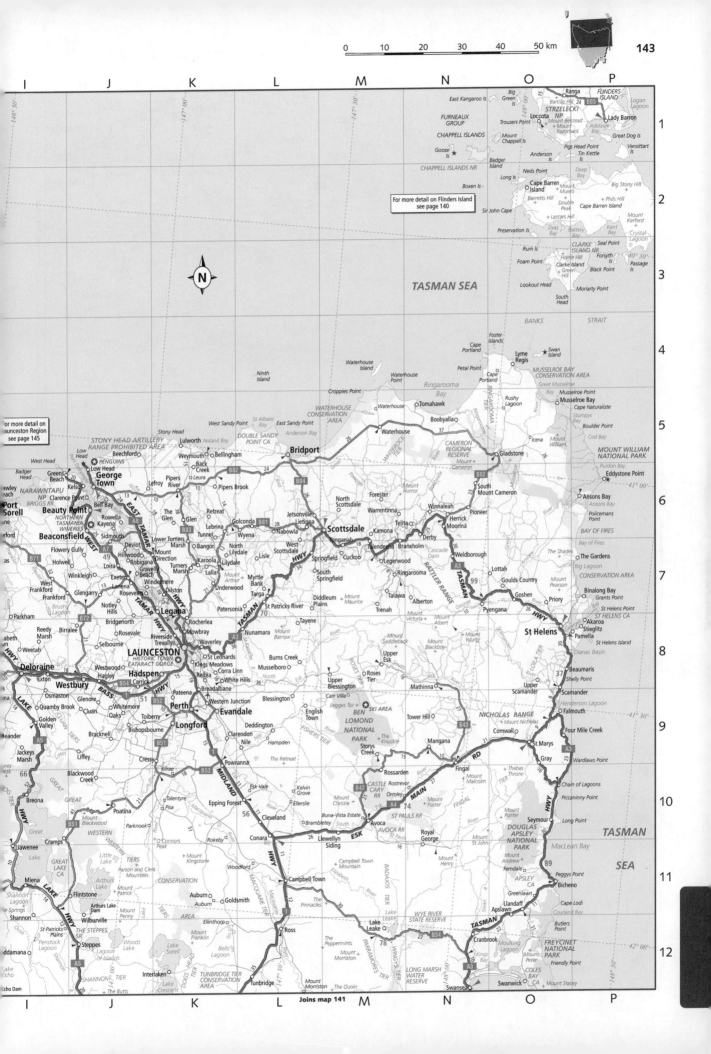

0 10 20 30 40 50 km

TASMAN SEA

For more detail on Flinders Island see page 140

For more detail on Launceston Region see page 145

TASMAN SEA

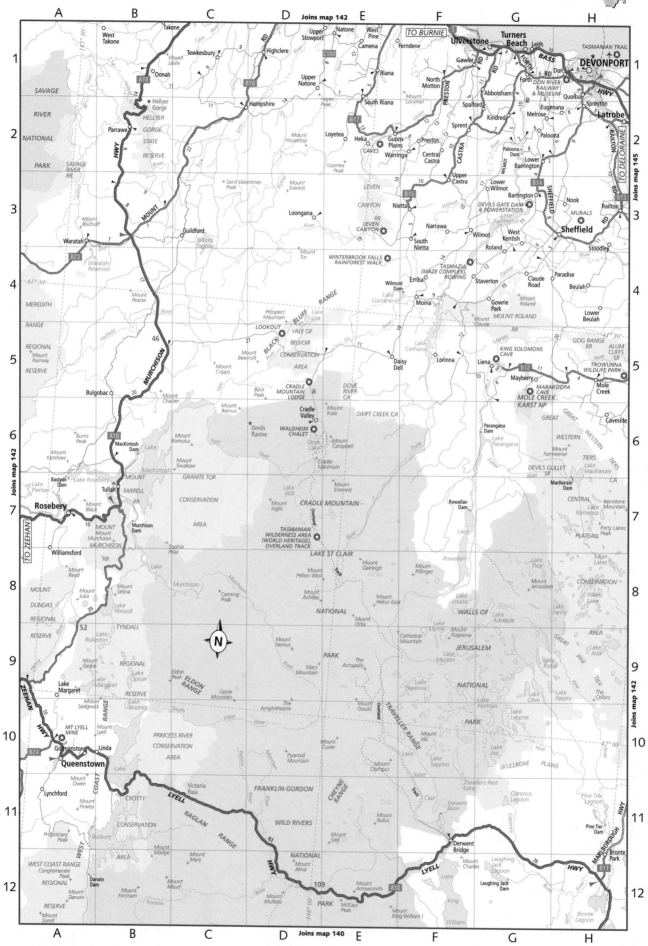

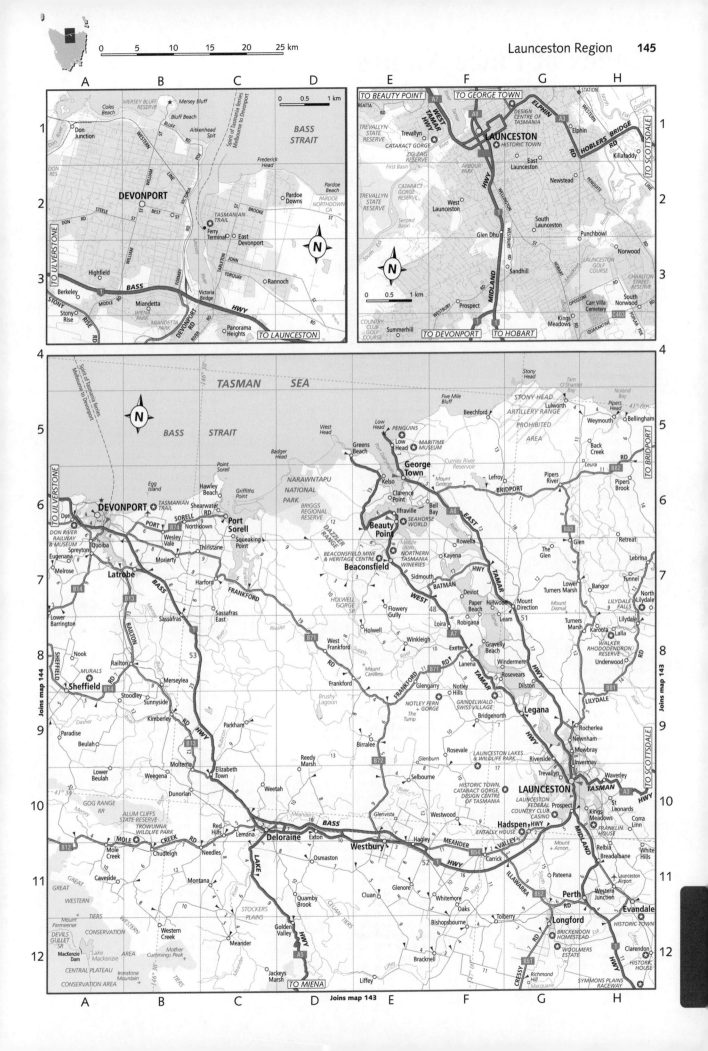

Index of Place Names

146

Ashfield WA xxv C4, 84 E5, 85 C5
Ashford NSW 27 I4
Ashford SA xx G7
Ashgrove Qld xxx D4, 114 D7
Ashley NSW 26 F4, 122 H12
Ashmore Qld 116 E6
Ashville SA 71 D5, 73 L11
Aspendale Vic. 43 J7, 45 K2, 52 C5
Aspendale Gardens Vic. 45 K2
Aspley Qld 114 E5, 115 D3, 117 F10
Asquith NSW 12 E4, 13 B10, 15 L6
Astrebla Downs NP Qld 130 G11
Atherton Qld 120 D3, 121 D9, 127 L7
Athlone Vic. 43 N9, 52 F7
Atitjere NT 109 K5
Atneltyey NT 109 J3
Attadale WA xxiv D10
Attunga NSW 26 H9
Aubrey Vic. 60 G7
Auburn NSW 12 D7, 13 A12, 15 K8
Auburn SA 73 J6
Auburn River NP Qld 123 K5
Auburn Tas. 141 K1, 143 K11
Auchenflower Qld xxx D7
Augathella Qld 122 C4, 133 P4
Augusta WA 86 C11, 88 B10, 90 B11
Auldana SA xxi P5
Aurora Kakadu Resort NT 103 M4, 104 G4
Aurukun Qld 128 B8
Auski Roadhouse WA 89 H3, 92 D4, 97 I9
Austinmer NSW 23 G4
Austins Ferry Tas. 137 B2
Austinville Qld 116 C9
Austral NSW 14 H9, 25 J7, 35 H1
Australia Plains SA 73 K7
Australind WA 86 E3, 88 C8, 90 C9
Avalon NSW 12 H3, 13 C10, 15 N6
Avalon Vic. 44 B2
Avenel Vic. 54 D10
Avenue SA 71 F9
Avoca Tas. 143 M10
Avoca Vic. 49 A6, 61 L12, 63 L1
Avoca Beach NSW 13 E8, 15 O3
Avoca Vale Qld 118 B11, 123 L7
Avon SA 69 G4, 71 B1, 73 J7
Avon Plains Vic. 61 J8
Avon Valley NP WA 84 G1, 85 E2, 88 C4, 90 C7
Avondale NSW 13 E4, 19 A10, 23 E5, 25 J8, 35 H3
Avondale Qld 118 C1
Avondale Heights Vic. xiv A1
Avonsleigh Vic. 41 C10, 45 O1
Awaba NSW 13 F14, 19 B10
Awonga Vic. 60 C10, 71 H9
Axe Creek Vic. 49 G4, 54 A9, 61 O10
Axedale Vic. 49 H3, 54 B9, 61 P10
Ayr Qld 119 B2, 124 H2, 127 O12
Ayrford Vic. 50 F8, 63 I8
Ayton Qld 127 L4

Baan Baa NSW 26 F7
Baandee WA 88 F3
Baarmutha Vic. 55 J8, 56 H4
Babakin WA 88 G5
Babinda Qld 120 E4, 121 G10, 127 M7
Bacchus Marsh Vic. 42 G4, 49 G11, 52 A3, 63 O5
Back Creek Tas. 143 K5, 145 H5
Baddaginnie Vic. 54 G8, 56 C5
Baden Tas. 141 L4
Badgerys Creek NSW 14 H8, 25 J7, 35 H1
Badgingarra WA 88 A1, 90 B5
Badgingarra NP WA 88 A1, 90 B5
Badjaling WA 88 F5
Baerami NSW 25 J2
Bagdad Tas. 139 I2, 141 K5
Bagnoo NSW 20 E6, 27 L11
Bago Bluff NP NSW 20 E6, 27 L11
Bagot NT 102 D3
Bagot Well SA 67 F2, 71 C1, 73 K7
Bagshot Vic. 49 G2, 54 A8, 61 O9
Bailieston Vic. 54 D9
Baird Bay SA 72 A4, 81 N11
Bairnsdale Vic. 53 M5
Bajool Qld 125 M11
Bakara SA 71 E2, 73 M8
Baker Vic. 60 E6

Bakers Creek Qld 119 G8, 125 K6
Bakers Hill WA 85 F3, 88 D4
Bakers Swamp NSW 24 F3
Baking Board Qld 123 J7
Balaclava Vic. xvii M11
Balaklava SA 69 H4, 73 J7
Balcatta WA xxiv D1, 84 D5
Balcombe Vic. 45 J6
Bald Hills Qld 114 E5, 115 D3, 117 F10
Bald Rock Vic. 29 I12, 54 A5, 61 O6
Bald Rock NP NSW 21 A4, 27 L3, 123 L12
Baldivis WA 84 D11, 85 C7
Baldry NSW 24 E3
Balfes Creek Qld 124 E3
Balfour Tas. 142 B6
Balga WA xxiv E1
Balgal Beach Qld 120 F9, 127 M11
Balgo Hills WA 95 N10
Balgowan SA 69 D4, 72 H7
Balgowlah NSW xi L4, 12 G6, 13 C12, 15 M8
Balgowlah Heights NSW xi L5
Balgownie NSW 22 C3, 23 F4
Balhannah SA 66 F8, 67 D9, 68 H3
Balingup WA 86 G6, 88 C9, 90 C10
Balintore Vic. 42 B8, 50 B1, 63 L8
Ball Bay Qld 119 G7, 125 K5
Balladonia WA 91 K7
Balladoran NSW 26 C11
Ballajura WA xxv A1, 84 D5, 85 C4
Ballalaba NSW 24 G11, 35 E5, 37 J5
Ballan Vic. 42 F3, 49 F11, 63 N4
Ballan North Vic. 42 F3, 49 F10, 63 N4
Ballandean Qld 21 A4, 27 K3, 123 K12
Ballangeich Vic. 50 D7, 62 H7
Ballarat Vic. 42 D3, 47, 49 C10, 63 M4
Ballarat North Vic. 47 E4
Ballarat South Vic. 47 C7
Ballark Vic. 42 E4, 49 E12, 63 N5
Ballaying WA 88 F8
Ballbank NSW 28 H10, 61 N3
Balldale NSW 29 N11, 55 J4
Ballendella Vic. 54 B6, 61 P8
Balliang Vic. 42 F5, 52 A4, 63 O5
Balliang East Vic. 42 F5, 52 A4, 63 O5
Ballidu WA 88 D1, 90 C5
Ballimore NSW 24 F1, 26 D12
Ballina NSW 21 G5, 27 O3, 123 N12
Ballyrogan Vic. 63 J3
Balmain NSW viii D3, x D10
Balmain East NSW viii E3, x E11
Balmattum Vic. 54 F9, 56 B6
Balmoral NSW xi K6, 13 F4, 19 B10
Balmoral Qld xxxi J6
Balmoral Vic. 60 E12, 62 E2
Balnarring Vic. 40 E12, 43 J10, 45 K8, 52 C7
Balnarring Beach Vic. 45 K9
Balook Vic. 53 I8
Balranald NSW 28 H7, 59 M9
Balrootan North Vic. 28 C12, 60 E7
Balumbah SA 72 E4, 74 D11
Bamaga Qld 128 C3
Bamawm Vic. 29 I12, 54 B6, 61 P7
Bamawm Extension Vic. 54 B6, 61 P7
Bambaroo Qld 120 E9, 127 M10
Bambill Vic. 28 C6, 58 E7, 73 P8
Bamboo Creek WA 92 F5, 94 F12, 97 L4
Bambra Vic. 42 D9, 50 E2, 63 M8
Bamganie Vic. 42 D6, 63 M6
Banana Qld 123 I2
Bancroft Qld 123 K3
Bandiana Vic. 24 A12, 55 K6, 57 I2
Bandon Grove NSW 19 D3, 20 B9, 25 M2
Banealla SA 71 F6, 73 N12
Bangadilly NP NSW 23 A4, 25 I8, 35 F2
Bangalow NSW 21 G4, 27 O3, 123 N12
Bangerang Vic. 60 H6
Bangham SA 60 B8, 71 G8
Bangor Tas. 143 K7, 145 H7
Baniyala NT 105 M6
Banksia NSW 15 L10
Banksia Beach Qld 114 G1, 117 G7
Banksia Grove WA 84 C3
Bankstown NSW 12 C8, 15 K9
Bannaby NSW 24 H8, 35 F2
Bannerton Vic. 28 F7, 59 J9

Bannister NSW 24 G8, 35 E2
Bannister WA 85 G9, 88 D6
Bannockburn Vic. 42 E7, 63 N7
Banora Point NSW 21 H2, 27 O2, 115 G12, 116 H11, 123 N11
Banyan Vic. 61 I3
Banyena Vic. 61 I9
Bar Beach NSW 18 C9
Barabba SA 67 B2, 69 H4
Baradine NSW 26 D8
Barakee NP NSW 20 B6, 27 J11
Barakula Qld 123 J6
Baralaba Qld 123 I1, 125 L12
Baranduda Vic. 55 K6, 57 I3
Barcaldine Qld 124 D10, 131 P10
Bardon Qld xxx C6
Barellan NSW 24 A7, 29 N7
Barellan Point Qld 114 B8
Barfold Vic. 49 H6, 54 A11, 61 P12, 63 P1
Bargara Qld 118 D2, 123 M3
Bargo NSW 23 D3, 25 J8, 35 G2
Barham NSW 29 I10, 54 A2, 61 O4
Baring Vic. 28 D9, 58 G12, 60 G2
Baringhup Vic. 49 D5, 61 N11, 63 N1
Barjarg Vic. 54 G10, 56 D8
Bark Hut Inn NT 102 H6
Barkers Creek Vic. 49 F6, 54 A10, 61 O11, 63 O1
Barkly Vic. 61 K11
Barkly Homestead NT 107 L9
Barkstead Vic. 42 E2, 49 E9, 63 N3
Barmah Vic. 29 J12, 54 D5
Barmah NP Vic. 29 K11, 54 D4
Barmedman NSW 24 C6, 29 P6
Barmera SA 28 A6, 71 G1, 73 N7
Barmundu Qld 123 K1
Barnadown Vic. 49 H2, 54 B8, 61 P9
Barnard Island Group NP Qld 120 F5, 121 H12, 127 M8
Barnawartha Vic. 24 A12, 29 N12, 55 J6, 56 H2
Barnawartha North Vic. 55 K6, 56 H2
Barnes NSW 29 J12, 54 C5
Barnes Bay Tas. 139 I8, 141 K8
Barongarook Vic. 42 B10, 50 B3, 63 L9
Barongarook West Vic. 42 B9, 50 B2, 63 K8
Barooga NSW 29 L11, 54 G4
Barool NP NSW 21 B8, 27 L5
Baroota SA 73 I3, 74 G11
Barpinba Vic. 42 B7, 63 L7
Barraba NSW 26 H7
Barrakee Vic. 61 L7
Barramunga Vic. 42 B11, 50 C4, 63 L9
Barranyi (North Island) NP NT 105 N10, 107 N1
Barraport Vic. 28 H11, 61 M6
Barringo Vic. 40 B1, 49 H9, 52 B2, 54 B12
Barrington NSW 20 C8, 25 M1, 27 J12
Barrington Tas. 142 H7, 144 G3
Barrington Tops NP NSW 19 C1, 20 A8, 25 L1, 27 I12
Barringun NSW 31 M2, 122 A11, 133 N11
Barron Gorge NP Qld 120 D2, 121 E6, 127 L6
Barrow Creek NT 109 I2
Barry NSW 24 G5, 27 I11
Barrys Reef Vic. 42 F2, 49 F9, 52 A2, 63 O3
Barton ACT 32 D10
Barton Vic. 63 I2
Barunga Gap SA 69 G2, 73 I6
Barunga NT 104 G8
Barwidgee Creek Vic. 55 K8, 56 H5
Barwo Vic. 54 D5
Barwon Downs Vic. 42 C10, 50 C3, 63 L9
Barwon Heads Vic. 42 G9, 44 C6, 50 H2, 52 A7, 63 O8
Baryulgil NSW 21 C6, 27 M4
Basin View NSW 23 C11, 37 O2
Basket Swamp NP NSW 21 B5, 27 L3, 123 L12
Bass Vic. 43 L11, 45 O11, 52 E8
Bass Landing Vic. 45 N11
Bassendean WA xxv C4
Batchelor NT 102 E7, 104 D5
Batchica Vic. 28 E12, 60 H6
Bateau Bay NSW 13 E8, 15 P2
Batehaven NSW 24 H12, 37 L6
Bateman WA xxiv F11
Batemans Bay NSW 24 H12, 35 F6, 37 L6
Bates SA 81 J3
Batesford Vic. 42 F7, 44 A2, 63 N7

147

Binginwarri Vic. 52 H9
Biniguy NSW 26 G4
Binjour Qld 123 K4
Binnaway NSW 26 E10
Binningup WA 86 D2, 88 C8
Binningup Beach WA 86 D2
Binnu WA 89 D11, 90 A2, 92 A12
Binnum SA 60 B9, 71 G8
Binya NSW 29 N7
Birany Birany NT 105 N5
Birchgrove NSW viii D2, x D10
Birchip Vic. 28 F11, 61 J5
Birchs Bay Tas. 138 H9, 141 J9
Birdsville Qld 77 K2, 132 D3
Birdwood NSW 20 E5, 27 L10
Birdwood SA 66 H5, 67 E8, 71 C2, 73 K9
Birdwoodton Vic. 58 G6
Biriwal Bulga NP NSW 20 D6, 27 K11
Birkdale Qld 114 G8, 115 F5, 117 G11
Birralee Tas. 143 J8, 145 E9
Birrego NSW 24 A9, 29 N9
Birregurra Vic. 42 G9, 50 D2, 63 L8
Birriwa NSW 24 H1, 26 E12
Birrong NSW 12 C8, 15 K9
Bishopsbourne Tas. 143 J9, 145 F12
Bittern Vic. 40 E12, 43 J10, 45 K8, 52 D7
Black Bobs Tas. 140 H4
Black Forest SA xx H9
Black Hill SA 71 D2, 73 L8
Black Hill Vic. 47 F4
Black Hills Tas. 138 G3, 141 J6
Black Mountain NP Qld 127 L3
Black Mountain NSW 27 J7
Black River Tas. 142 D4
Black Rock SA 69 E2, 72 H6, 73 J3, 75 I10
Black Springs NSW 24 H6, 26 H12, 27 I5
Black Springs SA 73 K6
Blackall Qld 122 A1, 124 D12, 131 P12, 133 O1
Blackberry Corner Vic. 45 I10
Blackbraes NP Qld 124 B1, 127 I11, 131 N1
Blackbull Qld 126 E8
Blackbutt Qld 118 A12, 123 L8
Blackdown Tableland NP Qld 125 J11
Blackfellow Caves SA 71 F12
Blackheath NSW 14 C4, 16 F6, 25 I6
Blackheath Vic. 60 G8
Blackmans Bay Tas. 139 I7, 141 K8
Blacksmiths NSW 13 G5, 19 C11
Blacktown NSW 12 B5, 15 J7, 25 J6
Blackville NSW 26 G11
Blackwarry Vic. 53 I8
Blackwater Qld 125 J11
Blackwood Creek Tas. 143 J10
Blackwood NP Qld 124 G6
Blackwood SA 66 C9, 67 B10, 68 F3
Blackwood Vic. 42 F2, 49 F10, 52 A2, 63 O3
Bladensburg NP Qld 131 L8
Blair Athol Qld 124 H9
Blairgowrie Vic. 40 B12, 42 H10, 44 F8, 52 B7, 63 P9
Blakeville Vic. 42 E3, 49 E10, 63 N4
Blampied Vic. 42 E2, 49 D9
Blanchetown SA 71 E1, 73 L7
Bland NSW 24 C6
Blandford NSW 26 H11
Blanket Flat NSW 24 G7, 35 D1
Blaxland NSW 14 G6, 17 K10, 25 J6
Blaxlands Ridge NSW 14 H3, 17 O4
Blayney NSW 24 G5
Bleak House Vic. 28 C12, 60 D7
Blessington Tas. 143 L9
Bletchley SA 66 H12, 67 E12
Blewitt Springs SA 66 C11, 67 B11, 68 F4
Bli Bli Qld 117 G3, 118 F11, 123 N7
Blighty NSW 29 K10, 54 E3
Blind Bight Vic. 45 N6
Blinman SA 70 C7, 75 I5
Bloomsbury Qld 119 E6, 125 J4
Blow Clear NSW 24 B5, 29 P5
Blue Lake NP Qld 115 H5, 123 N9
Blue Mountains NP NSW 14 E7, 16 G7, 17 J6, 23 A1, 24 H7, 25 I7, 35 F1
Blue Rocks Tas. 140 B10
Blue Water Springs Roadhouse Qld 120 D10, 124 E1, 127 L11

Bluewater Qld 120 F10, 124 G1, 127 N11
Blueys Beach NSW 20 E10, 25 O3
Bluff Qld 125 J11
Bluff Beach SA 69 D6, 72 H8
Bluff Rock NSW 21 A6, 27 L4
Blyth SA 69 H2, 73 J6
Boallia WA 86 C7
Boambee NSW 20 H1, 21 E12, 27 N8
Boat Harbour NSW 19 G8, 20 C12
Boat Harbour Tas. 142 E4
Boat Harbour Beach Tas. 142 E4
Boatswain Point SA 71 E9
Bobadah NSW 24 B1, 29 O1, 31 N12
Bobbin Head NSW 12 F4, 13 B10, 15 L6
Bobin NSW 20 D7, 25 N1, 27 K12
Bobinawarrah Vic. 55 I8, 56 G5
Bodalla NSW 35 E7, 37 L9
Bodallin WA 88 H3, 90 F6
Boddington WA 85 G10, 88 D7, 90 C8
Bogan Gate NSW 24 D3
Bogangar NSW 21 H3, 27 O2, 123 N11
Bogantungan Qld 124 G11
Boggabilla NSW 26 H2, 123 I11
Boggabri NSW 26 G8
Bogong Vic. 55 L10, 57 K8
Boho Vic. 54 G9, 56 B6
Boho South Vic. 54 G9, 56 C7
Boigbeat Vic. 28 F10, 61 J3
Boinka Vic. 28 C9, 58 E11, 60 E1, 73 P10
Boisdale Vic. 53 K5
Bolgart WA 88 D3, 90 C6
Bolinda Vic. 42 H2, 52 B2
Bolivar SA 66 C3, 67 B6
Bolivia NSW 21 A6, 27 K4
Bollon Qld 122 D9
Bolton Vic. 28 F8, 59 J10
Bolwarra NSW 13 G1, 19 C7, 20 A11
Bolwarrah Vic. 42 E3, 49 E10, 63 N4
Bomaderry NSW 23 D9, 25 I9, 35 G4, 37 O1
Bombala NSW 35 C9, 51 F7
Bombo NSW 23 F7
Bonalbo NSW 21 D4, 27 M3, 123 M12
Bonang Vic. 35 B10, 51 C8
Bonbeach Vic. 43 J7, 45 K3
Bondi NSW ix K8
Bondi Beach NSW ix L8
Bondi Junction NSW ix J8, 12 F8, 15 M9
Bondo NSW 24 E10, 35 B4, 36 E2
Bonegilla Vic. 24 A12, 55 L6, 57 J2
Boneo Vic. 40 C12, 43 I10, 44 H9, 52 C8
Bongaree Qld 114 G2, 115 F1, 117 G8, 123 N8
Bongil Bongil NP NSW 20 H1, 21 E12, 27 M8
Bonnells Bay NSW 13 F5, 19 B11
Bonnie Doon Vic. 54 G11, 56 C9
Bonnie Rock WA 88 G1, 90 E5
Bonny Hills NSW 20 F7, 27 M11
Bonogin Creek Qld 116 D9
Bonogin Qld 116 D9
Bonshaw NSW 27 J3, 123 J12
Bonville NSW 20 H1, 21 D12, 27 M8
Booborowie SA 73 K5, 75 I12
Booderee NP JBT 23 D12, 25 J10, 35 G4, 37 O3
Boodjamulla (Lawn Hill) NP Qld 107 P7, 129 A6
Bookabie SA 81 K7
Bookar Vic. 63 J7
Bookham NSW 24 E9, 35 B3
Boolading WA 88 D8
Boolaroo NSW 13 G3, 19 C9
Boolarra Vic. 43 P10, 52 H8
Boolba Qld 122 E9
Booleroo SA 73 J3, 74 H10
Booleroo Centre SA 73 J3, 74 H10
Boolgun SA 71 F1, 73 M8
Booligal NSW 29 K5
Boomahnoomoonah Vic. 54 H6, 56 E2
Boomi NSW 26 F2, 122 H11
Boonah Qld 21 D1, 27 M1, 115 A9, 123 M10
Boonah Vic. 42 D10, 50 E3, 63 M9
Boonarga Qld 123 J7
Boondall Qld 114 F5, 115 E3, 117 F10
Boonoo Boonoo NSW 21 B4, 27 L3, 123 L12
Boonoo Boonoo NP NSW 21 B4, 27 L3, 123 L12
Boonoonar Vic. 28 E7, 58 G8

Boorabbin NP WA 90 G6
Booragoon WA xxiv F10, 84 D7, 85 C6
Booral NSW 19 F5, 20 B10, 25 M3
Boorcan Vic. 50 G7, 63 I7
Boorhaman Vic. 55 I6, 56 F3
Boorindal NSW 31 M6
Boorongie Vic. 58 H11
Boorongie North Vic. 28 E8, 58 H11
Booroopki Vic. 60 C9, 71 H8
Booroorban NSW 29 J8
Boorowa NSW 24 E8, 35 C2
Boort Vic. 28 H12, 61 M6
Boosey Vic. 54 G5, 56 C1
Booti Booti NP NSW 20 E10, 25 N2
Booval Qld 115 B5, 117 D12
Booyal Qld 118 B3, 123 M4
Boppy Mountain NSW 31 M9
Borallon Qld 114 A7, 115 B4, 117 C11
Boralma Vic. 55 I6, 56 F3
Borambil NSW 25 I1, 26 F12
Borden WA 88 H9, 90 E10
Border Ranges NP NSW 21 E2, 27 N2, 115 B12, 123 M10
Border Store NT 103 P2, 104 H4
Border Village SA 80 C7, 91 P5
Bordertown SA 28 A12, 60 A7, 71 G7
Boree Creek NSW 24 A9, 29 N9
Boree NSW 13 B4, 24 F4, 25 K4
Boreen Point Qld 118 F9, 123 N6
Borenore NSW 24 F4
Boro NSW 24 G10, 35 E4, 37 J2
Boronia Vic. 41 B9, 43 K6, 52 D5
Boronia Heights Qld 114 D10, 115 D6
Bororen Qld 123 L2
Borrika SA 71 F3, 73 M9
Borroloola NT 105 M11, 107 M2
Borung Vic. 28 H12, 61 M7
Boscabel WA 88 E8, 90 D10
Bostobrick NSW 21 C11, 27 M7
Bostock Creek Vic. 50 G7, 63 J8
Botany NSW 12 F9, 15 L10, 25 K7
Botany Bay NP NSW 12 F10, 15 L11, 25 K7
Bothwell Tas. 141 J4
Bouddi NP NSW 13 D9, 15 O4, 25 L6
Bouldercombe Qld 125 M11
Boulia Qld 130 F8
Boulka Vic. 58 H11
Boundain WA 88 F7
Boundary Bend Vic. 50 G7, 59 K9
Bourke NSW 31 M5
Bournda NP NSW 35 E9, 51 H7
Bow NSW 25 J1, 26 G12
Bowan Park NSW 24 F4
Bowden SA xx H3, 65 A3, 66 C7, 67 B8, 68 F2
Bowelling WA 88 D8, 90 C9
Bowen Qld 119 E4, 125 J3
Bowen Hills Qld xxx H5
Bowen Mountain NSW 14 G4, 17 L6
Bowenfels NSW 14 B2, 16 D2
Bowenvale Vic. 49 B5, 61 L11, 63 L1
Bowenville Qld 123 K8
Bower SA 73 L7
Boweya Vic. 54 H7, 56 E3
Bowhill SA 71 E3, 73 L9
Bowling Alley Point NSW 27 I10
Bowling Green Bay NP Qld 119 B2, 120 G11, 124 H1, 127 O12
Bowman Vic. 55 J8, 56 G5
Bowmans SA 69 G4, 71 A1, 73 I7
Bowna NSW 24 B12, 29 O12, 55 L5, 57 K1
Bowning NSW 24 F9, 35 C3
Bowral NSW 23 C5, 25 I8, 35 G2
Bowraville NSW 20 G2, 27 M9
Bowser Vic. 55 I7, 56 F4
Box Hill Vic. 40 E6, 43 J6, 52 D4
Box Tank NSW 30 D11
Boxwood Hill WA 90 F10
Boxwood Vic. 54 G7, 56 C3
Boya WA xxv H3
Boyanup WA 86 E5, 88 C8, 90 C10
Boydtown NSW 35 E10, 51 H8
Boyeo Vic. 28 C12, 60 D7
Boyer Tas. 138 H4, 141 J6
Boykambil Qld 115 F8, 116 E3

149

Boyne Island Qld 123 L1, 125 N12
Boys Town Qld 115 C9
Boyup Brook WA 88 D9, 90 C10
Bracken Ridge Qld 114 E5
Brackendale NSW 20 B4, 27 J10
Bracknell Tas. 143 J9, 145 F12
Braddon ACT 32 D2
Bradvale Vic. 42 A5, 63 K5
Braefield NSW 26 H11
Braemar NSW 23 C4
Braeside Qld 21 A2, 27 L2, 119 E10, 123 L11, 125 J7
Braeside Vic. 45 K2
Braidwood NSW 24 H11, 35 E5, 37 K4
Bramfield SA 72 C5, 74 A12, 81 P12
Brampton Islands NP Qld 119 G6, 125 K5
Bramston Beach Qld 120 E4, 121 H10, 127 M7
Bramwell Junction Roadhouse Qld 128 D6
Brandon Qld 119 B2, 124 H2, 127 O12
Brandy Creek Vic. 41 G12, 43 N8, 52 G6
Branxholm Tas. 143 M7
Branxholme Vic. 62 E5
Branxton NSW 19 A6, 25 L3
Brawlin NSW 24 D8, 35 A2
Bray Junction SA 71 E10
Bray Park Qld 114 E5, 115 D3, 117 F9
Breadalbane NSW 24 G9, 35 E3
Breadalbane Tas. 143 K8, 145 H11
Break O Day Vic. 40 H1, 41 C2, 43 L2, 52 E2, 54 E12
Breakfast Creek NSW 24 F7, 25 I3, 35 C1
Breakwater Vic. 44 B4, 46 G11
Bream Creek Tas. 139 M5, 141 M7
Breamlea Vic. 42 F9, 44 B6, 50 H2, 52 A7, 63 O8
Bredbo NSW 24 F12, 35 C6, 36 G7, 51 F2
Breeza NSW 26 G10
Bremer Bay WA 90 G10
Brentwood SA 69 D7, 72 H9
Brentwood Vic. 28 D11, 60 G5
Brentwood WA xxiv G10
Breona Tas. 143 I10
Bretti NSW 20 C7, 25 M1, 27 K12
Brewarrina NSW 31 O5
Brewongle NSW 24 H5
Brewster Vic. 42 B2, 49 A9, 63 L3
Briagolong Vic. 53 K5
Bribbaree NSW 24 D7, 35 A1
Bribie Island NP Qld 114 G1, 115 F1, 117 G6, 118 F12, 123 N8
Bridge Creek Vic. 54 H10, 56 D9
Bridge Creek NP Qld 127 K2
Bridge Inn Vic. 61 I11, 63 I1
Bridgenorth Tas. 143 J7, 145 F9
Bridgetown WA 86 H8, 88 D9, 90 C10
Bridgewater On Loddon Vic. 49 D2, 61 N9
Bridgewater SA 66 E8, 67 D10, 68 G3, 71 C3, 73 J9
Bridgewater Tas. 139 I3, 141 K6
Bridport Tas. 143 L5
Brigalow Qld 123 J7
Bright Vic. 55 K9, 57 I7
Brighton Qld 114 F5, 115 E3, 117 F9, 123 N9
Brighton SA 66 B9, 67 B10, 68 E3, 69 H8, 73 J9
Brighton Tas. 139 I3, 141 K6
Brighton Vic. 40 D7, 43 J6, 52 C5
Brightwaters NSW 13 F5, 19 B11
Brim Vic. 28 E11, 60 H6
Brimbago SA 28 A11, 71 F7
Brimboal Vic. 62 C2, 71 H10
Brimin Vic. 55 I5, 56 E1
Brimpaen Vic. 60 G11
Brindabella NP NSW 24 E10, 33 A3, 34 A4, 35 C4, 36 F2
Bringagee NSW 29 L7
Bringalbert Vic. 60 C10, 71 H9
Bringelly NSW 14 H9
Brinkin NT xxvii D4
Brinkley SA 67 G12, 73 K10
Brinkworth SA 69 H1, 73 J5
Brisbane Qld xxx G7, 113, 114 E7, 115 D4, 117 F11, 123 N9
Brisbane Airport Qld xxxi M2
Brisbane Ranges NP Vic. 42 F5, 49 F12, 52 A4, 63 N5
Brisbane Water NP NSW 12 G1, 13 C8, 15 M3, 25 K5

Brit Brit Vic. 62 E3
Brittons Swamp Tas. 142 B4
Brixton Qld 124 C10, 131 O10
Broad Arrow WA 90 H4
Broad Sound Islands NP Qld 119 H10, 125 L7
Broadbeach Qld 21 G1, 27 O1, 115 G10, 116 F6
Broadford Vic. 43 J1, 52 D1, 54 D11
Broadmarsh Tas. 138 H2, 141 J6
Broadmeadows Vic. 40 D4, 43 I4, 52 C3
Broadview SA xxi K1
Broadwater NSW 21 G6, 27 O4
Broadwater Vic. 62 F6
Broadwater NP NSW 21 G6, 27 O4
Broadway NSW 10 A12
Brocklehurst NSW 24 F1, 26 C12
Brocklesby NSW 24 A11, 29 N11, 55 J4
Brockman NP WA 86 H11, 87 B3, 88 D11, 90 C11
Brocks Creek NT 102 G10, 104 E6
Brodies Plains NSW 27 J5
Brodribb River Vic. 35 A12, 51 B11
Brogo NSW 35 E8, 37 J12, 51 H5
Broke NSW 13 C1, 25 K3
Broken Hill NSW 30 B10, 73 P1, 75 O8
Bromelton Qld 21 E1, 115 C9
Bromley Vic. 49 C4, 61 M10
Brompton SA xx H2, 65 A2
Bronte NSW ix K9
Bronte Park Tas. 140 H2, 142 H12, 144 H11
Bronzewing Vic. 28 E9, 58 H11, 60 H1
Brook Islands NP Qld 120 F6, 127 M9
Brooker SA 72 D6
Brookfield NSW 19 E5, 20 B10, 25 M3
Brookfield Qld 114 C7, 115 C4, 117 E11
Brooklands Qld 115 C8
Brooklyn NSW 12 G2, 13 C9, 15 M4
Brooklyn Park SA xx E5
Brookside Vic. 55 K10, 57 I7
Brookstead Qld 123 K9
Brookton WA 88 E5, 90 D8
Brookvale NSW 12 G6, 13 C11, 15 M7
Brookville Vic. 53 N3, 57 M12
Brooloo Qld 117 E2, 118 D10
Broome WA 94 H8, 98 A11
Broomehill WA 88 F9, 90 E10
Broomfield Vic. 42 D2, 49 D9, 63 M3
Brooms Head NSW 21 F8, 27 N6
Brooweena Qld 118 C6, 123 M5
Broughton Vic. 28 C12, 60 D6, 71 H7
Broughton Island NSW 20 D11, 25 N3
Broula NSW 24 E6
Broulee NSW 24 H12, 35 F6, 37 L7
Brown Hill Vic. 42 D3, 47 H4, 49 C10
Brown Hill Creek SA xxi M11
Brownlow SA 67 H1, 69 E11, 71 D1, 72 H11, 73 L7
Browns Plains Qld 114 E10, 115 D6
Browns Plains Vic. 55 J6, 56 H2
Bruarong Vic. 55 K8, 57 I5
Bruce SA 73 I2, 74 H9
Bruce Rock WA 88 G4, 90 E7
Brucefield SA 69 E2, 72 H6
Brucknell Vic. 50 F9, 63 I9
Brukunga SA 66 H8, 67 E9
Brungle NSW 24 D10, 35 A4, 36 C1
Brunkerville NSW 13 F3, 19 B9
Brunswick Vic. xv K3, 40 D5, 43 I5, 52 C4
Brunswick East Vic. xv L4
Brunswick Heads NSW 21 H4, 27 O3, 123 N12
Brunswick Junction WA 86 E3, 88 C8
Brunswick West Vic. xv I3
Bruny Island Tas. 138 H11, 141 K10
Brushgrove NSW 20 A1, 21 E8, 27 I8
Bruthen Vic. 53 N5
Bryden Qld 115 A2, 117 C9
Brymaroo Qld 123 K8
Buangor Vic. 63 J3
Buaraba Qld 117 A9
Bucasia Qld 119 G7, 125 K5
Bucca Qld 118 C2, 123 M3
Buccan Qld 114 E11, 115 E7
Buccleuch SA 71 E4, 73 M10
Buchan Vic. 35 A11, 51 A10, 53 P4
Buchan South Vic. 53 O4
Bucheen Creek Vic. 55 N8, 57 M5
Buckenderra NSW 35 B7, 36 E8, 51 D3

Bucketty NSW 13 C4, 25 K4
Buckingham SA 28 A12, 71 G7
Buckingham WA 86 H3, 88 D8
Buckland Tas. 139 M2, 141 M5
Buckland Vic. 55 K10, 56 H8
Buckleboo SA 72 E3, 74 D10
Buckley Vic. 42 E8, 50 F1, 63 N8
Buckrabanyule Vic. 28 G12, 61 L7
Budawang NP NSW 24 H11, 35 F5, 37 L4
Buddabaddah NSW 31 O11
Budderoo NP NSW 23 D7, 25 J9, 35 G3
Buddigower NSW 24 B6, 29 O6
Buddina Qld 117 H4, 118 F12
Buderim Qld 117 G4, 118 F12, 123 N7
Budgeree Vic. 43 P11, 52 H8
Budgeree East Vic. 52 H8
Budgerum Vic. 61 L4
Budgewoi NSW 13 F6, 19 B12
Buffalo Vic. 43 O12, 52 G9
Buffalo Creek Vic. 55 J9, 56 H6
Buffalo River Vic. 55 J9, 56 H6
Bugaldie NSW 26 D9
Bugilbone NSW 26 D5
Bugong NP NSW 23 C8, 25 I9, 35 G3
Builyan Qld 123 L2
Bukalong NSW 35 C9, 51 E6
Bukkulla NSW 27 I5
Bulahdelah NSW 19 H4, 20 C10, 25 N3
Bulart Vic. 62 F3
Buldah Vic. 35 C10, 51 E9
Bulga NSW 25 K3
Bulgandramine NSW 24 E2
Bulgobac Tas. 142 E8, 144 B5
Bulimba Qld xxxi J6
Bull Creek WA xxiv G11, xxv A12
Bulla NT 95 P4, 99 P5, 104 C11, 106 C2
Bulla Vic. 40 C4, 43 I4, 52 B3
Bullaburra NSW 14 E6, 16 H9
Bullarah NSW 26 E4
Bullaring WA 88 F6, 90 E8
Bullarook Vic. 42 D3, 49 D10, 63 M4
Bullarto Vic. 42 F2, 49 F9, 63 N3
Bullarto South Vic. 42 F2, 49 F9
Bullengarook Vic. 42 G3, 49 H10, 52 A2, 63 O4
Bullengarook East Vic. 42 G3, 49 H10, 52 A2
Bulleringa NP Qld 127 I7
Bullfinch WA 88 H2, 90 F6
Bullhead Creek Vic. 55 M8, 57 K4
Bulli NSW 23 G4
Bullioh Vic. 55 M7, 57 L3
Bullock Creek Qld 120 A5, 127 J7
Bullocks Flat NSW 36 D10, 51 B4
Bullsbrook WA 88 E2, 85 C3, 88 C4, 90 C7
Bullumwaal Vic. 53 M4
Bulman NT 105 J6
Buln Buln Vic. 41 H12, 43 N8, 52 G6
Buln Buln East Vic. 41 H12, 43 O8, 52 G6
Bulwer Qld 115 G1, 123 N8
Bulyee WA 88 F5, 90 D8
Bumbaldry NSW 24 E6
Bumberry NSW 24 E4
Bumbunga SA 69 G2, 73 I6
Bunbartha Vic. 29 K12, 54 E6
Bunburra Qld 21 D1, 115 A9
Bunbury WA 86 D4, 88 C8, 90 C9
Bundaberg Qld 118 D2, 123 M3
Bundaburrah NSW 24 D5
Bundalaguah Vic. 53 K6
Bundalong Vic. 29 M12, 54 H5, 56 E1
Bundalong South Vic. 54 H6, 56 E2
Bundanoon NSW 23 A7, 25 I9, 35 G3
Bundarra NSW 27 I7
Bundeena NSW 12 E11, 15 L12, 25 K7
Bundella NSW 26 F10
Bunding Vic. 42 E3, 49 E10, 63 N4
Bundjalung NP NSW 21 F7, 27 O5
Bundook NSW 20 C8, 25 N1, 27 K12
Bundure NSW 29 M9
Bung Bong Vic. 49 A6, 61 L12, 63 L1
Bunga NSW 35 E8, 37 K12
Bungador Vic. 50 A2, 63 K8
Bungal Vic. 42 E4, 49 E11, 63 N5
Bungarby NSW 35 C9, 36 F12, 51 E5
Bungaree Vic. 42 D3, 49 D10, 63 M4

Bungawalbin NP NSW 21 F6, 27 N4
Bungeet Vic. 54 H7, 56 D3
Bungendore NSW 24 G10, 34 H5, 35 D4, 37 I3
Bungil Vic. 24 B12, 55 M6, 57 L2
Bungonia NSW 24 H9, 35 F3
Bungowannah NSW 24 A12, 55 K5, 57 I1
Bungulla NSW 21 A5, 27 L4, 123 L12
Bungulla WA 88 F4
Bunguluke Vic. 28 G12, 61 L6
Bungunya Qld 26 F1, 122 H10
Bungwahl NSW 20 D10, 25 N3
Buninyong Vic. 42 D4, 49 C11, 63 M4
Bunnaloo NSW 29 J11, 54 B3, 61 P5
Bunnan NSW 25 J1, 26 G12
Buntine WA 90 C5
Bunya Mountains NP Qld 123 K7
Bunyah NSW 20 D9, 25 N2
Bunyan NSW 35 C7, 36 G9, 51 F3
Bunyip Vic. 41 E12, 43 M8, 52 F6
Buraja NSW 29 M11, 55 I4
Burbank Qld 115 E5, 117 G12
Burbong NSW 33 H7, 34 G5, 36 H3
Burcher NSW 24 C5, 29 P5
Burekup WA 86 E3, 88 C8
Burgooney NSW 24 A4, 29 N4
Burke & Wills Roadhouse Qld 126 B10, 129 F8
Burkes Flat Vic. 49 A2, 61 L9
Burketown Qld 126 A7, 129 D4
Burleigh Head NP Qld 21 G1, 27 O1, 115 G10, 116 F8, 123 N11
Burleigh Heads Qld 21 G1, 27 O1, 115 G10, 116 F8, 123 N11
Burleigh Waters Qld 116 F8
Burnbank Vic. 49 A7, 61 L12, 63 L2
Burnett Heads Qld 118 D1, 123 M3
Burnie Tas. 142 F5
Burnley Vic. xv O12, xvii O4
Burns WA 84 B3, 85 B4
Burns Creek Tas. 143 L8
Burnside SA xxi O7
Burnt Yards NSW 24 F5
Buronga NSW 58 G6
Burpengary Qld 114 E2, 115 D1, 117 F8, 123 N8
Burra SA 73 K5
Burraboi NSW 29 I10, 54 A1, 61 O2
Burracoppin WA 88 G3, 90 E6
Burradoo NSW 23 B5
Burraga NSW 24 G6
Burragate NSW 51 G8
Burramine South Vic. 54 G5, 56 C1
Burrandana NSW 24 B10, 29 P10, 55 M2
Burrawang NSW 23 C6, 25 I9, 35 G3
Burrell Creek NSW 20 D8, 25 N1, 27 K12
Burren Junction NSW 26 D6
Burrereo Vic. 61 I8
Burrier NSW 23 B9, 37 N1
Burrill Lake NSW 25 I11, 35 G5, 37 N4
Burringbar NSW 21 G3, 27 O2, 123 N11
Burringurrah WA 89 F6, 92 C7
Burrinjuck NSW 24 E9, 35 B3
Burroin Vic. 28 E10, 60 H3
Burrowa–Pine Mountain NP Vic. 24 C12, 29 P12, 36 A7, 55 N6, 57 N2
Burroway NSW 26 B11
Burrowye Vic. 24 C12, 29 P12, 55 N6, 57 M2
Burrum Vic. 61 I9
Burrum Coast NP Qld 118 D3, 123 M4
Burrum Heads Qld 118 E4, 123 N4
Burrumbeet Vic. 42 C2, 49 B9, 63 L3
Burrumbuttock NSW 24 A11, 29 N11, 55 K4
Burswood WA xxiv H5, xxv A6, 84 E6, 85 C5
Burwood NSW 12 D7
Burwood Vic. 43 J6
Bushfield Vic. 50 C7, 62 G8
Bushy Park Tas. 138 F3, 141 I6
Bushy Park Vic. 53 K5
Busselton WA 86 C6, 88 B9, 90 B10
Butchers Ridge Vic. 35 A10, 51 A8, 53 P2, 57 P12
Bute SA 69 F2, 73 I6
Butler Tanks SA 72 E6
Butlers Gorge Tas. 140 G3
Butmaroo NSW 24 G10, 35 D4, 37 I2
Butterleaf NP NSW 21 A7, 27 K5
Buxton NSW 23 D3, 25 I8, 35 G2

Buxton Qld 118 D4, 123 M4
Buxton Vic. 41 F4, 43 N3, 52 F2, 56 B12
Byabarra NSW 20 E6, 27 L11
Byaduk Vic. 62 E5
Byaduk North Vic. 62 E5
Byawatha Vic. 55 J7, 56 G3
Byfield NP Qld 125 N10
Byford WA 84 F9, 85 D7, 88 C5
Bylands Vic. 40 D1, 43 J2, 52 C2, 54 C12
Bylong NSW 25 I2
Bymount Qld 122 F5
Byrne Vic. 55 I8, 56 F5
Byrneside Vic. 54 D7
Byrnestown Qld 118 A5, 123 L4
Byrneville Vic. 60 G8
Byrock NSW 31 N7
Byron Bay NSW 21 H4, 27 O3, 123 N12

Cabarita Vic. 28 D6, 58 G6
Cabarlah Qld 123 L9
Cabawin Qld 123 I8
Cabbage Tree Creek Vic. 35 B12, 51 C11
Caboolture Qld 114 E1, 115 D1, 117 F7, 123 N8
Caboonbah Qld 117 B7, 123 M8
Cabramatta NSW 12 B7, 15 J9, 25 J7, 35 H1
Cabramurra NSW 24 D12, 35 B6, 36 D7, 51 B1
Cadell SA 73 M6
Cadney Homestead SA 79 N7
Cadoux WA 88 E2, 90 D6
Cahills Crossing NT 103 P2, 104 H4
Caiguna WA 91 M7
Caiguna Roadhouse WA 91 M7
Cairns Qld 120 E2, 121 F7, 121 G2, 127 L6
Cairns Bay Tas. 138 F9, 141 I9
Calala NSW 27 I9
Calamvale Qld 114 E9, 115 D6
Calca SA 72 A3, 81 N11
Calder Tas. 142 E5
Caldermeade Vic. 45 P6
Caldwell NSW 29 I10, 54 B2, 61 P4
Calen Qld 119 F7, 125 J5
Calga NSW 13 C8, 15 M3
Calingiri WA 88 C3, 90 C6
Caliph SA 71 F2, 73 N8
Calivil Vic. 61 N7
Callala Bay NSW 23 D10, 25 J10, 35 G4, 37 O2
Callawadda Vic. 61 I10
Calleen NSW 24 B5, 29 O5
Callide Qld 123 J1
Callignee Vic. 53 I8
Callignee North Vic. 53 I8
Callington SA 67 F11, 71 C3, 73 K10
Calliope Qld 123 K1, 125 N12
Caloona NSW 26 E2, 122 G11
Caloote SA 67 H9, 73 K9
Caloundra Qld 117 H5, 118 F12, 123 N8
Caltowie SA 73 J4, 74 H11
Calulu Vic. 53 M5
Calvert Qld 117 B12
Calvert Vic. 63 I3
Camballin WA 95 J7, 98 E11
Cambarville Vic. 41 H5, 43 O4, 52 G3
Camberwell NSW 25 K2
Camberwell Vic. 40 E6, 43 J6
Cambewarra NSW 23 C8, 25 I9, 35 G3
Cambrai SA 67 H6, 71 D2, 73 L8
Cambrian Hill Vic. 42 C4, 49 C11
Cambridge Tas. 1 G2, 139 J5, 141 K7
Camdale Tas. 142 F5
Camden NSW 14 G11, 23 E1, 25 J7, 35 H1
Camden Park SA xx A9
Camena Tas. 144 E1
Camira Qld 114 C9, 115 C6, 117 E12
Camira Creek NSW 21 E7, 27 N4
Cammeray NSW x G6, 11 E1
Camooweal Qld 107 P10, 129 A9, 130 C1
Camooweal Caves NP Qld 107 P10, 129 A9, 130 C1
Camp Coorong SA 71 D5, 73 L12
Camp Hill Qld xxxi J10, 114 E8, 115 E5, 117 F11
Campania Tas. 139 J2, 141 K6
Campbell ACT 32 G6
Campbell Town Tas. 141 L1, 143 L11
Campbells Bridge Vic. 61 I10
Campbells Creek Vic. 49 F6, 61 N12, 63 N1

Campbells Forest Vic. 49 F2, 61 N9
Campbells Pocket Qld 114 C1, 117 E7
Campbelltown NSW 14 H11, 23 F1, 25 J7, 35 H1
Campbelltown SA xxi O1
Campbelltown Vic. 49 D7, 61 M12, 63 M2
Camperdown NSW viii D6
Camperdown Vic. 50 H7, 63 J7
Campwin Beach Qld 119 G8, 125 K6
Camurra NSW 26 G4
Canadian Vic. 42 D3, 47 H9, 49 C10
Canary Island Vic. 61 N6
Canary Island South Vic. 61 M6
Canbelego NSW 31 M9
Canberra ACT 24 F10, 32, 33 E5, 34 E5, 35 D4, 36 H3
Candelo NSW 35 D9, 51 H6
Cangai NSW 21 C7, 27 L5
Cania Gorge NP Qld 123 K2
Caniambo Vic. 54 F8, 56 B4
Cann River Vic. 35 C11, 51 E10
Canna WA 89 F12, 90 B3
Cannawigara SA 28 A12, 60 A6, 71 G7
Cannie Vic. 28 G11, 61 L4
Canning Vale WA xxv C12, 84 E8, 85 C6, 88 C5
Cannington WA xxv D9, 84 E7, 85 C5
Cannon Creek Qld 21 A3, 27 K2, 115 A9
Cannon Hill Qld xxxi L8
Cannons Creek Vic. 45 M6
Cannonvale Qld 119 F5, 125 J3
Cannum Vic. 60 G7
Canomodine NSW 24 F5
Canonba NSW 31 P9
Canoona Qld 125 M10
Canowie SA 73 K4, 75 I12
Canowindra NSW 24 F5
Canteen Creek NT 107 L11, 109 L1
Canterbury NSW 12 E8, 15 L9
Canunda NP SA 71 F11
Canungra Qld 21 F1, 115 E9, 116 A6
Capalaba Qld 114 G8, 115 E5, 117 G12
Cape Arid NP WA 91 J9
Cape Barren Island Tas. 140 B11, 143 O2
Cape Borda SA 69 A11, 72 F11
Cape Bridgewater Vic. 62 D6
Cape Clear Vic. 42 B5, 49 A12, 63 L5
Cape Hillsborough NP Qld 119 G7, 125 K5
Cape Jaffa SA 71 E9
Cape Jervis SA 68 A9, 69 F10, 71 A5, 73 I11
Cape Le Grand NP WA 91 I9
Cape Melville NP Qld 127 K1, 128 G11
Cape Nelson NP Vic. 62 D8
Cape Palmerston NP Qld 119 H9, 125 K6
Cape Paterson Vic. 43 L12, 52 E9
Cape Range NP WA 89 B3
Cape Schanck Vic. 44 H10
Cape Tribulation Qld 121 E1, 127 L4
Cape Upstart NP Qld 119 C3, 125 I2, 127 P12
Cape Woolamai Vic. 43 K11, 45 M11, 52 D8
Capel WA 86 D5, 88 B9, 90 C10
Capella Qld 125 I9
Capels Crossing Vic. 61 N4
Capertee NSW 25 I4
Capietha SA 72 B2, 74 A10, 81 O10
Capital Hill ACT 32 B10
Capoompeta NP NSW 21 A7, 27 K4
Capricorn Coast NP Qld 125 N10
Capricorn Roadhouse WA 92 E5, 97 L11
Capricornia Cays NP Qld 123 M1, 125 P11
Captain Billy Landing Qld 128 D4
Captains Flat NSW 24 G11, 34 G9, 35 D5, 37 I5
Carabost NSW 24 C11, 29 P11, 36 A4, 55 O4
Caragabal NSW 24 D6
Caralue SA 72 E4, 74 D12
Caralulup Vic. 49 B7, 61 L12, 63 L2
Caramut Vic. 62 H6
Carapooee Vic. 61 K9
Carapook Vic. 62 D3
Carawa SA 72 A1, 81 N9
Carbeen Qld 120 D3, 121 D8
Carboor Vic. 55 J9, 56 G6
Carboor Upper Vic. 55 J9, 56 G6
Carbunup River WA 86 B7
Carcoar NSW 24 G5
Cardiff NSW 13 G3, 19 C9
Cardigan Village Vic. 42 C3, 49 B10, 63 L3

151

Cardinia Vic. 40 H10, 41 C12, 43 L8, 45 O5, 52 E6
Cardross Vic. 58 G6
Cardstone Qld 120 D5, 127 L8
Cardwell Qld 120 E7, 127 M9
Cargerie Vic. 42 D5, 49 D12, 63 M5
Cargo NSW 24 F5
Carilla WA 84 G7
Carina Qld xxxi M10
Carina Heights Qld xxxi L11
Carinda NSW 26 A6
Carindale Qld xxxi N12, 114 F8
Carine WA xxiv B1
Caringbah NSW 12 D10, 15 K11
Carisbrook Vic. 49 C6, 61 M11, 63 M1
Carlingford NSW 12 D6, 15 K7
Carlisle WA xxv C7
Carlisle River Vic. 42 A11, 50 A4, 63 K9
Carlsruhe Vic. 42 G1, 49 H8, 52 A1, 54 A12, 63 O3
Carlton Tas. 139 L5, 141 L7
Carlton Vic. xv K9, xvii J1, 39 E2
Carlton North Vic. xv K7
Carlwood NSW 24 H5
Carmel WA 84 G6
Carmila Qld 119 G10, 125 K7
Carnamah WA 90 B4
Carnarvon WA 89 B7
Carnarvon NP Qld 122 E2
Carnegie Homestead WA 93 I8
Carngham Vic. 42 B3, 49 A10, 63 L4
Caroline SA 62 A5, 71 G12
Carool NSW 116 E11
Caroona NSW 26 G10
Carpa SA 69 A2, 72 F5
Carpendeit Vic. 50 H8, 63 J8
Carpenter Rocks SA 71 F12
Carrabin WA 88 H3
Carrai NP NSW 20 D3, 27 L9
Carrajung Vic. 53 I8
Carrajung South Vic. 53 J8
Carranballac Vic. 63 J4
Carraragarmungee Vic. 55 I7, 56 G4
Carrathool NSW 29 L7
Carrick Tas. 143 J8, 145 F11
Carrickalinga SA 68 C7, 69 G9, 71 B4, 73 I10
Carrieton SA 73 J2, 75 I9
Carrington NSW 18 B2, 19 F7, 20 C11
Carroll NSW 26 G9
Carron Vic. 28 F12, 61 I7
Carrum Vic. 40 E9, 43 J8, 45 K3, 52 D6
Carrum Downs Vic. 40 F9, 43 J8, 45 L3, 52 D6
Carseldine Qld 114 E5, 115 D3, 117 F10
Carwarp Vic. 28 E7, 58 G7
Cascade WA 90 H9
Cascade NP NSW 21 C11, 27 M7
Cascades Tas. 137 C9
Cashmore Vic. 62 D7
Casino NSW 21 B5, 27 N3, 123 M12
Cassilis NSW 25 I1, 26 F12
Cassilis Vic. 53 M2, 55 M12, 57 M12
Castella Vic. 40 H3, 41 C5, 43 L3, 52 E3
Casterton Vic. 62 C3, 71 H11
Castle Cove NSW x H2
Castle Forbes Bay Tas. 138 F8, 141 I8
Castle Hill NSW 12 D5, 13 A11, 15 K7
Castle Rock NSW 25 K2
Castle Tower NP Qld 123 L1, 125 N12
Castleburn Vic. 53 L4
Castlecrag NSW x H4
Castlemaine Vic. 49 F6, 61 N12, 63 N1
Castlereagh NSW 14 G5, 17 M8
Casuarina NT xxvii E4
Casula NSW 12 B8, 15 I9
Cataby Roadhouse WA 88 B2, 90 B6
Catamaran Tas. 141 I11
Catani Vic. 43 M9
Cathcart NSW 35 D9, 51 F7
Cathcart Vic. 63 I2
Cathedral Rock NP NSW 20 E1, 21 A12, 27 L8
Catherine Hill Bay NSW 13 F5, 19 C11, 25 L5
Cathkin Vic. 43 M1, 52 F1, 54 F11, 56 A10
Cathundral NSW 26 A11
Cattai NP NSW 12 B1, 15 J4, 25 K6
Cattai NSW 12 B1, 15 J4
Catumnal Vic. 28 G12, 61 L6
Caulfield Vic. 40 E6, 43 J6, 52 C5

Caulfield North Vic. xvii O11
Caveat Vic. 54 E11, 56 A9
Cavendish Vic. 62 F3
Caversham WA xxv D1
Caveside Tas. 142 H9, 144 H6, 145 A11
Cawdor NSW 14 G11, 23 E1
Cawongla NSW 21 F4, 27 N3, 123 N12
Cecil Park NSW 12 A7, 15 I8
Cecil Plains Qld 123 K9
Cedar Bay NP Qld 127 L3
Cedar Brush Creek NSW 13 D5
Cedar Grove Qld 115 D8
Ceduna SA 81 M8
Centennial Park NSW ix I8
Central Castra Tas. 142 G7, 144 F2
Central Colo NSW 15 I2, 17 P2, 25 J5
Central Mangrove NSW 13 C6, 15 N1, 25 K5
Central Tilba NSW 35 E8, 37 K10
Centreville Vic. 45 L4
Ceratodus Qld 123 K4
Ceres NSW 24 E1, 26 B12
Ceres Vic. 42 F8, 50 G1, 63 N7
Cervantes WA 88 A2, 90 A5
Cessnock NSW 13 E2, 19 A8, 25 L4
Chaelundi NP NSW 21 C9, 27 M6
Chain Valley Bay NSW 13 F6, 19 B11
Chakola NSW 35 C7, 36 G8, 51 F2
Challis WA 84 F8
Chandada SA 72 B2, 81 O10
Chandler SA 79 L4
Chandlers Creek Vic. 35 C11, 51 E9
Chapel Hill Qld xxx A9, 114 D7
Chapman Hill WA 86 C7, 88 B9
Chapple Vale Vic. 50 A4, 63 K10
Charam Vic. 60 D10
Chardons Bridge Qld 116 B2
Charles Darwin NT xxvii D9
Charles Darwin NP NT xxvii E8, 102 D3, 104 D4
Charleston SA 66 G7, 67 E9, 68 H2, 73 K9
Charlestown NSW 13 G4, 19 C10
Charleville Qld 122 B5, 133 P5
Charlotte Pass NSW 35 A8, 36 C10, 51 B4
Charlton NSW 24 H6, 31 O6
Charlton Vic. 28 G12, 61 K7
Charnocks Crossing NSW 116 C12
Charringa Qld 120 E3, 121 F8
Charters Towers Qld 124 F2
Chasm Creek Tas. 142 F5
Chatsbury NSW 24 H8, 35 E2
Chatswood NSW x F3, 12 F6, 13 B11, 15 L8
Chatswood West NSW x D3
Chatsworth NSW 21 F7, 27 N5
Chatsworth Vic. 60 H5
Cheepie Qld 133 M6
Cheesemans Creek NSW 24 F4
Chelmer Qld xxx C11
Chelsea Vic. 40 E8, 43 J7, 45 K2, 52 D6
Chelsea Heights Vic. 45 K2
Cheltenham NSW 12 D5, 13 A11
Cheltenham SA 67 B8, 68 E1
Cheltenham Vic. 40 E7, 43 J7, 45 J1, 52 C5
Chepstowe Vic. 42 B3, 49 A10, 63 L4
Cherbourg Qld 118 A9, 123 L6
Cherokee Vic. 42 H2, 52 B2
Cheshunt Vic. 55 I10, 56 F7
Chesney Vale Vic. 54 H7, 56 D4
Chesterton Range NP Qld 122 D5
Chetwynd Vic. 60 D12, 62 D2, 71 H10
Chewton Vic. 49 F6, 54 A10, 61 O12, 63 O1
Cheyne Beach WA 87 G10, 88 H11, 90 F11
Chidlow WA 84 H4, 85 E4
Chigwell Tas. 137 A3
Childers Qld 118 C4, 123 M4
Childers Vic. 43 O10, 52 G7
Chillagoe Qld 120 A3, 127 J6
Chillagoe Mungana Caves NP Qld 120 A3, 127 J6
Chillingham NSW 21 G2, 115 E12
Chillingollah Vic. 28 F9, 59 J12, 61 J1
Chilpanunda SA 72 A2, 81 O10
Chiltern Valley Vic. 55 J6, 56 G2
Chiltern Vic. 29 N12, 55 J6, 56 H2
Chiltern–Mt Pilot NP Vic. 24 A12, 29 N12, 55 J7, 56 G3
Chinaman Wells SA 69 D5, 71 E7, 72 H7

Chinbingina SA 72 A1, 81 N8
Chinchilla Qld 123 J7
Chinderah NSW 21 H2, 27 O2, 115 G12, 116 H12, 123 N11
Chinkapook Vic. 28 F9, 59 J11, 61 J1
Chippendale NSW viii E6
Chiswick NSW viii A1, x A9
Chittering WA 85 D1, 88 C4
Chorregon Qld 124 A8, 131 M8
Christie Downs SA 67 A11, 68 E4
Christies Beach SA 66 A10, 67 A11, 68 E4
Christmas Creek Qld 120 C9, 127 K11
Christmas Hills Tas. 142 C4
Christmas Hills Vic. 40 G4, 41 B6, 43 K4
Chudleigh Tas. 142 H8, 145 B11
Church Point NSW 12 H4, 13 C10, 15 N6
Churchill Qld 114 A9, 115 B6, 117 D12
Churchill Vic. 52 H8
Churchill Island Vic. 43 K11, 45 M11
Churchill NP Vic. 40 F7, 41 A10, 43 K7, 45 M1, 52 D5
Churchlands WA xxiv C4
Chute Vic. 42 A1, 63 K2
Chuwar Qld 114 B8, 115 B5, 117 D12
City Beach WA xxiv B5
Clackline WA 85 F3, 88 D4
Clairview Qld 119 H11, 125 L8
Clandulla NSW 25 I3
Clapham SA xxi J12
Clare Qld 119 B3, 120 H12, 124 H2
Clare SA 69 H2, 73 J6
Claremont Tas. xxxiv A1, 137 B2, 139 I4, 141 K6
Claremont Vic. 55 I9, 56 F6
Claremont WA xxiv C7, 84 C6, 85 B5, 88 B5
Claremont Isles NP Qld 128 F10
Clarence NSW 14 C2, 16 E2, 25 I5
Clarence Gardens SA xx H10
Clarence Park SA xx H9
Clarence Point Tas. 143 J6, 145 E6
Clarence Town NSW 19 E6, 20 B11, 25 M3
Clarendon NSW 15 I5, 17 O7
Clarendon Qld 117 B10
Clarendon SA 66 C10, 67 B11, 68 F4, 69 H8, 71 B3, 73 J9
Clarendon Tas. 143 K9, 145 H12
Clarendon Vic. 42 D4, 49 D11, 63 M5
Clarkefield Vic. 40 B2, 42 H3, 52 B2, 63 P4
Clarkes Hill Vic. 42 D3, 49 D10, 63 M3
Clarkson WA 84 B3
Claude Road Tas. 142 G8, 144 G4
Clay Wells SA 71 F10
Clayfield Qld xxxi J3
Clayton Qld 118 D2
Clayton SA 68 H8, 71 C4, 73 K11
Clayton Vic. 40 E7, 43 J6
Clear Lake Vic. 60 E10
Clear Ridge NSW 24 C5, 29 P5
Cleland SA xxi P10
Clematis Vic. 40 H7, 41 C10, 43 L7, 45 O1
Clermont Qld 119 B12, 124 H9
Cleve SA 69 A1, 72 F5
Cleveland Qld 114 H8, 115 F5, 117 H12, 123 N9
Cleveland Tas. 143 L10
Cliff Island NP Qld 128 F10
Clifton NSW 23 G3, 27 K3, 123 K12
Clifton Qld 123 L10
Clifton Beach Qld 120 D2, 121 F6, 127 L6
Clifton Beach Tas. 139 K7, 141 L8
Clifton Creek Vic. 53 M5
Clifton Gardens NSW ix J1, xi J9
Clifton Hill Vic. xv N7, 40 D5
Clifton Springs Vic. 42 G8, 44 D4, 52 A6, 63 O7
Clinton Centre SA 69 F4, 71 A1, 73 I7
Clintonvale Qld 21 B1, 27 L1, 123 L10
Clonbinane Vic. 43 J2, 52 D2, 54 D12
Cloncurry Qld 129 F11, 130 H3
Clontarf NSW xi K5
Clontarf Qld 123 K10
Closeburn Qld 114 C5, 115 C3, 117 E10
Clouds Creek NSW 21 C10, 27 M7
Clovelly NSW ix K10
Clovelly Park SA 67 B9, 68 F3
Cloven Hills Vic. 63 J6
Cloverdale WA xxv D6
Cloyna Qld 118 A8, 123 L6

Cluan Tas. 143 J9, 145 E11
Club Terrace Vic. 35 B11, 51 D10
Cluden Qld 119 A1, 120 G10, 124 G1
Clump Mountain NP Qld 120 E5, 127 M8
Clunes NSW 21 G4, 27 O3, 123 N12
Clunes Vic. 42 C1, 49 C8, 63 M2
Clybucca NSW 20 G4, 27 M9
Clyde Vic. 40 G9, 41 B12, 43 K8, 45 M4, 52 D6
Clyde North Vic. 45 N4
Clyde River NP NSW 24 H12, 35 F6, 37 L6
Clydebank Vic. 53 L6
Clydesdale Vic. 49 E7, 61 N12
Coal Creek Qld 117 B8
Coalcliff NSW 23 G3
Coaldale NSW 21 D7, 27 M5
Coalstoun Lakes Qld 118 A5, 123 L5
Coalstoun Lakes NP Qld 118 A5, 123 L5
Coalville Vic. 43 P9, 52 H7
Cobains Vic. 53 K7
Cobaki NSW 116 F11
Cobar NSW 31 L9
Cobargo NSW 35 E8, 37 K10
Cobaw Vic. 42 H1, 52 B1, 54 B12
Cobbadah NSW 26 H7
Cobbannah Vic. 53 L4
Cobboboonee NP Vic. 62 C6
Cobbora NSW 24 G1, 26 D12
Cobden Vic. 50 G8, 63 J8
Cobdogla SA 28 A6, 71 F1, 73 N7
Cobera SA 28 A7, 71 F2, 73 N9
Cobram Vic. 29 L12, 54 F4
Cobrico Vic. 50 G7, 63 I8
Cobungra Vic. 53 M1, 55 M12, 57 L10
Coburg Vic. xv J1, 40 D5, 43 I5
Cocamba Vic. 28 F9, 59 J11
Cochranes Creek Vic. 49 B2, 61 L9
Cockaleechie SA 72 D7
Cockatoo Vic. 40 H7, 41 D10, 43 L7, 45 P1, 52 E5
Cockburn SA 30 A10, 73 O1, 75 N8
Cockle Creek Tas. 141 I11
Cocklebiddy WA 91 M6
Coconut Grove NT xxvii B5
Cocoparra NP NSW 29 M6
Codrington Vic. 62 E7
Coen Qld 128 E10
Coffin Bay SA 72 D8
Coffin Bay NP SA 72 C8
Coffs Harbour NSW 20 H1, 21 E12, 27 N8
Coghills Creek Vic. 42 C2, 49 B9, 63 M3
Cohuna Vic. 29 I11, 54 A3, 61 O5
Coimadai Vic. 42 G4, 49 G11, 52 A3, 63 O4
Colac Colac Vic. 36 A8, 55 O7, 57 N4
Colac Vic. 42 B9, 50 B2, 63 L8
Colbinabbin Vic. 54 C8
Colbinabbin West Vic. 54 C8
Coldstream Vic. 40 H5, 41 C7, 43 L5, 52 E4
Coleambally NSW 29 M8
Colebrook Tas. 139 J1, 141 K5
Coledale NSW 23 G3
Coleraine Vic. 62 E3
Coles Bay Tas. 141 O3
Colignan Vic. 28 E7, 58 H8
Colinroobie NSW 24 A7, 29 N7
Colinton NSW 24 F12, 34 D12, 35 C6, 36 G7, 51 F1
Collarenebri NSW 26 D4
Collaroy NSW 25 I1, 26 F12
Collaroy Plateau NSW 12 H5, 13 C11, 15 N7
Collector NSW 24 G9, 35 D3
College Park SA xxi K4
Collendina Vic. 44 D6
Collerina NSW 31 O4
Colley SA 72 B3, 81 O11
Collie NSW 26 B10
Collie WA 86 G3, 88 D8, 90 C9
Collie Burn WA 86 G4
Collie Cardiff WA 86 H4, 88 D8
Collier Range NP WA 89 H6, 92 E7
Collingullie NSW 24 B9, 29 O9
Collingwood Vic. xv M9, xvii M1
Collins Cap Tas. 138 H5
Collinsfield SA 69 G1, 73 I5
Collinsvale Tas. 138 H4, 141 J7
Collinsville Qld 119 C5, 125 I4
Collinswood SA xxi J1

Collombatti Rail NSW 20 G4, 27 M10
Colly Blue NSW 26 G10
Colo NSW 15 I2, 17 P3, 25 J5
Colo Heights NSW 15 I1, 17 O1, 25 J5
Colo Vale NSW 23 C4, 25 I8, 35 G2
Colonel Light Gardens SA xxi I11
Colquhoun Vic. 53 O5
Colton SA 72 B5, 74 A12, 81 P12
Comara NSW 20 E3, 27 L9
Comaum SA 60 B12, 62 B1, 71 G10
Combara NSW 26 C9
Combienbar Vic. 35 C11, 51 D9
Comboyne NSW 20 E6, 27 L11
Come-By-Chance NSW 26 C6
Comet Qld 125 I11
Como NSW 12 D10, 15 K10, 23 H1
Como WA xxiv G8, xxv A9
Compton Downs NSW 31 N6
Conara Tas. 141 L1, 143 L10
Conargo NSW 29 K10, 54 E1
Concord NSW 12 D7, 15 K8
Condah Vic. 62 E5
Condamine Qld 123 I7
Condingup WA 91 J9
Condobolin NSW 24 B3, 29 P3
Condong NSW 21 G2, 27 O2, 115 F12
Condowie SA 69 G2, 73 J5
Congo NSW 35 F7, 37 L8
Congupna Vic. 54 E7, 56 A3
Conimbla NP NSW 24 E6
Coningham Tas. 139 I8, 141 K8
Coniston NSW 22 C11, 23 F5
Conjola NSW 23 B12, 25 I11, 35 G5, 37 N3
Conjola NP NSW 23 B12, 25 I10, 35 G5, 37 N3
Conmurra SA 71 F9
Connangorach Vic. 60 F10
Connellys Marsh Tas. 139 L5, 141 L7
Connemarra NSW 26 F10
Conondale Qld 117 D4, 118 D12, 123 M7
Conondale NP Qld 117 C4, 118 D11, 123 M7
Conway Beach Qld 119 F5, 125 J4
Conway NP Qld 119 F5, 125 J4
Coober Pedy SA 76 A10, 79 O10
Coobowie SA 69 E8, 72 H9
Coochin Creek Qld 117 F5, 118 E12
Cooee Tas. 142 F5
Coogee NSW ix J12
Coogee WA 84 C8
Coojar Vic. 62 E2
Cook SA 80 F4
Cookamidgera NSW 24 E4
Cookardinia NSW 24 B11, 29 O11, 55 M3
Cooke Plains SA 71 D4, 73 L10
Cooks Gap NSW 24 H2
Cooks Hill NSW 18 D7, 19 D9
Cooktown Qld 127 L3
Cookville Tas. 139 I11, 141 K10
Coolabah NSW 31 N8
Coolac NSW 24 D9, 35 A3
Cooladdi Qld 122 A6, 133 N6
Coolah NSW 26 F11
Coolah Tops NP NSW 26 F11
Coolalie NSW 24 F9, 35 C3
Coolalinga NT 102 E3
Coolamon NSW 24 B8, 29 O8
Coolana Qld 117 B11
Coolangatta Qld 21 H2, 27 O1, 115 G11, 116 G10, 123 N11
Coolatai NSW 27 I4, 123 I12
Coolbellup WA xxiv E12
Coolbinia WA xxiv F3
Coolcha SA 71 D3, 73 L9
Coolgardie WA 90 H5
Coolimba WA 90 A5
Coolongolook NSW 20 D9, 25 N2
Cooltong SA 28 A5, 58 A5, 73 O7
Coolum Beach Qld 117 G3, 118 F11, 123 N7
Coolup WA 85 D10, 88 C7
Cooma NSW 35 C7, 36 G9, 51 E3
Cooma Tas. 140 B11
Cooma Vic. 54 D7
Cooma West NSW 35 C7, 36 G9, 51 E3
Coomalbidgup WA 90 H9
Coomandook SA 71 E4, 73 L11

Coomba NSW 20 E10, 25 N2
Coombabah Qld 116 E4
Coombah Roadhouse NSW 28 C2, 75 O11
Coombe SA 71 F6, 73 M12
Coombell NSW 21 E5, 27 N4
Coomberdale WA 88 B1, 90 C5
Coomera Qld 115 F8, 116 D3
Coominya Qld 117 B10, 123 M9
Coomoora Vic. 42 E1, 49 E8, 63 N3
Coonabarabran NSW 26 E9
Coonalpyn SA 71 E5, 73 M11
Coonamble NSW 26 C8
Coonarr Qld 118 D2, 123 M3
Coonawarra NT xxvii F8
Coonawarra SA 60 A12, 62 A2, 71 G10
Coonerang NSW 35 C8, 36 G10, 51 F4
Coongie Lakes NP SA 77 M5, 132 E6
Coongulla Vic. 53 J5
Coongulmerang Vic. 53 L5
Coonong NSW 29 M9
Coonooer Bridge Vic. 61 K8
Coopernook NSW 20 E8, 25 O1, 27 L12
Coopers Creek Vic. 53 I6
Cooplacurripa NSW 20 C6, 27 K11
Coopracambra NP Vic. 35 C11, 51 F9
Coorabakh NP NSW 20 E7, 25 O1, 27 L12
Coorabie SA 81 J8
Cooran Qld 118 E10, 123 N6
Cooranbong NSW 13 E4, 19 A10, 25 L4
Cooranga North Qld 123 K7
Coorong NP SA 68 H9, 71 D6, 73 K11
Coorow WA 90 B4
Cooroy Qld 117 F1, 118 E10, 123 N7
Coorparoo Qld xxxi M11, 114 E7, 115 D4, 117 F11
Cootamundra NSW 24 D8, 35 A2
Cooya Beach Qld 120 D1, 121 D3, 127 L5
Cooyal NSW 24 H2
Cooyar Qld 123 L8
Copacabana NSW 13 D9, 15 O4
Cope Cope Vic. 61 J8
Copeland NSW 20 B8, 25 M1, 27 J12
Copeville SA 71 E2, 73 M9
Copley SA 70 B4, 75 I4
Copmanhurst NSW 21 D8, 27 M5
Coppabella Qld 119 D10, 125 I7
Copping Tas. 139 M5, 141 M7
Coppins Crossing ACT 33 C5, 34 D5, 36 G3
Cora Lynn Vic. 41 D12, 43 M8, 52 E6
Corack East Vic. 28 F12, 61 J6
Corack Vic. 28 F12, 61 J7
Coragulac Vic. 42 A8, 50 B1, 63 K8
Coraki NSW 21 F6, 27 O4, 123 N12
Coral Bank NSW 55 L9, 57 J6
Coral Bay WA 89 B5
Coram Vic. 42 B9, 50 B2, 63 L8
Coramba NSW 21 D11, 27 M7
Corang NSW 24 H10, 35 F4, 37 L2
Corattum SA 71 F12
Cordalba Qld 118 C3, 123 M4
Cordering WA 88 E8
Coreen NSW 29 M11, 55 I4
Corfield Qld 124 A6, 131 M6
Corinda Qld 114 D8, 129 B4
Corindhap Vic. 42 C5, 63 L6
Corindi NSW 21 E10, 27 N7
Corindi Beach NSW 21 E10, 27 N7
Corinella Vic. 43 L10, 45 N9, 52 E8
Corinna Tas. 142 C8
Corio Vic. 42 F7, 44 B2, 52 A6, 63 O7
Corlette NSW 19 G7
Corner Store Qld 30 B1, 77 N11, 132 F10
Cornwall Tas. 143 O9
Corny Point SA 69 C7, 72 G9
Corobimilla NSW 29 N8
Coromby Vic. 60 H8
Coronation Beach WA 89 D12, 90 A3
Coronet Bay Vic. 43 L11, 45 O10, 52 E8
Corop Vic. 54 C7
Cororooke Vic. 42 A9, 50 B1, 63 K8
Corowa NSW 29 M12, 55 I5, 56 F1
Corra Linn Tas. 143 K8, 145 H10
Corrigin WA 88 F5, 90 E8
Corrimal NSW 22 F1, 23 G4
Corringle NSW 24 C5, 29 P5
Corroboree Park Tavern NT 102 G5, 104 E5

153

Corryong Vic. 36 A8, 55 O7, 57 O3
Corunna NSW 37 L10
Cosgrove Vic. 54 F7, 56 B3
Cosmo Newbery WA 91 I1, 93 I11
Cossack WA 89 F1, 92 B2, 94 B12, 96 E4
Costerfield Vic. 54 C9
Cottan–Bimbang NP NSW 20 C5, 27 K10
Cottesloe WA xxiv B9, 84 C7, 85 B5
Cottles Bridge Vic. 41 A6, 43 K4
Cottonvale Qld 21 A3, 27 L2, 123 L11
Couangalt Vic. 40 A2, 42 H3, 49 H10, 52 B3, 63 P4
Cougal NSW 21 E2, 27 N2, 115 C12
Coulson Qld 115 A8
Coulta SA 72 D7
Countegany NSW 35 D7, 37 I9, 51 G3
Couridjah NSW 23 D2
Couta Rocks Tas. 142 A5
Coutts Crossing NSW 21 D9, 27 M6
Cow Bay Qld 121 E2, 127 L4
Cowabbie West NSW 24 A8, 29 O8
Cowan NSW 12 F2, 13 B9, 15 M5, 25 K6
Cowan Cowan Qld 115 G1
Cowandilla SA xx F6
Cowangie Vic. 28 C9, 58 D11, 60 D1, 73 P10
Cowaramup WA 86 B8, 88 B9
Cowell SA 69 B1, 72 G5
Cowes Vic. 43 K11, 45 L10, 52 D8
Cowley Beach Qld 120 F5, 127 M8
Cowleys Creek Vic. 50 G9, 63 J9
Cowper NSW 21 E8, 27 N5
Cowra NSW 24 F6
Cowwarr Vic. 53 J6
Coyrecup WA 88 G8
Crabbes Creek NSW 21 G3, 27 O2, 123 N11
Crabtree Tas. 138 G6, 141 J7
Cracow Qld 123 I4
Cradle Mountain–Lake St Clair NP Tas. 140 F1, 142 F10, 144 D7
Cradle Valley Tas. 142 F9, 144 D6
Cradoc Tas. 138 G8, 141 J8
Cradock SA 73 J1, 75 I8
Crafers West SA xxi O12
Craigie NSW 35 C10, 51 E8
Craigie Vic. 49 C6, 61 M12, 63 M1
Craigieburn Vic. 40 D3, 43 I4, 52 C3
Craiglie Qld 120 D1, 121 D4, 127 L5
Cramenton Vic. 28 E8, 58 H9
Cramps Tas. 141 I1, 143 I10
Cranbourne Vic. 40 G9, 41 A12, 43 K8, 45 M4, 52 D6
Cranbourne North Vic. 45 M3
Cranbourne South Vic. 40 F9, 41 A12, 43 K8, 45 L4, 52 D6
Cranbourne West Vic. 45 M4
Cranbrook Tas. 141 N2, 143 N12
Cranbrook WA 88 F10, 90 E10
Crater Lakes NP Qld 120 D3, 121 E9, 127 L7
Craven NSW 19 G2, 20 C9, 25 M2
Cravensville Vic. 55 N8, 57 M5
Crawford Qld 118 A10, 123 L7
Crawley WA xxiv E7
Crayfish Creek Tas. 142 D4
Creek Junction Vic. 54 G9, 56 C7
Creighton Vic. 54 E9, 56 A7
Cremorne NSW x H7
Cremorne Tas. 139 K6, 141 L8
Cremorne Vic. xvii M5
Cremorne Point NSW ix I1, xi I9
Crescent Head NSW 20 G5, 27 M10
Cressy Tas. 143 K9
Cressy Vic. 42 B7, 63 L6
Crestmead Qld 114 E10, 115 D6
Creswick Vic. 42 D2, 49 C9, 63 M3
Crib Point Vic. 40 F12, 43 J10, 45 L8, 52 D7
Croajingolong NP Vic. 35 C12, 51 E11
Croftby Qld 21 D1, 27 M1, 123 M10
Cronulla NSW 12 E11, 15 L11, 25 K7
Crooble NSW 26 H4, 123 I12
Crooked River Vic. 53 K3
Crookwell NSW 24 G8, 35 E2
Croppa Creek NSW 26 H3, 123 I12
Crossdale Qld 115 A1, 117 C8, 123 M8
Crossley Vic. 50 B7, 62 G8

Crossover Vic. 41 H12, 43 O8, 52 G6
Crowdy Bay NP NSW 20 F7, 25 O1, 27 L12
Crowlands Vic. 61 J12, 63 J1
Crows Nest NSW x G7, 11 B1
Crows Nest Qld 123 L8
Crows Nest NP Qld 123 L8
Crowther NSW 24 E7, 35 B1
Croxton East Vic. 62 F5
Croydon NSW 15 L9
Croydon Qld 126 F8
Croydon SA xx G2, 67 B8, 68 F2
Croydon Vic. 40 G6, 41 B8, 43 K5
Croydon Park SA xx G1
Crymelon Vic. 28 E12, 60 G6
Cryon NSW 26 D5
Crystal Brook SA 73 I4, 74 H12
Cuballing WA 88 E6, 90 D8
Cubbaroo NSW 26 E6
Cucania Qld 120 E3, 121 G9
Cuckoo Tas. 143 M7
Cudal NSW 24 F4
Cuddell NSW 29 N8
Cudgee Vic. 50 D8, 62 H8
Cudgen NSW 115 G12, 116 H12
Cudgera Creek NSW 21 H3
Cudgewa Vic. 36 A8, 55 O7, 57 N3
Cudgewa North Vic. 36 A7, 55 O6, 57 N3
Cudmirrah NSW 23 C12, 37 O3
Cudmore NP Qld 124 F9
Cue WA 89 H10, 90 D1, 92 D11
Culbin WA 88 E7
Culburra NSW 23 E10, 25 J10, 35 H4, 37 P1
Culburra SA 71 E5, 73 M12
Culcairn NSW 24 B11, 29 O11, 55 L4
Culgoa Vic. 28 F10, 61 K4
Culgoa NP NSW 26 A2, 31 P2, 122 C11, 133 P11
Culgoa Floodplain NP Qld 26 A2, 31 P2, 122 C11, 133 P11
Cullacabardee WA 84 D4
Cullen Bullen NSW 25 I5
Cullendulla NSW 24 H12, 37 M6
Culloden Vic. 53 K5
Cullulleraine Vic. 28 C6, 58 E6, 73 P7
Cumberland Park SA xx H10
Cumborah NSW 26 B4
Cummins SA 72 D7
Cumnock NSW 24 F3
Cundeelee WA 91 J5
Cunderdin WA 88 E4, 90 D7
Cundletown NSW 20 E8
Cungena SA 72 B2, 81 O9
Cungulla Qld 119 B1, 120 H11, 124 H1, 127 O12
Cunjurong NSW 37 N3
Cunliffe SA 69 E3, 72 H6
Cunnamulla Qld 122 A9, 133 N9
Cunnawarra NP NSW 20 D2, 21 A12, 27 K8
Cunningar NSW 24 E8, 35 B2
Cunningham Qld 21 A1, 27 K1, 123 K10
Cunningham SA 69 E5, 72 H7
Cunninyeuk NSW 28 H9, 59 N12, 61 N1
Cuprona Tas. 142 F6
Curara WA 85 F11, 88 D7, 89 E12, 90 B3
Curban NSW 26 C10
Curdie Vale Vic. 50 E9, 63 I9
Curl Curl NSW xi O1
Curlewis NSW 26 G9
Curlewis Vic. 44 C4
Curlwaa NSW 28 D5, 58 G5
Currabubula NSW 26 H10
Currambine WA 84 B3
Curramulka SA 69 E6, 72 H8
Currarong NSW 23 E11, 25 J10, 35 H4, 37 P2
Currawang NSW 24 G10, 35 E4, 37 J1
Currawarna NSW 24 B9, 29 O9
Currawinya NP Qld 31 I1, 133 L10
Currency Creek SA 68 G7, 71 C4, 73 J10
Currie Tas. 141 O11
Currowan Creek NSW 24 H12, 35 F6, 37 L5
Currumbin Qld 21 H2, 27 O1, 115 G11, 116 F9, 123 N11
Currumbin Beach Qld 116 G9
Currumbin Waters Qld 116 F10
Curtin Springs NT 108 F10
Curtis Island NP Qld 125 N11

Curyo Vic. 28 F11, 61 I5
Custon SA 28 B12, 60 B7, 71 G7
Cuttabri NSW 26 E6
Cygnet River SA 69 D11, 72 H11
Cygnet Tas. 138 G8, 141 J9
Cynthia Qld 123 K4

Daceyville NSW viii G12
Dadswells Bridge Vic. 60 H10
Daglish WA xxiv D6
D'Aguilar NP Qld 114 A1, 115 B1, 117 D7
Dagaragu NT 106 D5
Dahlen Vic. 60 G9
Dahwilly NSW 29 J10, 54 D1
Daintree Qld 121 D2, 127 L4
Daintree NP Qld 120 C1, 121 B2, 127 K4
Daisy Dell Tas. 142 G8, 144 E5
Daisy Hill Qld 114 F9, 115 E6
Daisy Hill Vic. 49 B6, 61 M12, 63 M1
Dajarra Qld 130 F5
Dakabin Qld 114 E3, 115 D2, 117 F9
Dalbeg Qld 119 B4, 124 H3
Dalby Qld 123 K8
Dalgety NSW 35 B8, 36 E11, 51 D4
Dalkeith WA xxiv D8
Dallarnil Qld 118 B4, 123 M4
Dalmalee Vic. 28 D11, 60 G5
Dalmeny NSW 35 F7, 37 L9
Dalmore Vic. 45 O5
Dalmorton NSW 21 B9, 27 L6
Dalrymple NP Qld 120 E12, 124 F2, 127 M12
Dalton NSW 24 F9, 35 D3
Dalveen Qld 21 A2, 27 L2, 123 L11
Dalwallinu WA 88 D1, 90 C5
Daly River NT 102 C12, 104 D7
Daly Waters NT 104 H12, 106 H3
Dalyellup WA 88 C8
Dalyston Vic. 43 L12, 45 P12, 52 E9
Dalyup WA 91 I9
Dampier WA 89 E1, 92 B2, 94 B12, 96 D5
Dandaloo NSW 24 D1, 26 A12, 31 P12
Dandaragan WA 88 B2, 90 B6
Dandenong Vic. 40 F8, 41 A10, 43 K7, 45 L1, 52 D5
Dandenong North Vic. 45 L1
Dandenong Ranges NP Vic. 40 G6, 41 B8, 43 K6, 45 N1, 52 D5
Dandenong South Vic. 45 L2
Dandongadale Vic. 55 J10, 56 G8
Dangarfield NSW 25 K1, 26 H12
Dangarsleigh NSW 20 B1, 27 J8
Dangin WA 88 E5
Danyo Vic. 28 C9, 58 D11, 60 D1, 71 H4, 73 P10
Dapto NSW 23 F5
Darby Falls NSW 24 F6
Darbyshire Vic. 55 M6, 57 L3
Dardadine WA 88 E8
Dardanup WA 86 E4, 88 C8
Dareton NSW 28 D5, 58 G5
Dargo Vic. 53 L3
Dargo High Plains Vic. 53 L1
Dark Corner NSW 24 H5
Darkan WA 88 E8, 90 D9
Darke Peak SA 72 E5, 74 D12
Darkwood NSW 20 F1, 21 C12, 27 M8
Darley Vic. 42 G4, 49 G11, 52 A3, 63 O4
Darling Harbour NSW 10 B9
Darlinghurst NSW viii G6, 10 G10
Darlington NSW viii E7
Darlington Point NSW ix I5, xi I12, 29 M7
Darlington Tas. 139 P2, 141 N5
Darlington Vic. 63 J6
Darlington WA 84 G5, 85 D4
Darnick NSW 28 H2
Darnum Vic. 43 O9, 52 G7
Daroobalgie NSW 24 D4
Darr Qld 124 B9, 131 N9
Darra Qld 114 D8, 115 D5, 117 E12
Darraweit Guim Vic. 40 D1, 43 I2, 52 C2, 54 C12
Darriman Vic. 53 J9
Dart Dart Vic. 28 D12, 60 G7
Dartmoor Vic. 62 C5, 71 H12
Dartmouth Qld 124 C10, 131 O10
Dartmouth Vic. 55 M9, 57 L6

Darwin NT xxvii C10, 101, 102 C3, 104 D4
Dattuck Vic. 28 E10, 60 G3
Davenport Range NP (Proposed) NT 107 K11, 109 K1
Davidson NSW 12 F5, 15 M7
Davis Creek NSW 25 L2
Davies Creek NP Qld 120 D3, 121 E7, 127 L6
Davistown NSW 13 D8, 15 O4
Daw Park SA xx H12
Dawes Qld 123 J2
Dawes Point NSW viii F3, x F10, 10 C2, 11 D11
Dawson SA 73 K3, 75 J10
Dawson Vic. 53 J6
Dawsons Hill NSW 25 L2
Dayboro Qld 114 C3, 115 C2, 117 E8
Daylesford Vic. 42 E1, 49 E8, 63 N3
Daymar Qld 26 E1, 122 G11
Daysdale NSW 29 M11, 55 I3
Daytrap Vic. 28 F9, 59 J12, 61 J1
Daytrap Corner Vic. 28 F9, 59 I12, 61 I2
Deakin ACT 32 A12
Deakin WA 80 C4, 91 P4
Dean Vic. 42 D2, 49 D9, 63 M3
Deanmill WA 86 H10, 87 B1, 88 D10
Deans Marsh Vic. 42 C10, 50 D3, 63 M8
Deception Bay Qld 114 E3, 115 E2, 117 F8, 123 N8
Deddick Vic. 35 A10, 51 B7
Deddington Tas. 143 L9
Dederang Vic. 55 L8, 57 J5
Dee Lagoon Tas. 140 H3
Deep Lead Vic. 61 I11
Deepwater NSW 27 K5
Deepwater NP Qld 123 M2
Deer Park Vic. 40 B5, 42 H5, 52 B4, 63 P5
Deeral Qld 120 E3, 121 G9, 127 M7
Delacombe Vic. 47 A10
Delamere SA 68 B9, 69 G10, 71 A5, 73 I11
Delaneys Creek Qld 117 E6
Delatite Vic. 43 P1, 52 H1, 54 H11, 56 D10
Delburn Vic. 43 P10, 52 H8
Delegate NSW 35 C10, 51 D7
Delegate River Vic. 35 B10, 51 D8
Dellicknora Vic. 35 B10, 51 C8
Deloraine Tas. 143 I8, 145 C10
Delta Qld 119 D4, 125 J3
Delungra NSW 27 I5
Denham WA 89 B9
Denham Group NP Qld 128 E4
Denicull Creek Vic. 63 I2
Deniliquin NSW 29 J10, 54 D2
Denison Vic. 53 J6
Denman NSW 25 J2
Denman SA 80 E4
Denmark WA 87 A11, 88 F11, 90 E11
Dennes Point Tas. 139 I7, 141 K8
Dennington Vic. 50 C8, 62 G8
D'Entrecasteaux NP WA 86 E11, 87 A3, 88 C11, 90 C11
Denver Vic. 42 F1, 49 F8, 52 A1, 54 A12, 63 O2
Deptford Vic. 53 N4
Derby Tas. 143 N6
Derby Vic. 49 E2, 61 N9
Derby WA 95 I7, 98 D9
Dereel Vic. 42 C5, 49 B12, 63 L5
Dergholm Vic. 62 C2, 71 H10
Dering Vic. 28 D9, 58 G12, 60 G2
Deringulla NSW 26 E10
Derrinal Vic. 54 B9, 61 P11
Derrinallum Vic. 63 J6
Derriwong NSW 24 C3, 29 P3
Derwent Bridge Tas. 140 G2, 142 G12, 144 F11
Derwent Park Tas. xxxiv D6, 1 A1, 137 C5
Detpa Vic. 28 D12, 60 F6
Deua NP NSW 24 G12, 35 D7, 37 K7, 51 H1
Devenish Vic. 54 G7, 56 C3
Deviot Tas. 143 J7, 145 F7
Devon Vic. 53 I9
Devon Meadows Vic. 45 M5
Devon Park SA xx H1
Devondale Vic. 50 H11, 63 J10
Devonport Tas. 142 H6, 144 H1, 145 B2
Dewars Pool WA 85 F1, 88 C4
Dharug NP NSW 13 B7, 15 L2, 25 K5

Dhulura NSW 24 B9, 29 P9
Dhuragoon NSW 29 I9, 59 O12, 61 O1
Diamantina NP Qld 130 H10, 131 I10
Diamond Beach NSW 20 E9, 25 O2
Diamond Creek Vic. 40 F4, 41 A6, 43 K4
Dianella WA xxiv G2, xxv A3, 84 D5, 85 C5
Diapur Vic. 28 C12, 60 D7
Diddleum Plains Tas. 143 L7
Digby Vic. 62 D5
Diggers Rest Vic. 40 B3, 42 H4, 52 B3, 63 P4
Diggora Vic. 54 B7, 61 P8
Dilston Tas. 143 K7, 145 G8
Dimboola Vic. 60 F8
Dimbulah Qld 120 C3, 121 B8, 127 K6
Dingee Vic. 54 A7, 61 O8
Dingley Village Vic. 45 K1
Dingo Qld 125 K11
Dingwall Vic. 28 H11, 61 M5
Dinmont Vic. 42 B11, 50 B4, 63 K10
Dinner Plain Vic. 53 L1, 55 L11, 57 K10
Dinninup WA 88 D9
Dinoga NSW 26 H6
Dinyarrak Vic. 28 B12, 60 B7, 71 H7
Dipperu NP Qld 119 E10, 125 J7
Direk SA 66 C3, 67 B6
Dirk Hartog Island WA 89 B8
Dirk Hartog NP WA 89 B8
Dirranbandi Qld 26 C1, 122 E10
Dixie Vic. 50 F7, 63 I8
Dixons Creek Vic. 40 H4, 41 C6, 43 L4, 52 E3
Djukbinj NP NT 102 G4, 104 E4
Dobie Vic. 63 J2
Docker Vic. 55 I8, 56 F5
Docklands Vic. xiv G11, xvi G2, 39 A8
Doctors Flat Vic. 53 N2, 57 M12
Dodges Ferry Tas. 139 L5, 141 L7
Don Junction Tas. 145 A1
Don Tas. 142 H6, 144 H1, 145 A6
Don Valley Vic. 41 E8, 43 M5
Donald Vic. 28 F12, 61 J7
Doncaster Vic. 40 E5, 43 J5, 52 D4
Dongara–Denison WA 90 A4
Donnybrook Qld 117 G7
Donnybrook Vic. 40 D3, 43 J3, 52 C3
Donnybrook WA 86 F5, 88 C9, 90 C10
Donovans Landing SA 62 B6, 71 G12
Doo Town Tas. 139 N8, 141 M8
Dooboobetic Vic. 61 K8
Doodlakine WA 88 F4, 90 E7
Dooen Vic. 60 G9
Dookie Vic. 54 F7, 56 B3
Doomadgee Qld 129 C5
Doomben Qld 115 E4, 117 F11
Doonside NSW 12 A5, 15 I7, 17 P11
Dooragan NP NSW 20 F7, 25 O1, 27 L12
Dooralong NSW 13 D5
Dopewora Vic. 60 C9, 71 H8
Dora Creek NSW 13 E5, 19 B10
Dorodong Vic. 60 B12, 62 B2, 71 H10
Dorrien SA 67 F4
Dorrigo NSW 20 G1, 21 C12, 27 M8
Dorrigo NP NSW 20 G1, 21 D12, 27 M8
Double Bay NSW ix I6
Doubleview WA xxiv B3
Douglas Qld 119 A1, 120 G10
Douglas Apsley NP Tas. 141 O1, 143 O10
Douglas Daly Tourist Park NT 102 G12, 104 E7
Douglas Park NSW 23 E2
Douglas Vic. 60 E11
Dover Tas. 138 F10, 141 J10
Dover Heights NSW ix M6
Doveton Vic. 45 M1
Dowerin WA 88 E3, 90 D6
Dowlingville SA 69 F4, 71 A1, 73 I7
Dowsings Point Tas. xxxiv D4, 137 C4
Doyalson NSW 13 F6, 19 B12, 25 L5
Drake NSW 21 C5, 27 L3, 123 L12
Dreeite Vic. 42 A8, 63 K7
Drik Drik Vic. 62 C6, 71 H12
Drillham Qld 123 I6
Dripstone NSW 24 G2
Dromana Vic. 40 D11, 43 I10, 45 I7, 52 C7
Dromedary Tas. 138 H3, 141 J6
Dropmore Vic. 54 E11

Drouin Vic. 43 N8, 52 F6
Drouin South Vic. 43 N9, 52 F7
Drouin West Vic. 41 G12, 43 N8, 52 F6
Drovers Cave NP WA 88 A1, 90 A5
Drumborg Vic. 62 D6
Drumcondra Vic. 44 B3, 46 D2
Drummartin Vic. 54 A7, 61 O8
Drummond Vic. 42 F1, 49 F7, 52 A1, 54 A11, 63 O2
Drummond Cove WA 89 D12, 90 A3
Drummoyne NSW viii B1, x A9, 12 E7, 13 B12, 15 L8
Drung Drung Vic. 60 G9
Drung Drung South Vic. 60 G10
Dry Creek SA 66 C5, 67 B8, 68 F1
Dry Creek Vic. 54 G10, 56 C8
Dryander NP Qld 119 E4, 125 J3
Drysdale Vic. 40 A9, 42 G8, 44 D4, 52 A6, 63 O7
Drysdale River NP WA 95 M3, 99 J3
Duaringa Qld 125 K11
Dubbo NSW 24 F1, 26 C12
Dublin SA 69 G5, 71 B1, 73 J8
Duchess Qld 129 D12, 130 F5
Duckenfield NSW 13 G1, 19 D7
Duddo Vic. 28 C9, 58 D11, 71 H4, 73 P10
Dudinin WA 88 G6, 90 E8
Dudley Vic. 43 L12, 52 E9
Dudley Park SA xx H1, 66 C6
Duffholme Vic. 60 E9
Duffys Forest NSW 12 F4, 13 B10, 15 M6
Dulacca Qld 122 H6
Dularcha NP Qld 117 F5, 118 E12, 123 N7
Dulcie Range NP NT 109 L4
Dulcot Tas. 137 H3
Dulguigan NSW 116 E12
Dululu Qld 125 L12
Dulwich SA xxi L6
Dumbalk Vic. 43 O12, 52 G9
Dumberning WA 88 E7, 90 E9
Dumosa Vic. 28 G11, 61 K5
Dunach Vic. 49 B7, 61 M12, 63 M2
Dunalley Tas. 139 M6, 141 M7
Dunbogan NSW 20 F7
Dundas Qld 115 A2, 117 C9, 123 M9
Dundas Tas. 142 D10
Dundee NSW 27 K5
Dundee Beach NT 102 A5, 104 C5
Dundonnell Vic. 63 I5
Dundurrabin NSW 21 C11, 27 L7
Dunedoo NSW 24 H1, 26 E12
Dungay NSW 116 D12
Dungog NSW 19 E4, 20 B10, 25 M2
Dungowan NSW 27 I10
Dunk Island Qld 120 F6, 127 M8
Dunkeld NSW 24 G5
Dunkeld Vic. 62 G4
Dunluce Vic. 49 B4, 61 L11
Dunmarra NT 104 H12, 106 H3
Dunneworthy Vic. 61 J12, 63 J2
Dunnstown Vic. 42 D3, 49 D10, 63 M4
Dunolly Vic. 49 C4, 61 M10
Dunoon NSW 21 G4, 27 O3
Dunorlan Tas. 142 H8, 145 B10
Dunrobin Vic. 62 C3, 71 H11
Dunsborough WA 86 B6, 88 B9, 90 B10
Dunwich Qld 115 G5, 123 N9
Dural NSW 12 D4, 13 A10, 15 K6
Duranillin WA 88 E8, 90 D9
Durdidwarrah Vic. 42 E5, 63 N5
Durham Lead Vic. 42 D4, 49 C11, 63 M5
Durham Ox Vic. 28 H12, 61 N6
Duri NSW 26 H10
Duroby Creek NSW 116 F12
Durong Qld 123 K6
Durran Durra NSW 24 H11, 35 E5, 37 K3
Durras NSW 25 I12, 35 F6, 37 M6
Dutson Vic. 53 K7
Dutton SA 67 G3, 71 D1, 73 K7
Dutton Park Qld xxx G9
Duverney Vic. 42 B6, 63 L6
Dwarda WA 85 H10
Dwellingup WA 85 E10, 88 C7, 90 C8
Dwyers NSW 31 M6
Dynnyrne Tas. 1 A10, 136 C12, 137 D9

156

Fairlies Knob NP Qld 118 C5, 123 M5
Fairlight NSW xi M4
Fairneyview Qld 115 A4, 117 C11
Fairview Vic. 28 G12, 61 K6
Fairy Dell Vic. 54 C7
Fairy Hill NSW 21 E4, 27 N3
Fairy Meadow NSW 22 F4, 23 F4
Falls Creek NSW 23 C10, 25 I10, 35 G4, 37 O1
Falls Creek Vic. 55 L10, 57 K8
Falmouth Tas. 143 O9
Family Islands NP Qld 120 F6, 127 M8
Fannie Bay NT xxvii B8
Faraday Vic. 49 F6, 54 A10, 61 O12, 63 O1
Farleigh Qld 119 G7, 125 K5
Farnborough Qld 125 M10
Farnham NSW 24 G3
Farrell Flat SA 73 K6
Faulconbridge NSW 14 F5, 17 K9
Fawcett Vic. 52 F1, 54 F11, 56 B10
Fawkner Vic. 40 D5, 43 I5, 52 C4
Feilton Tas. 138 F4, 141 I6
Felton East Qld 123 K9
Fentonbury Tas. 138 E2, 141 I5
Fentons Creek Vic. 49 A1, 61 L9
Fenwick Vic. 44 C5
Ferguson Vic. 42 A11, 50 B4, 63 K10
Fern Hill Vic. 42 G2, 49 G9, 52 A2, 54 A12
Fern Tree Tas. 137 A10, 139 I6, 141 K7
Fern Tree Bower Tas. 137 A10
Fernbank Vic. 53 L5
Ferndale NSW 24 A11, 29 N11, 55 J3
Ferndale WA xxv C10, 86 G7
Ferndene Tas. 142 G6, 144 E1
Fernhill NSW 22 D2
Fernihurst Vic. 61 M7
Fernlees Qld 125 I11
Ferntree Creek NP Qld 117 F3, 118 E11, 123 N7
Ferntree Gully Vic. 40 G7, 41 B9, 43 K6, 52 D5
Fernvale Qld 115 A4, 117 C10, 123 M9
Ferny Glen Qld 116 A7
Ferny Grove Qld 114 D6, 115 D4, 117 E10
Ferny Hills Qld 115 D3, 117 E10
Fiery Flat Vic. 61 M8
Fifield NSW 24 C2
Fig Tree NSW 24 F4
Fig Tree Pocket Qld xxx A12, 114 D8
Figtree NSW 22 A10, 23 F5
Figtree Creek Qld 120 E3, 121 G9
Finch Hatton Qld 119 E7, 125 J5
Findon SA xx D2
Fingal Tas. 143 N9
Fingal Vic. 44 H9
Fingal Bay NSW 19 H8, 20 C12
Fingal Head NSW 116 H11
Finke NT 109 J10
Finke Gorge NP NT 108 H7, 110 C6
Finley NSW 29 L11, 54 F3
Finniss SA 68 H7, 71 C4, 73 K10
Finucane Island NP Qld 126 A7, 129 E4
Firle SA xxi N3
Fish Creek Vic. 52 G10
Fish Point Vic. 28 H10, 61 M2
Fisher SA 80 G4
Fishermans Paradise NSW 23 B12, 37 N3
Fishery Falls Qld 120 E3, 121 G9, 127 M6
Fiskville Vic. 42 F4, 49 F11, 63 N5
Fitzgerald Tas. 138 D3, 140 H6
Fitzgerald River NP WA 90 F10
Fitzroy SA xxi I2, 65 C2
Fitzroy Vic. xv L9, xvii L1
Fitzroy Crossing WA 95 K8, 98 H11
Fitzroy Island NP Qld 120 E2, 121 H7, 127 M6
Fitzroy North Vic. xv M6
Five Ways NSW 24 A10, 29 O10, 31 O11, 55 L2
Five Ways Vic. 45 L10
Fiveways Vic. 45 M5
Flaggy Rock Qld 119 G10, 125 K7
Flagstaff Gully Tas. 137 F6
Flagstone Creek Qld 118 C1, 123 M3
Flat Tops NSW 19 E5, 20 B10
Flaxton Qld 117 F3
Flemington Vic. xiv F6
Fletcher Qld 21 A4, 27 K3

Flinders Vic. 43 I11, 45 I10, 52 C8
Flinders Chase NP SA 69 A12, 72 F12
Flinders Group NP Qld 128 G10
Flinders Island Tas. 140 B10, 143 P1
Flinders Park SA xx E3
Flinders Ranges NP SA 70 C8, 75 I6
Flinton Qld 122 H9
Flintstone Tas. 141 J1, 143 J11
Floreat WA xxiv C5, 84 C6, 85 B5
Florida NSW 31 M9
Florida WA 85 B10, 88 B6, 90 B8
Florieton SA 73 L6
Flowerdale Tas. 142 E4
Flowerdale Vic. 41 B2, 43 K2, 52 D2, 54 D12
Flowerpot Tas. 138 H9, 141 K9
Flowery Gully Tas. 143 J7, 145 E7
Flying Fish Point Qld 120 E4, 121 H11, 127 M7
Flying Fox Qld 21 F1, 115 E10
Flynn Vic. 53 J7
Flynns Creek Vic. 53 I7
Footscray Vic. xiv C8, xvi D1, 40 D5, 43 I5, 52 C4
Forbes Islands NP Qld 128 E6
Forbes NSW 24 D4
Forcett Tas. 139 L4, 141 L7
Fords SA 67 E3
Fords Bridge NSW 31 L4
Fordwich NSW 25 K3
Forest Den NP Qld 124 D7, 131 P7
Forest Glen NSW 12 D1, 13 A9, 15 K4
Forest Glen Qld 117 G4, 118 F12
Forest Grove WA 86 B9, 88 B10
Forest Hill NSW 24 C10, 29 P10, 55 N1
Forest Hill Qld 117 A11
Forest Lake Qld 114 D9, 115 D6
Forest Lodge NSW viii D6
Forest Reefs NSW 24 G5
Forest Tas. 142 D4
Forester Tas. 143 M6
Forestville SA xx H8
Forge Creek Vic. 53 M6
Formartin Qld 123 K8
Forrest ACT 32 B11
Forrest Beach Qld 120 F8, 127 M10
Forrest Vic. 42 B10, 50 C3, 63 L9
Forrest WA 80 A5, 91 O4
Forrestdale WA 84 E8
Forrestfield WA xxv F7, 84 F6
Forreston SA 66 G5, 67 E7, 68 H1
Forsayth Qld 126 H9
Forster SA 71 D2, 73 L8
Forster–Tuncurry NSW 20 E9, 25 O2
Fort Lytton NP Qld 114 F6, 115 E4, 117 G11, 123 N9
Fortescue Roadhouse WA 89 E2, 92 A3, 96 C6
Forth Tas. 142 G6, 144 G1
Fortis Creek NP NSW 21 D7, 27 M5
Fortitude Valley Qld xxx H6, 113 G1
Forty Mile Scrub NP Qld 120 B6, 127 K8
Foster Vic. 52 G9
Fosterville Vic. 49 H3, 54 B8, 61 P10
Fountain Gate Vic. 45 M2
Fountaindale NSW 13 D7, 15 O2
Four Mile Creek Tas. 143 O9
Fowlers Bay SA 81 J8
Fox Ground NSW 23 E8, 25 J9, 35 H3
Fox Trap Roadhouse Qld 122 A6, 133 N6
Foxeys Hangout Vic. 45 J7
Foxhow Vic. 42 A7, 63 K6
Framlingham Vic. 50 E7, 62 H7
Framlingham East Vic. 62 H7
Frampton NSW 24 D8, 35 A2
Frances SA 60 B9, 71 G8
Francistown Tas. 138 F10, 141 I9
Francois Peron NP WA 89 B8
Frank Hann NP WA 90 G8
Frankford Tas. 143 I7, 145 E8
Frankland WA 87 G1, 88 F10, 90 D11
Frankland Group NP Qld 120 F3, 121 H9, 127 M7
Franklin Tas. 138 G7, 141 J8
Franklinford Vic. 42 E1, 49 E7, 63 N2
Franklin–Gordon Wild Rivers NP Tas. 138 A1, 140 G4, 142 E12, 144 D11
Frankston Vic. 40 E9, 43 J8, 45 K4, 52 D6
Frankton SA 67 H2, 71 D1, 73 K7

Fraser Island Qld 118 H4, 123 O4
Frederickton NSW 20 G4, 27 M10
Freeburgh Vic. 55 K10, 57 J7
Freeling SA 67 D4, 71 C1, 73 K8
Freemans Reach NSW 12 A1, 15 I4, 17 O6, 25 J6
Freestone Qld 21 B1, 27 L1
Fregon SA 79 I4
Fremantle WA xxiv C11, 84 C8, 85 B6, 88 B5, 90 B8
French Island NP Vic. 40 G12, 43 K10, 45 N8, 52 E7
Frenchs Forest NSW 12 F5, 13 B11, 15 M7, 25 K6
Freshwater Creek Vic. 42 E9, 50 G2, 63 N8
Freshwater NP Qld 114 E3, 115 D1, 117 F8, 123 N8
Frewville SA xxi L8
Freycinet NP Tas. 141 O3, 143 O12
Frogmore NSW 24 F7, 35 C1
Fryerstown Vic. 49 F7, 54 A11, 61 O12, 63 O2
Fulham SA xx C5
Fulham Vic. 53 K7
Fulham Gardens SA xx C4
Fullarton SA xxi L8
Fullerton NSW 24 G7, 35 E1
Fumina Vic. 43 P7, 52 G5
Furner SA 71 F10
Furnissdale WA 85 C9, 88 C6
Fyansford Vic. 42 F8, 44 A3, 50 G1, 63 N7
Fyshwick ACT 33 F6, 34 E5, 36 H3

Gaffneys Creek Vic. 43 P3, 52 H3
Gagebrook Tas. 139 I3, 141 K6
Galah Vic. 28 D8, 58 G11
Galaquil Vic. 28 E11, 60 H5
Galaquil East Vic. 60 H5
Galga SA 71 E2, 73 M8
Galiwinku NT 105 L3
Gallanani Qld 117 A8
Gallangowan Qld 117 A1, 118 C10, 123 M7
Galong NSW 24 E8, 35 B2
Galston NSW 12 D3, 13 A10, 15 K5, 25 K6
Gama Vic. 28 E10, 60 H3
Ganmain NSW 24 B8, 29 O8
Gapsted Vic. 55 J8, 56 H5
Gapuwiyak NT 105 L4
Garah NSW 26 F3, 122 H12
Garbutt Qld 119 A1, 120 G10, 124 G1
Garden Island Creek Tas. 138 H9, 141 J9
Gardens of Stone NP NSW 25 I4
Gardners Bay Tas. 138 G9, 141 J9
Garema NSW 24 D5
Garfield Vic. 41 E12, 43 M8, 52 F6
Garfield North Vic. 41 E11, 43 M8, 52 F6
Gargett Qld 119 F7, 125 J5
Garibaldi Vic. 42 D4, 49 C12, 63 M5
Garig Gunak Barlu NP NT 104 F2
Garigal NP NSW x H1, xi I1, 12 F5, 13 B11, 15 M7, 25 K6
Garra NSW 24 F4
Garrthalala NT 105 N5
Garvoc Vic. 50 E7, 63 I8
Gary Junction WA 93 K3
Gascoyne Junction WA 89 D7, 92 A8
Gatton Qld 123 L9
Gatum Vic. 62 E2
Gaven Qld 116 D4
Gawler SA 66 E2, 67 D5, 71 C2, 73 J8
Gawler Tas. 142 G6, 144 F1
Gawler Ranges NP SA 72 C1, 74 B9, 81 P9
Gayndah Qld 123 L5
Gaythorne Qld xxx E2
Geebung Qld 114 E6
Geehi NSW 35 A8, 36 B10, 51 A4, 55 P8, 57 P5
Geelong Vic. 42 F8, 44 B4, 46, 50 G1, 52 A6, 63 O7
Geelong East Vic. 44 B4, 46 H8
Geelong North Vic. 44 B3, 46 C1
Geelong South Vic. 44 A4, 46 E9
Geelong West Vic. 46 C4
Geeralying WA 88 E7
Geeveston Tas. 138 F8, 141 I9
Geikie Gorge NP WA 95 L7, 98 H11
Geilston Bay Tas. xxxiv H6, 1 D2, 137 F6
Gelantipy Vic. 35 A10, 51 A8, 53 P2, 57 P12
Gellibrand Vic. 42 A10, 50 B3, 63 K9
Gelliondale Vic. 53 I9

157

Gelorup WA 86 D4
Gembrook Vic. 41 D10, 43 M7, 52 E5
Gemtree NT 109 J5
Genoa Vic. 35 D11, 51 G10
George Town Tas. 143 J6, 145 E6
Georges Creek Vic. 55 M6, 57 K3
Georges Heights NSW xi K8
Georges Plains NSW 24 H5
Georges River NP NSW 12 C9, 15 J10, 23 H1,
   25 K7, 35 H1
Georgetown Qld 126 H9
Georgetown SA 73 J4, 74 H12
Georgica NSW 21 F4, 27 N3
Geraldton WA 89 D12, 90 A3
Gerang Gerung Vic. 28 D12, 60 F7
Gerangamete Vic. 42 C10, 50 C3, 63 L9
Geranium SA 71 F4, 73 M10
Geranium Plain SA 73 K6
Germantown Vic. 55 K10, 57 I7
Gerogery NSW 24 A12, 29 O12, 55 L5
Gerogery West NSW 24 A12, 29 O12, 55 L5
Gerringong NSW 23 F8, 25 J9, 35 H3
Gerroa NSW 23 E8
Geurie NSW 24 F2
Gheringhap Vic. 42 E7, 63 N7
Ghin Ghin Vic. 43 L1, 52 E1, 54 E11
Ghin-Doo-Ee NP NSW 19 H3, 20 C9, 25 M2
Gibraltar Range NP NSW 21 B7, 27 L5
Gibson WA 91 I9
Gibsonvale NSW 24 A5, 29 O5
Gidgegannup WA 84 H3, 85 E4, 88 C4
Gidginbung NSW 24 C7, 29 P7
Giffard Vic. 53 K8
Gilbert River Qld 126 G8
Gilbert Spring NT 110 B5
Gilberton SA xxi K2, 65 G3
Gilberts SA 68 G7
Giles Corner SA 67 C1, 71 C1, 73 J7
Gilgai NSW 27 I6
Gilgandra NSW 26 C10
Gilgooma NSW 26 C8
Gilgunnia NSW 29 M1, 31 M12
Gillenbah NSW 24 A8, 29 N8
Gilliat Qld 129 H11, 131 I3
Gillieston Vic. 54 E7
Gillingarra WA 88 C2, 90 C6
Gilmore NSW 24 D10, 35 A4, 36 C2
Gilston Qld 21 G1, 115 F10, 116 D6
Gin Gin NSW 26 B11
Gin Gin Qld 118 B2, 123 L3
Gindie Qld 125 I11
Gingin WA 85 C1, 88 B3, 90 C7
Ginninderra ACT 33 D3, 34 E3, 36 G2
Gipsy Point Vic. 35 D11, 51 G10
Girgarre Vic. 54 D7
Girilambone NSW 31 O9
Girral NSW 24 B5, 29 O5
Girraween NP Qld 21 A4, 27 K3, 123 K12
Girringun NP Qld 120 D7, 127 L9
Giru Qld 119 A2, 120 H11, 124 H1, 127 O12
Gisborne Vic. 40 A2, 42 H3, 49 H10, 52 B2, 63 P4
Gladfield Qld 21 B1
Gladfield Vic. 28 H12, 61 N6
Gladstone NSW 20 G4, 27 M10
Gladstone Qld 123 K1, 125 N12
Gladstone SA 73 J4, 74 H12
Gladstone Tas. 143 O5
Gladstone WA 89 C8
Gladysdale Vic. 41 E8, 43 M6, 52 F5
Glandore SA xx G9
Glanmire NSW 24 H5
Glass House Mountains Qld 117 F6, 123 N8
Glass House Mountains NP Qld 117 F6, 118 E12,
   123 N8
Glaziers Bay Tas. 138 F8, 141 J8
Glebe NSW viii D5, x D12
Glebe Tas. xxxiv F10, 1 A6, 136 E3, 137 D8
Glen Alice NSW 25 I4
Glen Aplin Qld 21 A4, 27 K3, 123 K12
Glen Creek Vic. 55 K8, 57 I5
Glen Davis NSW 25 I4
Glen Dhu Tas. 145 F2
Glen Forbes Vic. 43 L11, 45 P10, 52 E8
Glen Geddes Qld 125 M10

Glen Helen Resort NT 108 G7, 110 C3
Glen Huon Tas. 138 F7, 141 I8
Glen Innes NSW 27 K5
Glen Iris Vic. 40 E6
Glen Martin NSW 19 E5, 20 B11
Glen Oak NSW 19 D6, 20 A11, 25 M3
Glen Osmond SA xxi M9
Glen Tas. 143 K6, 145 G7
Glen Valley Vic. 55 M10, 57 L9
Glen Waverley Vic. 40 F6, 43 J6, 52 D5
Glen William NSW 19 E5, 20 B10
Glen Wills Vic. 55 M10, 57 L9
Glenaire Vic. 42 A12, 50 A6, 63 K10
Glenaladale Vic. 53 L5
Glenalbyn Vic. 49 C1, 61 M8
Glenalta SA 66 C8, 67 B10, 68 F3
Glenariff NSW 31 N7
Glenaroua Vic. 54 C11
Glenbrae Vic. 42 B1, 49 A8, 63 L3
Glenbrook NSW 15 K6, 17 L10, 25 J6
Glenburn Vic. 40 H2, 41 C3, 43 L3, 52 E2
Glenburnie SA 62 A5, 71 G12
Glencoe NSW 27 K6
Glencoe SA 71 G11
Glencoe West SA 71 F11
Glendalough WA xxiv D4, 84 D6, 85 C5
Glendambo SA 74 C5
Glenden Qld 119 D8, 125 I6
Glendevie Tas. 138 F9, 141 I9
Glendon Brook NSW 19 A5, 25 L3
Gleneagle Qld 115 C8
Glenelg SA xx C11, 66 B8, 67 B9, 68 E2, 69 H7,
   71 B3, 73 J9
Glenelg East SA xx D11
Glenelg North SA xx C10
Glenelg South SA xx B12
Glenfern Tas. 138 G4, 141 J6
Glenfyne Vic. 50 F8, 63 I8
Glengarrie NSW 116 E11
Glengarry Tas. 143 J7, 145 E8
Glengarry Vic. 53 I7
Glengower Vic. 49 C7, 61 M12, 63 M2
Glengowrie SA xx D12
Glenhaven NSW 12 C4, 13 A10, 15 K6
Glenisla Vic. 60 G12, 62 G1
Glenlee Vic. 28 D12, 60 E7
Glenlofty Vic. 61 K12, 63 K1
Glenloth Vic. 28 G12, 61 K6
Glenluce Vic. 49 F7, 61 N12, 63 N2
Glenlusk Tas. 138 H4
Glenlyon Vic. 42 F1, 49 F8, 63 N2
Glenmaggie Vic. 53 J5
Glenmore NSW 14 F11, 23 D1
Glenmore Vic. 42 F4, 49 F12, 51 A8, 52 A3, 53 O2,
   57 O12, 63 O5
Glenmorgan Qld 122 H8
Glenora Tas. 138 F2, 141 I6
Glenorchy Tas. xxxiv A6, 137 B5, 139 I4, 141 K7
Glenorchy Vic. 60 H10
Glenore Crossing Qld 126 D7, 129 G5
Glenore Grove Qld 117 A11
Glenore Tas. 143 J9, 145 E11
Glenorie NSW 12 D2, 13 A9, 15 K4
Glenormiston Vic. 63 I7
Glenormiston North Vic. 63 I7
Glenpatrick Vic. 61 K12, 63 K1
Glenreagh NSW 21 D10, 27 M7
Glenrowan Vic. 54 H8, 56 E5
Glenrowan West Vic. 54 H8, 56 E5
Glenroy NSW 14 B3, 16 D4, 24 C11, 25 I5, 35 A6,
   36 B5, 55 O4
Glenroy SA 60 A12, 62 A1, 71 G10
Glenshee Vic. 61 K12, 63 K1
Glenside SA xxi L7
Glenthompson Vic. 62 H4
Glenunga SA xxi L8
Glenvale Vic. 40 F2, 43 J3, 52 D2
Glossodia NSW 15 I3, 17 O5
Glossop SA 28 A6, 58 A6, 73 N7
Gloucester NSW 20 C5, 25 M1, 27 K12
Gloucester Island NP Qld 119 E4, 125 J3
Gloucester NP WA 86 H11, 87 B2, 88 D10, 90 C11
Glynde SA xxi N2
Gnangara WA 84 D4, 85 C4

Gnarming WA 88 G6, 90 E8
Gnarwarre Vic. 42 E8, 50 F1, 63 N7
Gnotuk Vic. 50 G7, 63 J7
Gnowangerup WA 88 G9, 90 E10
Gobondery NSW 24 C2
Gobur Vic. 54 F11, 56 A9
Gocup NSW 24 D10, 35 A4, 36 C2
Godfreys Creek NSW 24 F7, 35 C1
Godwin Beach Qld 114 G2, 115 E1, 117 G8
Gogango Qld 125 L11
Gol Gol NSW 28 E6, 58 G6
Golconda Tas. 143 L6
Golden Beach Vic. 53 L7
Golden Point Vic. 49 F6, 54 A10, 61 M12
Golden Valley Tas. 143 I9, 145 D12
Goldfields Woodlands NP WA 90 G5
Goldsborough Vic. 49 B3, 61 L10
Goldsmith Tas. 141 K1, 143 K11
Goldsworthy WA 92 E1, 94 E11, 97 J3
Gollan NSW 24 G1, 26 D12
Golspie NSW 24 H8, 35 E2
Goneaway NP Qld 131 J10
Gongolgon NSW 31 O6
Gonn Crossing Vic. 61 N3
Goobang NP NSW 24 E3
Goobarragandra NSW 24 E11, 35 B5, 36 D3
Good Night Scrub NP Qld 118 A4, 123 L4
Goodedulla NP Qld 125 L10
Goodings Corner Qld 116 E7
Goodna Qld 114 C9, 115 C5, 117 E12
Goodnight NSW 28 G8, 59 L10
Goodooga NSW 26 A2, 122 D11
Goodwood Qld 118 D3, 123 M4
Goodwood East SA xxi I8, 66 C7, 67 B9, 68 F2
Goodwood Tas. xxxiv D5, 137 C5
Googa Googa Qld 118 A12
Goold Island NP Qld 120 F6, 127 M9
Goolgowi NSW 29 L6
Goolma NSW 24 G2
Goolmangar NSW 21 F4, 27 N3
Gooloogong NSW 24 E5
Goolwa SA 68 G8, 71 C4, 73 J11
Goomalibee Vic. 54 G8, 56 C4
Goomalling WA 88 D3, 90 C6
Goombungee Qld 123 L8
Goomburra Qld 27 L1
Goomeri Qld 118 B8, 123 L6
Goon Nure Vic. 53 M6
Goondah NSW 24 E9, 35 C3
Goondiwindi Qld 26 H1, 123 I11
Goondooloo SA 71 E3, 73 M9
Goonengerry NP NSW 21 G4, 27 O3, 123 N12
Goongarrie WA 90 H4
Goongarrie NP WA 90 H4
Goongerah Vic. 35 B11, 51 C9
Goonumbla NSW 24 E3
Gooram Vic. 54 F10, 56 A8
Goorambat Vic. 54 G7, 56 C4
Goornong Vic. 49 H2, 54 B8, 61 P9
Gooroc Vic. 61 K8
Gooseberry Hill WA xxv H5
Gooseberry Hill NP WA xxv H4, 84 F5, 85 D5,
   88 C5, 90 C7
Goovigen Qld 123 J1, 125 L12
Goowarra Qld 125 K11
Gorae Vic. 62 D7
Gorae West Vic. 62 D7
Gordon SA 73 J1, 74 H8
Gordon Tas. 138 H10, 141 J9
Gordon Vic. 42 E3, 49 E10, 63 N4
Gordon Park Vic. xxx H2
Gordonvale Qld 120 E3, 121 F8, 127 L6
Gormandale Vic. 53 J8
Gormanston Tas. 140 E1, 142 E11, 144 A10
Gorokan NSW 13 E6, 15 P1, 19 B12
Goroke Vic. 60 D9
Gosford NSW 13 D8, 15 O3, 25 L5
Goshen Tas. 143 O7
Gosnells WA xxv F12, 84 F7, 85 D6
Goughs Bay Vic. 43 P1, 52 H1, 54 H12, 56 D10
Goulburn NSW 24 H9, 35 E3
Goulburn River NP NSW 24 H1, 25 I1, 26 F12
Goulburn Weir Vic. 54 D9
Goulds Country Tas. 143 O7

Gourock NP NSW 24 G12, 34 G12, 35 D6, 37 I7, 51 G1
Gowanford Vic. 28 G10, 61 K2
Gowangardie Vic. 54 F8, 56 B4
Gowar Vic. 49 E5, 61 N11, 63 N1
Gowar East Vic. 61 K9
Gowrie Park Tas. 142 G8, 144 G4
Goyura Vic. 28 E11, 60 H4
Grabben Gullen NSW 24 G8, 35 D2
Grabine NSW 24 F6
Grace Vic. 45 L4
Gracemere Qld 125 M11
Gracetown WA 86 A8, 88 B9, 90 B10
Graceville Qld xxx C12
Gradgery NSW 26 B9
Gradule Qld 26 E1, 122 G10
Grafton NSW 21 D9, 27 M6
Graman NSW 27 I4
Grampians NP Vic. 60 G12, 62 G2
Grandchester Qld 117 A12
Grange Qld xxx G3
Grange SA xx A3, 66 B7, 67 A8, 68 E2
Granite Flat Vic. 55 M9, 57 L6
Grantham Qld 123 L9
Granton Tas. 139 I3, 141 K6
Grantville Vic. 43 L10, 45 P9, 52 E8
Granville NSW 12 C6, 13 A12, 15 K8
Granville Harbour Tas. 142 B9
Granya Vic. 24 B12, 29 O12, 55 M6, 57 L2
Grasmere NSW 14 G11, 23 E1
Grass Flat Vic. 60 E9
Grass Patch WA 91 I8
Grassdale Vic. 62 D5
Grassmere Vic. 50 D7
Grassmere Junction Vic. 50 D7, 62 H8
Grasstree Qld 119 G8, 125 K6
Grasstree Hill Tas. xxxiv H1, 137 F2, 139 J4
Grassy Tas. 141 P12
Gravelly Beach Tas. 143 J7, 145 F8
Gravesend NSW 26 H5
Grawin NSW 26 B4
Grawlin NSW 24 D5
Grawlin Plains NSW 24 D5
Gray Tas. 143 O9
Graytown Vic. 54 C9
Gre Gre Vic. 61 J9
Great Australian Bight Marine NP SA 80 C7, 81 I7, 91 P6
Great Barrier Reef Marine Park Qld 119 F2, 120 H7, 121 G6, 125 K2, 127 M3, 128 F6
Great Basalt Wall NP Qld 120 B12, 124 D2, 127 L12, 131 P2
Great Keppel Island Qld 125 N10
Great Northern Vic. 55 J6, 56 G1
Great Otway NP Vic. 42 A11, 50 B5, 63 K10
Great Palm Island Qld 120 G8, 127 N10
Great Sandy NP Qld 117 D12, 118 G4, 123 O4
Great Western Vic. 61 I12, 63 I1
Greater Bendigo NP Vic. 49 G1, 54 A8, 61 O9
Gredgwin Vic. 28 G11, 61 L5
Green Fields SA 66 C5, 67 B7
Green Head WA 90 A5
Green Hill NSW 20 G4, 27 M10
Green Hill Creek Vic. 49 A7, 61 K12, 63 K2
Green Island Marine Park Qld 120 E2, 121 H6
Green Island NP Qld 120 E2, 121 H6, 127 M6
Green Point NSW 13 D8, 15 O3, 20 E10, 25 O2
Greenbank Qld 114 C10, 115 C9
Greenbushes WA 86 G7, 88 C9
Greendale Vic. 42 F3, 49 F10, 52 A3, 63 O4
Greenethorpe NSW 24 E6
Greenhill SA xxi P8
Greenhills WA 88 E4
Greenmantle NSW 24 F6
Greenmount Qld 123 L9
Greenmount Vic. 53 I9
Greenmount WA xxv G2, 84 F5, 85 D4
Greenmount NP WA xxv H3, 84 F5, 85 D5, 88 C5, 90 C7
Greenock SA 67 E4, 71 C1, 73 K8
Greenough WA 90 A3
Greens Beach Tas. 143 I6, 145 D5
Greens Creek Vic. 61 J11
Greensborough Vic. 40 E4, 43 J5, 52 D4

Greenslopes Qld xxx H11
Greenvale Qld 120 B9, 127 K10
Greenwald Vic. 62 C5, 71 H12
Greenways SA 71 F10
Greenwell Point NSW 23 E9, 25 J10, 35 G4, 37 P1
Greenwich NSW viii D1, x E7
Greg Greg NSW 24 D12, 35 A6, 36 B7, 51 A2, 55 P6, 57 P2
Gregors Creek Qld 117 B6
Gregory Qld 125 I10
Gregory WA 89 D12
Gregory NP NT 95 P4, 99 P6, 104 C12, 106 C3
Greigs Flat NSW 35 E10, 51 H7
Grenfell NSW 24 D6
Grenville Vic. 42 D5, 49 C12, 63 M5
Gresford NSW 19 C4, 20 A10, 25 L2
Greta Vic. 55 I8, 56 E5
Greta South Vic. 54 H9, 56 E6
Greta West Vic. 54 H8, 56 E5
Gretna Tas. 138 F2, 141 J6
Grevillia NSW 21 E3, 27 N2, 123 M11
Grey Peaks NP Qld 120 E2, 121 G8, 127 M6
Greymare Qld 21 A1, 27 K1, 123 K10
Griffith NSW 29 M7
Griffiths Island Vic. 50 B8
Grimwade WA 86 G6
Gringegalgona Vic. 62 E2
Gritjurk Vic. 62 E3
Grogan NSW 24 D7, 35 A1
Grong Grong NSW 24 A8, 29 O8
Grose Vale NSW 14 G4, 17 M6
Grosvenor Qld 123 K4
Grove Tas. 138 G6, 141 J7
Grovedale Vic. 42 F8, 44 A4, 50 G1, 63 O8
Gruyere Vic. 40 H5, 41 C7, 43 L5
Gubbata NSW 24 A5, 29 N5
Guilderton WA 88 B4, 90 B7
Guildford NSW 12 C7, 15 J8
Guildford Tas. 142 E7, 144 C3
Guildford Vic. 49 E7, 61 N12, 63 N2
Guildford WA xxv D3, 84 E5, 85 C4
Gulaga NP NSW 35 E8, 37 K10
Gular NSW 26 C9
Gulargambone NSW 26 C9
Gulf Creek NSW 26 H7
Gulgong NSW 24 H2
Gulnare SA 73 J5, 74 H12
Guluguba Qld 123 I6
Gum Lake NSW 28 G1, 30 F12
Gumble NSW 24 F4
Gumbowie SA 73 K3, 75 I11
Gumdale Qld xxxi P11
Gumeracha SA 66 G5, 67 E8, 68 H1, 71 C3, 73 K9
Gumlu Qld 119 C3, 125 I2
Gumly Gumly NSW 24 C9, 29 P9, 55 N1
Gunalda Qld 118 D8, 123 M6
Gunbar NSW 29 L6
Gunbower Vic. 29 I11, 54 A4, 61 O6
Gunbower NP Vic. 29 I11, 54 A3, 61 O5
Gundabooka NP NSW 31 L6
Gundagai NSW 24 D9, 35 A3, 36 C1, 55 P1
Gundaring WA 88 F7
Gundaroo NSW 24 G10, 34 F2, 35 D4, 36 H1
Gundary NSW 24 H9, 35 E3
Gunderman NSW 13 B8, 15 L3
Gundiah Qld 118 D7, 123 M5
Gundillion NSW 24 G12, 35 E6, 37 J6, 51 H1
Gundowring Vic. 55 L8, 57 J5
Gundowring North Vic. 55 L7, 57 J4
Gundowring Upper Vic. 55 L8, 57 J5
Gundy NSW 25 K1, 26 H12
Gunebang NSW 24 A3, 29 O3
Gungahlin ACT 24 F10, 33 E3, 34 E3, 36 H2
Gungal NSW 25 J2
Gunnary NSW 24 F7, 35 C2
Gunnedah NSW 26 G9
Gunnewin Qld 122 F5
Gunning NSW 24 G9, 35 D3
Gunningbland NSW 24 D4
Gunns Plains Tas. 142 G6, 144 E2
Gunpowder Qld 129 D9, 130 F1
Gunyangara NT 105 N4
Gurley NSW 26 F5
Gurrai SA 28 A8, 58 A10, 71 G4, 73 N10

Gurrumuru NT 105 M4
Gurrundah NSW 24 G9, 35 D3
Guthalungra Qld 119 D3, 125 I2
Guthega NSW 35 A8, 36 C10, 51 B4
Guy Fawkes River NP NSW 21 A9, 27 L6
Guyong NSW 24 G5
Guyra NSW 27 J7
Guys Forest Vic. 24 C12, 55 N6, 57 M2
Gwabegar NSW 26 D7
Gwalia WA 90 H2
Gwandalan NSW 13 F5, 19 B11
Gwandalan Tas. 139 L7, 141 L8
Gwelup WA xxiv C2
Gwynneville NSW 22 C7
Gymbowen Vic. 60 D9
Gympie Qld 118 D9, 123 M6
Gypsum Vic. 28 E9, 58 H12, 60 H1

Haasts Bluff NT 108 F6
Haberfield NSW viii A4, x A12
Hackney SA xxi K4
Haddon Vic. 42 C3, 49 B10, 63 L4
Haden Qld 123 L8
Hadspen Tas. 143 K8, 145 G10
Hagley Tas. 143 J8, 145 E11
Hahndorf SA 66 F9, 67 D10, 68 H3, 71 C3, 73 K9
Haig WA 91 M5
Haigslea Qld 115 A5, 117 C11
Halbury SA 69 H3, 73 J6
Hale Village Qld 21 F1, 115 D9
Half Tide Qld 119 G8, 125 K6
Halfway Creek NSW 21 E10, 27 N6
Halfway Mill Roadhouse WA 88 A1, 90 B5
Halidon SA 71 F3, 73 M9
Halifax Qld 120 F8, 127 M10
Halifax Bay Wetlands NP Qld 120 F9, 127 M10
Hall ACT 33 D2, 34 D3, 36 G2
Hallam Vic. 40 F8, 41 A11, 43 K7, 45 M2
Hallett SA 73 K5, 75 I12
Halliday Point NSW 20 E9, 25 O2
Halls Creek WA 95 N7, 99 L11
Halls Gap Vic. 60 H12, 62 H1
Halls Head WA 85 B9
Hallston Vic. 43 O10, 52 G8
Halton NSW 19 C3, 20 A9, 25 L2
Hamel WA 85 D11, 88 C7
Hamelin Bay WA 86 B10, 88 B10
Hamersley WA xxiv C1, 85 H3, 89 G3, 92 C4, 96 G8
Hamilton NSW 19 D9
Hamilton Qld xxxi J4
Hamilton SA 67 E1, 71 C1, 73 K7
Hamilton Tas. 138 F1, 141 I5
Hamilton Vic. 62 F4
Hamilton East NSW 18 A6
Hamilton Island Qld 119 G5, 125 K4
Hamley Bridge SA 67 C3, 71 B1, 73 J7
Hamlyn Heights Vic. 44 A3, 46 A2
Hammond SA 73 J2, 74 H9
Hampden SA 73 K7
Hampshire Tas. 142 F6, 144 C2
Hampton NSW 14 A4, 16 B6, 25 I6
Hampton Qld 123 L9
Hampton Vic. 43 J6
Hampton Park Vic. 41 A11, 43 K7, 45 M2
Hanging Rock Vic. 51 B7, 53 P1, 55 P12
Hann River Roadhouse WA 127 I2
Hann Tableland NP Qld 120 C2, 121 B6, 127 K6
Hannahs Bridge NSW 26 E11
Hannan NSW 24 A5, 29 N5
Hansborough SA 67 F1, 73 K7
Hanson SA 73 K6
Hansonville Vic. 55 I8, 56 E6
Hanwood NSW 29 M7
Happy Valley Qld 118 G5, 123 O4, 125 L8
Happy Valley Vic. 28 F7, 42 B4, 49 A12, 55 K9, 57 I6, 59 I9, 63 L5
Harbord NSW xi N2
Harcourt Vic. 49 F5, 54 A10, 61 O11, 63 O1
Harcourt North Vic. 49 F5, 54 A10, 61 O11, 63 O1
Harden NSW 24 E8, 35 B2
Hardwicke Bay SA 69 D7, 72 H9
Harefield NSW 24 C9, 29 P9
Harford Tas. 143 I6, 145 C7
Hargraves NSW 24 H3

Harkaway Vic. 40 G8, 41 B10, 43 K7, 45 N2
Harlin Qld 117 A6, 123 M8
Harrietville Vic. 55 L10, 57 J9
Harrington NSW 20 F8, 25 O1, 27 L12
Harrismith WA 88 G7
Harrisville Qld 115 A7
Harrogate SA 67 F9
Harrow Vic. 53 L6, 60 D11, 62 D1
Harrys Creek Vic. 54 F9, 56 B6
Harston Vic. 54 D7
Hart SA 69 H2, 73 J6
Hartley NSW 14 B3, 16 D4, 25 I5
Hartley SA 66 H12, 67 F12
Hartley Vale NSW 14 C3, 16 F4
Hartz Mountains NP Tas. 138 D9, 141 I9
Harvey WA 86 F2, 88 C7, 90 C9
Harwood NSW 21 F8, 27 N5
Haslam SA 72 A2, 81 N9
Hassell NP WA 87 F8, 88 H10, 90 F11
Hasties Swamp NP Qld 120 D3, 121 D9, 127 L7
Hastings Tas. 138 F11, 141 I10
Hastings Vic. 40 F11, 43 J9, 45 K7, 52 D7
Hastings Point NSW 21 H3, 27 O2, 123 N11
Hat Head NSW 20 G4, 27 M10
Hat Head NP NSW 20 G4, 27 M10
Hatches Creek NT 107 K12, 109 K1
Hatfield NSW 28 H5, 59 N4
Hatherleigh SA 71 F10
Hattah Vic. 28 E7, 58 H9
Hattah–Kulkyne NP Vic. 28 E7, 58 H8, 59 I9
Hatton Vale Qld 117 A11
Havelock Vic. 49 C5, 61 M11
Haven Vic. 60 G9
Havilah Vic. 55 K9, 57 I6
Hawker SA 70 A12, 74 H8
Hawkesbury Heights NSW 14 G5, 17 L8
Hawkesdale Vic. 62 G6
Hawks Nest NSW 19 H7, 20 C11, 25 N3
Hawley Beach Tas. 143 I6, 145 C6
Hawthorn SA xxi J10
Hawthorn Vic. xv P12, xvii P3, 40 E6
Hawthorne Qld xxxi I7
Hay NSW 29 J7
Haydens Bog Vic. 35 B10, 51 D8
Hayes Creek NT 102 G10, 104 E6
Hayes Tas. 138 G3, 141 J6
Haymarket NSW viii F6, 10 C11
Haysdale Vic. 28 G8, 59 K10
Hazel Park Vic. 43 P12, 52 H9
Hazelbrook NSW 14 E6, 17 I9
Hazeldene Vic. 40 G1, 41 B2, 43 K2, 52 D2, 54 D12
Hazelmere WA xxv G4, 85 D4
Hazelwood Vic. 52 H7
Hazelwood Park SA xxi N7
Healesville Vic. 41 D6, 43 L4, 52 E4
Heartbreak Hotel NT 105 L12, 107 L3
Heath Hill Vic. 43 M9, 52 F7
Heathcote NSW 12 C11, 15 J11, 23 H1, 25 K7, 35 H1
Heathcote Vic. 54 B10, 61 P11
Heathcote–Graytown NP Vic. 54 C9
Heathcote Junction Vic. 40 E1, 43 J2, 52 C2, 54 C12
Heathcote NP NSW 12 B11, 15 J12, 23 G2, 25 J7, 35 H1
Heatherton Vic. 45 K1
Heathfield SA 66 E9, 67 C10, 68 G3
Heathmere Vic. 62 D7
Heathmont Vic. 40 F6, 41 A8
Heathpool SA xxi M6
Hebden NSW 25 K2
Hebel Qld 26 B2, 122 D11
Hector Qld 119 G8, 125 K6
Hectorville SA xxi O2
Heddon Greta NSW 13 F2, 19 B8, 20 A12
Hedley Vic. 53 I9
Heidelberg Vic. 40 E5, 43 J5
Heka Tas. 142 F7, 144 E2
Helena Valley WA xxv H4, 84 F5
Helensburgh NSW 23 H2, 25 K8, 35 H2
Helensvale Qld 21 G1, 27 O1, 115 F9, 116 D4, 123 N10
Helenvale Qld 127 L3
Helidon Qld 123 L9
Hell Hole Gorge NP Qld 133 L3
Hells Gate Roadhouse Qld 129 B3

Hellyer Tas. 142 D4
Hemmant Qld xxxi O7, 114 F7, 115 E4, 117 G11
Hendon SA 67 B8, 68 E1
Hendra Qld xxxi K3, 114 E6
Henley Beach SA xx A4
Henley Beach South SA xx B5
Henley Brook WA 85 D4
Henrietta Tas. 142 E6
Hensley Park Vic. 62 F4
Henty NSW 24 B11, 29 O11, 55 L3
Henty Vic. 62 D4
Hepburn Springs Vic. 42 E1, 49 E8, 63 N2
Herberton Qld 120 C4, 121 C10, 127 L7
Herdsman WA xxiv D4
Hermannsburg NT 108 H7, 110 D5
Hermidale NSW 31 N10
Hernani NSW 21 B11, 27 L7
Herne Hill Vic. 46 A3
Herons Creek NSW 20 F7, 27 L11
Herrick Tas. 143 N6
Herston Qld xxx G5
Hervey Bay Qld 118 F4, 123 N4
Hesket Vic. 42 H2, 52 B2, 54 B12, 63 P3
Hesso SA 72 H1, 74 F8
Hexham NSW 13 G2, 19 D8, 20 A12, 25 L4
Hexham Vic. 62 H6
Heybridge Tas. 142 F5
Heyfield Vic. 53 J6
Heywood Vic. 62 D6
Hi Way Inn Roadhouse NT 104 H12, 106 H3
Hiamdale Vic. 53 J7
Hiawatha Vic. 53 I9
Hidden Valley NP WA 95 O4, 99 M5, 104 A11, 106 A2
Hidden Valley NT xxvii G9
High Camp Vic. 52 C1, 54 C11
High Range NSW 23 B4, 25 I8, 35 G2
High Wycombe WA xxv F5
Highbury WA 88 E7
Highclere Tas. 142 F6, 144 D1
Highcroft Tas. 139 L9, 141 M9
Highett Vic. 43 J7
Highfield Tas. 145 A3
Highfields Qld 123 L9
Highgate SA xxi K9
Highgate WA xxiv G5, 83 F2
Highgate Hill Qld xxx F9, 113 C12
Highlands Vic. 54 E11
Highton Vic. 44 A4, 46 A10
Highvale Qld 114 B5, 115 C3, 117 D10
Hilgay Vic. 62 D4
Hill End NSW 24 G4
Hill End Vic. 43 P7, 52 H6
Hillarys WA 84 B4, 85 B4, 88 B5
Hillcrest Vic. 42 B3, 49 A11
Hilldale NSW 19 D5, 20 A10
Hillgrove NSW 20 C1, 27 K8
Hillman WA 88 B8
Hillside Vic. 53 M5
Hillston NSW 29 L4
Hilltop NSW 23 C4, 25 I8, 35 G2
Hilltown SA 73 J5
Hillview Qld 21 F2, 27 N1, 115 C11
Hillwood Tas. 143 J7, 145 F7
Hilton SA xx G6
Hilton WA xxiv D12
Hinchinbrook Island NP Qld 120 F7, 127 M9
Hindmarsh SA xx G3
Hindmarsh Valley SA 68 F8, 69 H10
Hines Hill WA 88 G3
Hinnomunjie Vic. 53 N1, 55 N11, 57 M10
Hinton NSW 13 G1, 19 C7
Hirstglen Qld 123 L10
Hivesville Qld 123 L6
HMAS Cerberus Vic. 45 K8
Hobart Tas. xxxiv F11, 1 A7, 136, 137 D8, 139 I5, 141 K7
Hobbys Yards NSW 24 G6
Hoddle Vic. 52 G10
Hoddles Creek Vic. 41 E9, 43 M6, 52 E5
Hodgson River Station NT 105 J10, 107 J1
Holbourne Island NP Qld 119 E3, 125 J2
Holbrook NSW 24 B11, 29 O11, 55 M4
Holgate NSW 13 D8, 15 O2
Holland Park Qld xxxi I12

Hollow Tree Tas. 141 J5
Holly WA 88 F9
Hollydeen NSW 25 J2
Hollywell Qld 116 F4
Holmview Qld 114 F11, 115 E7
Holmwood NSW 24 F6
Holwell Tas. 143 J7, 145 E8
Home Hill Qld 119 B2, 124 H2, 127 O12
Homebush NSW 12 D7
Homebush Qld 119 G8, 125 K6
Homebush Vic. 49 A5, 61 L11, 63 L1
Homecroft Vic. 28 E12, 60 H7
Homerton Vic. 62 E6
Homestead Qld 124 E3
Homevale NP Qld 119 E8, 125 J6
Homewood Vic. 43 L1, 52 E1, 54 E11
Hook Island Qld 119 G4, 125 K3
Hope Islands NP Qld 121 E2, 127 L4
Hope Vale Qld 127 K2
Hopetoun Vic. 28 E10, 60 H4
Hopetoun WA 90 G10
Hopetoun West Vic. 28 D10, 60 G3
Hopevale Vic. 28 E11, 60 G4
Hoppers Crossing Vic. 40 B6, 42 H6, 52 B5, 63 P6
Hordern Vale Vic. 42 A12, 50 B6, 63 K10
Hornsby NSW 12 E4, 13 B10, 15 L6, 25 K6
Hornsby Heights NSW 12 E4, 13 B10, 15 L6
Hornsdale SA 73 J4, 75 I11
Horrocks WA 89 D12
Horse Lake NSW 30 D11, 75 P9
Horseshoe Bay Qld 120 G10, 127 N11
Horseshoe Bend Vic. 45 P2
Horsham Vic. 60 G9
Horsley Park NSW 12 A6, 15 I8
Horsnell Gully SA xxi P7
Hoskinstown NSW 24 G11, 34 H7, 35 D5, 37 I4
Hotham Heights Vic. 53 L1, 55 L11, 57 J9
Hotspur Vic. 62 D5
Houghton SA 66 E5, 67 D8, 68 G1
Houtman Abrolhos Island WA 89 C12
Hove SA 66 B8, 67 B10, 68 E3
Hovell Park Vic. 44 B2
Howard Qld 118 D4, 123 M4
Howard Springs NT 102 E3, 104 D4
Howden Tas. 139 I7, 141 K8
Howes Valley NSW 25 K3
Howick Group NP Qld 128 H11
Howlong NSW 24 A12, 29 N12, 55 J5, 56 H1
Howqua Vic. 43 P1, 52 H1, 54 H12, 56 D11
Howrah Tas. 1 H9, 137 G8, 139 J5
Howth Tas. 142 G5
Hoya Qld 115 A8
Hoyleton SA 69 H3, 73 J6
Huddleston SA 73 J4, 74 H12
Hughenden Qld 124 B4, 131 N4
Hughes SA 80 D4
Hull River NP Qld 120 E6, 127 M8
Humevale Vic. 41 A4, 43 K3, 52 D3
Humpty Doo NT 102 E4, 104 D4
Humula NSW 24 C11, 36 A3, 55 O3
Hungerford Qld 31 J1, 133 L11
Hunter Vic. 54 B7, 61 P8
Hunter Island Tas. 142 B1
Hunters Hill NSW x B7
Hunterston Vic. 53 J9
Huntingdale Vic. 40 E7
Huntingdale WA xxv F12
Huntleys Cove NSW x A7
Huntleys Point NSW x A8
Huntly Vic. 49 G2, 54 A8, 61 O9
Huon Vic. 55 L7, 57 J3
Huonville Tas. 138 G7, 141 J8
Hurstbridge Vic. 40 F4, 41 A6, 43 K4, 52 D3
Hurstville NSW 12 D9, 15 K10
Huskisson NSW 23 D11, 25 J10, 35 G4, 37 O2
Hutt WA 89 D11, 90 A2
Hyams Beach NSW 23 D11, 37 O2
Hyde Park SA xxi J8
Hyden WA 88 H5, 90 F8
Hyland Park NSW 20 H2, 27 M9
Hynam SA 60 A10, 71 G9

Icy Creek Vic. 43 O6, 52 G5
Ida Bay Tas. 138 E12, 141 I10

Idalia NP Qld 124 B12, 131 N12, 133 M2
Ilbilbie Qld 119 G9, 125 K7
Ilford NSW 24 H4
Ilfracombe Qld 124 B10, 131 N10
Ilfraville Tas. 145 E6
Ilkurlka Roadhouse WA 91 N1, 93 N11
Illabarook Vic. 42 B5, 49 A12, 63 L5
Illabo NSW 24 C9
Illalong Creek NSW 24 E9, 35 C3
Illawarra Vic. 61 I11, 63 I1
Illawong NSW 12 C9, 15 J10
Illawong WA 90 A4
Illowa Vic. 50 C7, 62 G8
Iluka NSW 21 F7, 27 O5
Imangara NT 107 K12, 109 K1
Imanpa NT 108 G9
Imbil Qld 117 D1, 118 D10, 123 M7
Imintji Store WA 95 K6, 98 G9
Impimi NSW 28 H8, 59 M9
Inala Qld 114 D9
Indaringinya NT 109 K3
Indented Head Vic. 40 B9, 42 H8, 44 F4, 52 B6,
   63 P7
Indigo Vic. 55 J6, 56 G2
Indigo Upper Vic. 55 K7, 57 I3
Indooroopilly Qld xxx C10, 114 D7, 115 D4,
   117 E11
Indwarra NP NSW 27 J6
Ingham Qld 120 E8, 127 M10
Ingleby Vic. 42 C9, 50 D2, 63 M8
Ingleside NSW 12 G4, 13 C10, 15 N6
Ingleside Qld 21 G2, 115 F11, 116 E10
Inglewood Qld 27 J1, 123 J11
Inglewood Tas. 141 L4
Inglewood Vic. 49 D1, 61 M9
Inglewood WA xxiv G4, xxv A5
Ingliston Vic. 42 F4, 49 F11, 63 O4
Ingoldsby Vic. 123 L9
Injinoo Qld 128 C3
Injune Qld 122 F4
Inkerman Qld 119 C3, 124 H2
Inkerman SA 69 G4, 71 A1, 73 I7
Innaloo WA 84 C5, xxiv C3
Innamincka SA 77 N7, 132 F8
Innes NP SA 69 B8, 72 F10
Inneston SA 69 B9, 72 F10
Innisfail Qld 120 E4, 121 G11, 127 M7
Innot Hot Springs Qld 120 C5, 121 B12, 127 K7
Interlaken Tas. 141 K2, 143 K12
Inverell NSW 27 I5
Invergordon Vic. 54 F6, 56 B2
Inverleigh Vic. 42 D7, 63 M7
Inverloch Vic. 43 M12, 52 F9
Invermay Tas. 145 G10
Invermay Vic. 42 D3, 47 D2, 49 C10
Iona Vic. 41 E12, 43 M8
Ipolera NT 108 G7, 110 A5
Ipswich Qld 114 A9, 115 B5, 117 D12, 123 M9
Irishtown Tas. 142 C4
Irishtown Vic. 49 F7, 61 N12, 63 N2
Iron Baron SA 72 G3, 74 F11
Iron Knob SA 72 G2, 74 F10
Iron Range Qld 128 E7
Iron Range NP Qld 128 E7
Irrewarra Vic. 42 B9, 50 C2, 63 L8
Irrewillipe Vic. 42 A9, 50 A2, 63 K8
Irrwelty NT 109 K3
Irvinebank Qld 120 C4, 121 B10, 127 K7
Irymple Vic. 28 E6, 58 G6
Isabella NSW 24 H7, 35 E1
Isisford Qld 124 B11, 131 N11
Isla Gorge NP Qld 123 I3
Island Bend NSW 36 D9, 51 C3
Islington NSW 13 H3, 19 D9
Ivanhoe NSW 29 I2
Ivory Creek Qld 117 A6
Iwantja (Indulkana) SA 79 L4
Iwupataka NT 109 I7, 110 G4

Jabiru NT 103 O4, 104 G5
Jabuk SA 71 F4, 73 M10
Jack River Vic. 53 I9
Jack River NP Qld 127 J1, 128 H12
Jackadgery NSW 21 C8, 27 M5

Jackeys Marsh Tas. 143 I9, 145 C12
Jackie Junction WA 93 M8
Jackson Qld 122 H6
Jacobs Well Qld 114 H12, 115 F7, 116 E1, 123 N10
Jacobs Well WA 88 E5
Jalloonda Qld 120 G10, 124 G1, 127 N11
Jallumba Vic. 60 F10
Jam Jerrup Vic. 45 P8
Jamberoo NSW 23 E7, 25 J9, 35 H3
Jambin Qld 123 J1, 125 M12
Jamestown SA 73 J4, 75 I11
Jamieson Vic. 43 P2, 52 H2, 54 H12, 56 D11
Jan Juc Vic. 44 A7
Jancourt Vic. 50 G8, 63 J8
Jancourt East Vic. 50 H8, 63 J8
Jandakot WA xxiv H12, 84 D8, 85 C6, 88 C5
Jandowae Qld 123 K7
Jane Brook WA xxv H1
Jannali NSW 12 D10
Japoon NP Qld 120 E5, 127 M8
Jardee WA 86 H10, 87 B1, 88 D10
Jardine River NP Qld 128 D4
Jarklin Vic. 28 H12, 61 N7
Jarra Jarra NT 106 H12, 108 H1
Jarrahdale WA 84 G11, 85 D7, 88 C6
Jarrahmond Vic. 51 B11, 53 P5
Jarrahwood WA 86 E7, 88 C9
Jarvis Creek Vic. 55 L6, 57 K3
Jaurdi WA 90 G5
Jeffcott Vic. 28 F12, 61 J7
Jeffcott North Vic. 61 J7
Jellat Jellat NSW 51 H6
Jemalong NSW 24 D4
Jennacubbine WA 85 G1
Jenolan Caves NSW 16 A11, 25 I6
Jeogla NSW 20 D1, 21 A12, 27 K8
Jeparit Vic. 28 D12, 60 F6
Jerangle NSW 24 F12, 34 F12, 35 D6, 36 H7, 51 G1
Jericho Qld 124 E10
Jericho Tas. 141 K4
Jericho Vic. 52 H4
Jerilderie NSW 29 L10, 54 G1
Jerrabomberra NSW 33 F8, 34 E6, 36 H3
Jerramungup WA 90 F10
Jerrawa NSW 24 F9, 35 D3
Jerrawangala NP NSW 23 B11, 25 I10, 35 G4,
   37 N2
Jerrys Plains NSW 25 K2
Jerseyville NSW 20 G4, 27 M9
Jervis Bay JBT 23 D12, 25 J10, 35 G4, 37 O3
Jervis Bay NP NSW 23 D10, 25 J10, 35 G4, 37 O2
Jervois SA 71 D4, 73 L10
Jetsonville Tas. 143 L6
Jigalong WA 92 G5, 97 N11
Jil Jil Vic. 61 J4
Jilliby NSW 13 D6, 19 A12
Ji-Marda NT 105 J3
Jimaringle NSW 29 I9, 54 A1, 59 O12, 61 O2
Jimboomba Qld 114 D12, 115 D8, 123 N10
Jimbour Qld 123 K7
Jimna Qld 117 B3, 118 C11, 123 M7
Jindabyne NSW 35 B8, 36 E10, 51 C4
Jindera NSW 24 A12, 29 O12, 55 K5, 57 I1
Jindivick Vic. 41 G11, 43 N8, 52 G6
Jindong WA 86 B7
Jingalup WA 88 E9, 90 D10
Jingellic NSW 24 C12, 29 P12, 55 N5, 57 N1
Jingili NT xxvii D5
Jitarning WA 88 G6, 90 E8
Joanna SA 60 A11, 71 G9
Jodetluk (George Camp) NT 104 G8
Joel Joel Vic. 61 J11, 63 J1
Joel South Vic. 61 J11, 63 J1
Johanna Vic. 42 A12, 50 A5, 63 K10
John Forrest NP WA xxv H1, 84 F4, 85 D4, 88 C5,
   90 C7
Johnburgh SA 73 J2, 75 I9
Johns River NSW 20 F7, 25 O1, 27 L12
Johnsonville Vic. 53 N5
Jolimont WA xxiv D5
Jondaryan Qld 123 K8
Joondalup WA 84 C3, 85 B4, 88 B4
Joondanna WA xxiv E3
Josbury WA 88 E7, 90 D9

Josephville Qld 21 E1, 27 N1, 115 C9
Joskeleigh Qld 125 M11
Joslin SA xxi L2
Joyces Creek Vic. 49 D6, 61 N12, 63 N1
Judbury Tas. 138 F6, 141 I8
Jugiong Vic. 24 E9, 35 B3
Julatten Qld 120 D1, 121 D5, 127 L5
Julia SA 73 K7
Julia Creek Qld 129 H11, 131 J3
Jumbuk Vic. 53 I8
Jumbunna Vic. 43 M11, 52 F8
Junction Hill NSW 21 D8, 27 M6
Junction Village Vic. 45 M4
Jundah Qld 133 J1
Junee NSW 24 C9, 29 P9
Junee NP Qld 119 F12, 125 J9
Junee Reefs NSW 24 C8, 29 P8
Jung Vic. 60 G9
Junortoun Vic. 49 G3, 54 A9, 61 O10
Junuy Juluum NP NSW 20 G1, 21 C11, 27 M7
Jura WA 88 G4
Jurien Bay WA 90 A5
Jurunjung Vic. 40 A4, 42 H4, 49 H11, 52 B3, 63 P5

Kaarimba Vic. 29 K12, 54 E6
Kabra Qld 125 M11
Kadina SA 69 E3, 72 H6
Kadnook Vic. 60 C11, 62 C1, 71 H10
Kadungle NSW 24 D2
Kagaru Qld 114 C12, 115 C8
Kaimkillenbun Qld 123 K8
Kain NSW 24 G12, 34 H11, 35 D6, 37 I6, 51 H1
Kainton SA 69 F3, 73 I7
Kairi Qld 120 D3, 121 E9, 127 L7
Kajabbi Qld 126 B12, 129 E9, 130 G2
Kakadu NP NT 103 L5, 104 G4
Kalamunda WA xxv H7, 84 F6, 85 D5
Kalamunda NP WA 84 F6, 85 D5, 88 C5, 90 C7
Kalangadoo SA 62 A3, 71 G11
Kalannie WA 88 D1, 90 D5
Kalaru NSW 35 E9
Kalbar Qld 115 A8, 123 M10
Kalbarri WA 89 C11
Kalbarri NP WA 89 D11, 90 A2, 92 A12
Kaleentha Loop NSW 28 G1, 30 F12
Kalgan WA 87 E10, 88 G11, 90 E11
Kalgoorlie–Boulder WA 90 H5
Kalimna Vic. 53 O6
Kalimna West Vic. 53 N6
Kalinjarri NT 107 J11
Kalka SA 78 C2, 93 P8, 108 B11
Kalkallo Vic. 40 D2, 43 I3, 52 C3
Kalkarindji (Wave Hill) NT 106 D5
Kalkee Vic. 60 G8
Kalkite NSW 36 E9, 51 C3
Kallangur Qld 114 E4, 115 D2, 117 F9
Kallista Vic. 41 B9
Kalorama Vic. 40 G6, 41 B8
Kalpienung Vic. 28 G11, 61 K4
Kalpowar Qld 123 K2
Kaltukatjara (Docker River) NT 93 P6, 108 B9
Kalumburu WA 95 L2, 99 I2
Kalumpurlpa NT 107 I8
Kalunga Qld 120 C4, 121 C10, 127 L7
Kalyan SA 71 E3, 73 M9
Kamarah NSW 24 A7, 29 O7
Kamarooka Vic. 49 G1, 54 A7, 61 O8
Kambalda WA 90 H5
Kamballup WA 87 D8, 88 G10, 90 E11
Kameruka NSW 35 D9, 51 H6
Kamma Qld 120 E3, 121 F8
Kamona Tas. 143 M6
Kanangra–Boyd NP NSW 14 A7, 16 B11, 23 A1,
   24 H7, 25 I7, 35 F1
Kancoona South Vic. 55 K9, 57 I6
Kandanga Qld 117 D1, 118 D10
Kandiwal WA 95 K3, 98 H3
Kandos NSW 25 I3
Kangaloon NSW 23 C6
Kangarilla SA 66 D11, 67 C11, 68 F4, 69 H8, 71 B3,
   73 J10
Kangaroo Flat NSW 24 F6
Kangaroo Flat SA 66 D1, 67 C5
Kangaroo Flat Vic. 49 F3, 54 A9, 61 O10

Kangaroo Island SA 68 A11, 69 C11, 71 A5, 72 G12
Kangaroo Point Qld xxx H7, 113 H7
Kangaroo Valley NSW 23 C8, 25 I9, 35 G3
Kangawall Vic. 60 D10
Kangiara NSW 24 F8, 35 C2
Kaniva Vic. 28 B12, 60 C7, 71 H7
Kanmantoo SA 67 F10
Kanumbra Vic. 54 F11, 56 B9
Kanya Vic. 61 J10
Kanyapella Vic. 29 J12, 54 C6
Kanypi SA 78 E2, 108 D11
Kaoota Tas. 138 H7, 141 J8
Kapinnie SA 72 D7
Kapooka NSW 24 B10, 29 P10, 55 M1
Kapunda SA 67 E2, 71 C1, 73 K7
Karabeal Vic. 62 F3
Karadoc Vic. 28 E6, 58 H6
Karalee Qld 114 B8, 115 C5, 117 D12
Karalundi WA 89 H8, 92 E9
Karama NT xxvii G5
Karana Downs Qld 114 B8, 115 B5, 117 D11
Karanja Tas. 138 F2, 141 I6
Karara Qld 27 K1, 123 K10
Karatta SA 69 E12, 72 G12
Karawara WA xxiv G8, xxv A9
Karawinna Vic. 28 D6, 58 E7
Kardinya WA xxiv E12, 84 D8, 85 C6
Kariah Vic. 63 J7
Karijini NP WA 89 G3, 92 D5, 96 H10, 97 I9
Karingal Vic. 45 K4
Kariong NSW 13 C8, 15 N3
Karkoo SA 72 D6
Karlamilyi NP WA 92 H4, 93 I3, 97 P8
Karlgarin WA 88 H5, 90 F8
Karn Vic. 54 H9, 56 D6
Karnak Vic. 60 D10
Karonie WA 91 I5
Karoola Tas. 143 K7, 145 H8
Karoonda SA 71 E3, 73 M10
Karoonda Roadhouse Vic. 35 A10, 51 A8, 53 P2, 57 P12
Karrakatta WA xxiv D7, 84 C6, 85 B5
Karratha WA 89 E1, 92 B2, 94 B12, 96 D5
Karratha Travel Stop Roadhouse WA 89 E1, 92 B2, 94 B12, 96 D5
Karridale WA 86 B10, 88 B10
Karrinyup WA xxiv B2
Kars Springs NSW 25 J1, 26 G12
Karte SA 28 A8, 58 A10, 71 G3, 73 N9
Karuah NSW 19 F7, 20 B11, 25 M3
Karumba Qld 126 C7, 129 G4
Karween Vic. 28 C6, 58 C6, 71 H1, 73 P8
Katamatite Vic. 29 L12, 54 F5, 56 B1
Katandra Vic. 54 F6, 56 B3
Katandra West Vic. 54 F6, 56 A2
Katanning WA 88 F8, 90 E9
Katherine NT 104 F8
Katoomba NSW 14 D5, 16 F9, 25 I6
Katunga Vic. 29 K12, 54 F5
Katyil Vic. 60 G7
Kawarren Vic. 42 B10, 50 B3, 63 L9
Kayena Tas. 143 J6, 145 F7
Kedron Qld xxx H1, 114 E6
Keep River NP NT 95 O4, 99 N5, 104 A11, 106 A2
Keep River NP Extension (Proposed) NT 95 P3, 99 N4, 104 B10, 106 B1
Keilor Vic. 40 C5, 43 I5, 52 B4
Keiraville NSW 22 A7, 23 F5
Keith SA 71 F6
Kellalac Vic. 28 E12, 60 H7
Kellatier Tas. 142 E5
Kellerberrin WA 88 F4, 90 D7
Kellevie Tas. 139 M4, 141 M7
Kelmscott WA 84 F8, 85 D6
Kelso Tas. 143 J6, 145 E6
Kelvin NSW 26 G8
Kelvin Grove Qld xxx F5
Kelvin View Vic. 54 F9, 56 B7
Kempsey NSW 20 G4, 27 M10
Kempton Tas. 139 I1, 141 K5
Kendall NSW 20 F7, 27 L11
Kendenup WA 87 B8, 88 G10
Kenebri NSW 26 D8

Kenilworth Qld 117 E3, 118 D11, 123 M7
Kenmare Vic. 28 D11, 60 G5
Kenmore NSW 24 H9, 35 E3
Kenmore Qld xxx A11, 114 D7, 115 D5, 117 E11
Kenmore Hills Qld 114 D7, 115 D4, 117 E11
Kennedy Qld 120 E6, 127 M9
Kennedy Range NP WA 89 D6, 92 A8
Kennedys Creek Vic. 50 H10, 63 J9
Kennett River Vic. 42 C12, 50 D5, 63 M10
Kennys Creek NSW 24 F8, 35 C2
Kensington NSW viii G10
Kensington SA xxi M5
Kensington Vic. xiv F7
Kensington WA xxiv G7, xxv A8
Kensington Gardens SA xxi N4
Kensington Park SA xxi N4
Kent Town SA xxi K5, 65 G8
Kentbruck Vic. 62 C6
Kenthurst NSW 12 D3, 13 A10, 15 K5
Kentlyn NSW 12 A10, 15 I11, 23 G1
Kentucky NSW 20 A2, 27 J8
Kenwick WA xxv F9, 84 E7, 85 D5
Keperra Qld xxx B1, 114 D6, 115 D4, 117 E10
Keppel Bay Islands NP Qld 125 N10
Keppel Sands Qld 125 N11
Keppoch SA 71 G8
Kerang Vic. 28 H11, 61 N4
Kerang East Vic. 28 H11, 61 N4
Kerang South Vic. 28 H11, 61 N5
Kergunyah Vic. 55 L7, 57 J4
Kergunyah South Vic. 55 L8, 57 J4
Kernot Vic. 43 L10, 45 P10, 52 E8
Kerrabee NSW 25 J2
Kerrie Vic. 40 B1, 52 B2, 54 B12
Kerrisdale Vic. 52 D1, 54 D11
Kerrs Creek NSW 24 G4
Kerry Qld 21 F1, 27 N1, 115 D10
Kersbrook SA 66 F5, 67 D7, 71 C2, 73 K9
Keswick SA xx H7, 65 A12, 66 C7, 67 B9, 68 F2
Keswick Terminal SA xx H6
Kettering Tas. 138 H8, 141 K8
Kevington Vic. 43 P2, 52 H2, 56 D12
Kew NSW 20 F7, 27 L11
Kew Vic. xv P10, xvii P2
Kewdale WA xxv D7, 84 E6
Kewell Vic. 60 H8
Keyneton SA 67 G5, 71 C2, 73 K8
Keysborough Vic. xvii B2
Keysbrook WA 84 F12, 85 D8, 88 C6
Khancoban NSW 35 A7, 36 B8, 51 A3, 55 P7, 57 P4
Ki Ki SA 71 E5, 73 M11
Kiah NSW 35 E10, 51 H8
Kialla NSW 24 G8, 35 E2
Kialla Vic. 54 E7, 56 A4
Kialla West Vic. 54 E7
Kiama NSW 23 F7, 25 J9, 35 H3
Kiamil Vic. 28 E8, 58 H10
Kiana SA 72 C6
Kiandra NSW 24 E12, 35 B6, 36 D6, 51 C1
Kianga NSW 37 L9
Kiara WA xxv C2
Kiata Vic. 28 C12, 60 E7
Kidman Park SA xx D4
Kidston Qld 127 I10
Kielpa SA 72 E5, 74 D12
Kiewa Vic. 55 L7, 57 J3
Kikoira NSW 24 A5, 29 O5
Kilburn SA 66 C6, 67 B8, 68 F1
Kilcoy Qld 117 C6, 123 M8
Kilcunda Vic. 43 L11, 45 O12, 52 E9
Kilkenny SA xx F1
Kilkivan Qld 118 C8, 123 M6
Killabakh NSW 20 E7, 25 N1, 27 L12
Killafaddy Tas. 145 H1
Killara NSW 12 F5, 15 L7
Killara NSW x B1
Killarney Qld 21 C2, 27 L1, 123 L11
Killarney Vic. 50 B7, 62 G8
Killarney Heights NSW xi I1
Killawarra Vic. 55 I6, 56 E3
Killiecrankie Tas. 140 A9
Killingworth NSW 13 F3, 19 B9
Killora Tas. 139 I8, 141 K8
Kilmany Vic. 53 J7

Kilmany South Vic. 53 J7
Kilmore Vic. 43 J1, 52 C1, 54 C12
Kilpalie SA 71 F3, 73 M9
Kimba SA 72 F4, 74 D11
Kimberley Tas. 142 H7, 145 B9
Kinalung NSW 30 D10, 75 P8
Kincaid Vic. 42 A11, 50 B5, 63 K10
Kinchega NP NSW 28 E1, 30 D12, 75 P10
Kinchela NSW 20 G4, 27 M10
Kincumber NSW 13 D8, 15 O3, 25 L6
Kindred Tas. 142 G6, 144 G2
King Island Tas. 141 O11
King River WA 87 D10, 88 G11, 90 E11
King Valley Vic. 55 I9, 56 F7
Kingaroy Qld 118 A10, 123 L7
Kinglake Vic. 40 G3, 41 B5, 43 L3, 52 E3
Kinglake Central Vic. 40 G2, 41 B4, 43 K3, 52 E3
Kinglake East Vic. 41 C5, 43 L3
Kinglake NP Vic. 40 F1, 41 A3, 43 K2, 52 D2, 54 D12
Kinglake West Vic. 40 G2, 41 B4, 43 K3, 52 D2
Kingoonya SA 74 B5, 81 P5
Kingower Vic. 49 C2, 61 M9
Kings Camp SA 71 E9
Kings Canyon Resort NT 108 F8
Kings Cross NSW 10 H8, 12 F8, 13 B12, 15 M9
Kings Meadows Tas. 143 K8, 145 H10
Kings Park SA xxi I9
Kings Park WA xxiv E6
Kings Plains NP NSW 27 J5
Kings Point NSW 25 I11, 35 G5, 37 N4
Kingsborough Qld 120 C2, 121 A7, 127 K6
Kingscliff NSW 21 H2, 27 O2, 115 H12, 116 H12, 123 N11
Kingscote SA 69 E10, 72 H11
Kingsdale NSW 24 H9, 35 E3
Kingsford NSW viii H12, 12 F8, 15 M10
Kingsthorpe Qld 123 L9
Kingston ACT 32 F12
Kingston Qld 114 F10, 115 E6
Kingston S.E. SA 71 E8
Kingston Tas. 139 I6, 141 K8
Kingston Vic. 42 D2, 49 D9, 63 M3
Kingston-On-Murray SA 28 A6, 71 F1, 73 N7
Kingstown NSW 27 I8
Kingsvale NSW 24 E8, 35 B2
Kingsville Vic. xiv A9, xvi A1
Kingswood NSW 14 H6, 17 N11
Kingswood SA xxi J10, 73 I2, 74 H9
Kinimakatka Vic. 60 D7
Kinka Qld 125 N10
Kinnabulla Vic. 28 F11, 61 I5
Kinrara NP Qld 120 B7, 127 K9
Kintore NT 93 P4, 108 B6
Kioloa NSW 25 I12, 35 F6, 37 M5
Kiora NSW 37 L7
Kippa-Ring Qld 114 F4, 115 E2, 117 G9
Kirkstall Vic. 50 B7, 62 G7
Kirra Qld 115 G11, 116 H10
Kirrawee NSW 12 D10, 15 K11
Kirribilli NSW viii G2, x G10, 11 G9
Kirup WA 86 F6, 88 C9
Kitchener NSW 13 E2, 19 A8
Kitchener WA 91 K5
Kithbrook Vic. 54 F10, 56 B7
Kiwirrkurra WA 93 N4
Klemzig SA xxi M1
Knockrow NSW 21 G5, 27 O3
Knockwood Vic. 43 P3, 52 H3, 56 E12
Knowsley Vic. 54 B9, 61 P10
Knuckey Lagoon NT xxvii H7
Koah Qld 121 D6, 127 L6
Kobble Qld 114 C4, 115 C2, 117 E9
Koetong Vic. 55 N6, 57 M3
Kogan Qld 123 J8
Kogarah NSW 12 E9, 15 L10
Koimbo Vic. 28 F8, 59 J10
Kojonup WA 88 F9, 90 D10
Koloona NSW 26 H5
Kolora Vic. 63 I7
Komungla NSW 24 G9, 35 E3
Konagaderra Vic. 40 C3, 43 I3
Kondalilla NP Qld 117 E4, 118 E11, 123 N7
Kondinin WA 88 G5, 90 E8

Kongal SA 28 A12, 71 G7
Kongorong SA 71 F12
Kongwak Vic. 43 M11, 52 F8
Konnongorring WA 88 D3, 90 C6
Konong Wootong Vic. 62 E3
Konong Wootong North Vic. 62 E2
Kookynie WA 90 H3
Koolan WA 95 I5, 98 D7
Koolewong NSW 13 D8, 15 N3
Kooljaman WA 94 H5, 98 B7
Kooloonong Vic. 28 G8, 59 K10
Koolunga SA 69 G1, 73 J5, 74 H12
Koolyanobbing WA 90 F5
Koolywurtie SA 69 E6, 72 H8
Koonda Vic. 54 F8, 56 B5
Koondrook Vic. 29 I10, 54 A2, 61 O4
Koongamia WA xxv G3
Koongarra NT 103 O5, 104 G5
Koongawa SA 72 D4, 74 C11
Koonibba SA 81 L7
Kooninderie SA 67 F1
Koonoomoo Vic. 29 L11, 54 F4
Koonwarra Vic. 43 N12, 52 G9
Koonya Tas. 139 M8, 141 M8
Kooraban NP NSW 35 E7, 37 K10, 51 H3
Kooralbyn Qld 21 E1, 27 N1, 115 B10, 123 M10
Koorawatha NSW 24 E6
Koorda WA 88 E2, 90 D6
Kooreh Vic. 61 K9
Kooringal Qld 115 G4, 123 N9
Koorkab Vic. 28 G8, 59 K9
Koorlong Vic. 58 G6
Kootingal NSW 27 I9
Koo-Wee-Rup Vic. 40 H10, 43 L9, 45 O6, 52 E7
Koo-Wee-Rup North Vic. 45 P5
Koppio SA 72 D7
Korbel WA 88 G4
Koreelah NP NSW 21 C2, 27 M1, 123 L11
Koriella Vic. 43 M1, 52 F1, 54 F11, 56 B10
Korobeit Vic. 42 F3, 49 F11, 52 A3, 63 O4
Koroit Vic. 50 C7, 62 G7
Korong Vale Vic. 61 M8
Koroop Vic. 61 N4
Korora NSW 20 H1, 21 E11, 27 N7
Korumburra Vic. 43 N11, 52 F8
Korweinguboora Vic. 42 E2, 49 E9, 63 N3
Kosciuszko NP NSW 24 E11, 34 A6, 35 A7, 36 E4, 51 B2, 55 P6, 57 P3
Kotta Vic. 29 I12, 54 B6, 61 P7
Kotupna Vic. 29 K12, 54 D6
Koumala Qld 119 G9, 125 K6
Kowanyama Qld 126 E2
Kowrowa Qld 121 E6
Koyuga Vic. 54 C6
Krambach NSW 20 D8, 25 N2
Kringin SA 28 A8, 58 B10, 71 G3, 73 O9
Krongart SA 62 A3, 71 G10
Kroombit Tops NP Qld 123 K2
Krowera Vic. 43 M11, 52 F8
Kukerin WA 88 G7, 90 E9
Kulgera NT 79 L1, 109 I11
Kulgun Qld 115 A8
Kulikup WA 88 E9
Kulin WA 88 G6, 90 E8
Kulkami SA 71 F4, 73 N10
Kulkyne Vic. 28 E7, 58 H8
Kulla (McIlwraith Range) NP (CYPAL) Qld 128 E9
Kulnine Vic. 28 C6, 58 E6, 73 P7
Kulnine East Vic. 28 C6, 58 E6, 73 P7
Kulnura NSW 13 C6, 25 K5
Kulpara SA 69 F3, 73 I6
Kulpi Qld 123 K8
Kulwin Vic. 28 E8, 59 I10
Kumarina Roadhouse WA 92 E7
Kumarl WA 91 I8
Kumbarilla Qld 123 J8
Kumbatine NP NSW 20 F4, 27 L10
Kumbia Qld 123 L7
Kumorna SA 71 F6, 73 M12
Kunama NSW 24 D11, 35 A5, 36 B4, 55 P3
Kunat Vic. 61 L3
Kundabung NSW 20 G5, 27 M10
Kunghur NSW 21 F3, 27 O2, 123 N11

Kunjin WA 88 F5, 90 E8
Kunlara SA 71 E2, 73 M8
Kununoppin WA 88 F2, 90 E6
Kununurra WA 95 O4, 99 M5, 104 A11, 106 A2
Kunwarara Qld 125 L10
Kupingarri WA 95 L6, 98 H8
Kuraby Qld 114 E9, 115 E6
Kuranda Qld 120 D2, 121 E6, 127 L6
Ku-Ring-Gai Chase NP NSW 12 G3, 13 C10, 15 M5, 25 K6
Kuringup WA 88 H8
Kurmond NSW 14 H4, 17 N5
Kurnell NSW 12 F10, 15 L11, 25 K7
Kurraca Vic. 49 B1, 61 L9
Kurraca West Vic. 49 B1, 61 L8
Kurrajong NSW 14 G4, 17 M5
Kurrajong Heights NSW 14 G3, 17 L5, 25 J5
Kurralta Park SA xx G8
Kurri Kurri NSW 13 F2, 19 B8, 25 L4
Kurrimine Beach Qld 120 E5, 127 M8
Kurrimine Beach NP Qld 120 E5, 127 M8
Kurting Vic. 49 C1, 61 M9
Kurumbul Qld 26 H2, 123 I11
Kuttabul Qld 119 F7, 125 K5
Kweda WA 88 F5
Kwiambal NP NSW 27 I3, 123 J12
Kwinana WA 84 D10, 85 C7, 88 B5, 90 C8
Kwolyin WA 88 F4
Kyabram Vic. 54 D6
Kyalite NSW 28 G8, 59 L10
Kyancutta SA 72 D4, 74 B11
Kybeyan NSW 35 D8, 36 H10, 51 G4
Kybunga SA 69 H3, 73 J6
Kybybolite SA 60 B10, 71 G9
Kydra NSW 35 D8, 36 H11, 51 F4
Kyeamba NSW 24 C10, 29 P10, 55 N3
Kyndalyn Vic. 28 F7, 59 J9
Kyneton Vic. 42 G1, 49 G8, 52 A1, 54 A11, 63 O2
Kynuna Qld 131 J5
Kyogle NSW 21 E4, 27 N3, 123 M12
Kyup Vic. 62 F3
Kyvalley Vic. 54 D6
Kywong NSW 24 A9, 29 N9

L aanecoorie Vic. 49 D4, 61 M10
Laang Vic. 50 E8, 63 I8
Labertouche Vic. 41 F11, 43 N8, 52 F6
Labrador Qld 21 G1, 27 O1, 115 G9, 116 F5
Lachlan Tas. 138 G4, 141 J7
Lackrana Tas. 140 B10
Lady Barron Tas. 140 B11, 143 P1
Lady Bay Tas. 138 F11, 141 I10
Lady Elliot Island Qld 123 N2
Lady Julia Percy Island Vic. 62 F8
Lady Musgrave Island Qld 123 N1
Ladysmith NSW 24 C10, 29 P10, 55 N1
Laen Vic. 61 I8
Laen North Vic. 61 I7
Laggan NSW 24 G8, 35 E2
Lah Vic. 28 E12, 60 H6
Laharum Vic. 60 G10
Laheys Creek NSW 24 G1, 26 D12
Laidley Qld 117 A12, 123 M9
Lajamanu (Hooker Creek) NT 106 D7
Lake Bathurst NSW 24 G10, 35 E4, 37 J1
Lake Biddy WA 90 F8
Lake Bindegolly NP Qld 133 L8
Lake Boga Vic. 28 H10, 61 M3
Lake Bolac Vic. 63 I4
Lake Buloke Vic. 28 F12, 61 J7
Lake Cargelligo NSW 24 A4, 29 N4
Lake Cathie NSW 20 F6, 27 M11
Lake Charm Vic. 28 H10, 61 M4
Lake Clifton WA 85 C11, 88 B7, 90 C9
Lake Condah Vic. 62 E6
Lake Conjola NSW 25 I11, 35 G5, 37 N3
Lake Cowal NSW 24 C5, 29 P5
Lake Eildon NP Vic. 41 H1, 43 O1, 52 G1, 54 G12, 56 C11
Lake Eppalock Vic. 49 H4, 54 B9, 61 P11
Lake Eyre NP SA 74 F1, 76 F9, 132 A8
Lake Gairdner NP SA 72 E1, 74 A6, 81 P6
Lake Goldsmith Vic. 42 A3, 63 K4
Lake Grace WA 88 H7, 90 E9

Lake Hindmarsh Vic. 28 D11, 60 E6
Lake King WA 90 G8
Lake Leake Tas. 141 M2, 143 M12
Lake Margaret Tas. 140 D1, 142 D11, 144 A9
Lake Marmal Vic. 28 G12, 61 L6
Lake Mundi Vic. 62 B3, 71 H11
Lake Munmorah NSW 13 F6, 19 B12, 25 L5
Lake Rowan Vic. 54 G7, 56 D3
Lake Torrens NP SA 74 G4
Lake Tyers Vic. 53 O6
Lake View SA 69 G1, 73 I5
Lakefield NP Qld 127 I1, 128 F12
Lakeland Qld 127 K3
Lakes Entrance Vic. 53 O6
Lakeside Vic. 45 O1
Lakesland NSW 14 E12, 23 D2
Lal Lal Vic. 42 D4, 49 D11, 63 M4
Lalbert Vic. 28 G10, 61 L4
Lalbert Road Vic. 28 G10, 61 L3
Lalla Tas. 143 K7, 145 H8
Lallat Vic. 61 I8
Lalor Vic. 43 J4
Lama Lama NP Qld 128 E11
Lameroo SA 28 A9, 71 G4, 73 N10
Lamington Qld 21 F2, 27 N1, 115 C11, 123 M11
Lamington NP Qld 21 F2, 27 N2, 115 D11, 116 A10, 123 N11
Lamplough Vic. 49 A6, 61 L12, 63 L1
Lancaster Vic. 54 D6
Lancefield Vic. 42 H1, 52 B1, 54 B12, 63 P2
Lancelin WA 88 A3, 90 B6
Lands End Qld 116 F4
Landsborough Qld 117 F5, 118 E12, 123 N8
Landsborough Vic. 61 J11, 63 J1
Landsdale WA 84 D4, 85 C4
Lane Cove NSW x C5, 12 E6, 13 B12, 15 L8
Lane Cove NP NSW x B1, 12 E5, 13 B11, 15 L7, 25 K6
Lane Cove North NSW x C3
Lane Cove West NSW x B4
Lanena Tas. 143 J7, 145 F8
Lang Lang Vic. 43 L9, 45 P7, 52 E7
Langford WA xxv D10
Langhorne Creek SA 71 C4, 73 K10
Langi Logan Vic. 63 I2
Langkoop Vic. 60 B11, 62 B1, 71 H9
Langley Vic. 49 H7, 54 A11, 61 P12, 63 P2
Langlo Crossing Qld 122 A5, 133 O5
Langloh Tas. 141 I5
Langsborough Vic. 53 I10
Langville Vic. 28 H11, 61 M5
Langwarrin Vic. 40 E10, 43 J8, 45 K5
Lankeys Creek NSW 24 C12, 29 P12, 55 N5
Lannercost Qld 120 E8, 127 M10
Lansdowne NSW 20 E7, 25 O1, 27 L12
Lapoinya Tas. 142 E5
Lapstone NSW 14 G7, 17 L11
Lara Vic. 42 F7, 44 B1, 52 A5, 63 O7
Lara Lake Vic. 44 B1
Laramba NT 108 H4
Laravale Qld 21 E1, 27 N1, 115 C10
Largs North SA 66 B5, 67 A7, 68 E1, 71 B2, 73 J9
Larpent Vic. 42 A9, 50 B2, 63 K8
Larrakeyah NT xxvii A10, 102 C3
Larras Lee NSW 24 F3
Larrimah NT 104 H10, 106 H1
Lascelles Vic. 28 E10, 60 H3
Latham WA 90 C4
Lathlain WA xxiv H6, xxv B7
Latrobe Tas. 142 H6, 144 H2, 145 B7
Lauderdale Tas. 139 K6, 141 L7
Laughtondale NSW 13 A7, 15 K2
Launceston Tas. 143 K8, 145 F1
Launching Place Vic. 41 D8, 43 M5, 52 E4
Laura Qld 127 J3
Laura SA 73 J4, 74 H11
Laurel Hill NSW 24 D11, 35 A5, 36 B4, 55 P4
Laurieton NSW 20 F7, 25 O1, 27 L12
Lauriston Vic. 42 F1, 49 G8, 52 A1, 54 A11, 63 O2
Lavender Bay NSW viii G1, x G9
Lavers Hill Vic. 42 A12, 50 A5, 63 K10
Laverton Vic. 40 B6, 42 H6, 52 B4, 63 P6
Laverton WA 91 I2, 93 I12
Lawler Vic. 28 E12, 61 I7

163

Lawley River NP WA 95 L3, 98 H3
Lawloit Vic. 28 C12, 60 D7
Lawnton Qld 114 E4, 115 D2, 117 F9
Lawrence NSW 21 E8, 27 N5
Lawrence Vic. 42 D1, 49 D8, 63 M2
Lawrence Road NSW 21 E7, 27 N5
Lawrenny Tas. 141 I5
Lawson NSW 14 E6, 16 H9, 25 I6
Layard Vic. 42 E9, 50 F1, 63 N8
Le Roy Vic. 53 I8
Leabrook SA xxi N6
Leadville NSW 24 H1, 26 E12
Leaghur Vic. 28 H11, 61 M5
Leam Tas. 145 F8
Leanyer NT xxvii F4
Learmonth Vic. 42 C2, 49 B9, 63 L3
Learmonth WA 89 B3
Leasingham SA 73 J6
Leawarra Vic. 45 K4
Leawood Gardens SA xxi O10
Lebrina Tas. 143 K6, 145 H7
Leda WA 84 D10, 85 C7
Ledge Point WA 88 A3
Lee Point NT xxvii F2
Leederville WA xxiv E5
Leeka Tas. 140 A9
Leeman WA 90 A5
Leeming WA xxiv H12, xxv A12
Leeor Vic. 28 B12, 60 B7, 71 H7
Leeton NSW 29 N8
Leets Vale NSW 13 A7, 15 J2
Leeville NSW 21 E5, 27 N4
Lefroy Tas. 143 J6, 145 G6
Legana Tas. 143 K7, 145 G9
Legerwood Tas. 143 M7
Legume NSW 21 C2, 27 L2, 123 L11
Leichardt Vic. 49 E2, 61 N10
Leichhardt NSW viii A5, x A12, 12 E8
Leichhardt Qld 114 A9, 115 B5, 117 C12, 125 J11
Leigh Creek SA 70 B4, 74 H4
Leigh Creek Vic. 42 D3, 49 D10, 63 M4
Leighton SA 73 K5
Leighton WA 84 C7
Leinster WA 90 G1, 92 G11
Leitchville Vic. 29 I11, 54 A4, 61 O5
Leith Tas. 142 H6, 144 G1
Lemana Tas. 145 C10
Lemnos Vic. 54 E7, 56 A3
Lemon Tree Passage NSW 19 G8, 20 C12, 25 M4
Lemont Tas. 141 L4
Lenah Valley Tas. xxxiv B10, 137 C7
Leneva Vic. 55 K6, 57 I3
Lennox Head NSW 21 H5, 27 O3, 123 N12
Leongatha Vic. 43 N11, 52 G8
Leongatha South Vic. 43 N11, 52 F9
Leonora WA 90 H2
Leopold Vic. 42 G8, 44 C4, 50 H1, 52 A6, 63 O7
Leppington NSW 14 H9
Leprena Tas. 141 I11
Leschenault WA 86 E3
Leslie Manor Vic. 42 A7, 63 K7
Leslie Vale Tas. 138 H6, 141 K7
Lesmurdie WA xxv H8, 84 F7
Lesmurdie Falls NP WA xxv H7, 84 F6, 85 D5, 88 C5, 90 C7
Lesueur NP WA 88 A1, 90 A5
Lethbridge Vic. 42 E6, 63 N6
Leumeah NSW 14 H11, 23 F1
Leura NSW 14 D5, 16 G9, 25 I6
Levendale Tas. 139 L1, 141 L5
Lewis Ponds NSW 24 G4
Lewisham NSW viii A7, 12 E8
Lewisham Tas. 139 L5, 141 L7
Lewiston SA 66 C1, 67 B5, 69 H6
Lexton Vic. 42 B1, 49 A7, 63 L2
Leyburn Qld 123 K10
Liawenee Tas. 141 I1, 143 I11
Licola Vic. 53 J4
Lidcombe NSW 15 K8
Liena Tas. 142 G8, 144 G5
Lietinna Tas. 143 L6
Liffey Tas. 143 J9, 145 E12
Lightning Ridge NSW 26 B3, 122 E12
Likkaparta NT 107 J9
Lileah Tas. 142 C4

Lilli Pilli NSW 37 M7
Lillicur Vic. 49 A6, 61 L12, 63 L1
Lillimur Vic. 28 B12, 60 C7, 71 H7
Lillimur South Vic. 28 B12, 60 C7, 71 H7
Lilydale Tas. 143 K7, 145 H8
Lilydale Vic. 40 G5, 41 B7, 43 L5, 52 E4
Lilyfield NSW viii C4, x B11
Lima Vic. 54 G9, 56 C7
Lima East Vic. 54 G9, 56 C7
Lima South Vic. 54 G10, 56 D7
Limeburners Creek NSW 19 F6, 20 B11, 25 M3
Limekilns NSW 24 H4
Limestone Vic. 41 D1, 43 M1, 52 E1, 54 E12, 56 A11
Limestone Ridge Qld 114 A12, 115 B7
Limevale Qld 27 J2, 123 J11
Limmen NP (Proposed) NT 105 K9, 107 L2
Limpinwood NSW 116 A12
Lincoln NP SA 72 D9
Lincolnfields SA 69 F2, 73 I6
Lind NP Vic. 35 B11, 51 D10
Linda Tas. 140 E1, 142 E11, 144 B10
Lindeman Islands NP Qld 119 G5, 125 K4
Linden NSW 14 F6, 17 J9
Linden Park SA xxi M7
Lindenow Vic. 53 M5
Lindenow South Vic. 53 M5
Lindfield NSW x C1
Lindisfarne Tas. xxxiv H7, 1 E3 , 137 F6, 139 J5, 141 K7
Lindsay Point Vic. 28 B5, 58 C5, 71 H1, 73 O7
Lindum Qld 114 F7
Linga Vic. 28 C9, 58 E11
Linley Point NSW x B6
Linton Vic. 42 B4, 49 A11, 63 L4
Linville Qld 117 A4, 118 B12, 123 M7
Linwood SA 67 D3, 73 J7
Lipson SA 72 E7
Lisarow NSW 13 D7, 15 O2
Lisle Tas. 143 L7
Lismore NSW 21 F5, 27 O3, 123 N12
Lismore Vic. 42 A6, 63 K6
Liston NSW 21 B3, 27 L2, 123 L11
Litchfield Vic. 28 F12, 61 I7
Litchfield NP NT 102 D9, 104 D6
Littabella NP Qld 118 C1, 123 M2
Little Billabong NSW 24 C11, 29 P11, 55 N3
Little Desert NP Vic. 28 B12, 60 C8, 71 G8
Little Grove WA 87 D11, 88 G12, 90 E11
Little Hampton Vic. 42 F2, 49 F9, 52 A2, 54 A12, 63 O3
Little Hard Hills Vic. 42 C4, 49 B12
Little Hartley NSW 14 C3, 16 E5
Little Jilliby NSW 13 D6
Little Mulgrave Qld 120 E3, 121 F8
Little River Vic. 42 G6, 52 A5, 63 O6
Little Snowy Creek Vic. 55 L8, 57 K6
Little Swanport Tas. 141 N4
Little Topar Roadhouse NSW 30 D9
Littlehampton SA 66 G9, 67 D10, 68 H3
Liverpool NSW 12 B8, 15 J9, 25 J7, 35 H1
Livingstone NP NSW 24 B10, 29 P10, 55 M2
Lizard Island NP Qld 127 L1
Llandaff Tas. 141 O2, 143 O11
Llandeilo Vic. 42 E3, 49 E11, 63 N4
Llanelly Vic. 49 D3, 61 M10
Llangothlin NSW 27 K7
Llewellyn Siding Tas. 141 M1, 143 M10
Loccota Tas. 140 B11, 143 O1
Loch Vic. 43 M10, 52 F8
Loch Sport Vic. 53 M6
Lochern NP Qld 131 L11
Lochiel NSW 51 H7
Lochiel SA 69 G3, 73 I6
Lochinvar NSW 13 F1, 19 B7, 25 L3
Lochnagar Qld 124 D10, 131 P10
Lock SA 72 D5, 74 C12
Lockhart NSW 24 A10, 29 N10, 55 K1
Lockhart River Qld 128 E7
Lockington Qld 124 H11
Lockington Vic. 29 I12, 54 B6, 61 P7
Lockleys SA xx D5
Lockridge WA xxv C2
Locksley NSW 24 H5

Locksley Vic. 54 E9
Lockwood Vic. 49 F4, 61 N10
Lockwood South Vic. 49 F4, 61 N10
Loddon Vale Vic. 28 H11, 61 N6
Loftus NSW 12 C10, 15 K11, 23 H1
Logan Vic. 49 A2, 61 L9
Logan Village Qld 114 E11, 115 E7
Loganlea Qld 114 F10, 115 E6
Logie Brae NSW 29 L10, 54 F2
Loira Tas. 143 J7, 145 F8
Lombadina WA 94 H6, 98 B8
Londonderry NSW 14 H5, 17 N8
Londrigan Vic. 55 I7, 56 F4
Long Beach NSW 35 F6, 37 M6
Long Flat NSW 20 E6, 24 G11, 25 I8, 27 L11, 35 F2, 37 J5
Long Jetty NSW 13 E7, 15 P2, 25 L5
Long Plains SA 67 A2, 69 H5, 71 B1, 73 J7
Long Plains Vic. 61 J2
Long Pocket Qld 127 L12
Longerenong Vic. 60 G9
Longford Tas. 143 K9, 145 G12
Longford Vic. 53 K7
Longlea Vic. 49 G3, 54 A9, 61 O10
Longley Tas. 138 H6, 141 J7
Longreach Qld 124 B10, 131 N10
Longueville NSW x C7
Longwarry Vic. 41 F12, 43 N8, 52 F6
Longwood Vic. 54 E9
Longwood East Vic. 54 E9
Lonnavale Tas. 138 E6, 141 I7
Lonsdale SA 66 B10, 67 A11, 68 E4, 69 H8, 73 J9
Looma WA 95 J7, 98 E11
Loongana Tas. 142 F7, 144 D3
Loongana WA 91 N5
Loorana Tas. 141 O11
Lorinna Tas. 142 G8, 144 F5
Lorne NSW 20 E7, 27 L11
Lorne Vic. 42 D11, 50 E4, 63 M9
Lorquon Vic. 28 C12, 60 E6
Lorquon West Vic. 60 E6
Lostock NSW 19 B3, 20 A9, 25 L2
Lota Qld 114 G7
Lottah Tas. 143 O7
Louisville Tas. 139 N1, 141 M5
Louth Bay SA 72 D8
Louth NSW 31 K6
Loveday SA 73 N7
Lovely Banks Vic. 44 A2
Low Head Tas. 143 J6, 145 E5
Lowaldie SA 71 E3, 73 M9
Lowan Vale SA 28 A12, 60 A6, 71 G7
Lowanna NSW 21 D11, 27 M7
Lowbank SA 71 F1, 73 M7
Lowden WA 86 F5, 88 C8
Lowdina Tas. 139 J2, 141 K5
Lower Acacia Creek NSW 21 B2, 27 L2
Lower Barrington Tas. 142 H7, 144 G2, 145 A7
Lower Beulah Tas. 142 H8, 144 H4, 145 A10
Lower Boro NSW 24 H10, 35 E4, 37 K2
Lower Bucca NSW 21 E11, 27 N7
Lower Chittering WA 85 D2, 88 C4
Lower Creek NSW 20 E2, 27 L9
Lower Gellibrand Vic. 50 H11, 63 J10
Lower Glenelg NP Vic. 62 B6, 71 H12
Lower Goulburn NP Vic. 54 D5
Lower Heytesbury Vic. 50 F10, 63 I9
Lower Mangrove NSW 13 B8, 15 M2
Lower Marshes Tas. 141 K4
Lower Mitcham SA xxi J11
Lower Mookerawa NSW 24 G3
Lower Mount Hicks Tas. 142 F5
Lower Norton Vic. 60 F10
Lower Quipolly NSW 26 H10
Lower Sandy Bay Tas. 137 E10
Lower Turners Marsh Tas. 143 K6, 145 G7
Lower Wilmot Tas. 144 G3
Lowesdale NSW 29 M11, 55 I4
Lowlands NSW 14 H4, 17 O6, 29 L3
Lowmead Qld 123 L2
Lowood Qld 115 A4, 117 B10, 123 M9
Lowther NSW 14 B4, 16 C6, 25 I6
Loxton SA 28 A6, 58 A7, 71 G2, 73 N8
Loxton North SA 28 A6, 58 A7, 71 G1, 73 N8
Loyetea Tas. 142 F7, 144 E2

Lubeck Vic. 60 H9
Lucas Heights NSW 12 B10, 15 J11, 23 H1
Lucaston Tas. 138 G6, 141 J7
Lucinda Qld 120 F8, 127 M10
Lucindale SA 71 F9
Lucknow NSW 24 G5
Lucknow Vic. 53 M5
Lucky Bay SA 69 C1, 72 G5
Lucyvale Vic. 55 N7, 57 M4
Luddenham NSW 14 G8
Ludlow WA 86 D6, 88 B9
Ludmilla NT xxvii B7
Lue NSW 24 H3
Lughrata Tas. 140 B10
Lulworth Tas. 143 K5, 145 G5
Lunawanna Tas. 138 H11, 141 J10
Lune River Tas. 138 E12, 141 I10
Lurg Vic. 54 H8, 56 E6
Lurg Upper Vic. 54 H8, 56 E6
Lutana Tas. xxxiv E6, 1 A2 , 137 D5
Lutwyche Qld xxx H3
Lyiltjarra NT 110 C5
Lyme Regis Tas. 143 O4
Lymington Tas. 138 G9, 141 J9
Lymwood Tas. 141 P12
Lynchford Tas. 140 D2, 142 D11, 144 A11
Lynchs Creek NSW 21 E3, 27 N2
Lyndhurst NSW 24 F5
Lyndhurst SA 70 A2, 74 H3
Lyndhurst Vic. 40 F8, 41 A11, 43 K7, 45 M3,
    52 D6
Lyndoch SA 66 G2, 67 E5, 71 C2, 73 K8
Lynton SA xxi J12
Lynwood WA xxv C11
Lyons NT xxvii E3
Lyons Vic. 62 D6, 71 H12
Lyonville Vic. 42 F2, 49 F9, 63 O3
Lyrup SA 28 A6, 58 A6, 71 G1, 73 N7
Lysterfield Vic. 40 G7, 41 B9, 43 K6, 52 D5
Lysterfield Lake Park Vic. 40 G8, 43 K7, 45 M1
Lytton Qld xxxi P5

Maaroom Qld 118 F6, 123 N5
McAlinden WA 86 H5, 88 D8
Macalister Qld 123 J8
Macarthur Vic. 62 F6
Macclesfield SA 66 F11, 67 D11, 68 H5, 71 C4, 73 K10
Macclesfield Vic. 41 C9, 43 L6, 52 E5
McCrae Vic. 44 H8
McCullys Gap NSW 25 K2
Macdonnell NT 111 I4
McDonnell Creek Qld 120 E3, 121 G9
Macedon Vic. 40 A1, 42 G2, 49 H9, 52 B2, 54 B12,
    63 P3
McGraths Hill NSW 12 A2, 15 I5, 17 P7
Machans Beach Qld 120 E2, 121 F6
McIntyre Vic. 49 B2, 61 M9
Mackay Qld 119 G8, 125 K5
McKees Hill NSW 21 F5
McKenzie Creek Vic. 60 G9
McKinlay Qld 129 G12, 131 I4
Macks Creek Vic. 53 I9
Macksville NSW 20 G2, 27 M9
Maclagan Qld 123 K8
McLaren Flat SA 66 C12, 67 B12, 68 F5
McLaren Vale SA 66 B12, 67 B12, 68 E5, 69 H9,
    71 B4, 73 J10
Maclean NSW 21 F8, 27 N5
McLoughlins Beach Vic. 53 J9
McMahons Creek Vic. 41 G7, 43 N5, 52 F4
McMahons Point NSW viii F2, x F9, 11 B9
McMahons Reef NSW 24 E8, 35 B2
McMillans Vic. 29 I11, 54 A4, 61 O5
Macorna Vic. 28 H11, 61 N5
Macquarie Fields NSW 12 A9, 15 I10
Macquarie Park NSW x A2
Macquarie Pass NP NSW 23 D6, 25 J9, 35 G3
Macquarie Plains Tas. 138 F3, 141 I6
Macrossan Qld 120 F12, 124 F2
Macs Cove Vic. 43 P1, 52 H1, 54 H12, 56 D11
Madalya Vic. 53 I9
Maddington WA 84 F7, 85 D6
Maddington WA xxv F11
Madora WA 85 C9, 88 B6
Madura Roadhouse WA 91 N6

Madura WA 91 N6
Mafeking Vic. 62 H2
Maffra Vic. 53 K6
Maggea SA 71 F2, 73 M8
Magill SA xxi O3
Magnetic Island NP Qld 119 A1, 120 G10, 124 G1,
    127 N11
Magpie Vic. 42 C3, 49 C11
Magra Tas. 138 G3, 141 J6
Magrath Flat SA 71 D6, 73 L12
Mahogany Creek WA 84 G5
Maianbar NSW 12 D11, 15 K12
Maida Vale WA xxv G6
Maiden Gully Vic. 49 F3, 61 O10
Maidenwell Qld 123 L7
Maidstone Vic. xiv A5
Mailors Flat Vic. 50 C7, 62 G7
Maimuru NSW 24 D7, 35 B1
Main Beach Qld 21 G1, 27 O1, 115 G9, 116 F6,
    123 N10
Main Lead Vic. 42 A1, 63 K3
Main Range NP Qld 21 C1, 27 M1, 123 L10
Main Ridge Vic. 45 I9
Maindample Vic. 54 G11, 56 C9
Maitland NSW 13 F1, 19 C7, 20 A11, 25 L3
Maitland SA 69 E5, 72 H7
Major Plains Vic. 54 G7, 56 C4
Majorca Vic. 49 C6, 61 M12, 63 M1
Majors Creek NSW 24 G11, 35 E5, 37 J5
Malaga WA xxiv G1, xxv A1
Malak NT xxvii F5
Malanda Qld 120 D4, 121 E10, 127 L7
Malbina Tas. 138 H4, 141 J6
Malbon Qld 129 E12, 130 G4
Malcolm WA 90 H2
Maldon NSW 14 F12, 23 E2
Maldon Vic. 49 E5, 61 N11, 63 N1
Maleny Qld 117 E4, 118 E12, 123 N7
Malinong SA 71 D5, 73 L11
Mallacoota Vic. 35 D11, 51 G11
Mallala SA 67 B3, 69 H5, 71 B1, 73 J7
Mallan NSW 28 H9, 59 M11, 61 M1
Mallanganee NSW 21 D5, 27 M3, 123 M12
Mallanganee NP NSW 21 D5, 27 M3, 123 M12
Mallee Cliffs NP NSW 28 E5, 58 H5, 59 I6
Mallum Vic. 54 H9, 56 D7
Malmsbury Vic. 49 G7, 52 A1, 54 A11, 61 O12,
    63 O2
Malpas SA 28 A7, 58 A8, 71 G2, 73 N9
Malua Bay NSW 24 H12, 35 F6, 37 M7
Malvern SA xxi J9
Malyalling WA 88 F6
Mambray Creek SA 73 I3, 74 G10
Manangatang Vic. 28 F8, 59 J11
Manara NSW 29 I11, 30 H12
Mandagery NSW 24 E4
Mandalong NSW 13 E5, 19 A11
Mandorah NT 102 C3, 104 D4
Mandurah WA 85 C9, 88 B6, 90 C8
Mandurama NSW 24 F5
Mandurang Vic. 49 G4, 54 A9, 61 O10
Mangalo SA 69 A1, 72 F5, 74 E12
Mangalore Tas. 139 I2, 141 K6
Mangalore Vic. 54 D10
Mangana Tas. 143 N9
Mangerton NSW 22 C10
Mango Hill Qld 114 E4, 115 E2, 117 F9
Mangoola NSW 25 J2
Mangoplah NSW 24 B10, 29 O10, 55 M2
Mangrove Creek NSW 13 B7, 15 M1, 25 K5
Mangrove Mountain NSW 13 C6, 15 M1, 25 K5
Manguri SA 79 N10
Manildra NSW 24 F4
Manilla NSW 26 H8
Maningrida NT 105 J3
Manjimup WA 86 H10, 87 B1, 88 D10, 90 C10
Manly NSW xi O5, 12 G6, 13 C12, 15 M8, 25 K6
Manly Qld 114 G7, 115 E4, 117 G11
Manly Vale NSW xi M2
Manmanning WA 88 E2, 90 D6
Manmoyi NT 105 J4
Mannahill SA 73 M2, 75 L9
Mannanarie SA 73 J3, 75 I11
Mannerim Vic. 42 G8, 44 D5, 52 A6
Mannering Park NSW 13 F5, 19 B11, 25 L5

Mannibadar Vic. 42 A4, 63 K5
Manning WA xxiv G9, xxv A10
Manning Point NSW 20 E8, 25 O1, 27 L12
Manns Beach Vic. 53 J10
Mannum SA 67 H9, 71 D3, 73 L9
Manobalai NSW 25 J1, 26 H12
Manoora SA 73 K6
Mansfield Vic. 54 H11, 56 D9
Mantung SA 71 F2, 73 M8
Manumbar Qld 118 C10, 123 M6
Many Peaks Qld 123 L2
Manyallaluk NT 104 G8
Manyana NSW 37 N3
Manypeaks WA 87 F10, 88 H11
Mapleton Qld 117 F3, 118 E11
Mapleton Falls NP Qld 117 E3, 118 E11, 123 N7
Mapoon Qld 128 B5
Mara NT 105 M11, 107 M2
Maralinga SA 80 H3
Marama SA 71 F4, 73 M10
Maranboy NT 104 G8
Marangaroo WA 84 C4, 85 C4
Marathon Qld 124 A4, 131 M4
Maraylya NSW 12 B2, 15 J4
Marbelup WA 87 C11, 88 G11
Marble Bar WA 92 E2, 94 E12, 97 K5
Marburg Qld 115 A5, 117 B11, 123 M9
Marchagee WA 90 B5
Marcoola Qld 117 G3, 118 F11
Marcus Vic. 44 D5
Marcus Beach Qld 117 H2, 118 F10
Marcus Hill Vic. 42 G9, 44 D5, 52 A7
Mardella WA 84 F11, 85 D7
Marden SA xxi L2
Mareeba Qld 120 D2, 121 D7, 127 L6
Marengo NSW 21 B11, 27 L7
Marengo Vic. 42 B12, 50 C6, 63 L11
Margaret River WA 86 B8, 88 B10, 90 B10
Margate Tas. 139 I7, 141 K8
Maria NP NSW 20 G5, 27 M10
Maria Creek NP Qld 120 E5, 127 M8
Maria Island NP Tas. 139 O3, 141 N6
Maria NP NSW 20 G5, 27 M10
Mariala NP Qld 133 N4
Marian Qld 119 F7, 125 K5
Maribyrnong Vic. xiv B4
Mariginiup WA 84 C3
Marion Bay SA 69 B9, 72 G10
Marion SA 66 B8, 67 B9, 68 E3, 69 H8
Marion Bay Tas. 139 N5, 141 M7
Markwell NSW 19 H4, 20 C10, 25 N2
Markwood Vic. 55 I8, 56 G5
Marla SA 79 M5
Marlborough Qld 125 L9
Marlee NSW 20 D7, 25 N1, 27 K12
Marleston SA xx F7
Marlo Vic. 35 A12, 51 B11
Marma Vic. 60 H9
Marmion WA xxiv A1
Marmor Qld 125 M11
Marnoo Vic. 61 I9
Marong Vic. 49 E3, 61 N10
Maroochydore Qld 117 G4, 118 F11, 123 N7
Maroon Qld 21 D1, 27 N1, 115 A10, 123 M10
Maroona Vic. 63 I3
Maroota NSW 13 A8, 15 K3, 25 K5
Marp Vic. 62 C5, 71 H12
Marrabel SA 71 C1, 73 K7
Marradong WA 85 G11, 88 D7
Marralum NT 95 P3, 99 N4, 104 B10, 106 B1
Marramarra NP NSW 12 E1, 13 B9, 15 K3, 25 K5
Marrangaroo NSW 14 B1, 16 C1, 25 I5
Marrar NSW 24 B9, 29 P9
Marrara NT xxvii E6
Marrawah Tas. 142 A4
Marraweeny Vic. 54 F9, 56 B7
Marree SA 74 H1, 76 H12, 132 A12
Marrickville NSW viii A9, 12 E8, 15 L9
Marrinup WA 85 E10
Marryatville SA xxi M6
Marsden NSW 24 C5, 29 P5
Marshall Vic. 42 F8, 44 A4, 50 G1, 52 A6, 63 O7
Marshdale NSW 19 E4, 20 B10, 25 M3
Martin WA xxv H12
Martindale NSW 25 J2

165

Martins Creek NSW 19 C5, 20 A11, 25 L3
Martinsville NSW 13 E4, 19 A10
Marton Qld 127 L3
Marulan NSW 24 H9, 35 F3
Marulan South NSW 24 H9, 35 F3
Marungi Vic. 29 L12, 54 F6, 56 A2
Marvel Loch WA 90 F6
Mary River NP (Proposed) NT 102 H1, 103 I4, 104 E4
Mary River Roadhouse NT 103 L10, 104 F6
Maryborough Qld 118 E6, 123 N5
Maryborough Vic. 49 C5, 61 M11, 63 M1
Marybrook WA 86 B6
Maryfarms Qld 120 C1, 121 B4, 127 K5
Maryknoll Vic. 41 D11, 43 M7, 52 E6
Maryland NP NSW 21 B3, 27 L2, 123 L11
Marysville Vic. 41 F5, 43 N3, 52 F3
Maryvale NSW 24 F2
Maryvale Qld 21 C1
Maryville NSW 18 A2
Mascot NSW viii E12, 12 F8, 15 L9
Maslin Beach SA 66 A12, 67 A12, 68 E5
Massey Vic. 28 F12, 61 I7
Matakana NSW 29 M3
Mataranka NT 104 H9
Matcham NSW 13 D8, 15 O3
Matheson NSW 27 J5
Mathinna Tas. 143 N8
Mathoura NSW 29 J11, 54 D4
Matlock Vic. 43 P4, 52 H4
Matong NSW 24 B8, 29 O8, 35 B9, 36 E12, 51 D6
Maude NSW 29 I7, 59 P8
Maude Vic. 42 E6, 63 N6
Maudsland Qld 115 F9, 116 C4
Mawbanna Tas. 142 D4
Mawson WA 88 E5, 90 D7
Maxwelton Qld 131 K3
Mayanup WA 88 D9, 90 D10
Mayberry Tas. 142 H8, 144 G5
Maydena Tas. 138 D3, 140 H6
Maylands SA xxi L4
Maylands WA 84 D6, 85 C5
Maylands WA xxiv H4, xxv A5
Mayrung NSW 29 K10, 54 E2
Mazeppa NP Qld 119 A10, 124 G7
Meadow Creek Vic. 55 I8, 56 F6
Meadowbank NSW 15 K8
Meadows SA 66 E11, 67 D11, 68 G5, 71 C4, 73 J10
Meandarra Qld 122 H8
Meander Tas. 143 I9, 145 C12
Meatian Vic. 28 G10, 61 K3
Mebbin NP NSW 21 F3, 27 N2, 123 N11
Meckering WA 88 E4, 90 D7
Medindie SA xxi J2, 65 E2
Medindie Gardens SA xxi J1
Medlow Bath NSW 14 C5, 16 F8, 25 I6
Medowie NSW 19 E7
Meeandah Qld 114 F7
Meekatharra WA 89 H9, 92 E10
Meelon WA 85 D10
Meeniyan Vic. 43 O12, 52 G9
Meerawa Qld 120 E3, 121 G9
Meerlieu Vic. 53 L6
Meerschaum Vale NSW 21 G5, 27 O4, 123 N12
Megalong NSW 14 C5, 16 E8
Megan NSW 21 C11, 27 M7
Melaleuca Tas. 140 F10
Melbourne Vic. xv J11, xvii J2, 39, 40 D6, 43 I5, 52 C4
Meldale Qld 114 F1, 117 G7
Mella Tas. 142 C4
Mellis Vic. 60 H7
Melros WA 85 B10
Melrose SA 73 I3, 74 H10
Melrose Tas. 142 H6, 144 G2, 145 A7
Melrose Park SA xx H11
Melsonby Gaarraay NP Qld 127 K2
Melton SA 69 F3, 73 I6
Melton Vic. 40 A4, 42 G4, 49 H12, 52 B3, 63 P5
Melton Mowbray Tas. 141 K4
Melton South Vic. 40 A4, 42 G4, 49 H12, 52 B4, 63 P5
Melville WA xxiv D10, 84 D7, 85 C6, 87 D11
Melville Forest Vic. 62 E3

Melville Island NT 104 D2
Memana Tas. 140 B10
Memerambi Qld 118 A10, 123 L6
Mena Creek Qld 120 E5, 121 G12, 127 M8
Mena Park Vic. 42 A3, 63 K4
Menai NSW 12 C10, 15 J11, 23 H1
Menangle NSW 14 G12, 23 F2, 25 J7, 35 H1
Menangle Park NSW 14 H11, 23 F1
Mendooran NSW 26 D11
Mengha Tas. 142 D4
Menindee NSW 30 E11
Meningie SA 71 D5, 73 L11
Menora WA xxiv F4
Mentone Vic. 40 E8, 43 J7, 45 J1, 52 C5
Menzies WA 90 H3
Menzies Creek Vic. 40 H7, 41 C9, 43 L6
Mepunga East Vic. 50 E8, 62 H8
Mepunga West Vic. 50 D8, 62 H8
Merah North NSW 26 E6
Merbein SA 28 D6, 58 G6
Merbein South Vic. 28 D6, 58 G6
Merbein West Vic. 58 G5
Mercunda SA 71 F2, 73 M8
Merebene NSW 26 D7
Meredith Vic. 42 E5, 63 N5
Mereenie NT 111 I5
Merewether NSW 13 H3, 18 A10, 19 D9
Meribah SA 28 B7, 58 B8, 71 G2, 73 O8
Merildin SA 73 K6
Merimal Qld 125 M10
Merimbula NSW 35 E9, 51 H7
Merinda Qld 119 D4, 125 I3
Meringa Qld 120 E3, 121 F8
Meringo NSW 35 F7, 37 L8
Meringur Vic. 28 C6, 58 D7, 73 P8
Meringur North Vic. 28 C6, 58 D6, 73 P7
Merino Vic. 62 D4
Mermaid Beach Qld 21 G1, 115 G10, 116 F7
Mernda Vic. 40 E3, 43 J4, 52 D3
Meroo NP NSW 25 I11, 35 F5, 37 N4
Merredin WA 88 G3, 90 E6
Merriang Vic. 55 J8, 56 H6
Merriang South Vic. 55 J9, 56 H6
Merricks Vic. 45 J9
Merricks Beach Vic. 45 J9
Merricks North Vic. 40 E12, 43 J10, 45 J8, 52 C7
Merrigum Vic. 54 D7
Merrijig Vic. 52 H1, 54 H11, 56 E10
Merrimac Qld 115 F10, 116 E7
Merrinee Vic. 28 D6, 58 F7
Merrinee North Vic. 28 D6, 58 F6
Merriton SA 73 I5, 74 H12
Merriwa NSW 25 J1, 26 G12
Merriwa WA 84 B2
Merriwagga NSW 29 L5
Merrygoen NSW 26 D11
Merrylands NSW 15 J8
Merseylea Tas. 142 H7, 145 B8
Merton Tas. 137 B6
Merton Vic. 54 F10, 56 B9
Metcalfe Vic. 49 G6, 54 A11, 61 O12, 63 O1
Metricup WA 86 B7
Metung Vic. 53 N6
Meunna Tas. 142 D5
Mia Mia Vic. 49 H5, 54 B10, 61 P11, 63 P1
Miallo Qld 120 D1, 121 D3, 127 L5
Miami Qld 21 G1, 115 G10, 116 F8
Miami Keys Qld 116 F7
Miandetta NSW 31 O10
Miandetta Tas. 145 B3
Michael Creek Qld 120 E8, 127 L10
Michaelmas and Upolu Cays NP Qld 120 E1, 121 H5, 127 M5
Michelago NSW 24 F12, 34 E10, 35 C6, 36 H5
Mickleham Vic. 40 D3, 43 I3, 52 C3
Middle Cove NSW x H3
Middle Creek Vic. 63 K3
Middle Dural NSW 12 D3, 13 A10, 15 K5
Middle Indigo Vic. 55 J6, 56 H2
Middle Park Vic. xvii J8
Middle Point NT 102 F3, 104 E4
Middle Swan WA xxv F1, 84 F4, 85 D4
Middlemount Qld 125 J9
Middleton Qld 131 I7

Middleton SA 68 G8
Middleton Tas. 138 H9, 141 J9
Middlingbank NSW 35 B7, 36 E9, 51 D3
Midge Point Qld 119 F6, 125 J4
Midgee Qld 125 M11
Midgee SA 72 G4, 74 F12
Midland WA xxv F2, 84 F5, 85 D4, 88 C5, 90 C7
Midvale WA xxv G2
Midway Point Tas. 139 K4, 141 L7
Miena Tas. 141 I1, 143 I11
Miepoll Vic. 54 E8, 56 A5
Miga Lake Vic. 60 D10
Mil Lel SA 62 A4, 71 G11
Mila NSW 35 C10, 51 E8
Milabena Tas. 142 E5
Milang SA 71 C4, 73 K10
Milawa Vic. 55 I8, 56 F5
Milbrulong NSW 24 A10, 29 O10, 55 K1
Mildura Vic. 28 E6, 58 G6
Mile End SA xx G5
Mile End South SA xx G6
Miles Qld 123 I7
Milguy NSW 26 G4, 122 H12
Milikapiti NT 104 D2
Miling WA 88 C1, 90 C5
Milingimbi NT 105 K3
Millaa Millaa Qld 120 D4, 121 E11, 127 L7
Millaroo Qld 119 B4, 124 H3
Millbrook Vic. 42 E3, 49 D11
Millers Point NSW viii F3, x F11, 10 B4
Millfield NSW 13 D2, 25 L4
Millgrove Vic. 41 E8, 43 M5, 52 F4
Millicent SA 71 F11
Millie NSW 26 F5
Millmerran Qld 123 K9
Millner NT xxvii D5
Milloo Vic. 54 A6, 61 O8
Millstream–Chichester NP WA 89 F2, 92 B3, 96 E6
Millstream Falls NP Qld 120 D5, 121 D12, 127 L7
Millswood SA xxi I9
Millthorpe NSW 24 G5
Milltown Vic. 62 D6
Millwood NSW 24 B9, 29 O9
Milman Qld 125 M10
Milparinka NSW 30 D3, 75 P2, 132 H12
Milsons Point NSW viii G2, x G10
Miltalie SA 69 B1, 72 F5, 74 E12
Milton NSW 25 I11, 35 G5, 37 N4
Milton Qld xxx F7, 114 E7
Milvale NSW 24 D7, 35 A1
Milyakburra NT 105 M7
Mimili SA 79 K5
Mimmindie Vic. 28 H12, 61 M6
Mimosa NSW 24 B8, 29 P8
Mimosa Rocks NP NSW 35 E9, 37 K12, 51 H6
Minamia NT 105 J11, 107 J2
Mincha Vic. 28 H11, 61 N6
Mindarie SA 71 F3, 73 M9
Minden Qld 117 B11
Mindiyarra SA 71 E3, 73 M9
Miners Rest Vic. 42 C2, 49 C9, 63 M3
Minerva Hills NP Qld 124 H12, 125 I12
Mingary SA 30 A10, 73 O1, 75 M8
Mingay Vic. 42 A5, 63 K5
Mingela Qld 120 F12, 124 G2
Mingenew WA 90 B4
Mingoola NSW 27 K3, 123 K12
Minhamite Vic. 62 G6
Minilya Roadhouse WA 89 B6
Minimay Vic. 60 C9, 71 H8
Mininera Vic. 63 I4
Minjary NP NSW 24 D10, 35 A4, 36 C2, 55 P2
Minjilang NT 104 G1
Minlaton SA 69 E6, 72 H8
Minmi NSW 13 G3, 19 C9, 20 A12
Minnamurra NSW 23 F6
Minnie Water NSW 21 F9, 27 N6
Minniging WA 88 E7
Minnipa SA 72 C3, 74 A10, 81 P10
Minnivale WA 88 E3
Minore NSW 24 E1, 26 C12
Mintabie SA 79 L5
Mintaro SA 73 J6
Minto NSW 15 I10, 23 G1

Minyerri NT 105 J10, 107 J1
Minyip Vic. 60 H8
Miowera NSW 31 P10
Miralie Vic. 59 L11, 61 L1
Miram Vic. 28 C12, 60 C7, 71 H7
Miram South Vic. 60 D7, 71 H7
Miranda NSW 12 D10, 15 K11
Mirani Qld 119 F8, 125 K5
Mirannie NSW 19 B3, 25 L2
Mirboo Vic. 43 P11, 52 H8
Mirboo North Vic. 43 P11, 52 G8
Miriam Vale Qld 123 L2
Mirimbah Vic. 53 I1, 55 I11, 56 F10
Miriwinni Qld 120 E4, 121 G10, 127 M7
Mirrabooka WA xxiv F1
Mirranatwa Vic. 62 G3
Mirrngadja Village NT 105 K4
Mirrool NSW 24 B7, 29 O7
Missabotti NSW 20 G2, 27 M8
Mission Beach Qld 120 E5, 127 M8
Mistake Creek NT 95 O6, 99 N8, 106 A4
Mitcham SA xxi K11, 66 C8, 67 B9, 68 F2
Mitcham Vic. 40 F6, 41 A8
Mitchell ACT 33 E3, 34 E4, 36 H2
Mitchell Qld 122 E6
Mitchell River NP Vic. 53 L4
Mitchell River NP WA 95 K3, 98 G4
Mitchellville SA 69 C1, 72 G5, 74 F12
Mitchelton Qld xxx C1
Mitiamo Vic. 29 I12, 54 A6, 61 O7
Mitre Vic. 60 E9
Mitta Mitta Vic. 55 M9, 57 L6
Mittagong NSW 23 C5, 25 I8, 35 G2
Mittyack Vic. 28 F9, 59 I11, 61 I1
Miva Qld 118 D8
Moama NSW 29 J12, 54 C5
Moana SA 66 A12, 69 H9, 71 B4, 73 J10
Moats Corner Vic. 45 I7
Mockinya Vic. 60 F10
Moculta SA 67 G4
Modanville NSW 21 F4, 27 O3
Modella Vic. 43 M9, 52 F7
Modewarre Vic. 42 E9, 50 F1, 63 N8
Moe Vic. 43 P9, 52 H7
Moffat Vic. 62 H5
Mogendoura NSW 35 F6, 37 L7
Moggill Qld 114 C8, 115 C5, 117 D12
Mogil Mogil NSW 26 D3, 122 F12
Moglonemby Vic. 54 F8, 56 A6
Mogo NSW 35 F6, 37 L7
Mogriguy NSW 24 F1, 26 C12
Mogumber WA 88 C3
Moil NT xxvii E5
Moina Tas. 142 G8, 144 F4
Moira NSW 29 J11, 54 C4
Mokepilly Vic. 60 H11, 62 H1
Mokine WA 85 G3
Mole Creek Tas. 142 H8, 144 H5, 145 A11
Mole Creek Karst NP Tas. 142 G8, 144 G5, 145 A11
Mole River NSW 27 K4, 123 K12
Molendinar Qld 116 E5
Molesworth Tas. 138 H4
Molesworth Vic. 43 M1, 52 F1, 54 F11, 56 A10
Moliagul Vic. 49 B3, 61 L10
Molle Islands NP Qld 119 F5, 125 K3
Mollongghip Vic. 42 E2, 49 D9
Mollymook NSW 37 N4
Mologa Vic. 54 A5, 61 O7
Molong NSW 24 F4
Moltema Tas. 142 H8, 145 B10
Molyullah Vic. 54 H9, 56 E6
Mona SA 69 F2
Mona Vale NSW 12 H4, 13 C10, 15 N6, 25 K6
Monak NSW 58 H6
Monarto SA 67 G10, 73 K9
Monarto South SA 67 G11, 71 C3, 73 K10
Monash SA 28 A6, 58 A6, 71 G1, 73 N7
Monbulk Vic. 40 H7, 41 C9, 43 L6, 52 E5
Monea Vic. 54 E10
Monegeetta Vic. 40 C1, 42 H2, 52 B2, 54 B12, 63 P3
Monga NP NSW 24 H12, 35 E6, 37 K5
Monga NSW 24 H11, 35 E5, 37 K5
Mongarlowe NSW 24 H11, 35 E5, 37 K4
Monkey Mia WA 89 B8

Monomeith Vic. 43 L9, 45 P6, 52 E7
Montagu Tas. 142 B3
Montagu Bay Tas. xxxiv H10, 1 D5, 137 F7
Montana Tas. 143 I9, 145 C11
Monteagle NSW 24 E7, 35 B1
Montgomery Vic. 53 K6
Monto Qld 123 K3
Montrose Tas. xxxiv A5, 137 B5
Montumana Tas. 142 E4
Montville Qld 117 F4, 118 E11
Mooball NSW 21 G3
Mooball NP NSW 21 G3, 27 O2, 123 N11
Moockra SA 73 J2, 74 H9
Moodlu Qld 114 D1, 117 E7
Moogara Tas. 138 F4, 141 I6
Moogerah Qld 21 D1, 27 M1
Moogerah Peaks NP Qld 21 D1, 27 M1, 115 A8, 123 M10
Moola Qld 123 K8
Moolap Vic. 42 F8, 44 B4, 50 H1
Mooloolaba Qld 117 H4, 118 F12, 123 N7
Mooloolah Qld 117 F5, 118 E12
Mooloolah River NP Qld 117 G4, 118 F12, 123 N7
Moolort Vic. 49 D6, 61 M12, 63 M1
Moolpa NSW 28 H8, 59 M11
Moombooldool NSW 24 A7, 29 N7
Moombra Qld 117 B9
Moona Plains NSW 20 C3, 27 K9
Moonah Tas. xxxiv D7, 137 C6, 139 I5
Moonambel Vic. 61 K11
Moonan Flat NSW 25 L1, 27 I12
Moonbah NSW 35 B8, 36 D10, 51 C4
Moonbi NSW 27 I9
Moondarra Vic. 52 H6
Moonee Beach NSW 21 E11, 27 N7
Moonee Ponds Vic. xiv E3
Mooney Mooney NSW 12 G1, 13 C9, 15 M4
Moonford Qld 123 K3
Moonie Qld 123 I9
Moonlight Flat SA 72 C3, 74 A11, 81 P11
Moonta Bay SA 69 E3, 72 H6
Moonta SA 69 E3, 72 H6
Moora WA 88 B2, 90 B6
Moorabbin Vic. 40 E7, 43 J6, 52 C5
Moorabool Vic. 44 A2
Mooralla Vic. 62 F2
Moore Qld 117 A5, 118 B12, 123 M8
Moore Park NSW viii G3
Moore Park Qld 118 D1, 123 M3
Moore River NP WA 88 B3, 90 B6
Moores Flat Vic. 49 A6, 61 L11, 63 L1
Moorilda NSW 24 G5
Moorilim Vic. 54 E8
Moorina Tas. 143 N6
Moorine Rock WA 90 F6
Moorland NSW 20 E7, 25 O1, 27 L12
Moorlands SA 71 E4, 73 L10
Moorleah Tas. 142 E5
Moorngag Vic. 54 H9, 56 D7
Moorooduc Vic. 40 E10, 43 J9, 45 K6, 52 C7
Moorook SA 71 F1, 73 N7
Moorookyle Vic. 42 D1, 49 D8, 63 M2
Mooroolbark Vic. 41 B8, 43 K5
Mooroopna Vic. 54 E7
Moorrinya NP Qld 124 C5, 131 P5
Moppin NSW 26 F3, 122 H12
Moranbah Qld 119 C10, 125 I7
Morangarell NSW 24 C7
Morans Crossing NSW 35 D9, 37 I12, 51 G6
Morawa WA 90 B4
Morayfield Qld 114 E2, 115 D1, 117 F8
Morchard SA 73 J2, 75 I10
Mordialloc Vic. 40 E8, 43 J7, 45 K2, 52 C5
Morea Vic. 60 C9, 71 H8
Moree NSW 26 G4
Moree Vic. 60 D12, 62 D1
Morella Qld 124 A9, 131 M9
Moresby Range NP Qld 120 E4, 121 H11, 127 M7
Moreton Island NP Qld 115 H2, 123 N9
Morgan SA 73 L6
Moriac Vic. 42 E8, 50 F1, 63 N8
Moriarty Tas. 142 H6, 145 B7
Morisset NSW 13 E5, 19 B11, 25 L4
Morkalla Vic. 28 B6, 58 C6, 71 H1, 73 P8

Morley WA xxiv G2, xxv A3, 84 D5
Morningside Qld xxxi K7, 115 E4, 117 F11
Mornington Tas. 1 G5
Mornington Tas. 137 G7
Mornington Vic. 40 D10, 43 J9, 45 J5, 52 C7
Mornington Island Qld 129 D1
Mornington Peninsula NP Vic. 40 B12, 42 H10, 43 I10, 44 H9, 45 I9, 52 C8, 63 P9
Morongla NSW 24 F6
Morpeth NSW 13 G1, 19 C7, 20 A11, 25 L3
Morphett Vale SA 66 B10, 67 B11, 68 E4, 69 H8
Morphettville SA xx E11
Morri Morri Vic. 61 J10
Morrisons Vic. 42 E5, 49 E12, 63 N5
Mortat Vic. 60 D9, 71 H8
Mortchup Vic. 42 B3, 49 A11, 63 L4
Mortdale NSW 12 D9
Mortlake Vic. 63 I6
Morton NP NSW 23 A8, 24 H11, 25 I10, 35 F4, 37 M1
Morton Plains Vic. 28 F12, 61 J6
Morundah NSW 29 M9
Moruya Heads NSW 35 F7, 37 L7
Moruya NSW 35 F7, 37 L7
Morven NSW 24 B11, 29 O11, 55 L4
Morven Qld 122 D5
Morwell Vic. 52 H7
Morwell NP Vic. 52 H8
Mosman NSW ix J1, xi J8, 12 G7, 13 C12, 15 M8
Mosman Park WA xxiv C9, 84 C7, 85 B5
Moss Glen Tas. 141 I11
Moss Vale NSW 23 B6, 25 I9, 35 G3
Mossgiel NSW 29 J3
Mossiface Vic. 53 N5
Mossman Qld 120 D1, 121 D3, 127 L5
Mossy Point NSW 37 L7
Moulamein NSW 29 I9, 59 N11, 61 N1
Moulyinning WA 88 G7
Mount Aberdeen NP Qld 119 D4, 125 I3
Mount Adrah NSW 24 D10, 35 A4, 36 B1, 55 P1
Mount Alford Qld 21 D1, 27 M1, 123 M10
Mount Alfred Vic. 24 C12, 55 N6, 57 M1
Mount Archer NP Qld 125 M11
Mount Augustus NP WA 89 F6, 92 B7
Mount Barker SA 66 F10, 67 D10, 68 H3, 71 C3, 73 K9
Mount Barker WA 87 C9, 88 G11, 90 E11
Mount Barnett Roadhouse WA 95 L6, 98 H8
Mount Barney NP Qld 21 D2, 27 M1, 115 A11, 123 M11
Mount Bauple NP Qld 118 D7, 123 M5
Mount Baw Baw Vic. 43 P6, 52 H5
Mount Beauty Vic. 55 L10, 57 J7
Mount Beckworth Vic. 42 C1, 49 B8, 63 L2
Mount Benson SA 71 E9
Mount Beppo Qld 117 B7
Mount Best Vic. 43 P12, 52 H9
Mount Blue Cow NSW 36 C10, 51 B4
Mount Bryan SA 73 K5, 75 I12
Mount Bryan East SA 73 K5, 75 J12
Mount Buffalo NP Vic. 55 J9, 56 H7, 57 I7
Mount Buller Vic. 53 I1, 55 I12, 56 F10
Mount Burnett Vic. 45 P2
Mount Burr SA 71 F11
Mount Bute Vic. 42 A5, 63 K5
Mount Carbine Qld 120 C1, 121 B4, 127 K5
Mount Charlton Qld 119 F7, 125 J5
Mount Chinghee NP Qld 21 E2, 27 N2, 115 B12, 123 M11
Mount Claremont WA xxiv C6
Mount Clear Vic. 49 C11
Mount Clunie NP Qld 21 C2, 27 M1, 123 M11
Mount Colah NSW 12 E4, 13 B10, 15 L6
Mount Colosseum NP Qld 123 L2
Mount Compass SA 68 F6, 69 H9, 71 B4, 73 J10
Mount Cook NP Qld 127 L3
Mount Coolon Qld 119 B8, 124 H6
Mount Coolum NP Qld 117 G3, 118 F11, 123 N7
Mount Coot-Tha Qld xxx B7, 114 D7
Mount Cottrell Vic. 40 A5, 42 H5, 49 H12, 52 B4, 63 P5
Mount Crosby Qld 114 B8, 115 B5, 117 D11
Mount Damper SA 72 C4, 74 A11, 81 P11
Mount David NSW 24 H6

Mount Direction Tas. 143 K7, 145 G7
Mount Doran Vic. 42 D4, 49 D12, 63 M5
Mount Druitt NSW 12 A5, 15 I7, 17 O11
Mount Dunned Vic. 44 A5
Mount Ebenezer Roadhouse NT 108 G10
Mount Eccles Vic. 43 O10, 52 G8
Mount Eccles NP Vic. 62 E6
Mount Egerton Vic. 42 E4, 49 E11, 63 N4
Mount Eliza Vic. 40 E10, 43 J8, 45 K5, 52 C6
Mount Emu Vic. 42 A3, 63 K4
Mount Etna Caves NP Qld 125 M10
Mount Evelyn Vic. 40 H6, 41 C8, 43 L5
Mount Fairy NSW 24 G10, 35 E4, 37 J2
Mount Field NP Tas. 138 D2, 140 H5, 141 I5
Mount Frankland NP WA 87 E4, 88 E11, 90 D11
Mount Franklin Vic. 42 E1, 49 E8, 63 N2
Mount Gambier SA 62 A5, 71 G12
Mount Garnet Qld 120 C5, 121 A12, 127 K7
Mount George NSW 20 D8, 25 N1, 27 K12
Mount Glorious Qld 114 B5, 115 B3, 117 D9
Mount Gravatt Qld 114 E8, 115 E5, 117 F12
Mount Hallen Qld 117 A9, 123 M9
Mount Hawthorn WA xxiv E4
Mount Helen Vic. 42 D4, 49 C11, 63 M4
Mount Helena WA 84 H4, 85 E4
Mount Hope NSW 29 M2
Mount Hope SA 72 C6
Mount Horeb NSW 24 D10, 35 A4, 36 B1, 55 P1
Mount Hunter NSW 14 F11, 23 E1
Mount Hypipamee NP Qld 120 D4, 121 D10, 127 L7
Mount Imlay NP NSW 35 D10, 51 G8
Mount Irvine NSW 14 E2, 17 J3
Mount Isa Qld 129 D11, 130 F3
Mount Jerusalem NP NSW 21 G3, 27 O2, 123 N12
Mount Jim Crow NP Qld 125 M10
Mount Kaputar NP NSW 26 G6
Mount Keira NSW 22 A8
Mount Keith WA 92 G10
Mount Kembla NSW 23 F5
Mount Kuring-Gai NSW 12 E3, 13 B10, 15 L6
Mount Lambie NSW 14 A1, 16 A1, 25 I5
Mount Larcom Qld 125 N12
Mount Lawley WA xxiv F4, xxv A5
Mount Liebig NT 108 E6
Mount Lloyd Tas. 138 F4, 141 I7
Mount Lofty SA 66 D8, 67 C10, 68 G3
Mount Lonarch Vic. 61 K12, 63 K2
Mount Macedon Vic. 40 A1, 42 H2, 49 H9, 52 B2, 54 B12, 63 P3
Mount Magnet WA 89 H11, 90 D2, 92 D12
Mount Martha Vic. 40 D11, 43 I9, 45 I6, 52 C7
Mount Martin NP Qld 119 F7, 125 K5
Mount Mary SA 73 L7
Mount Mee Qld 114 B1, 117 D7
Mount Mercer Vic. 42 D5, 49 C12, 63 M5
Mount Molloy Qld 120 C1, 121 C5, 127 L5
Mount Morgan Qld 125 M11
Mount Moriac Vic. 42 E8, 50 F1, 63 N8
Mount Mulligan Qld 120 B2, 127 K6
Mount Nebo Qld 114 B6, 115 B3, 117 D10
Mount Nelson Tas. 1 A12, 137 D10
Mount Nothofagus NP Qld 21 D2, 27 M1, 115 A12, 123 M11
Mount O'Connell NP Qld 125 L9
Mount Ommaney Qld 114 D8, 115 C5, 117 E12
Mount Osmond SA xxi N9
Mount Ossa Qld 119 F7, 125 J5
Mount Ossa NP Qld 119 F7, 125 J5
Mount Ousley NSW 22 D5, 23 F4
Mount Perry Qld 118 A3, 123 L4
Mount Pikapene NP NSW 21 D5, 27 M4, 123 M12
Mount Pinbarren NP Qld 118 E10, 123 N6
Mount Pleasant NSW 22 A5
Mount Pleasant Qld 114 B2, 115 C1, 117 D8
Mount Pleasant SA 67 F6, 71 C2, 73 K9
Mount Pleasant Vic. 47 E9, 49 C10
Mount Pleasant WA xxiv F10, 89 D12, 90 H5
Mount Remarkable NP SA 73 I3, 74 H10
Mount Richmond Vic. 62 C7
Mount Richmond NP Vic. 62 C7
Mount Roe–Mt Lindesay NP WA 87 G4, 88 F11, 90 D11
Mount Rowan Vic. 42 D3, 49 C10, 63 M3
Mount Royal NP NSW 19 A1, 25 L2

Mount St Thomas NSW 22 B12
Mount Samson Qld 114 C4, 115 C2, 117 E9
Mount Schank SA 62 A5, 71 G12
Mount Seaview NSW 20 D5, 27 K11
Mount Seymour Tas. 141 L4
Mount Stuart Tas. xxxiv D10, 137 C7
Mount Surprise Qld 127 J8
Mount Tamborine Qld 21 G1, 115 E9, 116 B5
Mount Tarampa Qld 117 B10
Mount Taylor Vic. 53 M5
Mount Templeton NP SA 69 G3, 73 J6
Mount Thorley NSW 25 K3
Mount Tomah NSW 14 E3, 17 I4
Mount Torrens SA 66 H6, 67 E8, 71 C3, 73 K9
Mount Victoria NSW 14 C4, 16 E5, 25 I6
Mount Wallace Vic. 42 E5, 49 E12, 63 N5
Mount Walsh NP Qld 118 B5, 123 L5
Mount Warning NP NSW 21 G3, 27 O2, 123 N11
Mount Waverley Vic. 40 E6
Mount Webb NP Qld 127 L2
Mount Wedge SA 72 C5, 74 A12, 81 P12
Mount White NSW 13 C8, 15 M3, 25 K5
Mount William NP Tas. 143 P5
Mount Wilson NSW 14 D3, 16 H4, 25 I5
Mountain River Tas. 138 H6, 141 J7
Moura Qld 123 I2
Mourilyan Qld 120 E5, 121 H12, 127 M7
Moutajup Vic. 62 G4
Mowbray Tas. 143 K8, 145 G9
Mowbray NP Qld 120 D1, 121 D4, 127 L5
Mowbray Park NSW 14 E12, 23 D2
Mowen WA 86 B8, 88 B10
Moyhu Vic. 55 I8, 56 F6
Moyreisk Vic. 61 K10
Moyston Vic. 63 I2
Muchea WA 84 E1, 85 C2, 88 C4, 90 C7
Muckadilla Qld 122 F6
Mudamuckla SA 81 N8
Mudgee NSW 24 H2
Mudgeeraba Qld 21 G1, 27 O1, 115 F10, 116 E8, 123 N10
Mudgegonga Vic. 55 K8, 57 I5
Mudginberri NT 103 O3, 104 G4
Mudjimba Qld 117 G3, 118 F11
Muggleton Qld 122 G6
Muirhead NT xxvii F3
Mukinbudin WA 88 G2, 90 E6
Mulambin Qld 125 N10
Mulbring NSW 13 F3, 19 B9
Mulcra Vic. 28 B9, 58 C11, 71 H4, 73 O10
Mulgildie Qld 123 K3
Mulgoa NSW 14 G8, 25 J6
Mullaley NSW 26 F9
Mullalyup WA 86 F6, 88 C9
Mullaway NSW 21 E11, 27 N7
Mullenderee NSW 24 H12, 37 L7
Mullengandra NSW 24 B12, 29 O12, 55 L5, 57 K1
Mullengudgery NSW 26 A10, 31 P10
Mullewa WA 89 E12, 90 B3
Mulli Mulli NSW 21 D3, 27 M2, 123 M11
Mullindolingong Vic. 55 I9, 57 J7
Mullion Creek NSW 24 G4
Mullumbimby NSW 21 G4, 27 O3, 123 N12
Mulpata SA 28 A8, 71 F4, 73 N10
Mulwala NSW 29 M12, 54 H5, 56 D1
Mumballup WA 86 G5, 88 D8, 90 C10
Mumbannar Vic. 62 C5, 71 H12
Mumbil NSW 24 G3
Mumblin Vic. 50 F8, 63 I8
Mumdjin NSW 116 B11
Mummel Gulf NP NSW 20 C5, 27 J10
Mummulgum NSW 21 D5, 27 M3, 123 M12
Munbilla Qld 115 A8
Mundaring WA 84 G5, 85 E4, 88 C5, 90 C7
Mundaring Weir WA 84 G5, 85 E5
Mundijong WA 84 F10, 85 D7, 90 C8
Mundoona Vic. 54 E6
Mundoora SA 69 F1, 73 I5, 74 H12
Mundrabilla Roadhouse WA 80 A8, 91 O6
Mundubbera Qld 123 K4
Mundulla SA 28 A12, 60 A7, 71 G7
Mungalawurru NT 107 I9
Mungallala Qld 122 D6
Mungana Qld 120 A3, 127 J6

Mungar Qld 118 D6, 123 M5
Mungerannie Roadhouse SA 77 I8, 132 B8
Mungeribar NSW 24 E1, 26 B12
Mungery NSW 24 D2
Mungindi NSW 26 E2, 122 F11
Mungkan Kandju NP Qld 128 D9
Mungkarta NT 107 J11
Munglinup WA 90 H9
Mungo NP NSW 28 G4, 59 K1
Mungungo Qld 123 K3
Munro Vic. 53 L6
Munster WA 84 D9, 85 C6
Muntadgin WA 88 H4, 90 E7
Muradup WA 88 E9
Murarrie Qld xxxi M7, 114 F7
Murchison Vic. 54 D8
Murchison WA 89 E9, 92 B11
Murchison East Vic. 54 E8
Murdinga SA 72 D5
Murdoch WA xxiv F12
Murdunna Tas. 139 N6, 141 M8
Murga NSW 24 E4
Murgenella NT 104 G2
Murgheboluc Vic. 42 E7, 63 N7
Murgon Qld 118 A9, 123 L6
Murmungee Vic. 55 J8, 56 H5
Murphys Creek Vic. 49 C3, 61 M10
Murra Warra Vic. 60 G8
Murrabit Vic. 28 H10, 61 N3
Murradoc Vic. 44 E4
Murramarang NP NSW 24 H12, 25 I12, 35 F6, 37 M5
Murrami NSW 29 N7
Murrawal NSW 26 E10
Murray Bridge SA 67 H11, 71 D3, 73 K10
Murray River NP SA 28 A6, 58 A6, 71 G1, 73 N7
Murray Sunset NP Vic. 28 C7, 58 D9, 71 H2, 73 P9
Murray Town SA 73 I3, 74 H11
Murrays Run NSW 13 C4, 25 K4
Murrayville Vic. 28 B9, 58 C11, 60 C1, 71 H4, 73 O10
Murrindal Vic. 35 A11, 51 A9, 53 P3
Murrindindi Vic. 41 D2, 43 M2, 52 E2, 54 E12, 56 A11
Murringo NSW 24 E7, 35 B1
Murroon Vic. 42 C10, 50 D3, 63 L9
Murrumba Qld 117 B8
Murrumbateman NSW 24 F9, 34 D1, 35 C3
Murrumburrah NSW 24 E8, 35 B2
Murrungowar Vic. 35 B11, 51 C10
Murrurundi NSW 26 H11
Murtle Murula NT 107 O7
Murwillumbah NSW 21 G2, 27 O2, 115 F12, 123 N11
Musgrave Hill Qld 116 F5
Musgrave Roadhouse Qld 128 E12
Musk Vic. 42 E2, 49 E9, 63 N3
Muskerry East Vic. 54 B8, 61 P10
Musselboro Tas. 143 L8
Musselroe Bay Tas. 143 O5
Muswellbrook NSW 25 K2
Mutarnee Qld 120 F9, 127 M10
Mutawintji NP NSW 30 D7
Mutchilba Qld 120 C3, 121 B8, 127 K6
Mutdapilly Qld 115 A7, 123 M10
Mutitjulu NT 108 E10, 110 E10
Muttaburra Qld 124 C8, 131 O8
Muttama NSW 24 D9, 35 A3
Myall Vic. 28 H10, 61 N3
Myall Lakes NP NSW 19 H7, 20 D11, 25 N3
Myall Mundi NSW 26 B11
Myall Plains NSW 29 M10, 54 H2
Myalla Tas. 142 E5
Myalup WA 86 D2, 88 C8, 90 C9
Myamyn Vic. 62 E6
Myaree WA xxiv E11
Mylestom NSW 20 H1, 21 D12, 27 M8
Mylor SA 66 E9, 67 D10, 68 G3
Myola Qld 121 E6
Myola Vic. 54 B8, 61 P9
Mypolonga SA 67 H10, 71 D3, 73 L9
Myponga SA 68 E7, 69 H9, 71 B4, 73 J10
Myponga Beach SA 68 D7, 69 G9, 71 B4, 73 J10
Myrla SA 71 F2, 73 N8

168

Myrniong Vic. 42 F4, 49 F11, 52 A3, 63 O4
Myrrhee Vic. 43 P6, 52 H4, 55 I9, 56 F7
Myrtle Bank SA xxi L9
Myrtle Bank Tas. 143 L7
Myrtle Creek Vic. 49 G5, 54 A10, 61 O11, 63 O1
Myrtleford Vic. 55 J8, 56 H6
Myrtleville NSW 24 H8, 35 E2
Mysia Vic. 28 H12, 61 M7
Mystic Park Vic. 28 H10, 61 M3
Mywee Vic. 54 F4

Nabageena Tas. 142 C4
Nabawa WA 89 D12, 90 A3
Nabiac NSW 20 D9, 25 N2
Nabowla Tas. 143 L6
Nackara SA 73 L3, 75 J10
Nadda SA 28 B7, 58 B8, 71 H2, 73 O8
Nagambie Vic. 54 D9
Nagoorin Qld 123 K2
Nailsworth SA xxi J1
Nairana NP Qld 119 A8, 124 G6
Nairne SA 66 G9, 67 E10, 68 H3, 71 C3, 73 K9
Nakara NT xxvii E4
Nala Tas. 141 L4
Nalangil Vic. 42 A9, 50 B2, 63 K8
Nalinga Vic. 54 G7, 56 B4
Nalya WA 88 E5
Namadgi NP ACT 24 F12, 33 A11, 34 B5, 35 C5, 36 F5, 51 E1
Nambour Qld 117 F3, 118 E11, 123 N7
Nambrok Vic. 53 J6
Nambucca Heads NSW 20 H2, 27 M9
Nambung NP WA 88 A2, 90 A6
Nana Glen NSW 21 D11, 27 M7
Nanango Qld 118 A11, 123 L7
Nanarup WA 87 E11, 88 H11
Nandaly Vic. 28 F9, 59 I12, 61 I1
Nandi Qld 123 K8
Nanga WA 85 E11, 88 C7
Nangana Vic. 41 D9, 43 L6, 52 E5
Nangar NP NSW 24 E5
Nangari SA 28 B6, 58 B7, 71 H2, 73 O8
Nangeenan WA 88 G3, 90 E6
Nangiloc Vic. 28 E7, 58 H7
Nangkita SA 68 F6, 71 B4, 73 J10
Nangus NSW 24 D9, 35 A3, 55 P1
Nangwarry SA 62 A3, 71 G11
Nanneella Vic. 54 C6
Nannup WA 86 F8, 88 C10, 90 C10
Nanson WA 89 D12
Nantabibbie SA 73 K3, 75 J10
Nantawarra SA 69 G3, 73 I6
Nanutarra Roadhouse WA 89 D4, 92 A5, 96 B10
Napoleons Vic. 42 C4, 49 C11, 63 M4
Napperby SA 73 I4, 74 H11
Napranum Qld 128 B7
Nar Nar Goon Vic. 41 D12, 43 M8, 52 E6
Nar Nar Goon North Vic. 45 P2
Nara Qld 123 L8, 126 G11
Naracoopa Tas. 141 P11
Naracoorte SA 60 A10, 71 G9
Naracoorte Caves NP SA 60 A11, 71 G9
Naradhan NSW 29 N5
Naraling WA 89 D12, 90 A3
Narangba Qld 114 D3, 115 D2, 117 F9
Narara NSW 13 D8, 15 O2
Narawntapu NP Tas. 143 I6, 145 D6
Narbethong Vic. 41 E5, 43 M4, 52 F3
Nareen Vic. 62 D2
Narellan NSW 14 G10, 23 F1, 25 J7, 35 H1
Narembeen WA 88 G4, 90 E7
Naremburn NSW x F6
Naretha WA 91 L5
Nariel Vic. 36 A10, 55 O8, 57 N5
Naringal Vic. 50 E8, 62 H8
Naroghid Vic. 50 G7, 63 J7
Narooma NSW 35 F8, 37 L10
Narrabri NSW 26 F7
Narrabri West NSW 26 F7
Narracan Vic. 43 P10, 52 H7
Narrandera NSW 24 A8, 29 N8
Narraport Vic. 28 F11, 61 J5
Narrawa Tas. 142 G7, 144 F3
Narrawallee NSW 37 N4

Narraweena NSW 12 G5, 13 C11, 15 M7
Narrawong Vic. 62 D7
Narre Warren Vic. 40 G8, 41 B11, 43 K7, 45 M2, 52 D6
Narre Warren East Vic. 45 N1
Narre Warren North Vic. 41 B10, 43 K7, 45 N1
Narre Warren South Vic. 45 M3
Narrewillock Vic. 61 L6
Narridy SA 73 J5, 74 H12
Narrien Range NP Qld 124 G9
Narrikup WA 88 G11
Narrogin WA 88 E7, 90 D9
Narromine NSW 24 E1, 26 B12
Narrung SA 71 C5, 73 K11
Narrung Vic. 28 G8, 59 K9
Nashdale NSW 24 F4
Nathalia Vic. 29 K12, 54 E5
Natimuk Vic. 60 F9
National Park Tas. 138 E2, 141 I6
Natone Tas. 142 F6, 144 F1
Nattai NSW 14 D11, 23 C1, 25 I7, 35 G1
Nattai NP NSW 14 D12, 23 C2, 25 I8, 35 G2
Natte Yallock Vic. 49 A4, 61 L11
Natural Bridge Qld 21 G2, 27 O1, 115 E11, 116 B10
Natya Vic. 28 G8, 59 K10
Nauiyu NT 102 C12, 104 D7
Naval Base WA 84 D9, 85 C7
Navarre Vic. 61 J10
Navigators Vic. 42 D3, 49 D11, 63 M4
Nayook Vic. 41 H10, 43 O7, 52 G5
Neale Junction WA 91 M1, 93 M11
Neales Flat SA 67 G1, 71 D1, 73 K7
Neath NSW 13 E2, 19 A8
Nebo Qld 119 E9, 125 J7
Nectar Brook SA 73 I2, 74 G10
Nedlands WA xxiv D7
Neds Corner Vic. 28 C6, 58 E6, 73 P7
Needles Tas. 143 I8, 145 C11
Neerabup NP WA 84 B2, 85 B3, 88 B4, 90 B7
Neerdie Qld 118 E8, 123 N6
Neerim Vic. 41 H10, 43 O7, 52 G5
Neerim East Vic. 41 H11, 43 O7, 52 G6
Neerim Junction Vic. 41 H10, 43 O7, 52 G5
Neerim South Vic. 41 H11, 43 O7, 52 G6
Neeworra NSW 26 E3, 122 G12
Neika Tas. 138 H6, 141 K7
Neilborough Vic. 49 F1, 54 A8, 61 O9
Neilborough East Vic. 49 G1, 54 A7, 61 O9
Neilrex NSW 26 E11
Nelia Qld 131 K3
Nelligen NSW 24 H12, 35 F6, 37 L6
Nelly Bay Qld 119 A1, 120 G10, 124 G1, 127 N11
Nelshaby SA 73 I4, 74 H11
Nelson NSW 12 B3, 15 J5
Nelson Vic. 62 B6, 71 G12
Nelson Bay NSW 19 G8, 20 C12, 25 N4
Nelsons Plains NSW 13 H1, 19 D7, 20 A11
Nelungaloo NSW 24 D4
Nemingha NSW 27 I9
Nene Valley SA 71 F12
Nepabunna SA 70 E4, 75 J4
Nerang Qld 21 G1, 27 O1, 115 F9, 116 D6, 123 N10
Neranwood Qld 115 F11, 116 C8
Nerriga NSW 24 H10, 35 F4, 37 L2
Nerrigundah NSW 35 E7, 37 K9
Nerrin Nerrin Vic. 63 J5
Nerrina Vic. 42 D3, 47 H3, 49 C10, 63 M4
Nerring Vic. 42 A2, 63 K3
Netherby SA xxi K10
Netherby Vic. 28 C11, 60 E6
Nethercote NSW 35 E10, 51 H8
Netley SA xx E8
Neuarpurr Vic. 60 B9, 71 H8
Neurea NSW 24 F3
Neuroodla SA 74 H7
Neutral Bay NSW viii H1, x H8, 11 G5
Neutral Bay NSW
Nevertire NSW 26 A11, 31 P11
Neville NSW 24 G6
New Angledool NSW 26 B2, 122 E11
New Brighton NSW 21 H3
New Chum Qld 114 B9, 115 C5, 117 D12
New England NP NSW 20 E1, 21 A12, 27 L8
New Farm Qld xxxi I7

New Gisborne Vic. 40 A2, 42 H3, 49 H10, 52 B2, 63 P3
New Italy NSW 21 F6, 27 N4
New Lambton NSW 13 G3, 19 D9
New Mollyann NSW 26 E10
New Norcia WA 88 C2, 90 C6
New Norfolk Tas. 138 G4, 141 J6
New Residence SA 28 A6, 71 F1, 73 N7
New Town Tas. xxxiv E8, 1 A4, 136 A2, 137 C7, 139 I5
New Well SA 71 E1, 73 M7, 79 I2, 108 G11
Newborough Vic. 43 P9, 52 H7
Newbridge NSW 24 G5
Newbridge Vic. 49 D3, 61 M10
Newbury Vic. 42 F2, 49 F9, 52 A2, 54 A12, 63 O3
Newcastle NSW 13 H3, 18, 19 D9, 20 A12, 25 M4
Newcastle Waters (Marlinja) NT 106 H5
Newcastle West NSW 18 B6
Newdegate WA 90 F8
Newell Qld 120 D1, 121 D3
Newfield Vic. 50 G10, 63 I9
Newham Vic. 42 H1, 49 H8, 52 B1, 54 B12, 63 P3
Newhaven Vic. 43 K11, 45 M11, 52 D8
Newlands WA 86 F6, 88 C9
Newlyn Vic. 42 D2, 49 D9, 63 M3
Newman WA 92 E5, 97 L11
Newmarket Qld xxx F4, 114 E6, 115 D4, 117 F11
Newmerella Vic. 35 A12, 51 B11, 53 P5
Newnes Junction NSW 14 C2, 16 F2
Newnes NSW 25 I4
Newnham Tas. 145 G9
Newport NSW 12 H4, 13 C10, 15 N6, 25 K6
Newport Vic. xvi B6, 40 C6, 43 I6
Newry Vic. 53 J6
Newry Islands NP Qld 119 F7, 125 K5
Newrybar NSW 21 G4, 27 O3
Newstead Qld xxxi I6
Newstead Tas. 145 G2
Newstead Vic. 49 E6, 61 N12, 63 N1
Newton Boyd NSW 21 B9, 27 L6
Newton SA xxi P1
Newtown NSW viii C7, 12 F8, 15 L9
Newtown Vic. 42 B4, 46 B7, 49 B11, 63 L4
Ngangalala NT 105 K4
Nguiu NT 104 D3
Ngukurr NT 105 K9
Ngunarra NT 107 M7
Nhill Vic. 28 C12, 60 E7
Nhulunbuy NT 105 N4
Niagara Park NSW 13 D7, 15 O2
Niangala NSW 20 A4, 27 J10
Nicholls Point Vic. 58 G6
Nicholls Rivulet Vic. 138 H8, 141 J9
Nicholson Vic. 53 N5
Nicoll Scrub NP Qld 21 G2, 27 O1, 115 G11, 116 E10, 123 N11
Niemur NSW 29 I9, 59 O12, 61 O1
Nierinna Tas. 138 H7
Nietta Tas. 142 G7, 144 F3
Nightcap NP NSW 21 F3, 27 O2, 123 N12
Nightcliff NT xxvii B5, 102 C2
Nildottie SA 71 E2, 73 L8
Nile Tas. 143 L9
Nillahcootie Vic. 54 G11, 56 D9
Nilma Vic. 43 O9, 52 G7
Nimbin NSW 21 F4, 27 O3, 123 N12
Nimmitabel NSW 35 D8, 36 H11, 51 F5
Ninda Vic. 28 F10, 61 I2
Nindigully Qld 122 F10
Nine Mile Vic. 61 L8
Ningaloo Marine Park WA 89 B4
Ningi Qld 114 F1, 115 E1, 117 G7
Ninnes SA 69 F3, 73 I6
Ninyeunook Vic. 28 G11, 61 L5
Nipan Qld 123 I2
Nippering WA 88 F7
Nirranda Vic. 50 E9, 62 H9
Nirranda South Vic. 50 E9, 63 I9
Nitmiluk (Katherine Gorge) NP NT 103 M12, 104 F7
Noarlunga Centre SA 66 B11, 67 A11, 68 E4
Nobby Qld 123 L10
Nobby Beach Qld 116 F8
Nobbys Creek NSW 116 C12

169

Nobelius Vic. 45 O1
Noble Park Vic. 40 F7, 41 A10, 43 J7, 45 L1
Noccundra Qld 133 I8
Nollamara WA xxiv E2
Nonda Qld 131 K3
Noojee Vic. 41 H10, 43 O7, 52 G5
Nook Tas. 144 H3, 145 A8
Noonamah NT 102 E4, 104 D5
Noonameena SA 71 D5, 73 K11
Noonbinna NSW 24 E6
Noondoo Qld 26 D1, 122 F10
Noora SA 28 B6, 58 B7, 71 H2, 73 O8
Nooramunga Vic. 54 G7, 56 C4
Noorat Vic. 63 I7
Noorinbee Vic. 35 C11, 51 E10
Noorinbee North Vic. 35 C11, 51 E10
Noorong NSW 28 H9, 59 N12, 61 N2
Noorongong Vic. 55 L7, 57 K4
Noosa Heads Qld 117 H1, 118 F10, 123 N7
Noosa NP Qld 117 H2, 118 F10, 123 N7
Noosaville Qld 117 G1, 118 F10
Nora Creina SA 71 E10
Noradjuha Vic. 60 F10
Norah Head NSW 13 F7, 19 B12, 25 L5
Norahville NSW 13 F7, 19 B12
Noranda WA xxiv H1, xxv A2
Nords Wharf NSW 13 F5, 19 C11
Norlane Vic. 44 B2
Norman Park Qld xxxi I9
Normanhurst NSW 12 E5, 15 L6
Normanton Qld 126 D7, 129 G4
Normanville SA 68 C7, 69 G10, 71 B4, 73 I10
Normanville Vic. 61 M5
Nornakin WA 88 F5
Nornalup WA 87 G6, 88 E12
Norseman WA 91 I7
North Adelaide SA xxi J3, 65 C4, 66 C7, 67 B8, 68 F2
North Arm Cove NSW 19 G7, 20 C11
North Arm Qld 117 F2, 118 E11
North Balgowlah NSW xi K2
North Beach SA 69 E2, 72 H6
North Beach WA xxiv A1
North Bendigo Vic. 48 D1
North Bondi NSW ix L7, 12 G8, 13 C12, 15 M9
North Bourke NSW 31 M5
North Cremorne NSW xi I7, 11 H1
North Dandalup WA 85 D9, 88 C6, 90 C8
North Fremantle WA xxiv B11, 84 C7, 85 B6
North Haven NSW 20 F7, 27 M12
North Haven SA 66 B5, 67 A7
North Hobart Tas. xxxiv E10, 1 A6, 136 A3, 137 D7
North Jindong WA 86 B7
North Lake WA xxiv F12
North Lilydale Tas. 143 K7, 145 H7
North Maclean Qld 114 D11, 115 D7
North Manly NSW xi M1
North Melbourne Vic. xiv H9, xvii I1, 39 A3
North Motton Tas. 142 G6, 144 F1
North Perth WA xxiv F4
North Pinjarra WA 85 D9, 88 C6
North Plympton SA xx E8
North Richmond NSW 14 H4, 17 N6
North Rothbury NSW 19 A6, 25 L3
North Ryde NSW x B3
North Scottsdale Tas. 143 M6
North Shields SA 72 D8
North Shore Vic. 44 B3
North Star NSW 26 H3, 123 I12
North Stradbroke Island Qld 115 G6, 123 N9
North Sydney NSW viii G1, x G8, 11 C6, 12 F7, 15 M8
North Tamborine Qld 115 E9, 116 B4, 123 N10
North Tumbulgum NSW 116 F12
North Willoughby NSW x G3
North Wollongong NSW 22 F7, 23 F5
Northam WA 85 G2, 88 D4, 90 C7
Northampton WA 89 D12, 90 A3
Northbridge NSW x H5
Northbridge WA xxiv F5, 83 C4
Northcliffe WA 86 H12, 87 C4, 88 D11, 90 C11
Northcote Vic. xv O4
Northdown Tas. 142 H6, 145 B6
Northfield SA 66 C5, 67 B8, 68 F1

Northgate Qld xxxi L1
Northmead NSW 12 C5, 13 A11, 15 J7
Northumberland Islands NP Qld 119 H8, 125 L6
Northwood NSW x D7
Norval Vic. 61 I12, 63 I2
Norwin Qld 123 K9
Norwood SA xxi L5
Norwood Tas. 145 H3
Notley Hills Tas. 143 J7, 145 F9
Notting WA 88 G5, 90 E8
Notts Well SA 71 E1, 73 M8
Novar Gardens SA xx D9
Nowa Nowa Vic. 53 O5
Nowendoc NSW 20 B6, 27 J11
Nowendoc NP NSW 20 A5, 27 J11
Nowie North Vic. 59 L12, 61 L1
Nowingi Vic. 28 E7, 58 G8
Nowley NSW 26 E5
Nowra NSW 23 D9, 25 I10, 35 G4, 37 O1
Nowra Hill NSW 23 C10, 25 I10, 35 G4, 37 O1
Nturiya NT 108 H4
Nubba NSW 24 D8, 35 B2
Nubeena Tas. 139 L8, 141 L8
Nudgee Qld 114 F6, 115 E3, 117 F10
Nug Nug Vic. 55 J9, 56 H7
Nuga Nuga NP Qld 122 G2
Nugent Tas. 139 M3, 141 M6
Nuggetty Vic. 49 E5, 61 N11
Nulkaba NSW 13 E2, 19 A8
Nullagine WA 92 F3, 97 L7
Nullan Vic. 60 H8
Nullarbor NP SA 80 E6, 91 P5
Nullarbor Roadhouse SA 80 G6
Nullawarre Vic. 50 E9, 62 H9
Nullawil Vic. 28 G11, 61 K5
Numbla Vale NSW 35 B8, 36 E12, 51 D5
Numbugga NSW 35 D9, 37 I12, 51 H6
Numbulwar NT 105 L8
Numeralla NSW 35 D7, 36 H9, 51 F3
Numinbah NSW 116 B12
Numinbah Valley Qld 21 G1, 27 O1, 115 E11, 116 B9
Numurkah Vic. 29 K12, 54 F5, 56 A1
Nunamara Tas. 143 L8
Nunawading Vic. 41 A8
Nundah Qld xxxi K1, 114 E6
Nundle NSW 27 I10
Nundroo Roadhouse SA 81 J7
Nunga Vic. 28 E9, 58 H11
Nungarin WA 88 G2, 90 E6
Nungurner Vic. 53 N6
Nunjikompita SA 72 A1, 81 N9
Nurcoung Vic. 60 E9
Nurina WA 91 N5
Nurinda Qld 117 A5, 118 C12
Nuriootpa SA 67 F4, 71 C1, 73 K8
Nurom SA 73 I4, 74 H12
Nurrabiel Vic. 60 F10
Nutfield Vic. 40 F3, 41 A5, 43 K4, 52 D3
Nyabing WA 88 G8, 90 E9
Nyah Vic. 28 G9, 59 L11, 61 L1
Nyah West Vic. 28 G9, 59 L11, 61 L1
Nyarrin Vic. 28 F9, 59 I12, 61 I2
Nyirripi NT 108 D5
Nymagee NSW 31 M11
Nymboi–Binderay NP NSW 21 C10, 27 M7
Nymboida NSW 21 C10, 27 M6
Nymboida NP NSW 21 B8, 27 L5
Nyngan NSW 31 O10
Nyora Vic. 43 M10, 52 F7
Nypo Vic. 28 D10, 60 F4

Oak Beach Qld 120 D1, 121 E5, 127 L5
Oak Flats NSW 23 F6
Oak Forest Qld 121 E6
Oakbank SA 66 F8, 67 D9, 68 H3
Oakdale NSW 14 E11, 23 D1, 25 J7, 35 G1
Oakey Creek NSW 26 F11
Oakey Qld 123 K9
Oaklands NSW 29 M10, 55 I3
Oaklands SA 69 E7, 72 H9
Oakleigh Vic. 40 E7, 43 J6, 52 C5
Oaks Tas. 143 J9, 145 F11
Oakvale Vic. 28 G11, 61 L5

Oakwood Tas. 139 M8, 141 M9
Oasis Roadhouse Qld 120 A8, 127 J10
Oatlands Tas. 141 K3
Oatley NSW 12 D9, 15 K10
Ob Flat SA 62 A5, 71 G12
Oberne NSW 24 C10, 36 A3, 55 O3
Oberon NSW 24 H6
Obley NSW 24 F2
Obx Creek NSW 21 D9, 27 M6
Ocean Grove Vic. 42 G9, 44 C6, 50 H2, 52 A7, 63 O8
Ocean Shores NSW 21 H3, 27 O2, 123 N11
Ockley WA 88 F7
O'Connor WA xxiv D11
Oenpelli NT 103 P2, 104 H4
Officer Vic. 40 H9, 41 C11, 43 L8, 45 O3, 52 E6
Ogilvie WA 89 D11, 90 A2
Ogmore Qld 125 L9
Olary SA 73 N1, 75 M9
Old Adaminaby NSW 35 B7, 36 E7, 51 D2
Old Bar NSW 20 E8, 25 O1, 27 L12
Old Beach Tas. xxxiv E1, 137 B2, 139 I4, 141 K6
Old Bonalbo NSW 21 D4, 27 M3, 123 M12
Old Bowenfels NSW 14 B2, 16 C3
Old Farm Tas. 137 B9
Old Junee NSW 24 C9, 29 P9
Old Noarlunga SA 66 B11, 67 A11, 68 E5, 69 H8, 71 B4, 73 J10
Old Owen Springs NT 110 G5
Old Tallangatta Vic. 55 M7, 57 K3
Old Tyabb Vic. 45 L7
Old Warrah NSW 26 H11
Oldina Tas. 142 E5
Olinda NSW 25 I3
Olinda Vic. 40 G6, 41 B9, 43 L6, 52 E5
Olio Qld 131 L6
Olympic Dam Village SA 74 E3
O'Malley SA 80 G4
Ombersley Vic. 42 C8, 50 D1, 63 M7
Omeo Vic. 53 M1, 55 M12, 57 M11
Ondit Vic. 42 B8, 50 C1, 63 L8
One Arm Point WA 94 H5, 98 C8
One Tree NSW 29 J6
Ongerup WA 88 H9, 90 F10
Onkaparinga River NP SA 66 B11, 67 B11, 68 E4, 69 H8, 71 B3, 73 J10
Onslow WA 89 C2, 96 A8
Oodla Wirra SA 73 K3, 75 J10
Oodnadatta SA 76 B6
Oolambeyan NP NSW 29 K8
Ooldea SA 81 I3
Oombulgurri WA 95 N3, 99 L4
Oonah Tas. 142 E6, 144 B1
Oondooroo Qld 131 L7
Oonoonba Qld 119 A1, 120 G10
Oorindi Qld 129 G11, 131 I3
Ootann Qld 120 A4, 127 J7
Ootha NSW 24 C3, 29 P3
Opalton Qld 131 K9
Ophir NSW 24 G4
Opossum Bay Tas. 139 J7, 141 K8
Ora Banda WA 90 H4
Orange NSW 24 G4
Orange Grove WA xxv H10, 84 F7, 85 D5
Orangeville NSW 14 F10, 25 J7, 35 G1
Oranmeir NSW 24 G12, 35 E6, 37 J6
Orbost Vic. 35 A12, 51 B11
Orchid Beach Qld 118 H3, 123 O4
Orford Tas. 139 N2, 141 M5
Orford Vic. 62 F7
Organ Pipes NP Vic. 40 C4, 42 H4, 52 B3, 63 P5
Orielton Tas. 139 K3, 141 L6
Orient Point NSW 23 E10, 37 P1
Ormeau Qld 114 G12, 115 F7, 116 C1
Ormiston Qld 114 H8, 115 F5, 117 H12
Orpheus Island NP Qld 120 F8, 127 N10
Orroroo SA 73 J3, 75 I10
Orrtipa–Thurra NT 109 M5
Orton Park NSW 24 H5
Osborne SA 66 B5, 67 A7, 69 H7
Osborne Park NSW x E6
Osborne Park WA xxiv D3
Osbornes Flat Vic. 55 K7, 57 I4
Osmaston Tas. 143 I8, 145 D11
Osmington WA 86 C8, 88 B10

Osterley Tas. 141 I3
Otago Tas. xxxiv E2, 137 C4, 139 I4, 141 K7
Otford NSW 23 H3
Otway NP Vic. 42 A12, 50 B6, 63 K11
Oura NSW 24 C9, 29 P9, 55 N1
Ourimbah NSW 13 D7, 15 O2, 25 L5
Ournie NSW 24 C12, 36 A6, 55 O5, 57 O1
Ouse Tas. 141 I4
Outer Harbor SA 66 B4, 67 A7, 69 H6, 71 B2, 73 J8
Outtrim Vic. 43 M11, 52 F8
Ouyen Vic. 28 E8, 58 H11
Ovens Vic. 55 J9, 56 H6
Overland Corner SA 28 A5, 71 F1, 73 N7
Overlander Roadhouse WA 89 D9
Ovingham SA xx H2, 65 B2, 67 B8, 68 F2
Owanyilla Qld 118 D6, 123 M5
Owen SA 67 B2, 69 H4, 71 B1, 73 J7
Owens Gap NSW 25 K1, 26 H12
Oxenford Qld 115 F8, 116 D3
Oxley NSW 29 I6, 59 O6
Oxley Qld 114 D8, 115 D5, 117 E12
Oxley Vic. 55 I8, 56 F5
Oxley Wild Rivers NP NSW 20 C3, 21 A12, 27 K9
Oyster Cove Tas. 138 H8, 141 J8
Ozenkadnook Vic. 60 C10, 71 H9

Paaratte Vic. 50 F9, 63 I9
Pacific Palms NSW 20 E10, 25 N3
Packsaddle Roadhouse NSW 30 D6, 75 P4
Paddington NSW 10 H11, 31 K11
Paddington Qld xxx E6, 114 E7, 115 D4, 117 F11
Padthaway SA 71 F8
Pagewood NSW viii G12
Paignie Vic. 28 D8, 58 G11
Painswick Vic. 49 C3, 61 M10
Pakenham Vic. 40 H9, 41 C11, 43 L8, 45 O3, 52 E6
Pakenham South Vic. 45 P4
Pakenham Upper Vic. 45 P2
Palana Tas. 140 A9
Palgarup WA 86 H9, 87 B1, 88 D10
Pallamallawa NSW 26 G4
Pallara Qld 115 D5, 117 F12
Pallarenda Qld 119 A1, 120 G10, 124 G1, 127 N11
Palm Beach NSW 12 H3, 13 C10, 15 N5, 25 K6
Palm Beach Qld 21 H2, 27 O1, 115 G11, 116 F9
Palm Cove Qld 120 D2, 121 F6, 127 L5
Palm Dale NSW 15 O1
Palm Grove NSW 13 D7, 15 N1
Palmdale NSW 13 D7
Palmer SA 67 G8, 71 D3, 73 K9
Palmer River Roadhouse Qld 127 K4
Palmers Island NSW 21 F8, 27 N5
Palmers Oakey NSW 24 H4
Palmerston NT 102 D3, 104 D4
Palmerston Rocks NP Qld 120 E4, 121 G12, 127 M7
Palmgrove NP Qld 122 H3
Palmwoods Qld 117 F4, 118 E11
Palmyra WA xxiv D11
Paloona Tas. 142 H6, 144 G2
Paluma Qld 120 E9, 127 M11
Paluma Range NP Qld 120 E9, 127 M10
Pambula NSW 35 E10, 51 H7
Pambula Beach NSW 35 E10, 51 H7
Pampas Qld 123 K9
Panitya Vic. 28 B9, 58 B11, 60 B1, 71 H4, 73 O10
Panmure Vic. 50 E7, 62 H8
Pannawonica WA 89 E2, 92 A3, 96 D7
Panorama Heights Tas. 145 C4
Panorama SA xxi I12
Pantapin WA 88 F4
Panton Hill Vic. 40 G4, 41 A6, 43 K4
Paper Beach Tas. 145 F8
Pappinbarra NSW 20 E5
Papunya NT 108 F6
Para Hills SA 66 D5, 67 C7
Paraburdoo WA 89 G4, 92 C5, 96 G11
Parachilna SA 70 A7, 74 H5
Paradise Tas. 142 H8, 144 G4, 145 A9
Paradise Vic. 42 B12, 50 B5, 61 J10, 63 L10
Paradise Beach Vic. 53 L7
Paradise Point Qld 27 O1, 115 G8, 116 F3
Paradise Waters Qld 116 F6
Parafield SA 66 D5, 67 C7
Parafield Gardens SA 67 B7

Parap NT xxvii B8
Paraparap Vic. 42 E9, 50 F2, 63 N8
Parattah Tas. 141 L4
Pardoe Downs Tas. 145 D2
Pardoo Roadhouse WA 92 E1, 94 E11, 97 K2
Parenna Tas. 141 P11
Parilla SA 28 A9, 58 A11, 60 A1, 71 G4, 73 N10
Paringa SA 28 B5, 58 B5, 71 G1, 73 O7
Park Beach Tas. 139 L5
Park Holme SA xx F12
Parkdale Vic. 45 K1
Parkers Corner Vic. 52 H6
Parkerville WA 84 G4, 85 D4
Parkes ACT 32 D8
Parkes NSW 24 E4
Parkham Tas. 143 I7, 145 C9
Parkhurst Qld 125 M10
Parkside SA xxi K7, 65 G12
Parkville NSW 25 K1, 26 H12
Parkville Vic. xv I7, 39 B1
Parkwood WA xxv C11
Parndana SA 69 C11, 72 G11
Parnella Tas. 143 P8
Paroo–Darling NP NSW 30 G7, 31 I8
Parrakie SA 71 F4, 73 N10
Parramatta NSW 12 C6, 13 A12, 15 J8, 25 K6
Parrawe Tas. 142 E6, 144 B2
Paru 104 D3
Paruna SA 28 A7, 58 A8, 71 G2, 73 O8
Parwan Vic. 42 G4, 49 G12, 52 A4, 63 O5
Paschendale Vic. 62 D4
Pascoe Vale South Vic. xv I1
Paskeville SA 69 F3, 73 I6
Pata SA 28 A7, 58 A7, 71 G2, 73 N8
Patchewollock Vic. 28 D9, 58 G12, 60 G2
Pateena Tas. 143 K9, 145 G11
Paterson NSW 19 C6, 20 A11, 25 L3
Patersonia Tas. 143 L7
Patho Vic. 54 B5, 61 P6
Patonga NSW 12 H2, 13 C9, 15 N4
Patrick Estate Qld 115 A3, 117 B10
Patterson Lakes Vic. 45 K3
Patyah Vic. 60 C10, 71 H9
Paupong NSW 35 B8, 36 E11, 51 C5
Pawleena Tas. 139 L3, 141 L6
Pawtella Tas. 141 L3
Paxton NSW 13 D3
Payneham SA xxi M2
Payneham South SA xxi M3
Paynes Crossing NSW 13 B2, 25 K4
Paynes Find WA 89 H12, 90 D3
Paynesville Vic. 53 N6
Peaceful Bay WA 87 G6, 88 E12, 90 D11
Peachester Qld 117 F5, 118 E12
Peak Charles NP WA 90 H8
Peak Crossing Qld 114 A11, 115 B7, 123 M10
Peak Downs Qld 119 D11, 125 I8
Peak Hill NSW 24 E2, 116 G10
Peak Hill WA 89 H7, 92 E8
Peak Range NP Qld 119 C12, 124 H8, 125 I9
Peak View NSW 35 D7, 36 H8, 51 G2
Peake SA 71 E4, 73 M10
Pearcedale Vic. 40 F10, 43 K9, 45 L5, 52 D7
Pearl Beach NSW 12 H2, 13 C9, 15 N4
Pearshape Tas. 141 O12
Peats Ridge NSW 13 C7, 15 N1, 25 K5
Pebbly Beach NSW 25 I12, 35 F6, 37 M6
Peebinga SA 28 B8, 58 B9, 71 H3, 73 O9
Peechelba Vic. 29 M12, 55 I6, 56 E2
Peechelba East Vic. 55 I6, 56 E2
Peel NSW 24 H5
Peelwood NSW 24 G7, 35 E1
Pegarah Tas. 141 P11
Pekina SA 73 J3, 75 I10
Pelaw Main NSW 13 F2, 19 B8
Pelham Tas. 138 G1, 141 J5
Pella Vic. 28 D11, 60 F4
Pelverata Tas. 138 G7, 141 J8
Pemberton WA 86 H11, 87 B3, 88 D11, 90 C11
Pembroke NSW 20 F6, 27 L11
Penarie NSW 28 H7, 59 M7
Penderlea NSW 35 B8, 36 D10, 51 C4
Pendle Hill NSW 12 B6, 15 J7
Penguin Tas. 142 G6

Penguin Island WA 84 C11, 85 B8
Penna Tas. 139 K4
Pennant Hills NSW 12 D5, 13 A11, 15 K7
Penneshaw SA 69 F11, 71 A5, 73 I11
Pennyroyal Vic. 42 C10, 50 D3, 63 M9
Penola SA 62 A2, 71 G10
Penong SA 81 K8
Penrice SA 67 F4
Penrith NSW 14 H6, 17 M11, 25 J6
Penrose NSW 23 A7, 25 I9, 35 F3
Penshurst NSW 15 K10
Penshurst Vic. 62 G5
Pentland Qld 124 D3, 131 P3
Penwortham SA 73 J6
Penzance Tas. 139 N8, 141 M8
Peppermint Grove WA xxiv C9, 86 D5, 88 B9
Peppers Plains Vic. 28 D12, 60 G6
Peppimenarti NT 95 P2, 99 P1, 104 C8
Percy Isles NP Qld 125 M7
Percydale Vic. 61 K11, 63 K1
Peregian Beach Qld 117 H2, 118 F10, 123 N7
Perekerten NSW 28 H8, 59 N10
Perenjori WA 90 C4
Perenna Vic. 28 C11, 60 E5
Pericoe NSW 35 D10, 51 G8
Perisher NSW 35 A8, 36 C10, 51 B4
Perkins Reef Vic. 49 E5, 61 N11, 63 N1
Peronne Vic. 60 C9
Perponda SA 71 E3, 73 M9
Perroomba SA 73 J3, 74 H10
Perry Bridge Vic. 53 L6
Perth Tas. 143 K9, 145 H11
Perth WA xxiv F6, 83, 84 D6, 85 C5, 88 C5, 90 C7
Perth Airport WA xxv E6
Perthville NSW 24 H5
Petcheys Bay Tas. 138 F9, 141 J9
Peterborough SA 73 K3, 75 I11
Peterborough Vic. 50 F10, 63 I9
Peterhead SA 67 A8, 68 E1
Petersham NSW viii A7
Petersville SA 69 F5, 73 I7
Petford Qld 120 B3, 127 K7
Petina SA 72 A2, 81 N9
Petrie Qld 114 D4, 115 D2, 117 F9
Petrie Terrace Qld 113 B3
Pheasant Creek Vic. 40 G2, 41 B4, 43 K3, 52 D3
Phillip Island Vic. 43 K11, 45 L11, 52 D8
Pialba Qld 118 F4
Piallaway NSW 26 H9
Piambie Vic. 28 G8, 59 K9
Piangil Vic. 28 G8, 59 L11
Piangil North Vic. 59 L11
Piawaning WA 88 C2, 90 C6
Pickering Brook WA 84 G7
Pickertaramoor NT 104 D3
Picnic Bay Qld 119 A1, 120 G10, 127 N11
Picnic Point NSW 29 J11, 54 D4
Picola Vic. 29 K12, 54 D5
Picola North Vic. 29 K12, 54 D5
Picton NSW 14 F12, 23 D2, 25 J7, 35 G1
Picton WA 86 E4
Pier Millan Vic. 28 F9, 59 I12, 61 I1
Piesseville WA 88 F7
Pigeon Hole NT 106 E4
Pigeon Ponds Vic. 60 E12, 62 E2
Piggabeen NSW 21 G2, 115 G11, 116 F10
Piggoreet Vic. 42 B4, 49 A12, 63 L5
Pikedale Qld 27 K2, 123 K11
Pilchers Bridge Vic. 49 G5, 54 A10, 61 O11
Pile Siding Vic. 42 A11, 50 B4
Pillar Valley NSW 21 E9, 27 N6
Pilliga NSW 26 D6
Pilot Hill NSW 24 D11, 35 A5, 36 C4, 55 P4
Pimba SA 74 E6
Pimpama Qld 114 G12, 115 F8, 116 D2
Pimpinio Vic. 60 F8
Pindar WA 89 E12, 90 B3
Pine Creek NT 103 I12, 104 F7
Pine Gap NT 111 I4
Pine Lodge Vic. 54 F7, 56 A3
Pine Point SA 69 F5, 71 A2, 73 I8
Pine Ridge NSW 24 F4, 26 G10
Pine Scrub Tas. 140 A9
Pinery SA 67 A2, 69 H4, 71 B1, 73 J7

171

Ravenswood Vic. 49 F4, 61 N11
Ravenswood South Vic. 49 F5, 54 A10, 61 O11
Ravensworth NSW 25 K2
Rawdon Vale NSW 20 B8, 25 M1, 27 J12
Rawlinna WA 91 L5
Raymond Island Vic. 53 N6
Raymond Terrace NSW 13 H2, 19 D7, 20 A12, 25 M4
Raywood Vic. 49 F1, 54 A7, 61 O9
Red Banks SA 73 K5
Red Beach Qld 128 B5
Red Bluff WA 89 B6, 99 I2
Red Cliffs Vic. 28 E6, 58 G6
Red Hill Qld xxx E5
Red Hill Vic. 40 D12, 43 I10, 45 I8, 52 C7
Red Hill South Vic. 40 D12, 43 I10, 45 I8
Red Hills Tas. 143 I8, 145 C10
Red Jacket Vic. 52 H4
Red Range NSW 27 K6
Red Rock NSW 21 E10, 27 N7
Redan Vic. 42 C3, 47 C9, 49 C10
Redbank Qld 114 C9, 115 C5, 117 D12
Redbank Vic. 61 K11
Redbank Plains Qld 114 B9, 115 C6, 117 D12
Redbanks SA 67 B4, 69 H5, 71 B1, 72 F6, 73 J8
Redcastle Vic. 54 C9
Redcliffe Qld 114 F4, 115 E2, 117 G9, 123 N9
Redcliffe WA xxv C5
Redesdale Vic. 49 H6, 54 B10, 61 P11, 63 P1
Redfern NSW viii F7, 12 F8, 13 B12, 15 L9
Redhead NSW 13 G4, 19 D10
Redhill SA 69 G1, 73 I5, 74 H12
Redland Bay Qld 114 H9, 115 F6, 123 N9
Redmond WA 87 C10, 88 G11
Redpa Tas. 142 B4
Reedy Creek Qld 115 F10, 116 E8
Reedy Creek SA 71 E9
Reedy Creek Vic. 41 A1, 43 K1, 52 D1, 54 D12
Reedy Dam Vic. 28 E11, 61 I5
Reedy Flat Vic. 53 O3
Reedy Marsh Tas. 143 I8, 145 D10
Reef Hills Park Vic. 54 G8
Reefton NSW 24 C7, 29 P7
Reekara Tas. 141 O10
Regans Ford WA 88 B3, 90 B6
Regatta Point Tas. 140 C2, 142 C12
Regents Park NSW 12 C7, 13 A12, 15 K9
Reid ACT 32 F4
Reid WA 80 A5, 91 O4
Reid River Qld 119 A3, 120 G12, 124 G2, 127 N12
Reids Creek Vic. 55 J7, 56 H4
Reids Flat NSW 24 F7, 35 D1
Reidsdale NSW 24 H11, 35 E5, 37 K5
Rekuna Tas. 139 J3, 141 K6
Relbia Tas. 143 K8, 145 H11
Reliance Creek NP Qld 119 G7, 125 K5
Remine Tas. 142 C10
Rendelsham SA 71 F11
Renison Bell Tas. 142 D9
Renmark SA 28 A5, 58 B5, 71 G1, 73 O7
Renner Springs NT 107 I7
Rennie NSW 29 M11, 54 H4
Renown Park SA xx H2
Repulse Islands NP Qld 119 F6, 125 K4
Research Vic. 40 F5, 41 A7
Reservoir Vic. 40 E5, 43 J5
Restoration Island NP Qld 128 E7
Retreat Tas. 143 K6, 145 H6
Revesby NSW 12 C9, 15 J10
Reynella SA 66 B10, 67 B10, 68 E4
Rheban Tas. 139 N2, 141 M6
Rheola Vic. 49 B2, 61 M9
Rhodes NSW 12 D7, 13 A12, 15 K8
Rhyll Vic. 43 K11, 45 M10, 52 D8
Rhymney Reef Vic. 61 I12, 63 I2
Rhyndaston Tas. 141 K5
Rhynie SA 71 B1, 73 J7
Riachella Vic. 61 I10
Rialto Qld 116 E7
Riana Tas. 142 F6, 144 E1
Rich Avon Vic. 61 I8
Richlands NSW 24 H8, 35 E2
Richlands Qld 115 D5, 117 E12
Richmond NSW 14 H4, 17 N7, 25 J6

Richmond Qld 131 L3
Richmond SA xx F6
Richmond Tas. 139 J3, 141 K6
Richmond Vic. xv N12, xvii N4, 40 D6, 43 J5, 52 C4
Richmond Range NP NSW 21 D4, 27 M3, 123 M12
Riddells Creek Vic. 40 B2, 42 H3, 52 B2, 63 P3
Ridgelands Qld 125 M10
Ridgetop Qld 116 D11
Ridgeway Tas. 137 B10, 139 I6
Ridgley Tas. 142 F6
Ridleyton SA xx G2
Riggs Creek Vic. 54 F8, 56 A6
Ringa WA 85 F2, 88 D4
Ringarooma Tas. 143 M7
Ringwood Vic. 40 F6, 41 A8, 43 K6, 52 D4
Ripley Qld 114 B10, 115 B6
Ripplebrook Vic. 43 N9, 52 F7
Rippleside Vic. 44 B3
Ripponlea Vic. xvii M12
Risdon Tas. xxxiv G3, 1 B1, 137 D4, 139 I4
Risdon Vale Tas. xxxiv H4, 1 E1, 137 F4, 139 J4, 141 K7
River Heads Qld 118 F5, 123 N4
Riverside Tas. 143 K8, 145 G9
Riverstone NSW 12 A3, 15 I6, 17 P9
Riverton SA 71 C1, 73 J7
Riverton WA xxiv H10, xxv B10
Rivervale WA xxv C7
Riverview NSW x C6
Riverview Qld 114 B9, 115 C5, 117 D12
Riverwood NSW 15 K10
Roadvale Qld 115 A8
Rob Roy Vic. 41 B6, 43 K4
Robb Jetty WA 84 C8
Robe SA 71 E9
Robertson NSW 23 D6, 25 J9, 35 G3
Robertstown SA 73 K6
Robigana Tas. 143 J7, 145 F8
Robina Qld 115 G10, 116 E7
Robinson River NT 107 N4
Robinvale Vic. 28 F7, 59 J8
Rocherlea Tas. 143 K8, 145 G9
Rochester SA 69 H1, 73 J5
Rochester Vic. 54 C7
Rochford Vic. 42 H1, 52 B1, 54 B12, 63 P3
Rock Flat NSW 35 C8, 36 G10, 51 F4
Rockbank Vic. 40 B5, 42 H5, 52 B4, 63 P5
Rockdale NSW 12 E9
Rockhampton Qld 125 M11
Rockingham WA 84 C11, 85 B7, 88 B6, 90 B8
Rocklea Qld 114 E8, 115 D5, 117 F12
Rockleigh SA 67 F9
Rockley NSW 24 H6
Rocklyn Vic. 42 E2, 49 D9, 63 N3
Rocksberg Qld 114 C2, 115 C1, 117 E7
Rocky Cape Tas. 142 D4
Rocky Cape NP Tas. 142 E4
Rocky Creek NSW 26 G6
Rocky Creek Qld 120 D3, 121 D9
Rocky Crossing Qld 125 K9
Rocky Dam NSW 27 I3, 123 I12
Rocky Glen NSW 26 E9
Rocky Gully WA 87 G2, 88 E10, 90 D11
Rocky Hall NSW 35 D10, 51 G7
Rocky Islets NP Qld 127 L1
Rocky River NSW 20 B1, 27 J8
Rocky River SA 69 A12, 72 F12
Rodd Point NSW viii A3, x A11
Roe Creek NT 111 I4
Roebourne WA 89 F1, 92 B2, 94 B12, 96 E5
Roebuck Roadhouse WA 94 H7, 98 B11
Roelands WA 86 E3
Roger River Tas. 142 C4
Roger River West Tas. 142 C5
Rokeby Tas. 137 H9, 139 J5, 141 K7
Rokeby Vic. 41 G12, 43 N8, 52 G6
Rokewood Vic. 42 C6, 63 L6
Rokewood Junction Vic. 42 B5, 63 L5
Roland Tas. 142 G7, 144 G4
Roleystone WA 84 G8, 85 D6
Rollands Plains NSW 20 F5, 27 L10
Rolleston Qld 122 G1
Rollingstone Qld 120 F9, 127 M11
Roma Qld 122 G6

Romsey Vic. 42 H2, 52 B2, 54 B12, 63 P3
Rookhurst NSW 20 B8, 25 M1, 27 J12
Rookwood NSW 12 D7
Rooty Hill NSW 12 A5, 15 I7, 17 P11
Roper Bar Store NT 105 J9
Rorruwuy NT 105 M4
Rosa Glen WA 86 B9, 88 B10
Rosanna Vic. 40 E5
Rose Bay NSW ix L6, xi L12
Rose Bay Tas. xxxiv H9, 1 D5 , 137 F7
Rose Park SA xxi L6
Rosebery NSW viii F11
Rosebery Tas. 142 D9, 144 A7
Rosebrook NSW 19 B6, 20 A11
Rosebrook Vic. 50 B7, 62 G8
Rosebud Vic. 40 C12, 43 I10, 44 H8, 52 C7
Rosebud West Vic. 44 H8
Rosedale NSW 35 F6, 37 L7
Rosedale Qld 123 L2
Rosedale SA 66 G1, 67 D5
Rosedale Vic. 53 J7
Rosegarland Tas. 138 F2, 141 J6
Rosehill NSW 12 C6
Rosenthal NSW 19 H4, 20 C10, 25 N2
Roses Tier Tas. 143 M8
Rosetta Tas. 137 B4
Rosetta Tas. xxxiv A4
Rosevale Qld 123 M10
Rosevale Tas. 143 J8, 145 F9
Rosevears Tas. 143 J7, 145 F8
Roseville NSW x E1, 12 F6, 13 B11
Roseville Chase NSW x G1
Rosewall Vic. 44 B2
Rosewhite Vic. 55 K9, 57 I6
Rosewood NSW 24 C11, 36 A5, 55 O4
Rosewood Qld 115 A5, 117 B12, 123 M9
Roseworthy SA 67 D4, 71 C2, 73 J8
Roslyn NSW 24 G8, 35 E2
Roslynmead Vic. 29 I12, 54 B5, 61 P6
Rosny Tas. xxxiv H10, 1 D6, 137 E8
Rosny Park Tas. 1 E6, 137 F7, 139 J5, 141 K7
Ross Creek Vic. 42 C4, 49 B11, 63 L4
Ross Tas. 141 L2, 143 L12
Rossarden Tas. 143 M10
Rossbridge Vic. 63 I3
Rossi NSW 24 G11, 34 H7, 35 D5, 37 I4
Rosslyn Park SA xxi O5
Rossmore NSW 14 H9
Rossmoyne WA xxiv G10, xxv A11
Rossville Qld 127 L3
Rostrevor SA xxi P2, 66 D6, 67 C8, 68 G1
Rostron Vic. 61 J10
Rothbury NSW 13 E1, 19 A7, 25 L3
Rothwell Qld 114 F3, 115 E2, 117 F9
Rothwell Vic. 44 C1
Rottnest Island WA 84 A7, 85 A6, 88 B5, 90 B7
Roto NSW 29 L3
Round Corner NSW 12 D4, 13 A10, 15 K6
Round Top Island NP Qld 119 G8, 125 K5
Rowella Tas. 143 J6, 145 F7
Rowena NSW 26 D5
Rowland Flat SA 66 H1, 67 E5
Rowsley Vic. 42 F4, 49 G12, 52 A4, 63 O5
Rowville Vic. 40 F7, 41 A9, 43 K6
Roxburgh NSW 25 K2
Roxby Downs SA 74 E4
Royal George Tas. 141 N1, 143 N11
Royal NP NSW 12 C11, 15 K12, 23 H1, 25 K7, 35 H1
Royalla NSW 24 F11, 33 E10, 34 E7, 35 D5, 36 H4
Royston Park SA xxi L2
Rozelle NSW viii C3, x C11
Ruabon WA 86 D6
Rubicon Vic. 41 H3, 43 N2, 52 G2, 54 G12, 56 C11
Ruby Vic. 43 N11, 52 F8
Rubyvale Qld 124 H10
Rudall SA 72 E5
Ruffy Vic. 54 E10, 56 A8
Rufus River NSW 28 C5, 58 D5, 73 P7
Rugby NSW 24 F8, 35 C2
Rukenvale NSW 21 E3, 27 N2
Rules Point NSW 24 E12, 35 B6, 36 D5
Rum Jungle NT 102 E6
Rumula Qld 120 D1, 121 D4

Tewkesbury Tas. 142 E6, 144 C1
Texas Qld 27 J3, 123 J12
Thallon Qld 26 E1, 122 F11
Thanes Creek Qld 27 K1
Thangool Qld 123 J2
Tharbogang NSW 29 M7
Thargomindah Qld 133 K8
Tharwa ACT 24 F11, 33 C10, 34 D7, 35 C5, 36 G4
The Basin Vic. 40 G6, 41 B9, 43 K6, 53 M4
The Cascade Vic. 55 M7, 57 L3
The Caves Qld 125 M10
The Channon NSW 21 F4, 27 O3
The Cove Vic. 50 E9, 62 H9
The Entrance NSW 13 E7, 15 P2, 25 L5
The Entrance North NSW 13 E7, 15 P2
The Gap NSW 24 B9, 29 P9
The Gap Qld xxx A4, 114 D6, 115 D4, 117 E11, 131 L2
The Gap Vic. 40 B3, 42 H3, 52 B3, 63 P4
The Gardens NT xxvii B9, 101 C3
The Gardens Tas. 143 P7
The Glen Tas. 143 K6, 145 G7
The Gulf NSW 27 J4
The Gums Qld 123 I8
The Gurdies Vic. 43 L10, 45 P9, 52 E8
The Heart Vic. 53 K7
The Highlands Vic. 42 F4, 49 G11, 52 A3, 63 O4
The Hill NSW 18 E6
The Junction NSW 18 B8
The Lakes NP Vic. 53 N6
The Lea Tas. 137 C11
The Monument Qld 130 F5
The Narrows NT xxvii D7
The Oaks NSW 14 F11, 23 D1, 25 J7, 35 G1
The Palms NP Qld 123 L8
The Patch Vic. 41 C9, 43 L6
The Pines SA 69 C7, 72 G9
The Risk NSW 21 E3, 27 N2, 123 M11
The Rock NSW 24 B10, 26 G4, 29 O10, 55 L1
The Rocks NSW viii G3, x G11, 10 E3
The Sisters Vic. 63 I7
The Spit NSW xi K5
The Springs Tas. 137 A9
The Summit Qld 21 A3, 27 L2
The Vale NSW 13 A8
Thebarton SA xx G4
Theodore Qld 123 I3
Theresa Park NSW 14 G10
Thevenard SA 81 M8
Thirlmere NSW 14 F12, 23 D2, 25 J7, 35 G2
Thirlmere Lakes NP NSW 23 D2, 25 J8, 35 G2
Thirlstane Tas. 143 I6, 145 B7
Thirroul NSW 23 G4
Thologolong Vic. 24 B12, 29 P12, 55 M5, 57 L1
Thomas Plains SA 69 F3, 72 I6
Thomastown Vic. 40 E4, 43 J4, 52 C4
Thomson Vic. 42 F8, 44 B4, 46 G9, 50 H1, 53 I6
Thomson Bay WA 84 A7, 85 A6
Thoona Vic. 54 H7, 56 D4
Thora NSW 20 G1, 21 C12, 27 M8
Thornbury Vic. xv O3
Thorneside Qld 114 G8, 115 F5, 117 G11
Thorngate SA 65 D1
Thorngate SA xxi I2
Thornlands Qld 114 H9, 115 F5, 117 H12
Thornlie WA xxv E12
Thornton NSW 13 G2, 19 C8, 20 A12
Thornton Vic. 41 G2, 43 N1, 52 F1, 54 F12, 56 B11
Thorpdale Vic. 43 P10, 52 H7
Thowgla Vic. 36 A8, 55 O7, 57 O4
Thowgla Upper Vic. 36 A9, 55 O8, 57 O4
Thredbo NSW 35 A8, 36 C10, 51 B4
Three Bridges Vic. 41 E9, 43 M6, 52 F5
Three Islands NP Qld 127 L2
Three Springs WA 90 B4
Three Ways Roadhouse NT 107 J9
Thrushton NP Qld 122 D8
Thuddungra NSW 24 D7, 35 A1
Thulimbah Qld 21 A3, 27 L2
Thulloo NSW 24 A5, 29 O5
Thuringowa Qld 120 G10, 124 G1, 127 N11
Thurla Vic. 58 G6
Thursday Island Qld 128 C2
Tia NSW 20 C4, 27 J10

Tiaro Qld 118 D6, 123 M5
Tiberias Tas. 141 K4
Tibooburra NSW 30 D2, 132 H11
Tichborne NSW 24 D4
Tickera SA 69 E2, 72 H6
Tidal River Vic. 52 H12
Tiega Vic. 28 E8, 58 G11
Tieri Qld 125 I9
Tighes Hill NSW 18 A1
Tilba Tilba NSW 35 E8, 37 K10
Tilmouth Well Roadhouse NT 108 G5
Tilpa NSW 31 I7
Timbarra Vic. 53 O3
Timbarra NP NSW 21 B5, 27 L4, 123 L12
Timber Creek NT 104 D10, 106 D2
Timberoo Vic. 28 D9, 58 G11
Timberoo South Vic. 28 D9, 58 G11, 60 G1
Timbertown NSW 20 F6
Timbillica NSW 35 D11, 51 G10
Timboon Vic. 50 F9, 63 I9
Timmering Vic. 54 C7
Timor Vic. 49 B5, 61 M11, 63 M1
Timor West Vic. 49 B5, 61 L11
Tin Can Bay Qld 118 F8, 123 N6
Tinaburra Qld 120 D3, 121 E9, 127 L7
Tinamba Vic. 53 J6
Tinaroo Falls Qld 120 D3, 121 E9, 127 L6
Tincurrin WA 88 F7
Tindal NT 104 G8
Tinderbox Tas. 139 I7, 141 K8
Tingalpa Qld xxxi N9
Tingha NSW 27 I6
Tingoora Qld 118 A9, 123 L6
Tinonee NSW 20 D8, 25 N1, 27 L12
Tintaldra Vic. 24 C12, 36 A7, 55 O6, 57 O2
Tintinara SA 71 E6, 73 M12
Tiona NSW 20 E10, 25 N2
Tiparra West SA 69 E4, 72 H7
Tipton Qld 123 K8
Tirranna Roadhouse Qld 129 D4
Titjikala NT 109 J8
Ti-Tree NT 109 I4
Tittybong Vic. 61 K4
Tiwi NT xxvii E3
Tiwi (Bathurst and Melville) Islands NT 104 D2
Tjukayirla Roadhouse WA 93 K10
Tobermorey NT 109 P4, 130 C6
Tocal Qld 124 A11, 131 M11
Tocumwal NSW 29 L11, 54 F4
Togari Tas. 142 B4
Toiberry Tas. 143 J9, 145 F12
Tolga Qld 120 D3, 121 D9, 127 L7
Tolmans Hill Tas. 137 C10
Tolmie Vic. 54 H10, 56 E8
Tom Groggin NSW 35 A8, 36 B11, 51 A4, 55 P9, 57 P6
Tom Price WA 89 G3, 92 C5, 96 G10
Tomago NSW 13 G2, 19 D8, 20 A12
Tomahawk Tas. 143 N5
Tomahawk Creek Vic. 42 A9, 50 A2, 63 K8
Tomakin NSW 37 L7
Tomaree NP NSW 19 H8, 20 C12, 25 M4
Tombong NSW 35 C9, 51 D7
Tomerong NSW 23 C11, 37 O2
Tomewin Qld 21 G2, 115 F12, 116 D11
Tomingley NSW 24 E2
Tongala Vic. 29 J12, 54 D6
Tonganah Tas. 143 M7
Tonghi Creek Vic. 35 C11, 51 D10
Tongio Vic. 53 N2, 55 N12, 57 M12
Tongio West Vic. 53 N2, 57 M12
Tonimbuk Vic. 41 E11, 43 M7, 52 F6
Tooan Vic. 60 E9
Toobanna Qld 120 E8, 127 M10
Toobeah Qld 26 G1, 122 H10
Tooborac Vic. 54 C10
Toodyay WA 85 F2, 88 D4, 90 C7
Toogong NSW 24 F4
Toogoolawah Qld 117 A7, 123 M8
Toogoom Qld 118 E4, 123 N4
Tookayerta SA 28 A6, 58 A7, 71 G2, 73 N8
Toolamba Vic. 54 E8
Toolangi Vic. 41 D5, 43 L4, 52 E3
Toolern Vale Vic. 40 A3, 42 G4, 49 H11, 52 B3, 63 P4

Tooleybuc NSW 28 G8, 59 L11
Toolibin WA 88 F7
Tooligie SA 72 D6
Toolleen Vic. 54 B9, 61 P10
Toolondo Vic. 60 F11
Toolong Vic. 50 B7, 62 F8
Tooloom NSW 21 C3, 27 M2, 123 L11
Tooloom NP NSW 21 C2, 27 M2, 123 L11
Tooma NSW 24 D12, 35 A6, 36 B7, 51 A1, 55 P6, 57 P2
Toombul Qld 114 E6, 115 E4, 117 F10
Toombullup Vic. 54 H10, 56 E8
Toompine Roadhouse Qld 133 L7
Toongabbie Vic. 53 I6
Toongi NSW 24 F2
Toonumbar NSW 21 D3, 27 M2, 123 M11
Toonumbar NP NSW 21 D3, 27 M2, 123 M11
Tooperang SA 68 G7
Toora Vic. 52 H9
Tooradin Vic. 40 G10, 43 K9, 45 N6, 52 E7
Toorak Vic. xvii P7
Toorak Gardens SA xxi L6
Tooraweenah NSW 26 D10
Toorbul Qld 114 F1, 117 G7
Toorongo Vic. 43 P6, 52 H5
Tootgarook Vic. 44 G8
Tootool NSW 24 B10, 29 O10, 55 L1
Toowong Qld xxx D8, 114 D7, 115 D4, 117 F11
Toowoomba Qld 123 L9
Toowoon Bay NSW 13 E7, 15 P2
Top Springs NT 104 F12, 106 F3
Topaz Qld 120 D4, 121 F10
Topaz Road NP Qld 120 D4, 121 E10, 127 L7
Torbanlea Qld 118 E4, 123 M4
Torndirrup NP WA 87 E12, 88 G11, 90 E11
Toronto NSW 13 F4, 19 C10, 25 L4
Torquay Vic. 42 F9, 44 A7, 50 G2, 63 N8
Torrens Creek Qld 124 D4, 131 P4
Torrens Park SA xxi K12, 67 B9, 68 F2
Torrensville SA xx F4
Torrington NSW 27 K4
Torrita Vic. 28 D9, 58 F11
Torrumbarry Vic. 29 I12, 54 B5, 61 P6
Tostaree Vic. 35 A12, 51 A11, 53 O5
Tottenham NSW 24 C1, 29 P1, 31 P12
Tottington Vic. 61 J10
Toukley NSW 13 F6, 19 B12, 25 L5
Tourello Vic. 42 C1, 49 C8, 63 M3
Towallum NSW 21 D10, 27 M7
Towamba NSW 35 D10, 51 G8
Towaninny Vic. 28 G11, 61 L5
Towarri NP NSW 25 K1, 26 H11
Tower Hill Tas. 143 N9
Tower Hill Vic. 50 B7, 62 G8
Towitta SA 67 H5
Townsville Qld 119 A1, 120 F3, 120 G10, 124 G1, 127 N11
Towong Vic. 35 A7, 36 B8, 51 A2, 55 O7, 57 O3
Towong Upper Vic. 35 A7, 36 B8, 51 A2, 55 P7, 57 P4
Towradgi NSW 22 F3, 23 G4
Towrang NSW 24 H9, 35 E3
Tracy SA 73 K5, 75 J12
Trafalgar Vic. 43 P9, 52 G7
Tragowel Vic. 61 N5
Trangie NSW 26 B11
Tranmere SA xxi N3
Tranmere Tas. 1 H12, 137 H10
Traralgon Vic. 53 I7
Traralgon South Vic. 53 I7
Travancore Vic. xiv G5
Trawalla Vic. 42 B2, 63 K3
Trawool Vic. 54 D11
Trayning WA 88 F2, 90 D6
Traynors Lagoon Vic. 61 J9
Trebonne Qld 120 E8, 127 M10
Tregole NP Qld 122 D6
Trenah Tas. 143 M7
Trentham Vic. 42 F2, 49 F9, 52 A2, 54 A12, 63 O3
Trentham Cliffs NSW 58 H6
Trentham East Vic. 42 F2, 49 G9
Tresco Vic. 28 H10, 61 M3
Tresco West Vic. 61 M3
Trevallyn NSW 19 C5, 20 A10, 25 L3

Walbundrie NSW 24 A11, 29 N11, 55 K4
Walcha NSW 20 B3, 27 J9
Walcha Road NSW 20 A3, 27 J9
Walgett NSW 26 B5
Walgoolan WA 88 G3, 90 E6
Walhalla Vic. 53 I5
Walkamin Qld 120 D3, 121 D8, 127 L6
Walkaway WA 89 D12, 90 A3
Walker Flat SA 71 D2, 73 L9
Walkers Creek Qld 123 K7
Walkers Point Qld 118 E4, 123 M4
Walkerston Qld 119 G8, 125 K5
Walkerville SA xxi K2
Walkerville Vic. 52 G10
Walkerville South Vic. 52 G10
Walla Walla NSW 24 A11, 29 O11, 55 K4
Wallabadah NSW 26 H11
Wallabi Point NSW 20 E8, 25 O1
Wallabrook SA 60 A9, 71 G8
Wallace Vic. 42 E3, 49 D10, 63 N4
Wallace Rockhole NT 108 H7, 110 E6
Wallacedale Vic. 62 E5
Wallacia NSW 14 G8, 25 J7
Wallalong NSW 13 G1, 19 C7
Wallaloo Vic. 61 I9
Wallaloo East Vic. 61 J10
Wallan Vic. 40 E1, 43 J2, 52 C2
Wallangarra Qld 21 A4, 27 K3, 123 K12
Wallangra NSW 27 I4, 123 J12
Wallarah NP NSW 13 G5, 19 C11, 25 L5
Wallarobba NSW 19 D5, 25 M3
Wallaroo Qld 125 K11
Wallaroo SA 69 E3, 72 H6
Wallaville Qld 118 B3, 123 L3
Wallendbeen NSW 24 D8, 35 A2
Wallerawang NSW 14 A1, 25 I5
Walli NSW 24 F5
Wallinduc Vic. 42 B5, 63 K5
Wallingat NP NSW 20 D10, 25 N2
Wallington Vic. 42 G8, 44 C5, 50 H1, 52 A6, 63 O8
Walliston WA 84 F6
Walloon Qld 115 A5, 117 C12
Walloway SA 73 J2, 75 I10
Walls Of Jerusalem NP Tas. 140 G1, 142 G11, 144 F8, 145 A12
Wallsend NSW 13 G3, 19 C9, 20 A12
Wallumbilla Qld 122 G6
Wallup Vic. 28 D12, 60 G7
Walmer NSW 24 F2
Walmer Vic. 49 F5, 61 N11, 63 N1
Walpa Vic. 53 M5
Walpeup Vic. 28 D9, 58 F11
Walpole WA 87 F6, 88 E12, 90 D11
Walpole–Nornalup NP WA 87 F5, 88 E12, 90 D12
Walsall WA 86 C7
Walsh Qld 127 I5
Waltowa SA 71 D5, 73 L11
Walwa Vic. 24 C12, 29 P12, 36 A6, 55 O6, 57 N1
Walyunga NP WA 84 F2, 85 D3, 88 C4, 90 C7
Wamberal NSW 13 E8, 15 P3
Wambidgee NSW 24 D9, 35 A3
Wamboyne NSW 24 C5, 29 P5
Wamoon NSW 29 N7
Wampoony SA 28 A12, 71 G7
Wamuran Basin Qld 114 C1, 117 E7
Wamuran Qld 114 D1, 117 E7, 123 N8
Wanaaring NSW 31 I3, 133 L12
Wanalta Vic. 54 C8
Wanbi SA 71 F2, 73 N9
Wandana Heights Vic. 44 A4
Wandandian NSW 23 C11, 37 N2
Wandangula NT 105 M11, 107 M2
Wandearah SA 73 I4, 74 H12
Wandearah West SA 73 I4, 74 G12
Wandella NSW 35 E8, 37 J10, 51 H4
Wandering WA 85 H9, 88 D6, 90 D8
Wandiligong Vic. 55 K10, 57 I8
Wandilo SA 62 A4, 71 G11
Wandin North Vic. 40 H6, 41 C8, 43 L5, 52 E4
Wando Bridge Vic. 62 D3, 71 H11
Wando Vale Vic. 62 D3, 71 H11
Wandong Vic. 43 J2, 52 C2, 54 C12
Wandsworth NSW 27 J6

Wang Wauk NSW 20 D9, 25 N2
Wangara WA 84 C4, 85 B4
Wangarabell Vic. 35 D11, 51 F10
Wangaratta Vic. 55 I7, 56 F4
Wangary SA 72 D8
Wangenella NSW 29 J9
Wangerrip Vic. 50 A5, 63 K10
Wangi Wangi NSW 13 F5, 19 C10
Wangoom Vic. 50 D7, 62 H8
Wanguri NT xxvii E4
Wanilla SA 72 D8
Wanneroo WA 84 C3, 85 B4, 88 B4, 90 B7
Wannon Vic. 62 H3
Wanora Qld 115 A4, 117 C11
Wantabadgery NSW 24 C9, 55 O1
Wanwin Vic. 62 B6, 71 H12
Wapengo NSW 35 E9, 37 K12
Wappinguy NSW 25 J1, 26 G12
Warakurna WA 93 O7, 108 A9
Warakurna Roadhouse WA 93 O7, 108 A9
Warana Qld 117 H4, 118 F12
Waratah Tas. 142 E7, 144 A3
Waratah Bay Vic. 52 G10
Waratah North Vic. 52 G10
Warawarrup WA 86 E1, 88 C7
Warburton Vic. 41 F8, 43 M5, 52 F4
Warburton WA 93 M8
Warburton East Vic. 41 F8, 43 N5
Warburton Roadhouse WA 93 M8
Wardang Island SA 69 D5, 72 G8
Wardell NSW 21 G5, 27 O4, 123 N12
Wards River NSW 19 F2, 20 B9, 25 M2
Wareek Vic. 49 B5, 61 L11, 63 L1
Warialda NSW 26 H5
Warialda Rail NSW 26 H5
Warilla NSW 23 F6
Warkton NSW 26 E10
Warkworth NSW 25 K3
Warmga Qld 123 K8
Warmun WA 95 N6, 99 M8
Warmun–Turkey Creek Roadhouse WA 95 N6, 99 L8
Warncoort Vic. 42 C9, 50 C2, 63 L8
Warne Vic. 28 F11, 61 K4
Warneet Vic. 40 G10, 43 K9, 45 M6, 52 D7
Warner Qld 114 D5, 115 D3, 117 E10
Warners Bay NSW 13 G4, 19 C10
Warnertown SA 73 I4, 74 H11
Warooka SA 69 D7, 72 H9
Waroona WA 85 D11, 88 C7, 90 C9
Warra Qld 123 J7
Warra NP NSW 21 A9, 27 K6
Warra Yadin Vic. 61 J12, 63 J2
Warrabah NP NSW 27 I8
Warracknabeal Vic. 28 E12, 60 H7
Warradale SA 67 B10, 68 E3, 71 B3
Warraderry NSW 24 E6
Warragamba NSW 14 F8, 25 J7, 35 H1
Warragul Vic. 43 N9, 52 G7
Warrah Creek NSW 26 H11
Warrak Vic. 61 J12, 63 J2
Warralakin WA 88 G2, 90 E6
Warrambine Vic. 42 C6, 63 M6
Warramboo SA 72 D4, 74 B11
Warrandyte Vic. 40 F5, 41 A7, 43 K5, 52 D4
Warrane Tas. 1 F4, 137 G7
Warrawee NSW 13 B11, 15 L7
Warrawong NSW 23 F5
Warrayure Vic. 62 G4
Warrego NT 107 I9
Warrell Creek NSW 20 G3, 27 M9
Warren NSW 26 A10
Warren Qld 125 M11
Warren NP WA 86 G11, 87 A3, 88 C11, 90 C11
Warrenbayne Vic. 54 G9, 56 C6
Warrenmang Vic. 61 K11, 63 K1
Warrentinna Tas. 143 M6
Warrill View Qld 115 A7, 123 M10
Warrimoo NSW 14 G6, 17 K10
Warringa Tas. 142 G7, 144 F2
Warrion Vic. 42 B8, 50 B1, 63 L7
Warrnambool Vic. 50 C8, 62 G8
Warrong Vic. 62 G7
Warrow SA 72 C7

Warrumbungle NP NSW 26 D9
Warruwi NT 104 H2
Wartook Vic. 60 G11
Warup WA 88 E8
Warwick Qld 21 B1, 27 L1, 123 L10
Warwick WA 84 C5
Warwick Farm NSW 12 B8, 15 J9
Washpool SA 73 J4, 75 I12
Washpool NP NSW 21 B6, 27 L4
Wasleys SA 67 C4, 71 B1
Watagans NP NSW 13 D3, 19 A10, 25 L4
Watarrka NP NT 108 E7
Watchem Vic. 28 F12, 61 I6
Watchman SA 69 H3, 73 J6
Watchupga Vic. 28 F11, 61 I4
Waterfall Gully SA xxi O9, 72 H3, 74 G10
Waterfall NSW 12 B12, 15 J12, 23 H2, 25 K7
Waterford Qld 114 F10, 115 E6
Waterford Vic. 53 L3
Waterford WA xxiv H9, xxv B10
Waterford Park Vic. 43 J2, 52 D1, 54 D12
Waterhouse Tas. 143 M5
Waterloo NSW viii F8
Waterloo SA 73 K6
Waterloo Tas. 138 F9, 141 I9
Waterloo Vic. 42 A1, 63 K3
Waterloo WA 86 E3, 88 C8
Waterman WA xxiv A1
Watervale SA 73 J6
Waterview Heights NSW 21 D9, 27 M6
Watheroo WA 88 B1, 90 B5
Watheroo NP WA 88 B1, 90 B5
Watson SA 80 H3
Watsons Bay NSW ix M2, xi M9
Watsons Creek NSW 27 I8
Watsons Creek Vic. 40 G4, 41 B6, 43 K4
Watsonville Qld 120 C4, 121 C10, 127 L7
Wattamolla NSW 23 D8
Wattamondara NSW 24 E6
Wattle Flat NSW 24 B5, 29 P5, 35 F4, 37 L2
Wattle Glen Vic. 40 F4, 41 A6, 43 K4
Wattle Grove Tas. 138 F8, 141 J9
Wattle Grove WA xxv G8, 84 F7, 85 D5
Wattle Hill Tas. 139 L4, 141 L6
Wattle Hill Vic. 50 H1, 63 J10
Wattle Park SA xxi O6
Wattle Range SA 71 F10
Wattleup WA 84 D9, 85 C7
Waubra Vic. 42 B1, 49 B8, 63 L3
Wauchope NSW 20 F6, 27 L11
Wauchope NT 107 J11, 109 J1
Wauraltee SA 69 D6, 72 H8
Waurn Ponds Vic. 42 F8, 50 G1, 63 N8
Wave Hill NSW 31 N6
Wavell Heights Qld xxxi I1
Waverley NSW 12 G8, 15 M9
Waverley NSW ix J9
Waverley Tas. 143 K8, 145 H10
Waverton NSW viii F1, x F8, 11 A6
Wayatinah Tas. 140 H4
Waychinicup NP WA 87 G10, 88 H11, 90 F11
Waygara Vic. 51 A11, 53 P5
Wayville SA xxi I7, 65 B12
Webbs NSW 24 E1, 26 B12
Webbs Creek NSW 15 J1
Wedderburn NSW 14 H12, 23 F2
Wedderburn Vic. 61 L8
Wedderburn Junction Vic. 61 M8
Weddin Mountains NP NSW 24 D6
Wee Jasper NSW 24 E10, 34 A2, 35 B4, 36 F1
Wee Waa NSW 26 E6
Weeaproinah Vic. 42 A11, 50 B4
Weegena Tas. 142 H8, 145 B10
Weemelah NSW 26 E3, 122 G12
Weeragua Vic. 35 C11, 51 E9
Weerite Vic. 50 H7, 63 J7
Weetah Tas. 143 I8, 145 C10
Weetaliba NSW 26 E11
Weethalle NSW 24 A6, 29 N6
Weetulta SA 69 E4, 72 H7
Wehla Vic. 49 B1, 61 L9
Weipa Qld 128 B7
Weismantels NSW 19 F3, 20 B9, 25 M2
Weja NSW 24 B5, 29 O5

Welaregang NSW 24 C12, 36 B7, 51 A1, 55 O6, 57 O2
Weldborough Tas. 143 N7
Welford NP Qld 131 L12, 133 K2
Welland SA xx F3
Wellesley Island Qld 126 A4, 129 D1
Wellingrove NSW 27 J5
Wellington NSW 24 F2
Wellington NP WA 86 F3, 88 C8, 90 C9
Wellington Park Tas. xxxiv A11
Wellington Point Qld 114 G8, 115 F5, 117 H11
Wellington SA 71 D4, 73 L10
Wellstead WA 87 H7, 88 H10, 90 F10
Welshmans Reef Vic. 49 E6, 61 N12, 63 N1
Welshpool Vic. 52 H10
Welshpool WA xxv D8, 84 E6, 85 C5
Wembley WA xxiv D5
Wembley Downs WA xxiv C4
Wemen Vic. 28 F8, 59 I9
Wendouree Vic. 42 C3, 47 A2, 49 C10
Wentworth NSW 28 D5, 58 F5
Wentworth Falls NSW 14 D5, 16 G9, 25 I6
Wentworthville NSW 15 J8
Wepowie SA 73 J3, 75 I10
Werakata NP NSW 13 E1, 19 A7, 25 L3
Wereboldera NSW 24 D10, 35 A5, 36 C3
Werneth Vic. 42 B6, 63 L6
Werombi NSW 14 F9, 25 J7, 35 G1
Werona Vic. 42 E1, 49 D7
Werrap Vic. 28 D11, 60 F5
Werri Beach NSW 23 F8
Werribee Vic. 40 A6, 42 H6, 52 B5, 63 P6
Werribee South Vic. 40 B7, 42 H7, 44 F1, 52 B5, 63 P6
Werrikimbe NP NSW 20 D4, 27 K10
Werrimull Vic. 28 C6, 58 E7, 73 P8
Werris Creek NSW 26 H10
Wesburn Vic. 41 E8, 43 M5
Wesley Vale Tas. 142 H6, 145 B6
West Beach SA xx B7
West Burleigh Qld 21 G1, 115 G11, 116 F9
West Cape Howe NP WA 87 C12, 88 G12, 90 E12
West Creek Vic. 45 P12
West Croydon SA xx F1
West End Qld xxx E8, 114 E7
West Footscray Vic. xiv A8
West Frankford Tas. 143 I7, 145 D8
West Hill NP Qld 119 H10, 125 K7
West Hindmarsh SA xx G3
West Hobart Tas. 1 A7, xxxiv D11, 136 C6, 137 D8
West Kentish Tas. 142 G7, 144 G3
West Lakes SA xx A1
West Launceston Tas. 145 F2
West Leederville WA xxiv E5
West MacDonnell NP NT 108 H6, 109 I6, 110 C2, 111 I3
West Melbourne Vic. xiv E10, xvi E2, 39 A4
West Montagu Tas. 142 B3
West Moonah Tas. xxxiv C7, 137 C6
West Perth WA xxiv F5, 83 A1
West Pine Tas. 142 F6, 144 E1
West Richmond SA xx F6
West Ridgley Tas. 142 F6
West Scottsdale Tas. 143 L6
West Swan WA xxv D1
West Takone Tas. 142 E6, 144 B1
West Wallsend NSW 13 F3, 19 C9
West Waterhouse NT 110 E5
West Wollongong NSW 22 B9
West Wyalong NSW 24 B6, 29 P6
Westbourne Park SA xxi I10
Westbury Tas. 143 J8, 145 E11
Westbury Vic. 43 P9, 52 H6
Westby Vic. 28 H10, 61 N4
Westdale NSW 26 H9
Westdale WA 85 G7, 88 D5, 90 C8
Western Creek Tas. 142 H9, 145 B12
Western Flat SA 60 A8, 71 G8
Western Junction Tas. 143 K9, 145 H11
Westerway Tas. 138 E2, 141 I6
Westmar Qld 122 H9
Westmead NSW 12 C6
Westmere Vic. 63 I4
Westminster WA xxiv E1

Weston Creek ACT 33 C6
Weston NSW 13 E2, 19 B8, 25 L4
Westonia WA 88 H3, 90 E6
Westwood Qld 125 L11
Westwood Tas. 143 J8, 145 F10
Weymouth Tas. 143 K5, 145 H5
Wharminda SA 72 E6
Wharparilla Vic. 29 J12, 54 B5, 61 P7
Wharparilla North Vic. 54 B5, 61 P6
Wheatsheaf Vic. 42 F1, 49 F8
Wheeo NSW 24 G8, 35 D2
Whim Creek WA 89 G1, 92 C2, 94 C12, 96 G5
Whiporie NSW 21 E7, 27 N5
Whirily Vic. 61 J5
White Beach Tas. 139 L8, 141 L9
White Cliffs NSW 30 F7
White Flat SA 72 D8
White Gum Valley WA xxiv C12
White Hills Tas. 143 K8, 145 H11
White Mountains NP Qld 124 C3, 131 O3
White Rock Qld 120 E3, 121 F7
Whitefoord Tas. 141 L4
Whiteheads Creek Vic. 54 D10
Whiteman WA xxv B1, 85 C4
Whitemark Tas. 140 B10
Whitemore Tas. 143 J9, 145 F11
Whitewood Qld 124 A5, 131 M5
Whitfield Vic. 55 I9, 56 F7
Whitfords WA 84 C4
Whitlands Vic. 55 I9, 56 F7
Whittlesea Vic. 40 F2, 43 J3, 52 D3
Whitton NSW 29 M7
Whitwarta SA 69 G3, 73 J7
Whoorel Vic. 42 C9, 50 D2, 63 M8
Whorouly Vic. 55 J8, 56 G5
Whorouly East Vic. 55 J8, 56 G5
Whorouly South Vic. 55 J8, 56 G5
Whroo Vic. 54 D8
Whyalla SA 72 H3, 74 G11
Whyte Yarcowie SA 73 K4, 75 I11
Wialki WA 88 F1, 90 E5
Wiangaree NSW 21 E3, 27 N2, 123 M11
Wickepin WA 88 F6, 90 D8
Wickham NSW 13 H3, 18 A4, 19 D9
Wickham WA 89 F1, 92 B2, 94 B12, 96 E4
Wickliffe Vic. 62 H4
Widgiemooltha WA 90 H6
Widgiewa NSW 29 M9
Wilberforce NSW 12 A1, 15 I4, 17 P6, 25 J6
Wilburville Tas. 141 J2, 143 J11
Wilby Vic. 29 M12, 54 H6, 56 D2
Wilcannia NSW 30 G9
Wild Cattle Island NP Qld 123 L1, 125 N12
Wild Horse Plains SA 69 G5, 71 B1, 73 I7
Wiley Park NSW 15 K9
Wilga WA 86 H6, 88 D9
Wilgul Vic. 42 B6, 63 L6
Wilkawatt SA 71 F4, 73 N10
Wilkur Vic. 28 E11, 61 I6
Willa Vic. 28 E10, 60 G2
Willagee WA xxiv E11
Willalooka SA 71 F7
Willamulka SA 69 F3
Willandra NP NSW 29 K3
Willare Bridge Roadhouse WA 95 I7, 98 D10
Willatook Vic. 62 G7
Willaura Vic. 63 I3
Willawarrin NSW 20 F3, 27 L9
Willbriggie NSW 29 M7
Willenabrina Vic. 28 D11, 60 G6
Willetton WA xxiv H11, xxv B12
Willi Willi NP NSW 20 E4, 27 L10
William Bay NP WA 87 A12, 88 F12, 90 D11
William Creek SA 76 D10
Williams WA 88 E7, 90 D9
Williamsdale ACT 24 F11, 33 D11, 34 E8, 35 C5, 36 G5
Williamsford Tas. 142 D10, 144 A7
Williamstown SA 66 G3, 67 E6, 71 C2, 73 K8
Williamstown Vic. xvi D10, 40 C6, 43 I6, 52 C4
Williamstown North Vic. xvi A8
Williamtown NSW 19 E8, 20 B12
Willigulli WA 89 D12

Willina NSW 20 D9, 25 N2
Willoughby NSW 12 F6
Willoughby East NSW x G3
Willoughby NSW x F4
Willow Grove Vic. 43 P8, 52 H6
Willow Tree NSW 26 H11
Willowie SA 73 J2, 74 H10
Willowmavin Vic. 43 I1, 52 C1, 54 C12
Willowra NT 106 G12, 108 G2
Willows Qld 124 H11
Willows Gemfields Qld 124 H11
Willowvale Qld 21 B1, 27 L1
Willowvale Vic. 42 A5, 63 K5
Willung Vic. 53 J7
Willung South Vic. 53 J8
Willunga SA 67 B12, 68 E6, 69 H9, 71 B4, 73 J10
Wilmington SA 73 I2, 74 H10
Wilmot Tas. 142 G7, 144 F3
Wilora NT 109 I3
Wilpena SA 70 B10, 75 I6
Wilroy WA 89 E12, 90 B3
Wilson WA xxv C10
Wilsons Promontory NP Vic. 52 H11
Wilsons Valley NSW 36 D9, 51 C3
Wilston Qld xxx G4
Wilton NSW 23 E3, 25 J8, 35 H2
Wiltshire Junction Tas. 142 D4
Wiluna WA 92 F10
Wimba Vic. 42 B11, 50 B4, 63 K9
Wimbleton Heights Estate Vic. 45 L10
Winchelsea Vic. 42 D8, 50 E1, 63 M8
Windang NSW 23 F6, 25 J9, 35 H3
Windarra WA 91 I2, 93 I12
Windellama NSW 24 H10, 35 E4, 37 K1
Windermere Tas. 137 B3, 143 J7, 145 F8
Windermere Vic. 42 C2, 49 B9
Windermere Park NSW 13 F5, 19 B11
Windeyer NSW 24 H3
Windjana Gorge NP WA 95 K7, 98 F9
Windmill Roadhouse WA 88 B3, 90 B6
Windorah Qld 133 I3
Windowie NSW 24 D10, 35 A4, 36 C3, 55 P2
Windsor NSW 12 A2, 15 I5, 17 P7, 25 J6
Windsor Qld xxx G4
Windsor SA 69 G5, 71 B1, 73 J7
Windsor Vic. xvii M9
Windy Corner WA 93 K5
Windy Harbour WA 87 B5, 88 D11, 90 C11
Wingeel Vic. 42 C7, 63 M7
Wingello NSW 25 I9, 35 F3
Wingen NSW 25 K1, 26 H12
Wingham NSW 20 D8, 25 N1, 27 K12
Winiam Vic. 28 C12, 60 E7
Winiam East Vic. 60 E7
Winjallok Vic. 61 K10
Winkie SA 58 A6, 73 N7
Winkleigh Tas. 143 J7, 145 E8
Winmalee NSW 14 G5, 17 L8
Winnaleah Tas. 143 N6
Winnambool Vic. 28 F8, 59 I10
Winnap Vic. 62 C5, 71 H12
Winnellie NT xxvii E8, 102 D3
Winnindoo Vic. 53 J6
Winninowie SA 73 I2, 74 G10
Winnunga NSW 24 B5, 29 O5
Winslow Vic. 50 C7, 62 G7
Winthrop WA xxiv F11
Winton Qld 131 L7
Winton Vic. 54 H8, 56 D5
Winton North Vic. 54 H8, 56 E5
Winulta SA 69 F4, 71 A1, 73 I7
Wirha SA 28 A8, 71 G4, 73 N10
Wirlinga NSW 24 A12, 55 L6, 57 J2
Wirrabara SA 73 J3, 74 H11
Wirrega SA 28 A12, 60 A6, 71 G7
Wirrida SA 79 O12, 81 O1
Wirrimah NSW 24 E7, 35 B1
Wirrinya NSW 24 D5
Wirrulla SA 72 B1, 81 O9
Wiseleigh Vic. 53 N5
Wisemans Creek NSW 24 H6
Wisemans Ferry NSW 13 A7, 15 K2, 25 K5
Wishbone WA 88 G7
Wistow SA 66 G10, 67 E11, 68 H4

Witchcliffe WA 86 B9, 88 B10
Withersfield Qld 124 H10
Witjira NP SA 76 C2, 79 P2, 109 L12
Wittenoom WA 89 G3, 92 D4, 96 H8
Wivenhoe Tas. 142 F5
Wivenhoe Pocket Qld 115 A4, 117 C10
Woden Valley ACT 33 D6
Wodonga Vic. 24 A12, 29 N12, 55 K6, 57 I2
Wogyala NT 107 K8
Wokalup WA 86 E2, 88 C8
Woko NP NSW 20 B7, 25 M1, 27 J11
Wokurna SA 69 F2, 73 I5
Wolfe Creek Meteorite Crater NP WA 95 N9
Wollar NSW 25 I2
Wollemi NP NSW 13 A1, 14 G1, 15 I2, 17 M3, 25 J4
Wollert Vic. 40 E3, 43 J4, 52 C3
Wolli Creek NSW viii A11
Wollombi NSW 13 C3, 25 K4
Wollomombi NSW 20 D1, 27 K8
Wollongbar NSW 21 G5, 27 O3, 123 N12
Wollongong NSW 22, 23 F5, 25 J8, 35 H2
Wollstonecraft NSW x F8, 11 A4
Wollumbin NP NSW 21 G2, 27 O2, 123 N11
Wollun NSW 20 A2, 27 J9
Wolseley SA 28 B12, 60 B7, 71 G7
Wolumla NSW 35 E9, 51 H7
Womalilla Qld 122 E6
Wombarra NSW 23 G3
Wombat NSW 24 D8, 35 B2
Wombelano Vic. 60 D11
Wombeyan Caves NSW 24 H8, 35 F2
Womboota NSW 29 J11, 54 B4, 61 P5
Won Wron Vic. 53 I9
Wonboyn NSW 35 E11
Wonboyn Lake NSW 51 H9
Wondai Qld 118 A9, 123 L6
Wondalga NSW 24 D10, 35 A5, 36 C3, 55 P3
Wondul Range NP Qld 123 J10
Wonga Qld 121 D3, 127 L5
Wongaling Beach Qld 120 E6, 127 M8
Wongan Hills WA 88 D2, 90 C6
Wongarbon NSW 24 F1, 26 C12
Wongawilli NSW 23 E5
Wongulla SA 71 D2, 73 L8
Wonthaggi Vic. 43 L12, 52 E9
Wonwondah East Vic. 60 G10
Wonwondah North Vic. 60 F10
Wonyip Vic. 52 H9
Wood Wood Vic. 28 G9, 59 L11, 61 L1
Woodanilling WA 88 F8, 90 D9
Woodbridge Tas. 138 H9, 141 J9
Woodbridge WA xxv E2
Woodburn NSW 21 F6, 27 O4
Woodbury Tas. 141 L3
Woodchester SA 66 H12, 67 E12, 71 C4, 73 K10
Woodenbong NSW 21 D2, 27 M2, 123 M11
Woodend Vic. 42 G2, 49 H9, 52 B2, 54 B12, 63 P3
Woodfield Vic. 54 G11, 56 B9
Woodford NSW 14 E6, 17 I9
Woodford Qld 117 E6, 123 M8
Woodford Vic. 50 C7, 62 G8
Woodforde SA xxi P3
Woodgate Qld 118 E3, 123 M4
Woodglen Vic. 53 L5
Woodhill Qld 115 C8
Woodhouselee NSW 24 G8, 35 E2
Woodlands WA xxiv C4, 87 D9, 88 G11
Woodleigh Vic. 43 M10, 52 E8
Woodridge Qld 114 E10, 115 E6
Woods Point SA 71 D4, 73 L10
Woods Point Vic. 43 P4, 52 H3
Woods Reef NSW 26 H7
Woods Well SA 71 D6, 73 L12
Woodsdale Tas. 141 L5
Woodside Beach Vic. 53 J9
Woodside SA 66 G8, 67 E9, 68 H2, 71 C3, 73 K9
Woodside Vic. 53 J9
Woodstock NSW 24 F6
Woodstock Qld 119 A2, 120 G11, 124 G2, 127 N12
Woodstock Tas. 138 G7, 141 J8
Woodstock Vic. 40 E3, 43 J3, 52 C3
Woodvale Vic. 49 F2, 54 A8, 61 O9
Woodville NSW 13 G1, 19 C7, 20 A11, 27 J5

Woodville SA 67 B8, 68 E1, 69 H7
Woodville South SA xx E1
Woodville West SA xx D1
Woody Point Qld 114 F4, 115 E2, 117 G9
Wool Bay SA 69 E7, 72 H9
Wool Wool Vic. 42 A8, 50 A1, 63 K7
Woolamai Vic. 43 L11, 45 O11, 52 E8
Woolamai Waters Vic. 45 M11
Woolaning NT 102 C7, 104 D5
Woolbrook NSW 20 A3, 27 I9
Woolgoolga NSW 21 E11, 27 N7
Wooli NSW 21 F10, 27 N6
Woollahra NSW ix I7
Woolloomooloo NSW viii G5, 10 G8
Woolloongabba Qld xxx H10, 113 G12
Woolner NT xxvii C8
Woolomin NSW 27 I10
Woolooga Qld 118 C8, 123 M6
Woolooware NSW 12 E11, 15 L11
Wooloowin Qld xxxi I2
Woolshed Flat SA 73 I2, 74 G9
Woolshed Vic. 55 J7, 56 H4
Woolsthorpe Vic. 62 G7
Woolwich NSW viii C1, x D8
Woomargama NSW 24 B12, 29 O12, 55 M5
Woomargama NP NSW 24 B12, 29 P12, 55 N5, 57 L1
Woombye Qld 117 F4, 118 E11
Woomelang Vic. 28 E10, 61 I4
Woomera SA 74 E5
Woongoolba Qld 114 H11, 115 F7
Woonona NSW 23 G4
Wooragee Vic. 55 J7, 56 H3
Woorak Vic. 28 C12, 60 E7
Woorak West Vic. 60 E6
Wooramel Roadhouse WA 89 C8
Woorarra Vic. 52 H9
Wooreen Vic. 43 O11, 52 G8
Woori Yallock Vic. 41 D8, 43 M5, 52 E4
Woorim Qld 114 H2, 115 F1, 117 H8
Woorinen Vic. 28 G9, 59 L12, 61 L2
Woorinen North Vic. 59 L12, 61 L1
Woornack Vic. 28 E9, 58 H11, 60 H1
Woorndoo Vic. 63 I5
Wooroloo WA 85 E4, 88 C4
Wooroolin Qld 118 A9, 123 L6
Wooroonook Vic. 28 G12, 61 K7
Wooroonooran NP Qld 120 E4, 121 F9, 127 L7
Woosang Vic. 28 G12, 61 L7
Wootong Vale Vic. 62 E3
Wootton NSW 20 D10, 25 N2
Worongary Qld 116 D7
Woronora NSW 12 C10, 15 K11, 23 H1
Worsley WA 86 F3
Wowan Qld 125 L12
Woy Woy NSW 12 H1, 13 D8, 15 N3, 25 K6
Wrattonbully SA 60 B11, 62 B1, 71 G10
Wrightley Vic. 54 H10, 56 D7
Wroxham Vic. 35 D11, 51 F9
Wubin WA 90 C5
Wudinna SA 72 D3, 74 B11
Wujal Wujal Qld 127 L4
Wuk Wuk Vic. 53 M5
Wulagi NT xxvii F4
Wulgulmerang Vic. 35 A10, 51 A7, 53 P1, 55 P12, 57 P11
Wundowie WA 85 F3
Wunghnu Vic. 29 K12, 54 E6, 56 A2
Wunkar SA 71 F2, 73 N8
Wurankuwu NT 104 C3
Wurdiboluc Vic. 42 D9, 50 E2, 63 M8
Wutul Qld 123 L8
Wutunugurra NT 107 K11
Wy Yung Vic. 53 M5
Wyalkatchem WA 88 E3, 90 D6
Wyalong NSW 24 B6, 29 P6
Wyan NSW 21 E6, 27 N4
Wyandra Qld 122 B7, 133 O7
Wyangala NSW 24 F6
Wybalenna Tas. 140 A10
Wybong NSW 25 J2
Wycarbah Qld 125 L11
Wycheproof Vic. 28 G12, 61 K6
Wychitella Vic. 28 G12, 61 L7

Wycliffe Well Roadhouse NT 107 J11, 109 J1
Wye River Vic. 42 C11, 50 D5, 63 M10
Wyee NSW 13 E6, 19 B11, 25 L5
Wyee Point NSW 13 F5, 19 B11
Wyeebo Vic. 55 M7, 57 L4
Wyelangta Vic. 42 A11, 50 A5
Wyena Tas. 143 L6
Wyening WA 88 C3, 90 C6
Wylie Creek NSW 21 B3, 27 L2, 123 L11
Wymah NSW 24 B12, 55 M6, 57 L2
Wymlet Vic. 28 D8, 58 G10
Wynarka SA 71 E3, 73 L10
Wynbring SA 81 M4
Wyndham NSW 35 D10, 51 G7
Wyndham WA 95 N4, 99 L5
Wynnum Qld 114 G7, 115 E4, 117 G11, 123 N9
Wynnum West Qld xxxi P7
Wynyard Tas. 142 E5
Wyomi SA 71 E9
Wyoming NSW 13 D8, 15 O2, 20 D8, 25 N1, 27 K12
Wyong NSW 13 E7, 15 P1, 19 A12, 25 L5
Wyong Creek NSW 13 D6, 15 O1
Wyperfeld NP Vic. 28 C10, 58 E12, 60 E2, 71 H5, 73 P11
Wyrra NSW 24 B5, 29 P5
Wyrrabalong NP NSW 13 F7, 15 P3, 25 L5
Wyuna Vic. 29 K12, 54 D6

Yaamba Qld 125 M10
Yaapeet Vic. 28 D10, 60 F4
Yabba Vic. 55 L7, 57 K4
Yabba North Vic. 54 F6, 56 B2
Yabbra NP NSW 21 C3, 27 M2, 123 L12
Yabmana SA 69 A1, 72 F5
Yacka SA 69 H1, 73 J5, 74 H12
Yackandandah Vic. 55 K7, 57 I4
Yagoona NSW 12 C8, 13 A12
Yahl SA 62 A5, 71 G12
Yalangur Qld 123 L9
Yalata SA 81 I6
Yalata Roadhouse SA 81 I6
Yalboroo Qld 119 F6, 125 J5
Yalbraith NSW 24 H8, 35 E2
Yalgoo WA 89 F11, 90 C2
Yalgorup NP WA 85 B10, 86 D1, 88 B7, 90 C8
Yallakool NSW 29 I10, 54 B2, 61 P3
Yallaroi NSW 26 H3, 123 I12
Yalleroi Qld 124 D11
Yallingup WA 86 A6, 88 B9, 90 B10
Yallourn North Vic. 52 H7
Yallunda Flat SA 72 D7
Yaloak Vale Vic. 42 F4, 49 F12, 63 N5
Yalwal NSW 23 B9, 25 I10, 35 G4, 37 N1
Yamala Qld 125 I11
Yamanto Qld 114 A9, 115 B6, 117 C12
Yamba NSW 21 F8, 27 O5
Yamba Roadhouse SA 28 B6, 58 B6, 71 G1, 73 O7
Yambacoona Tas. 141 O10
Yambuk Vic. 50 A7, 62 F8
Yambuna Vic. 54 D5
Yan Yean Vic. 40 E3, 43 J4, 52 D3
Yanac Vic. 28 C12, 60 D6
Yanac South Vic. 60 D6
Yanakie Vic. 52 G10
Yanchep WA 84 A1, 85 A2, 88 B4, 90 B7
Yanchep NP WA 84 A1, 85 B2, 88 B4, 90 B7
Yanco NSW 29 N8
Yandaran Qld 118 C1, 123 M3
Yanderra NSW 23 D3, 25 J8, 35 G2
Yandeyarra WA 89 G1, 92 D3, 96 H6
Yandina Qld 117 F3, 118 E11, 123 N7
Yando Vic. 28 H12, 61 M6
Yandoit Vic. 49 E7, 61 N12, 63 N2
Yanerbie Beach SA 72 A3, 81 N10
Yanga NP NSW 28 H7, 59 N7
Yangan Qld 21 B1, 27 L1, 123 L10
Yaninee SA 72 C3, 74 B10, 81 P10
Yanipy Vic. 28 B12, 60 C7, 71 H7
Yankalilla SA 68 D7, 69 G10, 71 B4, 73 J10
Yantabulla NSW 31 K3, 133 M12
Yantanabie SA 72 B2, 81 O9
Yanununbeyan NP NSW 24 G11, 34 G8, 35 D5, 37 I4
Yapeen Vic. 49 E6, 61 N12, 63 N1